T0180264

Lecture Notes in Computer Science 13709

Founding Editors

Gerhard Goos
Karlsruhe Institute of Technology, Karlsruhe, Germany

Juris Hartmanis
Cornell University, Ithaca, NY, USA

Editorial Board Members

Elisa Bertino
Purdue University, West Lafayette, IN, USA

Wen Gao
Peking University, Beijing, China

Bernhard Steffen
TU Dortmund University, Dortmund, Germany

Moti Yung
Columbia University, New York, NY, USA

More information about this series at https://link.springer.com/bookseries/558

Davide Taibi · Marco Kuhrmann ·
Tommi Mikkonen · Jil Klünder ·
Pekka Abrahamsson (Eds.)

Product-Focused Software Process Improvement

23rd International Conference, PROFES 2022
Jyväskylä, Finland, November 21–23, 2022
Proceedings

 Springer

Editors
Davide Taibi ⓘ
Tampere University
Tampere, Finland

Marco Kuhrmann ⓘ
Reutlingen University
Reutlingen, Germany

Tommi Mikkonen ⓘ
University of Jyväskylä
Jyväskylä, Finland

Jil Klünder ⓘ
Leibniz University Hannover
Hannover, Germany

Pekka Abrahamsson ⓘ
University of Jyväskylä
Jyväskylä, Finland

ISSN 0302-9743   ISSN 1611-3349 (electronic)
Lecture Notes in Computer Science
ISBN 978-3-031-21387-8   ISBN 978-3-031-21388-5 (eBook)
https://doi.org/10.1007/978-3-031-21388-5

© The Editor(s) (if applicable) and The Author(s), under exclusive license
to Springer Nature Switzerland AG 2022
This work is subject to copyright. All rights are reserved by the Publisher, whether the whole or part of the material is concerned, specifically the rights of translation, reprinting, reuse of illustrations, recitation, broadcasting, reproduction on microfilms or in any other physical way, and transmission or information storage and retrieval, electronic adaptation, computer software, or by similar or dissimilar methodology now known or hereafter developed.
The use of general descriptive names, registered names, trademarks, service marks, etc. in this publication does not imply, even in the absence of a specific statement, that such names are exempt from the relevant protective laws and regulations and therefore free for general use.
The publisher, the authors, and the editors are safe to assume that the advice and information in this book are believed to be true and accurate at the date of publication. Neither the publisher nor the authors or the editors give a warranty, expressed or implied, with respect to the material contained herein or for any errors or omissions that may have been made. The publisher remains neutral with regard to jurisdictional claims in published maps and institutional affiliations.

This Springer imprint is published by the registered company Springer Nature Switzerland AG
The registered company address is: Gewerbestrasse 11, 6330 Cham, Switzerland

Preface

On behalf of the PROFES Organizing Committee, we are proud to present the proceedings of the 23rd International Conference on Product-Focused Software Process Improvement (PROFES 2022). The conference was held during November 21–23, 2022.

Following the previous editions, the main theme of PROFES 2022 was professional software process improvement (SPI) motivated by product, process, and service quality needs. The technical program of PROFES 2022 was selected by a committee of leading experts in software process improvement, software process modeling, and empirical software engineering.

This year, we received 75 submissions. After a thorough evaluation that involved at least three independent experts per paper, 24 full technical papers were finally selected. As we had strong competition this year, many good papers did not make it in the pool of selected papers and, therefore, we invited several author teams to re-submit their papers as a short paper or poster paper. Eventually, we included nine short papers and six poster papers in the program. Each submission was reviewed by at least three members of the PROFES Program Committees.

Alongside the technical program, PROFES 2022 hosted a doctoral symposium, two workshops, and one tutorial. In total eight papers were accepted for the doctoral symposium. The workshop on Computational Intelligence and Software Engineering (CISE) aims to foster the integration between software engineering and AI communities, and to improve research results, teaching and mentoring, and industrial practice. The workshop on Processes and Practices for Quantum Software (PPQS) aims to establish a community, fostering academic research and industrial solutions, focused on quantum software engineering principles and practices for process-centric design, development, validation, and deployment and maintenance of quantum software systems and applications.

We are thankful for the opportunity to have served as chairs for this conference. The Program Committee members and reviewers provided excellent support in the paper evaluation process. We are also grateful to all authors of submitted manuscripts, presenters, keynote speakers, and session chairs, for their time and effort in making PROFES 2022 a success. We would also like to thank the PROFES Steering Committee members for their guidance and support in the organization process.

October 2022

Davide Taibi
Marco Kuhrmann
Tommi Mikkonen
Jil Klünder
Pekka Abrahamsson

Organization

Organizing Committee

General Chair

Tommi Mikkonen	University of Jyväskylä, Finland

Program Chairs

Davide Taibi	Tampere University, Finland
Marco Kuhrmann	Reutlingen University, Germany
Pekka Abrahamsson	University of Jyväskylä, Finland

Short-Paper Track Chairs

Valentina Lenarduzzi	Lappeenranta-Lahti University of Technology, Finland
Juan Manuel Murillo Rodríguez	University of Extremadura, Spain

Industry Paper Track Chairs

Ilenia Fronza	Free University of Bozen-Bolzano, Italy
Marcus Ciolkowski	QAware, Germany

Tutorial and Workshop Chairs

Arif Ali Khan	University of Oulu, Finland
Fabio Calefato	University of Bari, Italy

Poster Track Chairs

Pilar Rodriguez	Universidad Politécnica de Madrid, Spain
Fabiano Pecorelli	Tampere University, Finland

Panel Chair

John Noll	University of Hertfordshire, UK

Journal-First Chairs

Darja Smite	Blekinge Institute of Technology, Sweden
Fabian Fagerholm	Aalto University, Finland

PhD-Symposium Chairs

Paul Clarke	Dublin City University, Ireland
Andrea Janes	Free University of Bozen-Bolzano, Italy

Proceedings Chair

Jil Klünder	Leibniz Universität Hannover, Germany

Publicity Chairs

Gemma Catolino	Jheronimus Academy of Data Science, The Netherlands
Sami Hyrynsalmi	Lappeenranta-Lahti University of Technology, Finland

Program Committee

Pekka Abrahamsson	University of Jyväskylä, Finland
Sousuke Amasaki	Okayama Prefectural University, Japan
Andreas Birk	SWPM, Germany
Fabio Calefato	University of Bari, Italy
Gemma Catolino	Jheronimus Academy of Data Science, The Netherlands
Marcus Ciolkowski	QAware GmbH, Germany
Paul Clarke	Dublin City University, Ireland
Bruno da Silva	California Polytechnic State University, USA
Maya Daneva	University of Twente, The Netherlands
Michal Dolezel	Prague University of Economics and Business, Czech Republic
Fabian Fagerholm	Aalto University, Finland
Davide Falessi	University of Rome Tor Vergata, Italy
Michael Felderer	University of Innsbruck, Austria
Ilenia Fronza	Free University of Bozen-Bolzano, Italy
Lina Garcés	UNIFEI, Brazil
Carmine Gravino	University of Salerno, Italy
Noriko Hanakawa	Hannan University, Japan
Jens Heidrich	Fraunhofer IESE, Germany

Helena Holmström Olsson	University of Malmo, Sweden
Martin Höst	Lund University, Sweden
Frank Houdek	Mercedes-Benz AG, Germany
Sami Hyrynsalmi	LUT University, Finland
Andrea Janes	Free University of Bozen-Bolzano, Italy
Marcos Kalinowski	Pontifical Catholic University of Rio de Janeiro, Brazil
Kai-Kristian Kemell	University of Helsinki, Finland
Petri Kettunen	University of Helsinki, Finland
Arif Ali Khan	University of Oulu, Finland
Jil Klünder	Leibniz Universität Hannover, Germany
Marco Kuhrmann	Reutlingen University, Germany
Filippo Lanubile	University of Bari, Italy
Valentina Lenarduzzi	University of Oulu, Finland
Jingyue Li	Norwegian University of Science and Technology, Norway
Silverio Martínez-Fernández	Universitat Politècnica de Catalunya, Spain
Kenichi Matsumoto	Nara Institute of Science and Technology, Japan
Tommi Mikkonen	University of Jyväskylä, Finland
Rahul Mohanani	University of Jyväskylä, Finland
Sandro Morasca	Università degli Studi dell'Insubria, Italy
Maurizio Morisio	Politecnico di Torino, Italy
Jürgen Münch	Reutlingen University, Germany
Anh Nguyen Duc	University of Southeastern-Norway, Norway
John Noll	University of Hertfordshire. UK
Edson Oliveirajr	State University of Maringá, Brazil
Fabiano Pecorelli	University of Salerno, Italy
Dietmar Pfahl	University of Tartu, Estonia
Rudolf Ramler	Software Competence Center Hagenberg, Austria
Pilar Rodriguez	Universidad Politécnica de Madrid, Spain
Daniel Rodriguez	University of Alcalá, Spain
Juan Manuel Murillo Rodriguez	University of Extremadura, Spain
Bruno Rossi	Masaryk University, Czech Republic
Rebekah Rousi	University of Vaasa, Finland
Gleison Santos	Universidade Federal do Estado do Rio de Janeiro, Brazil
Kurt Schneider	Leibniz Universität Hannover, Germany
Ezequiel Scott	University of Tartu, Estonia
Outi Sievi-Korte	Tampere University, Finland
Darja Smite	Blekinge Institute of Technology, Sweden
Kari Systä	Tampere University of Technology, Finland
Davide Taibi	Tampere University of Technology, Finland

Marco Torchiano	Politecnico di Torino, Italy
Ville Vakkuri	University of Jyväskylä, Finland
Rini Van Solingen	Delft University of Technology, The Netherlands
Xiaofeng Wang	Free University of Bozen-Bolzano, Italy
Hironori Washizaki	Waseda University, Japan
Dietmar Winkler	Vienna University of Technology, Austria

Contents

Process Management

Refactoring and Technical Department

Software Business and Digital Innovation

Testing and Bug Prediction

Posters

Keynote

The End-Users of Software Systems Deserve Better
Experiences on the Obstacles on Providing Value and How Servitization Can Help

Aapo Koski[✉][ID]

61 NorthPoint Solutions Oy, Tampere, Finland
aapo.koski@61n.fi

Abstract. Failed software projects, delayed deliveries and unsatisfied users are topics that we read on almost daily basis on the media. We're so used to unsuccessful software projects that we do not even seem to expect projects to provide real value to the users. Simultaneously, the societies are more dependent on the software than ever and huge amount of people make their living out of software engineering related jobs. We are investing substantially in the education and training in the software domain and emphasize modern technologies and practices in the education. A consensus exists within the academia and industry on how to effectively develop information systems: with iterative and user-centered methodologies that focus on continuous improvement, i.e. agile methods. Somehow, still, these great ideas and principles do not materialize in practice in software projects; we seem to encounter failing projects and unhappy clients more than succeeding projects with happy end-users. My claim is that we are not doing the best we can, and we know better what we should do when creating and maintaining software intensive systems. The structures that inhibit us from providing the best value possible for the user are often related to bad communication and/or non-disciplined ways of working. Many of the obstacles can be avoided through servitization: better collaboration, more user-centered development methods and iterative approaches.

Keywords: Software development methods · Agile development · Co-operation and collaboration · Servitization

1 Introduction

The software engineering (SE) and the development of information systems is definitively complex and cumbersome. I've worked in the software industry for more than 20 years in various roles, and I've been lucky enough to have worked with great teams and people. I have seen true successes where the created software has been praised by the customers, the projects have been economically feasible and sometimes even on schedule. On the other hand, I've witnessed

© The Author(s), under exclusive license to Springer Nature Switzerland AG 2022
D. Taibi et al. (Eds.): PROFES 2022, LNCS 13709, pp. 3–18, 2022.
https://doi.org/10.1007/978-3-031-21388-5_1

that in the projects same mistakes are repeated; I've seen carelessness and mere disregard to good practices, causing delays, headaches, errors and especially disappointments in the expectations by the customers.

The obscurity around the factors affecting the likelihood of a software project to succeed or fail has bothered me all my career. At some point, encouraged by my friends in academia, I started to write down my thoughts on various aspects on the topic, and tried to look at the software industry from a researcher's point-of-view. One of the outcomes of this endeavour was my PhD thesis [9], but I do feel that much more research is needed.

In this keynote, I revisit the characteristics of a successful software projects by discussing what I've found are the hardest things in the SE projects, elaborate on the possible reasons behind the difficulties, state some lessons learned and finally provide some solutions to many of the problems through the idea of software servitization. In particular, the two fundamental things that will drastically improve the way we create software are simple but hard to implement, namely disciplined ways-of-working and better communication.

2   The Paradox

When discussing with the people working in the SE domain, no matter are they from the academia or industry, the same paradox surfaces: we agree on the solid principles and know very well how to do software engineering. A wide consensus prevails that the only sensible approach to build any larger scale software is through close collaboration with the presumed users in an iterative and incremental way, while paying close attention to the process and improving it gradually. At the same time, a large majority of the software projects struggle to meet the expectations and projects often fail in one way or the other. This paradox has been with us already for decades, as documented by "the software crisis" [13], as well as by the seminal works of Brooks [2] or DeMarco [4], for instance.

This paradoxical behavior may relate to the same phenomenon with doing sports or eating healthy. We all know that one should avoid non-healthy food and exercise regularly, but few of us actually do. Other possible reasons for the existence of this paradox might be the lack of understanding of the true nature of system development processes or lack of effective communication in general.

My claim here is that there is no easy part in the software development effort: everything is crucial, and one cannot leave some aspects of the work abandoned or out of focus. Success is never a coincidence [8], at least when dealing with large software projects, and success, or perhaps just survival, is not about doing most of the things about right, but doing each one of the things exactly right.

Let's look at what we do and the ways we act when doing SE.

3   The Easy Things: What We are Good at

Humans are wired to blame. We are inclined to say that the reason for a failure was in other people or circumstances when things go wrong. This behavior is partially psychological, related to the fundamental attribution bias [16]. We're so good at blaming and finding errors that we don't even notice how often we do it.

Often in software project disasters human error is the first explanation provided, ignoring all the other, like the systemic factors. Human error also feels the most satisfying explanation of the failure: if someone else is to blame for our problems, then there is a nice and easy way to improve by leaving that someone out of the next project, and there's no need to improve anything else.

Unfortunately, what we're naturally good at does not help much at all in improving the success rate of software projects.

4   The Hard Things: What We Should and Can Do Better

On a specific request of a former employer of me, quite some years ago, I started to construct a training course intended to onboard new talent to the software industry. The idea was to shed some light on the true difficulties and challenges one encounters in real-life software projects, aspects of the SE that we thought are never taught in universities. While working on this course, we started to realize that there seems to be no area in the SE domain that we could leave untouched in our "Hardest Things" course.

Most people, even the ones who are not software designers, developers or testers, assume that the job of developing software and information systems is hard. The troubling question that I've had in my mind already for long has been the following: how can it be possible for some individual or a group of novice programmers to write applications (although mostly mobile ones) when many serious large-scale information system projects fail, despite employing all the wisdom, skills, resources and experiences of large software companies?

The root causes why we fail on creating software naturally vary per project, but Fig. 1 gives an overview of the typical factors. The diagram is not, for sure, a comprehensive one, but shows the complexity and the interdependency of the factors affecting the outcomes.

4.1   Defining the Need and Requirements

I've worked a lot in projects that are initiated by public tenders. In public tenders, there's typically a specific phase of the process where the aim to create the requirements of the system or software to be created. Typically, the specification results in a list of requirements, where the number of the requirements for any non-trivial software system is several hundreds and for larger ones, like the EHR system Apotti of Helsinki, which has more than 6000 functional requirements, complemented with hundreds of non-functional requirements related to interfaces, architecture, data migration etc. [1].

The quality of the requirements vary a lot. Some of the requirements are easily understandable, not prone to misinterpretations and describe a feature that is

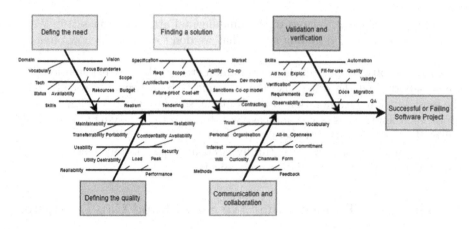

Fig. 1. Diagram on the factors affecting the success of any software project [10].

relatively straightforward to implement. On the other hand, some of the requirements use language that can be understood in totally different ways by different readers and leave large part of the described aspect open for interpretation and assumptions.

Although the good effort is spent on preparing, refining and tuning the requirements with all the best intentions, at least the following key problems remain unsolved:

– All the development efforts require learning between the starting point and the release of the system. What we know of the needs and on the potential solutions is often far from assumptions we have made in the beginning of the process. This problem is further emphasized with long lasting projects.
– The written list of requirements effectively prevents the new solutions that were not considered at the time the requirements were written.
– The requirements do not carry their history with them. This results in lost information as there are no means to understand where the requirement originally stems from and why it was written.
– Tacit knowledge is not transferred with the requirements. Those who have written the requirements have already had in their minds some sort of a solution and the requirements reflect that solution, even to the level of technologies used and architectures employed.
– A list of requirements underrates value of communication. From the requirements, it is next to impossible to derive the needs of the real end-users.
– The requirements are often not prioritized well and thus do not enable value-driven development, a must-have for an agile development process.

All the problems listed above point to the same direction: there needs to be a solid way communicate what the software under development should be able to do. The requirements give an idea, but the comprehensiveness and quality of the requirements is rarely, if ever, verified. As reported in, e.g. [6] and [7], low-quality requirements have been found to be the most common reason for the failure of software projects.

Furthermore, the requirements typically focus a lot on the functionalities of the system and the non-functional aspects, i.e. the quality aspects are overlooked. One improvement to this situation could be to start with the quality needs instead of functional requirements. This setup would give us a better chance to find the right solutions to the true needs. One crucial step towards being able to specify the non-functional requirements would be the usage of minimum viable architecture (MVA, [5]), as an intrinsic part amending the functional and other customer requirements.

The main lessons learned can be summarized as follows:

- Do not make the requirements the binding element in the contract. Instead, consider usage scenarios, user stories, or use cases. The IEEE 830 style of requirements do not make sense and do not communicate the intent well.
- Make sure that the usage scenarios are comprehensive and cover all the important use cases we need. Requirements may be still there, but only in a supporting and refining role for the usage-based specifications.

4.2 Design and Implementation

The challenge with the design and implementation is making sure that the design results in a solution that can be implemented and meets the customer's expectations. This calls for a design that needs to make sense to the customer to enable the customer to give feedback and adjust the design if required. The design must also allow the software to be built within the required time-frame.

In many projects I've worked, I have had the privilege to work with designers with a common characteristic: the designers want to please the customer and find designs that extend the original scope, resulting in feature creep. To increase the probability for the project success, however, the focus needs to be on the critical part of the system and to get it delivered as soon as possible. Any bloated or extended design risks this goal immediately.

Writing the code is not the hardest or most time-consuming part in the software development, which means that putting more manpower to do the coding does not help to achieve set goals sooner [2]. Too often, however, when things start to go wrong, the only solution the management finds is to hire more developers and testers.

The main lessons learned regrading design and implementation are:

- Start from the non-functional aspects and architecture.
- Make sure that the architecture will enable all the usage scenarios.
- While the architecture is designed, proceed with the user-centered discussions related to functional features with light prototypes.

4.3 Validation and Verification

For any software system, the functional quality must be understood in a broad sense and dependent on the specific context the system is used in. Functional quality does not just mean that a certain function is available for certain user to perform some action. High functional quality means that the functionality is for the user to use in all needed situations, informs the user in appropriate way about any issues related to the functionality and in case the functionality is somehow not fully available, offers the user options how to act to achieve wanted results.

To cope with the enormous amount of work involved in testing, the full automation of the release and build test cycles must be enabled from the start of the project. Emphasis needs to be on the automated testing, but the manual testing is also crucial. For example, ad hoc testing cannot be performed using automation and negative testing is done more rigorously with manual testing [15]. The skill-set required from an effective manual tester includes good scripting skills, ability to think critically and outside the box, ability to find out missing parts of information needed and true will to break the system under test.

A good question is that do we need to hire testers or are the people who do the testing, including both running automated tests and ad hoc testing, more like designers and developers with extended and broader skill-sets?

The lessons learned on testing can be summarized as follows:

– One should concentrate on the test automation from day one of the project, making sure that everything that can be automatized, will be automatized.
– One should regard the code-base related to the test automation as an artefact as valuable as the actual code-base and treat it accordingly - by refactoring, testing, maintaining and validating the test code on regular basis.
– One should not treat the testers as a necessary single part of the software construction process but as a crucial and irreplaceable function that inspects, ensures and improves the design and quality of the whole process. Test early and Shift left movements are good examples of this, but require careful planning and changes in the existing processes.
– The testers need to have a real tester attitude: passion to learn how things work and find ways to end in situations where things do not work anymore. The aim should always be to find what makes the system break. If we do not know how to break it, we do not know how to keep it safely running.

4.4 Performance, Reliability and Security

Any software development project faces the performance and reliability issues. Defining and knowing the limits of the performance cannot be overlooked.

Regarding reliability, the main question is, how reliable system needs to be and what is enough? For a critical system an availability of 100% is desirable but in practice this is not achievable by any cost. In addition to the cost of required redundancy mechanisms to enhance the reliability, the increased complexity of the redundant system comes into play. How are we able to say that certain mechanism intended for improving reliability make the system more reliable if we have not tested all possible scenarios?

The same that applies to performance and reliability, applies also to the security issues. What is enough when specifying the security measures and on what basis we can say that a software system is secure? Economic aspects related to the security cannot be overlooked and any security solution employed needs to be fully justified, tested and monitored.

Lessons learned on the performance, reliability and security can be summarized as follows:

- We need to understand what are the true performance and reliability requirements in the operative environment of the software.
- We should not waste time on testing performance and reliability in an environment that does not correspond to the actual operative environment.
- The performance test results must always be thoroughly analysed and resulting in modifications in the system, if required.
- There is no limit on the amount of time and resources that can be spent on the security issues. Therefore for any software system the threat modeling plays crucial role: what are the actual threats and with what budget can we do that. Having not enough money to secure the system does not free us from identifying the threats and risks involved.

4.5   Collaboration and Customer Care

Recently there has been a trend in the public tenders that the customer requires that customer representatives are involved in the software development project and customer's opinions are used to fine tune the direction the project is going [11]. The actual format and practicalities related to the collaboration are typically not described but are left to be negotiated between the customer and the software provider during the project.

While end users can be used as A/B, alpha, and beta testers of new features to refine the usability of the software design, the situation is radically different when developing enterprise software. Services provided by enterprise software are typically business-oriented, which are useless unless they are complete and reliable enough to fulfill their mission. Therefore, care must be taken what the end-users are allowed to test and what we expect from them.

A typical solution for a feedback channel for end-users that use software is to introduce a ticketing system in one form or another. For some contexts, like generic IT problem reporting, the helpdesk systems have proved to work well [12]. However, for many development projects similar ticketing systems are infamous for being ineffective in multiple ways. Firstly, the information provided in the created tickets is typically written by some customer representative, not necessarily the end user, and in the language of the customer, most probably not well understood by the developers trying to handle the problem at hand. Secondly, when the number of the tickets arise, the tickets are lost into the ticketing system, and neither appropriate prioritization nor aggregation and classification is possible without huge amount of time and effort.

In any case, to be successful in the development project some form of user monitoring is a must-have in the agile era to ensure customer satisfaction. Modern customers expect, quite legitimately, that they are utilized as a resource when software is designed, developed and tested and their voice is heard when they want to give feedback based on their points-of-view. There is, however, a great risk involved in the customer collaboration - listening to the customer feedback easily leads to situation where we start to ensure the customer satisfaction by giving in to wishes and nice-to-have improvements, which, in turn, cause feature creep and eventually extra costs and slips in the schedule.

Managing customer expectations is a prerequisite to a satisfied customer. The approach has long been to just meet customer expectations. However, appropriate shaping strategies could be employed and much neglected customer expectation shaping deserves attention, also from the research.

Lessons learned on collaboration and customer care are:

- Start building the trust between the customer and software provider from the very beginning.
- Accept that building trust takes time, and its seeds are planted long before any actual contracts are signed or development processes have started.
- Trust happens only between individuals, not that much on the company or organization level. Find people who get along with the customer representatives and give them enough time to get to know each other.

5   Possible Reasons Behind the Difficulties

Based on the discussion above, the reasons why building software is difficult touches almost every phase and aspect of software engineering. Thus, perhaps there are more fundamental, primary reasons behind them.

5.1   Primary Reason 1: Software Industry is Young

We have been building roads, bridges and houses for thousands of years. Presumably many projects have failed over the centuries, but we have learned and found solid building techniques. The software industry is only about 50 years old. We still have a long way to go before we have the body of experience behind us that the construction and manufacturing industries have.

5.2   Primary Reason 2: Software is Complex

Large part of software projects are custom built. From this it follows that the code is unproven and should be carefully and comprehensively tested. In the software projects, this is totally impractical. Only for some extremely rare projects, like space shuttle software, thorough testing can be performed.

The complexity of software means it is impossible to test every path. By testing we only try to find ways increase the likelihood of the software working in expected ways. Testing also comes at a cost. Every project must carefully asses how critical the software is and how much testing should we do to ensure the software is correct? Often the testing phase is rushed and the software goes out with an unacceptable level of defects.

5.3 Primary Reason 3: We Are Optimists

Given the premise that new projects are custom built, that the project will suffer from scope creep and that the development team is not be world's best, it should come as no surprise that estimating the duration of the project is not easy.

Experience guides us in estimating and the more experience we have the more likely we will be to anticipate the unknowns. Still, too many projects run over because overly optimistic estimates are set by inexperienced people who expect everything to flow smoothly and who make no allowance for the unknowns.

5.4 Primary Reason 4: The Wrong People are Doing This

It has been said that software development is so hard because programming is so easy. It is relatively easy to learn how to write code but there is a huge gap between that and being a great software engineer.

Various studies have shown that the productivity ratio between different developers can be huge and truly effective software teams are a very rare commodity. How do we know that we have the right people for our project? In my experience, only after working with them. And if you find good ones, keep them.

5.5 Primary Reason 5: We Do Not Understand the External Factors

Referring to building bridges and building, the physical structures obey physical laws. Through experience much is known about the physical world and can therefore be modelled and predicted.

Software does not obey physical laws to same extent. Software systems usually must conform to external constraints such as hardware, integration with other systems, government regulations, security, legacy data formats, performance criteria etc.

Understanding and catering for all of these external factors is a challenge and even if we count in the external factors, things happen.

5.6 Primary Reason 6: Lack of User Input

The Standish Group has surveyed companies on their IT projects for decades and the primary factor that has caused the software projects to become challenged has long been "Lack of User Input".

Reasons for this finding may be that the system is being promoted by the management and so the actual users have no buy-in, or that the users are too busy and have "more important" things to do than support the development of the new system.

Without the involvement and input of users the projects are doomed to fail. These persons should be subject matter experts with the authority to make decisions and a commitment to the development project timescales. However, user input is not an easy task, as the next topic explains.

5.7   Primary Reason 7: Customers Cannot Tell Us What They Need

Even with good input from the users no amount of analysis of user requirements can take away an immutable fact that users only think that they know what they want. Only when the users start using the software, they begin to understand what they actually need.

6   Servitization as a Solution

In this article, the servitization refers to the shift from traditional business models to an outcome-based, product as a service model [17]. A subset of the servitization is Software as a service (SaaS), a way of delivering applications over the network, as a service, freeing the customer from complex software and hardware management.

I feel that the rise in the interest to invest into SaaS and cloud solutions in general has resulted partly due to the challenges outlined earlier in this article.

6.1   Enabling Agility

With the servitization model, the roles of the customer and the system provider became clear. Customer pays for received value and provider provides the agreed service. In the picture, there are no third parties whose role are ambivalent and consequently there should not be situations where the responsibilities are not clear.

The servitization in the form of SaaS, with easier release and deployment scheme, enables us to focus on the right kind of MVP (valuable instead of viable) system. Increments and iterations are more easily reachable by the customer and end-users and confidence on the ability to deliver can be built. The SaaS model also supports true communication and true co-operation while making the feedback channels straight and the customer feedback easier to understand. Allowing the system provider to monitor and analyse the user behaviour in multitude of ways is the key [11].

Naturally the organizations procuring software need to ask themselves are they really looking for some company to deliver software or are they more into having a partner to help deliver results that need to be refined, modified and even totally transformed during the project. This calls for crafting the RFQ's accordingly to allow cooperation and building of trust.

6.2   Enabling Acceleration

The reason we need speed in the development processes is related to the ability to adjust, ability to invent and the ability to fail fast and learn. Furthermore, speed enables feedback to be received and to be used for further development and improvements of the services provided. The potential faster innovation of solutions to customer requests and wishes is not only a necessity for delivering high quality software on continuous basis but also a key differentiator when competing for customer projects and when trying to affect the customer expectations. Naturally, to be able to improve competitiveness we need to convince the customer on the advantages of the speed.

One of the biggest threats to the success of the software is time - the longer it takes to make the system delivered to the operative environment, the harder it will be to get the user acceptance to the system. Information systems become old surprisingly fast and the requirements become invalid even faster than that.

To-do: Start discussions with the customer from delivering new features as producing value to their end users. This helps them to understand that the right speed is a joint benefit. Accept also that the speed is not automatically a shared value. For instance, if the end users must be trained every time a change is made, this is clearly an obstacle for frequent releases.

6.3   Enabling Prioritization

A servitization model enables us to work more effectively in an iterative and incremental way and thus also the needs, let them be requirements, feature descriptions or user stories, must be prioritized and handled with disciplined way. In this regard, the following aspects need to be respected:

- Identifying the most valuable features. One of the downsides the continuous interaction with the customers and the end-users has, is that along with wide-band and frequent communication we inevitably also talk about features and qualities that the customer representatives or the end-users think they would like to have, the so called nice-to-have features and qualities. New features are extremely easy to invent and fun to discuss about. However, each feature should be associated with explicit stakeholder value and prioritized accordingly.
- Strict no to feature creep. When the software projects are executed in a close co-operation with the end-users and other customer-side stakeholders, the software provider receives easily a lot of feedback on the functional quality aspects of the system under development. When receiving the feed-back, the system provider should be very careful to avoid the feature creep. However, the responsibility on keeping the scope set by the system owner should not be on the development teams solely but on the customer representatives and end-users. To avoid feature creep, one needs to perform rigorous and visible change management. Learning to say "No" in a nice way to customers and end-users is obligatory.

6.4   Enabling Testability

Providing software as a service enables the software vendor to access the operative environment and observe the users doing their tasks in real-time – if only agreed with the customer.

To-do: Allows the developers to better understand the workflows, bottlenecks and pain-points, provided that the software is appropriately instrumented and monitored.

6.5   Making Availability Concrete

When providing any kind of service to a customer probably the most relevant question is how to measure the availability? Availability is the key in how much the service costs and most typically monthly service fees are directly based on some calculated availability measure defined in the service contract.

With pure servitization model, at least one thing is clear: who to blame when things go wrong. This is a major improvement from the traditional models where a considerable amount of time is potentially wasted when trying to find the party who is responsible for a fix to a problem or who has the knowledge to fix it.

In typical service scenarios, the availability is measured at the server side either polling the service with some predetermined set of requests or by relying on the heartbeat of the services needed by the customer. Both surely give us a measure of availability but leave a large part of the true situation into darkness as these measures do not reflect the experience obtained by a real use of the system.

Thus, if we want to define that the availability of the system is based on the opinion of the end-user now she is using the service, measuring the health or just existence of some process in a server not directly related to the functionalities a user is using, does not make much sense.

To-do: Focus measurements to the only relevant point to measure the availability of a service, the point-of-view of the end-user. If the user feels that she is given the promised service at the promised performance at the time she needs the service, the subjective availability is 100%.

6.6   Uncovering Security

One of the most common reasons not to take SaaS into use has traditionally been the concerns over data security. Security is naturally a key requirement that must be addressed when engineering any modern SaaS applications. Traditional security approaches do not fit with the multitenantcy application model where tenants and their security requirements emerge after the system was first developed. Enabling run-time, adaptable and tenant-oriented application security customization on single service instance is a key challenging security goal in multi-tenant application engineering.

To-do: Create a comprehensive security strategy, and communicate that clearly to the end users. The strategy should define the role of third parties and their potential systems that might be involved, as well as required security measures. Place special focus on following the strategy; it is easy to diverge from the strategy as the system and its environment evolve. Finally introduce scheduled security related processes, such as audits, to ensure that security continuously gets enough attention.

6.7   Enabling Continuous Delivery

The SaaS model emphasizes the needs and encourages us as the service providers to automate and make the operations more continuous. So, the move to continuous integration, deployment and delivery is natural since it is the easiest and preferred way to handle the software delivery process in the SaaS era.

However, while the situation seems to be strongly in favour of the continuous operations, not all customers are necessarily happy with the new continuous delivery model.

Not all customers are a good fit with the continuous mode of operation. The system providers need to carefully investigate to what customers the services provided on continuous delivery model are a good fit and to what kind of customers we do not provide the continuous services.

6.8   Enabling Customer Care

The SaaS model enables the service providers, if agreed appropriately with the customers, to monitor and analyse the end-user behaviour in ways that open a new repertory of opportunities to understand the end-users, to detect and assess their problems and to discern their true needs and priorities. Through smart and thorough analysis of the user information the service providers are enabled to provide the end-users, as customers, appropriate customer care. The key point in providing good customer service is to understand and consequently swiftly respond to the user expectations.

To-do: Managing customer expectations is prerequisite to create a satisfied customer. The approach to achieve this goal has long been to endeavour to meet customer expectations. However, we as practicing system providers many times under-utilize appropriate shaping strategies and therefore much neglected customer expectation shaping deserves close attention from both system providers and academician alike.

6.9   Enabling Continuous Improvement and Learning

I've often heard some manager or decision-maker, while adoring some new principle, practice or even set of tools that enable new ways-of-working, settling up with a blurt: "but that would not work in our project.". And that conclusion is solid – if you do not try it, it won't work.

If it hurts, try to do it more often.

6.10   Enabling Trust

By dictionary, trust is a firm belief in the reliability, truth, or ability of someone or something. What has trust to do with SE and why do we need it?

Simple graph, borrowed from John Cutler [3], tells it well (Fig. 2):

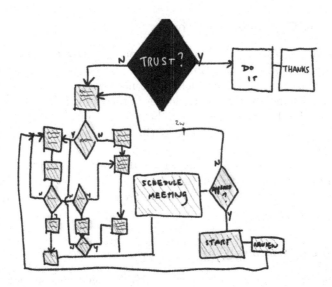

Fig. 2. Workflow of a decision with and without trust [3], courtesy of John Cutler, @cutlerfish, Twitter, 2021.

Without trust, things slow down, decisions became harder to make and all interactions are overshadowed by the thoughts that someone is cheating somehow.

7   Conclusions

By pointing out many of the serious challenges we have with complex systems, one could ask is it plausible to believe that in the near future we see better-constructed software projects and streamlined delivery processes which lead to deployment of systems in time and on budget? Based on my experience, it is hard to believe that such changes happen soon, but even so, the first step in the path of improving the current situation is to admit that there are serious problems. What this article aims for is to point out the fact that we should not continue as-is, but start thinking software delivery as a service and servitize the whole process.

As a take-away, and in addition to the aspects related to the idea of more service-oriented ways of working, there are two points that affect a lot how well software projects succeed:

1. There cannot be too much focus on the details: the more agile we want to be, the more disciplined the ways of working need to be and there is no room for unfounded optimism or lightly made assumptions. We need to be almost paranoid on checking that everything goes well and as planned, make sure we measure the right things in a right way and that everyone understands what is required. To be able to provide an efficient and effective development process, constant focus and continuous improvement are needed. It is not enough to do the tasks casually, everything needs to be done as well as we can and unfortunately, due to the complexity of software, even that might not be enough.

2. A good understanding on the domain and the users is a must. There is not much sense in developing anything if we are not sure that what is specified and developed has a chance to fulfill the needs it is developed for. If any assumptions are made, those need to be documented and discussed thoroughly, and revisited to verify that the they still hold. The first step to better communication is to admit that communication just often does not work very well. After that, we can start finding solutions that work better in a particular situation and for particular set of people.

Principles that enable the servitization of software systems include strong, wide-band and continuous customer collaboration. This calls for a new kind of customer-vendor relationship, something that has its roots far deeper than gained with typical customer relationships. In that relationship both parties, the software provider as well as the customer, must step away from looking at and playing with the requirements and set the needs and disciplined processes first. The processes involved must be a supporting and helping structure, not one that restricts or limits the design and development. Finding someone to blame when something goes is not essential, we're in this together. In other words, processes need to be seen as a living thing; they evolve over time as needs evolve and if the process does not work for some part, it should be changed.

What I have covered in this article is not all new, similar messages has been communicated in numerous articles, blog posts and books over the years. In his famous article from 1970 [14], Winston Royce already stated that the linear development method, later labeled as the waterfall method, won't work for any larger-scale information system project. But somehow and for some reason, we have been a bit deaf to all the valuable advice around us. Or, alternatively, we know what do to but in practice we do not know exactly how to accomplish what should be done. For these reasons, and since no-one was listening, the messages needs to be repeated.

Many of the points I've emphasized in the article seem trivial and something that should be considered self-evident on any software or information system project. But if anyone who has been involved with any larger scale information system can claim that all of these points were handled appropriately, without room for improvement, and still the project failed, it is hard to state what else we can do. Maybe complex software and information systems just cannot be developed effectively?

This keynote's message is that we are not doing the best we can, and we certainly know better what we should do when specifying and creating software and information systems. The end users of the systems deserve better.

> Toutes choses sont dites déjà; mais comme personne nécoute, il faut toujours recommencer.

> André Gideă/Traité du Narcisse

References

1. Apotti: Hankkeesta yritykseksi. https://www.apotti.fi/apotti/apotti-yrityksena/apotti-hankkeen-vaiheet/
2. Brooks Jr., F.P.: The Mythical Man-Month, Anniversary edn. (1995)
3. Cutler, J.: Trust? (2021). https://twitter.com/johncutlefish/status/1370298106319753219/photo/1
4. DeMarco, T., Lister, T.: Peopleware: Productive Projects and Teams. Addison-Wesley, Boston (2013)
5. Erder, M., Pureur, P.: Continuous Architecture: Sustainable Architecture in an agile and Cloud-Centric World. Morgan Kaufmann, Burlington (2015)
6. Hofmann, H.F., Lehner, F.: Requirements engineering as a success factor in software projects. IEEE Softw. 18(4), 58–66 (2001)
7. Jones, C.: Applied Software Measurement. McGraw-Hill Education, New York (2008)
8. Kahneman, D., Egan, P.: Thinking, Fast and Slow. Farrar, Straus and Giroux, New York (2011)
9. Koski, A.: On the Provisioning of Mission Critical Information Systems Based on Public Tenders. Universtity of Helsinki, Helsinki (2019)
10. Koski, A.: Software Engineering Methods and Tools. Seinäjoki University of Applied Sciences, Seinäjoki (2022, Unpublished)
11. Koski, A., Kuusinen, K., Suonsyrjä, S., Mikkonen, T.: Implementing continuous customer care: first-hand experiences from an industrial setting. In: 2016 42th Euromicro Conference on Software Engineering and Advanced Applications (SEAA), pp. 78–85. IEEE (2016)
12. Li, S.H., Wu, C.C., Yen, D.C., Lee, M.C.: Improving the efficiency of IT helpdesk service by six sigma management methodology (DMAIC) - a case study of C company. Prod. Plann. Control 22(7), 612–627 (2011)
13. Randell, B.: The 1968/69 Nato software engineering reports. Hist. Softw. Eng. 37 (1996)
14. Royce, W.W.: Managing the development of large software systems Dr. Winston W. Rovce introduction. In: IEEE Wescon, pp. 328–338 (1970)
15. Stobie, K.: Too much automation or not enough? When to automate testing. In: Pacific Northwest Software Quality Conference (2009)
16. Tetlock, P.E., Levi, A.: Attribution bias: on the inconclusiveness of the cognition-motivation debate. J. Exp. Soc. Psychol. 18(1), 68–88 (1982)
17. Vandermerwe, S., Rada, J.: Servitization of business: adding value by adding services. Eur. Manag. J. 6(4), 314–324 (1988)

Cloud and AI

Managing the Root Causes of "Internal API Hell": An Experience Report

Guillermo Cabrera-Vives[1,5], Zheng Li[2(✉)], Austen Rainer[2],
Dionysis Athanasopoulos[2], Diego Rodríguez-Mancini[3],
and Francisco Förster[4]

[1] Universidad de Concepción, 4070409 Concepción, Chile
`guillecabrera@inf.udec.cl`
[2] Queen's University Belfast, Belfast BT9 5AF, UK
`{zheng.li,A.Rainer,D.Athanasopoulos}@qub.ac.uk`
[3] Data Observatory Foundation, 7941169 Santiago, Chile
`diego.rodriguez@dataobservatory.net`
[4] Universidad de Chile, 8320000 Santiago, Chile
[5] Millennium Institute of Astrophysics (MAS), Santiago, Chile

Abstract. When growing the software infrastructure for a large-scale scientific project (namely ALeRCE, Automatic Learning for the Rapid Classification of Events), we observed an "internal API hell" phenomenon in which numerous and various API issues coexist and are inextricably interwoven with each other. Driven by this observation, we conducted a set of investigations to help both understand and deal with this complicated and frustrating situation. Through individual interviews and group discussions, our investigation reveals two root causes of the "internal API hell" in ALeRCE, namely (1) an internal API explosion and (2) an increased "churn" of development teams. Given the nature of the system and the software project, each root cause is inherent and unavoidable. To demonstrate our ongoing work on tackling that "hell", we discuss five API issues and their corresponding solutions, i.e., (1) using a multi-view catalog to help discover suitable APIs, (2) using a publish-subscribe channel to assist API versioning management and negotiation, (3) improving the quality of API adoption through example-driven delivery, (4) using operation serialisation to facilitate API development debugging and migration, and (5) enhancing the usability of long and sophisticated machine learning APIs by employing a graphical user interface for API instantiation. We also briefly consider the threats to validity of our project-specific study. On the other hand, we argue that the root causes and issues are likely to recur for other similar systems and projects. Thus, we urge collaborative efforts on addressing this emerging type of "hell" in software development.

Keywords: API · Dependency hell · Experience report · Internal API hell · Large-scale software system

© The Author(s), under exclusive license to Springer Nature Switzerland AG 2022
D. Taibi et al. (Eds.): PROFES 2022, LNCS 13709, pp. 21–36, 2022.
https://doi.org/10.1007/978-3-031-21388-5_2

1   Introduction

Modern software engineering principles advise organising a system into subsystems and making them communicate via reliable interfaces, and accordingly, application programming interfaces (APIs) have become an integral part of software projects [14]. When building up the software infrastructure for a large-scale scientific project (namely ALeRCE [10], Automatic Learning for the Rapid Classification of Events), we also develop single-responsibility APIs to expose highly cohesive and reusable components including machine learning models.

However, this API-oriented development strategy not only speeds up the growth of ALeRCE but in turn also leads to an "internal API hell" within the scope of the project. We define "internal API hell" as a situation where a large and varied number of API issues coexist and are inextricably interwoven with each other. These issues go beyond "dependency hell" [3] and cause various problems, e.g., for API debugging, maintenance, migration, discovery, delivery. Furthermore, addressing one issue can aggravate another. The consequences are that multiple issues need addressing concurrently, and that any single issue may require a sequence of incremental solutions over time.

To help comprehensively understand this situation, we conducted a project-specific investigation driven by a predefined research question *RQ1: What are the root causes of the "internal API hell" in ALeRCE?* To help address or at least relieve this situation, we investigated another research question *RQ2: How do we manage and mitigate an "internal API hell"?* This paper reports our investigations and especially our ongoing efforts on tackling that "hell". Considering that such a complicated and frustrating situation may commonly exist across large-scale software projects, our work makes a twofold contribution:

- For researchers, our experience of the emergence of "internal API hell" reveals new challenges and research opportunities other than that for the well-known "dependency hell".
- For practitioners, our developed solutions can be reused in, or adapted to, the other large-scale software projects for dealing with similar API issues.

In fact, we expect to use this experience report to raise the whole community's awareness of the "internal API hell" phenomenon, and we urge collaborative efforts of both practitioners and researchers to address such a "hell".

The remainder of this paper is organised as follows. Section 2 briefly explains different software situations in which the joyless term "hell" has been used. Section 3 introduces our ALeRCE project, and Sect. 4 explains the API-focused strategy and the "internal API hell" phenomenon in ALeRCE. Section 5 demonstrates five typical API issues and specifies how we have addressed them. The threats to validity of this project-specific work is discussed in Sect. 6. Section 7 draws conclusions and highlights our future work plans.

2   Background and Related Work

The usage of the joyless term "hell" in describing complicated situations of software development can be traced back to the "DLL hell" phenomenon endemic to the Microsoft Windows product in the mid-to-late 1990s [6]. To make software systems' development and run-time both efficient, Microsoft invented the dynamic-link library (DLL) technology to facilitate sharing common code/features among different Windows applications. In addition to the normal benefits (e.g., improved code reusability) from static programming libraries, the DLL technology further avoids loading multiple copies of a same functionality implementation into memory, which is particularly meaningful for large software ecosystems (e.g., the Windows software ecosystem).

Unfortunately, along with the development of DLLs (together with Windows updates), and especially after installing and uninstalling numerous applications on Windows, developers and users frequently encountered troubles such as incompatible DLL versions, missing DLLs, and increasingly accumulated legacy DLL copies. Among these troubles, the conflicts between DLL versions soon became a nightmare and were complained to be a "hell", because the update of DLLs would leave obsolete entries in the library registry on the machine. As a result, the installation of a new application that also installs and registers a new-version DLL will break the existing applications that rely on the DLL's old version. For the same reason, reinstalling the existing applications will make the new application fail, unless the old-version DLL is *forward compatible* [7].

After observing similar phenomena beyond the scope of Microsoft products, researchers and practitioners generalised the term "DLL hell" to "dependency hell" [6], in order to continuously indicate the significance of, and meanwhile imply the pervasiveness of, this problem. For example, dependency-related errors have been identified as the most common error type for C++ projects (up to 52.68%) and Java projects (up to 64.71%) at Google [21]. By distinguishing between *declared dependency* at design time and *actual dependency* at run-time, Fan et al. [9] categorised dependency problems into two groups, namely missing dependencies and redundant dependencies. A missing dependency will lead to failures due to an undeclared dependency that is actually needed, while a redundant dependency will result in performance degradation due to a useless dependency declaration. It should be noted that there can be cascade problems, because a dependency may also require its own dependencies (direct vs. transitive dependencies [5]).

Deinum et al. [5] further distinguished a "versioning hell" phenomenon from the "dependency hell": When a single application has multiple dependencies who need different versions of a same library, there will be additional challenges and troubles. In the extreme case, it will be impossible to reference multiple versions simultaneously, if the library vendor does not change the assembly filenames when growing product versions [13]. More generally, since versioning software applications and libraries has become a de facto practice with respect to the incremental development fashion [24], people also consider "versioning hell" or "version hell" as the frustrating situation of version conflicts and incompatibility between different libraries or applications. In addition to making troubles at the end-user side (e.g., the incompatible versions between an application and its underlying operating system [2]), such a "hell" seems to make software developers suffer more extensively in the era of DevOps. For example, a toolchain for CI/CD could be broken due to a new version of any tool at anytime [8, 15, 19].

Recall that APIs are widely employed to speed up development, conceal back-end complexity and heterogeneity, and reduce project overhead in the current software industry [12, 28, 29]. Given more and more focuses that are switched to APIs, it is claimed that the previous "hell" of DLL and dependency has been replaced by "API version hell" [25]. Besides the aforementioned dependency and version issues [27], people particularly noticed "API hell" as a result from the intricate connections among the explosively increasing number of APIs [14, 26]. It has been identified that the huge number of dependencies and interactions between relevant APIs will result in bloated runtimes, and will limit the ability of incremental software delivery [25].

The current discussions about "API hell" are generally related to the consumption of third-party APIs. More importantly, few of them focus on how to manage and mitigate such a "hell". In contrast, after observing various and numerous internal API issues within a large-scale system, we aim to manage their root causes and mitigate this "internal API hell". Note that in addition to the different controllability over some common problems (e.g., versioning), a distinctive feature of our work is: We argue the "hell" to be the diverse and interwoven issues along the whole life cycle of internal APIs, rather than the intricate connections between the involved third-party APIs, within a single software project.

3   The ALeRCE Project

Detecting and classifying astronomical events is a crucial part of space research that can not only help us understand the universe but may also save our planet and ourselves. Detection and classification requires multiple observatories across the planet and the information across these observatories needs managing. The Automatic Learning for the Rapid Classification of Events (ALeRCE) project (http://alerce.science/) was established to facilitate the detection and classification of astronomical events.

ALeRCE was initially funded in 2017 by the Millennium Institute for Astrophysics and the Center for Mathematical Modeling at the University of Chile. Since then it has grown into a large-scale scientific project in collaboration with researchers from over a dozen Chilean and international universities and organisations, including two strategic institutes, Data Observatory and University of Concepción, who joined ALeRCE in 2020 and 2022 respectively. The project's professional members include 37 researchers and engineers, with expertise mainly in Astronomy, Machine Learning, and Software Engineering. ALeRCE also offers thesis and internship opportunities to undergraduate and postgraduate students (currently 29 students). Currently, almost 70 people work on different components of ALeRCE.

ALeRCE has obtained outstanding achievements. For example, by implementing the Supernova Hunter service based on neural network classifiers, ALeRCE has reported 13017 supernovae candidates (11.8 candidates per day on average), of which 1635 are confirmed spectroscopically. Using Google Analytics, we estimate the ALeRCE service has supported more than 7000 external users from 125 countries. ALeRCE continues to grow rapidly, e.g., it is regularly developing new machine learning tools for subsequent deployment in production. At this moment, there are four active development teams, including one project kernel team and three feature teams.

4   ALeRCE's APIs and the "Internal API Hell" Phenomenon

To maximise development consistency, ALeRCE [10] employs an API-oriented strategy. The RESTful APIs are built on the Python web frameworks, Flask and Django. Some internal APIs are integrated as libraries to enable project-specific scaffolding. For legacy reasons, developed APIs are currently deployed in a hybrid and multi-cloud environment. ALeRCE intends to remain with its current cloud provider to further unify API deployment.

ALeRCE followed the single-responsibility principle [17] to wrap up highly cohesive and reusable components into APIs. At the early stage of the project, this API-focused strategy helped ALeRCE obtain multiple benefits, ranging from enhanced development efficiency to reduced management overhead. But with its rapid growth, ALeRCE encountered an increasing number of API-related issues within the project. The issues were interwoven, were related to both API provisioning and consumption, went beyond the known "dependency hell" [3] and caused various problems, e.g., to API development, debugging, delivery, maintenance, discovery, usage, etc.

To facilitate our discussion about this frustrating situation, we named this phenomenon as "internal API hell" in ALeRCE. To help understand this situation, we investigated the following research question:

RQ1: What are the root causes of the "internal API hell" in ALeRCE?

By conducting a wide range of individual interviews and by organising group discussions with team leaders, our investigation revealed two main root causes. First, the growth of ALeRCE leads to an internal API explosion. Except for a few APIs publicly available as ALeRCE services (http://alerce.science/services/), most APIs are developed for *internal* use only. For example, ALeRCE designed and created new APIs for newly included machine learning models, for data cleaning and preprocessing, and for accessing the data produced by those new models. Second, there is increasing "churn" in the development teams, arising from growth and frequent changes over the years to members of these development teams. Also, given the intensive collaborations with universities, ALeRCE increasingly hosts short-term student interns; these interns appear more likely to introduce disruptive technologies and hard-to-maintain codebases to the new APIs or new API versions. As with Brook's [4] *essential difficulties* of software, these root causes are inherent within the nature of the ALeRCE system and project.

5   The Typical Issues and How We Address Them

Given the identified root causes of our "internal API hell", a natural follow-up research question we investigated is:

RQ2: How do we manage and mitigate an "internal API hell"?

Since those two root causes are non-removable due to the nature of the ALeRCE project (see more discussions in Sect. 6), we decided to mitigate their negative influences, by addressing or relieving their resulting issues. For the purpose of conciseness and representativeness, this paper highlights five issues to exemplify the "internal API hell" in ALeRCE, as illustrated in Fig. 1 and listed below.

- *Issue #1:* More APIs, especially the internal APIs, are increasingly developed, and thus discovering suitable APIs (for further project development) becomes more difficult and time consuming.
- *Issue #2:* Some development teams seem to release new versions of APIs "impetuously", which triggers frequent cascade updates and troubleshooting.

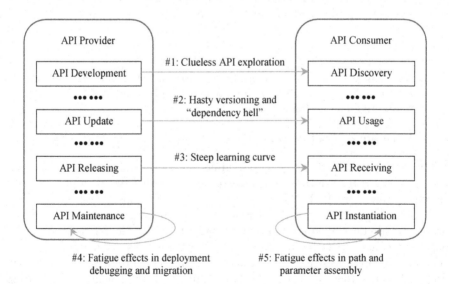

Fig. 1. Typical issues in the phenomenon of "internal API hell" in the ALeRCE project. (The red-colour texts describe the API issues; and each arrow indicates the corresponding issue "resulting from" one activity and "having impact on" another activity). (Color figure online)

- *Issue #3:* Newly developed APIs may have a steep learning curve, which also often results in a high communication overhead between API providers and consumers.
- *Issue #4:* Information on deployed APIs is incomplete or missing, which complicates API deployment debugging and migration, and eventually results in fatigue effects in API maintenance.
- *Issue #5:* Since different machine learning APIs have similar paths and multiple model-related parameters, it is confusing and tedious to assemble a particular machine learning API instance, by accurately locating the API and appropriately assigning values to the corresponding parameters.

These five issues reflect some of the major problems we faced and demonstrate the characteristics of the "internal API hell" (i.e. diverse and interwoven issues). For example, Issue #5 in API instantiation is also related to Issue #3 for improving the usability of sophisticated APIs; and Issue #2 in API update is also related to Issue #4 when providers need to clean up the environment of (e.g., retire) previously deployed APIs. In the following subsections, we report our workaround on each of these issues.

5.1 Solution to Issue #1: Using a Multi-view Catalog to Help Discover Suitable APIs

As mentioned previously, there is an increasing trend in API accumulation in our ALeRCE project. As a result, exploring and identifying reusable APIs become increasingly inconvenient for the new API teams and especially for the new developers. To relieve this situation, we firstly employed OpenAPI Specification (OAS)[1] to facilitate API recognition. Then, we developed a multi-view catalog to cross-index and organise the APIs. This paper does not repeat the well-known features and benefits of OAS, while mainly explaining our API organisation. In fact, using a hierarchical organisation to supplement OAS is a practical strategy for API discovery and management, e.g., [18]. We further argue to enable locating APIs via various entrances with respect to different concerns, i.e. using a multi-view API catalog.

The development of our multi-view API catalog is originally inspired by the "4+1" architectural view model [11]. Given different aspects of a software project, it is impossible to describe the software system and its components from a single angle only. Accordingly, we need different ways to categorise software components (APIs in this case) within different contexts. In ALeRCE, we classified APIs respectively according to their (1) usage scopes[2], (2) relevance to particular ALeRCE products, (3) corresponding steps in the processing pipeline[3], and (4) deployment environments, as illustrated in Fig. 2.

---

[1] https://swagger.io/specification/.

[2] There can be APIs used both internally and externally, e.g., https://api.alerce. online/ztf/v1 for accessing Alerts with the corrected magnitudes, object statistics and object data.

[3] The ALeRCE pipeline: http://alerce.science/alerce-pipeline/.

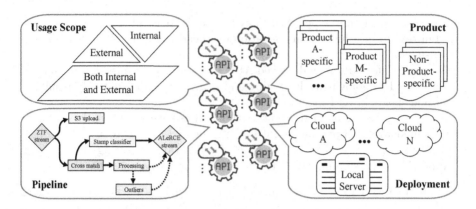

Fig. 2. The multi-view catalog for API discovery.

In practice, we categorise an API by conveniently attaching multiple labels to it, instead of registering the API in multiple places. Moreover, although inspired by the "4+1" model, we do not stick to fixed architectural views for categorising APIs. For example, our Usage Scope view may not reflect the software architecture of ALeRCE; and unlike the "4+1" model that requires depicting library dependencies in the Development View, we let the API teams figure out their dependencies via a publish-subscribe channel, as explained in the following subsection.

5.2   Solution to Issue #2: Using a Publish-Subscribe Channel to Assist API Versioning Management and Negotiation

Despite Roy Fielding's argument against using versions for APIs, versioning APIs has been a common practice in the software industry [20]. We also advocate versioning APIs, as enabling side-by-side versions has helped us implement blue-green deployment and asynchronous update of ALeRCE components. In particular, our versioning strategy is to include the version number as part of the URL path, for two reasons. First, this strategy is widely adopted in industry (e.g., by large companies like Twitter, Facebook and Google). Second, this is the most straightforward strategy for novice developers (e.g., student interns) to understand and employ.

However, the simplicity and flexibility of this URL versioning strategy seem to have encouraged ALeRCE's API developers to claim breaking changes and/or retire previous versions "rashly". To reduce the cost incurred by API changes [3], we introduced a negotiation mechanism to API versioning by setting up a publish-subscribe channel between the API providers and consumers, as illustrated in Fig. 3.

In practice, each API team publishes its developed APIs to, and subscribes its directly-consumed APIs from, the aforementioned multi-view catalog. As such, the open information about newly released updates will naturally flow to the

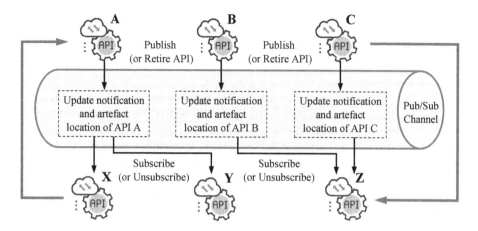

Fig. 3. The publish-subscribe channel for API versioning negotiation. (One API can be consumed by multiple APIs, for example, API A is consumed by both API X and API Y. One API can consume multiple APIs, for example, API Z consumes API B and API C together. Naturally, an API team can be both a publisher with respect to its developed APIs and a subscriber with respect to its consumed APIs).

relevant API consumers. In addition, plans about breaking changes of an API are also shared with the API's subscribers. When such a plan is communicated, the subscribers can negotiate with the publisher on whether or not the potential update deserves a major version.

The publish-subscribe channel essentially bridges the communication gap between the API developers and API users [14], at least internally to ALeRCE. Benefiting from this communication and negotiation mechanism, we saw that some tentative breaking changes eventually became minor updates, e.g., by supplementing new key-value pairs without modifying the existing parameters. When a major version is truly unavoidable, the negotiation will become a natural reminder for the API stakeholders to prepare/update examples in advance for delivering and receiving the new API version (explained in Sect. 5.3). This "extra workload" encourages the API providers to be more prudent about the backward compatibility and versioning in the future changes.

5.3 Solution to Issue #3: Using Example-Driven Delivery to Improve the Quality of API Adoption

Similar to the steep learning curve when employing third-party APIs [26], we also observed a frequent bottleneck in the adoption of internal APIs by other independent development teams at ALeRCE. Although our communication channel enables collaborative troubleshooting, and even supports adaptive changes after new APIs (or new versions) are received, the post-release troubleshooting and changes significantly increase the coordination overhead among the relevant teams. Since we did not obtain clear improvement by reinforcing the responsibility of API providers (e.g., addressing the documentation debt [22] in our previous workflow), we switched our focus to the consumer side to investigate how to improve the quality of development teams "receiving" new or changed APIs.

In switching our focus, we then realise that, previously, we *overstressed* the development independence and loose coupling between the individual API teams. As a result, the downstream API teams generally waited for and adapted to the upstream APIs, by viewing the upstream APIs as fixed artifacts. We (again) changed our development strategy by viewing API consumers as business domain experts. In principle, we wanted to involve the real-world context of use cases in the API development at the earliest opportunity. In practice, every API team is asked to figure out a minimal working example with each of its adjacent downstream counterparts, and use the examples to drive API development and to facilitate API delivery.

Compared with the methodology of example-driven development [1], our practice further emphasises the example-driven delivery and adoption of APIs, by including not only the source code but also the context stories, sample datasets and serialised deployment operations (explained in Sect. 5.4). It should be noted that the minimal examples are required to be always executable, to reduce the implicit descriptions or assumptions of their contexts. Since the API to be developed may not be functional or not even exist at the beginning, it can be replaced with a naive function or another API as a placeholder in the initial examples. For instance, we directly extracted our existing forecasting programme into a minimal example, for developing alternative Forecast APIs[4]. After that, the initial examples can gradually be updated whenever the developing API is testable.

Since such minimal working examples can often be merged into production programs directly, the API consumers can conveniently bypass the learning curve, and we have seen notable improvement of development in the ALeRCE project, for example: (1) the delivery and receiving of executable examples have largely reduced mutual complaints between partner API teams; and (2) the callback examples of async API usage have significantly benefited new developers who are not familiar with asynchronous programming.

5.4   Solution to Issue #4: Using Operation Serialisation to Facilitate API Deployment Debugging and Migration

We followed Infrastructure as Code (IaC) to implement continuous configuration automation, however, we still faced challenges in API deployment debugging and migration. On the one hand, it is unrealistic to have fully-fledged IaC during the

---

[4] A Forecast API uses a particular machine learning technique to make predictions on future supernova light curve brightness. Light curve is the variation of brightness of a star as time goes by. The prediction here shows how the light curve would behave in the future based on the existing measurements.

growth stages of the system, especially when changing physical infrastructure. For example, the scripts for utilising on-premises resources will not be reusable on the cloud platform, not to mention the learning curve of switching the infrastructural environment.

On the other hand, IaC is essentially a modeling approach to abstracting the objects and configuration processes of physical infrastructures, while abstract models inevitably sacrifice the complete reflection of the reality [16]. Thus, the implementation of IaC may lose some important environmental information. For example, when working on APIs deployed on the Amazon cloud, our engineers used to experience delays and even troubles in isolating API-specific EC2 instances from the whole system, especially when the engineers were not the original operators (e.g., the student operators who graduated and left the project).

The lesson we learned is that we cannot expect to replace human actions completely with IaC implementations. In fact, even if a "one click" automation pipeline is realised, the automated configurations would still require three manual steps at least, as specified by the comments within the pseudocode of IaC execution (see Algorithm 1).

Algorithm 1. Execution of IaC Artifacts

   Input: IaC artifacts.
   Output: IaC execution results.
1: ▷ Go to the place where the IaC artifacts will be executed.
2: *Locate(*IaC artifacts*)*;
3: ▷ Trigger the execution of the predefined IaC artifacts.
4: **for each** artifact unit **in** IaC artifacts **do**
5:     *Execute(*artifact unit*)*;
6: **end for**
7: ▷ Verify the results from executing the IaC artifacts.
8: *Return(*results*)*;

Consequently, we have tried to serialise the manual operations for APIs into cheat-sheet style documents.[5] Particularly, the verification steps and the contexts of some operations are captured by using screenshots in the document. Although preparing these documents can be time consuming, the later updates of available documents are generally convenient, fast, and of beneficial to the subsequent maintenance of the APIs.

Our practice also shows that the earlier operation serialisation can significantly facilitate the later IaC implementation in a divide-and-conquer fashion. In fact, before obtaining the ideal "one click" automation pipeline, a single document naturally acts as a one stop manual that indexes and organises the separate

---

[5] The snippets of some serialised operations are exemplified at https://doi.org/10.5281/zenodo.5914452.

IaC artifacts. Benefiting from the always up-to-date document, our engineers confirm that the straightforward operation serialisation is more efficient than the previous log tracing, for retrieving the environmental information of APIs.

5.5 Solution to Issue #5: Using a Graphical User Interface to Facilitate Path and Parameter Assembly for API Instantiation

As a machine learning-intensive project, ALeRCE is equipped with an increasing bunch of machine learning models, and we also employ APIs to hide technical details and to facilitate integrating machine learning solutions into functional features [28]. Given the same context of machine learning models in ALeRCE (e.g., classifying the astronomical events), different machine learning APIs have many similar and even overlapped paths and parameters (e.g., the learning activities, the number of hidden neurons, the size of training samples, etc.). Based on different expertise and experience, different development teams have used inconsistent mechanisms (i.e. path parameters vs. query parameters), naming conventions and abbreviations for those API paths and parameters, as shown in Fig. 4.

Consequently, assembling paths and parameters for API instantiation becomes a tedious task for the API consumers. It should be noted that the legacy machine learning APIs have not got chance to implement the example-driven delivery yet (see Sect. 5.3). In addition to the fatigue effects, we saw frequent typos or mismatches between parameters and their values when the consumer teams tried to instantiate sophisticated APIs to use. Since some of the machine learning APIs have already been used in various ALeRCE services, after conducting cost-benefit analyses, we are afraid that it is not worth refactoring those APIs for the terminology consistency issue. Besides, the potential refactoring will not reduce the length of the machine learning APIs, i.e. the model-specific parameters will not change.

To fix the problem here, we developed a graphical user interface (GUI) particularly to facilitate instantiating machine learning APIs. Firstly, we summarise and standardise the names of our machine learning models' activities and parameters. Then, we use predefined UI controls to make adaptation between the stan-

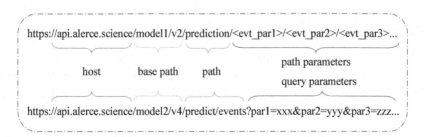

Fig. 4. The inconsistent mechanisms, naming conventions and abbreviations of API paths and parameters in ALeRCE.

dardised names and the original API elements. In detail, a cascading drop-down list is given to help users select wanted machine learning techniques and activities (e.g., classification or prediction), which decides the corresponding API paths. Once the selection is done, a set of text fields with labels will appear on the GUI, which indicates the needed parameters of the selected machine learning API (to be instantiated). Thus, users can conveniently input values (or variables) to those text fields according to the explanations in the labels, without worrying about the sequence and names of the parameters in the original API design. At last, the GUI can generate a well-assembled API for users to copy and paste into their programmes.

Although this is a recent improvement in ALeRCE, we have received extensive feedback that the GUI has made the legacy machine learning APIs more easy-to-use than in the past. It is also worth highlighting that, by playing an adapter role in the API instantiation, the GUI minimises the cost for enhancing the usability of those machine learning APIs.

6   Threats to Validity

The unique characteristics of ALeRCE raise questions about the wider applicability of our experiences. We consider two "threats" here. First, our experience may not apply to mature API services with relatively fixed functionalities and run-time environments, for which there is little, or less, need for API migration and discovery. Second, our experiences are mainly extracted from and for APIs *internal* to a system.

On the other hand, we believe that the two root causes we identified are likely to occur for large-scale software services of the type we describe here. For example, API explosion has become a common challenge in building artificial intelligence systems [23]. The popular microservices architecture may also result in (internal) API explosions, because a large system can involve thousands of microservices (e.g., Uber uses over 4000 microservices[6]), and one microservice can expose multiple APIs. Meanwhile, the decentralised development approach that is fashionable in the current software ecosystems would increase the cost of changes [3] and deepen the communication gap between API developers and consumers [14]. Consequently, "internal API hell" might be a common phenomenon across large-scale software services, even though different practitioners may experience, and focus on, contrasting subsets of the issues we've discussed here.

Furthermore, when it comes to the situation when external stakeholders (i.e. either API providers or consumers) are involved in the "API hell", we argue that our lessons and solutions may still be adapted and employed. Take *API versioning negotiation via a Publish-Subscribe channel* as an example, it could be impractical to build up a negotiation channel beyond the project scope. Similarly, for *example-driven delivery and receiving of APIs*, it is barely possible to work out minimal examples immediately with external API consumers. In this

---

[6] https://eng.uber.com/optimizing-observability/.

case, we have kept organising workshops[7] to communicate with our collaboration partners, in order to collect feedback and real-world contexts at least for the later development and updates of external APIs.

7 Conclusions and Future Work

As part of the development and maintenance of the ALeRCE system we encountered a phenomenon we called, "internal API hell". Compared with the existing usage of "hell" in describing the intricate connections between third-party APIs and libraries, we particularly emphasise the diverse and interwoven issues along the whole life cycle of internal APIs within a single software project. Based on our project-specific investigations, we report two root causes, demonstrate five API issues, and explain how we sought to address these issues. We hypothesise that the root causes and issues are likely to recur for other, similar systems and projects, with those systems also encountering an "internal API hell". Correspondingly, we urge collaborative efforts from both practitioners and researchers on addressing this emerging type of "hell" in software development.

We recognise that we report an experience report and have therefore suggested directions in which further, more formal research, might extend. An obvious direction for further research is to undertake a more formal analyses of the root causes and issues we've identified, e.g., to conduct a case study or interview study within the ALeRCE project or with other similar projects. A complementary approach would be to widen this investigation, e.g., through a survey of multiple systems and projects. A third approach is to conduct a systematic review of published work in this area. Finally, given the diversity of the interwoven API issues, it is likely to be impossible to come up with a one-size-fits-all solution. Therefore, we speculate (but have not yet investigated) there will be the need for a systematic suite of methods to deal with this situation. This suggests a further direction for research.

Acknowledgement. We want to thank the ALeRCE Engineering Team for their hard work and effort on developing and maintaining all the services, Alberto Moya, Javier Arredondo, Esteban Reyes, Ignacio Reyes, Camilo Valenzuela, Ernesto Castillo, Daniela Ruz and Diego Mellis. ALeRCE and this paper would not exist without them.

We acknowledge support from CONICYT/ANID through the grants FONDECYT Initiation Nž 11191130 (G.C.V.) and Nž 11180905 (Z.L.); BASAL Center of Mathematical Modelling (AFB-170001, ACE210010 and FB210005) and FONDECYT Regular Nž 1200710 (F.F). This work has been partially funded by ANID -Millennium Science Initiative Program - ICN12_009 awarded to the Millennium Institute of Astrophysics (MAS). Powered@NLHPC: This research was partially supported by the supercomputing infrastructure of the NLHPC (ECM-02). This work has been possible thanks to the use of AWS credits managed by the NLHPC.

---

[7] http://workshops.alerce.online/lsst-enabling-science-2020-broker-workshop/.

References

1. Adzic, G.: Specification by Example: How Successful Teams Deliver the Right Software. Manning Publications, Shelter Island (2011)
2. Bajaj, G.: PowerPoint version hell, 04 March 2009. https://www.indezine.com/products/powerpoint/ppversionhell.html. Accessed 3 Aug 2022
3. Bogart, C., Kästner, C., Herbsleb, J., Thung, F.: How to break an API: cost negotiation and community values in three software ecosystems. In: Proceedings of the 24th ACM SIGSOFT International Symposium on Foundations of Software Engineering (FSE 2016), pp. 109–120. ACM Press, Seattle, 13–18 November 2016
4. Brooks, F.P., Bullet, N.S.: Essence and accidents of software engineering. IEEE Comput. **20**(4), 10–19 (1987)
5. Deinum, M., Serneels, K., Yates, C., Ladd, S., Vanfleteren, C.: Configuring a spring development environment. In: Pro Spring MVC: With Web Flow, chap. 1, pp. 1–23. Apress, Berkeley (2012)
6. Dick, S., Volmar, D.: DLL Hell: Software dependencies, failure, and the maintenance of Microsoft Windows. IEEE Ann. Hist. Comput. **40**(4), 28–51 (2018)
7. Eisenbach, S., Sadler, C., Jurisic, V.: Feeling the way through DLL Hell. In: Proceedings of the First International Workshop on Unanticipated Software Evolution (USE 2002) Co-located with ECOOP 2002, Malaga, Spain, pp. 1–11, 11 June 2002
8. Esch-Laurent, P.: Versioning hell, 19 February 2021. https://paul.af/versioning-hell. Accessed 3 Aug 2022
9. Fan, G., Wang, C., Wu, R., Xiao, X., Shi, Q., Zhang, C.: Escaping dependency hell: finding build dependency errors with the unified dependency graph. In: Proceedings of the 29th ACM SIGSOFT International Symposium on Software Testing and Analysis (ISSTA 2020), pp. 463–474. ACM Press, Los Angeles, 18–22 July 2020
10. Förster, F., Cabrera-Vives, G., Castillo-Navarrete, E., et al.: The automatic learning for the rapid classification of events ALeRCE alert broker. Astronom. J. **161**(5) (2021). Article no. 242
11. Garcia, J., Kouroshfar, E., Ghorbani, N., Malek, S.: Forecasting architectural decay from evolutionary history. IEEE Trans. Softw. Eng. (2022). Early access
12. Ginsbach, P., Remmelg, T., Steuwer, M., Bodin, B., Dubach, C., O'Boyle, M.F.P.: Automatic matching of legacy code to heterogeneous APIs: an idiomatic approach. In: Proceedings of the 23rd International Conference on Architectural Support for Programming Languages and Operating Systems (ASPLOS 2018), pp. 139–153. ACM Press, Williamsburg, 24–28 March 2018
13. Goodyear, J.: Welcome to multiple version hell, 26 March 2004. https://visualstudiomagazine.com/articles/2004/05/01/welcome-to-multiple-version-hell.aspx. Accessed 3 Aug 2022
14. Lamothe, M., Shang, W.: When APIs are intentionally bypassed: an exploratory study of API workarounds. In: Proceedings of the 42nd IEEE/ACM International Conference on Software Engineering (ICSE 2020), pp. 912–924. ACM Press, Seoul, 23–29 May 2020
15. Markan, Z.: Android versioning hell in the CI-land, 6 May 2014. https://markan.me/android-versioning-hell/. Accessed 3 Aug 2022
16. Mellor, S., Clark, A., Futagami, T.: Model-driven development - guest editor's introduction. IEEE Softw. **20**(5), 14–18 (2003)
17. Nesteruk, D.: Design Patterns in .NET Core 3, 2nd edn. APress (2021)
18. Nevatech: API discovery and description (2022). https://nevatech.com/api-management/api-discovery-description. Accessed 3 Aug 2022

19. Ofosu-Amaah, K.: Version hell revisited, 01 July 2020. https://koranteng.blogspot.com/2020/07/version-hell-revisited.html. Accessed 3 Aug 2022

20. Sabir, F., Gueheneuc, Y.G., Palma, F., Moha, N., Rasool, G., Akhtar, H.: A mixed-method approach to recommend corrections and correct REST antipatterns. IEEE Trans. Softw. Eng. (2022). Early access

21. Seo, H., Sadowski, C., Elbaum, S., Aftandilian, E., Bowdidge, R.: Programmers' build errors: a case study (at Google). In: Proceedings of the 36th International Conference on Software Engineering (ICSE 2014), pp. 724–734. ACM Press, Hyderabad, 31 May–7 June 2014

22. Shmerlin, Y., Hadar, I., Kliger, D., Makabee, H.: To document or not to document? An exploratory study on developers' motivation to document code. In: Persson, A., Stirna, J. (eds.) CAiSE 2015. LNBIP, vol. 215, pp. 100–106. Springer, Cham (2015). https://doi.org/10.1007/978-3-319-19243-7_10

23. Stoica, I.: Systems and ML at RISELab, 13 July 2020. https://www.usenix.org/system/files/hotcloud20_hotstorage20_slides_stoica.pdf. Keynote speech at the 12th USENIX Workshop on Hot Topics in Cloud Computing (HotCloud 2020)

24. Tanabe, Y., Aotani, T., Masuhara, H.: A context-oriented programming approach to dependency hell. In: Proceedings of the 10th International Workshop on Context-Oriented Programming: Advanced Modularity for Run-time Composition (COP 2018), pp. 8–14. ACM Press, Amsterdam, 16 July 2018

25. Thomas, D.: The API field of dreams - too much stuff! It's time to reduce and simplify APIs! J. Object Technol. 5(6), 23–27 (2006)

26. VanSlyke, T.: API hell: the rise of application frameworks and the fall of sanity (2021). http://www.teejayvanslyke.com/api-hell-the-rise-of-application-frameworks-and-the-fall-of-sanity.html. Accessed 3 Aug 2022

27. de Villamil, F.: Always broken, inconsistent and non versioned, welcome to API hell, 22 August 2014. https://thoughts.t37.net/always-broken-inconsistent-and-non-versioned-welcome-to-api-hell-a26103b31081. Accessed on 3 Aug 2022

28. Wan, C., Liu, S., Hoffmann, H., Maire, M., Lu, S.: Are machine learning cloud APIs used correctly? In: Proceedings of the 43rd IEEE/ACM International Conference on Software Engineering (ICSE 2021), pp. 125–137. IEEE Press, Madrid, Spain, 22–30 May 2021

29. Zibran, M.F., Eishita, F.Z., Roy, C.K.: Useful, but usable? Factors affecting the usability of APIs. In: Proceedings of the 18th Working Conference on Reverse Engineering (WCRE 2011), pp. 151–155. IEEE Computer Society, Limerick, 17–20 October 2011

Requirements for Anomaly Detection Techniques for Microservices

Monika Steidl[1(✉)] ⓘ, Marko Gattringer[2] ⓘ, Michael Felderer[1] ⓘ,
Rudolf Ramler[3] ⓘ, and Mostafa Shahriari[3] ⓘ

[1] University of Innsbruck, 6020 Innsbruck, Austria
{Monika.Steidl,Michael.Felderer}@uibk.ac.at
[2] Gepardec, Europaplatz 4 - Eingang C, 4020 Linz, Austria
Marko.Gattringer@gepardec.com
[3] Software Competence Center Hagenberg GmbH, 4232 Hagenberg am Mühlkreis,
Austria
{Rudolf.Ramler,Mostafa.Shahriari}@scch.at

Abstract. Version configurations of third-party software are essential
to ensure a reliable and executable microservice architecture. Although
these minor version configurations seem straightforward as the functionality does not need to be adapted, unexpected behaviour emerges due to
the complex infrastructure and many dependencies. Anomaly detection
techniques determine these unexpected behaviour changes during runtime. However, the requirements anomaly detection algorithms need to
fulfil are unexplored. Thus, this case study collects experiences from practitioners and monitoring datasets from a well-known benchmark system
(Train Ticket) to identify five requirements - namely: (1) early detectability, (2) reliability, (3) risk analysis, (4) adaptability, and (5) root causes
analysis. In this work, we additionally evaluate three anomaly detection
techniques on their practical applicability with the help of these identified requirements and extracted monitoring data.

Keywords: Anomaly detection · Monitoring data · Logs · Traces ·
KPI · Microservice · Practical requirements · Root cause analysis

1 Introduction

Frequent software updates are necessary to improve and enhance the software's
functionality. One specific case is the update to new versions of third-party
libraries and frameworks to minimise the accumulation of maintenance debt
resulting from deferred updates [26]. However, such updates' impact on the
system's behaviour is often unpredictable due to complex dependencies, and
incompatible legacy configurations [5]. Version configurations in a microservice
architecture are even more challenging because microservices show characteristics of distributed systems. An empirical case study conducted in 2021 with

This work was supported by the Austrian Research Promotion Agency (FFG) in the
frame of the project ConTest [888127] and the COMET competence center SCCH
[865891].

© The Author(s), under exclusive license to Springer Nature Switzerland AG 2022
D. Taibi et al. (Eds.): PROFES 2022, LNCS 13709, pp. 37–52, 2022.
https://doi.org/10.1007/978-3-031-21388-5_3

five service systems in the commercial banking sector identified that the third most common reason for anomalies is incompatible software versions (11%) [39]. In addition, compatibility issues may not reveal themselves when compiling the software but result in failures, negative side-effects or deviations from expectations at runtime, which are called anomalies [11]. Developers often need to manually inspect heterogeneous monitoring and log data to identify the reason for such failures when performing root cause analysis [31]. One extensively researched solution to reduce the effort involved in this cumbersome work is the application of automated anomaly detection techniques. Although research puts a high emphasis on anomaly detection techniques, research is missing a set of requirements an anomaly detection technique should fulfil to be used in an industrial setting. This paper defines requirements based on IEEE [11], where requirements describe (1) capabilities required by the user to achieve an objective, (2) which must be met by the system and (3) are documented accordingly. In addition, anomalies due to version configurations are not used to evaluate the proposed anomaly detection techniques. Section 1.1 identifies these research gaps, which are the main contributions of this paper.

1.1 Related Work

Several different anomaly detection techniques have been proposed in the related work based on microservices' logs, traces, and Key Performance Indicator (KPI) data. These approaches were quantitatively evaluated using case-specific datasets or comparisons to other techniques as depicted in Table 1. However, anomaly detection techniques provide no consensus on what requirements they need to fulfil. The existing related work does not include research that qualitatively evaluates anomaly detection techniques based on such requirements.

Table 1. Summary of related work where authors quantitatively evaluate the efficiency of their anomaly detection technique for microservices

Input of anomaly detection techniques	Specific use case evaluation	Result comparison with other techniques
Logs	[12, 13, 21]	[10](monolithic systems)
Traces	[1, 2, 7, 14, 20, 22, 23, 35, 40]	[17]
KPIs	[4, 8, 18, 19, 24, 29, 37]	[3, 16, 30, 34, 38]

In addition, related work does not consider anomalies specifically based on version configurations. Artificial faults are mostly injected into the datasets for evaluating the applied anomaly detection techniques. Zhou et al. [41] identified several anomalies in microservices via an industrial survey. They did not focus on version configurations but on improper parameter settings and asynchronous interaction faults [40, 41]. Other non-version configuration-dependent faults are multi-instance faults [40], packet loss [4, 8, 18, 19, 35], configuration faults [35, 40], and delay and delete faults [2]. Memory leaks [4, 8, 18, 19, 24, 37], CPU hog

[3, 18, 19, 37, 38], CPU stress [4, 8, 37, 38], decreased network bandwidth [8], and increased network latency [4, 8, 38] are also among the injected anomalies.

The **contribution** of this paper is twofold. Firstly, we conduct a case study to identify anomalous behaviour in a company's context and to summarize and collect a dataset with anomalies occurring due to version configurations from a benchmark system. Based on this information, we derive requirements that anomaly detection techniques for microservices need to fulfil in practice. Secondly, we use these requirements to evaluate three anomaly detection technologies described in the literature and for which the implementations have been made available as open-source projects.

The remainder of this paper is organised as follows. Section 2 illustrates the research questions and applied methodology. The next Sect. 3 focuses on the anomalies in a software company, followed by the collection of monitoring data with a benchmark system in Sect. 4. Section 5 specifies the requirements and Sect. 6 evaluates anomaly detection algorithms with these requirements. The paper discusses threats to validity in Sect. 7, and the conclusions in Sect. 8.

2 Methodology

Several techniques exist to detect anomalies in logs, traces and KPI data. However, a consensus is missing on what requirements anomaly detection techniques should fulfil to be applicable in practice. Thus, the main objective of this paper is to collect information about anomalies due to version configurations and base respective requirements on these anomalies. The following research questions further refine our main research objective:

RQ1 What are potential anomalies due to version configurations?
RQ2 What are the requirements regarding anomaly detection techniques in practice?
RQ3 Do open-source anomaly detection techniques for microservices fulfil the identified requirements?

2.1 Methods

This work is based on a descriptive case study following the guidelines of Runeson and Höst [27, 28]. Firstly, we defined the objectives, prepared and executed the data collection procedure, and analysed and reported the data. This type of study not only allows us to take the complex and dynamic characteristics of the case company into consideration but also gathers evidence in a planned and consistent way [28].

Figure 1 depicts the steps necessary to answer the three research questions. This work's first and second steps describe the proposed data collection procedures using data triangulation to answer RQ1. Thus, the first step collects experienced anomalies in a software company via first-degree observations proposed by Lethbridge [15] (3). We used the focus group approach with two experienced software developers that lasted 60 min to gain an overview of the company's

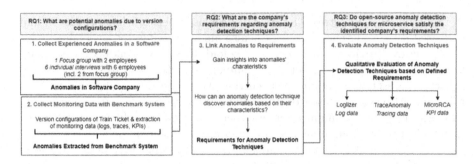

Fig. 1. Study design for this paper's case study.

domain and experienced anomalies. We collected the statements via careful note-taking. We further refined the statements via six individual open-ended interviews with company employees with five to twelve years of experience in software development, DevOps and automation and configuration. The second step cross-checks and extends the accumulated statements via collecting a dataset based on an established benchmark system (4)[1]. The test suite to automatically trigger Application Programming Interface (API) requests is created with Postman to ensure that the same execution always provides reproducible results. To further automate the data retrieval process, a respective Python script collects and transforms logs, traces, and KPIs. In the third step, we answer RQ2 by applying the requirements engineering principles established by Pohl and Rupp [25] and Ebert [6]. Firstly, we analysed the collected anomalies to provide insights into the anomalies' characteristics (3.1 and 4.1). Secondly, we focused on how techniques discover these characteristics, and we reported the requirements based on these insights (5). However, we kept them general enough that other unanticipated anomalies could also get detected. In addition, we established further requirements by looking at anomaly detection techniques explained in the related work section. Then, the fourth step answers RQ3 by evaluating three selected open-source anomaly detection techniques using the collected monitoring data from the second step to evaluate whether the proposed anomaly detection techniques can fulfil the established requirements.

2.2 Selected Anomaly Detection Techniques

Soldani et al. [31] identified anomaly and respective root cause detection techniques for microservice-based software. The techniques under evaluation were selected based on two requirements. Firstly, the case company requires easy adaptability to new data sets and cannot guarantee that these are labelled. Thus, we selected techniques based on unsupervised learning algorithms for evaluation in this work. Secondly, we selected techniques that have been made available as open-source because we follow a white-box view by inspecting the system's behaviour and adaptability with the generated input.

---

[1] Train Tickets API documentation: https://github.com/FudanSELab/train-ticket/wiki/Service-Guide-and-API-Reference, accessed 07.07.2022.

In total, we found three techniques that fulfil these requirements. We selected **Loglizer**[2] [9,10,43], although it is for monolithic systems since Soldani et al. [31] did not provide an open-source technique for microservices with logs as input. Loglizer extracts static parts of the logs, counts its occurrences within a session or time frame and applies several Artificial Intelligence (AI) models for anomaly detection. This work focuses on the provided Principal Component Analysis (PCA) model. **TraceAnomaly**[3] [17] uses traces and extracts the request-response times for each service call path and trains a deep Bayesian neural network with posterior flow. **MicroRCA**[4] [38] uses traces and KPI data and represents request-response times via a graph and KPIs as vectors for each service, where the BIRCH algorithm clusters the vectors to identify anomalies.

3 Experienced Anomalies in a Software Company

The case study is based on the industrial context of a software company that offers to develop, integrate, and maintain custom Java and Jakarta EE (JEE) solutions and cloud technologies, such as Kubernetes, Rancher, and OpenShift. As the company also provides operations and support services, they identified the need that their customers frequently require software updates due to deprecated third-party software and library versions. The company runs a suite of regression tests to ensure the quality of the customers' software after such updates and performs continuous automated system monitoring.

The remainder of this and the following section answers RQ1 by reporting the company's experience concerning frequently encountered anomalies, followed by a summary of identified anomalies when executing version configurations in the benchmark system. These gathered anomalies form the basis to answer RQ2 by identifying the requirements an anomaly detection technique needs to fulfil.

3.1 Anomalies in Software Company

This section describes five typical instances of anomalies that have been experienced by the case company in practice; see also Table 2.

A1 - After an update of the JBoss version part of a complex software system, the response time diminished continuously. After some time, requests were not handled anymore due to an out-of-memory exception. The identified root cause was that the session instances did not terminate and were not deleted, resulting in increasing memory allocation and worsening runtime behaviour.

A2 - Another encountered anomaly was that a library version changed its threat handling so that jobs were not executed in parallel but consecutively. The company became aware of this anomaly due to deteriorating system performance.

---

[2] https://github.com/logpai/loglizer, accessed 25.07.2022.

[3] https://github.com/NetManAIOps/TraceAnomaly, accessed 25.07.2022.

[4] https://github.com/elastisys/MicroRCA, accessed 25.07.2022.

A3 - A different JBoss and Hibernate configuration caused performance issues when writing a large amount of data to the database. The identified root cause was that a new version of Hibernate changed the DirtyCheck strategy.

A4 - After upgrading JSF and JBoss, Context and Dependency Injection (CDI) issues occurred. The JBoss injection configuration was incorrect, resulting in an undiscovered instance and, as an issue directly observable by end users, links referring from one to the next page did not work anymore.

A5 - Due to a new JBoss version's new garbage collection strategy, performance deteriorated, and out-of-memory issues occurred.

Table 2. Summary of company's experienced anomalies

ID	Anomaly	Root cause	Effect
A1	JBoss updates with Session Bean	Session instances did not terminate/were not deleted	Out-of-memory
A2	Threat handling	Threats are handled consecutively versus parallel	Slower execution, change in metrics
A3	Dirty checks	Database handling of dirty checks	Slow write access
A4	CDI injection	Wrong configuration setting	Required instance not found, broken links
A5	Garbage collection	Different garbage collection strategy	Performance deterioration, out-of-memory

4   Collect Monitoring Data with Benchmark System

This work uses a popular and well-established microservice benchmark system (Train Ticket [42][5]) to identify anomalies, establish requirements, and evaluate the anomaly detection techniques. It is a train booking system based on 41 microservices. It has been built using Java as the main programming language and Spring, Node.js, Python, WebGo, and it includes Mongo and MySql as databases.

This benchmark system allows for repeatably, transparently, and automatically extracting the necessary monitoring data throughout different version configuration combinations. The benchmark system also reduces the complexity that a real-world system usually contains. Thus, we better identify anomalies and more precisely investigate and validate the requirements as effects. Knowledge about the characteristics of anomalies is essential to evaluate if the techniques can find an anomaly with specific attributes. In addition, monitoring data, especially logs, contain personal data for which restrictions such as strict privacy protection rules apply. Therefore, as an additional bonus, this work contributes to an openly available dataset regarding anomalies in version updates in microservices that allows others to perform their research with this dataset. The case company's OpenShift cluster has been used to host the benchmark system under typical conditions, such as realistic monitoring settings and other software running in parallel that generates additional load.

---

[5] https://github.com/FudanSELab/train-ticket, accessed 20.07.2022.

4.1 Anomalies Extracted from Benchmark System

This section summarizes the anomalies extracted from ten version configurations of Train Ticket's microservices, also depicted in Table 3. For further information on the version configurations and resulting datasets, see [32].

B1 - Anomalies may produce unexpected values. The issue is that an anticipated positive value became negative, depicted in 1.1 in line 2:

Listing 1.1. B1: different value in line 2 than anticipated

```
1   2022−07−11  20:09:09.559   INFO 1 ──── [io−12031−exec−7]  order.service.OrderServiceImpl
          : [Order  Create]  Success.
2   2022−07−11  20:09:09.559   INFO 1 ──── [io−12031−exec−7]  order.service.OrderServiceImpl
          : [Order  Create]  Price: −50.0
```

B2 - Intermittent time deterioration also occurred during the reservation request. These types of failures were not explicitly stated in the logs, but are moderately visible in the response times of each microservice.

B3 - A database value cannot be loaded or updated because the request does not pass on the user authorization correctly. Thus, the logs indicate this anomaly with an exception and a 403 error.

B4 - Functional behaviour changes due to the database version did not allow the user to log in. When logging in unsuccessfully, the logs do not store the token, whereas a successful login request stores the token in the logs (see 1.2)

Listing 1.2. B4: successful login where generated token was documented

```
1   2022−07−13  19:45:23.861    INFO 1 ──── [io−12340−exec−8]  auth.service.impl.
          TokenServiceImpl        :  eyJhbGciOiJIUzI1NiJ9.
      eyJzdWIiOiJmZHN1X21pY3Jvc2VydmljZSIsInJvbGVsIjpbIlJPTEVfVVNFUiJdLCJpZCI6Ij
2   RkMmE0NmM3LTcxY2ItNGNmMS1iNWJiLWI2ODQwNmQ5ZGE2ZiIsImlhdCI6MTY1NzcxMjcyMywiZXhwIjoxNjU3NzE2MzIzfQ
      .9JaOnHz8i7pADuy5y1MJRYGhwVVP46GXpttMC2IxogsUSER TOKEN
```

Moreover, Table 4 shows seemingly anomalous behaviour concerning version configurations, but it is not version specific.

No-B1 - Logging in requires longer than in previous test runs with the same version configuration. Thus, the issue is not version specific but depends on the node's workload.

No-B2 - Train Ticket does not display some requested data. The issue is not version specific because the database never had to store these values.

In summary, the collection of anomalies shows that anomalies heavily hinge on unknown and restricted implementation changes of the third-party software providers. Based on these changes and resulting dependencies, the behaviour of the software changes unpredictably. In addition, the anomalies do not follow a consistent pattern and affect the root cause and the behaviour unpredictably and individually.

5 Requirements for Anomaly Detection Techniques

Based on the gathered knowledge of Sects. 3.1 and 4.1, this section answers RQ2 by identifying requirements that an anomaly detection technique needs to fulfil. These requirements need to be defined broadly enough to encompass all related

Table 3. Summary of identified anomalies with Train Ticket

ID	Anomaly	Version	Configured microservice	Root cause	Effect
B1	Unexpected value	Spring Boot Starter Data MongoDB 1.5.22	ts-order-service	Unknown	Positive value became negative
B2	Request not handled in time	Spring Boot MongoDB Driver 3.0.4	ts-order-service	Server did not handle request in time	504 Gateway Time-out
B3	Forbidden Access	MongoDB 4.4.15	ts-auth-service	Authorization not correctly handled	User is not updated as required
B4	Unexpected function behaviour	MongoDB 4.4.15	ts-auth-service	Unknown	Login failure

Table 4. Anomalous behaviour not resulting from a version configuration

ID	Anomaly	Version	Service	Root cause	Effect
No-B1	Performance deterioration with login	Spring Boot Starter Data MongoDB 2.0.0	ts-order-service	Higher workload in node	Performance deteriorates when logging in via UI
No-B2	Values not loaded from database	MongoDB 4.2.2	ts-order-service	Values not available in database	Missing values

instances of anomalies, and they must be comprehensive enough to provide a foundation to evaluate anomaly detection techniques.

1. *Early detectability*
   Anomalies may not be apparent at the system start but evolve during runtime. Identified examples in the previous section are deteriorating performance, such as **A1** and **A5**. Thus, anomaly detection techniques must recognise slight hints before the main issue occurs.
2. *Reliability*
   Anomalies vary in their appearances and symptoms. Thus, a seemingly anomalous behaviour may not be an anomaly. Although performance changes are the most common identified effect (**A1**, **A5**, and **B2**), it does not necessarily indicate an anomaly that requires attention [31]. For example, external reasons, such as the node experiencing an increased workload, can also cause performance deterioration, as described by **No-B1**. In addition, anomalies usually occur rarely, as identified with the determined anomaly **B2**. Thus, it is essential that the anomaly detection technique works reliably and does not provide too many false positive alarms to avoid desensitizing developers.

3. *Risk Analysis*

Anomalies vary in their impact on the whole software and their associated risk level. For example, a slower execution of tasks as in **A2** due to threat handling may decrease the performance but does not interrupt system execution or falsify results as in **A1**, **A4** or **B4**, where users cannot log in anymore. Thus, the anomaly detection technique must help to identify how critical the effect of an anomaly is for the software's functionality.

4. *Adaptability*

As indicated in the previous section, anomaly detection techniques must be adaptable to different data with many different anomalies. In addition, monitoring the software under test should require reasonable effort and expenses.

- *Unlabelled data:* In a real-life application, labelled datasets are impractical as it is challenging to pinpoint unknown anomalies in a vast dataset. Moreover, new anomalies may occur unforeseeably.
- *Adaption of anomaly detection technique:* The anomaly detection technique should work with heterogeneous systems. Extensive configuration effort should not be necessary. Hence, a clear guideline for usage, limitations, and potential advantages is necessary.
- *Adaption of monitored software:* The monitored software should not require specific monitoring instruments because the customers decide on the monitoring set-up. Thus, extracting and transforming data from integrated monitoring instruments should be possible.

5. *Root Cause Analysis*

Anomalies may have the same symptoms, such as in example **A1** and **A5** with an out-of-memory anomaly, but they differ in their root cause. Thus, it is not only sufficient to identify an anomaly, but the technique should also provide information on the root cause or provide information on where to start the troubleshooting.

6   Evaluation of Anomaly Detection Techniques

This section answers RQ3, i.e., whether the selected anomaly detection techniques Loglizer, TraceAnomaly, and MicroRCA satisfy the identified requirements (see 5) by providing a qualitative analysis.

Table 5. Fulfilment of requirements by the selected anomaly detection techniques

Anomaly detection technique	(1) Early detectability	(2) Reliability	(3) Risk analysis	(4) Adaptability	(5) Root cause analysis
Loglizer	~	✗	✗	~	✗
Trace anomaly	~	~	✗	~	✓
MicroRCA	~	~	~	~	✓

1. *Early detectability*

   For performance-related issues, early detectability occasionally prevents more serious anomalies because, as in example **A1** and **A5**, performance deterioration is an early sign of out-of-memory issues. Other identified anomalies indicate the worst case immediately and do not exacerbate over time. Thus, the further argumentation focuses on performance-related anomalies.

   Loglizer does not consider the execution time and, ultimately, the response time of each microservice when the logs are grouped based on session identifiers. Thus, it does not identify deterioration in performance.

   TraceAnomaly considers the response-request times of a microservice which can identify deteriorating performance. However, it ignores that the execution time of different methods within one microservice may vary heavily. For example, Train Ticket's methods within one specific microservice require between 23 ms and 206 ms.

   MicroRCA also does not consider the varying time due to different methods in a microservice. In addition, it depends on MicroRCA's parameter setting if it identifies slowly deteriorating response times. For example, if the last five minutes are considered, and performance only slightly decreases, all activities may fall within the same cluster.

2. *Reliability*

   Loglizer achieved a high accuracy with our ten datasets. However, the calculated precision and recall are low. Thus, we assume that Loglizer is inapplicable when identifying several types of anomalies because it only counts the static part's occurrences. Consequently, Loglizer does not detect changes in variables, as in **B1** or any response time-related issues. In addition, the low precision and recall may result from the PCAs dimension reduction that overlooks or parses a critical event [10].

   TraceAnomaly works well with differences in the microservice execution sequence as, for example, in **A4** not being able to call the required instance or in **B3** not being able to add new order details. In addition, TraceAnomaly also identifies deviations in the response time as an anomaly, although it does not identify changes in a value as described in **A4**.

   MicroRCA assumes that a service's anomalies may influence other services running on the same node. However, this should not be the case with a correctly initialized OpenShift platform. OpenShift configures how many resources it distributes to each service via resource quotas and limit ranges. Thus, this assumption is suitable for identifying configuration errors, but they may not depend on version updates.

3. *Risk Analysis*

   Loglizer does not consider the degree of severity of an anomaly. The PCA analysis identifies that an anomaly occurred. However, the results cannot be reliably interpreted concerning where it happened because the PCA model works as black-box.

   TraceAnomaly uses the mean and standard deviation of the extracted response times to identify if a response time deviates from the normal behaviour. By modifying the implementation of the detection technique, one can use this value to identify the severity of the deviation. However, these measurements do not signify how much this anomaly influences the software. **MicroRCA** calculates the most likely faulty service by using monitoring data of container and node resource utilization. This measurement just indicates the likelihood of the microservice is the root cause but does not consider how severely the anomaly influences the whole system.

4. *Adaptability*

All three anomaly detection techniques require some additional documentation. It is challenging to adapt and understand the source code within a reasonable time if the code is not sufficiently documented and only an example implementation is provided.

– *Unlabelled data:* All three algorithms provide unsupervised learning algorithms that do not require labelled data.

– *Adaption of anomaly detection technique:* **Loglizer** provides several different AI models and allows an easy exchange.

  TraceAnomaly requires excessive hyperparameter tuning, which is always essential for Deep Learning algorithms. However, to adapt TraceAnomaly, we required documentation to understand the reasons for the provided parameter setting in their example.

  MicroRCA requires perfectly tuned hyperparameters for the clustering of response times. The technique identifies up to four clusters when applying the predefined clustering to one extracted dataset, although no apparent anomalies are present in the dataset. One of the reasons for this unexpected behaviour is that the response times deviate more than in the authors' test dataset. According to Liu et al. [17], it is ubiquitous for functions in microservices to have highly distributed response times without any anomaly. However, fewer clusters may exist when choosing a too high threshold, but these clusters are too inaccurate and may miss anomalies.

– *Adaption of monitored software:* For all three anomaly detection techniques, we were able to extract the required data from the available monitoring instruments. However, transforming the data to the demanded format requires extensive knowledge about the dataset itself, while essential documentation regarding the necessary data representation is missing.

  Loglizer provides a Logparser[6] to extract static and variable content of the log, which does only need moderate adaption specifying the structure of the log. We had to implement a function adapted to our input dataset for the event count vector, counting the number of occurrences within a time or session.

  TraceAnomaly required a moderate amount of time to transform the traces into a call sequence of traces with the associated execution time. The challenge is to have the same order of the call sequence in every single file. Thus, all potential call sequences need to be known in advance.

  MicroRCA assumes that the monitored system uses Istio to store the traces. However, Train Ticket uses Jaeger, which collects all the necessary information in a different structure. Thus essential preprocessing was required.

---

[6] https://github.com/logpai/logparser, accessed 08.08.2022.

5. *Root Cause Analysis*

Loglizer does not identify the root cause because the PCA algorithm does not provide interpretable results but only identifies whether an anomaly exists or not. If **TraceAnomaly** identifies an anomaly, it assumes that the longest call path with diverging performance (due to time propagation) is the failed microservice. **MicroRCA** can identify a ranked list of identified root causes based on a computed anomaly score.

7 Threats to Validity

This section discusses the four possible main threats to validity according to Wohlin et al. [36] as well as how we mitigated these threats.

We avoid a lack of **internal validity** by not only collecting experiences from the company and monitoring data via a benchmark system. With this benchmark system, we only change one independent variable at a time and keep the other variables constant. So it is possible to observe if and how a change in one specific version configuration of one component affects the software's behaviour. We control and reduce confounding and intervening variables to a minimum by extracting monitoring data with a fixed and automated setting.

External validity may suffer because we collected the dataset via a benchmark system in a semi-lab setting. Thus, the automated tests sent only a request at a time to the benchmark system. Therefore, generalizability is limited in multi-usage scenarios, as it may happen with real-world applications. Thus, we carefully considered the company's experiences to counteract this threat.

To minimize **construct validity**, we mitigated the mono-method bias by identifying anomalies via experience reports and experimenting with a benchmark system. In addition, we further mitigated the mono-operation bias by choosing a specific microservice for version configurations that are frequently used in different requests and have the most functionalities. In addition, we selected various versions based on their documentation, such as MongoDB's documentation[7].

Regarding **conclusion validity**, Wagstaff [33] indicated that performance measurement scores, such as accuracy, precision, recall or the loss function, are abstract and remove problem-specific details. Thus, we qualitatively discuss anomaly-specific details to counteract this threat. It allows us to conclude if a technique identifies a type of anomaly, even if the specific anomaly is unknown.

8 Conclusion

Version configuration due to deprecated third-party software and library versions are essential to minimize the accumulation of maintenance debt. Although these minor version configurations seem straightforward because the functionality does not need to be adapted, we still observed unexpected behaviour, also called anomalies, in this case study.

---

[7] https://www.mongodb.com/docs/drivers/java/sync/current/upgrade/.

The identified anomalies and respective causes and effects are heterogeneous, and anomaly detection techniques cannot identify them easily. Thus, we collected different anomalies from an industrial setting as well as from a benchmark system to derive five requirements an anomaly detection technique needs to fulfil: (1) *Early detectability*, such as performance deterioration should be detected before severe faults occur, and (2) *reliability*, indicating that the anomaly detection technique should reliably identify anomalies although they do not follow a consistent pattern, affect the root cause and behaviour unpredictably and individually or may not indicate an anomaly at all. In addition, (3) *risk analysis* should be possible to estimate how much an anomaly influences the system, and (4) *adaptability* is necessary due to different unlabelled data sets, monitoring systems, and monitored software. Finally, (5) *root cause analysis* should speed up the troubleshooting process by providing at least an idea of where the anomaly may have happened.

Using these requirements as basis, we evaluated three anomaly detection techniques based on logs (**Loglizer**), traces (**TraceAnomaly**) and KPI data (**MicroRCA**). Our evaluation showed that none of the three techniques thoroughly fulfilled the stated requirements.

Thus, for future work, we propose to adapt and enhance the proposed anomaly detection techniques to improve (1) early detectability and (2) reliability by considering more types of anomalies in advance. This is critical because anomalies are heterogeneous, and the root causes or symptoms are unpredictable. (3) Risk analysis requires further research on identifying the anomaly's influence on the observed system. One of the possible directions is to provide a risk calculation based on the identified root cause. In addition, (4) establishing preprocessing guidelines which are not only adapted to a specific dataset may improve adaptability.

All identified microservice techniques use logs, traces, and KPI data to identify anomalies. Further research may also look into new techniques that use other inputs, such as Heapdump, power usage, memory, and request-response data.

References

1. Bogatinovski, J., Nedelkoski, S., Cardoso, J., Kao, O.: Self-supervised anomaly detection from distributed traces. In: Proceedings - 2020 IEEE/ACM 13th International Conference on Utility and Cloud Computing, UCC 2020, pp. 342–347, Dec 2020. https://doi.org/10.1109/UCC48980.2020.00054
2. Chen, H., Chen, P., Yu, G.: A framework of virtual war room and matrix sketch-based streaming anomaly detection for microservice systems. IEEE Access **8**, 43413–43426 (2020). https://doi.org/10.1109/ACCESS.2020.2977464
3. Chen, P., Qi, Y., Hou, D.: CauseInfer?: Automated end-to-end performance diagnosis with hierarchical causality graph in cloud environment. IEEE Trans. Serv. Comput. **12**(2), 214–230 (2016). https://doi.org/10.1109/TSC.2016.2607739
4. Du, Q., Xie, T., He, Yu.: Anomaly detection and diagnosis for container-based microservices with performance monitoring. In: Vaidya, J., Li, J. (eds.) ICA3PP 2018. LNCS, vol. 11337, pp. 560–572. Springer, Cham (2018). https://doi.org/10.1007/978-3-030-05063-4_42

5. Dumitraş, T., Narasimhan, P.: Why do upgrades fail and what can we do about It? In: Bacon, J.M., Cooper, B.F. (eds.) Middleware 2009. LNCS, vol. 5896, pp. 349–372. Springer, Heidelberg (2009). https://doi.org/10.1007/978-3-642-10445-9_18

6. Ebert, C.: Systematisches Requirements Engineering: Anforderungen ermitteln spezifizieren, analysieren und verwalten. dpunkt.verlag, 6. edn. (2019)

7. Gan, Y., et al.: Seer: leveraging big data to navigate the complexity of performance debugging in cloud microservices. In: Proceedings of the Twenty-Fourth International Conference on Architectural Support for Programming Languages and Operating Systems, pp. 19–33 (2019). https://doi.org/10.1145/3297858, https://doi.org/10.1145/3297858.3304004

8. Gulenko, A., Schmidt, F., Acker, A., Wallschlager, M., Kao, O., Liu, F.: Detecting anomalous behavior of black-box services modeled with distance-based online clustering. In: IEEE International Conference on Cloud Computing, CLOUD 2018-July, pp. 912–915, Sep 2018. https://doi.org/10.1109/CLOUD.2018.00134

9. He, P., Zhu, J., He, S., Li, J., Lyu, M.R.: An evaluation study on log parsing and its use in log mining. In: Proceedings - 46th Annual IEEE/IFIP International Conference on Dependable Systems and Networks, DSN 2016, pp. 654–661, Sep 2016. https://doi.org/10.1109/DSN.2016.66

10. He, S., Zhu, J., He, P., Lyu, M.R.: Experience report: system log analysis for anomaly detection. In: Proceedings - International Symposium on Software Reliability Engineering, ISSRE, pp. 207–218, Dec 2016. https://doi.org/10.1109/ISSRE.2016.21

11. IEEE: IEEE Standard 610.12-1990. IEEE Standard Glossary of Software Engineering Terminology (1990)

12. Jia, T., Chen, P., Yang, L., Li, Y., Meng, F., Xu, J.: An approach for anomaly diagnosis based on hybrid graph model with logs for distributed services. In: Proceedings - 2017 IEEE 24th International Conference on Web Services, ICWS 2017, pp. 25–32, Sep 2017. https://doi.org/10.1109/ICWS.2017.12

13. Jia, T., Yang, L., Chen, P., Li, Y., Meng, F., Xu, J.: LogSed: anomaly diagnosis through mining time-weighted control flow graph in logs. In: IEEE International Conference on Cloud Computing, CLOUD 2017-June, 447–455, Sep 2017. https://doi.org/10.1109/CLOUD.2017.64

14. Jin, M., et al.: An anomaly detection algorithm for microservice architecture based on robust principal component analysis. IEEE Access (2020). https://doi.org/10.1109/ACCESS.2020.3044610

15. Lethbridge, T.C., Sim, S.E., Singer, J.: Studying software engineers: data collection techniques for software field studies. Empir. Softw. Eng. 10(3), 311–341 (2005). https://doi.org/10.1007/S10664-005-1290-X

16. Lin, J., Chen, P., Zheng, Z.: Microscope: Pinpoint performance issues with causal graphs in micro-service environments. In: Pahl, C., Vukovic, M., Yin, J., Yu, Q. (eds.) ICSOC 2018. LNCS, vol. 11236, pp. 3–20. Springer, Cham (2018). https://doi.org/10.1007/978-3-030-03596-9_1

17. Liu, P., et al.: Unsupervised detection of microservice trace anomalies through service-level deep bayesian networks. In: Proceedings - International Symposium on Software Reliability Engineering, ISSRE 2020, pp. 48–58, Oct 2020. https://doi.org/10.1109/ISSRE5003.2020.00014

18. Mariani, L., Monni, C., Pezze, M., Riganelli, O., Xin, R.: Localizing faults in cloud systems. In: Proceedings - 2018 IEEE 11th International Conference on Software Testing, Verification and Validation, ICST 2018, pp. 262–273, May 2018. https://doi.org/10.1109/ICST.2018.00034

19. Mariani, L., Pezzè, M., Riganelli, O., Xin, R.: Predicting failures in multi-tier distributed systems. J. Syst. Softw. **161**, 110464 (2020). https://doi.org/10.1016/J.JSS.2019.110464

20. Meng, L., Ji, F., Sun, Y., Wang, T.: Detecting anomalies in microservices with execution trace comparison. Future Generat. Comput. Syst. **116**, 291–301 (2021). https://doi.org/10.1016/J.FUTURE.2020.10.040

21. Nandi, A., Mandal, A., Atreja, S., Dasgupta, G.B., Bhattacharya, S.: Anomaly detection using program control flow graph mining from execution logs. In: Proceedings of the ACM SIGKDD International Conference on Knowledge Discovery and Data Mining 13–17-Aug, pp. 215–224 (2016). https://doi.org/10.1145/2939672.2939712

22. Nedelkoski, S., Cardoso, J., Kao, O.: Anomaly detection and classification using distributed tracing and deep learning. In: Proceedings - 19th IEEE/ACM International Symposium on Cluster, Cloud and Grid Computing, CCGrid 2019, pp. 241–250, May 2019. https://doi.org/10.1109/CCGRID.2019.00038

23. Nedelkoski, S., Cardoso, J., Kao, O.: Anomaly detection from system tracing data using multimodal deep learning. In: IEEE International Conference on Cloud Computing, CLOUD 2019-July, pp. 179–186. Jul 2019. https://doi.org/10.1109/CLOUD.2019.00038

24. Pitakrat, T., Okanović, D., van Hoorn, A., Grunske, L.: Hora: Architecture-aware online failure prediction. J. Syst. Softw. **137**, 669–685 (2018). https://doi.org/10.1016/J.JSS.2017.02.041

25. Pohl, K., Rupp, C.: Basiswissen requirements engineering: Aus-und Weiterbildung nach IREB-Standard zum certified professional for requirements engineering foundation level. dpunkt. verlag (2021)

26. Raemaekers, S., Van Deursen, A., Visser, J.: Measuring software library stability through historical version analysis. In: IEEE International Conference on Software Maintenance, ICSM, pp. 378–387 (2012). https://doi.org/10.1109/ICSM.2012.6405296

27. Runeson, P.: Case study research in software engineering: guidelines and examples. Wiley (2012), https://www.wiley.com/en-ie/Case+Study+Research+in+Software+Engineering%3A+Guidelines+and+Examples-p-9781118104354

28. Runeson, P., Höst, M.: Guidelines for conducting and reporting case study research in software engineering. Empirical Softw. Eng. 14(2), 131–164, Apr 2009. https://doi.org/10.1007/s10664-008-9102-8

29. Samir, A., Pahl, C.: DLA: Detecting and localizing anomalies in containerized microservice architectures using markov models. In: Proceedings - 2019 International Conference on Future Internet of Things and Cloud, FiCloud 2019, pp. 205–213, Aug 2019. https://doi.org/10.1109/FICLOUD.2019.00036

30. Shan, H., et al.: ϵ-Diagnosis: Unsupervised and real-time diagnosis of small-window long-tail latency in large-scale microservice platforms. In: The Web Conference 2019 - Proceedings of the World Wide Web Conference, WWW 2019, pp. 3215–3222 (2019). https://doi.org/10.1145/3308558.3313653

31. Soldani, J., Brogi, A.: Anomaly detection and failure root cause analysis in (Micro) service-based cloud applications: a survey. ACM Comput. Surv. (CSUR) **55**, 39 (2022). https://doi.org/10.1145/3501297

32. Steidl, M., Felderer, M.: Anomalies in Microservice Arcitecture (train-ticket) based on version configurations, Aug 2022. https://doi.org/10.5281/zenodo.6979726

33. Wagstaff, K.L.: Machine learning that matters. In: Proceedings of the 29th International Conference on Machine Learning, ICML 2012, vol. 1, pp. 529–534, Jun 2012. https://doi.org/10.48550/arxiv.1206.4656

34. Wang, P., et al.: CloudRanger: Root cause identification for cloud native systems. In: Proceedings - 18th IEEE/ACM International Symposium on Cluster, Cloud and Grid Computing, CCGRID 2018, pp. 492–502, Jul 2018. https://doi.org/10.1109/CCGRID.2018.00076

35. Wang, T., Zhang, W., Xu, J., Gu, Z.: Workflow-aware automatic fault diagnosis for microservice-based applications with statistics. IEEE Trans. Netw. Service Manag. **17**(4), 2350–2363 (2020). https://doi.org/10.1109/TNSM.2020.3022028

36. Wohlin, C., Runeson, P., Höst, M., Ohlsson, M.C., Regnell, B., Wesslén, A.: Experimentation in software engineering, vol. 9783642290. Springer Science & Business Media (2012). https://doi.org/10.1007/978-3-642-29044-2

37. Wu, L., Bogatinovski, J., Nedelkoski, S., Tordsson, J., Kao, O.: Performance diagnosis in cloud microservices using deep learning. In: Hacid, H., et al. (eds.) ICSOC 2020. LNCS, vol. 12632, pp. 85–96. Springer, Cham (2021). https://doi.org/10.1007/978-3-030-76352-7_13

38. Wu, L., Tordsson, J., Elmroth, E., Kao, O.: MicroRCA: root cause localization of performance issues in microservices. In: Proceedings of IEEE/IFIP Network Operations and Management Symposium 2020: Management in the Age of Softwarization and Artificial Intelligence, NOMS 2020, Apr 2020. https://doi.org/10.1109/NOMS47738.2020.9110353

39. Zhao, N., et al.: Identifying bad software changes via multimodal anomaly detection for online service systems; identifying bad software changes via multimodal anomaly detection for online service systems. In: Proceedings of the 29th ACM Joint Meeting on European Software Engineering Conference and Symposium on the Foundations of Software Engineering, vol. 21 (2021). https://doi.org/10.1145/3468264, https://doi.org/10.1145/3468264.3468543

40. Zhou, X., et al.: Latent error prediction and fault localization for microservice applications by learning from system trace logs. In: Proceedings of the 2019 27th ACM Joint Meeting on European Software Engineering Conference and Symposium on the Foundations of Software Engineering, vol. 19 (2019). https://doi.org/10.1145/3338906, https://doi.org/10.1145/3338906.3338961

41. Zhou, X., et al.: Fault Analysis and Debugging of Microservice Systems: Industrial Survey, Benchmark System, and Empirical Study. IEEE Trans. Softw. Eng. **4**(8) (2018)

42. Zhou, X., et al.: Fault analysis and debugging of microservice systems: industrial survey, benchmark system, and empirical study. IEEE Trans. Softw. Eng. **47**(2), 243–260 (2021). https://doi.org/10.1109/TSE.2018.2887384

43. Zhu, J., et al.: Tools and benchmarks for automated log parsing. In: Proceedings - 2019 IEEE/ACM 41st International Conference on Software Engineering: Software Engineering in Practice, ICSE-SEIP 2019, pp. 121–130, May 2019. https://doi.org/10.1109/ICSE-SEIP.2019.00021, https://github.com/logpai/logparser

Towards a DSL for AI Engineering Process Modeling

Sergio Morales[1]([⊠])(iD), Robert Clarisó[1](iD), and Jordi Cabot[1,2](iD)

[1] Universitat Oberta de Catalunya, Barcelona, Spain
{smoralesg,rclariso,jcabot}@uoc.edu
[2] ICREA, Barcelona, Spain
jordi.cabot@icrea.cat

Abstract. Many modern software products embed AI components. As a result, their development requires multidisciplinary teams with diverse skill sets. Diversity may lead to communication issues or misapplication of best practices. *Process models*, which prescribe how software should be developed within an organization, can alleviate this problem. In this paper, we introduce a *domain-specific language* for modeling AI engineering processes. The DSL concepts stem from our analysis of scientific and gray literature that describes how teams are developing AI-based software. This DSL contributes a structured framework and a common ground for designing, enacting and automating AI engineering processes.

Keywords: Domain-specific language · AI engineering · Process modeling

1 Introduction

Modern business applications usually embed Machine Learning (ML) and other Artificial Intelligence (AI) components as core of their logic [3,6]. The engineering of AI components requires the introduction of new development activities and profiles in development teams beyond software engineers, *e.g.*, data scientists, psychologists and AI experts. As a result, there is a need for more support and guidance when developing AI projects, as reported in recent studies [2,8,15]. Enterprises need to revise their practices and adopt a clear process for building AI products.

A *process model* provides full visibility and traceability about the work decomposition within an organization, along with the responsibilities of their participants and the standards and knowledge it is based on. Process models are guidelines for configuration, execution and continuous improvement.

In this sense, we propose a *domain-specific language* (DSL) to facilitate the specification of AI engineering processes. The motivation for a DSL is to have a shared language in a particular problem space that can foster communication and collaboration. Our DSL encompasses standard process modeling concepts plus AI-specific process primitives based on the analysis of research and gray literature. We currently have introduced concepts from Machine Learning and leave other AI activities and facets for future work.

© The Author(s), under exclusive license to Springer Nature Switzerland AG 2022
D. Taibi et al. (Eds.): PROFES 2022, LNCS 13709, pp. 53–60, 2022.
https://doi.org/10.1007/978-3-031-21388-5_4

Our DSL facilitates the definition of AI engineering processes by enabling stakeholders to discuss and specify a single and formalized representation of such processes. This also brings additional benefits. For instance, it opens the door to automatic processing, *e.g.*, as part of a process execution scenario, it facilitates the detection of hidden or conflicting practices, and simplifies the onboarding of new team members.

The remainder of this paper is organized as follows. Section 2 reviews existing proposals for AI processes. In Sect. 3 we introduce our DSL, while in Sect. 4 we present an example of its usage, leading to Sect. 5 where we analyze other related work. Finally, Sect. 6 concludes and outlines the future work.

2   Background

There are several scientific papers and gray literature describing the development of real AI projects. Among those, we have selected the most cited research publications and influential contributions from the industry as inspiration for our DSL.

In particular, we have chosen 3 industrial methods: CRISP-DM [5] as the de facto standard process for data science projects; and Microsoft Team Data Science Process [14] and IBM AI Model Lifecycle Management [9] as two major players in the field. We have also included 3 scientific references that discuss the Machine Learning lifecycle in actual applications [2,4,10]; and 1 paper that blueprints a maturity framework for AI model management [1].

Each of those proposals has a slightly different grouping, distribution and granularity of activities, but all share the following high level structure:

1. *Business Understanding*, to set the business objectives and criteria linked to an AI project, and produce a plan along with an initial assessment of tools and techniques.
2. *Data Collection & Preparation*, to perform activities to gather and clean data, and prepare datasets and features for creating AI models.
3. *AI Model Training & Evaluation*, to select AI modeling techniques, optimize hyperparameters and train the AI models, which will be evaluated and ranked according to evaluation and business criteria.
4. *Production & Operation*, to finally make the AI models available for consumption and to build a monitoring system and pipelines for continuous improvement.

Our DSL generalizes and unifies these concepts to enable the specification of end-to-end AI engineering processes.

3   DSL Design

A DSL is commonly defined through a metamodel that represents its domain entities and their relationships. As shown in Fig. 2, at its core, our DSL contains the generic description of activities, the relationships between them, and the main elements they are related to. Based on the analysis of existing literature, we predefine four main activities (see Fig. 1): (1) *BusinessActivity*, (2) *DataActivity*, (3) *AIModelingActivity*, and (4) *AIModelDeploymentActivity*.

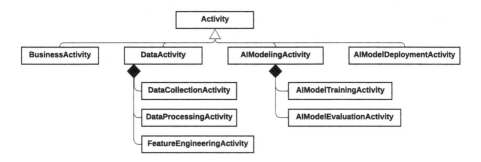

Fig. 1. High-level view of activities and subactivities.

In the next sections, we focus on the two most AI-specific ones: *DataActivity* and *AIModelingActivity*. We only briefly cover the *AIModelDeploymentActivity* and leave the *BusinessActivity* for future work. Due to lack of space, we describe an excerpt of the DSL. The complete metamodel is available online[1].

Note that our DSL does not prescribe any concrete AI engineering process model. Instead, it offers the modeling constructs so that each organization can easily define its own process.

3.1 Activity Core Elements

An *Activity* constitutes the core element of any process. Activities are composed of other activities (association *composedOf*). Completing an activity may require completing all subactivities (attribute *requiresAllSubactivities*). Process creators define if an activity is mandatory (attribute *isOptional*). There may also be a precedence relationship between activities (association *next*).

Several *Roles* perform the activities during development. Their *participation* could be specified according to the organization's levels of responsibility, *e.g.*, as responsible or accountable (class *Participant*).

Activities consume (*inputs*) and produce (*outputs*) *Artifacts*. An artifact could be a document that is generated as an output of an activity and is consumed as an input by the following one. Other examples of artifacts will be studied in the following sections.

Finally, *Resources* might be helpful to complete an activity. Resources are not consumed nor produced by the process – they are supporting components. An example would be a template for the document from the previous paragraph.

---

[1] http://hdl.handle.net/20.500.12004/1/C/PROFES/2022/422.

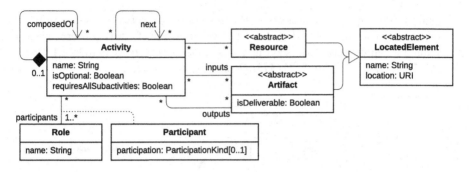

Fig. 2. Generic elements of an activity.

3.2 Data Activity

The *DataCollectionActivity* is the acquisition of *DataInstances* from *Data-Sources*. The participants move data from internal or external data sources (attribute *isExternal*) into a destination (attribute *location*) for further processing.

In the *DataProcessingActivity*, data is cleaned and transformed via different *techniques* (*e.g.*, dummy substitution for cleaning empty values in relevant attributes, and data reduction or augmentation) to overcome deficiencies that might result in bad predictions if used for training an AI model. Additionally, data could be labelled to help AI models identify concepts in production data.

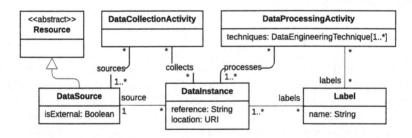

Fig. 3. An excerpt of activities and other elements of the *DataActivity*.

The *FeatureEngineeringActivity* (not included in Fig. 3) comprehends the tasks and statistical techniques used to transform data attributes of a *DataInstance* into features that can be used by an AI model and enhance its prediction accuracy. During this activity, correlations between features are identified. As a result of this activity, a set of features are extracted from the data instances.

Data is then usually split into three disjoint sets: a training dataset, a validation dataset and a test dataset.

3.3 AI Modeling Activity

The *AIModelTrainingActivity* is the activity for creating, training and validating new AI models from the collected and prepared data. An *AIModel* is trained by an AI algorithm using the observations held in the *TrainingDataset*.

Once an AI model is initially trained, a data scientist tunes its *Hyperparameters* looking for the *OptimalValues* that yield its best performance. The *ValidationDataset* is applied in this procedure. Finally, the hyperparameter values that maximize an AI model performance are fixed for production.

The *AIModelPerformanceCriteria* will drive the AI model training and will be used to pursue an AI model or discard it; in other words, they dictate when it is not worthwhile to keep improving an AI model.

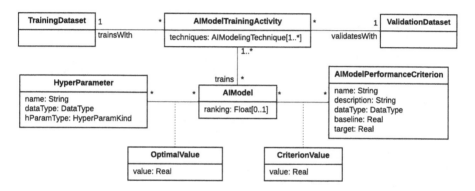

Fig. 4. An excerpt of the *AIModelingActivity* and its elements.

In the *AIModelEvaluationActivity* (not part of Fig. 4), a data scientist checks if an AI model satisfies the AI model success criteria, along with its adequacy to its AI model requirements. A test dataset is used to assess this. Data scientists then set a *ranking* for each AI model.

3.4 AI Model Deployment Activity

In the *AIModelDeploymentActivity*, an AI model is deployed to a production *Platform* to serve end users or other systems (Fig. 5). It may be useful to run *Scripts* to automate its installation and setup. An AI model can be deployed (attribute *pattern*) statically, dynamically (on the user's device or on a server), or via streaming. An AI model can make its *inferences* either: (a) in batch mode, periodically making predictions offline and serving the results to a repository; or (b) in real-time, making and serving predictions whenever requested to.

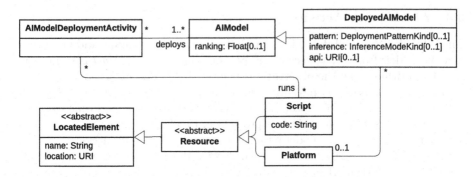

Fig. 5. An excerpt of elements of the *AIModelDeploymentActivity*.

4   Tool Support

We have implemented our DSL on top of Sirius Web[2], an open-source subproject of Eclipse Sirius. Given a metamodel and its mapping to a set of visual notation elements, Sirius Web generates a modeling environment that can then be used by modelers to design new graphical models conforming to that metamodel.

As an example, Fig. 6 depicts an excerpt of the *DataActivity* of a simple process model with four subactivities: (1) *Ingest the data*, (2) *Clean the data*, (3) *Reduce the data*, and (4) *Set the data pipeline*. The first one is an instance of the *DataCollectionActivity* and employs a technique (*Load data to SQL Server on Azure VM*) for transferring data from the data source *Employees ERP* into the data instance *Extraction ref A00451*. The activity *Ingest the data* has one participant, a *Data engineer*, who is *responsible* for its execution. The activities *Clean the data* and *Reduce the data* are instances of the *DataProcessingActivity*, and each of them performs different techniques to process the data instance.

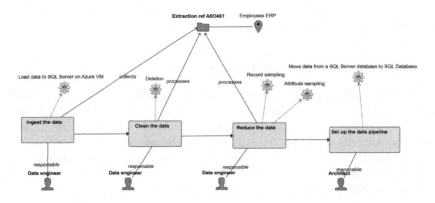

Fig. 6. A sample process model created with our DSL on Sirius Web.

---

[2] https://www.eclipse.org/sirius/sirius-web.html.

The DSL provides flexibility for adding elements that are specific to a method. In the example, *Set up the data pipeline* does not correspond to any predefined AI activity described in our DSL. Therefore, it is based on the generic *Activity*.

5   Related Work

There are dozens of process modeling languages, *e.g.*, BPMN & SPEM and their extensions, UML profiles, and formal languages [7]. Specifically, SPEM is an OMG standard for describing software development processes, but it purposely does not include any distinct feature for particular domains or disciplines – like Artificial Intelligence. To the best of our knowledge, none of the process modeling languages includes AI specific extensions.

Regarding DSLs for AI, there are languages to model certain AI activities such as OptiML [13], ScalOps [16], Arbiter [18] or Pig Latin [11]. There are also DSLs for creating AI artifacts like ML-Schema [12], an ontology for interchanging information on ML experiments, or DeepDSL [17] for the creation of deep learning networks. Nevertheless, none of those DSLs focus on process aspects.

Therefore, as far as we know, our DSL is the first that provides elements for describing AI-specific activities and enables modeling AI engineering processes.

6   Conclusions and Future Work

In this paper, we have presented a first version of a DSL to model AI engineering processes. Our language covers the needs for such type of processes as described in academic and industry proposals. We believe this DSL is a step forward towards the adoption of software engineering practices in the AI area.

Our DSL will facilitate the formalization of AI processes within organizations. Moreover, this formalization will also enable the manipulation of the models via any of the existing model-driven tools – especially the EMF-based ones, which will be directly compatible with our DSL implementation.

As further work, we plan to create a tool set that would enable enacting and automating these modeled AI processes, thus providing real-time information of running processes and guidance for intervention.

Additional future work will involve extending the DSL. In particular, we will dive deep into the *BusinessActivity* for contextualizing and setting business purposes to AI projects. Similarly, we plan to enrich the *AIModelDeploymentActivity* to incorporate monitoring elements to ensure the performance of deployed AI models remains within acceptable limits. Besides, we will go beyond ML and include other AI methods. We will also add process snippets and templates that would help companies to create their own process without starting from scratch. Finally, we will empirically validate the usability of our DSL.

Acknowledgements. This work has been partially funded by the Spanish government (PID2020-114615RB-I00/AEI/10.13039/501100011033, project LOCOSS) and the AIDOaRt project, which has received funding from the ECSEL Joint Undertaking (JU) under grant agreement No 101007350. The JU receives support from the European Union's Horizon 2020 research and innovation programme and Sweden, Austria, Czech Republic, Finland, France, Italy and Spain.

References

1. Akkiraju, R., et al.: Characterizing machine learning processes: a maturity framework. In: Fahland, D., Ghidini, C., Becker, J., Dumas, M. (eds.) BPM 2020. LNCS, vol. 12168, pp. 17–31. Springer, Cham (2020). https://doi.org/10.1007/978-3-030-58666-9_2
2. Amershi, S., et al.: Software engineering for machine learning: a case study. In: ICSE-SEIP, pp. 291–300 (2019)
3. Anthes, G.: Artificial intelligence poised to ride a new wave. Commun. ACM **60**(7), 19–21 (2017)
4. Ashmore, R., Calinescu, R., Paterson, C.: Assuring the machine learning lifecycle: desiderata, methods, and challenges. ACM Comput. Surv. **54**(5), 1–39 (2021)
5. CRISP-DM. https://cordis.europa.eu/project/id/25959. Accessed 6 June 2022
6. Deng, L.: Artificial intelligence in the rising wave of deep learning: the historical path and future outlook. IEEE Signal Proc. Mag. **35**(1), 180–187 (2018)
7. García-Borgoñón, L., Barcelona, M., García-García, J., Alba, M., Escalona, M.: Software process modeling languages: a systematic literature review. Inf. Softw. Technol. **56**(2), 103–116 (2014)
8. Hill, C., Bellamy, R., Erickson, T., Burnett, M.: Trials and tribulations of developers of intelligent systems: a field study. In: 2016 IEEE Symposium on VL/HCC, pp. 162–170 (2016)
9. IBM Ai Model Lifecycle Management. https://www.ibm.com/blogs/academy-of-technology/ai-model-lifecycle-management-white-paper. Accessed 6 June 2022
10. Nascimento, E.D.S., Ahmed, I., Oliveira, E., Palheta, M.P., Steinmacher, I., Conte, T.: Understanding development process of machine learning systems: challenges and solutions. In: ESEM 2019, pp. 1–6 (2019)
11. Olston, C., Reed, B., Srivastava, U., Kumar, R., Tomkins, A.: Pig latin: a not-so-foreign language for data processing. In: SIGMOD, pp. 1099–1110. ACM (2008)
12. Publio, G.C., et al.: ML-schema: exposing the semantics of machine learning with schemas and ontologies. arXiv preprint arXiv:1807.05351 (2018)
13. Sujeeth, A.K., et al.: OptiML: an implicitly parallel domain-specific language for machine learning. In: ICML, pp. 609–616 (2011)
14. What is the Team Data Science Process? https://docs.microsoft.com/en-us/azure/architecture/data-science-process/overview. Accessed 6 June 2022
15. Wan, Z., Xia, X., Lo, D., Murphy, G.C.: How does machine learning change software development practices? IEEE Trans. Softw. Eng. **47**(9), 1857–1871 (2021)
16. Weimer, M., Condie, T., Ramakrishnan, R., et al.: Machine learning in ScalOps, a higher order cloud computing language. In: NIPS, vol. 9, pp. 389–396 (2011)
17. Zhao, T., Huang, X.: Design and implementation of DeepDSL: a DSL for deep learning. Comput. Lang. Syst. Struct. **54**, 39–70 (2018)
18. Zucker, J., d'Leeuwen, M.: Arbiter: a domain-specific language for ethical machine learning. In: AAAI/ACM Conference on AI, Ethics, and Society, pp. 421–425 (2020)

Classification of Changes Based on API

Masashi Iriyama[⊠], Yoshiki Higo, and Shinji Kusumoto

Graduate School of Information Science and Technology,
Osaka University, Suita, Japan
{m-iriyam,higo,kusumoto}@ist.osaka-u.ac.jp

Abstract. In software maintenance process, software libraries are occasionally updated, and their APIs may also be updated. API changes can be classified into two categories: changes that break backward compatibility (in short, breaking changes) and changes that maintain backward compatibility (in short, maintaining changes). Detecting API changes and determining whether each is a breaking or maintaining change is useful for code reviews and release note generations. Since it is burdensome to check API changes manually, research on automatic detection of API changes has been conducted. APIDiff is a tool that automatically detects API changes and classifies the detected changes into breaking and maintaining ones. APIDiff takes two versions of a Java library as input, and it detects API changes based on the similarity of the input code. Each detected change is classified into the two kinds of changes. However, since APIDiff identifies breaking changes for each type of change, it tends to fail to correctly classify changes if multiple changes were conducted to a single API. On the other hand, our proposed technique in this paper groups changes by APIs and checks whether each group contains changes that break backward compatibility. Classifying API changes more correctly by our technique will be helpful for release note generations in maintenance process. We conducted experiments on eight open-source software and confirmed that our technique could detect API changes more correctly than APIDiff. We also confirmed that the proposed technique could classify API changes more correctly into breaking and maintaining ones than APIDiff.

Keywords: API Evolution · Breaking changes · Mining software repositories

1 Introduction

Libraries have been used in many software applications [6]. Libraries provide functionality through application programming interfaces (in short, APIs). In software maintenance process, software libraries are occasionally updated, and their APIs may also be updated; API changes may include additions of new features, removals of unnecessary features, or refactoring to improve maintainability [4]. Those changes can be categorized as those that break backward compatibility (in short, *breaking changes*) and those that maintain backward compatibility (in short, *maintaining changes*). Detecting API changes and determining

© The Author(s), under exclusive license to Springer Nature Switzerland AG 2022
D. Taibi et al. (Eds.): PROFES 2022, LNCS 13709, pp. 61–70, 2022.
https://doi.org/10.1007/978-3-031-21388-5_5

MPChartLib/src/main/java/com/github/mikephil/charting/components/YAxis.java

```
     public class YAxis extends AxisBase {
        ...
-        public void setValueFormatter(YAxisValueFormatter f) {
-            if (f == null)
-                mYAxisValueFormatter = new DefaultYAxisValueFormatter(mDecimals);
-            else
-                mYAxisValueFormatter = f;
-        }
     }
```

MPChartLib/src/main/java/com/github/mikephil/charting/components/AxisBase.java

```
     public abstract class AxisBase extends ComponentBase {
        ...
+        public void setValueFormatter(AxisValueFormatter f) {
+            if (f == null)
+                mAxisValueFormatter = new DefaultAxisValueFormatter(mDecimals);
+            else
+                mAxisValueFormatter = f;
+        }
     }
```

https://github.com/PhilJay/MPAndroidChart/commit/1482f9331e6d47c2e255be1cb95b3e91133aabc0

Fig. 1. An example of an issue in APIDiff

whether the changes maintain backward compatibility of the API is useful for code reviews and release note generations [7].

Since manually detecting API changes is burdensome, research has been conducted on automatically detecting API changes. APIDiff is a tool that automatically detects API changes and classifies them into breaking and maintaining ones [1]. A variety of research has been conducted using APIDiff. For example, research has been conducted to clarify the stability of libraries [10], the impact of breaking changes on client code [10], reasons why developers made breaking changes [2], and developers' awareness of the dangers of breaking changes [11].

However, APIDiff tends to fail to correctly classify changes if multiple changes were conducted to a single API since it identifies breaking changes for each type of change. As a result, API developers (library developers) and API users (library users) may have wrong perceptions of API changes. Figure 1 shows an example of the issue in APIDiff. APIDiff should classify the API changes of setValueFormatter into *Pull Up Method* and *Change in Parameter List*. Users of setValueFormatter can no longer use it after the API changes because the parameter of the API has been changed. That is, the backward compatibility of setValueFormatter is broken by the changes, but APIDiff classifies *Pull Up Method* incorrectly into the maintaining change based on its change type.

Our proposed technique groups changes by APIs and checks whether each group contains API changes that break backward compatibility. Classifying API changes more correctly by our technique will be helpful for release note generations in maintenance process. We conducted experiments on eight open-source software and confirmed that our technique could detect API changes more correctly than APIDiff. We also confirmed that our technique could classify API changes more correctly into breaking and maintaining ones than APIDiff.

2   Preliminaries

2.1   Catalog of API Changes

The backward compatibility considered in this paper is in the context of syntactic changes and not semantic changes. The catalog of breaking changes is shown in Table 1. The catalog of maintaining changes is shown in Table 2. Those catalogs are based on the README file of APIDiff[1] and the README file of RefactoringMiner[2]

2.2   APIDiff

APIDiff internally utilizes a refactoring detection tool called RefDiff [8]. RefDiff outputs a list of refactoring operations applied to the later version of the two input versions based on the similarity of the code.

The two versions of a Java library given as input to APIDiff are passed to RefDiff, and classes, methods, and fields are extracted for each version. RefDiff obtains a list of refactoring operations applied to the later version. Then refactoring operations that are not related to APIs are discarded. APIDiff itself extracts classes, methods, and fields for each version. APIDiff matches APIs between the two versions based on the list of refactoring operations and information such as fully qualified names of classes, APIs' names, and sequences of parameters. Based on the results of the API matching and information such as API qualifiers and annotations, API changes are detected. The detected changes are classified

Table 1. Catalog of breaking changes

Type	Rename, Move, Move and Rename, Remove, Lost Visibility, Add Final Modifier, Remove Static Modifier, Change in Supertype, Remove Supertype, Extract Type, Extract Subtype
Method	Move, Rename, Remove, Push Down, Inline, Change in Parameter list, Change in Exception List, Change in Return Type, Lost Visibility, Add Final Modifier, Remove Static Modifier, Move and Rename
Field	Remove, Move, Push Down, Change in Default Value, Change in Field Type, Lost Visibility, Add Final Modifier, Rename, Move and Rename

Table 2. Catalog of maintaining changes

Type	Add, extract supertype, Gain Visibility, Remove Final Modifier, Add Static Modifier, Add Supertype, Deprecated
Method	Pull Up, Gain Visibility, Remove Final Modifier, Add Static Modifier, Deprecated, Add, Extract
Field	Pull Up, Add, Deprecated Field, Gain Visibility, Remove Final Modifier, Extract

---

[1] https://github.com/aserg-ufmg/apidiff.
[2] https://github.com/tsantalis/RefactoringMiner.

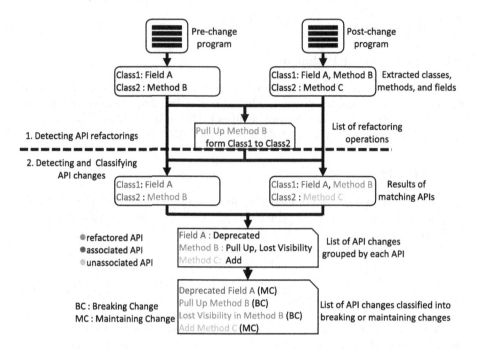

Fig. 2. Overview of the proposed technique

into breaking or maintaining changes based on their change types. Then APIDiff creates a list of API change operations, including information such as its change type, the API before and after the change, and the result of determining whether the change breaks backward compatibility.

3   Proposed Technique

An overview of our technique is shown in Fig. 2. It is important to detect API changes with high accuracy in our technique in advance to classify API changes. The proposed technique detects API refactorings using RefactoringMiner [9] instead of RefDiff. RefactoringMiner (in short, RMiner) is a tool that detects refactorings with high accuracy because of syntax-aware replacements of abstract syntax trees nodes and heuristics defined to match statements. Our proposed technique matches APIs between versions based on the output of RMiner. Our technique detects and groups changes by APIs and checks whether each group contains changes that break backward compatibility.

3.1   Detection API Refactorings

The two versions of a Java library given as input to our technique are passed to RMiner. The tool extracts classes, methods, and fields for each version. RMiner outputs a list of refactoring operations applied to the later version. Then refactoring operations that are not related to APIs are discarded.

3.2   Detecting and Classifying API Changes

The API changes detection and classification procedure consists of the following steps:

Step-1 matching APIs between versions,
Step-2 detecting/grouping API changes for each API, and
Step-3 classifying API changes into breaking or maintaining changes.

In Step-1, the classes having identical fully qualified names are associated between the two versions. The methods having identical fully qualified names of the class, method names, sequences of parameters, and return types are associated. The fields having identical fully qualified names of the class, field names, and field types are associated. The unassociated APIs are classified into refactored, deleted, or added APIs based on the list of refactoring operations. In Step-2, based on the results of the API matching in Step-1 and information such as API qualifiers and annotations, API changes are detected. Then changes are grouped for each API based on the combination of the API before and after the change. In Step-3, each detected change is classified into breaking or maintaining changes based on its change type. Then our technique checks whether each group includes at least a breaking change. If the group includes at least a breaking change, our technique determines that the API is broken and reclassifies all the changes included in the group into breaking changes. Then a list of API change operations is created in the same way as APIDiff.

4   Experiment

We evaluated our technique in terms of the number of detected API changes, the precision of classifying API changes, and execution time. Our tool and datasets are available[3].

4.1   Target Projects

In order to experiment with projects that are frequently updated and popular, we selected eight open source software for the experiment from the experimental targets of the longitudinal study using RMiner [3]. The eight projects were selected because their repositories included enough commits, and many users gave stars to the repositories. The target projects are shown in Table 3.

4.2   The Number of Detected API Changes

We applied our technique and APIDiff to all the commits on the master branch of the projects and compared the number of detected changes. The results are shown in the column of Number in Table 3. While APIDiff detected 4,180 (=2,943+1,237) changes, our technique detected 7,883 (=2,943+4,940) changes. In all the projects, our technique detected more API changes than APIDiff.

---

[3] https://github.com/kusumotolab/APIMiner.

4.3   The Precision of Classifying API Changes

We used MPAndroidChart to calculate the precision because its calculation required manual checking of detected API changes. MPAndroidChart was also used in the experiment of APIDiff [1]. Due to the large number of API changes detected by our technique and APIDiff, we visually checked 165 API changes of which classification results are different from our technique and APIDiff. Due to the large number of API changes detected by our technique alone, 311 were sampled to achieve a tolerance of 5% and a confidence level of 95%. All the API changes detected only by APIDiff were visually checked. The results are shown in Table 4. The column of Num shows the number of detected API changes. The column of Prec1 shows whether each change is correct in change type. The column of Prec2 shows whether each change is correct in both change type and classification results. The overall precision of APIDiff alone is the number of API changes visually checked to be correct divided by 165, the number of API changes detected by APIDiff alone. The overall precision of ours alone is the number of API changes visually checked to be correct divided by the sample size, 311. Although for *Inline Method* and *Move Method*, the precision of APIDiff was higher than that of our technique, the overall precision of our technique was 89.7%, compared to 44.8% for APIDiff. The difference between Prec1 and Prec2 in the column of APIDiff alone indicates that APIDiff detected *Pull up Method* correctly but classified some of them into breaking or maintaining changes incorrectly. On the other hand, our technique detected *Pull up Method* correctly and classified them into breaking or maintaining changes correctly.

4.4   Execution Time

We applied our technique and APIDiff to all the commits on the master branch of the projects and measured execution time. Then we compared the total execution time between our technique and APIDiff. The results are shown in the column of Execution Time of Table 3. In five out of the eight projects, the execution time of our technique was shorter than that of APIDiff. In three projects out of the

Table 3. Target projects, the number of detected API changes, and execution time

Project name	LOC	Commits	Number			Execution time			
			Both	Ours Alone	APIDiff Alone	Total		Detect Refactorings	
						Ours	APIDiff	Ours	APIDiff
OkHttp	72,696	4,839	675	460	396	11 min53 s	12 min30 s	11 min49 s	6 min20 s
Retrofit	26,995	1,865	243	338	84	2 min36 s	3 min07 s	2 min35 s	1 min19 s
MPAndroidChart	25,232	2,068	1,120	1,607	116	2 min08 s	4 min18 s	1 min59 s	2 min00 s
LeakCanary	26,269	1,609	41	79	51	24 s	2 min59 s	24 s	18 s
Hystrix	50,510	2,108	292	722	183	19 min58 s	4 min36 s	19 min56 s	2 min10 s
Iosched	23,550	2,757	91	143	44	3 h16 min39 s	6 min57 s	3 h16 min38 s	1 min53 s
Fresco	7,194	2,897	452	1,514	359	2 min25 s	20 min18 s	2 min18 s	5 min46 s
Logger	1,441	144	29	77	3	11 s	8 s	11 s	3 s
Sum			2,943	4,940	1,237				

eight projects, our technique took less time to detect API changes than APIDiff, even though RMiner took more time to detect refactorings than RefDiff.

5   Discussion

Figure 3 shows an example of API change detected by APIDiff alone. APIDiff detected and classified the API change of `cloneEntry` into *Rename Method* correctly, but our technique classified the API change into *Remove Method* and *Add Method* incorrectly. Our technique matches APIs between two versions using the

Table 4. The precision of classifying API changes

API change type	Both				Ours alone			APIDiff alone		
	Num	Prec1	Ours Prec2	APIDiff Prec2	Num	Prec1	Prec2	Num	Prec1	Prec2
Change in field default Value	107				18	100	100	1	100	100
Change in return type method	125				56	100	100	3	100	100
Extract method	0				133	78.6	78.6	4	25.0	25.0
Inline method	5				19	84.6	76.8	4	100	100
Lost visibility in method	19				32	38.5	38.5	44	0.0	0.0
Pull up method	115	100	100	0.0	107	100	100	20	100	70.0
Push down field	6				2	100	100	1	100	100
Push down method	28				29	100	100	2	100	100
Move field	45				75	100	100	1	100	100
Move method	60				46	15.4	15.4	12	66.7	66.7
Rename method	147				67	100	100	22	68.2	68.2
Rename type	27				2	100	100	2	100	100
Add static modifier in method	1				3	100	100	0		
Change in field type	53				10	100	100	0		
Change in supertype	132	100	100	0.0	2	100	100	0		
Deprecated method	6				48	100	100	0		
Deprecated type	3				2	100	100	0		
Gain visibility in field	43				35	100	100	0		
Gain visibility in method	47				56	100	100	0		
Gain visibility in type	2				4	100	100	0		
Lost visibility in field	8				18	100	100	0		
Move and rename type	3				2	100	100	0		
Move type	69				8	100	100	0		
Pull up field	28	100	100	0.0	45	100	100	0		
Change in parameter list	0				626	100	100	0		
Extract field	0				3	100	100	0		
Extract subtype	0				2	100	100	0		
Extract supertype	0				36	92.3	92.3	0		
Extract type	0				25	100	100	0		
Move and rename field	0				4	75.0	75.0	0		
Move and rename method	0				32	84.6	84.6	0		
Remove static modifier in method	0				2	100	100	0		
Rename field	0				58	84.6	84.6	0		
Add final modifier in field	1				0			0		
Add supertype	28				0			0		
Remove final modifier in field	5				0			0		
Remove supertype	7				0			0		
Overall	1,120	100	100	0.0	1,607	90.0	89.7	116	50.0	44.8

Pre-change

```
protected Entry cloneEntry() {
  Entry entry = new Entry(mVal, mXIndex);
  return entry;
}
```

Post-change

```
public Entry copy() {
  return new Entry(mVal,mXIndex);
}
```

https://github.com/PhilJay/MPAndroidChart/commit/30e54a3aa3a7a35fcd1b33f98df471c231a8740e

Fig. 3. An example of API change detected by APIDiff alone

output of RMiner. RMiner did not detect the change, so our technique classified cloneEntry into a removed API and classified copy into an added API incorrectly.

In the column of Ours alone in Table 4, the precision of *Move Method* was as low as 15.4%. That is because RMiner classified some of *Pull up Method* and *Push Down Method* into *Move Method* incorrectly. Our technique determines the type of refactoring based on the output of RMiner. Even if our technique classifies an API as a refactored API correctly, the type of refactoring may not be correctly determined.

In the column of Execution Time in Table 3, our technique took a much longer time to detect API changes than APIDiff in the project iosched. The majority of our tool's execution time was spent detecting refactorings by RMiner. RMiner constructs abstract syntax trees of changed files and compares subtrees of them between two versions to detect refactorings. If many files are changed in a single commit, there will be more subtrees to compare between versions, and it will take more time to detect refactorings.

6 Threats to Validity

We considered classes, methods, and fields with the access level of public or protected as APIs. The access level may be set to public or protected for internal processing rather than for exposing as an API. If such classes, methods, and fields are excluded, the experiment results may change.

In order to calculate the precision, we visually check the detected changes. Some API changes may not have been classified correctly.

Since some API change types were not detected so much, their precisions may not have been correctly calculated.

7 Related Works

RefDiff [8] and RMiner [9] are refactoring detection tools. Those tools themselves neither detect other changes (i.e., adding or removing API, etc.) nor classify detected changes into breaking or maintaining changes.

Android applications, like libraries, are suffered from API-related compatibility issues. Li et al. proposed an automated approach named CiD for systematically modeling the lifecycle of the Android APIs and analyzing app bytecode to flag usages that can lead to potential compatibility issues [5]. Our technique is for detecting API changes of Java libraries, not Android APIs.

8   Conclusions and Future Work

We proposed a new technique to classify API changes into breaking and maintaining ones automatically. Our proposed technique groups changes by APIs and checks whether each group contains changes that break backward compatibility. Classifying API changes more correctly by our technique will be helpful for release note generations in maintenance process.

By increasing the number of OSSs to be evaluated, we are going to visually check a sufficient number of API change types that were not detected so much in this experiment. We are also going to integrate our technique with CI platforms.

Acknowledgment. This research was supported by JSPS KAKENHI Japan (JP20H04166, JP21K18302, JP21K11820, JP21H04877, JP22H03567, JP22K11985)

References

1. Brito, A., Xavier, L., Hora, A., Valente, M.T.: APIDiff: detecting API breaking changes. In: Proceedings of International Conference on Software Analytics, Evolution, Reengineering, pp. 507–511 (2018)
2. Brito, A., Xavier, L., Hora, A., Valente, M.T.: Why and how Java developers break APIs. In: Proceedings of International Conference on Software Analytics, Evolution, Reengineering, pp. 255–265 (2018)
3. Cedrim, D., et al.: Understanding the impact of refactoring on smells: a longitudinal study of 23 software projects. In: Proceedings of Joint Meeting on Foundations of Software Engineering, pp. 465–475 (2017)
4. Dig, D., Johnson, R.: How do APIs evolve? A story of refactoring. Softw. Maint., Evol. Res. Pract. **18**(2), 83–107 (2006)
5. Li, L., Bissyandé, T.F., Wang, H., Klein, J.: CiD: automating the detection of API-related compatibility issues in android apps. In: Proceedings of ACM SIGSOFT International Symposium on Software Testing and Analysis, pp. 153–163 (2018)
6. Michail, A.: Data mining library reuse patterns in user-selected applications. In: Proceedings of International Conference on Automated Software Engineering, pp. 24–33 (1999)
7. Moreno, L., Bavota, G., Penta, M.D., Oliveto, R., Marcus, A., Canfora, G.: ARENA: an approach for the automated generation of release notes. IEEE Trans. Softw. Eng. **43**(2), 106–127 (2017)
8. Silva, D., Valente, M.T.: RefDiff: detecting refactorings in version histories. In: Proceedings of IEEE/ACM International Conference on Mining Software Repositories, pp. 269–279 (2017)
9. Tsantalis, N., Ketkar, A., Dig, D.: RefactoringMiner 2.0. IEEE Trans. Softw. Eng. 1–21 (2020)

10. Xavier, L., Brito, A., Hora, A., Valente, M.T.: Historical and impact analysis of API breaking changes: a large-scale study. In: Proceedings of International Conference on Software Analysing, Evolution, Reengineering, pp. 138–147 (2017)
11. Xavier, L., Hora, A., Valente, M.T.: Why do we break APIs? First answers from developers. In: Proceedings of International Conference on Software Analysing, Evolution, Reengineering, pp. 392–396 (2017)

Empirical Studies

Defining Requirements Strategies in Agile: A Design Science Research Study

Amna Pir Muhammad[1]([✉]) [iD], Eric Knauss[1]([✉]) [iD], Odzaya Batsaikhan[1],
Nassiba El Haskouri[1], Yi-Chun Lin[1], and Alessia Knauss[2]

[1] Deprtment of Computer Science and Eng., Chalmers, University of Gothenburg,
Gothenburg, Sweden
amnap@chalmers.se
[2] Zenseact AB, Gothenburg, Sweden

Abstract. Research shows that many of the challenges currently
encountered with agile development are related to requirements engineering. Based on design science research, this paper investigates critical
challenges that arise in agile development from an undefined requirements strategy. We explore potential ways to address these challenges
and synthesize the key building blocks of requirements strategies. Our
design science research rests on a multiple case study with three industrial cases in the domains of communication technology, security services,
and automotive. We relied on a total of 20 interviews, two workshops,
participant observation in two cases, and document analysis in each of
the cases to understand concrete challenges and workflows. In each case,
we define a requirements strategy in collaboration with process managers
and experienced engineers. From this experience, we extract guidelines
for defining requirements strategies in agile development.

Keywords: Requirements strategy · Design science research ·
requirements engineering · Large-scale agile development

1 Introduction

Agile development methodologies aim to shorten the time to market and incorporate maximum changes during the sprint to meet customer needs [21] and
have been adapted at small-scale as well as large-scale organizations [18]. With
its' focus on interactions and working software over rigid processes and extensive
documentation, traditional well established Requirements Engineering (RE) processes have been neglected. Research shows that many of the challenges currently
encountered with agile development are related to requirements engineering [14]
for example, misunderstanding customer needs, missing high-level requirements,
and difficulty to achieve having just enough documentation.

In this study, we identify specific RE-related challenges and related solution
strategies in agile development. Based on this knowledge, we derive necessary
building blocks as different viewpoints that should be considered when thinking

© The Author(s), under exclusive license to Springer Nature Switzerland AG 2022
D. Taibi et al. (Eds.): PROFES 2022, LNCS 13709, pp. 73–89, 2022.
https://doi.org/10.1007/978-3-031-21388-5_6

strategically about RE in agile development. In this, we are inspired by test strategies, which guide testing activities to achieve the quality assurance objectives [8] and which mandate that each project must have its test plan document that clearly states the scope, approach, resources, and schedule for testing activities [20]. We argue that defining a so called *requirements strategy* similar to a test strategy for RE can be critical for successful agile development.

In this paper, we aim to establish the concept of *requirements strategy for agile development* by investigating the following research questions based on iterative design science research in three industrial case studies.

RQ1 Which challenges arise from an undefined requirements strategy?
RQ2 How do companies aim to address these challenges?
RQ3 Which potential building blocks should be considered for defining a requirements strategy?

Since we particularly target agile development, we aimed to investigate requirements challenges independent from process phases or specific documents. Instead, we took the lens of *shared understanding* [7] to investigate different RE activities (i.e., elicitation, interpretation, negotiation, documentation, general issues). According to Fricker and Glinz, an investigation of *shared understanding* may primarily target how such shared understanding is *enabled* in an organization, how it is *built*, and how it is *assessed* for relevance [7].

Therefore, our contribution are guidelines on how requirements strategies should be described for agile development. Through building three complementary perspectives, we see that the requirement strategy guidelines capture relevant information and provide a useful overview. We suggest that a strategy defines the structure of requirements to create a shared language, define the organizational responsibilities and ownership of requirements knowledge, and then map both structure and responsibilities to the agile workflow.

In the next section, we provide the related work for our study. In Sect. 3 we elaborate on our design science research method before revealing our findings in Sect. 4 in order to answer our research questions. Then, in Sect. 5, we present our artifact - guidelines on how to define a requirements strategy for RE in agile development. Finally, we discuss and conclude our paper in Sect. 6.

2   Related Work

Literature shows that many companies adopt agile methods [13,17] due to its numerous benefits, for example, flexibility in product scope which improves the success rate of products [3], in contrast to traditional development methods [27]. Furthermore, agile methods incorporate maximum change and frequent product delivery [13], encourage changes with low costs, and provide high quality products in short iterations [21]. Due to its success, agile methodologies are become widely popular and adopted by both small and large companies [18]. The term *large-scale agile* refers to agile development, which includes large teams and large multi-team projects [4]. Dikert et al. define large-scale agile development as agile development that includes six or more teams [3].

However, despite the success of agile methods, large-scale companies also still face several challenges. Dikert et al. (2016) [3] conducted a systematic literature review of empirical studies. The authors identified several challenges and success factors for adopting agile on a large scale. The most mentioned challenges are change resistance, integrating non-development functions, difficulty to implement agile methods (misunderstanding, lack of guidance), requirement engineering challenges (e.g., high-level requirements management largely missing in agile methods, the gap between long and short term planning). Based on a literature review, Dumitriu et al. (2019) [5] identified 12 challenges of applying large-scale agile methods at the organization level. The most cited challenge is the coordination of several agile teams. Kasauli et el. (2021) [14] identified 24 challenges through multiple case studies across seven large-scale companies. Some of the identified challenges are building long lasting customer value, managing experimental requirements, and documentation to complete tests and stories. The authors conclude that strong RE approaches are needed to overcome many identified challenges.

When it comes to RE in agile development, challenges that have been identified include lack of documentation, project budget, time estimation, and shared understanding of customer values [1,6,12,15,24] First attempts have been made to tackle some of the challenges of RE in agile development, e.g., Inayat et al. and Paetsch et al. [12,22]. suggest combining traditional RE with agile methods and encounter challenges like how much documentation is just enough documentation [11] to have a shared understanding of customer values.

Considering that there are many challenges related to RE that can be solved through RE approaches, this paper proposes to use the concept of a requirements strategy as a method to define requirements engineering practices to tackle challenges related to requirements engineering in agile development.

3 Design Science Research Method

Our research aims to design suitable ways of defining requirements strategies for organizations with agile software development. Such requirements strategies should be suitable for addressing real-world needs, incorporating state-of-the-art knowledge, and ideally being empirically evaluated in practice. Thus, we decided that design science research [10,28,29] is a good fit.

Design Science Research. Our research questions are targeted towards design science research, with RQ1 focusing on the problem domain, RQ2 investigating potential solutions, and RQ3 targeting towards deriving the artifact. Our artifact are guidelines on how to define a requirements strategy in agile development. Refining on well-known challenges with RE in agile development, we needed to gain in-depth insights into those challenges related to a lack of a clear requirements strategy throughout the agile development organization (RQ1). Throughout our cases, we discuss those challenges with respect to potential mitigation strategies (RQ2) for those challenges. Finally, we systematically synthesize the building blocks of requirements strategies (RQ3) from solution strategies.

Table 1. Research questions in relation to cases and research cycles

	Case 1	Case 2			Case 3
	Cycle 1	Cycle 2	Cycle 3	Cycle 4	Cycle 5
Identify challenges (RQ1)	■■■■■■	■■■■■■	■■■■□□	■■□□□□	■■■□□□
Identify solutions (RQ2)	■■■■□□	■■□□□□	■■■■■■	■■■■□□	■■■□□□
Building blocks (RQ3)	■■□□□□	□□□□□□	■□□□□□	■■□□□□	■■■■■■
Data source	11 Interviews, document analysis	9 Interviews, participant observation, document analysis, 1 workshop			Participant observation, document analysis, 1 workshop

Inspired by the regulative cycle [29], the artifact (guidelines for defining a requirements strategy based on good practices from our cases) has iteratively evolved, allowing to refine the knowledge with respect to each research question. Table 1 provides an overview of our research method. As can be seen, we relied on three case studies over which we distribute a total of five research cycles. The cycles differ in how much focus is given to each of our three research questions:

Case 1 - Exploring the problem through the lens of requirements engineering and shared understanding: Case 1, an information and communication technology company, focuses on a strategy to achieve a shared understanding about customer value throughout the development organization. Our research aims were two-fold: understand the real world problem and conceptualize a design artifact that may address this problem. Within a Master's thesis [2], we developed an appropriate lens that combined both the concept of shared understanding (as expressed by Glinz and Fricker through enabling, building, and assessing shared understanding [7]) and commonly used RE activities (such as elicitation, interpretation, negotiation, and documentation). We then relied on 11 interviews to understand customer value and its common understanding, information sharing, tools and channels for sharing, and tools and methods for documenting. Since our first cycle focuses on the exploration of the problem we locally relied on the case study research method for our research with respect to Case 1 [2]. As Table 1 shows, we complemented the interviews with document analysis to produce an overview of challenges and related solution strategies.

Case 2 - Refining the requirements strategy artifact iteratively: We then followed up in *Case 2*, a company producing security smart alarms and services. In this case, the focus was on a more general requirements strategy that covers both stakeholder and system requirements. Again, through a Master's thesis [8], we investigated concrete requirements challenges of an agile team, defined a requirements strategy along the lines of the result from Case 1, and investigated in depth to what extent it could help with the challenges in practice. At this point, we further focused on investigating whether there are reusable building blocks for a requirements strategy.

Case 3 - Applying and evaluating the artifact: Finally, we brought our experience from the previous two cases into *Case 3*, an automotive supplier, focusing on complex safety critical and software intense systems. Here, we focus less on challenges and solution strategies, in particular, since the case company already had compiled a good overview. Instead, our focus is to refine the artifact (guidelines for requirements strategies) by discussing, applying, and improving our understanding of the building blocks of a requirements strategy. At the time of the research, the first author of this paper did an internship with this automotive supplier and helped to make the requirements strategy explicit. The company did already identify some of the challenges and making a first step towards implementing their solution strategies. Thus, she was able to investigate the phenomenon as a participant observer, contrasting it with documents and ways of working in the practical context, allowing us to fine-tune our guidelines for requirements strategies to provide an overview of challenges and solution strategies for continuous process improvement.

Data Collection. We relied on a mix of different methods for data collection, including interviews, participant observation, document analyses, and workshops.

Interviews - We relied on interviews in Case 1 and Case 2, in particular, to understand the problem (RQ1) in each specific case. 20 interviews were conducted using interview guides (details in [2,8]), relying on a mix of closed and open-ended questions. Interviews were recorded, transcribed, and then coded. In both cases, we recruited interviewees through purposeful sampling [23]. We relied on convenience sampling so that interviewees were both available and knowledgeable. We employed diversity sampling to capture the views of multiple relevant roles and stakeholders and similarity sampling to ensure that we received multiple views for each relevant perspective for triangulation.

Participant Observation - The fourth author was very familiar with Case 2, in which she had worked for several years before starting her Master thesis [8]. Her work included defining a testing strategy, which provided intimate knowledge about the agile ways of working in the case company, which were also helpful for understanding the requirements-related challenges, defining a requirements strategy, and conducting the evaluation in Case 2. The first and last authors did work with RE and the continuous improvement of requirements processes of Case 3. Through this work, we were able to verify that previously identified challenges in Case 3, as well as initiatives to address them, were of similar nature and matched well with our recent work on requirements strategies. Both co-authors relied on our requirements strategy work to support the ongoing initiatives on requirements processes and on integrating RE practices into agile ways of working. This allowed us to evaluate the suitability of our requirements strategy concept. Knowledge from these activities was collected through field notes, presentations given at the case company, and discussions with other co-authors.

Document Analysis - In all three cases, a subset of the authors studied the documents related to the flow of requirements (Case 1: Author 3 and 5, Case 2: Author 4, Case 3: Author 1 and 6). Since all three cases embraced agile ways of working, we considered that not all relevant information might be found in formal documents. However, we ensured that documentation did match or at least not contradict our data. We found relevant documentation of requirements, e.g., as user stories, in all three cases to match and support our other data sources. Document analysis also allowed us to better understand the implied requirements strategy and processes.

Workshops - We relied on two workshops in cases 2 and 3 to evaluate the proposed requirements strategies and, by that, also our requirements strategy guidelines. In case 2, a workshop was conducted to present the challenges identified, the proposed solution candidates, and different versions of the specific requirements strategy of each case. In case 3, a workshop was used to understand the requirements strategy that was used to address certain challenges. Expert participants were sampled similarly as for interviews. They were asked to bring up additional challenges that we may have missed, give feedback on the criticality of the challenges that we had found, provide their opinion about the solution candidates, and evaluate the structure, presentation, and concrete advice on the requirements strategies. Depending on the circumstances in each case, we recorded and transcribed, took live notes for all participants to see, or shared our notes after the workshop for validation.

Data Analysis. In order to analyze interview transcripts, field notes from participatory observation and document analysis, and workshop notes/transcripts, we relied on typical coding approaches for qualitative research [26]. This allowed us to report on challenges that relate to a missing or undefined requirements strategy. For example, the following quote from Case 1 contributed to identifying the challenge *d) lack of communication with customers*: *"The thing that sometimes does not work as it should, is communication with some of the customer units. It heavily depends on the competence of the customer unit people."*

In each case, we had access to an industry champion from the respective company, who helped to suggest practical solutions. For example, the following quote suggested a solution for challenge above as *c) ability to initiate on demand meetings with customer representatives*: *"The right people to nail down a requirement should be put together in the meeting to have a requirement handshake."* In addition, the second author was involved as an academic supervisor in all three cases, providing pointers toward relevant published knowledge. We regularly presented and discussed our findings at the case companies, focusing on strong tracing between challenges, solution candidates, and the proposed requirements strategies. Together with iterative refinements, this allowed us to analyze the data in depth.

Threats to Validity. *Internal validity* aims to reveal factors that affect the relationship between variables, factors investigated, and results. A key threat to internal validity of this study is the risk of misinterpretations, particularly during the interviews and observations. *Construct validity* defines the extent to which the investigated measures describe what the researchers analyze and what is studied according to research questions [25]. We mitigated threats to internal and construct validity through interacting closely with industry partners in study design and interpretation of results. We also worked iteratively and triangulated across our iterations and cycles as well as different data sources. *External validity* relates to identifying to what extent our findings can be generalized [19]. We identified common challenges in all three case companies. Thus, we expect that in particular the structure and perspectives of our requirements strategy guidelines can be transferred to other contexts. *Reliability* reflects to what extent other researchers can produce the same results repeating the same study methodology. In a qualitative study, it is always hard to achieve *reliability* since one cannot argue based on statistical significance. We mitigate this threat by elaborating our research method in detail to support other researchers in replicating our research and in recovering from any possible differences in results.

4   Findings

4.1   RQ1: Which Challenges Arise from an Undefined Requirements strategy?

The left column of Table 2 depicts RE challenges identified based on our three cases that are encountered without a clear requirements strategy existing for agile development. The challenges are categorized in RE practices and related to Glinz and Fricker's [7] practices of shared understanding, grouped in three categories, i.e., enable, build, and assess. Enable practices describe what is needed to form and establish a common foundation of knowledge. Building practices aim to provide the structured knowledge that can be communicated within the team or company through explicit artifacts or by constructing a body of implicit knowledge for shared understanding. Assessing methods determine how all team members have a shared understanding of a topic or artifact. Some methods can be used for both building and assessing practices. Indices indicate in which of the cases a challenge was relevant.

   a) Teams struggle to integrate RE in their agile work efficiently[1,2,3] - Agile development enables organizations to respond to change. If there is a change in code and tests, the requirements should usually be updated. Or if requirements change, then the code and tests need to be adjusted accordingly. Teams struggle with this since requirements tools do not integrate well with agile software development work and do not support parallel changes from several teams. Thus, it is hard to integrate RE work into the agile work effectively.

   b) No formal event to align on customer value[1] - There were no formal events to create awareness of customer value in Case 1. Even when the customer unit took the initiative and organized some events, there were only a few participants. Such events must be better integrated in the organization and workflow.

   c) Insufficient customer feedback[1,2] - In Case 1 and 2, developers lack customer feedback, which is crucial for agile workflows. This can be due to a lack of formal events, or due to scale and distance to customers. It impacts the ability of an organization to assess whether shared understanding has been reached. Customer feedback should be integrated into the workflow across organizational levels and take into account the specific needs of product owners and developers.

d) Lack of communication with customer[1] - Customer-facing units have a key role and are on the boundary between development teams and customers. We encounter difficulties with communication in both directions: between customer-facing teams and development teams and between customer-facing teams and the customers. These challenges are mainly due to a lack of systematic guidance on how such communication should take place, thus depending completely on the individual skills of those involved. Companies would have to find a way to ensure good and transparent communication, for example by having product owners moderating direct meetings between developers and customers.

e) Who owns customer value[1] - Requirements enter the development organization mainly through the hierarchy of product owners (PO) in Case 1. However, a significant amount of requirements originate from other sources, e.g., development teams or system managers, and in those cases, it is less clear who is able to define or who owns the customer value.

f) Inconsistent elicitation[2] - POs or application specialists collect requirements when needed and apply techniques such as interviews. There is, however, no systematic strategy to elicitation integrated into the workflow.

g) Lack of feedback on elicitation[2] - Without a systematic validation of elicitation results, misunderstandings will only surface late in the agile workflow, e.g. during acceptance testing and result in additional costs and effort.

h) Unclear why requirement is needed[2] - Due to scale, distance to customers, or because a customer value description is not available for developers (see Challenge o), application specialists and POs may lack information on why specific low-level requirements are needed. This can result in a gap between what product owners want and how the development teams interpret their requirements.

i) Wrong assumptions about customer value[1] - Interviewees highlighted that one of the significant challenges is that people assume customer value based on their tacit knowledge, leading to the development of faulty assumptions.

j) Unclear and volatile customer needs[2] - Requirements change, for example when the customer changes their mind or did not have a detailed opinion in the beginning. When assessing the interpretation of requirements, this can cause friction, since the team tries to "hit a moving target".

k) Decentralized knowledge building[3] - Different teams develop requirements, architecture, and also processes at the same time. This decentralized way of working is needed to yield the benefits of agile work at scale, but requires some infrastructure to enable knowledge sharing and alignment. Otherwise, conflicting decisions will be made throughout the organization.

l) Focus on technical details[1,2] - Often customer value is not explicitly described; instead, customer needs and technical solutions are more explicit. When we asked participants in Case 1 and 2 to describe the customer value of specific requirements, they explained the technical solutions rather than customer values. This finding is consistent with documentation, where often technical details are described instead of linking to a business reason for motivating the requirement.

m) Requirements open for comments[3] - In agile development, everyone who has access to the system can create issues related to requirements in the requirements management tool. While it is positive to include as many stakeholders as possible

Table 2. Overview of Challenges in Relation to the Solution Strategies. Indices ([1],[2],[3]) show in which case study a challenge or strategy was encountered.

RE	Shared understanding			Solution Strategy
	Enable	*Build*	*Assess*	
General issues	a) Teams struggle to integrate RE in their agile work efficiently[1,2,3]	b) No formal event to align on customer value[1]	c) Insufficient customer feedback[1,2]	a) Tools that allow developers to take ownership of req.[1,2,3] b) Regular meetings with customer representat.[1,2]
Elicitation	d) Lack of communication with customer[1] e) Who owns customer value[1]	f) Inconsistent elicitation[2]	g) Lack of feedback on elicitation[2]	c) Ability to initiate on demand meetings with customer representatives[1,2]
Interpretation	h) Unclear why requirement is needed[2]	i) Wrong assumptions about customer value[1]	j) Unclear and volatile customer needs[2]	d) Fast feedback cycles[1,2]
Negotiation	k) Decentralized knowledge building[3]	l) Focus on technical details[1,2] m) Req. open for comments[3]	n) No time for stakeholder involvement[2]	e) Req. template includes customer value & goals[1,2] f) Define team respon- sibilities for different parts of req. and review updates regularly[2,3]
Documentation	o) Customer value description lost between systems[1] p) Lack of knowledge about writing requirements[1,2,3] q) No dedicated time for requirements[1,2,3]	r) Too much/not enough document.[1,2] s) Trace the requirements to all levels, (test, and code)[3]	t) Inconsistency b/c of requirements change[3]	g) Rationale must always be provided[1] h) Just enough documentation[1,2] i) Plan time for requirements updates[3] j) Educate and train the development teams[2,3] k) Tools need to be setup to support traceability[3]

in discussions, without a defined process that respects the development lifecycle, this can result in an unstructured discussion and very late changes.

n) No time for stakeholder involvement[2] - Getting stakeholders' feedback after interpreting the elicited requirements is challenging since stakeholders do not have time for several meetings.

o) Customer value description lost between systems[1] - At the scale of Case 1, it is not unusual to use several different tools to manage requirements at various abstraction layers. Customer-facing units use one tool, in which they define stakeholder requirements and customer value. Development teams interact with different tools, and it is the task of the POs to refine and decompose the stakeholder requirements from tool 1 into work items for the agile teams in tool 2. At this step, documentation about customer value is often not transferred and thus not available to the developers.

p) Lack of knowledge about writing requirements[1,2,3] - Throughout our cases, we found that those who are responsible for documenting requirements often do not have the right training. In addition, we frequently saw a lack of structure and no requirements information model. Thus, teams mix stakeholder and system requirements and are challenged with writing high-quality user stories, system requirements, and in particular quality requirements. In particular, the quality requirements might not get documented at all and teams will work on them without making them visible on the sprint dashboard.

q) No dedicated time for requirements[1,2,3] - Since agile methods focus on reducing time to market, spending time on writing formal requirements is not considered. Instead, agile teams rely on verbal requirements. Dedicated time to work on requirements should be integrated in the agile workflow, e.g. each sprint.

r) Too much/not enough documentation[1,2] - Because agile focuses on less documentation, some essential information could be missing (e.g., such as the "why" part of the requirement). Thus, in agile development, determining the right amount or sweet spot of documentation is challenging.

s) Trace the requirements to all levels, (test, and code)[3] - Due to ISO26262 and ASPICE compliance, the automotive company needs to guarantee full traceability between all requirements levels, (tests, and code). This places a big challenge on the entire company, since most teams work on something related to requirements, tests, or code and those artifacts evolve in parallel.

t) Inconsistency because of requirements change[3] - Agile methods embrace change and, consequently, teams will make changes on requirements during their work. However, it is challenging to handle sudden change requests and opinions from different team members, especially at scale. The consequence can be that teams inconsistently change related requirements, or that the scope is increased without central control. The problem is known, yet there is a lack of guidance on how to handle this in large-scale agile development to avoid expensive rework.

4.2   RQ2: How Do Companies Aim to Address These Challenges?

The last column of Table 2 summarizes the answers to RQ2 on solution strategies associated with the challenges with each phase of RE in respective rows, derived from interviews, literature, or workshops and confirmed by experts in each case.

a) Tools that allow developers to take ownership of requirements[1,2,3] - In order to allow developers to take ownership of requirements, we need to find requirements tooling that integrates into the mindset and the development environment of developers to provide an efficient way of manipulating requirements. For instance, developers work closer to the code, so the requirements tool that supports commit/git is highly encouraged.

b) Regular meetings with customer representatives[1,2] - The customer-facing unit should arrange regular meetings with customers. These meetings should be well integrated in the agile workflow and mandatory for team members.

c) Ability to initiate on demand meetings with customer representatives[1,2] - There should be a setup to initiate meetings with customers whenever developers need feedback. Since access to customer representatives is a sparse and valuable resource, a strategy for such meetings should be well aligned with the organizational structure and the agile workflow.

d) Fast feedback cycles[1,2] - All teams use direct communication with stakeholders and fast feedback cycles as a baseline to get the correct interpretation. Customer insight is abstract knowledge and could be hard to write down. There is a need to arrange events where people can meet, interact, and share customer values and feedback.

e) A requirements template that includes customer value and goals[1,2] - To avoid challenges related to a lack of awareness of customer value, there should be specific fields or tracelinks that show how each requirement adds customer value. It is important to check their usage regularly.

f) Define team responsibilities for different parts of requirements and review updates/comments regularly[2,3] - In order to yield benefits from agile workflows, RE must be integrated into the agile workflow. This means that agile teams need to take responsibility of maintaining requirements and to monitor changes of requirements that are potentially related. This allows to manage requirements updates in parallel and at scale. However, responsibilities have to be carefully delegated and clearly assigned.

g) Rationale must always be provided[1] - The rationale for the requirement should mandatorily be provided by the role/person writing the requirement. Moreover, it should effectively be passed on from tool to tool.

h) Just enough documentation[1,2] - Balancing sufficient communication and documentation is crucial in agile development. We should not spend too much time documenting; however, it should have all the necessary information. Developers need clear guidelines to achieve this balance.

i) Plan time for requirements updates[3] - Teams should plan (update, change, review) the requirements in time to align with the updated scope. Such a plan should consider that updating requirements in the scope of one team may imply also requirements updates in other scopes.

j) Educate and train the development teams[2,3] - If development teams should take more responsibility of requirements, they need to be trained in RE as well as in the specifics of the overall requirements processes in their organization. A clear requirements strategy can be a good starting point to plan such training.

k) Tools need to be setup to support traceability[3] - Requirements are usually represented in different forms (e.g., textual requirements, user stories) and on different levels (e.g., system level and software level). Teams could get requirements at higher level and then derive the lower level requirements (e.g., software/technical requirements). Tracing requirements could be hard in a large complex system. Tools are needed and they should be aligned with a requirements strategy for agile workflows, i.e. allow parallel work for many teams.

4.3   RQ3: Which Potential Building Blocks Should Be Considered for Defining a Requirements Strategy?

This section systematically develops the building blocks of a requirements strategy from our findings in all three cases.

In Case 1, the company was challenged to establish a shared understanding. Proposed solution strategies for specific challenges in Case 1 can be categorized as ***structural***, ***organizational***, or related to the ***work and feature flow***. For example, for the challenge *l) focus on technical details)*, a related solution strategy is *e) requirements template includes customer value and goals*. This strategy explains that, to avoid the lack of awareness about customer value, there should be specific fields related to customer value in the requirements templates. This solution shows that there is a need for improvement at the ***structural level***. In contrast, *b) no formal event to align on customer value* is a challenge related to stakeholders' roles and responsibilities that needs to be well integrated into the ***organization***. The last column in Table 2 provides a solution strategy related to this challenge as *b) regular meetings with customer representative*, which relates not only to the ***organizational perspective***, but also to the ***work and feature flow***.

In Case 2, we found the same perspectives (***structural, organizational***, as well as ***work and feature flow***) in in solution strategies for their specific challenges. As in Case 1, the solution strategy to introduce *e) requirements templates that include customer value and goals* is a ***structural*** example. In contrast, the challenge *g) lack of feedback on elicitation* can lead to misunderstandings late in an agile workflow. The solution strategy is to establish the *c) ability to initiate on-demand meetings with customer representatives*. Providing access to a sparse and valuable resources such as a customer representative relates to the ***organizational*** perspective. Another related solutions strategy, *d) fast feedback cycles*, for the challenge *j) unclear and volatile customer needs* falls into the ***work and feature flow*** perspective, by arranging events where people can meet, interact, and share customer values and feedback.

After looking deep into the concrete solution strategies in Case 1 and Case 2 (see Table 2), we found that many of these strategies were already successfully implemented in Case 3. However, the company still faced some RE challenges in agile development, allowing us to check whether the same building blocks are also applicable in Case 3. For example, the challenge *s) trace the requirements to all levels* can be addressed with the ***structural*** solution strategy *k) tools to set up traceability*. Similarly, the challenge *k) decentralized knowledge building* can be addressed by the ***organizational*** solution strategy *define team responsibilities for different parts of requirements and review updates/comments regularly*. Finally, an example of a ***work and feature flow*** related solutions strategy is to *i) plan time for requirements updates* in agile sprints to counter the challenge of having *q) no dedicated time for requirements*.

In summary, in order to address specific challenges related to enabling, building, and assessing shared understanding of requirements in agile development, specific solution strategies fall into three distinct categories: ***structure, organiza-***

tion, as well as *work and feature flow*. Thus, a requirements strategy that bundles solution strategies for a concrete case should cover all three perspectives.

5 Artifact: Guidelines for Defining a Requirements Strategy

Our artifact is a set of guidelines for defining a *Requirements Strategy* as a means to define RE activities in agile development. As a design science research study, we built this artifact in parallel to answering our research questions iteratively. In particular, RQ3 provides empirical validation of the building blocks. At the time of research, the term "requirements strategy" has not been widely used. This is in contrast to, for example, "test strategy", which has quite widely been accepted to describe how testing practices can be integrated in development workflows, such as in agile ways of working. In our work, we refer to "requirements strategy" as a general strategy for including RE practices in agile methods.

Definition: Requirements Strategy. A requirements strategy is an outline that describes the requirements engineering approach in systems or software development cycles. The purpose of a requirements strategy is to support decision makers with a rational deduction from organizational, high-level objectives to actual requirements engineering activities to meet those objectives and to build a shared understanding about the problem space and requirements.

The creation and documentation of a requirements strategy should be done in a systematic way to ensure that all objectives are fully covered and understood by all stakeholders. It should also frequently be reviewed, challenged, and updated as the organization, the ways of working, and the product evolve over time. Furthermore, a requirements strategy should also aim at aligning different requirements stakeholders in terms of terminology, requirements types and abstraction levels, roles and responsibilities, traceability, planning of resources, etc.

Table 3. Building blocks of a requirements strategy

| Perspective | Support for shared understanding of requirements | | |
	Common language	Knowledge flow	Examples
Structural	Define reqts. levels	Define structural decomp.	Stakeholder, System, Component Requirements
	Define reqts. types	Define traceability demands	Requirements and Traceability Information Model
	Define templates		User stories include customer value and goal
Organizational	Define ownership of reqts. types	Define roles and responsibilities	Training plan per type/role; Team responsibility sheet
Work and feature flow	Define lifecycle of types	Map structure to workflow	Elicitation strategy, definition of done
		Map organization to workflow	Stakeholder map, requirements review strategy

Therefore, our contribution is a model of how requirements strategies should be described for agile development. Through providing three complementary perspectives, the proposed guidelines help to capture relevant information and provide an useful overview. Our guidelines are summarized in Table 3 , including reoccurring examples and good practices abstracted from the three case studies. We propose that a requirements strategy should include the following building blocks: a structural perspective, an organizational perspective, and a work and feature flow perspective. Across these perspectives, a requirement strategy aims to support a shared understanding of requirements, in particular with respect to establishing a *common language* (i.e., enabling perspective in Table 2) and with respect to facilitating the exchange and *flow of knowledge* (i.e., building and assessing perspective in Table 2).

We suggest to start with a structural view to create a common language. A good starting point can be the artifacts in the development lifecycle model, for example the requirements information model in the Scaled-Agile Framework SAFe [16], or to define templates for user stories including customer value. Based on these initial definitions, refinements can be provided based on experience, e.g., after sprint reflections.

As a second step, we propose to make the organizational perspective explicit. Define the roles and responsibilities with respect to the definitions in the structural view. This can, for example, be done with a one-pager that describes the responsibilities of a team. Also, state who owns which part of requirements (e.g., requirements on certain subsystems) to determine specific training needs.

Finally, the work and feature flow perspective needs to be defined. A good starting point can be a lifecycle model for each critical type, which is then mapped to the intended workflow. In agile development, this can partially be provided by defining done criteria. In particular, it needs to be defined when and by whom certain information must be provided. If requirements elicitation efforts are anticipated, guidance should be given on obtaining the information from stakeholders. The workflow should be related to the roles and responsibilities as well as ownership. A stakeholder map can provide valuable information: who owns an artifact, who should be kept informed, and who needs to review it. An explicit review strategy can be very valuable, affecting not only the requirements quality but also keeping reviewers informed about recent changes.

6   Discussion and Conclusion

In this design science research study, we identified challenges related to agile requirements engineering in three case companies. Based on these three case studies, we identified solution strategies for resolving the identified challenges and derived building blocks as substantial parts of a requirements strategy. For each case we investigated a concrete requirements strategy. The individual requirements strategies have been well received by experts in each case company. Specifically, we recognize the need to enable, build, and assess shared understanding of requirements in agile development. As our experience grew, we noticed reoccurring building blocks on what should be part of such a requirements strategy. For our design science research, we choose therefore *guidelines for creating requirements strategies* as our artifact, which we develop in parallel to investigating our knowledge questions Our results suggest that a requirements strategy should describe how requirements are structured, how work is organized, and how RE is integrated in the agile work and feature flow.

Building on previously published challenges and solution proposals for RE in agile development (e.g. [1, 14]), our contribution is to enable organizations to define a holistic approach to RE that integrates with their agile development. Since our guidelines shall be applicable in agile development, they do not primarily relate to explicit documentation or a dedicated requirements phase within a development lifecycle, as for example custom in waterfall processes. Instead, we rely on the theory of shared understanding to embrace RE as a knowledge management problem and give suggestions on how organizations can approach it in their agile development.

Ideally, such a strategy should be documented concisely and made available to all stakeholders. Our requirements strategy can be interpreted as an instance of situational method engineering [9] where we focus on the context of agile system development and requirements methods in particular. By this, we aim to make it easier for practitioners to integrate RE in their agile workflows. This supports its evolution through the reflection opportunities built into agile methods. We hope that our requirements strategy guidelines facilitate future research on how to manage knowledge related to requirements in agile development.

References

1. Alsaqaf, W., Daneva, M., Wieringa, R.: Quality requirements challenges in the context of large-scale distributed agile: an empirical study. Inf. Softw. Technol. **110**, 39–55 (2019)
2. Batsaikhan, O., Lin, Y.C.: Building a Shared Understanding of Customer Value in a Large-Scale Agile Organization: A Case Study. Master's thesis, Department of Computer Science and Engineering, Chalmers | University of Gothenburg (2018). https://hdl.handle.net/20.500.12380/304465
3. Dikert, K., Paasivaara, M., Lassenius, C.: Challenges and success factors for large-scale agile transformations: a systematic literature review. J. Syst. Softw. **119**, 87–108 (2016)
4. Dingsøyr, T., Moe, N.B.: Towards principles of large-scale agile development. In: Dingsøyr, T., Moe, N.B., Tonelli, R., Counsell, S., Gencel, C., Petersen, K. (eds.) XP 2014. LNBIP, vol. 199, pp. 1–8. Springer, Cham (2014). https://doi.org/10.1007/978-3-319-14358-3_1
5. Dumitriu, F., Mesniță, G., Radu, L.D.: Challenges and solutions of applying large-scale agile at organizational level. Inform. Econ. **23**(3), 61–71 (2019)
6. Elghariani, K., Kama, N.: Review on agile requirements engineering challenges. In: International Conference on Computer and Information Sciences, pp. 507–512 (2016)
7. Glinz, M., Fricker, S.A.: On shared understanding in software engineering: an essay. Comput. Sci. Res. Dev. **30**(3), 363–376 (2015)

8. Haskouri, N.E.: Requirement Strategy in Large-Scale Agile Development: A Design Science Research. Master's thesis, Department of Computer Science and Engineering, Chalmers | University of Gothenburg (2021). https://gupea.ub.gu.se/bitstream/2077/69096/1/gupea_2077_69096_1.pdf
9. Henderson-Sellers, B., Ralyté, J.: Situational method engineering: state-of-the-art review. J. Univ. Comput. Sci. **16**, 424–478 (2010)
10. Hevner, A.R., March, S.T., Park, J., Ram, S.: Design science in information systems research. MIS Q. **28**(1), 75–105 (2004)
11. Hoda, R., Noble, J., Marshall, S.: How much is just enough? Some documentation patterns on agile projects. In: Proceedings of the 15th European Conference on Pattern Languages of Programs, pp. 1–13 (2010)
12. Inayat, I., Salim, S.S., Marczak, S., Daneva, M., Shamshirband, S.: A systematic literature review on agile requirements engineering practices and challenges. Comput. Hum. Behav. **51**, 915–929 (2015)
13. Jorgensen, M.: Relationships between project size, agile practices, and successful software development: results and analysis. IEEE Softw. **36**(2), 39–43 (2019)
14. Kasauli, R., Knauss, E., Horkoff, J., Liebel, G., de Oliveira Neto, F.G.: Requirements engineering challenges and practices in large-scale agile system development. J. Syst. Softw. **172**, 110851 (2021)
15. Kasauli, R., Liebel, G., Knauss, E., Gopakumar, S., Kanagwa, B.: Requirements engineering challenges in large-scale agile system development. In: International Requirements Engineering Conference (RE), pp. 352–361 (2017)
16. Knaster, R., Leffingwell, D.: SAFe 4.0 distilled: applying the Scaled Agile Framework for lean software and systems engineering (2017)
17. Lagerberg, L., Skude, T., Emanuelsson, P., Sandahl, K., Ståhl, D.: The impact of agile principles and practices on large-scale software development projects: a multiple-case study of two projects at ericsson. In: International Symposium on Empirical Software Engineering and Measurement, pp. 348–356 (2013)
18. Larman, C.: Practices For Scaling Lean & Agile Development: Large, Multisite, and Offshore Product Development with Large-scale Scrum. Pearson Education, London (2010)
19. Maxwell, J.: Understanding and validity in qualitative research. Harv. Educ. Rev. **62**(3), 279–301 (1992)
20. Méndez, E.M., Pérez, M.A., Mendoza, L.E.: Improving software test strategy with a method to specify test cases (MSTC). In: ICEIS vol. 1, pp. 159–164 (2008)
21. Meyer, B.: The ugly, the hype and the good: an assessment of the agile approach. In: Agile! pp. 149–154. Springer, Cham (2014). https://doi.org/10.1007/978-3-319-05155-0_11
22. Paetsch, F., Eberlein, A., Maurer, F.: Requirements engineering and agile software development. In: International Workshops on Enabling Technologies: Infrastructure for Collaborative Enterprises, pp. 308–313. IEEE (2003)
23. Palinkas, L.A., Horwitz, S.M., Green, C.A., Wisdom, J.P., Duan, N., Hoagwood, K.: Purposeful sampling for qualitative data collection and analysis in mixed method implementation research. Admin. Policy Mental Health Mental Health Serv. Res. **42**(5), 533–544 (2015)
24. Ramesh, B., Cao, L., Baskerville, R.: Agile requirements engineering practices and challenges: an empirical study. Inf. Syst. J. **20**(5), 449–480 (2010)
25. Runeson, P., Höst, M.: Guidelines for conducting and reporting case study research in software engineering. Empir. Softw. Eng. **14**(2), 131–164 (2009)
26. Saldaña, J.: The Coding Manual For Qualitative Researchers, 3rd edn. Sage, Thousand Oaks (2015)

27. Serrador, P., Pinto, J.K.: Does Agile work? A quantitative analysis of agile project success. Int. J. Project Manage. **33**(5), 1040–1051 (2015)
28. Vaishnavi, V., Kuechler, W.: Design Science Research Methods and Patterns: Innovating Information and Communication Technology. Taylor & Francis, Milton Park (2007)
29. Wieringa, R.J.: Design science as nested problem solving. In: International Conference on Design Science Research in Information Systems and Technology, pp. 1–12. Philadelphia (2009)

Analysing the Relationship Between Dependency Definition and Updating Practice When Using Third-Party Libraries

Kristiina Rahkema[✉][iD] and Dietmar Pfahl[iD]

University of Tartu, Tartu, Estonia
{kristiina.rahkema,dietmar.pfahl}@ut.ee

Abstract. Using third-party libraries is common practice when developing software. Package managers have made it easy to add third-party libraries as dependencies and to keep dependency versions up to date. Nevertheless, research shows that developers are prone to not updating their dependencies. We study how the type of version requirements used in the package manager manifest files affect dependency updating lag time (measured in days) and how this lag affects dependencies to vulnerable library versions. We focus on the package managers commonly used in iOS development, i.e., CocoaPods, Carthage and Swift PM. We first measure how the dependency updating lag time evolves over time for each package manager. Then we analyze whether and how the chosen type of version requirement affects the dependency updating lag time. Third, we investigate how not re-running package manager version resolution affects library updates. Lastly, we analyse how many vulnerable dependencies could have been fixed by updating the dependency. We found that dependency updating lag time differs between package managers but grows over time for all of them. We also found that the preferred version requirement types differ between package managers. As expected, version requirement types that are less restrictive produce less dependency updating lag. Moreover, we found that keeping library dependency versions up to date results in less vulnerable dependencies. Interestingly, some of the vulnerable dependencies could have been fixed by simply rerunning the package manager version resolution.

Keywords: Package manager · Dependency requirement · Third-party libraries · iOS

1 Introduction

Using third-party libraries can speed up development and, therefore, it is a common practice when developing software. Solutions in the form of third-party libraries are often better vetted and tested than custom implementations. For example, security organizations such as the Open Web Application Security

© The Author(s), under exclusive license to Springer Nature Switzerland AG 2022
D. Taibi et al. (Eds.): PROFES 2022, LNCS 13709, pp. 90–107, 2022.
https://doi.org/10.1007/978-3-031-21388-5_7

Project (OWASP), strongly recommend against the use of custom encryption algorithms [6].

Sometimes, however, even well tested and popular libraries can introduce security vulnerabilities. Therefore, it is important for developers to keep library dependency versions up to date to guarantee that security updates are included.

Decan et al. [1] found that, for npm packages, 24% of library dependencies are not up to date with dependency updates lagging behind from 215 to 267 days on average. Kula et al. [5] analyzed how developers update their library dependencies in Java projects and found that 81.5% of projects use outdated library dependencies. They also investigated reasons for developers to not update their library dependencies and found that developers feared high cost of updating and that developers were unaware of possible issues. Similarly Salza et al. [9] found that developers rarely update the dependencies of their Android apps. The reason might be that updating a library carries the risk of introducing incompatibilities through changes in the new library version.

Package managers have made it very easy to update library dependency versions. Using semantic versioning makes it possible to set version requirements and within these requirements the package manager finds and updates the dependency to a suitable new version. Semantic versioning makes it possible to communicate through version numbers if the new version of a library is a small or significant change. For example, a change from version 1.2.3 to 1.2.4 is expected to be small while a change from 1.2.3 to 2.0.0 is so fundamental that it might introduce incompatibilities.

Kikas et al. [4] studied the evolution of three library dependency networks. When looking at the dependency version requirement types, they found that the most popular requirement types were different for the three ecosystems. JavaScript libraries preferred the ˆ notation (up to next major version), Ruby libraries preferred the *any* notation (allowing any version of a library) while Rust libraries mostly required an exact version of a library.

Our expectation is that the choice of the version requirement type affects how library dependencies are updated. We investigate this expectation by answering four research questions (RQs) using a previously created library dependency network dataset.

The paper is structured into seven sections. Section 2 lists related work regarding analysis of dependency updates, vulnerable library dependencies and library version requirements. Section 3 explains necessary background, such as the dataset, the three relevant package managers, dependency requirement types and dependency updating lag. Section 4 describes the method. Section 5 gives results and discusses them. Section 6 describes the threats to validity and Sect. 7 concludes the paper.

2   Related Work

In this section, we summarize related work about analysis of dependency updates, vulnerable library dependencies and library version requirements.

2.1 Analysis of Dependency Updates

Kula et al. [5] analysed 4600 GitHub projects and found that 81.5% of the projects still keep their outdated library dependencies. They asked developers why they were reluctant to update. Some of the answers included fear of incompatibilities and lack of time to perform the migration.

Derr et al. [2] analysed third-party libraries in Android apps and found that 49.2% of the library dependencies could be updated to the latest version and 85% of the library dependencies could be upgraded at least by one version without any modification to the code. Salza et al. [9] analysed how developers update library dependencies in Android apps and found that in 63% of the cases developers did not update the library dependency after it was added to their project. They found that some categories of libraries, e.g., UI libraries, are updated more often.

Decan et al. [1] analysed the evolution of dependency updating lag in the npm library dependency network. They found that every fourth dependency suffers from dependency updating lag and that the mean dependency updating lag time ranges from 7 to 9 months.

We build on existing research by analysing the dependency updating lag time (defined in Subsect. 3.4) for libraries available through CocoaPods, Carthage and Swift PM, the three package managers used in iOS development. Analysing the dependency updating lag for these package managers gives us insight into a new ecosystem. Additionally we analyse if dependency updating lag only differs between ecosystems or if there are behavioural differences between users of package managers within the same ecosystem.

2.2 Vulnerable Library Dependencies

Derr et al. [2] looked at vulnerable dependencies in Android apps and found that vulnerable dependencies of 97.9% active library versions could be fixed by upgrading to the fixed library dependency version. Similarly, Kula et al. [5] found that many developers do not update their library dependency version even if a vulnerability in the library dependency is made public.

Decan et al. [1] found that 54% of vulnerabilities in npm libraries are fixed in a patch and 30% are fixed in a minor release indicating that even restrictive version requirements such as $\sim$ > would help including vulnerability fixes.

Similarly to Derr et al. [2] we report how many vulnerable dependencies could be fixed by a dependency version upgrade. Additionally we analyse how many of these dependencies could have been fixed by simply rerunning the package manager version resolution giving insights of how developers could mitigate risks from third party libraries.

2.3 Library Version Requirements

Kikas et al. [4] studied the evolution of three library dependency ecoystems. They also looked at the library version requirement types and found that they differ depending on the ecosystem.

Zerauli et al. [10] analysed dependency updating lag in npm and found that there is a reluctance to upgrade library dependencies. They found that there is a strong preference for specific use of version requirement types. They found that the most often used version requirement type allows updates up to the next major version (excluded).

We build on existing research by analysing the library version requirements used through CocoaPods, Carthage and Swift PM. We analyse how the choice of dependency version requirement type affect dependency version updates and dependency updating lag. We compare results for the three package managers and analyse if there are differences in version requirement type choice between package managers in the same ecosystem.

3   Background

Below we describe the used dataset, the analyzed package managers (CocoaPods, Carthage, Swift Package Manager), the types of dependency requirements and dependency updating lag.

3.1   Dataset

Rahkema et al. [8] published a library dependency network dataset for the Swift ecosystem. The dataset provides information on libraries available through the package managers CocoaPods, Carthage and Swift Package Manager, in total over 60 thousand libraries. The dataset is provided as a neo4j database consisting of nodes and relationships between these nodes.

The dataset contains *Project*, *App* (analyzed project version), *Library*, *LibraryDefinition* and *Vulnerability* nodes. To answer our RQs we query App, Library and LibraryDefinition nodes and the DEPENDS_ON relationships from App nodes to Library and LibraryDefinition nodes. The LibraryDefinition node contains information on the library dependency and the version requirement from the package manager manifest file. The Library node contains information on the actual library version matched as a dependency.

3.2   Package Managers

When developing iOS or Mac OS applications three package managers can be used: CocoaPods, Carthage and Swift Package Manager (Swift PM).

CocoaPods is the oldest package manager (released in 2011[1]). It has a central repository. Library dependencies are defined in a Podfile. When CocoaPods is run, it generates a new Xcode workspace and embeds the libraries specified as dependencies. Developers then have to use the Xcode workspace instead of the original Xcode project, but they do not need to perform any additional steps to embed the library dependency. Dependencies in CocoaPods are listed as pods with an optional version requirement:

---

[1] https://cocoapods.org.

```
pod 'AFNetworking'
pod 'FBSDKCoreKit', '~> 4.9'
```

A pod declaration following a pod name results in a dependency requirement where the latest possible library version is used. The following requirements can be used in a Podfile: ~ >, >=, =, <=, <, :tag, :branch.

Carthage was released in 2014[2] and was developed as a lightweight alternative to the more heavyweight CocoaPods. Library dependencies are defined in a Cartfile. When Carthage is run, it downloads and compiles the libraries specified as dependencies, but developers need to add these libraries manually to the project's Xcode project. Dependencies in Carthage are listed as origin, library name or repo path and optional version requirement:

```
github "Alamofire/Alamofire" ~> 5.5
git https://repository-url/project
```

Carthage allows three types of origin: github, git and binary. The github option requires a project name, the git option requires a path to a git repository and the binary option requires a path to a json file, that specifies where to get specific versions of the library. If no version requirement is specified the latest possible version of the library is used. The following requirements can be used in a Cartfile: ~ >, ==, >=, :branch, :version.

Swift Package Manager (Swift PM) is the official package manager for Swift (released by Apple in 2017[3]). It has no central repository. Library dependencies are defined in a Package.swift file. Running Swift PM not only downloads and adds the libraries specified as dependencies but also serves as project build file. In the Package.swift file the developer creates a new Package object and adds library dependencies as a list under the dependencies argument:

```
let package = Package(
    name: "TestPackage",
    products: [
        .library(name: "TestPackage", targets: ["TestPackage"]),
    ],
    dependencies: [
        .package(url: "https://github.com/Alamofire/Alamofire.git",
                     .upToNextMajor(from: "5.6.1"))
    ],
    targets: [
        .target(name: "TestPackage", dependencies: ["Alamofire"])
    ]
)
```

---

[2] https://github.com/Carthage/Carthage.
[3] https://www.swift.org/package-manager/.

A dependency package declaration consists of a URL and a version requirement. The following version requirements are supported: `exact`, `upToNextMajor`, `upToNextMinor`, `branch`, `revision`, `..<`, `version`.

3.3 Dependency Version Requirement Types

CocoaPods, Carthage, and Swift PM support different types of dependency version requirements. Generally, there are eight different kinds of version requirements: `latest`, `==`, $\sim$ `>`, `>=`, `>`, `<=`, `<` and `..<`. The version requirement types `latest`, `>=` and `>` behave similarly, by requiring the latest possible version with the only difference that `latest` does not define a minimum version. The version requirement types `<=`, `<` provide an upper bound for the version number, while `..<` provides both an upper bound, as well as, a lower bound for the version number. The version requirement $\sim$ `>` behaves similarly to `..<` where the version following $\sim$ `>` is the lower bound and the next minor or major version is the upper bound for the version number.

Each package manager has slightly different ways of declaring the version requirements. Table 1 lists how the dependency requirement types were unified in the Swift library dependency network dataset used in our study. A blank entry signifies, that this version requirement type is not supported by the package manager. Entry "empty" means that this version requirement type is used if no version requirement is listed in the manifest file.

Table 1. Unification of version requirement types

Requirement type	CocoaPods	Carthage	Swift PM
`latest`	empty	empty	
`==`	`=`	`==`	`exact`
$\sim$ `>`	$\sim$ `> x.y`	$\sim$ `> x.y`	`upToNextMajor`
$\sim$ `>`	$\sim$ `> x.y.y`	$\sim$ `> x.y.z`	`upToNextMinor`
`==`	`branch`	`branch`	`branch`
`==`	`tag`	`version`	`revision`
`>=`	`>=`	`>=`	`from`
`>`	`>`		
`<=`	`<=`		
`<`	`<`		
`..<`			`..<`

3.4 Dependency Updating Lag

When defining dependency version requirements developers can choose the exact version that should be used for a library dependency. They can, however, also choose a version requirement type that allows the package manager to update the library dependency version if a new version is available.

If a project is using a library dependency version where a newer version is available we consider the project to have dependency updating lag. If a project version uses the most up to date library dependency versions available at the time of the project version release then there is no dependency updating lag. If, however, the most recent library dependency version available at that time is not used, the dependency updating lag time is measured as the difference between the project version release time and the most recent library dependency version release time. The dependency updating lag time is measured in days.

4   Method

In our study, we investigate whether the version requirement used affects the updating of library dependencies. In the following, we first present and motivate our RQs. Then we describe how we analyse our dataset to answer them.

4.1   Research Questions

We formulate the following four RQs:

- RQ1: How long is the dependency updating lag time?
- RQ2: Does the version requirement type affect the dependency updating lag time?
- RQ3: How does not rerunning the package manager version resolution affect library updating?
- RQ4: How many vulnerable dependencies could be fixed by upgrading the library dependency?

To answer RQ1, we measure the dependency updating lag time for each package manager. Since developers seem to be reluctant to update their library dependencies our expectation is that this is also the case in the Swift ecosystem. We do, however, not know to what extent. Given that Swift is a relatively new language and not backwards compatible [3], we expect the lag time to be lower than, e.g., for Java projects. Since all three analyzed package managers belong to the same ecosystem, we do not expect big differences between them.

To answer RQ2, we analyze how a chosen version requirement type affects the dependency updating speed. Previous work has shown that developers are reluctant to update library dependencies [1,9]. Thus, our expectation is that $\sim$ > is the most often used version requirement type for all package managers. This requirement type allows updating until (but not including) the next minor or major version. This provides benefits from updating, such as including security fixes, while avoiding problems from major changes to the library functionality. Furthermore, we expect that version requirements that do not provide an upper bound result in a smaller updating lag time. If our assumption holds, it provides a good incentive for developers to use such version requirements.

To answer RQ3, we analyze whether rerunning the package manager version resolution affects the updating of dependency versions. We expect that when developers do not rerun the package manager version resolution then library dependency versions are not updated although the version requirement would allow an update, yielding increased dependency updating lag time.

To answer RQ4, we investigate how often a vulnerable library dependency could be fixed by upgrading the library dependency version. Additionally, we check how often the vulnerable library dependency could be fixed by simply rerunning the package manager version resolution. Previous research shows that most vulnerable dependencies could be fixed by upgrading the library dependency version [2]. Our expectation is that this should also be the case in the Swift ecosystem. We also expect that in some cases these vulnerable dependencies could already be fixed by rerunning the package manager version resolution without changing the version requirement itself.

4.2   RQ1: Dependency Updating Lag

For each analyzed project version, i.e., App node, we find library versions it depends on. We then find the latest version of each dependent library that was released before the analyzed project version. If the latest library version is already used as a dependency then the dependency updating lag time is zero. If a newer library version exists, then the dependency updating lag time is calculated by subtracting the commit timestamp of the newest library version from the analyzed project version. We record how many dependencies have a dependency updating lag and calculate the mean dependency updating lag time for dependencies that are not up to date.

Next, we calculate monthly snapshots of the library dependencies and calculate the mean dependency updating lag time for each month. We then plot the mean dependency updating lag time in days for each package manager.

4.3   RQ2: Version Requirement vs Dependency Updating Lag

First, we analyze the frequency of dependency version requirements used with each of the package managers by finding all

```
(App)-[DEPENDS_ON]->(LibraryVersion)
```

chains. The LibraryVersion node contains information on the version requirement type and the DEPENDS_ON relationship contains information on the package manager used. Then, we group the version requirements by package manager and version requirement type and plot the frequencies for each package manager.

To investigate how the used version requirement affects the dependency updating lag, we first need to match the correct LibraryDefinition and Library nodes. The App-to-LibraryDefinition node relationship corresponds to how the developer defined the library dependency in the package manager manifest file. The App-to-Library node relationship corresponds to which actual library version was resolved by the package manager a the given time.

We match LibraryDefinition and Library nodes by first finding the Library and LibraryDefinition nodes connected to the same App node. We then pair the Library and LibraryDefinition nodes where the name of the Library node ends with the name of the LibraryDefinition node. We use the ends with match instead of an exact match to account for cases where the LibraryDefinition only contains a shorter version of the library name.

To analyze the relationship between version requirement types and the dependency updating lag, we first find the percentage of dependencies with lag for each version requirement type and package manager. Then we calculate the mean dependency updating lag time for each version requirement type over all dependencies that are not up to date.

We plot the dependency updating lag time for each version requirement type. To take into account possible differences between package managers we plot the dependency updating lag time per version requirement type additionally for each package manager.

4.4   RQ3: Version Resolution Effect on Version Updating

To analyze whether or not rerunning the package manager version resolution affects version updating, we check whether the library dependency versions between two consecutive versions of a project changed. We then distinguish between (i) library dependency versions that were directly extracted from package manager resolutions files in the project repositories and (ii) library dependency versions that were calculated based on the version requirement in the package manager manifest file. For the latter case, the calculation is done as if the developers of the library had rerun the package manager version resolution for each new library version [8].

As for RQ2, we match App nodes connected to matching LibraryDefinition and Library node pairs. We then find the consecutive version of the App node and check if it is connected to the same Library node as the previous version. If the Library node changed and it is a previous version of the same library we record this as a downgrade. If the Library node is a later version of the library we record this as an upgrade. If the Library node remains the same we record this as no change. In addition, we check whether the Library node was originally extracted from the package manager resolution file.

Once having found all upgrades, downgrades and no changes in versions, we plot the difference between version changes where the library version was extracted from the package manager resolution file and version changes that were calculated based on the package manager manifest file.

4.5   RQ4: Dependency Updating Lag Effect on Vulnerability

The library dependency dataset we use includes, in addition to data on library dependencies, data on vulnerable library versions. For each project version with a dependency to a vulnerable library version we check if the vulnerable library dependency could be fixed by upgrading the library dependency version. Additionally we check if simply rerunning package manager version resolution would have resulted in fixing the vulnerable dependency.

For this we find App-Library-Vulnerability chains which indicates that the project version depends on a vulnerable library version. For each of these App, Library pairs we find the corresponding LibraryDefintion. We then check if there is a Library node that is a future version of the previously found Library node, but which is not connected to a vulnerability and where the library version was released before the App commit time. In other words we find the next library version that does not have a publicly reported vulnerability. We then check if the LibraryDefintion is connected to the new Library node. If yes, then it means that the vulnerable library dependency could be fixed by rerunning the package manager version resolution. If not, then the vulnerable library dependency could be fixed by upgrading the library dependency version. If no such Library node was found then it means that the vulnerable library dependency could not be fixed at the time of the project version release.

We then plot the number of projects with vulnerable library dependencies that could have been fixed by a version update, that could have been fixed by rerunning the version resolution and that could not have been fixed through a version update.

5   Results and Discussion

In the following we present for each RQ our results with a brief discussion.

5.1   RQ1: Dependency Updating Lag

For RQ1, we studied to what extent dependency updates were lagging behind. The proportions of dependencies having a lag was similar for all package managers, i.e., 43% of dependencies in CocoaPods, 32% of dependencies in Carthage and 39% of dependencies in Swift PM. For dependency updates that had a lag, the mean lag time was 92 days for CocoaPods, 45 days for Carthage and 58 days for Swift PM, as shown in Table 2.

Table 2. Lag time in days for dependencies with updating lag.

Package manager	count	mean	std	min	25%	50%	75%	max
CocoaPods	52975	91.6	170.5	0.000046	10.6	34.4	97.2	2625.4
Carthage	19957	44.8	86.1	0.000023	4.7	17.4	50.0	1827.0
Swift PM	7863	58.2	86.8	0.000266	6.2	25.6	75.5	869.8

The mean lag time for monthly snapshots are shown in Fig. 1. The data indicates that the lag time has been growing over time for all package managers. In 2022, the mean dependency updating lag time for CocoaPods is over 80 days, for Carthage it is over 40 days and for Swift PM around 50 days.

The lag time is similar for Carthage and Swift PM, but considerably larger for CocoaPods. For all package managers, the lag time is growing linearly with

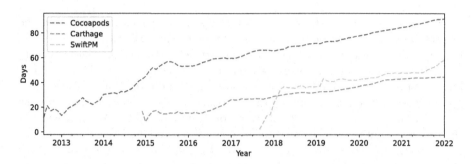

Fig. 1. Mean dependency updating lag time per package manager.

approximately the same speed. When Swift PM was released in the second half of 2017 it understandably started out with a near zero lag time which then quickly rose to the same level as that of Carthage. A possible explanation for the growing lag time is that there are projects that never update their dependencies.

5.2 RQ2: Version Requirement vs Dependency Updating Lag

For RQ2, we investigated the relationship between version requirements and the dependency updating lag. Our expectation was that version requirements without an upper bound would have a smaller lag time than version requirements with an upper bound or strict version requirements.

First, we analysed which version requirements are used through CocoaPods, Carthage and Swift PM. Figure 2 shows the proportion of each version requirement type. The analysis showed that when using CocoaPods, developers use the latest version option almost exclusively. For Carthage the most often used requirement type is ∼ >, followed by exact version and latest version. For Swift PM the most common requirement types is >=, which is very similar to latest, followed by ∼ > and exact version.

It is surprising that the version requirement type used with CocoaPods is almost always `latest`. In terms of how requirements are declared in the Podfile, this means that developers simply declare the library name without a version requirement. The official documentation for CocoaPods[4] suggest the use of ∼ >, but it seems that developers prefer to use an even simpler notation.

For Carthage, version requirements are more restrictive. Over half of the time, a version requirement specifying the major or minor version is given. This corresponds to the recommendation in the Carthage documentation[5]. Surprisingly, an exact version is used relatively often (20%). Perhaps developers using Carthage prefer to be more in control of when a library version is installed and they update the exact version requirement manually when needed.

---

[4] https://guides.cocoapods.org/using/using-cocoapods.html.
[5] https://github.com/Carthage/Carthage.

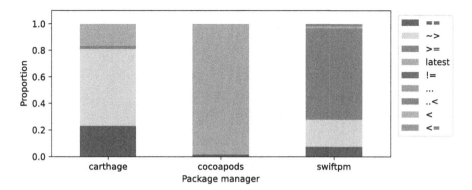

Fig. 2. Proportion of requirement type

Most library dependencies in Swift PM are declared with the >= requirement. This is the version requirement type suggested by the official documentation[6]. It can be seen as equivalent to the latest requirement in terms of potential dependency updating lag, as it does not limit new updates. We checked the version requirement types used in the README files of 30 popular libraries and found no connection between the version requirement type in the README and how developers declared library version requirements for these libraries.

A possible explanation for the difference between the version requirement choices for CocoaPods and Carthage are that Carthage was created as an alternative to CocoaPods. Some developers did not like that using CocoaPods forced them to use the Xcode workspace generated by the package manager. Carthage was introduces as a more lightweight alternative that gave the developers more control over the app project and how the library dependencies were integrated. It might be that the desire for more control carried over to how developers declare their dependency requirements.

Table 3 presents for each package manager the percentages of dependencies with updating lag of the four most popular version requirement types. For CocoaPods types ∼ > and >= were excluded as there were no or too few such dependencies. For all three package managers we see that the more restrictive version requirement types have a larger percentage of dependencies with lag than the less restrictive requirement types. For Carthage and Swift PM this difference is particularly big, as for the most restrictive == version requirement type almost 50% of dependencies experience lag, while for the least restrictive requirement type latest the percentage is only 25%.

Table 4 presents information on the lag time for each dependency requirement type and package manager. We excluded version requirement types with less than 50 uses (!= with 10 uses and ∼ > with 4 uses for CocoaPods; ..< with 30 uses for Swift PM). The overall trend for CocoaPods and Carthage is that dependencies with more restrictive version requirement types inhibit longer updating lag time.

---

[6] https://www.swift.org/package-manager/.

Table 3. Percentage of dependencies with updating lag per package manager and version requirement type.

Package manager	==	~ >	>=	latest
CocoaPods	52%	-	-	44%
Carthage	46%	29%	27%	25%
Swift PM	47%	40%	38%	25%

Exceptions to this rule are requirement types that are used relatively little, i.e., >= for Carthage. These results confirm the initial expectation that less restrictive version requirement types yield smaller lag time.

The results for Swift PM are not as conclusive. The lag times seem to be relatively similar for all four version requirement types. It might be that the nature of Swift PM - not being solely a package manager but a build system - results in it being used differently than the other package managers.

Table 4. Lag time in days for dependencies with updating lag.

Package manager	type	count	mean	std	min	25%	50%	75%	max
CocoaPods	==	907	207.5	280.6	0.002199	16.6	69.4	296.8	1268.2
	latest	52054	89.6	167.3	0.000046	10.5	34.0	96.1	2625.4
Carthage	==	5527	62.0	118.8	0.000590	8.7	28.7	71.2	1827.0
	~ >	11535	38.5	68.3	0.000116	3.9	14.3	42.4	1146.8
	>=	299	48.8	68.6	0.003970	3.6	15.3	53.3	270.4
	latest	2596	35.5	69.5	0.000023	3.0	11.8	35.0	751.7
Swift PM	==	695	63.9	101.8	0.002326	7.7	29.0	70.8	671.4
	~ >	2232	55.6	67.0	0.000868	8.0	30.1	81.1	613.3
	>=	4777	58.4	91.5	0.000266	5.4	23.2	74.2	869.8
	latest	121	65.8	84.0	0.010046	12.9	33.7	90.6	390.7

Figure 3 (a) shows the evolution of lag time for the four most used version requirement types over all package managers. The biggest lag time can be observed for the latest and the exact version requirements.

Figures 3 (b)–(d), however, indicate that looking at each package manager separately, the latest requirement has one of the smallest lag times. For all package managers the largest lag time corresponds to the exact version requirement. The results for Swift PM, again, are less conclusive and the lag time seems to converge for all version requirement types. Results for CocoaPods and Carthage, however, show that the choice of version requirement type has a noticeable effect on the lag time. This is an indication that developers should prefer less strict version requirements, where possible. If a less strict version requirement is not possible, then developers should update library dependency versions manually on a regular bases to keep the lag time low.

5.3 RQ3: Version Resolution Effect on Version Updating

For RQ3, we investigated how often library dependency versions are updated depending on the version requirement and if the library dependency version was extracted directly from the package manager resolution file or if it was resolved based on the manifest file.

Figure 4 shows the proportions of library *upgrade*, *downgrade* and *no change* for Carthage and Swift PM. We chose the most frequent library version requirement types for the respective package managers. From the data of both package managers it is evident that library versions are upgraded more often when the package manager version resolution is rerun for each new project version (left column of each column pair). We have no results for CocoaPods, as all library dependency versions were extracted from package manager resolution files.

Our results indicate that it is not enough, if developers choose a library dependency version requirement type that allows for frequent automatic updates, potentially resulting in shorter lag time for dependency updates. It is also necessary to rerun the library dependency version resolution by running the package manager more often.

There might be different reasons for developers not wanting to rerun the package manager version resolution, e.g., fear of incompatibilities, no time to check if everything works correctly, forgetting about the need to rerun the package manager. Although sometimes problems can be introduced by upgrading library dependency versions, some of these concerns could be alleviated by using a more restrictive version requirement such as ∼ >.

5.4 RQ4: Dependency Updating Lag Effect on Vulnerability

For RQ4, we investigated how not updating library dependency versions can lead to more vulnerable projects. Figure 5 shows the number of projects with a direct dependency to a vulnerable library over time that could have been and could not have been fixed by a library dependency version upgrade. We found that 30% of the projects with a direct dependency to a vulnerable library could have been fixed by simply rerunning the package manager version resolution (3%) or by updating the library version in the manifest file and then rerunning the package manager version resolution (27%).

These results show that, at least in terms of vulnerable dependencies, keeping the library dependency versions up to date results in safer projects. In this analysis we did not consider transitive dependencies, but it is possible that the dependency updating lag accumulates over dependencies of dependencies and therefore results in even less projects that include the necessary security fixes.

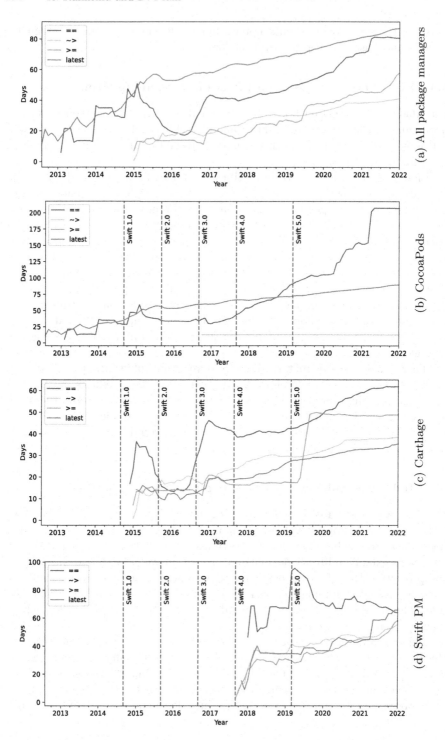

Fig. 3. Mean dependency updating lag time per requirement type for (a) all package managers combined, (b) CocoaPods, (c) Carthage and (d) Swift PM.

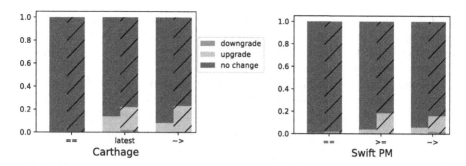

Fig. 4. Proportions of downgrades and upgrades for each new project version for dependencies through Carthage and Swift PM (library version taken from resolution file is shown in left column of each column pair).

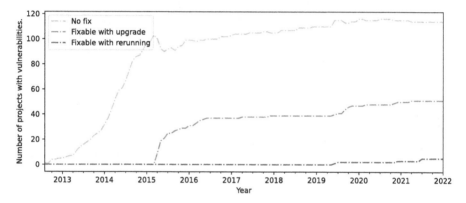

Fig. 5. Number of projects with dependencies to vulnerable libraries that could not have been fixed by an upgrade of the dependency (red line) versus those that could have been fixed (blue and green lines). (Color figure online)

6   Threats to Validity

Only partial results for RQ2 (counting of version requirement types specified in manifest files) were based on all library dependencies in the dataset, encompassing dependency information for 8674 libraries. All other results were based on a subset of 6329 libraries which included the package manager resolution file so that it was possible to match the library dependency definition from the manifest file to the actual library definition from the package manager resolution file. Out of these libraries, 4250 libraries had at least one version that had dependency updating lag. We have no reason to expect major differences between libraries that included the package manager resolution file and the ones that did not.

Our results are based on libraries that are open source. There might be differences in libraries that are open source and closed source. Most of the libraries used through the three package managers in our analysis [7], however, are open source. Further, our analysis only looked at libraries and not applications. There might be differences in how dependency requirements are defined and dependencies are updated as was shown by Kikas et al. [4] who reported version requirement types separately for JavaScript and Ruby libraries versus applications.

Due to the dependency updating lag definition used, our analysis only takes into account library updating lag times in libraries that are actively developed. The updating lag time is calculated based on the library dependency versions that were available at the time the project version was released. This means that if a project is no longer updated its dependency lag time is not growing. The advantage of this approach is that projects that have been discontinued will not inflate the dependency updating lag time. Nevertheless, it is possible that some of these projects are still being used and could therefore result it other projects having outdated transitive dependencies.

We use an existing library dependency network dataset [8]. The correctness of the used dataset was validated by manually checking suspicious data subsets. In each case there existed an explanation that made the correctness of the suspicious data plausible. The description and code to reproduce the dataset is open source and can be checked.

7   Conclusion

We show that the dependency updating lag time is growing steadily for all three analyzed package managers. We analyzed how version requirement types can affect dependency updating lag. As expected, more restrictive version requirements seem to yield longer lag time. The exception is Swift PM, where the dependency updating lag time is relatively similar for all version requirement types.

We recommend that developers choose less restrictive version requirements where possible. Additionally, it is important to regularly run package manager updates so that library dependency versions can be updated. One reason to keep up to date with library dependency versions is to include security fixes. We showed that around 30% of projects could fix their vulnerable dependencies by upgrading the library dependency version and 3% of the projects could include a fix by simply rerunning the package manager version resolution.

The version requirements of choice for package managers differ. It would be interesting to find out why developers choose a certain version requirement type.

Acknowledgments. Funding of this research came from the Estonian Center of Excellence in ICT research (EXCITE), European Social Fund via IT Academy program, the Estonia Research Council grant (PRG 1226), the Austrian ministries BMVIT and BMDW, and the Province of Upper Austria under the COMET (Competence Centers for Excellent Technologies) Programme managed by FFG.

References

1. Decan, A., Mens, T., Constantinou, E.: On the evolution of technical lag in the NPM package dependency network. In: 2018 IEEE International Conference on Software Maintenance and Evolution (ICSME), pp. 404–414. IEEE (2018)

2. Derr, E., Bugiel, S., Fahl, S., Acar, Y., Backes, M.: Keep me updated: an empirical study of third-party library updatability on android. In: Proceedings of the 2017 ACM SIGSAC Conference on Computer and Communications Security, pp. 2187–2200 (2017)

3. Ilseman, M.: Swift ABI Stability Manifesto (2022), github.com. https://github.com/apple/swift/blob/main/docs/ABIStabilityManifesto.md. Accessed 17 Aug 2022

4. Kikas, R., Gousios, G., Dumas, M., Pfahl, D.: Structure and evolution of package dependency networks. In: 2017 IEEE/ACM 14th International Conference on Mining Software Repositories (MSR), pp. 102–112 (2017). https://doi.org/10.1109/MSR.2017.55

5. Kula, R.G., German, D.M., Ouni, A., Ishio, T., Inoue, K.: Do developers update their library dependencies? Empir. Softw. Eng. **23**(1), 384–417 (2018)

6. OWASP: M5: Insufficient Cryptography (2016). https://owasp.org/www-project-mobile-top-10/2016-risks/m5-insufficient-cryptography. Accessed 3 Mar 2022

7. Rahkema, K., Pfahl, D.: Analysis of Dependency Networks of Package Managers Used in iOS Development, June 2022. https://doi.org/10.36227/techrxiv.20088539.v1

8. Rahkema, K., Pfahl, D.: Dataset: dependency networks of open source libraries available through CocoaPods, Carthage and Swift PM. In: 2022 IEEE/ACM 19th International Conference on Mining Software Repositories (MSR), pp. 393–397. IEEE (2022)

9. Salza, P., Palomba, F., Di Nucci, D., D'Uva, C., De Lucia, A., Ferrucci, F.: Do developers update third-party libraries in mobile apps? In: Proceedings of the 26th Conference on Program Comprehension, pp. 255–265 (2018)

10. Zerouali, A., Constantinou, E., Mens, T., Robles, G., González-Barahona, J.: An empirical analysis of technical lag in NPM package dependencies. In: Capilla, R., Gallina, B., Cetina, C. (eds.) ICSR 2018. LNCS, vol. 10826, pp. 95–110. Springer, Cham (2018). https://doi.org/10.1007/978-3-319-90421-4_6

On the Limitations of Combining Sentiment Analysis Tools in a Cross-Platform Setting

Martin Obaidi[(✉)][ID], Henrik Holm, Kurt Schneider[ID], and Jil Klünder[ID]

Software Engineering Group, Leibniz University Hannover,
Welfengarten 1, 30167 Hannover, Germany
{martin.obaidi,jil.kluender,kurt.schneider}@inf.uni-hannover.de,
hello@henrikholm.de

Abstract. A positive working climate is essential in modern software development. It enhances productivity since a satisfied developer tends to deliver better results. Sentiment analysis tools are a means to analyze and classify textual communication between developers according to the polarity of the statements. Most of these tools deliver promising results when used with test data from the domain they are developed for (e.g., GitHub). But the tools' outcomes lack reliability when used in a different domain (e.g., Stack Overflow). One possible way to mitigate this problem is to combine different tools trained in different domains. In this paper, we analyze a combination of three sentiment analysis tools in a voting classifier according to their reliability and performance. The tools are trained and evaluated using five already existing polarity data sets (e.g. from GitHub). The results indicate that this kind of combination of tools is a good choice in the within-platform setting. However, a majority vote does not necessarily lead to better results when applying in cross-platform domains. In most cases, the best individual tool in the ensemble is preferable. This is mainly due to the often large difference in performance of the individual tools, even on the same data set. However, this may also be due to the different annotated data sets.

Keywords: Sentiment analysis · Cross-platform setting · Majority voting · Development team · Machine learning

1 Introduction

The application of sentiment analysis in software engineering (SE) has many purposes and facets ranging from identifying the actual mood in a team to extracting information from app-reviews [9,18]. These tools usually analyze statements for the pre-dominant sentiment and classify them according to their polarity (*positive*, *negative* and *neutral*). Sentiment analysis tools are frequently applied to investigate the social component of a developer team (e.g., [5,21]).

These sentiment analysis tools are most often trained on data emerging from frequently used data bases such as Stack Overflow or GitHub [9,18]. Within these

© The Author(s), under exclusive license to Springer Nature Switzerland AG 2022
D. Taibi et al. (Eds.): PROFES 2022, LNCS 13709, pp. 108–123, 2022.
https://doi.org/10.1007/978-3-031-21388-5_8

different SE specific domains (e.g., GitHub), tools like Senti4SD [2] or RoBERTa [11] achieve high accuracies [13,25].

For a tool to be widely used in practice, it is important that it performs sufficiently well among different SE specific domains, and not just within one. Otherwise, it would be necessary to develop or train a separate tool for each domain, complicating the use in practice and reducing the number of application scenarios to a minimum.

However, several papers indicate that SE specific sentiment analysis tools perform worse in domains in which they were not trained (e.g., [10,13,25]), meaning that a tool trained and tested in one SE specific domain (e.g., GitHub data) performs worse in another domain (e.g., JIRA data). Cabrera-Diego et al. [1] identified that tools trained with JIRA did not perform well on Stack Overflow. Novielli et al. [13] investigated the performance of pre-trained sentiment analysis tools in different, unknown domains, in a so called cross-platform setting. They overall observed a poor cross-platform performance of the tools. For example, they observed a 26% difference in the macro average F1 score in a cross-platform setting with the tool Senti4SD [2].

One possible solution suggested by Obaidi et al. [18] and Zhang et al. [25] is to combine different tools by using a majority vote. The basic idea is that by combining different tools, a majority vote may be able to classify correctly, if a well-performing tool alone misclassifies. Moreover, such an ensemble combining different "domain expert knowledge" would allow the use in all domains instead of needing a separate tool for each domain – if the approach works.

In this paper, we analyze how such a combination of different tools performs compared to single tools and compared to different settings of training and test data. That is, we present combinations of three different sentiment analysis tools in a voting classifier (VC). In a first step of our approach, we combine three sentiment analysis tools and train them with three data sets. In this scenario, one tool at a time is an "expert" for a SE specific domain (as the tools are specifically designed to be trained with one of the data sets). We first investigated whether the tools achieve a better accuracy on the within-platform when they are combined. Then, based on a quantitative approach, we tried several combinations of pre-trained tools to investigate their accuracy in a cross-platform setting in two different experiments.

Outline. The rest of the paper is structured as follows: In Sect. 2, we present related work and background details. The concept of the voting classifier and its application in the study is introduced in Sect. 3. Section 4 summarizes the results that are discussed in Sect. 5, before concluding the paper in Sect. 6.

2   Background and Related Work

In this section, we present related work on sentiment analysis tools in general, voting classifiers and on SE specific data sets used for sentiment analysis.

2.1 Sentiment Analysis

For the field of software engineering, several sentiment analysis tools have been developed or evaluated.

Calefato et al. [2] developed the tool Senti4SD and thus enabled training and classification of models specific to the domain of SE. To do this, they used a specialized word lexicon in combination with a support-vector machine. With this approach, they were able to classify an input document in one of the three polarities *positive, negative, and neutral.*

Zhang et al. [25] compared the performance of different pre-trained neural network models with those tools using more classical machine learning approaches (but without training and thus without adapting them for each domain). These included four neural network models like RoBERTa [11], and five other existing tools (e.g., Senti4SD [2]). They found that the performance of these tools changes depending on the test data set [25]. They observed that the RoBERTa model [11] most often had the highest scores on average among the pre-trained transformer models.

Novielli et al. [13] investigated in their cross-platform study to what degree tools that have been trained in one domain perform in another unknown domain. They used three data sets and four tools and concluded that supervised tools perform significantly worse on unknown domains and that in these cases a lexicon-based tool performs better across all domains.

In their replication study, Novielli et al. [16] explained some sentiment analysis tools (e.g. Senti4SD [2]) in great detail and described the underlying data. They also investigate the agreement between sentiment analysis tools with each other and with manual annotations with a gold standard of 600 documents. Based on their results, they suggest platform-specific tuning or retraining for sentiment analysis tools [16].

All these mentioned tools perform well within one domain, but significantly worse in cross-platform domains [13,25]. One possibility to counteract this is to use a combination of several tools. To the best of our knowledge, this approach has not yet been used for a cross-platform settings.

2.2 Voting Classifier

To the best of your knowledge, the concept of majority voting has been applied in the context of sentiment analysis in SE in only three papers.

Herrmann and Klünder [6] applied a voting classifier (SEnti-Analyzer) consisting of three machine learning methods for German texts especially for meetings [6]. They used three different machine learning algorithms and an evolutionary algorithm.

Uddin et al. [22] used different sentiment analysis tools in a majority voting ensemble. They combined tools such as Senti4SD [2], or RoBERTa [11] in an ensemble and investigated whether majority voting can improve the performance of this ensemble compared to the best individual tool. In doing so, they combined several data sets into one large benchmark data set. Overall, they conclude that while ensembles can outperform the best individual tool in some cases, they cannot outperform it overall.

However, neither paper specifically examined how tools trained in several different domains perform together in a cross-platform setting.

2.3 SE Data Sets for Sentiment Analysis

Several papers highlight the need of domain adaptation to the field of SE (e,g., [2]), leading to some SE specific data sets. Recent SMSs and SLRs about sentiment analysis in SE show an overview of the data sets used [9,18]

Novielli et al. [15] collected 4,800 questions asked on the question-and-answer site Stack Overflow and assigned emotions to each sentence of the collected communication. Afterwards, they labeled these sentences based on these emotions with three polarities *positive*, *negative* and *neutral*. This labeling process was done by a majority decision of three raters.

Another gold standard data set crawled from GitHub was developed by Novielli et al. [14]. This data set contains over 7,000 sentences. Similar to the Stack Overflow data set [15], they first assigned emotions to each sentence and labeled polarities based on these emotions.

Ortu et al. [19] developed a data set consisting of about 6,000 comments crawled from four public JIRA projects. They assigned each statement an emotion label based on the Parrott emotion model [20].

Lin et al. [10] collected 1,500 discussions on Stack Overflow tagged with Java. Five authors labeled the data supported by a web application they built. In their paper no emotion model or guidelines for labeling were mentioned.

Uddin et al. [23] developed the API data set. It consists of 4,522 sentences from 1,338 Stack Overflow posts regarding API aspects. The authors did not follow an emotion model or any guidelines, but in their coding guide, an example sentence was mentioned for each polarity with focus on the opinion expressed in the text.

The APP reviews data set, labeled by Lin et al. [10], consists of 341 mobile app reviews. No emotion model or guidelines for labeling are mentioned.

3 Study Design

In this section, we present our research questions, our voting classifier approach and the used data sets. Afterwards, we describe our training methods, the used metrics for evaluation and for the quantitative analysis.

3.1 Research Questions

We chose five different data sets and developed a tool which combines three different sentiment analysis tools in a voting classifier. For this investigation, we pose the following research questions:

RQ1: *How does the classification accuracy of an ensemble of sentiment analysis tools vary in comparison to the individual tools trained and tested within the same domain?*

This allows us to evaluate whether a voting classifier in an already known domain offers any additional benefit in terms of performance. Based on the outcome of this research question, it would be conceivable to take an ensemble of individual tools for a certain domain in order to achieve a better classification accuracy.

RQ2: *How does the classification accuracy of the voting classifier vary in a cross-platform setting?*

To explore this research question in more detail, we split it into two parts:

RQ2.1: *Do different tools, pre-trained on different domains, perform better in a cross-platform setting in an ensemble than the best individual tool?*

In this first experiment, we consider all possible combinations of tools and pre-trained three data sets, testing them on two other data sets.

RQ2.2: *Do the best tools for different domains in an ensemble perform better in a cross-platform setting than the best individual tool?*

In the second experiment, we determine the best tool for each data set and then test different combinations of these tools, in a cross-platform setting. It can therefore happen that a tool occurs several times in an ensemble.

We call the analysis for the research questions RQ2.1 and RQ2.2 "experiment" so that we can simply refer to it in the further course of our study.

3.2   Selection of Sentiment Analysis Tools

For our voting classifier, we selected three tools with different machine learning approaches which we described in Sect. 2. Therefore, it is likely that they complement each other well regarding the strengths and weaknesses of these methods.

- *Senti4SD* [2], a machine learning based tool which uses support-vector machine and heuristics. It was originally developed for the analysis of Stack Overflow data.
- *RoBERTa* [11], which is a BERT-based model, using a neural network. RoBERTa was trained with several data sets consisting of, among others, Wikipedia articles, books and news.
- *SEnti-Analyzer* [6], which implements different machine learning algorithms (random forest, naive Bayes, support-vector machine) and an evolutionary algorithm. This tool was developed specifically for software project meetings and trained with student communication data from software projects.

Senti4SD [2] and SEnti-Analyzer [6] were trained and fine tuned with their default settings. The settings for RoBERTa [11] were adopted from the previous work of Zhang et al. [25] as they yielded the best accuracies.

Each of the tools is combined in a majority voting. If there was a disagreement between all of them (and therefore no majority voting possible), the output label is set randomly.

3.3 Data Sets

We used a total of five different data sets for training and testing. The data sets are described in Table 1. #Docs stands for the number of statements in the respective data set.

Table 1. Overview of the used data sets

Data set	#Docs	#Positive (%)	#Neutral (%)	#Negative (%)
API	4522	890 (19.7%)	3136 (69.3%)	496 (11%)
APP	341	186 (54.5 %)	25 (7.3%)	130 (38.1%)
GitHub (G)	7122	2013 (28.3%)	3022 (42.4%)	2087 (29.3%)
JIRA (J)	3974	290 (7%)	3058 (77%)	626 (16%)
Stack Overflow (SO)	4423	1527 (35%)	1694 (38%)	1202 (27%)

Unlike the other data sets, the JIRA statements [19] have emotions as a label. We took this data set and assigned polarities for each document similar to Calefato et al. [2] corresponding to emotions. Since there were multiple duplicates in the data set, we ended up with a total of 3974 statements.

3.4 Training

We trained each tool with 5-fold cross-validation. The data sets were shuffled and then split into five stratified folds. These stratified folds were balanced just like the data set. By using this kind of validation, we have decided against balancing the data sets, because it seems to be "realistic" that there is a lot of neutral in many data sets, which is the case for most data sets we use. The tools themselves implemented certain procedures to deal with unbalanced data as well.

3.5 Evaluation Metrics

When evaluating a model, accuracy is considered as the first relevant measurement value, since it represents the overall classification accuracy of a model [12]. Therefore, we present the accuracy in our results. However, for the choice of the best tool or model, we also consider the macro average F1 value ($F1_{macro}$), because it considers both the precision and the recall of all classes.

3.6   Interrater Agreement

To measure the extent to which the individual classification tools used within the voting classifier agree in their decisions, we calculated *Fleiss' Kappa* (κ) [3] as agreement value. Fleiss' kappa measures the interrater reliability between more than two raters [3]. We classify the kappa value based on Landis and Koch [8].

3.7   Combination of the Tools

Table 2 shows all the combinations of tools and training data sets we used for the evaluation of RQ1. Here we test the voting classifier in a within domain setting.

Table 2. Tested combinations of tools in a within domain setting with the same pre-trained data set

ID	Senti4SD	RoBERTa	SEnti-Analyzer
1	GitHub	GitHub	GitHub
2	JIRA	JIRA	JIRA
3	Stack Overflow	Stack Overflow	Stack Overflow
4	API	API	API
5	APP	APP	APP

We assigned an ID to each of the different combinations of tools so that we can reference them in the results later.

For the research questions RQ2.1 and RQ2.2, we opted for a quantitative approach to ensure the widest possible coverage of combinations. The different combinations for the first experiment (RQ2.1) are presented in Table 3.

Table 3. First experiment for testing combinations of tools with the respective cross-platform domains for RQ2.1

ID	Senti4SD	RoBERTa	SEnti-Analyzer
6	GitHub	Stack Overflow	JIRA
7	GitHub	JIRA	Stack Overflow
8	Stack Overflow	GitHub	JIRA
9	Stack Overflow	JIRA	GitHub
10	JIRA	GitHub	Stack Overflow
11	JIRA	Stack Overflow	GitHub

Here we selected three different tools and then permuted the respective domains within these tools.

In the second experiment (RQ2.2), we chose a deeper analysis and selected the best performing tool per domain, regardless of whether it was already selected for another domain as well. Table 4 presents the list of combinations. Because in all evaluations RoBERTa was the best performing tool, we listed the three tools as "RoBERTa1", "RoBERTa2" and "RoBERTa3".

Table 4. Second experiment for testing combinations of tools with the respective cross-platform domains for RQ2.2

ID	RoBERTa1	RoBERTa2	RoBERTa3
12	GitHub	JIRA	Stack overflow
13	GitHub	API	JIRA
14	GitHub	Stack Overflow	API
15	Stack Overflow	JIRA	API

We marked each usage of a combination of tools with a number after the ID, separated by a dot. For example, if the combination with ID 2 was used 3 times, we wrote ID 2.1, 2.2 and 2.3 in the tables and in the text. This ensures that we can definitively identify each run.

4 Results

We conducted the data analysis as described in Sect. 3. In the following, we present the results for the different analysis steps.

4.1 Within-Domain Classification

The results of the analysis related to RQ1 can be found in Table 5. As mentioned before, disagreement means that all three tools have assigned a different label (see 3.2).

Table 5. Classification accuracy within the same domain

ID	#Data	VC	Senti4SD	RoBERTa	SEnti-Analyzer	Disagreement	κ
1.1 (G)	1426	**0.93**	0.92	0.92	0.88	0.8%	0.83
2.1 (J)	796	**0.89**	0.85	0.87	0.88	0.1%	0.68
3.1 (SO)	885	**0.90**	0.87	**0.90**	0.86	1.2%	0.80
4.1 (API)	904	**0.91**	0.87	0.89	0.86	0.9%	0.68
5.1 (APP)	69	**0.88**	0.87	0.87	0.86	0.0%	0.84

For four out of five data sets, the VC achieved an accuracy 1–2% higher than the best individual tool in its ensemble (ID 1.1, 2.1, 4.1 and 5.1). Only on Stack Overflow (ID 3.1), the accuracy of 90% is identical between the voting classifier and the RoBERTa model.

The Fleiss' κ value for these combinations range from 0.68 to 0.84, which shows that the tools have a substantial to almost perfect agreement. The relative amount of disagreements per document are under 1.2%.

4.2   Cross-Platform Domains

To answer RQ2.1 and RQ2.2 we conducted an experiment for each research question.

First Experiment The results of the evaluation on API [23] and APP [10] are summarized in Table 6.

Table 6. Classification accuracies for RQ2.1. The best accuracy for each ID is highlighted in bold.

ID	Testset	#Data	VC	Senti4SD	RoBERTa	SEnti-Analyzer	Disagreement	κ
6.1	API	4522	**0.72**	**0.72** (G)	**0.72** (SO)	0.70 (J)	0.4%	0.33
7.1	API	4522	0.73	0.72 (G)	0.70 (J)	**0.74** (SO)	0.9%	0.33
8.1	API	4522	**0.72**	**0.72** (SO)	0.70 (G)	0.70 (J)	1.0%	0.23
9.1	API	4522	**0.73**	0.72 (SO)	0.70 (J)	**0.73** (G)	1.5%	0.29
10.1	API	4522	0.73	0.70 (J)	0.70 (G)	**0.74** (SO)	1.0%	0.28
11.1	API	4522	0.72	0.70 (J)	0.72 (SO)	**0.73** (G)	0.9%	0.28
6.2	APP	341	0.55	0.57 (G)	**0.70** (SO)	0.25 (J)	6.5%	0.20
7.2	APP	341	0.61	0.57 (G)	0.50 (J)	**0.62** (SO)	7.0%	0.39
8.2	APP	341	0.60	0.59 (SO)	**0.77** (G)	0.25 (J)	11.7%	0.14
9.2	APP	341	**0.62**	0.59 (SO)	0.50 (J)	0.61 (G)	4.7%	0.42
10.2	APP	341	0.52	0.35 (J)	**0.77** (G)	0.62 (SO)	12.0%	0.24
11.2	APP	341	0.61	0.35 (J)	**0.70** (SO)	0.61 (G)	5.9%	0.31

Overall, the voting classifier is either worse or exactly as good as the best of the used individual tools within the ensemble. The highest accuracy achieved by the voting classifier for API is 73% (IDs 9.1 and 10.1), and thus 1% worse than the best individual tool. All individual tools trained with JIRA achieve notably worse accuracy values compared to the other two data sets for the APP domain. Only in one run (ID 9.2), the voting classifier is more accurate (62%) than the three individual tools used in its ensemble. The RoBERTa model pre-trained with GitHub data achieves an accuracy of 77% (ID 8.2 and 10.2) and, thus, has the highest overall accuracy, beating the best VC by 15%.

The Fleiss' κ values range from 0.14 to 0.42, which corresponds to slight to fair agreement. The random label assignment per data point (disagreement) is higher compared to RQ1. For ID 8.2 (11.7%) and 10.2 (12%.), they are even above 10%, whereas the highest disagreement value in the API data set was 1.5%, the lowest was even 0.4%. Thus, the tools are less likely to agree on other domains which they have not been trained with.

Second Experiment In the second experiment, instead of three different tools, we selected the best tool for each domain. For this purpose, we calculated the average of accuracy and F1 score across all folds and chose the best ones. The combination IDs are presented in Table 4 of Sect. 3.7 and the results are presented in Table 7.

Table 7. Classification accuracies of the tools for each SE domain on multiple data sets. The best accuracy for each ID is highlighted in bold.

ID	Testset	#Data	VC	RoBERTa1	RoBERTa2	RoBERTa3	Disagreement	κ
12.1	API	4522	**0.71**	0.70 (G)	0.70 (J)	0.70 (SO)	0.3%	0.41
12.2	APP	341	0.70	**0.77** (G)	0.50 (J)	0.65 (SO)	6.2%	0.40
13.1	SO	4423	0.82	**0.85** (G)	0.73 (API)	0.67 (J)	2.5%	0.49
13.2	APP	341	0.73	**0.77** (G)	0.67 (API)	0.50 (J)	7.9%	0.39
14.1	J	3976	**0.79**	**0.79** (G)	0.76 (SO)	0.73 (API)	0.9%	0.51
14.1	APP	341	0.76	**0.77** (G)	0.65 (SO)	0.67 (API)	3.2%	0.50
15.1	G	7122	0.75	**0.79** (SO)	0.67 (J)	0.63 (API)	3.8%	0.42
15.2	APP	341	**0.67**	0.65 (SO)	0.50 (J)	**0.67** (API)	7.9%	0.32

In one out of eight runs, the voting classifier has the highest accuracy (ID 12.1), in two other cases (ID 14.1 and 15.2), it shares the first place with another tool. In the other five cases, it is second place.

Overall, the tools in experiment two performed the most robustly with a range of 0.67 to 0.82 (0.74 in average), compared to experiment one with a range of 0.55 to 0.73 (0.66).

4.3   Comparison of Results from RQ1 and RQ2

To study in more detail how the voting classifier performed among these two experiments, we built Table 8 based on the results from RQ1 and RQ2. It shows the performance of the best voting classifier from RQ1 (VC RQ1). In contrast, it also shows the performance of the best individual tool from the first two experiments (Tool RQ2) as well as best the voting classifier (VC RQ2).

The largest difference of accuracy between the voting classifier (0.91) and the best VC from RQ2 (0.73) is 15% for API. The lowest is 8% for Stack Overflow. Every single tool was better than the best voting classifier except for JIRA, where the best voting classifier and individual tool had 79% accuracy. The deviations for the rest are between 1% and 4%. In three out of five cases, a tool pre-trained with GitHub performed best, for the other two it is Stack Overflow. No tool performed best pre-trained with JIRA or API.

Table 8. Performance of the best tools from RQ1 and RQ2 for each data set. The best accuracy for each data set is highlighted in bold.

Data set	VC RQ1	Tool RQ2	VC RQ2
GitHub (G)	**0.93**	0.81 (SO)	0.78
JIRA (J)	**0.89**	0.79 (G)	0.79
Stack Overflow (SO)	**0.90**	0.86 (G)	0.82
API	**0.91**	0.74 (SO)	0.73
APP	**0.88**	0.77 (G)	0.76

5   Discussion

5.1   Answering the Research Questions

Based on the results and the findings of Sect. 4, we answer the research questions as follows.

RQ1: The results show that in most cases, we achieve higher classification accuracies using a voting classifier rather than using the individual tools in its ensemble. For four of the five data sets considered, the voting classifier achieves a 1–2% higher accuracy than the best individual tool and 2–5% higher than the worst tool.

RQ2: The use of a voting classifier does not lead to an increase of accuracy in a cross-platform setting in most cases. For a voting classifier, it is most often better to choose the best performing tool for each SE domain (RQ2.2). However, in most cases, the best individual tool should be preferred.

5.2   Interpretation

The basic idea of using a voting classifier can be useful, as our results showed with respect to RQ1. Hence, if the domain is already known and data sets exist for it, it is often useful to combine different, well-performing tools in one voting classifier, since the implementation of a voting classifier is quite simple.

However, based on the results of RQ2, there is not always an improvement by such a combination with different tools. Comparing RQ2.1 and RQ2.2, it can be concluded that the best method to achieve a good, robust performance of the voting classifier is to assemble the best tools for different data sets (RQ2.2).

It seems that the pre-trained data set plays a role in the performance of the single tool in an ensemble. This is not surprising at first glance. However, even though the API data contains statements from the Stack Overflow platform [23], tools pre-trained with API performs worse on the data set Stack Overflow [15] than tools pre-trained with the GitHub data set [14] (e.g. ID 13.1). One reason could be the different labeling process and the subjectivity of it, as mentioned by many papers (e.g., [7,10,23,25]).

Our results also indicate that labels from some data sets were subjectively labeled and may differ from labels from other data sets. For example, the tools that were trained with JIRA in the first experiment all received the worst accuracies in both cross-platform domains. It is reasonable to assume that the JIRA data set is very different from the APP review data set. The JIRA data set is the oldest data set among the ones considered in our study (published with labels 2016 [19]), so the labeling rigor back than might not have been the same. Another indication is the good performance of the tools, which were pre-trained by gold standard data sets. RoBERTa pre-trained with GitHub achieved the best accuracies in experiment two. For all four other cross-platform data sets (API, APP, Stack Overflow and JIRA), it was the best single tool. The GitHub data set differs from the other data sets as it is by far the largest data set and was first labeled by a guideline emotion model and then mapped to the polarities. This is also true for the Stack Overflow and JIRA data sets, but the JIRA data set is with 3974 statements smaller than GitHub (7122 statements) by almost 44% and is very unbalanced in regard to the distribution of polarities(cf. Table 1). 77% of the statements are neutral, which is much more compared to GitHub (42.4%). The Stack Overflow data set has almost 40% less data (4423). Unsurprisingly, RoBERTa pre-trained with Stack Overflow is the second best performing tool for three out of four other cross-platform data sets. Therefore, one reason for the good performance could be the large amount of data as well as the balanced distribution and the annotation process. This supports the need for consistent, noise-free gold standard sets [13,17]. These two assumptions (much data and emotion guidelines annotation) is also supported by the fact that in the comparison of all tools and voting classifiers in RQ2, only those pre-trained with GitHub or Stack Overflow performed best (cf. Table 8).

On the other hand, while the JIRA data set is poorly balanced, it was labeled based on the Parrott emotion model [20], but by other authors [19] compared to GitHub or Stack Overflow. However, RoBERTa pre-trained with JIRA performed the worst compared to RoBERTa pre-trained with API in all cross-platform data sets, except for GitHub. Therefore, another explanation could be that people communicate differently on JIRA and during reviews, e.g., we observe different levels of politeness. Another reason could be the unbalanced distribution of the JIRA data set.

The performance of the voting classifier in the cross-platform setting shows the tendency that it rather does not matter whether we choose different tools and thus different machine learning approaches or not. Surprisingly, RQ2.1 has shown that different tools, pre-trained in the same domain, have larger accuracy differences among themselves in a cross-platform setting. As soon as one or two tools in an ensemble perform significantly worse compared to the others, the voting classifier will accordingly not perform better than the best individual tool, and vice versa. Since we do not necessarily know the accuracies of individual tools in a cross-platform setting (e.g., new unlabeled data), it is a matter of luck whether the voting classifier performs better or a single tool. Therefore, we can conclude that if the domain is unknown, a voting classifier may well be an alternative to the dictionary-based tools that have been proposed so far for these cases [13]. But, our results do not show that a voting classifier can solve the problem of poor cross-platform performance, but rather show the limitations of such an approach in our setting.

5.3   Threats to Validity

In the following, we present threats to validity according to our study. We categorize the threats according to Wohlin et al. [24] as internal, external, construct, and conclusion validity.

The 1–2% better performance of the voting classifier compared to the best single tool observed in RQ1 is not high and thus could have occurred rather by coincidence (construct validity). However, the performance was 2–5% higher than the worst tool in the ensemble and we performed the evaluation multiple times to minimize this threat.

For RQ2, we used two different cross-platform domains for testing. One of them is the API data set from Uddin et al. [23]. This data is also from the platform Stack Overflow like the data set from Novielli et al. [15], which we used for training (internal validity). However, the API data set only includes comments regarding API. Moreover, based on the results of RQ2, we found indications that a tool being pre-trained with Stack Overflow had not resulted in an advantage regarding the API data set.

In the second experiment (RQ2.2), we only used RoBERTa. This makes the results of the voting classifier dependent on only one tool (construct validity). However, for each domain, based on the evaluation metrics, RoBERTa was the best performing tool.

In some circumstances it is possible that the results of this work are specific to the data sets used (construct validity). The API data set of Uddin et al. [23] and the APP review data set by Lin et al. [10] were presumably labeled ad hoc. The label assignment may not be representative (construct validity). By using the three data sets from Novielli et al. [14,15] and Ortu et al. [19], we attempted to minimize this threat, as these three data sets were labeled based on the same emotion model.

5.4   Future Work

Based on the results, interpretation, and to minimize the previously mentioned threats, we propose the following:

Evaluating other data sets is a possible approach to possibly improve the overall accuracy of the voting classifier. It would be beneficial to build more gold standard data sets for as many different SE specific domains as possible. Besides, the data sets should be examined for subjective labels. It should be investigated whether these labels were assigned consistently and to what extent subjectivity plays a role. Is a meaningful assignment of polarities possible at all? Or is the degree of subjectivity too great? In addition, factors such as the context of sentences should be considered. Do developers pay more attention to the perceived tone (e.g. "@Mark Not you again...") or more to the content (e.g. "I don't like this phone")? Here it could be researched in the direction of linguistics and psychology, like Gachechiladze et al. [4] conducted.

Furthermore, it may also be interesting to expand the number of tools within the voting classifier to allow for even greater domain coverage.

Our goal in this work was to combine pre-trained experts, because it was already found by Novielli et al. [13] that dictionary tools often performed worse compared to pre-trained tools in the same domain. Nevertheless, it is possible that a mix of pre-trained tools as well as dictionary-based tools perform even better, since dictionary-based tools have the advantage of hardly performing very badly since they use a dictionary [13].

The statements of our results do not necessarily have to be limited to the field of sentiment analysis. An similar analysis on other classification areas (such as classification to bugs or feature requests) would also be interesting.

6 Conclusion

To successfully complete a software project, it's important that developers are satisfied. To be able to measure the sentiment in teams, sentiment analysis tools have been developed. To train these machine learning tools to be used in the SE domains, data from platforms such as GitHub or Stack Overflow were crawled and manually assigned to sentiments.

However, tools trained in one of these SE specific domains perform notably worse in another, cross-platform domain. We analyzed this issue in detail. We first investigated whether a voting classifier can improve the accuracy of the classification in the same domain. Our evaluation showed that a voting classifier could improve the accuracy in three cases by 1% compared and in one case by 2% to the best performing tool of its ensemble.

Afterwards, we have examined the behavior of the voting classifier in a cross-platform setting. For this purpose, we conducted two experiments. In both experiments, we observed that the use of the voting classifier did not lead to an increase in accuracy compared to the individual tools in most cases. There were constellations in which the voting classifier was better than the individual tools within this ensemble. However, the voting classifier was not able to prove itself in terms of accuracy in an overall comparison.

When the three individual tools performed similarly well in the ensemble, the voting classifier was often the best performing. However, if one or two tools performed significantly worse than the rest in the ensemble, this had a corresponding influence on the voting classifier. Surprisingly, this deviation in performance was also observed and had a respective influence on the voting classifier when the individual tools were pre-trained with the same data. The influence of the data set chosen for pre-training has a more significant influence on the performance of the individual tools and thus on the voting classifier.

Acknowledgment. This research was funded by the Leibniz University Hannover as a Leibniz Young Investigator Grant (Project *ComContA*, Project Number *85430128*, 2020–2022).

References

1. Cabrera-Diego, L.A., Bessis, N., Korkontzelos, I.: Classifying emotions in stack overflow and JIRA using a multi-label approach. Knowl. Based Syst. **195**, 105633 (2020). https://doi.org/10.1016/j.knosys.2020.105633
2. Calefato, F., Lanubile, F., Maiorano, F., Novielli, N.: Sentiment polarity detection for software development. Empir. Softw. Eng. **23**(3), 1352–1382 (2017). https://doi.org/10.1007/s10664-017-9546-9
3. Fleiss, J.L.: Measuring nominal scale agreement among many raters. Psycholog. Bull. **76**(5), 378–382 (1971). https://doi.org/10.1037/h0031619
4. Gachechiladze, D., Lanubile, F., Novielli, N., Serebrenik, A.: Anger and its direction in collaborative software development. In: Proceedings of the 39th International Conference on Software Engineering: New Ideas and Emerging Results Track, ICSE-NIER 2017, pp. 11–14. IEEE Press (2017). https://doi.org/10.1109/ICSE-NIER.2017.18
5. Graziotin, D., Wang, X., Abrahamsson, P.: Do feelings matter? On the correlation of affects and the self-assessed productivity in software engineering. J. Softw. Evol. Process **27**(7), 467–487 (2015). https://doi.org/10.1002/smr.1673
6. Herrmann, M., Klünder, J.: From textual to verbal communication: towards applying sentiment analysis to a software project meeting. In: 2021 IEEE 29th International Requirements Engineering Conference Workshops (REW), pp. 371–376 (2021). https://doi.org/10.1109/REW53955.2021.00065
7. Herrmann, M., Obaidi, M., Chazette, L., Klünder, J.: On the subjectivity of emotions in software projects: how reliable are pre-labeled data sets for sentiment analysis? J. Syst. Softw. **193**, 111448 (2022). https://doi.org/10.1016/j.jss.2022.111448
8. Landis, J.R., Koch, G.G.: The measurement of observer agreement for categorical data. Biometrics **33**(1), 159–174 (1977). https://doi.org/10.2307/2529310
9. Lin, B., Cassee, N., Serebrenik, A., Bavota, G., Novielli, N., Lanza, M.: Opinion mining for software development: a systematic literature review. ACM Trans. Softw. Eng. Methodol. **31**(3) (2022). https://doi.org/10.1145/3490388
10. Lin, B., Zampetti, F., Bavota, G., Di Penta, M., Lanza, M., Oliveto, R.: Sentiment analysis for software engineering: how far can we go? In: Proceedings of the 40th International Conference on Software Engineering, ICSE 2018, pp. 94–104. Association for Computing Machinery, New York (2018). https://doi.org/10.1145/3180155.3180195
11. Liu, Y., et al.: RoBERTa: a robustly optimized BERT pretraining approach (2019). https://doi.org/10.48550/ARXIV.1907.11692
12. Manning, C.D., Raghavan, P., Schütze, H.: Introduction to Information Retrieval, reprinted Cambridge University Press, Cambridge (2009)
13. Novielli, N., Calefato, F., Dongiovanni, D., Girardi, D., Lanubile, F.: Can we use se-specific sentiment analysis tools in a cross-platform setting? In: Proceedings of the 17th International Conference on Mining Software Repositories, MSR 20220. Association for Computing Machinery, New York (2020). https://doi.org/10.1145/3379597.3387446

14. Novielli, N., Calefato, F., Dongiovanni, D., Girardi, D., Lanubile, F.: A gold standard for polarity of emotions of software developers in GitHub (2020). https://doi.org/10.6084/m9.figshare.11604597.v1

15. Novielli, N., Calefato, F., Lanubile, F.: A gold standard for emotion annotation in stack overflow. In: 2018 IEEE/ACM 15th International Conference on Mining Software Repositories (MSR), MSR 2018, pp. 14–17. Association for Computing Machinery, New York (2018). https://doi.org/10.1145/3196398.3196453

16. Novielli, N., Calefato, F., Lanubile, F., Serebrenik, A.: Assessment of off-the-shelf SE-specific sentiment analysis tools: an extended replication study. Empir. Softw. Eng. **26**(4), 1–29 (2021). https://doi.org/10.1007/s10664-021-09960-w

17. Novielli, N., Girardi, D., Lanubile, F.: A benchmark study on sentiment analysis for software engineering research. In: Proceedings of the 15th International Conference on Mining Software Repositories, MSR 2018, pp. 364–375. Association for Computing Machinery, New York (2018). https://doi.org/10.1145/3196398.3196403

18. Obaidi, M., Nagel, L., Specht, A., Klünder, J.: Sentiment analysis tools in software engineering: a systematic mapping study. Inf. Softw. Technol. **151**, 107018 (2022). https://doi.org/10.1016/j.infsof.2022.107018

19. Ortu, M., et al.: The emotional side of software developers in JIRA. In: Proceedings of the 13th International Conference on Mining Software Repositories, MSR 2016, pp. 480–483. Association for Computing Machinery, New York (2016). https://doi.org/10.1145/2901739.2903505

20. Parrott, W.G.: Emotions in Social Psychology: Essential Readings. Psychology Press (2001)

21. Schneider, K., Klünder, J., Kortum, F., Handke, L., Straube, J., Kauffeld, S.: Positive affect through interactions in meetings: the role of proactive and supportive statements. J. Syst. Softw. **143**, 59–70 (2018). https://doi.org/10.1016/j.jss.2018.05.001

22. Uddin, G., Guéhénuc, Y.G., Khomh, F., Roy, C.K.: An empirical study of the effectiveness of an ensemble of stand-alone sentiment detection tools for software engineering datasets. ACM Trans. Softw. Eng. Methodol. **31**(3) (2022). https://doi.org/10.1145/3491211

23. Uddin, G., Khomh, F.: Automatic mining of opinions expressed about APIS in stack overflow. IEEE Trans. Software Eng. **47**(3), 522–559 (2021). https://doi.org/10.1109/TSE.2019.2900245

24. Wohlin, C., Runeson, P., Höst, M., Ohlsson, M.C., Regnell, B., Wesslén, A.: Experimentation in Software Engineering. Springer, Berlin (2012). https://doi.org/10.1007/978-3-642-29044-2

25. Zhang, T., Xu, B., Thung, F., Haryono, S.A., Lo, D., Jiang, L.: Sentiment analysis for software engineering: How far can pre-trained transformer models go? In: 2020 IEEE International Conference on Software Maintenance and Evolution (ICSME), pp. 70–80 (2020). https://doi.org/10.1109/ICSME46990.2020.00017

Marine Data Sharing: Challenges, Technology Drivers and Quality Attributes

Keila Lima[1]([✉]), Ngoc-Thanh Nguyen[1], Rogardt Heldal[1],
Eric Knauss[2,3], Tosin Daniel Oyetoyan[1], Patrizio Pelliccione[4],
and Lars Michael Kristensen[1]

[1] Western Norway University of Applied Sciences, Bergen, Norway
keila.lima@hvl.no
[2] Chalmers University of Technology, Gothenburg, Sweden
[3] University of Gothenburg, Gothenburg, Sweden
[4] Gran Sasso Science Institute, L'Aquila, Italy

Abstract. *Context*: Many companies have been adopting data-driven applications in which products and services are centered around data analysis to approach new segments of the marketplace. Data ecosystems rise from data sharing among organizations premeditatedly. However, this migration to this new data sharing paradigm has not come that far in the marine domain. Nevertheless, better utilizing the ocean data might be crucial for humankind in the future, for food production, and minerals, to ensure the ocean's health. *Research goal*: We investigate the state-of-the-art regarding data sharing in the marine domain with a focus on aspects that impact the speed of establishing a data ecosystem for the ocean. *Methodology*: We conducted an exploratory case study based on focus groups and workshops to understand the sharing of data in this context. *Results*: We identified main challenges of current systems that need to be addressed with respect to data sharing. Additionally, aspects related to the establishment of a data ecosystem were elicited and analyzed in terms of benefits, conflicts, and solutions.

Keywords: Data sharing · IoUT · Data ecosystems

1 Introduction

Nowadays, we are observing an increasing interest of companies in data sharing and data ecosystems, as part of a transition towards data-driven applications, in which business value and innovation involves around data usage [30]. Limited and restricted sharing of data can be catastrophic not only to national interests but also to companies' revenues. In the marine context, what happened in the salmon aquaculture disease spread reported in 2009 in Chile [3] is a showcase of the consequences of such limitations. Signs of the outbreak were misinterpreted as single occurrences, combining unwillingness to report from some companies and lack of regulations, which led the country to substantial losses in the sector.

© The Author(s), under exclusive license to Springer Nature Switzerland AG 2022
D. Taibi et al. (Eds.): PROFES 2022, LNCS 13709, pp. 124–140, 2022.
https://doi.org/10.1007/978-3-031-21388-5_9

Marine data is produced by a network of underwater sensors. This network is referred to as Internet-of-Underwater-Things (IoUT) [7] and is resembling to Internet-of-Things (IoT) [19]. The collected marine data is transmitted to the shore via cabled or wireless communication. While the former is reliable, it is expensive to install. The latter is more affordable but has many technical limitations affecting data integrity. Other issues are also observable on underwater nodes such as limited power supply and high costs for deployment and maintenance. We refer the readers to [7,8,20] for detailed discussions. Those issues make collecting marine data costly and challenging; explaining why not much marine data is publicly available as pointed out in [26].

Concerning data sharing in other domains, products based on blockchain technology and its smart contracts are considered to be enabling transparency in sharing information among public and private stakeholders [21]. At the same time, data workflows are being operationalized for optimizing big data applications [15]. These solutions are being deployed in the transition to the new paradigm of data sharing called data ecosystems. In short, data ecosystems are defined as systems constituted by actors which can either produce, provide, or consume data. They do not necessarily depend on an explicitly shared data platform [17]. Data ecosystems are now present in many domains, such as supply chain and transportation [13], social media [24], and manufacturing [6]; but not in the marine domain. Once established, it would facilitate collaboration among stakeholders, improving operations and management of the oceans.

On the other hand, transitions to data ecosystem are strongly influenced by sector-specific demands [11]. In the BYTE European project[1], the relationship between stakeholders from different sectors was analyzed to identify external factors that can help increase the market share of this paradigm.

Before conducting this study, we held several meetings and discussions with experts and practitioners in the marine domain. The purpose was to understand technological challenges of marine data sharing. Interestingly, we identified conflicting views regarding data sharing by public and private stakeholders. Therefore, we conducted this exploratory case study by following the guidelines of Runeson et al. [22] to understand challenges, and benefits and drawbacks of sharing data in the marine sector. To overcome the challenges, we identified the need of a data ecosystem in the marine domain. Accordingly, this work aims to address the following research questions:

RQ1. What are the current challenges that organizations in the marine domain face when sharing data? Aspects such as barriers or limitations can contribute to the understanding of the constraints and be considered as opportunities to foster innovative solutions. All these domain characteristics represent current open challenges and influence architectural choices and thus, must be taken into account in the system development and evaluation processes.

RQ2. What could be the potential benefits or drawbacks of adopting the data ecosystem paradigm for sharing marine data? We want to investigate motivating reasons that can bring added values to participating organizations of

---

[1] https://cordis.europa.eu/project/id/619551.

the newly established data ecosystem. Additionally, we show potential draw-backs or hindrance that originates from the realization of this goal.

RQ3. What characteristics can accelerate this adopting process? We are focusing on high-level goals for the overall systems that can help address current challenges in marine data workflows towards the realization of a data ecosystem. We aim to determine technology drivers, system properties, and associated quality attributes that can help add value to software products and services in the marine domain.

The rest of this paper is structured as follows: Section 2 discusses related works at the intersection of this study, i.e. the marine data sharing and data ecosystems. Section 3 describes the research methodology of this study. In Sect. 4, we present our results, answering RQ1-3 in Sects. 4.1–4.3, respectively. Section 5 discusses our findings. Finally, Sect. 6 concludes the study and presents our future plans to extend this work.

2   Related Work

In the ocean context, the systems are divided into components with three main roles: data acquisition, communication, and services for applications [7,20]. The first two greatly influence the availability and quality of data along the delivery chain from sensing sites to cloud platforms, which are essential in understanding some of the technological challenges in the field. The last component is responsible for the accessibility of the data collected in the sensor network and typically provides endpoints for different data-driven applications. Regarding the sharing of data in this context, in the literature, there are some examples of practices that encompass common data infrastructures that rely on open data provided by public organizations [1,10,14]. These solutions result from the open-data principles adopted at regional levels and target marine and other earth observation data [27]. Inter-agencies collaborations allowed the adoption of common data exchange formats, nomenclature conventions, and retrieval services APIs in the different data management infrastructures, bringing together the marine community [18]. Nevertheless, these type of data and platforms are mostly understandable by expert users that know the context of these databases and what to retrieve from them [4]. Additionally, the applications are mainly focusing on providing data for marine science purposes and related scientific fields. In this study, we expanded the stakeholders' group to understand the views of organizations operating in the oceans for different purposes, but that are still considered to be marine data producers.

When it comes to data ecosystems, the concept is formalized in [17] based on a literature survey on the topic. The authors specify data ecosystems as being composed by *actors* (data producers, providers and consumers), with a set of *roles* that exchange *data-related resources* defined in the actor's *relationship*. Additionally, self-organization with feedback loops and actors networks (instead of value chain) are identified as one of the main properties of these systems.

In the supply chain domain (which includes maritime operations) data ecosystems are being deployed among different stakeholders to expedite processes and logistics around cargo shipping [13,21]. This is an example of data ecosystems implementation and deployment in production scenarios enabling transparent and automated transactions bridging the gap between governmental and industry organizations interactions.

Other examples of such ecosystems from different domains (Industry 4.0, automotive, and labor market) were also reported in [23], where three cases were studied in depth w.r.t. their collaboration around data, considered the business driver in the data ecosystems context. The authors suggest a conceptual model based on four high-level aspects to consider in open-data ecosystems: value, data intrinsic, the governance of the ecosystem, and its evolution. When it comes to data intrinsics, aspects such as standards, domain models, quality, and common procedures should be considered. Nevertheless, properties such as trust in the ecosystems can depend on multiple aspects. In the specific case in the supply chain domain, blockchain infrastructure enables traceability and access control [21], contributing to the overall trust of the system. In turn, trust is also being used as an alternative heuristic for data quality in data sharing in IoT settings [5]. These examples can illustrate the interdependencies of data ecosystem properties.

In this study, we investigate how these data ecosystem characteristics manifest in marine data sharing workflows and organizations' relationships. In addition, we aim to understand which aspects and mechanisms are to be taken into account to capture domain's constraints and ease the migration process.

3 Research Methodology

We followed the exploratory case study approach [22] and employed qualitative methods for data collection. The studied case is marine data sharing that encompasses organizations currently collecting ocean data and related stakeholders regarding the usage and sharing of data. Particularly, we are interested in organizations that did not initiate the adoption of data ecosystems; helping to understand the challenges, needs, and improvements around marine data workflows.

Regarding the data collection, we combined focus group interviews (direct observations) with workshops (participant observations) going for a deeper understanding of issues on marine data sharing from the product management point of view to data-centric discussion with practitioners and team leaders. By having these two types of participants we were able to have top-down and bottom-up views on data sharing in the marine domain, which lead us to investigate not only the technical aspects but also the business-related aspects.

The study had a total of twenty participants from ten different Norwegian organizations, and details are presented in Tables 1 and 2. We combined the editing approach from [22] and the thematic approach from [29] for data analysis. The editing approach allowed us to have an initial set of categories in the coding, based on our interview guide (both coding categories and interview guide are available in the companion package in [12]). In turn, the thematic approach allowed us to cluster all the resulting sub-categories in broader themes, as presented in the next sections. The research methodology process is illustrated in Fig. 1, where in the first analysis step we gathered the observable conclusions regarding the challenges and implications. In the second stage, system properties, quality attributes, and technology drivers were derived.

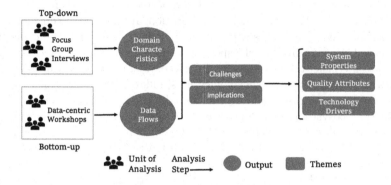

Fig. 1. Overview of the research process

Focus Groups. We requested each of the organizations listed in Table 1 to nominate 1–2 representatives. We specifically wanted to have people with a profile towards the management of the products, which should include some decision making roles but also some knowledge about the details of the products. We ended up with 14 participants from five research institutes, five companies, and a marine company cluster to technology innovation and synergies in the marine sector. The subjects were divided into three focus groups used as units of analysis. The data collection for the study was conducted between March and April of 2022. The data collection and recording for the study was performed online using Zoom, complemented with the Miro[2] tool. We have collected around 6 h of data, having an average of 122 min per focus group interview.

Workshops. For the working sessions, we relied on notes that were validated by different participants that took part in the working sessions. The data collection for the workshops occurred on two occasions between May and June of 2022 and took around two and a half hour each. The participants collaborated to discuss the data flow among the different components ranging from data collection to the data transmission, forwarding, and storage. There were ten subjects from six different organizations. The profile of these subjects were more towards systems design and development, which also included some of the subjects from the previous round due to their technical background and expertise.

---

[2] https://miro.com/.

Table 1. Organizations involved in the study.

ID	Size (empl.)	Profile	Sector	Operations scope
RI1	4000	University with research focused on marine, climate and energy	Public	International
RI2	800	Research institute on technology development for sensors and decision support	Public	Regional (Europe)
RI3	75	Research institute in climate change and sea ice	Public	Regional (Arctic)
RI4	1700	Applied Sciences University focused on sustainable development and technology	Public	International
P1	1100	Marine Research Institute	Public	National
C1	70	Oceanographic sensors manufacturer and sensor services provider	Industry	Global
C2	7600	Supplier of products and systems for underwater communication and marine robotics	Industry	Global
C3	200	Offshore telecommunications carrier (wireless and fiber communication)	Industry	Global
C4	1477	IT consultancy in software products for environmental monitoring	Industry	Regional (Scandinavia)
C5	10	Integration of sensors and monitoring services providers	Industry	Global
O1	N/A	Marine Companies Cluster to foster technology synergies	Industry	National

Threats to Validity. *Construct Validity:* The semi-structured interview guide [12] was the instrument used in focus group data collection, to foster discussions among participants. Here we started with closed questions targeting each participant towards open-ended ones, leaving space to additional questions on the way. Although the questions were handed to the interview subjects in advance, we proceeded to explain them along with our goals in the beginning of each one of the meetings. We also relied on the Miro online tool as a virtual emulator for stick notes to support the interview session, which allowed to have a better picture of the panel ideas for each topic and triggered follow-up questions to further understand each point of view.

Internal Validity: we do not aim to establish a cause-effect relation for data sharing in the marine domain, but, instead, clarify how data sharing is performed in the marine context, by eliciting aspects that influence the transition to data ecosystems.

External Validity: our findings can help explain the case of data sharing in the marine context. These findings can be limited to this specific context since we focused on the particularities of the ocean domain and organizations at the beginning of the transition. Thus, the recommendations might not hold for organizations that are more advanced in the transition, and neither they can be generalized for other domains.

Table 2. Demography of the participants in data collection.

ID	Organization	Current role	Experience	Obs. Method
1	RI1	Chief scientist related to sensors	15	Focus group
2	RI2	Underwater and WSN researcher director	34	Both
3	RI2	Development manager related to sensors	33	Both
4	P1	Ocean senior research scientist	33	Both
5	RI4	Underwater and WSN senior researcher	26	Workshop
6	RI3	Ocean research scientist	10	Focus group
7	RI2	Senior researcher on digital systems	N/A	Workshop
8	P1	Software development director	15	Workshop
9	P1	Ocean research director	27	Focus group
10	P1	Marine data senior software developer	7	Workshop
11	C1	R&D Manager	21	Focus group
12	C4	Marine systems software consultant	4	Workshop
13	C1	Software development director & architect	30	Both
14	C2	Product manager related to sensors	20	Focus group
15	C3	Offshore network communication researcher	31	Focus group
16	C1	Marine systems engineer	14	Workshop
17	RI1	Principal investigator	40	Focus group
18	C4	Software development manager	10+	Focus group
19	C5	CEO	14	Focus group
20	O1	R&D manager	20	Focus group

Abbreviation: WSN – Wireless Sensor Network.

Reliability: we had a panel of observers, co-authors of this work, who took turns during the interview and the workshops and they were responsible for the validation of the findings to reduce the risk of bias in the analysis stage. Moreover, to increase the validation of the study, we have adopted the following measures: (i) we combined two data sources based on different observational methods, extending the level of detail of our findings, especially on the technical side; (ii) we opted to have a balance between different types of stakeholders in the marine domain, which includes industry, public/government, and research institutes; and (iii) a companion package to support the evidence chain of the findings presented throughout this work is provided in [12], adopting the open science principles. The package includes excerpts of raw data, coding details, summary of the workshops, and the focus group interview guide, preserving the confidentiality of the subjects and organizations.

4   Results

In Sects. 4.1, 4.2, and 4.3, we provide our answers for RQ1, RQ2, and RQ3.

4.1   RQ1: Challenges in Marine Data Sharing

In relation to **RQ1**, in this section, we present various aspects that need to be addressed in order to improve the sharing processes and bring added value to current solutions. Figure 2 shows all challenges that we identified; they are divided into limitations and risks, which are described in more detail below.

Fig. 2. Summary of challenges in marine data sharing (**RQ1**).

Limitations. We identified three sources of limitations from our data set (see the right-hand branch in the diagram in Fig. 2). Firstly, as previously mentioned and related to the surrounding environment in the data acquisition stage, the communication bandwidth in IoUT is one of the major obstacles to data availability in real-time in the marine domain.

Secondly, there is a lack of automated procedures in quality control and assurance. These solutions currently rely on expert knowledge, which makes the task difficult to automate; this is a need when local data processing is performed or there is a high volume of data. As a consequence, there is a demand for processing data locally to fit important information on the available bandwidth and to prioritize what is to be stored, as depicted by interviewee 19: *"there's a lot of data captured and most of it is thrown away because there is not enough bandwidth to send it to surface or somewhere it can be used."*. On the other hand, communication devices are one of the main sources of battery consumption on standalone systems, which implies that a thorough management is required to balance the endurance and the data availability in (near) real-time.

Lastly, we were also able to capture challenges when it comes to the usage of data from long-term observations (historical data). This is related to the volume and variety of data, but it is in contrast to the challenges that come from the need to have data in (near) real-time. An example of this challenge was mentioned by interviewee 9: *"...the data centers can be overflowed by data that nobody knows what they actually have found."*. The main challenge resides in the data co-relation since each sensor provider can have its associated visualization and data handling tools making it difficult to have a uniform semantics.

Risks. As shown in the left-hand branch of Fig. 2, two aspects (liabilities and information disclosure) are tightly coupled to the risks in the sense that they are perceived as a weakness when it comes to data sharing.

Concerning liabilities, some legal barriers are not negotiable and need to be solved before the data producing system engages with the ecosystem. The legal barriers range from national regulations to data ownership and stock market-sensitive information. National regulations laws impose which and what type of data can be shared by systems operating under certain territories. Examples of such restrictions are bathymetry data used to produce navigational maps, including underwater navigation which lays into the national defense category. Imagery data are also another type of concern for territorial security and need to be filtered carefully. In contrast, on the regulations side, there is data that is required to be shared from companies by regulatory organizations, which is an aspect counterbalancing legal barriers to data sharing. Another aspect closely related to the risks is the breaches that can arise from the data sharing process and that are seen as a fragility by the organizations. These risks concern the organization's footprint and its responsibility towards society since the operations are held in an important part of our global ecosystem: the oceans. Another concern that is related to the organization's reputation is the down-service exposure by engaging a service shared with others. Lastly, regarding the market position, the exposure of business or market critical information is a concern with respect to cyber-security threats. Some of these concerns were referenced by interviewee 15, who has been working in the telecommunication field, which is responsible for providing data from remote locations: *"If you suddenly leak out the data that the customers are transporting, this makes big headlines."* On the other hand, the lack of data sharing also comes with some counterpointing risks. Current practices can lead to data bias due to the shortage of available data. As a consequence, decisions can be sub-optimal; this can also be a consequence of having those made upon imprecise or incorrect data. These decisions, at a regulatory level, can also negatively affect industry organizations in the correspondent sector.

Summary of RQ1: Several factors hinder the sharing process of marine data. Technical limitations include restricted resources, lack of data understandability, and automatic data quality control. Fear of business disclosure and legal liabilities contribute to the hesitations of marine data producers for data sharing.

4.2   RQ2: Implications of Adopting Data Ecosystems

In this section, we address **RQ2** by discussing the main characteristics that can help the adoption of data ecosystems for marine data sharing. First, we present results regarding the advantages that arise from the adoption process (see upper branch in Fig. 3). Second, we analyze characteristics of the adoption process to detect possible conflicts in materializing marine data ecosystems (see lower branch in Fig. 3).

Benefits. We have identified some benefits or reasons to adopt this new way of sharing data by having the different stakeholders in the same ecosystem; see the upper branch in the diagram in Fig. 3. These benefits apply not only at a societal level, which includes the environmental and political aspects, but also applies to organizations operating at the oceans. On the industry side, data concerning sea state conditions can be used to improve safety of operations by its incorporation in the forecasting models to have more accurate predictions (data assimilation). This models can be especially useful for those locations in which *in situ* data can be sparse or non-existing. There are many services that currently rely on marine sea state and its forecasts such as navigation, climate predictions, and even human-recreational activities. As a result, the benefits bring value to both intra- and inter-organizational levels and across sectors.

On the governmental side, data sharing more transparently can aid resource management and regulations for the targeting sectors. The latter can also influence data producers, as mentioned by interviewee 9: "...*if they (fishing fleet) don't report their catches we cannot calculate our fish-stories and we won't give a good quota next time.*" This has an implication on decision-making, which can be data-driven. By having more data, there is also a contribution to the understanding of the ocean which can be used in the marine science fields and ultimately can help explain political decisions and regulations to the general public.

Overall, in terms of benefits, there could be improvements in operations within and across industries, fact-based and data-driven decision making, fostering a better understanding of the oceans for different research-based studies. The benefits are aspects that can help explain the relationship among stakeholders and their associated value in the ecosystem.

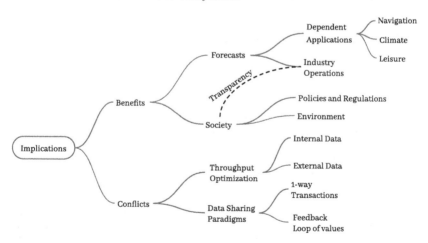

Fig. 3. Summary of the implications of adopting data ecosystem (**RQ2**).

Conflicts. On the management side, as shown in the lower branch in Fig. 3, many interviewees perceive data sharing only as an additional cost to their organization, where factors such as lack of resources or incentives are expressed as limiting reasons for not sharing data. This process, as it is seen currently is not perceived as an investment, but instead as an expense by some of these companies and can present a great barrier to adherence to the ecosystem. There seems to be a conflict between the data producers and third-party data consumers when the sharing is perceived in the traditional transnational way, where the former bears the risk and costs and the latter carries the benefits of using the data.

Additionally, regarding the data availability, this type of data can represent value at the ecosystem level, but can be irrelevant for internal operations. However, as we identified previously, a conflict arises when it comes to prioritization of the transmission of the data from sensing sites in real-time, or even in the storage of such data. This is a consequence of the physical limitations and constraints of data transmission in the marine domain.

Although these are issues that directly affect the data producers, the decision made at this level influences the overall system and consequently, the resulting applications, the availability of data to be shared, and the relations in the ecosystem.

Summary of RQ2. There are advantages and disadvantages to promoting marine data ecosystems. In terms of benefits, sharing more marine data will improve understanding and facilitate the management of the ocean, leading to its sustainable use. Regarding the drawbacks, data sharing processes can be seen as an effort or expense for marine data producers in the ecosystem. This can occur if the relationship among the ecosystem actors is not well defined, and there is no value transferred back to data producers. Furthermore, this can also raise some conflicts regarding the data provided to the ecosystem.

4.3   RQ3: Factors for Marine Data Ecosystem Adoption

In Sect. 4.2, we have shown that adopting the data ecosystem paradigm for marine data sharing is beneficial in various ways when there is value shared among all actors. In this section, we address **RQ3**, identifying factors (depicted in Fig. 4) that can accelerate the adoption of a marine data ecosystem.

System Properties: The first step to embrace this adoption is to have the data workflow automated. As one of the main drivers for the realization of a marine data ecosystem, we identified **automation** of the following processes in data sharing:

– **Access Control** - marine data varies both in parameters (e.g., environment, structural integrity) and formats (e.g., time series, multimedia). It is often difficult and time-consuming to find a suitable data sources, as indicated by interviewee 4: "*In this national marine data center, there is a lot of data. I think many are struggling to access.*" In addition, there are different confidential levels that marine data producers want to impose. For some types of data (e.g., oil drilling), open data access is not preferred. Others, such as sea state conditions do not entails risks and can be openly shared. Therefore,

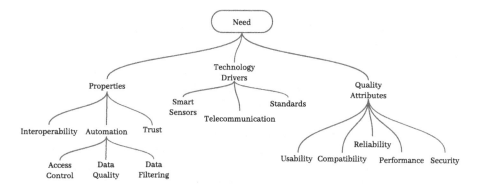

Fig. 4. Summary of the migration process analysis (**RQ3**).

automatic data access control should be realized, which is not available in conventional data platforms.

- **Data Quality Control** - most of marine data producers have to perform data quality control (i.e., mark and remove suspicious and bad data) in a semi-automated manner. This process is time-consuming and costly due to the required labor resources. In addition, data sharing is prolonged as this process takes time. The possibility to integrate automatic data quality control procedures in a data ecosystem would eliminate current issues of marine data sharing.
- **Data Filtering** - the automation of mechanisms to indicate which data can be shared and with which entities is of high importance. This property fulfills not only privacy constraints, but also complies with regulations, and represents a valuable component in the sharing system taking into account the specificity of the domain described in the previous section.

Interoperability. Another fundamental property for the interchange of data on the ecosystem is the specifications. All the information that helps make sense of the data shared, i.e. the metadata, is relevant to the interoperability of the ecosystem actors. Currently, marine data producers apply proprietary data formats for data collection and storage, hindering interoperability. Interviewee 3 stressed that: "...*subsea survey data often comes as a separate time series of one for each instrument. The tricky part is how to merge these different time series together so that you get a useful dataset out of it.*". The adoption of standard data and metadata formats is one way to achieve a certain level of interoperability. Furthermore, to have this interchangeability among different heterogeneous data sources, besides the formats, their meanings must also be agreed upon among all actors.

Trust. Taking into account the identified conflict among some stakeholders regarding the risks for their businesses against the footprint and reporting responsibilities to others, as referred by interviewee 19: "...*if an oil company shares data, that data can be mined. For example for blaming them for a different environmental contamination, ecosystem impact, etc. So I think there's probably legal liability risk that they're also avoiding to share data...*"; the trust in the data ecosystem becomes another crucial property in this context.

Quality Attributes. We identified related quality attributes to be taken into account in the development and evaluation processes of marine data sharing, in the light of the ISO/IEC 25010 model [25]. The following five quality attributes are identified to be taken into account in the development and evaluation processes of the data ecosystem.

In terms of **usability**, as mentioned in Sect. 4, there are clear needs with respect to the integration and understanding of data being shared. Additionally, the efforts that have to be made to engage the ecosystem will affect its usability in terms of operability of the data ecosystem. Furthermore, **compatibility** is another relevant attribute that will drive the whole ecosystem because of the data format standards, conventions, and specifications for data quality assessment. These attributes must be fine tuned in order to enable interoperability between the stakeholders. Taking into account the nature of the participant stakeholders in marine data ecosystems, **reliability** also comes into the picture. Aspects such as the credibility and transparency are a reflection of the system's maturity and availability of the involved actors. Also related to reliability, in the marine domain, there is a need to encompass fault-tolerance because of the nature of the IoUT, particularly its devices which operate autonomously in remote and harsh underwater locations and thus can experience down periods for various reasons (e.g., maintenance, malfunction, damage). Concerning the volume of data provided, the bandwidth usage optimization must also be considered, which in other words is captured by the throughput of the **performance** attribute. Lastly, comes the **security** attribute. As we analysed in the previous section, guaranteeing that only the legitimate entities have access to the resources in the ecosystem is another important property. This attribute is also transversal to the whole data sharing ecosystem, starting from integrity of the data through the traceability and filtering. The importance of this attribute is critical considering territorial security threats which are associated with some types of data being collected at the oceans.

Technology Drivers. Considering the limitations mentioned in Sect. 4.1 and topics discussed in the Data-Centric Workshops (available in [12]), technology solutions to address data availability and flow reliability in underwater and marine deployment in the IoUT context are crucial to capture missing pieces of data. Furthermore, these drivers also refer to other technical solutions regarding the quality of data, the specification, and the meaning of fields, which are important factors to the data relationships definition in the ecosystem. The technologies' needs extracted, identified below, are crucial to different stages of data sharing processing, becoming valuable to the whole ecosystem:

– **Smart Sensors** - with the increase of sensor capabilities related to resources such as processing, storage, and battery life, the incorporation of most recent advances in data analytics-related fields such as numerical models or artificial intelligence can be brought into the early stages of the sensor network, helping to improve the entire workflow.

- **Standards and Conventions** - on the software side, the creation, maturation, and adoption of existing data, metadata specifications, and exchange formats address the interoperability among different stakeholders and data sources and types.
- **Telecommunication** - it is crucial for transmission devices used underwater or in links to remote and coastal areas to get access to data as close as possible to its acquisition. This technology driver is particularly important in time-critical applications such as oil spill control, offshore structural safety, or tsunami alerts, to name a few.

Summary of RQ3. There are multiple factors that need to be considered for a data ecosystem. Automation, interoperability, and trust are crucial system properties. Considering the domain characteristics, five suitable quality attributes from the ISO/IEC 25010 model were indicated for the design and evaluation of newly established marine data ecosystems: usability, compatibility, reliability, performance, and security. Finally, smart sensors, standards and conventions, and telecommunication are three main technology drivers to help address current challenges while also addressing some of the data ecosystem characteristics, accelerating the adoption process.

5 Discussion

In the marine domain, there are constraining factors and limitations that depict and explain how complex the sharing process is.

Firstly, there are strict liabilities that must be handled carefully by all parties. Secondly, there is a clear conflict when it comes to management views on data sharing paradigms. Thirdly, there are risks related to the disclosure of sensitive information. While technology based on blockchain is being deployed in production to address transparency and traceability on public-private data sharing [21], a comprehensive survey on privacy and security challenges performed in [2], recognizes the need for more practical end-to-end solutions in this field. The authors investigated the challenges' interdependencies, mapping those to possible solutions to be considered by practitioners in the implementation of data ecosystems. As also pointed out in [23], the licenses, the legal framework, and liabilities must also be considered when establishing such ecosystems. In this study, we took one step forward into specific legal liabilities in the domain and associated processes such as data filtering, complementing the requirements for the migration to data ecosystems in this specific context. Concerning the access control models on data sharing, and to help formalize these systems, some implicit relationships among the different actors were identified in Sect. 4.2, followed by procedures and technology needed to address express such constraints in Sect. 4.3. Such models should reflect contractually-dependent constraints to data usage, covering processes from the engagement, update, as well as disengagement of the ecosystem. All these aspects will be relevant to the security attributes of the system.

IoUT-related limitations, including the lack of interoperability, affect data availability and prevent these processes to be further automated, having an impact in the way the integration of the systems in the ecosystem paradigm. Viewed as a long-term issue in the IoT field, at the application layer, interoperability encompasses common specifications for data exchange and systems interactions [28]. The adoption of standard data and metadata formats is one way to achieve a certain level of interoperability, in this case, it refers to synthetic interoperability, for ensuring common data structures for information exchange [18]. Despite the existing standards with good levels of acceptance for historical/long-term observation data, when it comes to real-time data, the scenario is similar to other IoT domains since these existing standards present high redundancy that translates into the overhead of this type of transmission. Furthermore, solutions are needed in order to combine the different data sources improving the situational awareness regarding different types of data being shared, either from heterogeneous sources or different processing levels. One solution is to introduce a list of control vocabularies [9]. This requires marine data ecosystem actors to agree on the data field's meanings. These aspects are closely related to the technology drivers identified in the previous section and can be reflected in the usability, compatibility, and performance of the system.

There are some benefits starting to be recognized in the sharing process. It is considered a 2-way process, having a feedback loop of values that can propagate back into the ecosystem. The existence of values shared among ecosystem's actors make data quality and trust central properties in a marine data ecosystem because it has implications on both management and technical sides. And it reflects the value and the confidence in the data sources, influencing its further usage inside the ecosystem. The quality assessment also influences whether or not the data can be trusted in decision-making processes [16]. Nevertheless, the definition of data quality across different IoT deployments and applications is not trivial because of the existence of various metrics, and thus additional heuristics such as trust are also being proposed to overcome this limitation [5].

6   Conclusion and Future Work

We have shown the need of adopting the data ecosystem paradigm to facilitate the data sharing process in the marine domain. We have covered different dimensions of the problem, starting from a management view from various stakeholders to workflow solutions with respect to data sharing, uncovering aspects that need improvement to help organizations in the domain transition to a data sharing paradigm. Furthermore, we identified properties to help address the current limitations in the data workflow and help foster new applications to underpin new knowledge regarding the oceans and the operations that are held there. Finally, a major challenge on the management side of these ecosystems is that the business model does not seem clear to all stakeholders. In the data ecosystem paradigm, there is supposed to be shared values among the actors, allowing data producers to get something back out of the ecosystem as well. More research in this direction is needed, but falls out of the aims of this paper.

As a matter of future work, we will investigate the feasibility of existing solutions in other domains in this context to identify which innovative approaches are needed to address the particularities of this domain introduced. More specifically, we are interested in investigating how data can be filtered automatically, data flow relationships, and how these solutions can be combined with the remaining components such as access control and data quality assessment for the overall system architecture. To materialize the migration, another crucial aspect will be to identify the business goals of the ecosystem. This aspect can lead to more concrete definitions in terms of the governance model, which will influence the data sharing properties as access control and legal framework.

Acknowledgements. We would like to thank the participants in the study. This work was supported by SFI SmartOcean NFR Project 309612/F40.

References

1. Ansari, S., et al.: Unlocking the potential of NEXRAD data through NOAA's big data partnership. Bull. Am. Meteor. Soc. **99**(1), 189–204 (2018)
2. Anwar, M.J., Gill, A.Q., Hussain, F.K., Imran, M.: Secure big data ecosystem architecture: challenges and solutions. EURASIP J. Wirel. Commun. Netw. **2021**(1), 1–30 (2021). https://doi.org/10.1186/s13638-021-01996-2
3. Asche, F., Hansen, H., Tveteras, R., Tveterås, S.: The salmon disease crisis in Chile. Mar. Resour. Econ. **24**(4), 405–411 (2009)
4. Buck, J.J., et al.: Ocean data product integration through innovation-the next level of data interoperability. Front. Mar. Sci. **6**, 32 (2019)
5. Byabazaire, J., O'Hare, G., Delaney, D.: Using trust as a measure to derive data quality in data shared IoT deployments. In: ICCCN, pp. 1–9 (2020)
6. Cui, Y., Kara, S., Chan, K.C.: Manufacturing big data ecosystem: a systematic literature review. Rob. Comput. Integr. Manuf. **62**, 101861 (2020)
7. Domingo, M.C.: An overview of the internet of underwater things. J. Netw. Comput. Appl. **35**(6), 1879–1890 (2012)
8. Fattah, S., Gani, A., Ahmedy, I., Idris, M.Y.I., Targio Hashem, I.A.: A survey on underwater wireless sensor networks: requirements, taxonomy, recent advances, and open research challenges. Sensors **20**(18), 5393 (2020)
9. Hankin, S., et al.: NetCDF-CF-OPeNDAP: standards for ocean data interoperability and object lessons for community data standards processes. In: Oceanobs 2009, Venice Convention Centre, 21–25 September 2009, Venise (2010)
10. Hansen, H.S., Reiter, I.M., Schröder, L.: A system architecture for a transnational data infrastructure supporting maritime spatial planning. In: Kő, A., Francesconi, E. (eds.) EGOVIS 2017. LNCS, vol. 10441, pp. 158–172. Springer, Cham (2017). https://doi.org/10.1007/978-3-319-64248-2_12
11. ul Hassan, U., Curry, E.: Stakeholder analysis of data ecosystems. In: Curry, E., Metzger, A., Zillner, S., Pazzaglia, J.-C., García Robles, A. (eds.) The Elements of Big Data Value, pp. 21–39. Springer, Cham (2021). https://doi.org/10.1007/978-3-030-68176-0_2
12. Lima, K., et al.: Marine data sharing companion package (2022). https://doi.org/10.5281/zenodo.6901964

13. Louw-Reimer, J., Nielsen, J.L.M., Bjørn-Andersen, N., Kouwenhoven, N.: Boosting the effectiveness of Containerised supply chains: a case study of TradeLens. In: Lind, M., Michaelides, M., Ward, R., Watson, R.T. (eds.) Maritime Informatics. PI, pp. 95–115. Springer, Cham (2021). https://doi.org/10.1007/978-3-030-72785-7_6

14. Míguez, B.M., et al.: The European marine observation and data network (EMODnet): visions and roles of the gateway to marine data in Europe. Frontiers Mar. Sci. **6**, 1–24 (2019)

15. Munappy, A.R., Mattos, D.I., Bosch, J., Olsson, H.H., Dakkak, A.: From ad-hoc data analytics to dataOps. In: ICSSP 2020, pp. 165–174. ACM (2020)

16. Nakhkash, M.R., Gia, T.N., Azimi, I., Anzanpour, A., Rahmani, A.M., Liljeberg, P.: Analysis of performance and energy consumption of wearable devices and mobile gateways in IoT applications. In: Proceedings of the International Conference on Omni-Layer Intelligent Systems, pp. 68–73 (2019)

17. Oliveira, M.I.S., Lóscio, B.F.: What is a data ecosystem? In: Proceedings of the 19th Annual International Conference on Digital Government Research: Governance in the Data Age, pp. 1–9 (2018)

18. Pearlman, J., Schaap, D., Glaves, H.: Ocean data interoperability platform (ODIP): addressing key challenges for marine data management on a global scale. In: Oceans 2016 MTS/IEEE Monterey, pp. 1–7. IEEE (2016)

19. Peña-López, I., et al.: ITU Internet report 2005: the internet of things. Technical report, International Telecommunication Union (2005)

20. Qiu, T., Zhao, Z., Zhang, T., Chen, C., Chen, C.P.: Underwater internet of things in smart ocean: system architecture and open issues. IEEE Trans. Industr. Inf. **16**(7), 4297–4307 (2019)

21. Rukanova, B., et al.: Realizing value from voluntary business-government information sharing through blockchain-enabled infrastructures: The case of importing tires to The Netherlands using TradeLens. In: DG.O2021, pp. 505–514 (2021)

22. Runeson, P., Höst, M.: Guidelines for conducting and reporting case study research in software engineering. Empir. Softw. Eng. **14**(2), 131–164 (2009)

23. Runeson, P., Olsson, T., Linåker, J.: Open data ecosystems-an empirical investigation into an emerging industry collaboration concept. J. Syst. Softw. **182**, 111088 (2021)

24. Schubert, R., Marinica, I.: Facebook data: sharing, caring, and selling. In: 2019 International Conference on Cyber Situational Awareness, Data Analytics And Assessment (Cyber SA), pp. 1–3 (2019)

25. Systems and Software Engineering: ISO/IEC 25010: Systems and software quality requirements and evaluation (SQuaRE) (2011)

26. Tanhua, T., et al.: What we have learned from the framework for ocean observing: evolution of the global ocean observing system. Front. Mar. Sci. **6**, 471 (2019)

27. Tanhua, T., et al.: Ocean FAIR data services. Frontiers Mar. Sci. **6** (2019)

28. Tayur, V.M., Suchithra, R.: Review of interoperability approaches in application layer of Internet of Things. In: ICIMIA 2017, pp. 322–326 (2017)

29. Vaismoradi, M., Jones, J., Turunen, H., Snelgrove, S.: Theme development in qualitative content analysis and thematic analysis. Nurs. Educ. Pract. **6**, 100–110 (2016)

30. Wixom, B.H., Sebastian, I.M., Gregory, R.W.: Data sharing 2.0: new data sharing, new value creation. CISR-Res. Briefings **20**(10) (2020)

The Viability of Continuous Experimentation in Early-Stage Software Startups
A Descriptive Multiple-Case Study

Vihtori Mäntylä⬦, Bettina Lehtelä(✉)⬦, and Fabian Fagerholm⬦

Aalto University, P.O. Box 15400, Espoo, Finland
vihtori.mantyla@protonmail.com,
{bettina.lehtela,fabian.fagerholm}@aalto.fi

Abstract. Background: Continuous experimentation (CE) has been proposed as a data-driven approach to software product development. Several challenges with this approach have been described in large organisations, but its application in smaller companies with early-stage products remains largely unexplored. **Aims:** The goal of this study is to understand what factors could affect the adoption of CE in early-stage software startups. **Method:** We present a descriptive multiple-case study of five startups in Finland which differ in their utilisation of experimentation. **Results:** We find that practices often mentioned as prerequisites for CE, such as iterative development and continuous integration and delivery, were used in the case companies. CE was not widely recognised or used as described in the literature. Only one company performed experiments and used experimental data systematically. **Conclusions:** Our study indicates that small companies may be unlikely to adopt CE unless 1) at least some company employees have prior experience with the practice, 2) the company's limited available resources are not exceeded by its adoption, and 3) the practice solves a problem currently experienced by the company, or the company perceives almost immediate benefit of adopting it. We discuss implications for advancing CE in early-stage startups and outline directions for future research on the approach.

Keywords: Continuous experimentation · New product development · Startup · Continuous software engineering · Case study

1 Introduction

A mismatch between product features and customer needs is one of the most common reasons for software startup failure [15]. While agile methods emphasise customer value [6], building the right product appears to be a feat that few startups achieve. Continuous experimentation (CE) is a software engineering method where product development is driven by field experiments with real users [2,8,9,29,41]. It strives to establish virtuous feedback loops between business, development, and operations [11], and reportedly improves product quality and business performance [7,8], with promising implications for startups.

© The Author(s), under exclusive license to Springer Nature Switzerland AG 2022
D. Taibi et al. (Eds.): PROFES 2022, LNCS 13709, pp. 141–156, 2022.
https://doi.org/10.1007/978-3-031-21388-5_10

Previous studies have found that startups tend to run experiments as part of their product development process [21, 22]. However, the experiments are usually neither planned nor run in the organised and systematic manner characteristic of CE [21, 25]. Startups are often reluctant to incorporate industry best practices, methods, and frameworks proposed by researchers into their business and product development processes [15]. This raises the question of whether CE, as envisioned in different frameworks and models in the literature, fits the needs of small companies with early-stage products, such as software startups.

This paper aims to elucidate possible reasons for why adopting CE in early-stage startup (ESS) settings might be difficult. Rather than producing a general theory of adoption of CE in startups, we develop propositions that can be extended and validated in future studies, and that can point to novel directions for research. Specifically, we address the following research questions:

R1: Do ESS companies integrate experimentation into their software development practices?

R2: How do ESS companies utilise user data in their software product development process?

R3: What factors influence the adoption of CE in ESS companies?

We study these questions in the context of five startup companies. We contribute 1) a description of the state of experimentation and overall mode of operation in the case companies from the perspective of CE, providing insight into what product development practices startups tend to adopt and why; and 2) a set of factors that affect the adoption of CE in startup companies, partly supporting earlier findings from startups (e.g., [13, 21, 22, 25, 26]) and larger companies (e.g., [41]), but with new and more detailed factors relevant to adoption of CE. The paper builds on results obtained in a Master's thesis [23].

2   Background

CE approaches software product development through experiments with real users [2, 8, 9, 29, 41]. This includes collecting and analysing experimental data to test product hypotheses, gaining insights for new feature ideas to be evaluated in subsequent experiments. CE comes with various implications on organisational structure and culture [11, 19, 41], product and software development processes [9, 29], and software architecture, construction, and deployment [9, 34].

2.1   Scientific and Online Controlled Experiments

Scientific experiments can provide causal descriptions of what consequences varying a treatment has on a subject of interest [35]. Experimental setups vary with the study they are used for, but they all share the same basic elements: 1) a hypothesis to be tested, including evaluation criteria for its acceptance or rejection; 2) sufficient control of independent variables; 3) means for collecting data; and 4) experimental subject(s) under investigation [35].

Online controlled experiments (OCE) [17] leverage the ease of access to users through the Internet to deploy field experiments. These are often performed as A/B tests where two different user groups receive a different treatment, e.g., the old versus new version of a feature. The treatments are usually assigned randomly to the target groups and statistical analysis is used to determine which of the tested implementations produced better results in terms of improved metrics. OCEs can be arranged into an ongoing process to implement CE.

2.2 Implementing Continuous Experimentation

CE can be seen as arising from advances in the use of experimentation in product development [37], agile software development practices, and continuous software engineering [11] practices such as continuous integration, continuous delivery, and continuous deployment. Modern software engineering practices like these are behind the experimentation processes in pioneering companies such as Microsoft [18,19], Netflix [1,12], and others [10,36,38]. Applying experimentation to product development reportedly gives increased customer satisfaction, improved and quantified business goals, and a transformation to a continuous development process [4]. Holmström Olsson et al. [29] position experimentation as the last step of an organisational evolution ladder, where agile software development, continuous integration, delivery, and deployment are prerequisites.

Realising CE requires arranging experiments across time. A number of models have been proposed to prescribe how CE can be implemented as a method. For example, the HYPEX model describes a detailed experimentation process model spanning the complete product development cycle [30]. A minimum viable feature (MVF) is implemented and deployed, usage data is collected, and gap analysis is applied to determine the next course of action. Experimental results are fed back into the business strategy function, completing the feedback loop.

The RIGHT model describes an experimentation framework in detail [9]. It features a continuous experimentation cycle encompassing business and product vision, strategy, experiment design, and software construction activities. It also describes an architectural model for the experimentation infrastructure and related stakeholder roles. Furthermore, it covers experiment objects in the form of minimum viable products (MVPs) and MVFs, which are used to rapidly test product hypotheses. The RIGHT model assumes that CE capabilities can be built little by little. Once multiple simultaneous experiments are running, the full model becomes critical.

While other models are available, they share most of their essential characteristics with HYPEX and RIGHT, and the latter is considered a reference model in the literature [2].

2.3 Software Startups and Experimentation

Software startups are often characterised as being innovative and driven by small teams, operating under high uncertainty and rapidly evolving, and being challenged by a lack of resources, time pressure to deliver a product to market, and only little working and operating history [3,27,31]. Startups are thus distinctly different from traditional enterprises, in which new product development is only one concern alongside concerns related to existing products and customers.

Startups commonly fail [31], often by not achieving product-market fit [20,32] – they create the wrong product [14]. To increase the chances of success, the Lean Startup method proposes Build-Measure-Learn loops: testing hypotheses about how users will react to software changes based on predefined metrics, and using the results to make an MVP [32]. Many ideas from the Lean Startup model can be found in continuous software engineering [11] and CE [9,30]. Camuffo et al. [5] conducted a randomised study and concluded that the scientific experimentation approach is beneficial for startups.

Research indicates that while experimentation in general is common in startups, systematic experimentation is not widely adopted [22,25]. Previous studies addressing CE adoption (e.g., [22,29,40,41]) acknowledge that it requires high levels of skill and coordination, and advanced technological and organisational capabilities. Auer et al. [2] identified six categories of challenges: 1) cultural, organisational and managerial challenges, 2) business challenges, 3) technical challenges, 4) statistical challenges, 5) ethical challenges, and 6) domain specific challenges. However, few studies address CE specifically for software startups. Although some CE models allow for gradual adoption (e.g., the RIGHT model [9]), knowledge about systematic adoption strategies and application of the practice in software startups is scarce. Research on CE often describes the benefits, but most studies rely on examples from a small number of industry leaders whose methods are not necessarily suitable for, e.g., smaller companies [34] or companies whose products do not share the same characteristics of flexibility. Open questions thus revolve around the circumstances under which CE is suitable for startups and what characteristics of the product development and user data practices of startups are compatible with CE.

3   Research Method

We conducted a descriptive multiple-case study [42] to investigate product development practices in our case companies. Through semi-structured interviews [28], we obtained insights into the product development practices, utilisation of user data, and experimentation used in the companies, which we analysed to develop propositions that address the research questions. We used interviews because they provide relatively quick access to key information, and because other data sources can be scarce in startup companies; for example, extensive process documentation may not exist. Confidentiality requirements prevent us from publishing the full set of collected data, but excerpts are given in this paper. An online supplement gives details on the study design and results [24].

3.1   Case Companies

We selected case companies (see Table 1) from two startup communities in the capital region of Finland: *Maria 01* (https://maria.io/), with over 175 startups residing in Kamppi, Helsinki; and *A Grid* (https://agrid.fi/), with around 150 startups located on the Aalto University campus in Otaniemi, Espoo.

For the company selection we used purposeful sampling: a convenience sample guided by our research goals [28]. We sought to include companies at any stage of the early product development life-cycle and with different kinds of software-based products or services. Having a relaxed set of selection criteria provided a heterogeneous set of cases and varied qualitative data. All companies remain anonymous and we omit identifying information, such as product details.

Table 1. Case companies and their context at the time of the study.

ID	Location	Business model	Distribution channel	Product stage	Participant role
A	Maria 01	Free app, sell ads	Mobile app	V1.0 launch in progress	Product owner (PO)
B	Maria 01	B2B (provision[a])	API as a service	Released	COO
C	Maria 01	B2C (subscription)	Side-loaded application	Early access program live	CTO
D	A Grid	B2B (provision[a])	SaaS	Live for over a year	CEO
E	A Grid	B2C (subscription)	Physical	Live for over a year	Lead software engineer

[a]Provision business model: the company receives a provision of sales from their B2B customer.

3.2 Data Collection

Semi-structured interviews are suitable when the topic and expected data are not well understood before starting the data collection [28]. We expected startups to operate in varied ways that we could not fully anticipate. We designed a semi-structured interview format with open-ended questions based on the guide used by Lindgren & Münch [21]. We extended the question set with new questions on tool and practice selection and added CE as a distinct topic.

As shown in Table 1, we interviewed one expert participant from each case company, identified through discussion with company representatives, and based on their broad understanding of both the technical and business aspects of their company. In addition to the main interviews, follow-up data collection with the same or additional participants was conducted to verify and fill in some details. The interviews were performed in Finnish.

3.3 Data Analysis

The first author iteratively analysed the interview transcripts. Insights obtained from one case company often provided a new perspective into data from other companies. Multiple passes allowed building higher-order categories from topics that appeared across case companies. The analysis was supported by data review sessions with the two other authors. In these, each transcript was walked through and discussed, with the first author explaining the interview and preliminary insights obtained. Gradually, the sessions moved to discussions about transcript coding and emerging insights from the data. ATLAS.ti was used for the analysis task. Coding was performed in English although the transcripts were in Finnish.

First-Cycle Coding. The analysis started without any predefined categories. Codes produced from the first analysis iterations were long and descriptive, and multiple coding passes were used to group similar codes under a single parent code. Higher-level categories were built based on recurring themes.

Individual Case Analysis. After coding and category-building, each company was analysed as an individual case. Practices for software and product development and user data collection and use were extracted for closer inspection. The information flow within each company was represented graphically, giving a picture of the organisation and the interactions between different stakeholders. The graphics are provided in the supplementary material [24].

Cross-Case Analysis and Second-Cycle Coding. Combined data from all five cases were also analysed. Tools and practices used by the companies were analysed in tabular form. The coded interview data from all five individual cases were re-coded into common themes that permeate the whole data set. In this final phase, the analysis focused on uncovering categories that could potentially explain the tool and practice choices made by the companies.

4   Results

Systematic experimentation was rare in the case companies. Our results question the attractiveness of CE for startups as multiple factors detract from its use.

4.1   Case Company Descriptions

Company A. Lack of previous experience in mobile application development was a major bottleneck for data acquisition in Company A. Challenges involved understanding what data was possible to get, what data was valuable, and which tools were worth using. The application was instrumented to log some user actions, and the team was actively seeking to improve their data collection.

A feedback form was used to collect user data, and app store reviews were a regular feedback channel, with in-app prompts to request reviews. The product owner (PO) reviewed the collected data weekly, but would have wanted to better understand the real-world usage of the application, and have the capability to chat with individual users to gain insights on how and why they used the app.

The PO was not familiar with CE, but mentioned iterative user testing – resembling experimentation – for the application's on-boarding experience. Think-aloud user tests had been used with a small number of new users. Based on this, design adjustments were made and subsequent user testing indicated an improvement. The PO considered most of their development as some form of test.

> Well, almost everything we do is maybe more like tests. (Product owner, Company A)

However, it is not clear if these tests would qualify as planned experiments, and whether hypotheses and measurable goals were set before starting development.

Company B. There was only restricted access to user data in this company, as their service was used through a third-party UI. The company had to rely on the limited data available from their own systems, as the business partners owning the UI were not willing to share detailed user data. However, Company B closely collaborated with current and potential customers for requirements elicitation. Data from weekly customer meetings were used extensively from early on, and the products were engineered to meet partner-defined functional and non-functional requirements. Overall, the company appeared to base their product development decisions on the data received through their business partners and less on the scarcely available user data.

Although Company B would likely be technologically capable of running continuous experimentation, the company's B2B business model makes any experimentation involving user data very difficult. The company claimed that the pricing of their product was the only parameter they could adjust.

> We do not have resources at the moment to do anything repeatedly or as a process [...] this interest rate is the only parameter we could control. (COO, Company B, on A/B testing).

Adjusting the pricing was also considered to be difficult, since any changes would need to be coordinated with, and approved by, their business partners. These obstacles to experimentation for companies operating in the B2B domain are well recognised in earlier studies [2, 41].

Company C. This company was in a transition phase where they had just launched their application through an early access program (EAP). They used a form of repeated experimentation when building the EAP version, working closely with potential customers and industry experts to understand the requirements their future customers would have for the product. After establishing the initial set of requirements, they executed numerous Build-Measure-Learn iterations where each new version of the product was subjected to a user test by an expert user, including observation and an interview for feedback. The collected user data was then converted into software development tasks.

> It has been this [...] very tight develop and test type of work where we develop something and then go [try it out]. (CTO, Company C, on the development process).

However, there was no sign of predefined metrics or evaluation criteria which would have indicated a systematic approach for experimentation. The company had thought about possible future A/B testing and had recently implemented feature flags, but mainly for licensing purposes. Instrumentation data was not automatically sent to the company due to user privacy expectations and offline capability requirements. The company expected that most feedback would be received via email and discussing with the users. This was seen as good enough for now and they recognised that some other way of handling user feedback would need to be implemented once their customer base grows.

Company D. This company used a well-defined process for product development planning, following the Data-Insight-Belief-Bet (DIBB) framework [16]. The leadership defined a set of objective key results (OKR) for the next quarter, to be implemented by the product development teams. Each OKR contained a high-level goal and the metrics to evaluate whether or not the goal was reached at the end of the quarter. The focus was on meeting investor goals.

The development teams regularly built feature prototypes, mostly used internally, but occasionally presented to end users or customer representatives. An expert board reviewed the data from prototyping and selected the best implementation based on qualitative feedback. The data was used continuously as company D was not only reacting to negative feedback, but also actively trying to learn from the data and even predicting future needs based on historical data.

> Ten percent of the features [have come from when we analysed all feedback] and predicted what kind of things there would be coming. [We can say] we actually need to build this kind of feature because [customers] are going towards this kind of world. (CEO, Company D, on use of data).

The company employed numerous user data collection channels and used data extensively in all stages of product development. Event-level quantitative data was collected from different parts of the system and qualitative data was collected through a chat embedded in the service. Research ops, a dedicated business unit, analysed and refined all available data, and was responsible for the data to be available to all members of the organisation.

Company E. The last company offered a physical service; their software provided internal support. There was no instrumentation for quantitative data collection due to lack of interest in such feedback. To collect qualitative user data, the company mainly observed office staff and read feedback from chat channels. This internal feedback loop tied back to the development team's Kanban board where new input was entered as work items. A survey was used to collect feedback from company field workers, but it was not entirely clear how the data was used, suggesting a lack of systematic usage.

> We have sent our field workers these quick surveys just to see what is the general opinion about this app and such. We did not have any specific metrics like "rate this from 0 to 10" or anything. (Lead developer, Company E, on user surveys).

Feedback on the physical service was collected through a form and email, was handled by customer service agents, and was generally not available to everyone in the company. Overall, Company E did not systematically use data in the internal software product development. We found indications that data was seen as a way to detect problems rather than understanding users' needs.

[...] often not receiving any feedback about anything indicates that things are probably quite ok as there is nothing to complain about. (Lead developer, Company E, on negative feedback).

The team had envisioned doing A/B testing once they have released customer-facing applications. However, in its current state, the company lacked the capabilities to effectively use experimentation since the software development team was largely disconnected from the rest of the organisation.

4.2   Cross-Case Analysis

All case companies had an incremental software development process and used lean and agile practices such as continuous integration and delivery. They also had several prerequisites for continuous deployment in place but none of them actually deployed automatically to production.

Different forms of experimentation were used in four out of five companies. Company A did user testing with different UI implementations and a MVP feature implementation. A price change experiment was going on in Company B, prototyping and expert user testing in a continuous cycle in Company C, and extensive prototyping and user testing in Company D. Company C appeared to be using systematic prototyping, but their data collection and data analysis practices were not systematic: they simply let expert test users try the product without planning what data to collect. Company D had advanced data collection, storage, and refinement capabilities, used the data systematically, and would most likely be capable of continuous experimentation.

It appeared that the startups had set up their tools and practices based on previous experience of founders or employees. There was isolated use of practices such as user testing, prototyping, and even occasional A/B testing in the companies, but those seemed to originate from individuals with previous experiences with the techniques rather than the company actively adopting the practices.

Allocating resources to execute the product roadmap in the most efficient way was central to work planning in all case companies. Only Company B did not mention funding as a resource limitation. All companies had roadmaps with far more work than they could ever implement given their available schedule and resources. This chronic lack of resources forced the companies to prioritise work that would be beneficial in the next funding round, even at the expense of feature development with real value to customers.

There was a tendency in the companies to avoid advanced practices until a strong need emerged – a fiercely pragmatic stance towards method adoption. It became apparent that even experiencing problems was not enough to adopt better ways to operate. Even if the team would know a better way of doing their work, the effort to set up a new system and the opportunity cost of being unable to work on other, more important, tasks, could prevent change from taking place. Change was seen as a waste of resources unless a perceived tangible benefit was in sight within the time horizon that is currently relevant for the company.

5   Discussion

The descriptive account given above allows us to construct a number of propositions to address the research questions, which we now discuss.

5.1   CE and Software Development Methods (RQ1)

To address RQ1, we propose that *software startups do not generally integrate experimentation into their software development methods, but may use CE-support-ing methods*. Experimentation in a loose sense was present in our case companies, but systematic, statistically controlled experimentation was uncommon, in line with existing research showing a lack of systematic CE in startups [13,21,25]. Product domains and business models that limit the possibilities for experimentation further reduce integration. Maturing startups may introduce more structure into their methods, and we then expect systematic experimentation to be more frequent and deeply integrated into methods and practices.

Several practices supporting CE were in place in the case companies. All developed their products incrementally using agile or lean software development practices. Only Company A built their mobile app manually. The companies were similar in development practices, the single major difference being automated testing, used by only two. Version control and backlog were the only practices with an adoption rate above 35% in a prior study [14]. Compared to this, the case companies are fairly advanced in adopting key agile practices. However, a closer look reveals rather selective adoption of agile practices in three of our case companies, and some deviations were found in all. Method selectiveness has been reported before, with a warning that picking only some agile practices without supporting practices may lead to adverse effects [14].

The prerequisites for experimentation thus appear at first glance to be in place in the case companies, but they have picked methods selectively. Experimentation does not appear to be integrated with the methods. We found that only one company had a systematic approach to experimentation, which is in line with findings from a study with ten case companies [21] reporting that non-systematic experimentation was common, but systematic experimentation among startup companies was rare.

5.2   Use of Data (RQ2)

For RQ2, we propose that 1) *utilisation of user data in startups tends to begin with ad hoc collection and interpretation of rich, qualitative data when the user base is small and the startup is in its early stages*, but that 2) *transitioning to more systematic use of data, which allows reliable understanding of the effects of product decisions, requires deliberately building specific technical capabilities and adopting an experimentation framework.*

Four of the five companies had good access to user data and established ways for collecting qualitative feedback. Interviews, feedback forms, and email were the most common channels, but social media, application store feedback, and chat were also used. Company B's B2B model practically prevented access to qualitative end user data, and forced them to rely on data their business partners were willing to share. These are known issues of the B2B context [33].

Four of the companies had built instrumentation for collecting event-level quantitative data, but only companies A and D had automated access to UI level events; both demonstrated product improvement as a result of using this data. Company B was limited to backend data, and Company C had implemented an opt-in data collection mechanism primarily for debugging purposes.

Prior work suggests that CE adoption relies on initial awareness [13], and progresses through several stages, each with many challenges to overcome [26]. However, we add the consideration that CE in the form often proposed in the literature may be inadequate for startups as its costs may be too large. Our findings show that, in line with previous research on organisational development towards CE (e.g., [4,11,29]), the transition to systematic and advanced use of data in startups requires considerable investment in development of skills, procedures, data acquisition, and customer collaboration in different forms. It requires a mode of functioning that is not easily combined with the sparse resources of startups nor with the culture of fast-moving innovation and a sharp focus on realising the founders' product vision. Adopting a systematic experimentation approach may face resistance (c.f. [26]), pointing to the need for data acquisition and utilisation methods that work for very early-stage startups, and can scale up as they grow and mature.

5.3 The Appeal of Continuous Experimentation (RQ3)

The following three propositions concern conditions for adopting CE in startups.
P1. Adoption of a Practice Requires Previous Personal Experience. Only the interviewee from Company D had heard about continuous experimentation, but was unable to describe it in detail, which suggests that they had no prior experience with it. Our findings suggest that the strongest adoption pathway in this context is word of mouth and personal experience.
P2. The Practice Must Not Require Large Resources to Adopt or Use. Four out of the five companies mentioned funding as critical to their priorities. The fear of running out of time and money may prevent startups from taking risks in adopting practices, especially if large time and resource investments are perceived to be needed. It is unclear what resources are required to adopt CE. The case companies had already performed experiments, albeit in unstructured ways. Becoming more systematic could be a matter of educating the company employees. However, establishing an experimentation process and the required technical infrastructure requires upfront work. Additionally, more resources are

needed to make variants for experiments than to build a single version. These resource requirements may exceed what the companies believe they can afford. *P3. The Practice Must Solve a Serious Enough Problem within a Reasonable Amount of Time.* Whether CE solves a concrete enough problem and provides enough perceived value is a question beyond personal experience and resource requirements. From the company's perspective, an issue must be serious enough and timely, and the new practice must guide to a solution fast enough to keep up with the speed dictated by investors. At least companies A and C, which had not yet established a firm user base, were effectively looking for a product-market fit and trying to test their ideas with early versions of their application. These two companies seemed to be less inclined to do systematic experimentation than they were to develop features from the roadmap and see what users would say about the next version. Even though CE could have some benefits, these companies may be more interested in increasing the speed of development. Therefore, the companies would not recognise CE as a valuable solution for their problem.

Earlier studies covering CE adoption (e.g., [9,13,22,25,26,29,39]) indicate that notable skill and coordination from the whole organisation is required. They indicate that adopting CE is a journey that should be taken gradually, starting with small-scale experimentation, and building increased technical and organisational capabilities in each subsequent experimentation round [22,39]. Yaman et al. [39] propose having a CE champion with the required expertise and mandate to facilitate adoption. This idea aligns well with the identified need for prior experience, as well as the startup companies' suggested inability to see the value of systematic experimentation.

5.4   Implications for Practice

The propositions above suggest that CE is problematic for software startups. On one hand, the possible benefits, especially the validation of value hypotheses, are important for startups since they help avoid directions that do not lead to a viable product. On the other hand, the considerable resources required for full adoption, the many details and required rigour in currently existing methods, and the potential mismatch with fast-paced startup culture and the skills that startup employees currently have, mean that adopting CE risks depleting precisely those scarce resources that startups need to build their product.

As noted above, the current solution is to do a gradual, piecemeal adoption, and to find a person or small team to spearhead the practice, using minimal resources. However, we suggest that startups should consider CE without all the prerequisites that are usually listed. Simple means of observing user behaviour, such as sending back a single value from an app, and basic analyses in a spreadsheet, can enable startups to focus on product questions rather than the infrastructure. This turns the order of adoption around to provide immediate value: instead of large up-front investments in CI, CD, and other automation that must be constantly updated as the product changes, the focus should be on developing the capability to dress product development questions as simple experimental designs and finding the quickest and least resource-intensive ways to execute them. This leverages the key assets that startups have: knowledge about their product and customers, a sense of the product vision, and an aptitude for fast-paced innovation, turned towards the practice of experimentation itself.

5.5   Limitations

The credibility or internal validity [28] of this study is limited by the participation of only one main interviewee per company. To counter this threat, we sought to include participants who had the best possible knowledge of the questions we wanted to ask. We also included a small number of additional participants to provide missing details on, e.g., technical matters. Credibility, as well as consistency [28] is also strengthened by our use of researcher triangulation and the repeated data sessions carried out during the analysis. Given the small size of the companies, we argue that our study is credible and consistent in capturing the reality of each of the five companies.

In terms of transferability or external validity [28], the variation in case companies and the reporting of results and circumstances should help the reader determine the extent to which our findings can be applied in specific future cases. We have not sought to statistically validate the findings in a larger sample. Rather, the aim of this study is to develop a descriptive account of the case companies and develop propositions that could be used, for example, to design a larger survey study to examine the prevalence of the factors found here. We argue that the propositions obtained in this study enable future studies to examine CE in startups in more detail than what was possible based on existing studies to date, and that they can be used as points of reflection for practitioners if they are considering to adopt CE in a startup context.

6   Conclusions

We sought to understand the factors involved in adopting CE in software startups. Through a descriptive multiple-case study in five Finnish startups, we examined product development practices, and method choices, asking how these companies collected and utilised user data in product development.

All companies used agile or lean software development practices and continuous software development practices such as continuous integration and continuous deployment. Most companies were able to collect qualitative user data. Two were also doing automatic collection of user interface event level data from their services. The companies used the collected data mostly for validating that their services did not contain errors. Only one company appeared to be systematically using the data for predicting future user requirements.

Continuous experimentation was not commonly known: only one participant had heard about it and could not describe it in detail. Previous experience and expected short-term value seem to be important factors when startups select CE tools and practices. The companies struggled with limited resources, forcing them to carefully prioritise work and foregoing the adoption of complex methods.

A well-resourced company can afford dedicating an extra team to experimentation without negatively affecting the development work. This is not feasible for a startup with only a handful of developers, where the effort of doing an experiment might require halting other development. Thus, it is understandable that a startup company would prefer to simply continue executing their roadmap.

More awareness of continuous experimentation could improve the adoption rate of the practice among developers and entrepreneurs. Potential approaches include teaching the practice in university curricula or to prepare entrepreneurship training programs with CE-related material. The latter approach has been tried with promising results [5] and may be worth pursuing in further research.

However, the CE practice should also adapt to the requirements of different kinds of companies. The research community should seek ways to make CE more affordable for a larger variety of companies, to lower the adoption barrier on both organisational and individual levels, and to make it more attractive and easier to benefit from the practice's advantages.

Acknowledgements. We express our gratitude to the study participants and participating companies for their generous sharing of information.

References

1. Amatriain, X.: Beyond data: from user information to business value through personalized recommendations and consumer science. In: Proceedings of the 22nd ACM International Conference on Information & Knowledge Management, pp. 2201–2208. ACM, San Francisco (2013)
2. Auer, F., Ros, R., Kaltenbrunner, L., Runeson, P., Felderer, M.: Controlled experimentation in continuous experimentation: knowledge and challenges. Inf. Softw. Technol. **134**, 106551 (2021)
3. Berg, V., Birkeland, J., Nguyen-Duc, A., Pappas, I.O., Jaccheri, L.: Software startup engineering: a systematic mapping study. J. Syst. Softw. **144**, 255–274 (2018)
4. Bosch, J.: Building products as innovation experiment systems. In: Cusumano, M.A., Iyer, B., Venkatraman, N. (eds.) ICSOB 2012. LNBIP, vol. 114, pp. 27–39. Springer, Heidelberg (2012). https://doi.org/10.1007/978-3-642-30746-1_3
5. Camuffo, A., Cordova, A., Gambardella, A., Spina, C.: A scientific approach to entrepreneurial decision making: evidence from a randomized control trial. Manage. Sci. **66**(2), 564–586 (2020)
6. Dingsøyr, T., Lassenius, C.: Emerging themes in agile software development: introduction to the special section on continuous value delivery. Inf. Softw. Technol. **77**, 56–60 (2016)
7. Fabijan, A., Dmitriev, P., Olsson, H.H., Bosch, J.: The benefits of controlled experimentation at scale. In: 43rd Euromicro Conference on Software Engineering and Advanced Applications (SEAA), pp. 18–26. IEEE, Vienna (2017)
8. Fabijan, A., Dmitriev, P., Olsson, H.H., Bosch, J.: The evolution of continuous experimentation in software product development: from data to a data-driven organization at scale. In: IEEE/ACM 39th International Conference on Software Engineering (ICSE), pp. 770–780 (2017)

9. Fagerholm, F., Sanchez Guinea, A., Mäenpää, H., Münch, J.: The right model for continuous experimentation. J. Syst. Softw. **123**, 292–305 (2017)

10. Feitelson, D.G., Frachtenberg, E., Beck, K.L.: Development and deployment at Facebook. IEEE Internet Comput. **17**(4), 8–17 (2013)

11. Fitzgerald, B., Stol, K.J.: Continuous software engineering: a roadmap and agenda. J. Syst. Softw. **123**, 176–189 (2017)

12. Gomez-Uribe, C.A., Hunt, N.: The Netflix recommender system: algorithms, business value, and innovation. ACM Trans. Manage. Inf. Syst. **6**(4) (2016)

13. Gutbrod, M., Münch, J., Tichy, M.: How do software startups approach experimentation? empirical results from a qualitative interview study. In: Felderer, M., Méndez Fernández, D., Turhan, B., Kalinowski, M., Sarro, F., Winkler, D. (eds.) PROFES 2017. LNCS, vol. 10611, pp. 297–304. Springer, Cham (2017). https://doi.org/10.1007/978-3-319-69926-4_21

14. Klotins, E., et al.: Use of agile practices in start-up companies. e-Informatica Softw. Eng. J. **15**(1) (2021)

15. Klotins, E., Unterkalmsteiner, M., Gorschek, T.: Software engineering in start-up companies: an analysis of 88 experience reports. Empir. Softw. Eng. **24**(1), 68–102 (2019)

16. Kniberg, H.: Spotify Rhythm - how we get aligned (slides from my talk at agile Sverige), June 2016. https://blog.crisp.se/2016/06/08/henrikkniberg/spotify-rhythm. Accessed 29 Apr 2022

17. Kohavi, R., Deng, A., Frasca, B., Walker, T., Xu, Y., Pohlmann, N.: Online controlled experiments at large scale. In: Proceedings of the 19th ACM SIGKDD International Conference on Knowledge Discovery and Data Mining, KDD 2013, pp. 1168–1176. Association for Computing Machinery, New York (2013)

18. Kohavi, R., Henne, R.M., Sommerfield, D.: Practical guide to controlled experiments on the web: listen to your customers not to the hippo. In: Proceedings of the 13th ACM SIGKDD International Conference on Knowledge Discovery and Data Mining, p. 959. ACM Press, San Jose (2007)

19. Kohavi, R., et al.: Online experimentation at Microsoft. Data Mining Case Stud. **11**(2009), 39 (2009)

20. Kotashev, K.: Startup failure rate: how many startups fail and why? (2022). https://www.failory.com/blog/startup-failure-rate. Accessed 29 Apr 2022

21. Lindgren, E., Münch, J.: Software development as an experiment system: a qualitative survey on the state of the practice. In: Lassenius, C., Dingsøyr, T., Paasivaara, M. (eds.) XP 2015. LNBIP, vol. 212, pp. 117–128. Springer, Cham (2015). https://doi.org/10.1007/978-3-319-18612-2_10

22. Lindgren, E., Münch, J.: Raising the odds of success: the current state of experimentation in product development. Inf. Softw. Technol. **77**, 80–91 (2016)

23. Mäntylä, V.: Continuous experimentation in finnish startups - a descriptive case study of A Grid and Maria 01 communities. Master's thesis, Aalto University, School of Science (2022). http://urn.fi/URN:NBN:fi:aalto-202201301571

24. Mäntylä, V., Lehtelä, B., Fagerholm, F.: Supplementary material for "the viability of continuous experimentation in early-stage software startups" (2022). https://docs.google.com/document/d/1Gx5dkKAZD-_0L5uNP1pZWRaiceoDZDlDPpLxnyTtShc/edit?usp=sharing. Review version

25. Melegati, J., Chanin, R., Wang, X., Sales, A., Prikladnicki, R.: Enablers and inhibitors of experimentation in early-stage software startups. In: Franch, X., Männistö, T., Martínez-Fernández, S. (eds.) PROFES 2019. LNCS, vol. 11915, pp. 554–569. Springer, Cham (2019). https://doi.org/10.1007/978-3-030-35333-9_39

26. Melegati, J., Edison, H., Wang, X.: XPro: a model to explain the limited adoption and implementation of experimentation in software startups. IEEE Trans. Software Eng. **48**(6), 1929–1946 (2022)
27. Melegati, J., Guerra, E., Wang, X.: Understanding hypotheses engineering in software startups through a gray literature review. Inf. Softw. Technol. **133**, 106465 (2021)
28. Merriam, S.B., Tisdell, E.J.: Qualitative Research: A Guide to Design and Implementation. The Jossey-Bass Higher and Adult Education Series, 4 edn. Wiley, San Francisco (2015)
29. Olsson, H.H., Alahyari, H., Bosch, J.: Climbing the "stairway to heaven" - a mulitiple-case study exploring barriers in the transition from agile development towards continuous deployment of software. In: 38th Euromicro Conference on Software Engineering and Advanced Applications, pp. 392–399 (2012)
30. Olsson, H.H., Bosch, J.: The HYPEX model: from opinions to data-driven software development. In: Bosch, J. (ed.) Continuous Software Engineering, pp. 155–164. Springer, Cham (2014). https://doi.org/10.1007/978-3-319-11283-1_13
31. Paternoster, N., Giardino, C., Unterkalmsteiner, M., Gorschek, T., Abrahamsson, P.: Software development in startup companies: a systematic mapping study. Inf. Softw. Technol. **56**(10), 1200–1218 (2014)
32. Ries, E.: The Lean Startup: How Today's Entrepreneurs Use Continuous Innovation to Create Radically Successful Businesses, 1st edn. Crown Business, New York (2011)
33. Rissanen, O., Münch, J.: Continuous experimentation in the B2B domain: a case study. In: 2015 IEEE/ACM 2nd International Workshop on Rapid Continuous Software Engineering, pp. 12–18. IEEE, Florence (2015)
34. Schermann, G., Cito, J., Leitner, P.: Continuous experimentation: challenges, implementation techniques, and current research. IEEE Softw. **35**(2), 26–31 (2018)
35. Shadish, W.R., Cook, T.D., Campbell, D.T.: Experimental and Quasi-Experimental Designs for Generalized Causal Inference. Houghton Mifflin, Boston (2001)
36. Steiber, A., Alänge, S.: A corporate system for continuous innovation: the case of Google Inc. Eur. J. Innov. Manag. **16**(2), 243–264 (2013)
37. Thomke, S.H.: Managing experimentation in the design of new products. Manage. Sci. **44**(6), 743–762 (1998)
38. Wu, L., Grbovic, M.: How Airbnb tells you will enjoy sunset sailing in Barcelona? Recommendation in a two-sided travel marketplace. In: Proceedings of the 43rd International ACM SIGIR Conference on Research and Development in Information Retrieval, pp. 2387–2396 (2020)
39. Yaman, S.G.: Initiating the transition towards continuous experimentation: empirical studies with software development teams and practitioners. Doctoral thesis, University of Helsinki (2019). http://urn.fi/URN:ISBN:978-951-51-5543-6
40. Yaman, S.G., et al.: Transitioning towards continuous experimentation in a large software product and service development organisation - a case study. In: Abrahamsson, P., Jedlitschka, A., Nguyen Duc, A., Felderer, M., Amasaki, S., Mikkonen, T. (eds.) PROFES 2016. LNCS, vol. 10027, pp. 344–359. Springer, Cham (2016). https://doi.org/10.1007/978-3-319-49094-6_22
41. Yaman, S.G., et al.: Introducing continuous experimentation in large software-intensive product and service organisations. J. Syst. Softw. **133**, 195–211 (2017)
42. Yin, R.K.: Case Study Research: Design and Methods, 5th edn. SAGE, Los Angeles (2014)

Data-Driven Improvement of Static Application Security Testing Service: An Experience Report in Visma

Monica Iovan[1]([✉]) and Daniela Soares Cruzes[1,2]

[1] Visma Software, Romania, Norway
{monica.iovan,daniela.soares.cruzes}@visma.com
[2] Department of Computer Science, NTNU, Trondheim, Norway

Abstract. Security is increasingly recognized as an important aspect of software development processes. Improving processes for security in agile teams is very important to streamline the focus on security and keep the agility of the software development process. In Visma we use data to drive improvement of security services provided to the software teams. The improvement process involves changing the services or their structures after some period of usage and experience with it, driven by data collected during operations. We systematically identify the areas that need changes in order to become more valuable for the development teams and for the security program. In this paper we have described the improvement process used on the security static analysis service in Visma, the data we have used for that, how we extracted this data from the Static Application Security Testing (SAST) tool, the lessons learned and also provide some guidelines to other organizations that would like to use this method in their own services.

Keywords: Security defects · Static analysis · Static application security testing · Software security · Agile · Continuous software development

1 Introduction

Nowadays, security focus needs to become a natural part of a constantly improving development process, meaning that the security activities needs to be merged into the development lifecycle. Usually these activities are defined by the security team, in a top-down approach, after making an analysis of what to include in the lifecycle, and agreeing on what needs to be done to improve the security of the software. The Secure Software Development Lifecycle (SSDLC) generally refers to a systematic, multi-step process that streamlines software development from inception to release. Software companies need to establish processes, methods, technologies and proven standards to ensure their customers have secured

Supported by Visma.

© The Author(s), under exclusive license to Springer Nature Switzerland AG 2022
D. Taibi et al. (Eds.): PROFES 2022, LNCS 13709, pp. 157–170, 2022.
https://doi.org/10.1007/978-3-031-21388-5_11

services. In Visma, these security add-ons to the lifecycle are part of a security program and are provided as services to the software development teams.

Visma is currently a federation of around 200 individual companies with over 14,000 employees. Each company has one or more self-managed software development teams and each with its own way of working and culture. Since 2015 a centralized Product Security Team (PST) is driving the software security efforts creating a standardized way of working across teams [16]. Now after several years of offering this program, surged the need to evaluate the different strategies of approaching security and define program interventions based on the findings.

As the Static Application Security Testing (SAST) service is the oldest service offered in the program, we have decided to start the service improvement process from it. At the time of the writing, SAST was implemented in 155 teams regularly, with over 40000 snapshots (each build generates a snapshot, a report which contains the new discovered vulnerabilities or the ones that were fixed since the previous run). The SAST service was one of the first services provided by the PST as part of the security program. As also mentioned by Oyetoyan et al. [4] in their study, the adoption strategy for the security services plays a significant role in the end result. Therefore, as with all the other services in the security program, in Visma's SAST is offered free of charge to the development teams and the teams have the power to decide if they are using the offered service or if they want to use another similar tool. One of the benefits of using the offered SAST service is that the servers are centrally configured by the PST together with a centralized support team. The PST is responsible for the configuration and access to the servers but also for the continuous monitoring and improving of the SAST service. The service is provided using a commercial tool since September 2016.

SAST tools generates large amount of data that can be used to understand the dynamics of the service and to find points for improvement. The focus of this paper is not on the tool itself, but how the SAST data can help on improving the SAST service itself and also the other parts of the security program. In this paper we have described the DMAIC (an acronym for Define, Measure, Analyze, Improve and Control) for the SAST service. DMAIC refers to a data-driven improvement cycle used for improving, optimizing and stabilizing business processes and designs. The DMAIC improvement cycle is the core tool used to drive Six Sigma projects. Since an authoritative or uniform account of the DMAIC method does not exist, we have defined our steps to follow the improvement process.

The goal with this process was to improve the SAST service by innovating, making it more efficient and useful for the development teams. Since SAST tools generates large amount of data, we can use them to understand the efficiency of the tool, the development teams' behavior and possible ways to improvement the service. We aim to automate this process as much as possible to be able to reuse most of the analysis steps in future improvement.

We describe the process used on the security static analysis service, the data we have used for that, how we extracted this data from the Static Application Security Testing (SAST) tool, the lessons learned by doing the DMAIC process and also provide some guidelines to other organizations that would like to use this method in their own services.

2   Background

Almost every software organization nowadays have a security lifecycle in which SAST is an essential and fundamental part of it. SAST tools are reviewing the application' source code and check them for violations [9] and identify potential source code anomalies early in the software development lifecycle, anomalies that could lead to field failures [15]. The output of a SAST tool still requires human evaluation, which means the team has to follow a process. Therefore, using a SAST tool does not imply an automatic improvement in the security of the code [4,10,11,13].

Many research papers discuss the effectiveness of the tools on finding vulnerabilities or how to improve the tools to find less false positives. Excessive alert generation and a large proportion of unimportant or incorrect alerts may hinder the usage of SAST by developers [10–12]. Even if false positives are known concerns towards static analysis tools, Goseva-Popstojanovaa and Perhinschi [13] found that tools also suffer from a high number of false negatives, what is even more worrisome because they lead to a false sense of security [9].

The second category of research papers in SAST focus on the developers' perspective. Oyetoyan et al. [4] performed a study on the adoption of SAST on a large Telecom organization. In his study one of the goals was to understand the desired features in SAST tools that could increase the chance of adoption. The authors found that the developers fear the effort to setup a third party SAST tool and get it to work seamlessly in their development and build environments, but also fear that the tool may disrupt the flow of their work and acting on the issues reported from the tool depends on whether it overburden them or not.

The third category of papers focus on the SAST Tools as a "service", as the case reported in this paper. We found three main industrial cases (from Ericson, Google and Facebook) and a study on five open source projects. Imtiaz et al [5], empirically studied five open source projects as case studies that have been actively using Coverity, a static analysis tool, with an aim to understand how developers act on static analysis alerts. They found that the portion of total alerts that developers fix through code changes vary between 27.4% to 49.5% across projects; and that the developers generally take a long time to fix the alerts despite the fixes being low in complexity.

Baca et al. [6] performed an industry case study at Ericsson AB that is also using Coverity. The authors found out that just stating that SAST should be used was not enough to achieve wide adoption. The adoption strategy for the tools played a significant role in the end result. The authors conclude that a configuration management approach where the tool is integrated in the development process as a mandatory part is the best adoption strategy. That is efficient if developers are educated in order to make use of the tool to correctly identify vulnerabilities as soon as possible after detection. Using a configuration management approach had a good success rate as developers started on their own initiative to examine the tool's output.

Sadowski et. al. [7] when describing the lessons from building Static Analysis Tools at Google, affirms that for a static analysis project to succeed, developers must feel they benefit from and enjoy using it. The authors also recommend that SAST tools providers should focus on the developer and listen to their feedback; they also conclude that careful developer workflow integration is key for static analysis tool adoption. They recommend project-level customization and analyzing the results during the development workflow, like on compiling time, code review or presenting issues only when a developer is changing the code in question. They also suggest to measure success in terms of defects corrected, not the number presented to developers.

Distefano et. al. [8], describe the key lessons for designing static analyses tools in Facebook. Their approach is to invest in advanced static analysis tools that employ reasoning techniques similar to those from program verification. They use the concept of "bugs that matter", using static analysis to prevent bugs that would affect their products and rely on their engineers' judgment as well as data from production to highlight the bugs that matter the most. To analyze improvement needs to the SAST, they do analysis on actioned reports and observable missed bugs. The actioned reports and missed bugs are related to the classic concepts of true positives and false negatives from the academic static analysis literature.

3   DMAIC: Data-Driven Improvement Process in Security

Visma is using data collected from SAST tool, similar with the previous experiences of Google, Facebook and Ericsson and referring to DMAIC, process improvement methodology. The proposed process involves decisions that are supported by quantitative indicators and are shared among the involved stakeholders. The process is composed of five not linear, but more iterative steps (Fig. 1):

1. **Define** - The purpose of this step is to clearly pronounce the problem, goal, potential resources, project scope and high-level project timeline.
2. **Measure** - The purpose of this step is to measure the specification of problem/goal. This is a data collection step, the purpose of which is to establish process performance baselines;
3. **Analyze** - The purpose of this step is to identify, validate and select root cause for elimination.
4. **Improve** The purpose of this step is to identify, test and implement a solution to the problem; in part or in free of all whole.
5. **Control** - The purpose of this step is to embed the changes and ensure sustainability, this is sometimes referred to as making the change'stick'.

3.1   Defining the DMAIC Plan

The first step in the process is *defining the improvement plan*, determining what one wants and appropriate levels of relevant objectives. Before starting the improvement process it is important to understand the service, its history and the reputation of the service from the users' perspective, but also how the other services complements it. This is more a requirements collection based on the existing assumptions regarding the service, within a possible timeframe and with an estimated budget.

In Visma case, during the onboarding process the software development team and PST configures the SAST servers, the build agents and the build pipeline. The software development team receives then a short training regarding the usage of the tool with a link to the documentation pages on the tool's features. The development teams have the responsibility for running the automatic static analysis of the code through their build pipeline, while also triaging and fixing the discovered vulnerabilities. On the first time using the SAST tool, the team has the possibility to mark all initial discovered vulnerabilities as legacy. The PST advice the development teams to fix these legacy issues in time, prioritizing them based on criticality, but in the same period of time to fix any new issue that is discovered on the next runs.

Depending on the teams' needs and technology they use, SAST configuration can be adjusted, by creating project-level customization. Some of the teams, mostly the ones with smaller products or the ones using microservices, decided to run the SAST analyses on every commit. Other teams, with monolithic architecture, run the analyses on weekly bases due to time required for the analysis. The time used by the SAST tool to analyze the code is between 2 min to 150 h.

The DMAIC team is composed of 5 members as follows: two researchers, one developer, the SAST service owner, and the director of the PST. Regarding the timeline the plan was to finish in 6 months.

Fig. 1. Key phases in a DMAIC process

The plan includes:

- analyzing the development teams' onboarding experience
- analyzing the usage of the tool
- analyzing the follow up of the discovered vulnerabilities.
- finding patterns on the usage of the tool on company level
- identifying specifics of each team
- understanding where the teams see benefits or lack of benefits from using such a service
- understanding where teams would benefit from having more awareness.

3.2   Measuring the Existing Service

The second step is *measuring the existing service*. This is an iterative process where Service Owner together with the researchers run through the measurement and evaluation of the overall service. The scope is to identify the areas for improvement and key performance indicators of the service. The outputs of this step are:

- general information about the service;
- lists of data that can be collected;
- methods of collecting this data;
- performance indicators that can be measured;
- the pre-improvement values of these indicators, if exists.

The SAST service is now used by 155 development teams. Depending on the product' lifecycle phase and also the teams' decisions, SAST run daily, weekly or monthly independent for each product. The recommendation from the PST is to run SAST on every code commit, but in some cases, products that are in maintenance mode can run it once per month. It is important to run SAST even if no new code was added because new vulnerability types are discovered. Every run of the SAST service generates a snapshot, a report which contains the new discovered vulnerabilities or the ones that were fixed since the previous run. Last year over 40000 snapshots were taken in the company' codebase which consists of mostly C# and Java products, but also products that use different technologies such as C++, Visual Basic or Ruby.

We automated the data collection from the SAST servers through the tool' APIs:

- General service statistics: there are 155 projects, 84772 streams, 411 292 935 lines of code, 28 843 discovered issues and 17 463 fixed issues;
- Projects composition - for each project we extracted: total number of lines of code, total number of discovered issues and total number of fixed issues;
- Snapshots details - for each snapshot we extracted: commit date, number of new issues, number of fixed issues;
- Issues' details - for each discovered security issue we extracted: its type, criticality, classification, status.

In addition, we have collected information from other systems:

- Product dashboard - a system that stores and analyze information regarding the technology used for each product;
- Confluence - specific pages where the onboarding of each product to SAST is done;
- Build systems - status of the last run build.
- Security Maturity Index - a system designed to measure the security maturity level of the products. It collects data from different parts of the security program. The system is based on penalty points and it has four levels, called tiers (bronze, silver, gold and platinum). When a team is not following the activities designed to given security activity, they receive a penalty, and this affects their current tier.

We have created a database, specially designed for collecting and aggregating data from these different sources. In a first phase we created different queries and exported this aggregated data into Excel files. The data was aggregated based on the following identified performance indicators that can be measured:

- usage of the tool
  - number of snapshots per product per month - all teams create at least one snapshot a month for each part of their product' code;
  - time to fix per project - new discovered issues are fixed immediately if they are high severity, within 30 days if they are major severity and within 90 days if they are moderate severity;
  - number of vulnerabilities of the top 3 most common types - decrease the number of new discovered issues in the top 3 most common types;
  - costs of the service - costs to run and maintain the service should be reduced;
- catching errors
  - number of projects with low number of lines of code
  - number of projects with variations in number of lines of code - in every two consecutive snapshots of the same code there is less than 20% unjustified variations in number of lines of code (LOC);
  - number of projects that are missing security checkers
- trust
  - percentage of false positive - less than 20% false positive for each type of vulnerability;
  - teams' satisfaction - increase teams' satisfaction with the service;
  - teams' confidence - increase teams' confidence in the tool.

3.3   Analyzing the Data

The third step is about *analyzing and assessing the data*. The focus is on the implementation of manual and automatic data collection. After data is collected the research team pre-process (clean and validate) and analyze it, thinking on where the service needs to be modified to increase its value. Too much data is as bad as no data, therefore it is important to select relevant data, that give value for the DMAIC process. This data analyzes is iterated with identifying future improvement scenarios. Based on the collected data, multiple options for improvement are discovered. For this non linear process we can have different approaches: like, in less complex situations, we can use a trial and error approach or selecting the obvious solution approach. In more complex situations we can decide to divide up the problem (chunking) or brainstorm. The prioritization of these options is very important for the success of the improvement process, and should involve the service owner, as he is the one that understands the risks and consequences of each scenario and can identify better each benefit.

Once the improvement scenarios are prioritized, the *implementation of the improvement work* can start. Good scenarios alone does not ensure that the improvement will be successful. Additional sub-steps may be needed to implement the scenarios in a way that can increase the likelihood the improvement will achieve its intended outcomes. One important additional sub-step is identifying the resources (funding, staffing and infrastructure, etc.) that can help with the implementation.

After implementation, resources and other support from stakeholders may decrease. Therefore, as with any change, there is a need or a *controlled evaluation*, adding future monitoring of the service. The planning for sustainability can be achieved through good automation.

4   Improving the SAST Service in Visma

Analysis Based on Project Composition. When a team decides to onboard to SAST service they create a Confluence page based on a template and then to fill-up the form. In these pages we maintain the onboarding status as follows:

- INITIATED = the page is created and the implementation of SAST in the product has not started;
- IN PROGRESS = implementation has started;
- ENROLLED = implementation is done; usage is started;
- ON HOLD = language not yet supported or support is not good enough;
- CANCELLED = discontinued;

In our analysis, we compared the confluence status to the data extracted from the SAST servers. We discovered some deviations, such as products that had the status as ENROLLED in confluence but the analyses were missing from the server, or the other way around.

Then we checked the commands used to analyze the code during the build pipeline and one example of our findings is that 42.58% of the projects have disabled CSRF checkers. Although this type has the biggest number of issues discovered and one of the biggest percentages of false positives, only 2.16% are marked as bugs by the developers in the SAST tool.

Next we divided the projects based on the number of lines of code (LOC) covered by the tool, as follow:

- Large (L) - 14,19% of projects have more than 5.000.000 LOC covered;
- Medium (M) - 36,77% of projects have within 1.000.000–5.000.000 LOC covered;
- Small (S) - 31,19% of the projects have within 100.000–1.000.000 LOC covered;
- XSmall (XS) - 14,84% of the projects have less than 100.000 LOC covered.

We reviewed all the projects from the XSmall category to make sure they include the whole codebase of that product. This way we were able to discover some projects that had hidden build failures, undetected by the development teams or the PST. Then for each category we compared the number of vulnerabilities discovered with the number of vulnerabilities fixed by the teams. Table 1 shows the averages lines of code, discovered issues and fixed issues (issues that do not appear in the last snapshots) for each category of projects.

As overall each one of the 155 projects fixed in average 60.5% of the issues discovered. The medium size projects have a smaller ratio (49.39%) of fixed issues compared with the discovered ones. Our assumption when verifying the data is that projects with larger number of discovered issues tend to become overwhelmed by the number of vulnerabilities to analyze and take actions. These teams are more inclined to mark issues as false positive, intentional or to leave them unfixed. The projects with smaller amount of issues discovered by the SAST tool are more inclined to fix them because they have more time/issue to fix or because of the reduced complexity of the code to fix and test the findings.

Analysis Based on Ignored Vulnerabilities. Our concern was on the unwillingness of developers to act upon the suggestions of the SAST tool on changes in the software code that shall improve security. We believe that the perceived usefulness of the SAST tool is directly linked to the amount of issues that the developers believe are important to fix. The high number of "ignored" issues in the services is somehow alarming for the service. In the system, on the 4 years of the service, 5982 of the issues were marked as false positive, 5707 of the issues were marked as intentional. 9886 of the false positive and intentional were marked as "ignore". Ignored in this case is defined as: developers classified the issues as "False Positive" or "Intentional" and Action = "Ignore".

From the analysis of the "ignored" issues, we noticed that developers tend to ignore some types of issues were more than others. We then performed an analysis on the ratio of ignored (false positives and intentional) issues for the top 10 vulnerability types in our database (Fig. 2). One specific type of vulnerability

Table 1. Averages for different project sizes.

	Average lines of code	Average issues discovered	Average issues fixed
XSmall projects	39287	31.86	20.48
Small projects	501544	89.89	62.83
Medium projects	2655485	219.32	108.32
Large projects	10565673	492.95	340.36

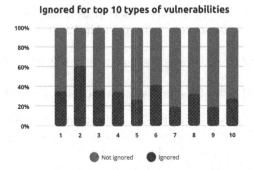

Fig. 2. Ratio of Ignored issues per Type.

reached to 61% of ignored issues and we decided to take a look further. The service owner of SAST was not sure if this behavior is because of lack of awareness on the risks and possible attacks that these vulnerabilities expose the systems to, or because the tool is not performing well on the detection of vulnerabilities for those types. We have recommended to create some awareness campaigns regarding those types of vulnerabilities.

For Cross-site request forgery type, after discussing with the service owner, we discovered that it was already known that that this SAST tool has problems to identify such vulnerabilities, and provides high ratio of false positives. The PST has previously given guidelines to the development teams to exclude this type from the analysis during the build. Also the testing for such vulnerabilities is provided by other security services.

4.1   Improving the SAST Service

The analysis done on the previous step helped us to identify different scenarios and areas of the service that needs retrofitting. We have performed other analysis using the collected data, and the definition of "done" on the analysis is not always clear, but we decided that the saturation and the number of actions we have found was enough for the analysis in this year. Based on the analysis done before we brainstormed what possible options can increase the value of the service and we drafted the retrofitting scenarios.

Next we will present some of the scenarios identified for each of the three main categories:

– changes in the security program;
– changes on the security activities from the development teams;
– changes on the SAST service.

Changes in the Security Program. On the scenario suggested for the security program in CompanyX, other stakeholders were involved in the process because it affected other services. For example, one proposal was to change the security training to better fits the teams needs. For that we have created a top 10 list for each technology, list that can be used as input into developers training, while presenting the most common types of issues in the company. We also created a list with types of vulnerability for each team. This way we can find types of vulnerabilities that appears only in one or very few teams. Using such an information the training can be tailored targeting a specific subject and specific teams. Other scenarios were about changes we need to do on the security program in order to mitigate deficiencies in the SAST service on detecting certain vulnerabilities. Lastly, we added scenarios that impact (directly or indirectly) other services like Software Composition Analysis, Manual Vulnerability Assessment or Bug Bounty. Our proposition is that the service owners of those services shall use this information for better planning in their services or for finding more vulnerabilities using the following testing principle: "Use defect clustering, as software problems tend to cluster around narrow areas or functions. By identifying and focusing on these clusters, testers can efficiently test the sensitive areas while concurrently testing the remaining "non-sensitive" areas."

Changes on the Development Teams. In these cases we needed to discuss with specific teams to correct and/or verify some of the findings. For example, as mentioned before, we discovered some deviations between the onboarding status and the projects from the SAST servers. In such cases we verified with the teams if those projects are still needed or what is the status from their point of view and then correct either the onboarding page or the projects configuration. Other scenarios included modification of the build pipeline to reduce the running time or to better identify failures, or of the project configuration to better use the SAST capabilities.

Changes on the SAST Service. The scenarios for the SAST service are focusing on improving the well-functioning of the SAST as a service for the software development teams. This includes automation of the onboarding process or adding automatic monitoring of different performance indicators. As example, one scenario is trying to improve the monitoring of the SAST usage therefore it is needed to measure that the last snapshot for each part of the product is not older than 30 days. This way we make sure that the code that is in production is patched when new vulnerabilities are discovered.

After the full list of retrofitting scenarios was created, each scenario was discussed with the service owner in order to understand the resources needed for the retrofitting work, but also reviewed in order to understand its benefits and risks.

4.2   Control

After discussion we decided which scenarios will bring benefits to the service and the development teams, and then we started to implement them immediately. We

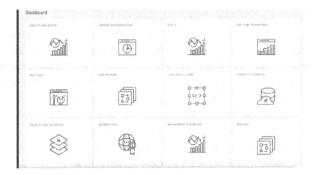

Fig. 3. Security Retrofitting Analysis solution.

started with the deviations between the onboarding status and the projects from the SAST servers, then we continued with some changes in the build template.

After implementing all the scenarios from the list we started improving the automatic monitoring of SAST, by implementing some relevant graphs into the Security Retrofitting Analysis solution (Fig. 3).

5   Discussion and Conclusions

The focus is improvement activities which should depend on the needs of the service. This may include:

- fine-tuning the service - the ongoing day-to-day operation, either by lowering the costs or for example creating a better image of the service;
- service innovation - the redesign of the service and the end-to-end processes used, increasing productivity and lowering the maintenance needed;
- making the security program anti-fragile - releasing the stress of team members and improving the serviceability.

Process improvement through DMAIC is a way to systematically identify the areas that need changes in order to become more valuable for the development teams and for the security program. As part of the service continuous improvement this improvement process can be repeated every second year or when big structural changes occur. In this case study we have identified improvement opportunities to the SAST service in Visma. With the work done we have identified the following benefits to the service:

- Lowered cost of the service by reducing the number of projects on the server which implicated lower costs on the maintenance and licenses;
- Better confidence/understanding of the service towards the stakeholders by understanding the limitations and possibilities of the tools further;
- Increase the usability of the service - using this process and paying attention to the way teams work we discover new ways of working and better ways of supporting work, to help them work smarter;

- Increasing productivity of the SAST tool usage by having focused awareness trainings and by eliminating the vulnerability types that have too higher percentage of false positives;
- Attracting more development teams to use the service - increasing the image of the service and showing the benefits of using such a tool can help other development teams decide to onboard on this service;
- Improved serviceability by improving how the service is provided to all stakeholders.

As future work we will focus on measuring quantitatively the benefits of the security retrofitting and run the process with other services in the security program.

Acknowledgments. We would like to thank Visma and all the participants of the Security process improvement.

References

1. Beck, K., Andres, C.: Extreme Programming Explained: Embrace Change, 2nd edn. Addison-Wesley, Boston (2004)
2. Martin, R.C.: Agile Software Development: Principles, Patterns, and Practices. Prentice Hall, Upper Saddle River (2003)
3. Abril, P.S., Plant, R.: The patent holder's dilemma: buy, sell, or troll? Commun. ACM **50**(1), 36–44 (2007). https://doi.org/10.1145/1188913.1188915
4. Oyetoyan, T.D., Milosheska, B., Grini, M., Cruzes, D.S.: Myths and facts about static application security testing tools: an action research at telenor digital. In: XP, pp. 86–103 (2018)
5. Imtiaz, N., Murphy, B., Williams, L.: How do developers act on static analysis alerts? an empirical study of coverity usage. In: ISSRE, pp. 323–333 (2019)
6. Baca, D., Carlsson, B., Petersen, K., Lundberg, L.: Improving software security with static automated code analysis in an industry setting. Softw. Pract. Exp. **43**(3), 259–279 (2013)
7. Sadowski, C., Aftandilian, E., Eagle, A., Miller-Cushon, L., Jaspan, C.: Lessons from building static analysis tools at google. Commun. ACM **61**(4), 58–66 (2018)
8. Distefano, D., Fähndrich, M., Logozzo, F., O'Hearn, P.W.: Scaling static analyses at Facebook. Commun. ACM **62**(8), 62–70 (2019)
9. Chess, B., McGraw, G.: Static analysis for security. IEEE Secur. Priv. **2**(6), 76–79 (2004). https://doi.org/10.1109/MSP.2004.111
10. Austin, A., Williams, L.: One technique is not enough: a comparison of vulnerability discovery techniques. In: ESEM, pp. 97–106 (2011)
11. Dukes, L.S., Yuan, X., Akowuah, F.: A case study on web application security testing with tools and manual testing. In: 2013 Proceedings of IEEE Southeastcon, pp. 1–6. IEEE (2013)
12. Satyanarayana, V., Sekhar, M.V.B.C.: Static analysis tool for detecting web application vulnerabilities. Int. J. Modern Eng. Res. (IJMER) **1**(1), 127–133 (2011)
13. Goseva-Popstojanova, K., Perhinschi, A.: On the capability of static code analysis to detect security vulnerabilities. Inf. Softw. Technol. **68**, 18–33 (2015)

14. Ma, Z., Cooper, P., Daly, D., Ledo, L.: Existing building retrofits: methodology and state-of-the-art. Energy Build **55**, 889–902 (2012). ISSN 0378–7788, https://doi.org/10.1016/j.enbuild.2012.08.018
15. Heckman, S., Williams, L.: A systematic literature review of actionable alert identification techniques for automated static code analysis. Inf. Softw. Technol. **53**(4), 363–387 (2011)
16. Cruzes, D.S., Johansen, E.A.: Building an ambidextrous software security initiative, to appear in balancing agile and disciplined engineering and management approaches for IT services and software products. In: Mora, M., Marx Gómez, J., O'Connor, R., Buchalcevova, A. (eds). IGI Global (2020)
17. Iovan, M., Cruzes, D.S., Johansen, E.A.: Empowerment of security engineers through security chartering in Visma. In: XP 2020, Experience Report (2020). https://www.agilealliance.org/wpcontent/uploads/2020/xxx

Near Failure Analysis Using Dynamic Behavioural Data

Masoumeh Taromirad$^{(\boxtimes)}$ (iD) and Per Runeson (iD)

Lund University, 221 00 Lund, Sweden
{masoumeh.taromirad,per.runeson}@cs.lth.se

Abstract. Automated testing is a safeguard against software regression and provides huge benefits. However, it is yet a challenging subject. Among others, there is a risk that the test cases are too specific, thus making them inefficient. There are many forms of undesirable behaviour that are compatible with a typical program's specification, that however, harm users. An efficient test should provide *most possible information* in relation to the resources spent. This paper introduces *near failure analysis* which complements testing activities by analysing dynamic behavioural metrics (e.g., execution time) in addition to explicit output values. The approach employs machine learning (ML) for classifying the behaviour of a program as *faulty* or *healthy* based on dynamic data gathered throughout its executions over time. An ML-based model is designed and trained to predict whether or not an arbitrary version of a program is at risk of failure. The very preliminary evaluation demonstrates promising results for feasibility and effectiveness of near failure analysis.

Keywords: Regression testing · Failure prediction · Dynamic metrics

1 Introduction

Automated testing (AT) is one of the cornerstones of agile software engineering, with its short development cycles. In continuous integration/deployment (CI/CD) pipelines, AT is a safeguard against software regression due to side effects, unintentional changes, or changes in the environment. To make testing faster, cheaper and more reliable, it is desirable to automate as much of the testing process as possible [3].

A risk of AT is that the typical test cases are too specific; only testing pairs of input-output makes them ineffective. There are many forms of undesirable program behaviour that are compatible with a typical program's specification, that however, impair users and/or are undesirable for developers, such as using excessive computational resources or unnecessary complexity in a program [17]. An efficient test should provide *most possible information* in relation to the resources spent.

This paper introduces *near failure analysis* (NFA) which complements testing activities (and their outcome) by considering behavioural metrics (e.g., time

© The Author(s), under exclusive license to Springer Nature Switzerland AG 2022
D. Taibi et al. (Eds.): PROFES 2022, LNCS 13709, pp. 171–178, 2022.
https://doi.org/10.1007/978-3-031-21388-5_12

and memory consumption) in addition to output values. In comparison to the standard tests, where test cases include assertions against a specific output value or condition, the approach considers implicit dynamic behavioural data and their variation, additionally. The outcome of this analysis is not only a binary pass/fail, but a *pass/fail risk distribution*. The proposal – inspired by near crash analysis in traffic monitoring [6] – is expected to provide more information throughout program executions.

The key idea is to employ machine learning to classify the behaviour of a program under test (PUT), as *Faulty* or *Healthy*, considering dynamic data (e.g., execution time, memory consumption). Using the execution data gathered from various faulty and healthy versions of a PUT, an ML-based model is designed and trained to predict whether or not an arbitrary (and possibly new) version of the PUT includes a defect. The prediction model is trained using a supervised learning classification technique. Tests executions are a potential source of labeled behavioural data, and hence, we assume that enough labeled training samples are available.

In addition to the aforementioned challenge, the proposed approach could also contribute to the "test oracle problem", i.e., the challenge of distinguishing between the correct and incorrect behaviour of a program. Recent surveys (e.g., [5,13]) show that automating the test oracle is still a challenging issue and existing automated oracles are not widely applicable and are difficult to use in practice. Our early experiment suggests that implicit behavioural data could be an indication of the faulty or correct behaviour. Having the dynamic behavioural model (pattern) of a program (w.r.t. various input values) would alleviate this problem, since there is no need to know the exact output values for all the inputs. In this context, when a program is executed with arbitrary inputs, for example in regression testing (RT) or within operational environment, the behaviour of the program can be analysed, regardless of the expected output values – that are not specified or not available.

Through an early experiment of applying the proposed approach, within the Math project from Defects4J repository [12], we found our approach effective and applicable when a program incorporates substantial computation. In particular, NFA is seemed to be useful for test case prioritisation. The results also show that the implementation of the ML process provides acceptable accuracy (average of 95%) in predicting faulty behaviour.

2   Near Failure Analysis

We propose a supervised failure prediction framework that classifies the program behaviour into two classes, namely *Faulty* and *Healthy*, based on dynamic behavioural data gathered throughout its execution. Using dynamic data (e.g., execution time) collected from various executions of different faulty and healthy versions of a PUT, a machine learning-based model is designed and trained to predict whether or not an arbitrary (and possibly new) version of the PUT includes a defect. An overview of the proposed approach is presented in Fig. 1.

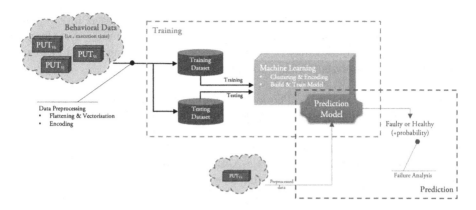

Fig. 1. Overview of the proposed approach.

A supervised approach could usually produce acceptable detection results; however, it requires enough labeled data. Tests executions are a potential source of labeled behavioural data, and thus, at this stage, we assume that enough labeled training samples (data correspondent to *healthy* and *faulty* versions) are available.

Behavioural Data. The behavioural data represents the behaviour of a PUT, w.r.t. a set of behavioural metrics (e.g., time, memory), throughout its executions. It is demonstrated as a *collection* of tuple $(Params, Bhv_{out}, l)$ that represents a single execution of the program, where

- *Params* is a map of values for the arguments and/or related parameters,
- Bhv_{out} is a map of values of the behavioural metric(s), and
- l is the label for the program: faulty or healthy.

The *Params* could be either the immediate input parameters passed to the program or other related parameters (e.g., global values) that involve in its execution. Also, this map could be hierarchical in that the parameters have been traced recursively to reach to primitive data types, i.e., the value of a parameter might be a map itself. This makes the values useful within the context of this work, for example a pointer to an array is not a meaningful value for learning algorithms.

2.1 Data Preprocessing

Data preprocessing is an essential stage for the success of any machine learning model. In almost all knowledge discovery tasks, this step takes the major part of the overall development effort [9]

Shape and size of the input data vary widely, leading to a fundamental challenge when designing a machine learning model that accepts fixed length vectors representing a single execution. To address this, we developed DATAPREP, a program that prepares the input behavioural (raw) data for training. DATAPREP flattens the data, encodes values (e.g., values of parameters), and then transform the variable-sized representations into fixed-length vectors.

Flattening and Vectorisation. The most preliminary task is to flatten the provided behavioural data through transforming the maps in the tuples, in particular the *Params* hierarchical map, into a flat representation. The resulting representation may have different sizes, e.g., when a parameter in the *Params* is a variable-length list. Therefore, the variable-sized sequences are also summarised and transformed into fixed-length vectors, employing heuristics, such as using the size of the list or the number of zeros (or negative values) in the list rather than the original values.

Encoding. Values within each execution record provide useful indications for classification. However, values – such as ints and strings – vary widely in shape and format. Therefore, the values are encoded into a similar representation, e.g., encode label-strings as numerical representations.

2.2   Prediction Model

In this phase, we perform the principal task of designing a model that trains to classify a program as *faulty* or *healthy* regarding the given *preprocessed* behavioural data (i.e., representing a set of executions of the program). The model consists of three components that are trained and used jointly and end-to-end: 1. CLUCENT that determines the clusters and their centroids with respect to the values of *Params*, 2. ENCOBE that encodes the behaviour of each version of the program, w.r.t the identified centroids, into a single vector, called *behaviour trace*, and finally, 3. CLASSICT that accepts *behaviour traces*, and builds a model that can predict whether a program is faulty or not.

Clustering. The values of the *Params* among all the input data (i.e., the input domain of the program), are grouped into clusters such that the data samples assigned to the same cluster are supposed to have similar (or close) values. In order to have better results, K-Means++ [4] is used as the initialisation scheme rather that the random initialisation. Note that this clustering is somehow aligned with test input data partitioning and, hence, the number of test cases for the program or input partitions are a promising, potential number for clusters.

   The main outcome of this task is the *centroids* of the clusters that are indexed and then used as the reference throughout the later steps. The *centroids* are represented as $C = \{c_1, c_2, ..., c_k\}$ where c_i is the centroid of cluster i.

Encoding the Behaviour. Based on the previously identified centroids, the behavioural data of each version of the PUT is summarized into a single trace throughout the following steps:

1. The execution data are grouped with respect to the centroids, considering its *Params* value.
2. For each group, the minimum and the maximum value of each behavioural metric are determined (a group may have multiple executions), and assigned to the group.
3. A single *behaviour trace* is generated by appending the label of the PUT (faulty or healthy), the data corresponding to each and every cluster (i.e., cluster's ID, the min value, and the max values) together. The high-level structure of a behaviour trace is illustrated in Fig. 2.
4. Finally, the *behaviour trace* is examined for missing clusters, in that for each missing cluster a particular sequence of values, representing 'Not Available' (e.g., $(m, -1, -1)$ when the data for cluster m is unavailable), is inserted into a proper position. In this way, all the behavioural traces have the same length.

Min and max value for cluster #1

Fig. 2. The structure of a behavioural trace, having k clusters and one behavioural metric (Bhv1). The *label* indicates a faulty or healthy behaviour.

Classification and Prediction. Once the behaviour traces are generated, *Random Forest* (RF) classification model [14] is employed; an RF classifier is trained over the generated behaviour traces. The classifier can then predict if a given (unseen) behaviour trace is faulty or healthy. Other classification models can also be used that is left as future work.

3 Early Experimental Result

The feasibility and effectiveness of the architecture proposed was preliminary investigated within the **Math** project from Defects4j, which provides the required setup and data for our early/limited experiment.

Data Collection. For this experiment, we consider the timing behaviour in that the time spent in a method w.r.t. different input values, were collected and made available for the experiment. The behavioural data was collected through running available test cases on different versions of the subject program. Using tests provides the required knowledge to label the execution records.

A set of test cases, that relate to a selected method, were executed on about 120 (faulty and healthy) versions of the program. Additionally, a random number of versions of the program was selected for which the selected method was executed with new arbitrary input values, providing a *validation set* of unseen behaviour traces for further evaluation.

Table 1. Experimental results of precision and recall using the validation set.

%Traces for test	n_estimator	Precision	Recall
15	50	0.86	1
20	50	0.86	0.86
15	100	0.87	0.93
20	100	0.93	0.94

Early Results. We applied our implementation on the experimental data, using different parameters for configuration, e.g., size of traces for test, n_estimator in the RF classifier. The cross validation reported 95% on average for training accuracy, with an average standard deviation of 0.06. Also, the experiment showed promising testing accuracy averaging to 95%. We additionally considered precision (the ratio of number of traces correctly classified as "faulty" to the total number of traces labelled as "faulty") and recall (the ratio of faulty traces that were correctly identified) achieved by the model on the validation set. We achieved acceptable precision and recall averaging to 88% and 93%, respectively. Table 1 shows the early results. Nevertheless, more complex experiments are required for a sound evaluation of the approach, e.g., how (much) would NFA contribute and improve regression testing? Our early experiment showed that NFA could provide a promising measure for test case prioritisation by considering the behavioural data collected alongside testing other parts, e.g., executions predicated as faulty would guide the selection/prioritisation of the next tests.

Feasibility and Applicability. We looked into different parts of the subject program and investigated the applicability of our approach within each part. In particular, we looked for specific characteristics, given the designated behavioural metric (i.e., execution time), that make the approach applicable and useful. We also studied project-specific tasks, for example, in the preprocessing step. An initial observation was that the proposed approach would work well if the PUT shows distinguishable behaviour in terms of the given dynamic metrics. For example, if the *execution time* is the target metric, then the timing behaviour of a program should vary with respect to different inputs, in order to be able to apply the proposed approach.

4   Related Work

Statistical analysis and machine learning techniques have been widely considered and applied for addressing different testing challenges [8]. In particular, they provide effective measures for understanding and specifying software behaviour (i.e., the test oracle problem) using data gathered from a large set of test executions. ML-based approaches were presented for classifying program behaviours using different types of data, such as frequency profile of single events in the execution trace [7], traces of input and output [2], and dynamic execution trace information including sequence of method invocations [18]. Neural networks were also used for generating test oracles (e.g., [1,11,19]) that were however applied to simple programs. The main difference between these works and our proposed approach is that, in addition to explicit and typical data used in testing, we consider implicit or indirect dynamic behavioural data.

Another relevant line of research is software defect prediction which predicts defective code regions and, hence, can improve software testing. More recently, defect prediction approaches extensively employ new and improved machine learning based techniques (e.g., [16,20,21]), to automatically learn features from the data extracted from source code, and then utilize these features to build and train defect prediction models. In contrast, traditional techniques manually design feature(s) or combination of features to effectively represent defects, and then build a prediction model (e.g., [10]). While there are similarities between these works and the proposed approach in this paper, our work basically differs from them since it uses dynamic metrics rather than static software metrics, e.g., McCabe features [15].

5 Conclusion

This paper introduced *near failure analysis*, alongside classical testing activities, which considers implicit dynamic behavioural data and their variation, in addition to explicit output values. Using behavioural data, an ML-based prediction model was designed that can predict whether or not an arbitrary version of a program is at risk of failure. The very preliminary evaluation demonstrated promising results for feasibility and effectiveness of near failure analysis. We are working on more and complex experiments in addition to improving the learning process and accordingly the implementation.

Acknowledgements. The work is funded by ELLIIT strategic research area (https:// elliit.se), project A19 Software Regression Testing with Near Failure Assertions.

References

1. Aggarwal, K.K., Singh, Y., Kaur, A., Sangwan, O.P.: A neural net based approach to test oracle. SIGSOFT Softw. Eng. Notes **29**(3), 1–6 (2004). https://doi.org/10. 1145/986710.986725
2. Almaghairbe, R., Roper, M.: Separating passing and failing test executions by clustering anomalies. Softw. Qual. J. **25**(3), 803–840 (2016). https://doi.org/10. 1007/s11219-016-9339-1
3. Ammann, P., Offutt, J.: Introduction to Software Testing, 2nd edn. Cambridge University Press, Cambridge (2016)
4. Arthur, D., Vassilvitskii, S.: K-means++: the advantages of careful seeding. In: Proceedings of the 18th Annual ACM-SIAM Symposium on Discrete Algorithms, pp. 1027–1035. Society for Industrial and Applied Mathematics, USA (2007). https://doi.org/10.1145/1283383.1283494

5. Barr, E.T., Harman, M., McMinn, P., Shahbaz, M., Yoo, S.: The oracle problem in software testing: a survey. IEEE Trans. Softw. Eng. **41**(5), 507–525 (2015). https://doi.org/10.1109/TSE.2014.2372785
6. Bornø Jensen, M., et al.: A framework for automated traffic safety analysis from video using modern computer vision. In: Transportation Research Board Annual Meeting (2019)
7. Bowring, J.F., Rehg, J.M., Harrold, M.J.: Active learning for automatic classification of software behavior. SIGSOFT Softw. Eng. Notes **29**(4), 195–205 (2004). https://doi.org/10.1145/1013886.1007539
8. Briand, L.C.: Novel applications of machine learning in software testing. In: Proceedings of the 8th International Conference on Quality Software, pp. 3–10 (2008). https://doi.org/10.1109/QSIC.2008.29
9. Cai, J., Luo, J., Wang, S., Yang, S.: Feature selection in machine learning: a new perspective. Neurocomputing **300**, 70–79 (2018). https://doi.org/10.1016/j.neucom.2017.11.077
10. Hassan, A.E.: Predicting faults using the complexity of code changes. In: Proceedings of the 31st International Conference on Software Engineering, pp. 78–88 (2009). https://doi.org/10.1109/ICSE.2009.5070510
11. Jin, H., Wang, Y., Chen, N.W., Gou, Z.J., Wang, S.: Artificial neural network for automatic test oracles generation. In: Proceedings of the International Conference on Computer Science and Software Engineering, vol. 2, pp. 727–730 (2008). https://doi.org/10.1109/CSSE.2008.774
12. Just, R., Jalali, D., Ernst, M.D.: Defects4j: a database of existing faults to enable controlled testing studies for java programs. In: Proceedings of the 2014 International Symposium on Software Testing and Analysis, pp. 437–440. ACM, USA (2014). https://doi.org/10.1145/2610384.2628055
13. Langdon, W.B., Yoo, S., Harman, M.: Inferring automatic test oracles. In: Proceedings of the 10th International Workshop on Search-Based Software Testing, pp. 5–6 (2017). https://doi.org/10.1109/SBST.2017.1
14. Liaw, A., Wiener, M.: Classification and regression by random forest. R News **2**(3), 18–22 (2002)
15. McCabe, T.J.: A complexity measure. IEEE Trans. Softw. Eng. SE **2**(4), 308–320 (1976)
16. Pradel, M., Sen, K.: Deepbugs: a learning approach to name-based bug detection. Proc. ACM Program. Lang. **2**(OOPSLA) (2018). https://doi.org/10.1145/3276517
17. Reichenbach, C.: Software ticks need no specifications. In: Proceedings of the 43rd International Conference on Software Engineering: New Ideas and Emerging Results, pp. 61–65. IEEE Press (2021). https://doi.org/10.1109/ICSE-NIER52604.2021.00021
18. Tsimpourlas, F., Rajan, A., Allamanis, M.: Supervised learning over test executions as a test oracle. In: Proceedings of the 36th Annual ACM Symposium on Applied Computing, pp. 1521–1531. ACM, USA (2021). https://doi.org/10.1145/3412841.3442027
19. Vanmali, M., Last, M., Kandel, A.: Using a neural network in the software testing process. Int. J. Intell. Syst. **17**, 45–62 (2002). https://doi.org/10.1002/int.1002
20. Walunj, V., Gharibi, G., Alanazi, R., Lee, Y.: Defect prediction using deep learning with network portrait divergence for software evolution. Empir. Softw. Eng. **27**(5), 118 (2022). https://doi.org/10.1007/s10664-022-10147-0
21. Wang, S., Liu, T., Nam, J., Tan, L.: Deep semantic feature learning for software defect prediction. IEEE Trans. Softw. Eng. **46**(12), 1267–1293 (2020). https://doi.org/10.1109/TSE.2018.2877612

Process Management

A Process Model of Product Strategy Development: A Case of a B2B SaaS Product

Bogdan Moroz[ID], Andrey Saltan[(⊠)][ID], and Sami Hyrynsalmi[ID]

LUT University, Lahti, Finland
mr.bogdan.moroz@gmail.com, {andrey.saltan,
sami.hyrynsalmi}@lut.fi

Abstract. A growing number of software companies nowadays offer their solutions using the SaaS model. The model promises multiple business-related benefits for these companies; however, existing software companies are forced to re-develop products and reconsider product strategies to address all the aspects of the new SaaS model. The existing literature provides a limited understanding of how product strategies for newly productized SaaS solutions should be developed. In this paper, we report the results of a longitudinal case study of a Finnish B2B software company experiencing a transition towards the SaaS model and developing the initial strategy for its newly productized SaaS solution. We introduce a six-phase process model aligned with the ISPMA SPM framework. Being implemented, the model created an initial shared understanding and vision among stakeholders for their SaaS solution and provided guidance in developing the required product strategy.

Keywords: Product strategy · Software-as-a-Service · Software industry · Business-to-Business · Productization · Software product management

1 Introduction

Inspired by the success of prominent Software-as-a-Service (SaaS) solutions offered by ambitious startups and tech giants, a growing number of software companies seek to productize their customer-specific software into SaaS solutions. This shift from customer-specific software to standard software products, offered using the cloud-based service model, calls for increased attention to software product management (SPM) [17]. However, quite often, the way processes and practices in companies should be reconsidered is unclear, and companies struggle to cope with these challenges and cannot make the transition coherent and systematic [13].

Software process improvement is defined as "understanding existing processes and changing these processes to increase product quality and/or reduce costs and development time" [15]. Companies look for process improvement approaches to accelerate product development, improve quality, and reduce costs. However, literature indicates that software companies often focus too much on project execution, technologies, and features, while neglecting a sufficient understanding of markets, value, and products [5].

© The Author(s), under exclusive license to Springer Nature Switzerland AG 2022
D. Taibi et al. (Eds.): PROFES 2022, LNCS 13709, pp. 181–200, 2022.
https://doi.org/10.1007/978-3-031-21388-5_13

As a result, products that were developed on time and within budget, but without proper value and market awareness, may not be received as well as expected or may fail to satisfy the customers [5].

SPM process improvement has received less focus in academic research than project execution until recently [10]. Maturity matrices and competence models have been developed to gauge the maturity of various SPM processes and practices within companies. An updated standardized product lifecycle with clear interfaces, milestones, and governance, is identified among the success factors for implementing the product manager role [5]. Core SPM activities with associated processes and practices can be divided into two distinct groups: software product strategy and software product planning [9]. Activities in the software product strategy group are performed to develop and implement a software product strategy, which is defined as a high-level plan that helps companies achieve the vision for their products [11]. The purpose of developing a product strategy is to determine the path to achieving a product vision that describes what the product will be at the end of a certain strategic timeframe [9]. This is an essential step, describing the value that the product will bring to the customers and the vendor. The product strategy defines how the product should evolve over a certain timeframe (often 1 to 5 years, varying based on industry). Product planning converts the strategy into an executable plan that a product team can follow day to day [9]. This study focuses on product strategy practices and processes, omitting product planning activities, such as roadmapping and setting milestones.

The SPM framework developed by the International Software Product Management Association[1] (ISPMA framework) consolidates multiple preceding frameworks and provides a holistic perspective on the product manager role [5, 10]. This framework was employed as a foundation for the development of the proposed process model. The ISPMA framework does not provide ready-made processes to its practitioners [10]. This paper aims to address this gap and design a process that guides the development of a comprehensive software product strategy at a company undergoing the productization of customer-specific software into a B2B SaaS solution. To achieve this goal, the study answers the following research questions:

RQ1: What process could be followed to develop an initial product strategy for a newly productized SaaS solution?
RQ2: How do the B2B and SaaS contexts affect the product strategy development process at the case company?

The rest of the paper is structured as follows. Section 2 provides the theoretical background of the study. Section 3 describes the research approach employed. Section 4 introduces the case company and describes the proposed process model for the initial product strategy development. Section 5 discusses the results of the study by providing answers to the research questions. Section 6 concludes the paper.

---

[1] https://ispma.org/framework/.

2   Background

The transformation of software tailored to the needs of specific customers into a standard software product is usually referred to as productization. Such transformation is driven by recognizing similar needs and wishes of multiple customers [2]. Nowadays, productization is closely related to the cloud computing paradigm. Encouraged by the wide range of benefits, companies try to productize their solutions into SaaS solutions – one of the forms of cloud computing which is defined as "providing a standard software solution to customers as a service over the Internet" [4, 13, 18]. The fast pace of technological innovation forces product managers to make long-lasting and financially impactful decisions about their products in the face of relative uncertainty. Having a clear strategy for several years into the future provides a basis for making those decisions and aligns the stakeholders involved in product development [9].

Several frameworks attempt to define elements of the product strategy, propose maturity phases, and define the competencies needed [9–11]. These include the Scaled Agile Framework (SAFe)[2], the Pragmatic Framework[3], Blackblot Product Manager's Toolkit (PMTK)[4], the ISPMA framework, and the AIPMM framework[5] [10] The frameworks aim to give structure to the SPM discipline, categorize SPM activities and define the responsibilities of software product managers [10]. Additionally, scholars and practitioners offer various tools and techniques for different product strategy components [9, 11]. A comparison of several frameworks applicable to SPM revealed the ISPMA framework to be the most balanced and purely focused on SPM, as opposed to addressing SPM alongside other company functions [10]. The framework is described in literature as the underlying knowledge area framework of the Software Product Management Body of Knowledge (SPMBOK) [5].

Product strategy development is a continuous process that spans a product's lifecycle and consists of multiple activities. Defining a coherent process for product strategy activities can be challenging [9]. This leaves product managers charged with developing a strategy for a new product in a perplexing position. They must develop a comprehensive product strategy, considering multiple interrelated aspects, and work closely with Marketing, Sales, and executive management [9]. Formally, according to the ISPMA SPM framework, the product strategy should address the development or evolution of the following eight elements: (1) Positioning and Product Definition, (2) Delivery model and Service strategy, (3) Sourcing, (4) Pricing, (5) Financial Management, (6) Ecosystem management, (7) Legal and IPR management, (8) Performance and Risk management [9].

---

[2] https://scaledagile.com/what-is-safe/.

[3] https://www.pragmaticinstitute.com/framework/.

[4] https://www.blackblot.com/methodology.

[5] https://aipmm.com.

3   Methodology

The research started with the awareness of a problem that became apparent while working with the case company. The company faced challenges in establishing a process for product strategy development while undertaking the productization of customer-specific software into B2B SaaS. The problem can be formulated as follows: "SPM is seen as a continuous activity with many separate tasks, and no formalized process exists to guide product managers in initial strategy development." To propose a process model aimed at supporting the company, we employed a mixed-method research design approach [1] and combined a case study with design science research. This allowed us to analyze the situation in a particular company and develop a design artifact that was successfully adopted by it and could be used by other companies with the same or similar profiles.

Design science research is defined as "the scientific study and creation of artifacts as they are developed and used by people with the goal of solving practical problems of general interest" [7]. The desired outcome is not only a novel artifact itself, but also knowledge about the artifact and its effects on its environment. We followed the design science framework and guidelines proposed by Hevner et al. [6]. During the research process, knowledge about the artifact is accumulated, including the influence of the B2B SaaS context and the productization context on product strategy decisions.

A case study is an integral part of our research in all the main stages. The case study can be classified as an exploratory single case study [12, 16] of a software company that faces the challenge of developing a product strategy for a B2B SaaS product, which is a productized version of a customer-specific software system. The required information on the case was collected through a series of semi-structured interviews, open-ended interviews, workshops, and surveys.

4   Process Model of Product Strategy Development

4.1   Case Description

The case company is a mid-sized Finnish company specializing in the development of situational awareness solutions for chemical, biological, radiological, and nuclear reconnaissance (CBRN), as well as environmental and industrial monitoring. The company has extensive experience in delivering customized solutions for a wide variety of organizations with different needs. The company's focus nowadays is the cloud-based modular software solution, Perception Cloud[6].

The first version of Perception was offered as a standalone vehicle installation in 2016. The system was designed to be installed in a CBRN vehicle to provide awareness to the operators inside. The measurements and status of the detectors were displayed on a desktop client UI, and visual and audio alarms were triggered when CBRN measurements exceeded certain thresholds.

---

[6] For the sake of anonymity, we used a fabricated name for the product instead of the real one.

In 2018, the company started a new vehicle project, with another shelter project on the horizon. It became apparent that splitting the codebase for each new project would not be sustainable long-term. Moreover, many completed features could be reused with enhancements and customizations for the new projects. A new desktop client application was created using a proprietary application model syntax. Using the syntax, it became possible to modify the contents of the client by adding and removing panels, windows, and components. A modular backend architecture allowed adding and removing services based on the project.

Another significant milestone was the creation of the Perception Go mobile app in 2019. The application allowed to pair portable CBRN detectors via Bluetooth and transmit measurement data to the central Perception system in real-time. The desktop client was enhanced to display the locations of smartphones running the app on a map and the readings of CBRN detectors paired to the app. Perception Go was received enthusiastically in the CBRN industry. In 2021, the company developed a web-based version of Perception for a customer. The project served as a learning experience for the upcoming Perception Cloud, including developing new features and a better understanding of customer and user needs.

4.2 Model Requirements

While the research started with the aim of solving a functional problem for the case company, the proposed model can be useful to other software organizations wishing to productize their customer-specific offerings and improve SPM practices.

The model itself is primarily a tool that is used to discuss critical decisions, consider crucial details, elicit feedback from stakeholders, and formulate a shared and accepted plan: "the final deliverable is not as valuable as the process you go through to write the documentation" [3]. The following requirements have been identified for the process model.

1. The model should provide direction to product managers in establishing a product strategy.
2. The model should lead to the creation of a product strategy.
3. The resulting strategy should incorporate all eight elements of the product strategy according to the ISPMA framework.
4. The resulting strategy should apply to a B2B SaaS software product.
5. The model should suggest effective methods and tools for strategy development.
6. The model should utilize company resources efficiently by ensuring that only the necessary stakeholders are required to attend certain phases.
7. The resulting strategy should be documented in a single product strategy document, which can be used to communicate the strategy across the organization.

With these requirements, the research aims to ensure that the resulting artifact is helpful to the case company while remaining sufficiently generalizable and applicable outside of the context of said company. Requirements 2, 4, 6, and 7 ensure that the problems of the lack of strategy and limited resources are solved for the case company. Requirements 1, 3, and 5 ensure that the artifact is developed according to the established knowledge base and may provide guidance to SPM practitioners in companies of the similar profile.

4.3 Model Structure

The proposed process model for initial product strategy development supporting the productization of customer-specific software is depicted in Fig. 1. The boxes at the center of the model are the eight elements of product strategy according to the ISPMA framework. The bubbles around the boxes indicate the phases of the process model. The dashed arrows from each bubble to the next indicate the order in which the phases should be executed.

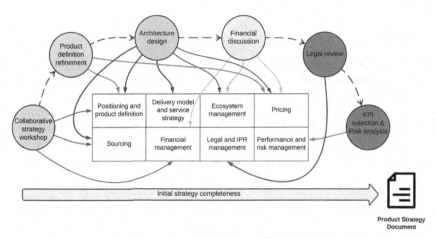

Fig. 1. Proposed process model of product strategy development

Each bubble is linked to one or more elements of product strategy. Each bubble and its arrows are color-coded to simplify the visual comprehension of the model. The process model is described in more detail in Table 1. For each phase, the key questions that need to be answered are specified, alongside the recommended tools and the strategy elements impacted during the phase.

Table 1. Phases of the process model

Questions	Tools	Strategy elements
Phase 1: Collaborative Strategy Workshop		
1. What is the motivation to create the product? What positive change will it bring? 2. Who are the target users? What are the market segments? 3. What problem will the product solve? 4. What is the product? What makes it stand out? 5. How will the product benefit the company? What are the business goals? 6. Who are the competitors? What are their strengths and weaknesses? 7. How will the product be monetized? 8. What are the main cost factors in developing, marketing, and selling the product? 9. How will the product be marketed and sold? What channels are needed to reach customers?	Product Vision Board Problem and position statement template	Positioning and product definition Sourcing Financial management
Phase 2: Product definition refinement		
1. What features will the product include? What quality attributes will the product possess? 2. How will the product compare to the competition in terms of functionality, user experience, and quality? 3. Does the product offer some feature or attribute that currently does not exist in the market?	Blue Ocean Strategy Canvas Blue Ocean Eliminate-Reduce-Raise-Create Grid	Positioning and product definition Pricing
Phase 3: Architecture design		

(*continued*)

Table 1. (*continued*)

Questions	Tools	Strategy elements
1. What is the defining technology for the software product? What technology enables our competitive edge and market differentiation over time? 2. What is the offering architecture? Meaning, what are the separately priced components of the product? 3. What is the tailorability architecture? Meaning: a. How configurable do we want the software to be? What parameters are configurable? b. How composable do we want the software to be? What components can be added or removed? c. How customizable do we want the software to be? 4. What is our desired place in the software ecosystem? a. What organizations could we partner with? b. What external systems could we integrate? Could we provide a way for third parties to integrate into our software? 5. What is the business architecture? a. What is the domain model of the new software? b. What business processes need to be created to support the new product?	UML Domain Model BPMN business process models	Positioning and product definition Delivery model and service strategy Ecosystem management Pricing Sourcing
Phase 4: Financial discussion		
1. Is there any reason to choose cost-based or competitor-based pricing over value-based pricing? 2. What is the upper pricing bound? What is the maximum value the product has for customers? 3. What is the lower pricing bound? What are the fixed and variable costs for the product? 4. Are there any reasons to charge less than the maximum value? 5. What will the pricing structure be for the product? What combination of freemium, consumption-based, and tiered pricing can the product have? Is a perpetual license an option?	Accion pricing framework	Pricing Financial management

(*continued*)

Table 1. (*continued*)

Questions	Tools	Strategy elements
Phase 5: Legal review		
1. Contracts. Who is responsible for formulating service contracts in the organization? What are the terms of the service-level agreement (SLA)? Does the organization have templates for such SLAs? Can any existing SLAs be reused? 2. IPR protection. How will the company protect the intellectual property rights related to the product? Does the company have patents or trademarks that apply to the product? Should the company obtain new trademarks or patents for the product? 3. Open-source. What open-source components may be used when developing and running the software? What are the distribution licenses for those components? Are there any restrictions or caveats? 4. Data protection. Who is responsible for formulating the privacy policy within the organization? What are the terms of the policy? Does the organization have templates for such policies? Can any existing policies be reused?	Checklist of legal aspects to review	Legal and IPR management
Phase 6: KPI selection and Risk analysis		
1. What are the business goals of the company? How can they be measured? What targets should we set for those goals? 2. What financial, customer, product, process, and people KPIs should we track to achieve the business goals? How should those KPIs be measured? 3. What elements of the overall product strategy are we least certain about?	Balanced Product Scorecard (BSC), "Digital Red Dot Game"	Performance and Risk management

4.4 Model Implementation

The proposed process model was implemented at the case company during the period between April and July 2022. Table 2 summarizes strategy development activities performed at the case company according to the model. The product manager participated in every session and is therefore not mentioned explicitly in the participants column.

Table 2. Model implementation schedule at the case company

Phase	Date	Participants
Collaborative Strategy Workshop	April 27th, 2022	Chief Operating Officer, Chief Technical Officer, Project Manager, Sales Representative
Product definition refinement	May 23rd, 2022	Project Manager and Sales Representative
Architecture design – session 1	June 1st, 2022	CTO and Software Engineer
Architecture design – session 2	June 7th, 2022	CTO and Software Engineer
Financial discussion	July 7th, 2022	Project Manager and Sales Representative
Legal review – data protection discussion	July 11th, 2022	Data Protection Officer
Legal review – open-source check-up	July 23rd, 2022	Done independently
Legal review - Contract discussion & IPR protection check-up	July 29th, 2022	Chief Operating Officer
KPI selection & risk analysis	July 24th, 2022	Chief Operating Officer, Chief Technical Officer, Project Manager, Sales Representative

Phase 1. The first step of the proposed process model was the collaborative strategy workshop. The COO and CTO of the company, as well as a project manager and a sales representative, were present in the meeting with the product managers. The discussion was structured using the Product Vision Board tool [11]. After each section of the board was introduced, participants were requested to share their ideas related to the section. The sections of the board were followed in this order: target group, needs, product, business goals, competitors, revenue streams, cost factors, and channels. After the meeting, the product managers summarized the discussion using a Problem and position statement template (see Table 3).

Table 3. Problem and position statement for Perception Cloud

Problem statement	
The problem of	Lack of complete vision of the operational picture during a CBRN incident
Affects	Civil defense, emergency services, and first responders
The impact of which is	Increased delay in response to incidents and increased harm to the wellbeing and lives of victims

(*continued*)

Table 3. (*continued*)

Problem statement	
A successful solution	Unifies data from multiple types of CBRN detectors to provide a comprehensive operational picture to decision makers, reducing the time necessary to make informed decisions that save lives

Position statement	
For	Civil defense members, emergency services, first responders, as well as border control and customs officials
Who	Respond to a CBRN incident to reduce the hazard and avoid harm to the population in the area of incident
The	Perception Cloud solution
That	Provides a centralized interface to view the collected measurements of a variety of CBRN detection devices
Unlike	The current approach of manually collecting and correlating data from multiple CBRN detection devices
Our product	Reduces response time to CBRN incidents by supporting informed decision-making based on a comprehensive operational picture

The participants agreed that the main business goal for the product is to unlock a new revenue source. The product will also simplify installation compared to an on-premises solution, thus reducing some of the customer acquisition costs. Several possible competitor products were identified. The revenue stream will come from recurring subscriptions. It was agreed that the product should be modular, with extra features available at extra cost. It is possible that for certain customers, the software will have to be extended with specific features and integrations, and the development of such custom modules can be billed separately as a professional software service. The main cost factor will be the development effort. Outsourcing customer support was agreed upon as a possibility. The company will utilize existing channels to reach customers, including expos, magazine ads, and private demonstrations.

Phase 2. The next phase of the process model involved product definition refinement. A project manager and a sales representative were present in the meeting with the product manager. The purpose of the phase is to advance the product definition. The new product is compared to existing market offerings to determine what features or attributes can be created, improved, reduced, or eliminated compared to competitor offerings. The phase is structured around the Strategy Canvas and the ERRC Grid from the Blue Ocean toolkit [8]. In preparation for this phase, the product manager studied competitor products to determine the features and quality attributes offered. The product manager also considered the existing customer-specific Perception system. The manager made a list of competing factors and added them to a Strategy Canvas template.

The product manager started the meeting by introducing the Strategy Canvas tool. The group went through each category and estimated the industry offering and the desired product offering. The product manager asked the participants whether any relevant categories were missing from the list and whether some could be eliminated from the new product or offered at a reduced level. The product manager also elicited possible new categories. During the meeting, several categories were eliminated, and several new ones were added (see Fig. 2). The red line in Fig. 2 represents the current value offered to buyers in the market space – the industry value curve [8, 11]. As established during the collaborative strategy workshop, the core purpose of the Perception Cloud product is to offer a comprehensive operational picture to enable informed decision-making quickly. Therefore, features related to real-time measurement communication and displaying were prioritized over features concerning the post-factum analysis of the data.

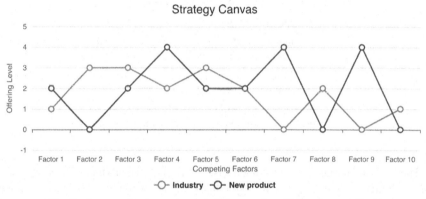

Fig. 2. Strategy Canvas at the end of the meeting. (Color figure online)

After the meeting, the product manager sorted the factors by their score from low to high. This combines the Strategy Canvas with the ERRC grid (see Fig. 3). The top right corner in Fig. 3 indicates the potential Blue Ocean for the product – competing factors that are offered by the product at an excellent level and not offered by the industry at all. For Perception Cloud, one factor was identified that is currently not offered by the competition at all, indicating a new opportunity.

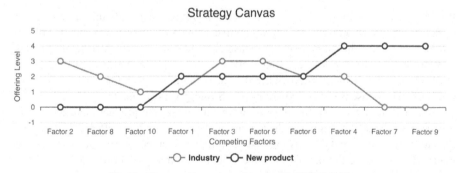

Fig. 3. Strategy Canvas combined with ERRC Grid

Phase 3. During this phase, the initial architecture design was done. The phase is split into two meetings where the offering architecture, business architecture, and tailorability architecture are discussed. The place of the product in software ecosystems is touched upon. The CTO and a software engineer participated in both meetings with the product manager. In the first meeting, overall architecture considerations, the offering architecture, and the place in the software ecosystem were discussed.

It was decided that the Perception Cloud product must be configurable and composable to have broad appeal in the target market. Customers should be able to configure, at minimum, the alarm limits for their detection equipment. Composability should be a major focus. The product shall support multiple separately priced plugins. Competing factors from the product definition refinement phase were discussed as possible plugins. Unique customer requests could be addressed by developing custom plugins. The company would seek to generalize such plugins to reuse them with other customers.

The company also wants to grow its role within the ecosystems of CBRN detector manufacturers and software providers. The company could make it easier for willing manufacturers to integrate devices into Perception Cloud by providing open APIs. APIs could also be created for third parties to make plugins, but this open-source plugin ecosystem will not be implemented in the early versions. At the end of the meeting, the overall architecture and technical constraints were discussed, with several open-source technologies agreed upon.

Based on this preliminary discussion, the product manager prepared a domain model for the new product and relevant business process models in BPMN. These models were presented in the second meeting of the phase to elicit further discussion and refine the strategy.

Phase 4. This phase was devoted to the financial discussion. The Accion pricing framework was followed[7]. Four questions about pricing needed to be answered as part of the discussion: (1) What is the upper bound? (2) What is the lower bound? (3) What are the reasons to charge less than the maximum value? (4) How to structure the pricing model as a compromise between the upper and lower bounds?

Based on the discussion, the product manager prepared a mockup of a pricing page for the new SaaS product. This page was presented to the stakeholders for feedback and approval. Based on the feedback, a second draft of the pricing page was made and accepted as the initial pricing structure for the product.

Phase 5. The legal review phase of the process model consists of discussing four legal aspects: contracts, IPR protection, open source, and data protection. The product manager held a one-on-one discussion with a Data Protection Officer (DPO). The product manager started the meeting by explaining the strategy so far, primarily focusing on aspects that may involve personal data processing. The product manager asked the DPO what existing templates could be reused and what documents needed to be created to ensure compliance with GDPR. The DPO proposed documenting all types of personal data processed in Perception Cloud, data retention policies, and transfers outside EEA. A Data Processing Agreement needs to be created and appended to the service-level agreement for the product.

---

[7] https://content.accion.org/wp-content/uploads/2018/08/Pricing-Your-SaaS-Product.pdf.

The open-source check-up was carried out independently. The product manager checked the licenses of open-source components selected for the product during the architecture design phase and found no restrictions. The contract and IPR protection discussions were conducted together, in a one-on-one meeting with the COO. It was agreed that the company should purchase trademarks for the product. However, obtaining patents was deemed unnecessary at this point. Obtaining a patent comes at a high cost, which increases with the geographical scope of the patent. Both trademarks and patents can be purchased via the Finnish Patent and Registration Office.

Phase 6. In the final phase, KPIs were selected. The product manager used the Balanced Product Scorecard, as well as a list of sample KPIs. The selected KPIs were added to the product strategy document and sent to the stakeholders from executive management, Development, and Sales. The participants were asked to comment on the product strategy overall, including the KPIs. The participants were also requested to participate in a "Digital Red Dot Game" and mark three statements or strategy elements that they were least confident about. The "Red Dot Game" is a risk identification and prioritization method where each stakeholder is asked to place a total of three red dots next to the segments or statements in the strategy that they are least sure about [11].

The product strategy document was reviewed and approved by the selected stakeholders. The KPI selection was also approved, but an important issue was raised regarding the selected targets for the business goals. Increasing annual revenue by 5% to 10% was deemed unrealistic. Now, the annual revenue of the company is tied to the number of contracts obtained for professional software services and the delivery of these services, which varies each year. The goal for the new SaaS is to provide a steady and growing source of revenue, but comparing it to the overall company revenue will not provide a meaningful measure of success. A long-term average of the annual Perception revenue was suggested as one possible point of comparison, but no decision was made. Selecting the proper target for the financial success of the product thus requires further consideration.

4.5 Model Evaluation

The case study described above could be considered a weak form of evaluation, suitable to present the artifact convincingly and vividly [7]. All phases of the model implementation were documented, including the meeting minutes and observations of participant behaviour. This documentation was used to develop coherent product strategy that meets all the requirements defined in Sect. 4.2. Additionally, a survey was used to collect feedback from the process model implementation participants. Collected feedback and the successfully developed strategy indicate the overall validity of the proposed process model.

For the 1st requirement, the process model guided the product manager in creating the product strategy. However, the process model was designed with the case company in mind. Because of this, there is a risk of "over-fitting" the model to the case company's processes and organizational structure. Independent implementation of the process could test whether the model is generalizable and illustrate how the model can be generalized further.

Regarding the 2nd requirement, the proposed process model produced an initial product strategy for the case company. The strategy was reviewed and approved by company stakeholders, creating alignment around the vision and priorities for the product. The strategy solidified and developed the productization ideas that had been suggested by various company stakeholders over the years but remained unrealized until now.

For the 3rd requirement, the strategy covered all the elements of product strategy as classified by the ISPMA framework.

To address the 4th and the 5th requirements, the recommendations in the process model were based on the academic and practitioner literature aimed at B2B SaaS. The process model produced a product strategy for the B2B SaaS product. Most steps and suggested tools also apply to licensed software products and hybrid models. Pricing and legal aspects, however, are tied to the SaaS nature of the product. The legal discussion was focused on the contract contents specific to SaaS (i.e., SLA) and the data protection concepts applicable for delivering a service over a network (i.e., the data controller and the data processor). An elaboration of the financial discussion and legal review phases can make the process model more applicable to products other than SaaS.

The Accion framework – the tool selected for the pricing discussion – helped quickly explain the SaaS pricing concepts and best practices to the stakeholders that were not used to managing pricing decisions. The tool helped select the value metrics and the price structure for the new product. The participants, however, could not determine an upper bound that could be charged to customers. The BSC tool alone resulted in a non-systematic KPI selection process, and the paper recommends a further study of rigorous step-by-step KPI selection methodologies. Nonetheless, the Accion framework and the BSC produced a useful starting point for further strategy work and illustrated which areas are well-understood and which need to be developed further.

Considering the 6th requirement, the selection of attendees for each phase was not fully systematic and relied on a tacit knowledge of the situation in the company. A generic stakeholder selection approach can complement the process model. For example, the Power-Interest Grid can be employed to determine the most influential participants [11]. RACI matrices can also be developed to map the responsibilities of the available stakeholders. The recommendations can also be adjusted depending on the size of the organization.

For the 7th requirement, the strategy was defined in a single document shared with stakeholders for feedback. The process model does not enforce a template for this document, allowing each product manager to define it in a way that fits their company best.

A questionnaire was created and shared with participants in the strategy development process. All 6 stakeholders who participated in the strategy development process responded to the questionnaire. All respondents agreed or strongly agreed that their understanding of the product improved after participating in the sessions (4 agreed, 2 strongly agreed). All 6 respondents agreed that their expertise and contributions influenced the results of the sessions, and they feel more confident in the product's success after attending the sessions (5 agreed, 1 strongly agreed). None of the participants thought the sessions they attended were too long (4 disagreed, 2 strongly disagreed), nor felt they had nothing to contribute (5 disagreed, 1 strongly disagreed).

In the open feedback section, the process model was commended as "good work", even "excellent work", and a "well arranged, well thought and professional take on the process". One respondent was glad that a strategy for the product was finally created: "This has been much-needed clarification of Perception product strategy for SaaS service provision". Another respondent praised the "well prepared sessions with clear agenda". Finally, one of the respondents liked the way the materials were prepared, and the way the product manager had a vision of how to move the discussion forward, especially given the fact that most participants did not prepare before attending the meetings.

The collected feedback shows that the participants better understood the product and its strategy after participating in the sessions, contributed with their expertise, and did not waste their time. Moreover, those who shared open feedback indicated they were happy with the resulting strategy.

5 Discussion

The prime goal of this study was to design a process that develops a comprehensive product strategy for a company undergoing the productization of customer-specific software into B2B SaaS. This aim is reflected in the two research questions being addressed.

5.1 What Process Could be Followed to Develop an Initial Product Strategy for a Newly Productized SaaS Solution?

The proposed process model for initial product strategy development is grounded in the established ISPMA SPM framework and consists of six phases: (1) Collaborative strategy workshop, (2) Product definition refinement, (3) Architecture design, (4) Financial discussion, (5) Legal review, and (6) KPI selection and Risk analysis. During each phase, one or several elements of the product strategy were discussed and refined. The results were combined into a product strategy document, which was evaluated by the key stakeholders in the company.

The evaluation showed the model to be an efficient tool for product strategy development within the productization context of the case company. It resulted in a detailed product strategy that aligned multiple company stakeholders regarding the direction of the new product. The participants of the process felt their time and expertise were used efficiently, and the company approved the resulting product strategy document.

However, a review by an SPM expert revealed limitations in the applicability of the process model for brand new B2B SaaS product development outside the productization context. At the case company, there was an initial understanding of the market requirement, which would be satisfied by the new product, and a general idea of the features that the product would offer. This helped follow the strategy development linearly. Brand new product development calls for iterative approaches involving extensive learning and prototyping, and the model could be enhanced by emphasizing this need for iteration.

Especially during the product definition refinement phase, it can be helpful for product managers to have some experience in the product or market domain. This helps evaluate competing products and existing software to create a list of competing factors for the industry value curve. However, this is not a requirement, and most phases can be executed without deep domain experience. Incidentally, it would be natural to expect that a manager assigned to a product in a certain domain has some relevant experience in the area, or the means to acquire it.

The process model suggested and demonstrated the usefulness of several tools that SPM and software business practitioners recommended, including Product Vision Board, Strategy Canvas, Accion Pricing Framework, Balanced Product Scorecard, and "Digital Red Dot Game." The study also suggested software engineering and business modelling tools – the domain model and BPMN business process models – to be used in the context of SPM. Testing the applicability of practitioner tools allows the incorporation of new tools into the knowledge base if they prove to be efficient. The demonstrated usefulness of these tools in an academic context contributes to developing a reliable SPM toolkit.

5.2 How do the B2B and SaaS Contexts Affect the Product Strategy Development Process at the Case Company?

The primary influence of the B2B and SaaS contexts is on the delivery model, tailorability architecture, pricing, legal, and performance management aspects of the product strategy. The impact on the delivery model is self-evident, since SaaS is a specific delivery model that requires the product to be offered on demand over a network, supporting scalability and multi-tenancy. The B2B SaaS context calls for the tailorability architecture to incorporate configurability and composability of the software. In the B2B area, customers often require customization to specific business needs, but the multi-tenant SaaS model does not allow to freely customize the software for one customer without impacting others. Companies customizing their SaaS products for customers that request it embark on a dangerous route that might negate the benefits of the SaaS delivery model and lead to isolated codebases for each customer. Focusing on a composable architecture and giving the customer configuration options to personalize their experience is the recommended approach for B2B SaaS vendors.

SaaS pricing is a complex area of research. At least 13 pricing frameworks can be identified, with sometimes confusing recommendations [14]. Regardless of the specific framework, the pricing model for SaaS products is subscription-based – companies pay for the right to use the software on a recurring basis. The subscription fee incorporates all or most product-related services, including maintenance, customer support, and data storage. The pricing approach recommended for all types of software, including B2B SaaS, is value-based, not market-based or cost-based [9]. In certain cases (e.g., when entering a mature market or aiming to undercut competitors), it is still necessary to understand the price offered by the competitors. In the B2B area this can be a challenge, as some vendors ask potential clients to contact their own sales departments to check the price.

In legal management, the B2B SaaS context determines the type of contract offered to customers and the data protection measures that need to be taken. A SaaS contract can be signed with individual customers but is often provided in the form of standard terms and conditions. The contract includes an SLA, which may clarify the functional scope, availability commitment, backup policies, and vendor liability should the terms be breached. Advanced data protection regulation, such as GDPR, also imposes restrictions on B2B SaaS software vendors, who host the server infrastructure where personal data may be stored and processed. In GDPR terms, the B2B SaaS vendor can make a Data Processing Agreement with customers, which describes the types of data processed and the legal basis for processing the data. As countries worldwide follow in the footsteps of GDPR, all B2B SaaS vendors must understand their regional data protection regulations.

In the performance management area, the process model recommends a balanced approach to KPI selection – considering the financial, customer, product and process, and people perspectives. However, most of the KPIs selected at the case company are focused on revenue, customer lifetime value, and monitoring customer activity to ensure retention and decrease the churn rate, another influence of the B2B SaaS context.

6 Conclusions

The paper proposes a process model for initial product strategy development for newly productized SaaS solutions. The proposed model consists of the following six phases: (1) Collaborative strategy workshop, (2) Product definition refinement, (3) Architecture design, (4) Financial discussion, (5) Legal review, and (6) KPI selection and Risk analysis. During each phase, one or several elements of software product strategy are developed and refined. The process model was implemented at a Finnish B2B software company, which is productizing its customer-specific system into a B2B SaaS solution. Following the steps of the proposed model allowed the company to develop an initial software product strategy for the SaaS solution and establish a shared understanding and an alignment between company stakeholders. The case company adopted the developed initial product strategy; various strategy elements will be revisited when more information becomes available and certain decisions change. The successful implementation of the process model at the case company calls for further testing of the model at other companies undergoing productization.

This study implies that the process model may provide prescriptive knowledge for developing initial product strategies for B2B SaaS, at least in the context of productization. This context implies that a company may know what the product should be and what the market is, based on experience in providing professional software services to that market. Product managers may use the model to introduce SPM practices in their organizations, which can be unaware of the state-of-the-art SPM practices that would benefit them immensely. The model proposed in this study could act as a template, and the described implementation of the model at the case company could serve as an example of its application. Following the process model, product managers can produce a strategy that addresses, in some capacity, all the product strategy knowledge areas, with no relevant aspects being overlooked during strategy design.

The process model was developed with the case company and its productized SaaS solution in mind, which might affect its generalization. The linear structure of the proposed model worked for the case company, which had an initial understanding of the market for the product and the functionality it may offer in the SaaS version. However, it is a limitation preventing the use of the model for new product development outside of the productization context. In the cases when the product and the market are entirely unknown at the beginning of the process, it is necessary to iterate and experiment, rapidly moving back and forth across the process and executing strategy design activities in a different order and in an ad hoc fashion. A possible future modification of the model that emphasizes iteration could make it more applicable for brand new product development outside the productization context.

Another limitation of the process is that it addresses some of the elements of product strategy to a lesser extent. In particular, the area of financial management is limited to the business model's revenue sources and cost factors. A business plan or cost management aspects are not yet addressed. The study calls for further development and testing of the process model and the continuous refinement of its phases. In the sphere of pricing and financial management, cross-disciplinary research with scholars of management and finance could further advance the model. A comprehensive toolkit for product strategy development can also be created.

References

1. Anguera, M.T., Blanco-Villaseñor, A., Losada, J.L., Sánchez-Algarra, P., Onwuegbuzie, A.J.: Revisiting the difference between mixed methods and multimethods: Is it all in the name? Qual. Quant. **52**(6), 2757–2770 (2018). https://doi.org/10.1007/s11135-018-0700-2
2. Artz, P., van de Weerd, I., Brinkkemper, S., Fieggen, J.: Productization: transforming from developing customer-specific software to product software. In: Tyrväinen, P., Jansen, S., Cusumano, M.A. (eds.) ICSOB 2010. LNBIP, vol. 51, pp. 90–102. Springer, Heidelberg (2010). https://doi.org/10.1007/978-3-642-13633-7_8
3. Bavaro, J., McDowell, G.L.: Cracking the PM career: the skills, frameworks, and practices to become a great product manager. CareerCup (2021)
4. Buxmann, P., et al.: The Software Industry: Economic Principles, Strategies, Perspectives. Springer, Heidelberg (2013). https://doi.org/10.1007/978-3-642-31510-7
5. Ebert, C., Brinkkemper, S.: Software product management – an industry evaluation. J. Syst. Softw. **95**, 10–18 (2014)
6. Bichler, M.: Design science in information systems research. Wirtschaftsinformatik **48**(2), 133–135 (2006). https://doi.org/10.1007/s11576-006-0028-8
7. Johannesson, P., Perjons, E.: An Introduction to Design Science. Springer, Heidelberg (2021). https://doi.org/10.1007/978-3-030-78132-3
8. Kim, W., Mauborgne, R.: Blue ocean strategy, expanded edition: how to create uncontested market space and make the competition irrelevant (2014)
9. Kittlaus, H.-B.: Software Product Management: The ISPMA®-Compliant Study Guide and Handbook. Springer, Heidelberg (2022). https://doi.org/10.1007/978-3-662-65116-2
10. Paajoki, A.: Best practices for and benefits from implementing ISPMA's SPM framework. University of Jyväskylä (2020)
11. Pichler, R.: Strategize: product strategy and product roadmap practices for the digital age (2016)
12. Runeson, P., et al.: Case Study Research in Software Engineering: Guidelines and Examples. John Wiley & Sons, Inc, Hoboken (2012)
13. Saltan, A., Seffah, A.: Engineering and business aspects of SaaS model adoption: insights from a mapping study. In: CEUR Workshop Proceedings (2018)
14. Saltan, A., Smolander, K.: Bridging the state-of-the-art and the state-of-the-practice of SaaS pricing: a multivocal literature review. Inf Softw Technol. **133**, 106510 (2021). https://doi.org/10.1016/j.infsof.2021.106510
15. Sommerville, I.: Software Engineering. Pearson Education Limited, Boston (2015)
16. Yin, R.: Case study research: design and methods (2009)

17. Yrjönkoski, T.: How to support transformation from on-premise products to SaaS?: position paper for future research. In: Proceedings of International Workshop on Software- intensive Business: Start-ups, Ecosystems and Platforms, pp. 144–157 (2018)
18. Yrjönkoski, T., Systä, K.: Productization levels towards whole product in SaaS business. In: Proceedings of the 2nd ACM SIGSOFT International Workshop on Software-Intensive Business: Start-ups, Platforms, and Ecosystems, pp. 42–47 (2019)

Communication Skills Requirements of Junior Software Engineers — Analysis of Job Ads

Anu Niva[(✉)] [iD] and Jouni Markkula[iD]

Empirical Software Engineering in Software, Systems and Services (M3S), University of Oulu, 90570 Oulu, Finland
anu.niva@oulu.fi

Abstract. Software engineering (SE) profession requires various technical and non-technical skills. The skills required are influenced by the changes in the field, industry, and global trends. The changes are also reflected in the recruitment. To understand the current situation and expectations from jobseekers, this study investigates how language, intercultural, and communication skills are presented in the job ads applicable to junior software engineers. The study is based on job ads published in the Vacancies job seeking service maintained by Public Employment and Business Service in Finland. Data contained 166 job ads of which 60% were published in Finnish and 40% in English. Data analysis was based on content and thematic analysis. Based on the job ads, language, both Finnish and English, and communication skills were largely presented and required from junior software engineers, but intercultural skills and multiculturalism were almost missing. The job ads described a multifaceted, multidisciplinary communication environment where junior software engineers work. Moreover, Finnish SE labor markets have needs for fluent Finnish and English speakers; Finnish SE working environment is almost bilingual in practice. Intercultural aspects of communication were not generally visible. The peculiarities of intercultural communication are either not understood or not been aware of in designing the job ads. Moreover, the language of the ad indicates the needs and awareness. The job ads written in English highlight English skills, present Finnish skills mainly as an advantage, and emphasize communication and intercultural skills.

Keywords: Software engineering · Junior software engineer · Job ads · Skill requirements · Language proficiency · Communication · Multiculturalism

1 Introduction

Software engineering (SE) profession requires various technical and non-technical knowledge and skills. Those skills are expected from the jobseekers when they are applying for jobs and hired by companies. The knowledge and skills should be taught, learned, and practiced in SE education.

SE discipline is international, and very often SE work is conducted in international teams. English is the de facto language. In many countries, such as in Finland, significant

© The Author(s), under exclusive license to Springer Nature Switzerland AG 2022
D. Taibi et al. (Eds.): PROFES 2022, LNCS 13709, pp. 201–216, 2022.
https://doi.org/10.1007/978-3-031-21388-5_14

part of employees is non-Finnish, and foreign SE professionals are needed and required, also due to skilled labor shortage.

In addition to the technical knowledge and skills, also other non-technical skills are essential in SE. These skills have been characterized in SWEBOK V3.0 [1] that contains knowledge areas significant to SE professionals. Professional Practice is one of the knowledge areas and contains Communication Skills. Non-technical skills are often referred as "soft skills".

To understand the current situation what expectations SE companies and other organizations have for language, intercultural, and communication skills and what skills jobseekers should possess and demonstrate when looking for a job, and have acquired during education, job ads targeted for junior software engineers were studied.

This study is based on online job ads applicable to junior software engineers. The job ads present skills and knowledge areas that are desired and required from graduates and other novice software engineers and what kind of communicative working environment these junior software engineers are hired for. This paper, especially, aims to specify the content and scope of the necessary language, intercultural, and communication skills required from junior software engineers.

As the SE working environment and its requirements are changing, there is a need to understand the current skill requirements set for junior software engineers and increase general understanding of the nature of communicative environmental factors considered relevant in SE organizations in present day. This is especially relevant from the perspective of graduates and other novice software engineers seeking and recruited to open SE jobs. Better understanding of the current communication skills requirements can also be utilized in revising and improving SE education.

The rest of the paper is organized as follows. Section 2 reviews related work on language, intercultural, and communication skills relevant to SE as well as skill identification based on job ads. Section 3 describes the research questions, data collection process, and data analysis. Section 4 presents the results of the study. In Sect. 5, the results obtained are discussed and compared with those found in previous studies. Section 6 discusses validity issues, and Sect. 7 concludes this article and gives an outline of future work.

2   Related Work

To succeed at work, a SE professional needs various language, intercultural, and communication skills. Studying skill requirements is possible using job ads and skill count, a skill identification method, to increase the understanding of the nature of essential communication skills.

2.1   SE Professional Communication Skills

Software engineers' work, characterized in SWEBOK [1], contains different software-related practices from software construction and processes to software quality, economics, and other foundations. Dealing with communication-related issues, SWEBOK highlights that SE professionals must possess skills to be able to work with others, both internally in teams and with customers and other stakeholders also in multidisciplinary environments. SWEBOK also highlights team members' tolerance, and rules and their dependence on societal norms. Moreover, pure communication skills enable clear understanding between a software engineer and customers, supervisors, coworkers, and suppliers. Effective communication covers face-to-face meetings and written communication such as documentation, emails, and collaboration tools. [1] Software engineers are required a variety of skills and knowledge to succeed in the field.

The role of soft skills has been emphasized, for instance in SWEBOS [2] that highlighted that soft skills are equally important as technical knowledge, because software is developed in teams and software engineers need to interact with each other and various stakeholders. SWEBOS highlights issues such as cooperation, willingness to communicate even across disciplinary boundaries, presenting ideas, and respect. [2] Furthermore, even if technical skills can be regarded as a prerequisite in IT industry, soft skills can bring commercial benefits: soft skills enable faster staff integration and happier, more productive teams. Moreover, soft skills are vital in creating relationships and building customer trust. IT industry calls for communication and interpersonal skills, and teamwork [3] which belong also to the most valued soft skills in SE along with analytic & problem-solving, commitment & responsibility, and eagerness to learn [4].

English Skills. English is used as a lingua franca in ICT and very often English is the main or one of the working languages in software companies. The importance of English proficiency appears generally in the industry of IT and Computer Services [5]: 73% of the employers in countries or territories where English is not an official language, stated that English is significant for their organization. Reading was the most important skill, followed by speaking, listening, and writing.

The importance of English proficiency is, naturally, emphasized when moving from a domestic environment to a more international environment i.e. when changing from a native language to a foreign language. Proficiency presupposes the understanding and use of English of a professionally oriented domain to a necessary level [6]. Despite the official working language(s), also other languages can be used in various contexts.

Intercultural Skills. While working together with practitioners of different cultural origins, a software engineer needs intercultural skills, where intercultural communication is regarded as interaction with people from different cultural backgrounds [7]. Cultural sensitivity plays a role at the workplace, along with linguistic matters [8].

Cultural sensitivity is significant when people from different cultural backgrounds collaborate. Business and social etiquette, meeting protocols, formality and rituals, orientation to time, communication style, working methods, and decision-making process are good examples demonstrating cultural differences that can be faced in international SE. Moreover, the actions influenced by cross-cultural matters can be carried out both online and onsite via emails and online meetings, as well as in face-to-face meetings. [9] Culture is an omnipresent part of any communication activity [10].

Communication Skills. A software engineer needs communication skills that are essential for personal but also for company success [11]. From the perspective of an organization, an employee needs organizational communication skills enabling interaction with a larger, external environment. Interpersonal communication skills are essential when two or more people exchange thoughts in face-to-face contexts. [12] These skills are significant for software engineers, who collaborate with people within and outside of their teams. Software engineers collaborate mostly with other software engineers, both on their team and other teams, but collaboration rates can also be high with engineering and project managers as well as scientists outside of the team and operations specialists of business and service operations. [13] Software developers can spend even 45% of their time collaborating with their colleagues [14].

Communication can, in fact, be regarded as one of the critical success factors for software projects. Failure in communication can prevent a team from achieving progress in a project. Communication as a success factor covers project communication, leadership, relationship between users and staff, ambiguity reduction, and stability maximization. The centrality of communication becomes evident because communication factors have impacts on other success factors such as team, technical, organizational, environmental, and product and project management. Moreover, the success of the project can depend on more elementary tasks such as user and customer involvement, documentation, team capability and competence, teamwork, selection of the right project team, personnel recruitment, progress meetings, project review, feedback, and well-defined project requirements. [15] Software development productivity can be extended by skills and competences, team cohesion, collaboration among team members, ease of communication, work environment regarding collaborative work and software processes, and stakeholder participation [16].

A software engineer's communication toolbox covers a broad range of interpersonal, professional, and team communication skills. Vital skills in SE could contain communication design, explaining, discussions, receiving communication, sharing information, nonverbal communication, usage of forms and tools, and presentations [17] as well as questioning, reinforcement, self-disclosure, listening, humor and laughter, and persuasion [18]. A software engineer's "career success is affected by the ability to consistently provide oral and written communication effectively and on time" [1]. Also, other studies have stressed the importance of written and verbal communication [19].

Communication is a significant part of collaboration. In fact, communication is one of the six facets in teamwork quality, covering the frequency of communication or time spent on communication, ways of formal and informal communication, directness of communication between team members, and openness in information sharing [20].

2.2 Skill Identification in Job Ads

"A job posting, also known as a job ad, is an announcement that informs people that a certain job position is available. This announcement is written, generally in an engaging tone, and describes the job position. It has a title and a description. The description provides details about the position, including skill requirements. "[21].

Skill count is one of four methods identified for skill identification from job ads. It is regarded as the most reliable and the most popular method for skill identification and is based on manual reading. Job ads are labelled and tagged manually with 0/1, to count the skills for statistical analysis. Skill counts can be based on skill bases using a defined list of skills, or alternatively, skill count methods can be used without skill bases relying on expert judgments. Other skill identification methods comprise topic modelling, skill embedding, and machine learning techniques. [21].

Skill identification can be based on three approaches. Skills can be identified as single words or multi-word phrases, skills expressed in sentences, and, thirdly, as their combinations. These methods can be used for many purposes such as skill extraction and job market analysis, curricula development, skill mismatch and alignment, competitive intelligence and talent search, and skill demand prediction. [21].

Various skill identification methods have been used before to identify in-demand job roles [3, 22, 23] but also knowledge and skills. Knowledge and skills required by software development industry including technical and non-technical skills revealed that communication skills were the most often demanded topic. Also, teamwork skills were significant along other identified topics: education, experience, technical skills, and knowledge. [22] A corresponding study on SE labor market revealed that communication skills are the most demanded soft skill, followed by teamwork, management skills, writing skills, leadership, and problem solving [24]. The results from similar studies [23, 25, 26] regarding communication-related topics were collected to Table 1. It is, however, important to notice that the skill bases were different in various studies.

Table 1. Skills identified on the job ads by their appearance.

Year (field)	2017 (RE) [26]	2018 (SD) [23]	2013 (SE) [25]
	%		
Communication skills	56	31	13
Interpersonal skills		8	15
English skills	41	36	65
Local native language	65		4
Other languages	9		

As Table 1 shows, there are considerable variations in rates, for instance in communication and local native skills. Identified communication skills requirements varied between 28% and 56%, including interpersonal skills. Local native skills were required only in the RE study [26] by 65%. English skills' appearance varied from 36% to 65%.

Job ads are different and the number of references to non-technical skills can vary. Based on the previous studies, it seems that soft skills play a significant role in job ads: soft skills were mentioned in 72% [25] or 86% of the job ads [26]. Moreover, about 60% of the employers were looking for two or more soft skills [3].

3 Methodology

This study aims to explore junior software engineers' employability-related language, intercultural, and communication skills requirements in SE. The study is reviewing the skills sought by companies based on the job ads. The ads reveal aspects of the employers, workplaces, and positions as well as needs, skill requirements, and working environment. The job ads describe the relevant issues employers consider important as well as indicate what kind of working environment the jobseekers are hired for. The ads are regarded to describe the requirements set for junior software engineers in job seeking.

3.1 Goals and Research Questions

For the purpose to investigate how language, intercultural, and communication skills are presented in the job ads applicable to junior software engineers, the following research questions (RQ) were formulated:

1. What language, intercultural, and communication skills are required from a junior software engineer?
2. How is the communicative working environment characterized?

These research questions belong partly together, providing both quantitative and qualitative views on the studied skill areas. Whereas RQ1 focuses mainly quantitatively on the skill requirements of all the studied skill areas, RQ2 concentrates more on qualitative working environment descriptions of communication and collaboration aspects.

3.2 Data Collection

Data for this study has been collected from the job ads published either in Finnish or in English in the TE Offices' Vacancies job seeking service maintained by Public Employment and Business Service in Finland during 27.1.-11.3.2022. Job ads were searched by various Finnish and English keywords referring to SE positions: software engineer, software developer, software designer, back-end developer, front-end developer, full stack developer, and web developer as well as their Finnish counterparts, considering subtle differences in their spelling.

The applicability of the job ad to this study was proved by reading. All the job ads outside the field of SE were excluded. Also, web developers who only create content for websites, without SE-related practices, were excluded.

The main inclusion criterion contained the requirement of having a job title listed above. At this phase, the job titles with developer, engineer or designer endings specified with a different technical prefix without the term 'software', 'back-end', 'front-end', 'full stack', or 'web' were disregarded.

Next, each job ad was inspected by reading, and thus, according to the second-level criteria, a position had to be permanent, or harnessed with a possibility of permanence, and applicable to junior software engineers. All the senior and expert level job ads were excluded, either based on the expert or senior term in the job title or secondly, based on a clearly specified requirement in the job description that the job was directed for more experienced jobseekers, either having at least three years' work experience or otherwise expert-level competence. Based on the inclusion criterion, a position is applicable to a junior if it is applicable to a jobseeker with work experience less than three years. The difficulty of the job position was not judged based on the presented job tasks for the inclusion purposes.

Lastly, all the summer job and trainee positions were excluded, as well as the SE positions overseas. Also, identical copies of the ads, published by the same employer, were excluded.

3.3 Data Analysis

The analysis of 166 job ads was based on content and thematic analysis. All the job ads were read and analyzed thoroughly two to four times for coding purposes. Manual coding was based on linguistic, cultural, and communicative elements, arising from both the skill requirements and working environment descriptions. The first rounds of analysis were conducted during the data collection process.

The codes covered the language of the ad, job title, skill requirements and working environmental descriptions for languages, multiculturalism, communication, and collaboration issues. The coding was conducted for two purposes: to enable skill identification and calculation of relative proportions and to uncover working environmental issues. Skill identification was based on judgments and manual labeling. The skills were counted, and statistical content analysis was performed, similarly to other calculations of relative proportions.

Skill identification was based on exact matches of skills in terms of exact names of the skill, the alternate labels, or aliases of the skills. The skill requirements were described as single words, multi-word phrases, and sentences. Importantly, this study separated skill requirements from the working environment descriptions, and only clear requirements were counted as requirements for the job. Judgments were also based on the location of the phrase in the job ad in relation to other requirements. Often, skill requirements were given as a list.

Generally, the analysis relied on skill identification and calculation of relative proportions with the support of qualitative descriptions. In addition to percentages, the study aimed to describe communicative working environment junior software engineers are hired for.

The conclusions drawn are based on the occurrences of the skill requirements and working environment descriptions in the ads. If an issue is mentioned in the job ad, then it is regarded as important for the job. All the findings, classifications, and comparisons made in the study are based on the occurrences of the issues. On the other hand, if an issue is omitted, it is not assumed to be insignificant for the job.

Data analysis was based on content and thematic analysis. The coding was conducted using NVivo, based on codes and case classifications. Later, data was exported to MS Excel, by copying code references and crosstab query results, to enable, first, analysis of the contents of the themes, and second, a statistical analysis using IBM SPSS Statistics. Originally the data collected for this study is bilingual. For reporting purposes, the job titles and extracts from the job ads written in Finnish were translated into English.

4   Research Results

Data chosen for this study contains 166 SE-related job ads published in Finland of which 60% were written in Finnish and 40% were written in English. Of the ads written in Finnish (n = 99), 33 had an English job title and 3 both English and Finnish titles. Correspondingly, 1 of the ads written in English (n = 67) had a Finnish job title and 4 job ads contained both Finnish and English titles. The job ads comprised various software engineer professional titles, as shown in Table 2.

Table 2. Job titles (n = 166)

Job title	%
Software Developer, Software Engineer, Software Designer	60
Junior Frontend, Backend, Full Stack, Software, Web Developer	13
Full Stack Developer	8
Frontend Developer	7
Web Developer	4
Backend Developer	4
Front-end/Back-End/Full Stack Developer (combinations)	3
Total	100

Most of the ads (60%) were looking for various software developers, engineers, and designers. The term 'Junior' was included in 13% of the job titles. Otherwise, the job titles contained a variety of different frontend, backend, full stack, and web developers.

4.1   Language Skills

Language skills requirements were presented in the job ads as clear demands, but also as the needs described more specifically. Along with clear language skills requirements, also the language of the job ad hints language needs: 40% of the ads were written in English.

Of all the job ads, 59% were looking for software engineers possessing English and 42% Finnish skills. Moreover, 4% of the ads contained requirements for other languages: 4 referred to Swedish, another domestic language in Finland, 2 to German, and 1 to multilingualism in general. Table 3 shows what kind of language skills combinations were presented in the job ads.

As Table 3 shows, employers' language skills requirements were mainly split in three main trends. Whereas one third of the employers (30%) required both English and Finnish skills, almost one third (26%) required only English, and lastly, one third

(31%) required no language skills at all. Additionally, the requirement of Finnish skills occurred rarely on its own. Eventually, 69% of the job ads were looking for at least one language skill.

Table 3. Language skills requirements (n = 166)

Skill	%
Both English skills and Finnish skills	30
Only English skills	26
Only Finnish skills	8
English, Finnish, and other language skills	3
Only other language or multilingualism	1
No language skills requirements	31
Total	100

The requirements for English skills were typically presented as list items in the job ads, as follows: "Fluency in English", "Excellent written and spoken communication skills in English", or "Full professional proficiency in English". Rather often, the requirement of English was specified, and connected to written (32%), verbal (31%), or communication skills (19%). Moreover, 62% of the job ads demanding English skills required fluency or excellent skill level. Sometimes, the specified requirement was connected to the situations where English is necessary such as English as a working language, test documents written in English, or need for technical English. Here, 4 of the ads described that English is used as a working language.

Finnish skills were required similarly to English, despite that 23% of the ads demanding Finnish skills described that Finnish skills are seen as an advantage, not mandatory for the job, as seen in the following extracts: "Finnish language skills are seen as an advantage" or "Fluent in either Finnish or English". Especially, the job ads written in English who demanded Finnish skills stated that proficiency in Finnish is not a prerequisite for the job, but a nice bonus, plus, or an advantage. In fact, almost three fourths (71%) of the job ads written in English considered demanded Finnish skills as an advantage, hinting that the job ads written in English seem partly to be targeted for non-Finnish speaking jobseekers. In Finnish, this was not expressed in the same way: only 1 job ad written in Finnish described Finnish skills as an asset. Of the job ads demanding Finnish skills, 54% demanded fluent or excellent skill level.

Considering the different language skills requirements, 2 job ads demanded fluency either in Finnish or English, in addition to that one job ad presented that some of the projects require fluent Finnish, unlike most projects; then, fluent English would be enough. The requirement of Finnish skills in a few job ads was established on the use of Finnish as a working language with customers.

Language Skills Requirements by the Language of the Job Ad. Presuming that the language of the job ad indicates language skills requirements, Finnish job markets have needs for both Finnish-speaking and English-speaking software engineers. The main emphasis based on the language of the ad seems to be in the Finnish language, because 60% of the job ads were published in Finnish. On the other hand, a high rate of the job ads published in English (40%) indicates a rather significant role of the English language in the Finnish job markets.

Secondly, also clearly presented language skills requirements indicate language needs. The impact of the language of the job ad on requirements is presented in Fig. 1.

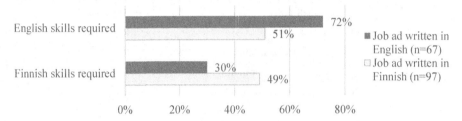

Fig. 1. Impact of the language of the job ad on language skills requirements

As Fig. 1 shows, the job ads written in both languages required more English than Finnish skills even though the difference between languages is clear. Of the job ads written in English, even 72% demanded English skills and 30% Finnish skills, whereas 51% of the job ads written in Finnish demanded English and 49% Finnish skills. The job ads written in English required noticeably more English than Finnish, in contrast to the ads written in Finnish whose requirements for English and Finnish were almost equal.

This figure reveals that the language of the job ad is associated with language skills requirements. English skills are required relatively more by the ads written in English and Finnish required more by the ads written in Finnish. Eventually, 75% of the ads written in English and 65% of the ads written in Finnish required at least one language skill. The job ads written in English required more language skills than the ads written in Finnish.

4.2 Intercultural Skills

The role of intercultural skills in the job ads was assessed both by skill requirements and working environmental descriptions, in terms of demands for intercultural skills and descriptions of multiculturalism.

First, intercultural skills were referred in 4 of 166 job ads (2%), including require-ments that a jobseeker is expected to demonstrate the "ability to work in Finnish and international networks" or must be "well-suited for an international work environment". Only 1 of the job ads contained a clear requirement for intercultural communication skills: "We expect you to be a professional — who is comfortable in communicating with different people with different backgrounds and cultures." Three of these four job ads demanding intercultural skills were written in English.

Secondly, multiculturalism appeared in 7% of the job ads, according to working environment descriptions. Only 4 job ads described their workplace as "a multicultural organization", "an international, diverse, and sociable workplace", or a diverse community. These job ads described how they value or aim to promote diversity, or provide "equal opportunities regardless of national origin", and they do not "discriminate on the basis of race, religion, color, or national origin". A job ad referred to "the right mix of people with diverse backgrounds, personalities, skills, and perspectives" by striving that "people of all backgrounds are treated equally, respected, and valued for who they are." Some job ads described that practices and methods used in projects vary by extremely diverse clients.

4.3 Communication Skills

Communication skills were already referred tangentially in company with language and intercultural skills requirements. As examined separately, communication issues appeared in many ways in the job ads. Skills requirements are presented in Table 4.

Table 4. Communication skills requirements (n = 166)

Skill	%
Communication skills	24
People/Social skills	8
Documentation skills	7
Interaction skills	4
Reporting skills	2

Of the job ads, 24% demanded communication skills, most of which were defined by a level such as good, great, or excellent. Moreover, some job ads specified demands for documentation (7%) and reporting (2%) skills, as well as customer and end user communication skills – also with non-technical persons, ability to bring up own viewpoints, receive feedback from experts, and courage to ask for help. Interaction skills were separately required by 4% of the job ads. Communication skills requirements were presented more by ads written in English (36%) than ads written in Finnish (16%).

People or social skills were demanded by 8% of the job ads of which one fourth referred directly to people or social skills. Other job ads described various characteristics a jobseeker should have such as outgoingness, caringness, outspokenness, and kindness, in addition to that some ads were just looking for nice persons and chaps.

The job ads contained a plenty of communication-related issues when the attention was shifted from skill requirements to working environmental descriptions. Based on these descriptions, a software engineer must cope with rather diverse communication situations at work. The job ads elucidate how software engineers are encouraged to share thoughts, opinions, and viewpoints, suggest solutions, participate in decision making, influence, and ask for help. More specifically software engineers need to innovate, brainstorm, discuss, share information and expertise, guide others, handle problems, and receive feedback.

Software engineers seem to 'work alongside customers' or closely with end users, but also with industrial leaders, manufacturers, technology partners, subcontractors, suppliers, and authorities as well as other internal customers and stakeholders. Software engineers' work includes encounters with rather diverse people occupying various roles, hinting at the diversity of communication situations in the working environment.

The investigation of communication skills raised the viewpoint of interrelatedness between communication and collaboration/teamwork. Based on the job ads, a software engineer collaborates closely with different professionals, such as product owners, Scrum Masters, team leads, customers and other developers in addition to different system analysts, developers, testers, application specialists, DevOps engineers, engineering leads, designers, hardware engineers, architects, UI/UX designers, security and network experts, project managers, quality assurance, R & D, product management, business operations, production, sales, marketing, service managers, graphics professionals, content creators, founders, and other experts. Collaboration with multidisciplinary actors set additional challenges for communication skills.

5 Discussion

This job ad-based study focused on junior software engineers' language, intercultural, and communication skills requirements, regarding differences based on the choice of the language of the job ad. The study aimed at exploring what skills employers present in the job ads indicating the skills demanded from the junior software engineers. The attention was also drawn to communicative working environment to describe what kind of working environment junior software engineers are hired for.

Qualitative data analysis using both content and thematic analysis for the purposes of relative proportions and qualitative descriptions turned out to be a good choice. Percentages, supported by working environment descriptions, offered a comprehensive view on the studied issues.

5.1 RQ1: What Language, Intercultural, and Communication Skills are Required from a Junior Software Engineer?

Regarding the role English plays in the global settings, this study confirms that English plays a significant role in SE and in Finnish SE labor markets. In addition to that 40% of the ads were written in English and that 36% of the ads written in Finnish have an English job title, English skills were mentioned as a requirement for the job in 59% of the job ads. This result seems to be in line with previous studies, 41% in [26], 36% in [23], and 65% in [25]. Rather often (62%) these demands for English were specified with the demand of fluency or the excellent skill level.

Local native language skills (Finnish) were required by almost half of the ads (42%), deviating from 65% in RE [26]. Although it seems that Finnish skills are significant, a remarkable part of these Finnish skills requirements, especially in the job ads written in English, regarded Finnish skills as an advantage, not as a requirement for the job, indicating the position to be open also for international jobseekers. Otherwise, the significance of Finnish skills appears in the job ads of which 60% were written in Finnish.

Intercultural skills requirements were almost missing. Surprisingly, only 2% of the job ads demanded intercultural skills, although the English language and its clear role in the ads could be seen as a reference to more intercultural working environment. It seems that awareness of the specificity of intercultural skills in the workplace is either rather low or that job ads just neglect intercultural skills. Previous job ad studies disregarded intercultural skills requirements – perhaps because they were not presented.

The greatest variation occurred in the ways how communication skills requirements were presented in the job ads. Communication skills were required but the need and the way how they were presented dispersed considerably. Communication (24%), documentation (7%), interaction (4%), and reporting (2%) skill requirements were extended by a set of specific skills. In the light of figures, this result corresponds the previous studies, 13% in [25] and 56% in [26].

This study shows that language and communication skills requirements are reasonably presented in the job ads, but intercultural skills requirements are almost missing.

5.2   RQ2: How is the Communicative Working Environment Characterized?

The job ads present SE working environment as multidisciplinary where junior software engineers communicate and collaborate with numerous parties, with team members, customers, and other stakeholders. The working environment requires a jobseeker to master a multifaceted variety of diverse communication situations. These numerous communicative situations – including, for instance, information sharing, decision making, brainstorming, discussing, and guidance – pose challenges for junior software engineers and their skill acquisition. Communication environment seems to be similar to [17]. This study confirms that software engineers deal with rather diverse people with whom they communicate and cooperate [13].

Multicultural aspect was almost disregarded in working environment descriptions. Only a minor part (7%) of the job ads referred to a multicultural working environment. These sparse descriptions referred either to a multicultural or diverse workplace, or respect for others regardless of origin.

High skill requirements for English and the number of job ads published in English implies that proficiency in English is significant and English is used for communication at work. Moreover, communication and multicultural aspects were emphasized in the ads published in English. It seems that the employer who writes a job ad in English is more aware of language, communication, and intercultural issues.

6   Validity Discussion

Data collection for this study took place on TE Offices' Vacancies online service that can still be regarded as one of the useful recruitment channels in Finland. Although job change can take place via other channels, too, and all open positions cannot be analyzed, the data source can be expected to provide relatively unbiased view of open job positions in Finland. The study could be replicated in other countries.

This study paid special attention to the selection of data. To reduce the dependence of the choice of the ad on the researcher, clear inclusion and exclusion criteria were created and applied. The inclusion was confirmed by thorough consideration of criteria.

Although analysis is based on free-form job descriptions different in length, content, and style, the language used in the job ads is primarily clear and concise. Despite that requirements are described in many ways, the information given should produce the same meaning for everyone. Special attention was drawn to the difference between skills requirements and working environment descriptions. The requirements specify what skills are expected from software engineers whereas descriptions of working environment describe where software engineers work. These two approaches support each other. Coding was conducted carefully and confirmed by re-reading by the same person.

The reasonable number of the job ads, 166, enabled both quantitative content analysis for skill identification and qualitative thematic analysis for working environment descriptions. The analysis was based on the job ads written in Finnish and in English. The extracts of the job ads written in Finnish were translated into English for reporting purposes. A special attention was paid on subtle differences in some of the concepts and translations from Finnish into English due to linguistic differences. The extracts were chosen with care, to preserve the original message.

The study relies on the job ads used to investigate the requirements set for junior software engineers. The results are based on the occurrences of the issues in the job ads even if the absence does not make an issue insignificant for the job. The job ads enable interpretations from many perspectives such as employers, workplace needs, job positions, and skill requirements, albeit jobseekers' perspective is the most significant.

The results can be regarded valid in Finland and could be generalized to the countries having rather similar linguistic and cultural environment. Generalization to English-speaking countries or the countries having remarkably greater multiculturalism and foreign population is controversial. Finnish working environment is characterized by the difficult Finnish language and relatively small proportion of foreign population.

7 Conclusions and Future Research Work

This study focused on junior software engineers' language, intercultural, and communication skills requirements, to explore the skills employers present in the job ads. The attention was also drawn to communicative working environment to describe what kind of working environment software engineers are hired for.

This study highlighted English skills and a multifaceted communication environment where software engineers collaborate with various parties. Communication skills were clearly visible in the job ads, referring to communication at work, as well as communication needs with various stakeholders and within the team. Software engineers' working environment is multidisciplinary. Labor markets have needs for skilled communicators and collaborators. Lack of communication and language skills weaken opportunities in job seeking.

The partition of language issues implies that Finnish SE working environment is almost bilingual in practice. Finnish SE labor markets seeks employees by publishing job ads in Finnish and in English with high rates for proficiency in English and moderate proficiency in Finnish. Finnish SE labor markets have needs for fluent Finnish and English speakers.

Intercultural aspects of communication were not, in any case, generally visible. The peculiarities and specific aspects of intercultural communication are either not understood or not been aware of in designing the job ads.

Moreover, the language of the job ad indicates the needs. The ads written in English highlight proficiency in English and presents Finnish skills as an advantage for the job. Also, communication and intercultural skills were emphasized in the ads written in English. The employer who writes a job ad in English is more aware of language, communication, and intercultural issues. Respectively, the ads written in Finnish regard English and Finnish skills as important; Finnish skills are regarded more important in the ads written in Finnish than in the ads written in English. There is no need for other languages is Finnish SE labor markets.

The study revealed that language and communication -related expectations are widely presented in the job ads. However, it was observed that, despite of the language requirements, other intercultural communication aspects are not explicated in the ads. This is an aspect that would require further research, to explore and explain the reasons for it: whether this aspect is just not well-understood by the employers or missed in the job ads. Moreover, internationality aspects, qualification requirements, and teamwork, which is culture-specific, would require further research and deeper investigation. The study of these questions would require going beyond the job ad analysis and going into companies to study the understanding of intercultural communication issues. In addition, an analysis of SE education would, possibly, be necessary, to understand how these aspects are considered in education.

This single study could be replicated in other countries where similar comparisons between job ads written in different languages could be made.

References

1. IEEE Computer Society: SWEBOK V3.0 Guide to the Software Engineering Body of Knowledge (2014). https://www.computer.org/education/bodies-of-knowledge/software-eng ineering
2. Sedelmaier, Y., Landes, D.: SWEBOS - Software engineering body of skills. In: IEEE Global Engineering Education Conference, EDUCON, pp. 395–401 (2014)
3. Stevens, M., Norman, R.: Industry expectations of soft skills in IT graduates a regional survey. In: ACM International Conference Proceeding Series, 01–05 February 2016, art. no. a13 (2016)
4. Matturro, G., Raschetti, F., Fontán, C.: Soft skills in software development teams: a survey of the points of view of team leaders and team members. In: Proceedings - 8th International Workshop on Cooperative and Human Aspects of Software Engineering, CHASE 2015, pp. 101–104 (2015)
5. Cambridge English: English at Work: global analysis of language skills in the workplace (2016). http://www.cambridgeenglish.org/english-at-work
6. Knoch, U., Macqueen, S.: Assessing English for Professional Purposes. Routledge, Abingdon (2020)
7. Patel, F., Li, M., Sooknanan, P.: Intercultural Communication Building a Global Community. SAGE, New Delhi, London (2011)

8. Lehtonen, T., Karjalainen, S.: University graduates' workplace language needs as perceived by employers. System **36**, 492–503 (2008)
9. Jaakkola, H., Heimbürger, A., Linna, P.: Knowledge-oriented software engineering process in a multi-cultural context. Software Qual. J. **18**, 299–319 (2010)
10. Chen, L.: Cultures, communication, and contexts of intercultural communication. In: Chen, L. (ed.) Intercultural Communication, pp. 3–15. De Gruyter Mouton, Boston/Berlin (2017)
11. Cress, J.A., Thomas, P.W.: Imbedding industry expectations for professional communication into the undergraduate engineering curricula. In: ASEE Annual Conference and Exposition, Conference Proceedings (2020)
12. Newberry, R., Conrad, D.: Identification of outcome based business communication skills. In: Allied Academies International Conference. Academy of Organizational Culture, Communications and Conflict. Proceedings, vol. 15, pp. 28–32 (2010)
13. Ford, D., Zimmermann, T., Bird, C., Nagappan, N.: Characterizing Software Engineering Work with Personas Based on Knowledge Worker Actions. In: International Symposium on Empirical Software Engineering and Measurement. pp. 394–403 (2017)
14. Gonçalves, M.K., de Souza, C.R.B., González, V.M.: Collaboration, information seeking and communication: an observational study of software developers' work practices. J. Univ. Comput. Sci. **17**, 1913–1930 (2011)
15. Sudhakar, G.P.: A model of critical success factors for software projects. J. Enterp. Inf. Manag. **25**, 537–558 (2012)
16. Canedo, E.D., Santos, G.A.: Factors affecting software development productivity: an empirical study. In: ACM International Conference Proceeding Series, pp. 307–316 (2019)
17. Ruff, S., Carter, M.: Communication learning outcomes from software engineering professionals: a basis for teaching communication in the engineering curriculum. In: Proceedings - Frontiers in Education Conference, FIE, art. no. 5350442 (2009)
18. Hargie, O. (ed.): The Handbook of Communication Skills. Routledge, Abingdon (2019)
19. Exter, M., Caskurlu, S., Fernandez, T.: Comparing computing professionals' perceptions of importance of skills and knowledge on the job and coverage in undergraduate experiences. ACM Trans. Comput. Educ. **18** (2018)
20. Hoegl, M., Gemuenden, H.G.: Teamwork quality and the success of innova-tive projects: a theoretical concept and empirical evidence. Organ. Sci. **12**, 435–449 (2001)
21. Khaouja, I., Kassou, I., Ghogho, M.: A survey on skill identification from online job ads. IEEE Access. **9**, 118134–118153 (2021)
22. Gurcan, F., Sevik, S.: Expertise roles and skills required by the software development industry. In: 1st International Informatics and Software Engineering Conference: Innovative Technologies for Digital Transformation, IISEC 2019 - Proceedings (2019)
23. Hiranrat, C., Harncharnchai, A.: Using text mining to discover skills demanded in software development jobs in Thailand. In: ACM International Conference Proceeding Series, pp. 112–116 (2018)
24. Papoutsoglou, M., Ampatzoglou, A., Mittas, N., Angelis, L.: Extracting knowledge from on-line sources for software engineering labor market: a mapping study. IEEE Access. **7**, 157595–157613 (2019)
25. Matturro, G.: Soft skills in software engineering: a study of its demand by software companies in Uruguay. In: 2013 6th International Workshop on Co-operative and Human Aspects of Software Engineering, CHASE 2013 – Proceedings, pp. 133–136 (2013)
26. Daneva, M., Wang, C., Hoener, P.: What the job market wants from requirements engineers? an empirical analysis of online job ads from the Netherlands. In: International Symposium on Empirical Software Engineering and Measurement, pp. 448–453 (2017)

Benefit Considerations in Project Decisions

Sinan Sigurd Tanilkan$^{(\boxtimes)}$ and Jo Erskine Hannay

Simula Metropolitan Center for Digital Engineering, Oslo, Norway
{sinan,johannay}@simula.no

Abstract. Software project success is often characterized in terms of time, cost and scope – despite that delivering benefit is the main purpose of a project. In this paper, we explore 1) to what degree benefit considerations influence major project decisions, 2) to what degree a specific set of benefits management challenge are handled and influence major project decisions and 3) if there is any realization (over time) that benefit considerations should receive greater attention. We investigate influence in projects with four types of problem severity: completed projects with only minor problems, completed projects with major problems, projects that were disrupted but completed, and projects that were terminated before completion. We asked 45 software professionals to what degree time, cost, scope, benefit and benefit/cost, as well as benefits management challenges, influence major project decisions. Our findings indicate that time, cost and scope have a significantly higher degree of influence on project decisions than benefit and benefit/cost. However, practitioners think that benefit and benefit/cost *should* have significantly more influence on decisions than cost. The benefits management challenges are found to have less influence in the more severe projects. We argue that giving benefits considerations a stronger voice in project decisions would be in line with the desire of practitioners and the prime objective of delivering benefit to stakeholders. We conclude that it is important to understand how to handle benefits management challenges at different stages of project life and that handling such challenges should be integrated with other prime drivers of project success.

Keywords: Time · Cost · Scope · Benefit · Benefits management challenges · Software project severity

1 Introduction

A central public sector agency in Norway terminated its information technology modernization program prematurely after about one and a half years' development. The total budget was about EUR 400 million, to be spent over six years. The sunk cost at termination was about EUR 180 million, of which EUR 36 million was spent on functionality that was never to be used [33,34]. Generally

© The Author(s), under exclusive license to Springer Nature Switzerland AG 2022
D. Taibi et al. (Eds.): PROFES 2022, LNCS 13709, pp. 217–234, 2022.
https://doi.org/10.1007/978-3-031-21388-5_15

presented by the press as yet another information technology scandal, the termination of the program was applauded in professional circles as a remarkably insightful decision [46]. When things went bad, program management took the bold decision to stop before further losses, thus countering the *escalation of commitment to a failing course of action* phenomenon [27] and *sunk cost effect* [1] otherwise so proliferant in high-stakes development initiatives. This, and other similar stories, give reasons for optimism; some programs and projects no longer simply spend up their allotted budget no matter what.

The reason, however, for taking action in the above program was, officially, a lack of cost control. Whether they were on track in delivering benefit was not explicitly evident in the decision to stop.

Delivering benefit is the prime reason for software development initiatives, and empirical studies suggest that organizations that engage in *benefits management* [43] perform better in terms of most success criteria [26]. Despite this, there is a tendency to focus on success understood as being on time, being on budget and delivering the specified functionality [18]. In other fields than software engineering, success measured in terms of time, cost and scope, does not correlate with client benefit and satisfaction [37]. This observation has lead researchers to call for further research on the relations between these dimensions for software projects [25].

In light of the above, we want to understand in more detail the extent to which considerations regarding benefit have, or should have, an impact on decisions to continue, disrupt or terminate projects, compared to the traditional control metrics time, cost and scope. To further understand how benefits considerations may play a role, we investigate the extent to which an identified set of benefits management challenges influence these project decisions and project flow. We also explore if there is a growing realization during projects that benefits considerations should have a greater influence. We investigate these topics in four types of projects, according to the severity of problems they encounter.

The next section presents relevant work for our discussion. We present our research questions in Sect. 3, the research method in Sect. 4 and the results in Sect. 5. After that, we discuss and conclude.

2   Background and Previous Work

Benefits Management, defined as "[t]he process of organizing and managing such that potential benefits arising from the use of IT are actually realized" [43], has been suggested to improve organizations' ability to successfully realize benefits of software investments [3,8,10,14,24,42,43], and benefits management practices have been reported to increase benefits realization [13,23]. Notable characteristics of projects that professionals perceived as "successful" are (a) the application of benefits management practices before and during project execution, (b) the application of core agile practices of frequent delivery to the client and scope flexibility, and (c) that their clients were deeply involved in these practices [25].

The uptake of benefit management practices has been conspicuously slow in light of the existing evidence and general consensus among IT professionals of its relevance. There have been calls for research into what practices in benefits management contribute to success, on how benefits management is actually performed and what challenges practitioners are facing [5,25]. It seems particularly pertinent to investigate what it is that is hampering benefits management. There have been efforts to understand challenges in benefits management [4,9,12,15,16,32] and barriers to benefits management [39]. However, there are few empirical studies on organizations applying benefits management in the context of software development [22], beyond professionals reporting a lack of methodological support for benefits management [25].

A recent in-depth analysis of public-sector projects revealed six sets of conceptual *benefits management challenges* [38]:

A: Identifying and describing the planned benefits of a solution
B: Ensuring that work in the project is aligned with the planned benefits
C: Ensuring the reception and acceptance of the planned benefits
D: Handling organizational issues related to realizing benefits
E: Maintaining an overview of whether the benefits can be realized by other solutions or mechanisms
F: Measuring and evaluating realized benefits

These challenges were uncovered in a *critical case study*: The investigated projects where critical cases [45] in that they had *explicit incentives* to employ benefits management practices. Benefits management challenges uncovered in these projects will arguably be accentuated in projects without such incentives. To increase our understanding of how these challenges influence project decisions, we use them in our further investigations in the next sections.

The so-called *iron triangle* of project management promotes time, cost and scope as control mechanisms to obtain technical quality. The *agile triangle* introduces benefit (extrinsic quality) as a goal together with technical quality; both of which are obtained by controlling, or constraining the bundle of time, cost and scope. However, it has been argued that benefit should be presented as a control mechanisms in its own right; not merely as a fuzzy goal to be obtained by controlling those other things [19, p. 17]. Further, the real control mechanism should be the ratio of benefit/cost, since the point is not to maximize benefit regardless, but to maximize benefit for the cost invested [21].

In the introductory anecdote, the program achieved project learning to the extent that it was possible to make an informed decision based on cost control in the midst of failure. The question arises as to what influence benefit has, or should have, and what influence do benefits management challenges have, both in plain sailing and when the going gets tough.

3   Research Questions

Our first objective is to study the extent to which considerations regarding benefit have, or should have, an impact on project decisions compared to the traditional control metrics time, cost and scope. We compare the standard control metrics from the "iron triangle" and metrics explicitly involving benefit. The compared control metrics are *time, cost, scope, benefit* and *benefit/cost*.

Our second objective is to understand further how benefits considerations may play a role, and we investigate the extent to which the identified set of benefits management challenges (A–F above) influence project decisions.

A third objective is to see how the influence of both the control metrics and the benefits management challenges might vary according to project problems. For the purpose of this paper, we define four project *severity* types (S1–S4):

(S1) completed projects with only minor problems
(S2) completed projects with major problems
(S3) projects that were disrupted but completed
(S4) projects that were terminated before completion

These severity types are based on the work experience of the authors and three experienced software project professionals.

Based on the above elaborations, we pose the following research questions. Although partly exploratory, we also present expectations with rationales that are not yet founded in theory, but rather, based on anecdotal evidence.

RQa *To what degree do the control metrics time, cost, scope, benefit and benefit/cost influence decisions on termination and disruption in a project?*
   Expectation: The measures time, cost and scope are more influential than the measures of benefit and benefit/cost. Moreover, they are more influential than the benefits management challenges, and more so for severe projects. There is a desire that benefit and benefit/cost should be more influential.
   Rationale: There is still a focus on the "iron triangle" when controlling projects, and especially when things get difficult, where salvaging cost may be perceived as the better face-saver. There is currently an increased focus and awareness on benefits management that raises awareness that benefit should ideally be the more prominent argument.

RQb *To what degree do the benefits management challenges influence decisions on termination or disruption of a project?*
   Expectation: The challenges have less influence on disruption or termination decisions in projects with more severe problems.
   Rationale: Benefits management is not used in crises.

RQc *Are there differences in how well benefits management challenges are handled?*
   Expectation: At early stages of a project, the challenges are handled less favorably, the more severe the project is.
   Rationale: The lack of handling benefits management challenges might have an adverse effect on a project.

RQd *To what degree do practitioners improve their handling of benefits management challenges during projects?*
   Expectation: The challenges are handled better at later stages than at early stages, and more so for severe projects.
   Rationale: Failure can create an opportunity for learning.

4   Research Method

We conducted a survey with an online questionnaire. A full list of survey questions and responses can be found at: https://tinyurl.com/becipd. Below, we include a subset of the survey questions that are directly relevant to answering the research questions. To sample the participants' personal experience, we prompted them to choose one concrete project, among the four types of project severity, from their experience in software development, and answer the subsequent questionnaire items for that project. Based on the authors' knowledge of the Norwegian IT industry, we assumed that respondents would have fewer terminated or disrupted projects to report on, compared to finished projects. To increase the probability of receiving close to equal amounts of responses in each severity group, the project selection question was phrased to promote selection of disrupted and terminated projects. Respondents were also prompted for their role in the project, as well as for their professional experience in terms of years in software development and the number of projects they had participated in.

4.1   Survey Questions

The survey questions directly relevant to answering the research questions are listed in Table 1 in the order they were posed on the questionnaire. This order was designed for survey comprehension and differs from the (logical) order of the research questions above.

Respondents were prompted for each benefits management challenge A–F (Sect. 2), indicated by <benefits management challenges> in the questions, and for each control metric (time, cost, scope, benefit and benefit/cost), indicated by <control metrics>. Respondents were given variant phrases indicated by the text in square brackets, according to their choice of project severity type.

The survey was piloted prior to data collection on five respondents (on two research colleagues and three experienced managers from the IT industry). The pilot resulted in changes to the wording of questions in the survey for better comprehension and alignment with current terminology in the field. This applied in particular to the project selection question. Minor adjustments were also done to SQ1–SQ5. The project severity groups (S1–S4) were also finalized and validated for meaningfulness and relevance during the pilot.

Data was collected during a webinar titled "Failed digitalization projects: A source of learning and improvement?" in October 2021. In the webinar a selection of IT professionals presented experiences from failed projects, including lessons learned from these projects. A total of 71 professionals were present at the webinar when the survey was conducted. A link to the questionnaire was given as part of the opening remarks to the webinar, and participants were given ten minutes to complete the questionnaire. Fifty-seven persons participated in the survey, but twelve did not complete the survey, leaving 45 complete responses.

The number of software development projects in which the respondents had participated ranged from two to 100 (median: 15, mean: 20.31). The number of years of experience within development of digital solutions ranged from under

Table 1. Survey questions

	In your opinion,	Answer options
SQ1	how were the following <benefits management challenges> handled in the early phases of the project?	seven-point ordinal (poorly 1–7 well)
SQ2	to what extent did the following <control metrics> of the project influence [decisions along the way], [the decision to change course], [the decision to stop]?	seven-point ordinal (minor 1–7 major)
SQ3	to what extent should the following <control metrics> of the project have influenced [decisions along the way], [the decision to change course], [the decision to stop]?	seven-point ordinal (minor 1–7 major)
SQ4	to what extent did problems in the following <benefits management challenges> influence [decisions along the way], [the decision to change course], [the decision to stop]?	seven-point ordinal (minor 1–7 major)
SQ5	compared to the early stages of the project, how [were], [would] the following <benefits management challenges> [handled at later stages of the project], [handled after changing course], [have been handled if the project had continued]?	seven-point ordinal (worse −3– +3 better)

a year to 40 (median: 20, mean: 18.04). The number of years of experience as a manager within this field ranged from zero to 30 (median: 5, mean: 7.78). The project that each participant chose as a reference for the subsequent questions was owned by a public sector organization in (68.9%) of the cases and the private sector in (31.1%) of the cases. The distribution per project severity type was as follows: completed projects with only minor problems (24.5%), completed projects with major problems (22.2%), projects that were disrupted but completed (28.9%), projects that were terminated before completion (24.4%).

4.2   Analysis

Ordinal data from the questionnaire was analyzed using percentile box-plots for descriptive statistics.[1] We used related-samples Friedman's two-way analysis of variance by ranks for comparison with and across benefits management challenges and control metrics. We used independent samples Jonckheere-Terpstra non-parametric tests for comparisons across the four types of project severity. Both tests are specifically for ordinal data. The Jonckheere-Terpstra test assumes directional comparisons and is one-tailed: We are expecting responses to be higher for one severity level than another; for example we expect handling to deteriorate from level S1 to level S4 (as described for RQc in Sect. 3). We

---

[1] Data analyses were conducted using IBM SPSS Statistics version 27 using test-wise deletion of missing data.

accept statistical significance at $p \leq \alpha = 0.05$. That is, we accept a 5% chance of rejecting the null hypothesis when it is, in fact, true.

Traditionally, one performs an omnibus test, with ensuing pairwise comparisons if the omnibus test is significant. Our primary interest lies with the pairwise comparisons, and we perform the pairwise comparisons even when the omnibus test is not significant. There can be significant pairwise differences, even when the omnibus test is not significant [40]. We are interested in single comparisons; for example if a challenge is handled worse between two levels of severity. We are also interested in composed comparisons; for example if a challenge intensifies across a chain of severities. When composing multiple comparisons, the probability of rejecting the null hypothesis for any one in the group of comparisons increases. If one intends to draw conclusions on a composed comparison on the basis of any one constituent comparison, one should therefore use a stricter α_{adj} using, e.g., the Bonferroni adjustment. In the composed comparisons we are interested in, the null hypotheses for all tests in the composition have to be rejected, and using a stricter α_{adj} is not relevant [2,17]. We do, however, also report the Bonferroni-adjusted probability (p_{adj}) to cater for other kinds of composed comparisons. For space reasons, we only display the significant results.

We wish to report effect sizes for the pairwise comparisons. The pairwise comparisons for the Jonckheere-Terpstra tests are based on the Mann-Whitney U statistic, and it is possible to report effect sizes estimates in terms of Cohen's d [30], where the following rules of thumb apply: <0.1 (very small), 0.1 – <0.3 (small), 0.3 – <0.5 (medium), 0.5 – <1.2 (large), 1.2 – <2.0 (very large) and >=2.0 (huge) [36]. Pairwise comparisons for the Friedman test are in terms of the Dunn-Bonferroni statistic with no straightforward effect size estimate, so for the Friedman tests, we report effect sizes in terms of Kendal's W for the omnibus test [41] in lack of anything better. Kendal's W ranges from 0 to 1, with the following rules of thumb for evaluating effect sizes: 0.1 – <0.3 (small), 0.3 – <0.5 (medium) and >=0.5 (large) [11].

With our small sample size, statistical power is expectedly low. That is, there is low probability of the data revealing (significant) effects, when, in fact, there are effects in the intended population, and the probability of revealing small effects is lower than that of revealing large effects. On the other hand, it is all the more promising for further studies if our data does reveal effects under low power. Given a sample size, one might calculate power for various effect sizes (small, medium, large) and see if the commonly acceptable level of $\beta = 0.8$ is achieved, but power calculations for non-parametric tests are not straightforward [35], and we omit them for this initial study.

5   Results

The Friedman omnibus tests are all significant with effect sizes ranging from very small to small. None of the Jonckheere-Terpstra omnibus tests are significant, while several of the pairwise comparisons are; and except for two of the results (on RQc), all significant results have large, very large or huge effect sizes. Larger effect sizes are generally more useful for practitioners [28]. Nevertheless, a study with higher statistical power would have a higher probability of finding significant results with also smaller effects sizes. This would be particularly interesting for establishing the expected linked relationships across all four severity types, which are only partially seen in our data. In the following, we report these, and other significant findings.

RQa: To What Degree Do the Control Metrics Time, Cost, Scope, Benefit and Benefit/cost Influence Decisions on Termination and Disruption in a Project? This research question is answered using the responses from survey questions SQ2 and SQ3. Figure 1a shows descriptive statistics, regardless of project severity, for the influence the control metrics time, cost, scope, benefit and benefit/cost (red shades) are reported to have on project decisions, and the influence practitioners report that the control metrics "should

(a) Influence of control metrics on project decisions – actual (red), should (green):

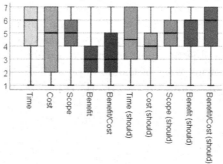

(b) **Sign. diff. in influence – actual:**
Omnibus test n: 41, p: .000, W: .19

Pair-wise two-sided tests		p	p_{adj}
Time	> Benefit	.000	.002
	> Benefit/Cost	.000	.003
Cost	> Benefit	.025	.254
	> Benefit/Cost	.028	.278
Scope	> Benefit	.000	.005
	> Benefit/Cost	.001	.005

(c) **Sign. diff. in influence – should:**
Omnibus test n: 41, p: .000, W: .14

Pair-wise two-sided tests		p	p_{adj}
Benefit	> Cost	.006	.058
Benefit/cost	> Time	.010	.098
	> Cost	.000	.002
Scope	> Cost	.043	.428

(d) **Sign. diff. in influence – actual versus should:** Omnibus test n: 38, p: .000, W: .17

Pairwise two-sided tests			p	p_{adj}
Benefit actual	< Benefit should		.000	.000
Benefit/Cost actual	< Benefit/Cost should	.000	.000

Fig. 1. Analysis for RQa of SQ2 and SQ3 – the influence of control metrics on project decisions – actual and should. Friedman tests. (Color figure online)

(a) Influence of control metrics on project decisions – by project severity:

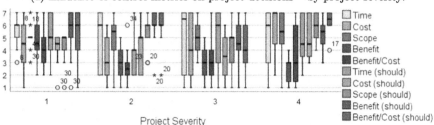

(b) Sign. diff. in influence of control metrics across severity (one-sided):

Actual	Severity	p	p_{adj}	d	Should	Severity	p	p_{adj}	d
Cost	S2<S4	.006	.039	1.250	Scope	S1<S2	.016	.096	1.017
Benefit	S1>S2	.011	.067	1.129		S1<S4	.035	.210	0.813
	S1>S3	.023	.136	1.297		S2>S3	.035	.208	0.821
	S1>S4	.017	.105	0.558		S3<S4	.041	.245	0.768
Benefit/Cost	S1>S2	.032	.194	0.888	Benefit	S2>S3	.045	.270	0.756
					Benefit/Cost	S2>S3	.019	.114	0.949
						S3<S4	.005	.028	1.264

Fig. 2. Analysis for RQa of SQ2 and SQ3 – the influence of control metrics on project decisions – by project severity. Jonckheere-Terpstra tests.

have" (green shades). It is immediately apparent that benefit and benefit/cost were perceived as less influential than the iron-triangle metrics (significant for time, cost and scope – Fig. 1b), but that the respondents thought that benefit and benefit/cost should have had more influence (significant for cost and time – Fig. 1c). Figure 1d shows significance for comparisons between the influence that a metric has, versus should have. The desire that benefit and benefit/cost should have more influence shows up highly significantly in the data.

Figure 2a shows descriptive statistics again, but now per project severity (S1–S4). One can see how respondents perceive that time, cost and scope were highly influential in terminating projects, and that benefit and benefit/cost considerations were not very influential (red boxplots for severity S4) in terminating projects. However, respondents think benefit and the benefit/cost ratio *should* have been highly influential when considering terminating the project (green boxplots for severity S4). Similar remarks hold for severities S3 and S2. For projects with minor problems, benefit and benefit/cost are perceived to have had more influence, with a desire to increase that influence further.

The expectation that benefit is less influential the more severe the project, is supported for project severities S1>S2, S1>S3 and S1>S4 (Fig. 2b). The notion of benefit/cost ratio looses influence for S1>S2. In contrast, cost is perceived to have greater influence the more severe the project (S2<S4). Thus, the difference in influence between cost and benefit clearly increases to the disadvantage of benefit, over project severities.

RQb: To What Degree Do the Benefits Management Challenges Influence Decisions on Termination or Disruption of a Project? For this, we analyzed responses for SQ4. From Fig. 3a and b, we see that challenge C has significantly more influence on decisions, regardless of severity, than challenges A, D, and F. Also, challenge B is significantly more influential than challenge A.

Comparing across project severity (Fig. 3c), we see that influence is uniformly higher for severity S1 (minor issues). Pairwise comparisons (Fig. 3d) support the expectation of less influence the more severe the project, with significant differences for all challenges in the expected direction. (The data exhibits the opposite direction, across severities S2 and S3, for challenge F.)

(a) Influence of benefits management challenges on project decisions:

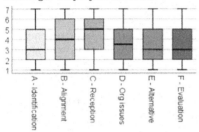

(b) Sign. diff. in influence of benefits management challenges:

Omnibus test n: 38, p: .011, W: .078

Pairwise two-sided tests	p	p_{adj}
B (Alignment) > A (Ident.)	.034	.516
C (Reception) > A (Ident.)	.008	.115
> D (Org issues)	.050	.746
> F (Evaluation)	.027	.409

(c) Influence of challenges on project decisions – by project severity:

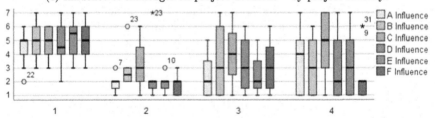

□ A Influence
■ B Influence
■ C Influence
■ D Influence
■ E Influence
■ F Influence

(d) Sign. diff. in influence of challenges across severities (one-sided):

Chal.	Severity	p	p_{adj}	d	Chal.	Severity	p	p_{adj}	d	Chal.	Severity	p	p_{adj}	d
A	S1>S2	.000	.002	2.185	C	S1>S2	.030	.183	0.872	F	S1>S2	.000	.001	2.911
	S1>S3	.002	.015	1.415	D	S1>S2	.012	.074	1.132		S1>S3	.010	.057	1.130
B	S1>S2	.017	.104	1.017	E	S1>S2	.001	.005	1.896		S1>S4	.030	.183	0.910
	S1>S4	.021	.123	0.974		S1>S3	.002	.011	1.564		S2<S3	.045	.272	0.764
						S1>S4	.039	.231	0.849					
						S2<S3	.045	.272	0.764					

Fig. 3. Analysis for RQb of SQ4– influence of benefits management challenges on project decisions. Friedman tests (a, b), Jonckheere-Terpstra tests (c, d).

RQc: Are There Differences in How Well Benefits Management Challenges Are Handled? To answer this research question, we used responses to SQ1. Figure 4a indicates that challenges C, D, E and F are handled poorer (at early stages) than A and B. Looking at Fig. 4b, we see that challenge A is handled significantly better than all the other challenges. Also, challenge B is handled significantly better than challenges D, E and F.

Our expectation that challenges are handled less favourably the more severe the project, is supported to some extent: Visual inspection of the boxplots (Fig. 4c) suggests a general tendency of decreasing early handling of challenges as project severity increases, which is supportive of our expectation. Pairwise comparisons (Fig. 4d) give significant differences for challenges A, B (small effect size), C, D and F, where early handling is better for severity S1 than for a variety of higher severities. Still, the data does not give evidence of a steadily decreasing trend through severities.

(a) How well benefits management challenges were handled early:

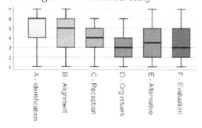

(b) **Sign. diff. in how well the benefits management challenges were handled early:** Omnibus test n: 39, p: .000, W: .27

Pairwise two-sided test		p	p_{adj}
A (Ident.)	> B (Alignment)	.032	.475
	> C (Reception)	.000	.003
	> D (Org issues)	.000	.000
	> E (Alternative)	.000	.000
	> F (Evaluation)	.000	.000
B (Alignment)	> D (Org issues)	.001	.018
	> E (Alternative)	.018	.274
	> F (Evaluation)	.009	.139

(c) How well benefits management challenges were handled early – by project severity:

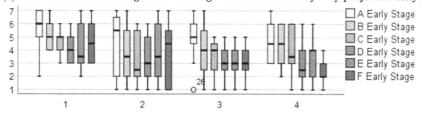

□ A Early Stage
□ B Early Stage
□ C Early Stage
□ D Early Stage
■ E Early Stage
■ F Early Stage

(d) **Sign. diff. in handling of each benefits management challenge across project severities (one-sided):**

Chal.	Severity	p	p_{adj}	d	Chal.	Severity	p	p_{adj}	d	Chal.	Severity	p	p_{adj}	d
A	S1>S4	.046	.277	0.747	C	S1>S4	.038	.226	0.799	D	S1>S4	.015	.089	1.002
B	S3<S4	.034	.202	0.214		S2<S4	.042	.251	1.956	F	S1>S4	.002	.0125	1.558
						S3>S4	.022	.131	0.275		S2>S4	.009	.052	2.437

Fig. 4. Analysis for RQc of SQ1 – handling of benefits management challenges in early stages of projects. Friedman tests (a, b), Jonckheere-Terpstra tests (c, d).

RQd: To What Degree Do Practitioners Improve Their Handling of Benefits Management Challenges During Projects? We analyzed responses on SQ5. The boxplots in Fig. 5a indicate that respondents perceive a weak improvement of the handling of the benefits management challenges at later stages, thus supporting the expectation of project learning on these challenges. Improvement is similar across challenge types, except for challenge E, where practitioners report significantly less improvement compared to challenges A, B and C (Fig. 5b).

When comparing improvement across severity types (Fig. 5c), pairwise comparisons (Fig. 5d) reveal that for some of the challenges, improvement in handling challenges was greater for severity S1 than for severity S2 and severity S3. There

(a) Improvement in handling of benefits management challenges:

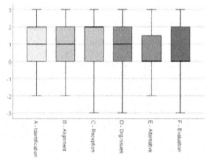

(b) Sign. diff. in improvement of handling benefits management challenges:

Omnibus test n: 36, p: .018, W: .076

Pairwise two-sided test		p	p_{adj}
A (Ident.)	> E (Altern.	.044	.657
B (Alignment)	> E (Altern.)	.038	.565
C (Reception)	> E (Altern.)	.044	.657

(c) Improvement in handling of benefits management challenges – by project severity:

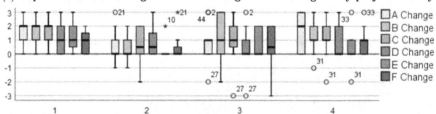

(d) Sign. diff. in improvement of handling benefits management challenges across project severities (one-sided):

Challenge	Severity	p	p_{adj}	d
A	S1>S2	.020	.121	1.090
	S1>S3	.048	.290	0.727
B	S1>S2	.015	.090	1.160
C	S1>S2	.027	.164	0.923
E	S1>S2	.035	.209	0.867

Fig. 5. Analysis for RQd of SQ5 – improvement in handling of benefits management challenges. Friedman tests (a, b), Jonckheere-Terpstra tests (c, d).

are also some indications in the data that improvement was lowest for severity S2 and that improvement increases from S2 to S3 and S4 (challenges A, B, E), in line with our expectations of increased improvement for severe projects, but these latter observations fail to be significant at our chosen level.

6   Discussion

The results above suggest clearly that practitioners think that more emphasis should be placed on benefit and benefit/cost when making project decisions, compared to the iron-triangle metrics of time, cost and scope. But given that practitioners seem to be aware of the importance of increasing the influence of benefit and benefit/cost considerations, the question arises as to how to make this happen. To provide actionable guidance to practitioners, we must understand what is keeping practitioners from prioritizing the right factors when making decisions. We observed that benefit considerations have less influence in more severe projects, and that challenges A, C and F are handled less favorably in more severe projects. These challenges may therefore be a good starting point to understanding why benefit does not get the attention it should in project decisions. In particular, it seems important to understand better the characteristics of challenges A, C and F that can affect practitioners ability to manage benefit, and therefore to employ considerations of benefit in project decisions.

The deterioration of the early handling of challenge A (Identifying and describing the planned benefits of a solution) as project severity increases, could be due to difference in predictability of benefits identification. Several papers have reported that practitioners find it challenging to identify all benefits before project initiation [3,14,25,38], but it is reasonable to assume that the identification of benefits of some projects are more predictable than others. As such, less favorable handling of challenge A in more severe projects, might be due to greater challenges in identifying benefits, rather than poor handling of the challenge. Also, it is reasonable to expect that some projects are more aware of the need to update planned benefits during the project [38]. If unpredictable changes to benefits is the underlying problem , then measures to handle such unpredictability are called for. The incremental and agile approach of not over-planning early then applies also to benefit, and it becomes correspondingly more important to open up the project to changes to planned benefits in addition to time, cost and scope. Techniques to declare and update benefits and monitor the progress in developing beneficial code may be useful [20,21,29]. Keeping track of realized benefit in terms of beneficial code, as one keeps track of the cost of code, can then aid in early and sound decisions on continuation, disruption or termination of projects. However, even with such techniques, organizational issues may add to the challenge, because updating the business case of the project often requires effort from people outside the project organization [39]. An agile approach to business cases is called for.

Challenge C (Ensuring the reception and acceptance of the planned benefits) is likely to be affected both by a difference in difficulty of the challenge and a difference in practitioners handling, which can help explain the deterioration in handling as severity increases. Difference in difficulty is likely to occur as a result of varying resistance to new solutions [8] and a varying interest in benefits themselves [9]. It is unclear if it is possible to predict the degree of difficulty that will be encounter in the reception and acceptance of benefits in different projects. There seems to be differences between benefits that are internal and external to the organization, but further research is needed to understand the characteristics of benefits and stakeholders, that affect the challenges of reception and acceptance of benefits [38]. Previous empirical research has documented a difference in effort put into handling of challenge C. Even when practitioners are aware that more work is needed in order to realize benefits, the extra needed effort is sometimes not spent [38]. Influencing stakeholders to receive and accept new solutions and benefits is a topic where we have not found any research in the field of benefits management, and it is likely that practitioners do not have much empirical or actionable guidance available, other than normative guidance to the effect that the problem is important to keep in mind [42].

Challenge F (Measuring and evaluating realized benefits) has gained much attention in research on benefits management [6,31], but the challenge still remains very much alive for practitioners [38]. Here we discuss three issues of measuring and evaluating realized benefits that are relevant to project decisions and the handling of challenge F.

First, while measures of time, cost and scope are fairly standardized, and fits nicely into business decisions, measures of benefits varies largely. The characteristics used to describe benefits, such as qualitative/quantitative [23] and financial/non-financial [44] is one example. It is reasonable that financial measures are easier to include in business decisions than qualitative evaluations.

Secondly, measures must be taken after benefits realization has started. This is usually in late phases of a project or after a project has ended. Hence, the necessary data is often not available to be used for project decisions. One mitigation is the use of leading measures [24] which are measurement of indicators that are available early. The problem with indicators, is that they are not measures of the actual benefit, and might not give a true representation of the benefits.

Third, it seems practitioners do not prioritize evaluation. Organization may put little emphasis on evaluation because their limited IT resources would be better spent on new projects, rather than on evaluating old projects [7].

7   Limitations

Statistical Conclusion Validity. The low statistical power decreases the probability of the data exhibiting effects where there might, in fact, be effects in the population. The opposite threat of the data exhibiting effects, when there might, in fact, be none, is handled by the significance tests. Even with this small a sample, the data exhibits significant effects. Replicating studies that use larger samples may find additional effects.

External Validity. Based on the characteristics of the sample itself one can generalize the results to similar groups (populations) of interest. This can be problematic for our sample for the following reasons:

1. The sampling strategy was designed to increase the number of disrupted and terminated projects (compared to the population of IT-projects).
2. We have limited information on the characteristics of the projects in the study. Some characteristics, such as the technology applied or the type of solution created, are less likely to influence the studied topics. Other characteristics, such as project size and organization, are likely to have an influence, but were not collected, due to time limitations duration the webinar.
3. It is possible that practitioners attending a seminar in Norway on failed projects have different experiences than other practitioners.

Experiences from this, and other similar webinars and seminars, suggests that participants represent a varied selection of IT professionals that together have a broad experience in many types of software project. We therefore hold that our results are genealizable to the situation of termination and disruption decisions, as long as one takes the above threats into consideration.

Construct Validity. Although response rates and pilots of the survey suggest that participants were able to relate to the given challenges, we do not know to what degree the challenges occurred or how difficult they were to handle. This is likely to have caused different perceptions of the challenges as concepts and of the concepts of "good" and "poor" handling. In retrospect, asking for success in handling, could have mitigated part of this problem. There are similar issues with the influence that challenges have on project decisions (e.g., a challenge that did not occur, is likely to be reported to have low influence on project decisions). Not asking about the occurrences of challenges was a conscious choice when designing the study, because we did not want to confuse the respondents with too many similar questions. However, this issues should be dealt with in later studies. We hold that our findings are relevant as a basis for further study and as initial advice to practitioners in software projects.

8   Conclusion and Further Research

We conclude that benefit and benefit/cost considerations should have more influence in project decisions than they currently have. This would help align project decisions with the primary objectives of projects – to deliver benefits. However, the characteristics of benefits together with benefits management challenges, seems to make considerations of benefit more difficult than time, cost and scope. As a result, we propose three topics for further improvement and research:

– Guidance to help practitioners handle changes to understanding of benefits
– Explore how practitioners can influence others to ensure benefits realization
– Improved guidance to practitioners on benefits evaluation

Further research in these topics is needed in order to understand the difficulties of benefit considerations and how practitioners can gain the information they need to make timely project decisions, influenced by benefit considerations.

Acknowledgments. The authors are grateful to experienced IT professionals Kjetil Strand, Hans Christian Benestad and Bjørn Olav Salvesen for feedback on the questionnaire. The authors are further grateful to the survey respondents.

References

1. Arkes, H.R., Ayton, P.: The sunk cost and concorde effects: are humans less rational than lower animals? Psychol. Bull. **25**(5), 591–600 (1999)
2. Armstrong, R.: When to use the bonferroni correction. Ophthal. Physiol. Opt. **34** (2014)
3. Ashurst, C., Doherty, N.F.: Towards the formulation of a 'best practice'framework for benefits realisation in it projects. Electr. J. Inf. Syst. Eval. **6**(2), 1–10 (2003)
4. Askedal, K., Flak, L.S., Aanestad, M.: Five challenges for benefits management in complex digitalisation efforts-and a research agenda to address current shortcomings. Electr. J. e-Govt. **17**(2), 64–78 (2019)
5. Aubry, M., Boukri, S.E., Sergi, V.: Opening the black box of benefits management in the context of projects. Proj. Manag. J. **52**(5), 434–452 (2021)
6. Ballantine, J.A., Galliers, R.D., Stray, S.J.: Information systems/technology evaluation practices: evidence from UK organizations. J. Inf. Technol. **11**(2), 129–141 (1996)
7. Berghout, E., Nijland, M., Powell, P.: Management of lifecycle costs and benefits: lessons from information systems practice. Comput. Ind. **62**(7), 755–764 (2011)
8. Bradley, G.: Benefit Realisation Management: A Practical Guide to Achieving Benefits through Change. Routledge, London (2016)
9. Breese, R.: Benefits realisation management: panacea or false dawn? Int'l J. Project Manag. **30**(3), 341–351 (2012)
10. Breese, R., Jenner, S., Serra, C.E.M., Thorp, J.: Benefits management: lost or found in translation. Int. J. Project Manage. **33**(7), 1438–1451 (2015)
11. Cohen, J.: Statistical Power Analysis for the Behavioral Sciences, 2nd edn. Routledge, London (1988)
12. Coombs, C.R.: When planned IS/IT project benefits are not realized: a study of inhibitors and facilitators to benefits realization. Int. J. Project Manag. **33**(2), 363–379 (2015)
13. Doherty, N.F., Ashurst, C., Peppard, J.: Factors affecting the successful realisation of benefits from systems development projects: findings from three case studies. J. Inf. Technol. **27**(1), 1–16 (2012)
14. Farbey, B., Land, F., Targett, D.: The moving staircase - problems of appraisal and evaluation in a turbulent environment. Inf. Technol. People **12**(3), 238–252 (1999)
15. Fernandes, G., O'Sullivan, D.: Benefits management in university-industry collaboration programs. Int. J. Project Manag. **39**(1), 71–84 (2021)
16. Flak, L.S., Eikebrokk, T.R., Dertz, W.: An exploratory approach for benefits management in e-government: Insights from 48 Norwegian government funded projects. In: Proceedings of 41st Annual Hawaii International Conference on System Sciences (HICSS) (2008), article no. 210

17. Gigerenzer, G.: Mindless statistics. J. Socio-Econ. **33**, 587–606 (2004)
18. Gingnell, L., Franke, U., Lagerström, R., Ericsson, E., Lilliesköld, J.: Quantifying success factors for it projects-an expert-based Bayesian model. Inf. Syst. Manag. **31**(1), 21–36 (2014)
19. Hannay, J.E.: Benefit/Cost-Driven Software Development with Benefit Points and Size Points. Springer, Simula Springer Briefs (2021). https://doi.org/10.1007/978-3-030-74218-8D
20. Hannay, J.E., Benestad, H.C., Strand, K.: Benefit points–the best part of the story. IEEE Softw. **34**(3), 73–85 (2017)
21. Hannay, J.E., Benestad, H.C., Strand, K.: Earned business value management–see that you deliver value to your customer. IEEE Softw. **34**(4), 58–70 (2017)
22. Hesselmann, F., Mohan, K.: Where are we headed with benefits management research? Current shortcomings and avenues for future research. In: Proceedings of 22nd European Conference on Information Systems (ECIS) (2014)
23. Holgeid, K.K., Jørgensen, M.: Benefits management and agile practices in software projects: how perceived benefits are impacted. In: IEEE 22nd Conference on Business Informatics (CBI), vol. 2 (2020)
24. Jenner, S.: Managing Benefits: Optimizing the Return from Investments. The Stationery Office, APMG-International, High Wycombe (2014)
25. Jørgensen, M.: A survey of the characteristics of projects with success in delivering client benefits. Inf. Softw. Technol. **78**, 83–94 (2016)
26. Jørgensen, M., Mohagheghi, P., Grimstad, S.: Direct and indirect connections between type of contract and software project outcome. Int. J. Project Manag. **35**(8), 1573–1586 (2017)
27. Keil, M., Mann, J., Rai, A.: Why software projects escalate: an empirical analysis and test of four theoretical models. MIS Q. **24**(4), 631–664 (2000)
28. Kirk, R.E.: Practical significance: a concept whose time has come. Educ. Psychol. Measur. **56**(5), 746–759 (1996)
29. Leffingwell, D.: Agile Software Requirements: Lean Requirements Practices for Teams. Addison Wesley, Programs and the Enterprise (2011)
30. Lenhard, W., Lenhard, A.: Computation of effect sizes (2016). https://www.psychometrica.de/effect_size.html Psychometrica. https://doi.org/10.13140/RG.2.2.17823.92329
31. Lin, C., Pervan, G.: Is/it investment evaluation and benefits realisation issues in a government organisation. In: ACIS 2001 Proceedings, vol. 49 (2001)
32. Lin, C., Pervan, G.: The practice of IS/IT benefits management in large Australian organizations. Inf. Manag. **41**(1), 13–24 (2003)
33. Lystad, J.: Det er ingen skam å snu - erfaringer fra Mattilsynet og NAV. Presentation given at Conference of the Agency for Public Management and eGovernment (DIFI), 6 December 2017
34. Olaussen, S., Tendal, Ø., et al.: KSP-rapport nr. 1 for Modernisering av IKT i NAV - Rapport til Finansdepartementet og Arbeids- og sosialdepartementet, Versjon: 1.0 (2015)
35. Rabbee, N., Coull, B.A., Mehta, C.: Power and sample size for ordered categorical data. Stat. Methods Med. Res. **12**, 73–84 (2003)
36. Sawilowsky, S.S.: New effect size rules of thumb. J. Mod. Appl. Stat. Methods **8**(2), 596–599 (2009)
37. Shenhar, A.J., Dvir, D., Levy, O., Maltz, A.C.: Project success: A multidimensional strategic concept. Long Range Plan. **34**(6), 699–725 (2001)

38. Tanilkan, S.S., Hannay, J.E.: Perceived challenges in benefits management–a study of public sector information systems engineering projects. In: 2022 IEEE 24th Conference on Business Informatics (CBI), June 2022
39. Terlizzi, M.A., Albertin, A.L., de Oliveira Cesar de Moraes, H.R.: IT benefits management in financial institutions: practices and barriers. Int'l J. Project Manag. **35**(5), 763–782 (2017)
40. Tian, C., Manfei, X., Justin, T., Hongyue, W., Xiaohui, N.: Relationship between omnibus and post-hoc tests: An investigation of performance of the F test in ANOVA. Shanghai Arch. Psychiatry **30**(1), 60–64 (2018)
41. Tomczak, M., Tomczak, E.: The need to report effect size estimates revisited. An overview of some recommended measures of effect size. Trends Sport Sci. **1**(21), 19–25 (2014)
42. Ward, J., Daniel, E.: Benefits Management: How to increase the Business Value of Your IT Projects, 2nd edn. Wiley, New York (2012)
43. Ward, J., Taylor, P., Bond, P.: Evaluation and realisation of IS/IT benefits: an empirical study of current practice. Eur. J. Inf. Syst. **4**, 214–225 (1996)
44. Williams, T., et al.: A cross-national comparison of public project benefits management practices - the effectiveness of benefits management frameworks in application. Prod. Plan. Control **31**, 1–16 (2020)
45. Yin, R.K.: Case Study Research: Design and Methods, Applied Social Research Methods Series, 3rd edn., vol. 5. Sage Publications 2003)
46. Zachariassen, E.: Nav stanser IT-prosjekt til 3,3 milliarder - Moderniseringsprogrammet var feil metode. Nav får skryt fra statlig ekspert, article published 25 October 2013

Towards Situational Process Management for Professional Education Programmes

Dennis Wolters[(✉)] and Gregor Engels

Department of Computer Science, Paderborn University, Paderborn, Germany
{dennis.wolters,engels}@uni-paderborn.de

Abstract. Designing and running professional education programmes involves various processes that responsible parties must manage. The knowledge gathered during development and with each new programme iteration is seldom externalized and it cannot be guaranteed that it will be applied in the next programme or iteration. This work-in-progress paper proposes a situational process management approach for professional education programmes. The basis for our approach is a modelling language to describe the high-level perspective of such programmes. Processes, best practices and existing content elements can be extracted from these models and added to a knowledge base alongside situational factors in which these items apply. If a relevant situation is observed in a model representing a professional education programme, the applicable items from the knowledge base are suggested to users. Our approach allows persisting the knowledge gained while developing/running professional education programmes and makes it accessible to others.

Keywords: Professional education · Process management

1 Introduction

Professional education is crucial in finding, developing and retaining highly skilled employees [12]. Companies turn towards education providers to develop and run professional education programmes. Examples of education providers are companies providing education on their products, companies focused on professional education or universities. Depending on the size, a company may even have a dedicated department that serves as an education provider. Education providers gain insights and refine their processes with each new programme and iteration. This gained knowledge is not always documented or taken into account when developing a new programme or doing another iteration of an existing one. For instance, a designer might not recall a lesson learned due to a high workload, or a different person is responsible for a programme.

Many instructional design processes exist [1,4,5,8] to develop education programmes and there is no one-size-fits-all. Instead processes have to selected and adapted based on the situation [3]. This selection and adaptation is often done based the experience of instructional designers. Unfortunately, not everybody

© The Author(s), under exclusive license to Springer Nature Switzerland AG 2022
D. Taibi et al. (Eds.): PROFES 2022, LNCS 13709, pp. 235–242, 2022.
https://doi.org/10.1007/978-3-031-21388-5_16

developing and running a professional education programme is an experienced instructional designer or even educated in the field [14]. Hence, standard practices maybe unknown and learning from more experienced colleagues, literature and past projects is crucial.

In this paper, we present our ongoing work in assisting with the design and management of professional education programmes. Our research follows the design science research method from Kuechler and Vaishnavi [11], which is structured into "Awareness of Problem", "Suggestion", "Development", "Evaluation" and "Conclusion". The awareness of the problem of missing process management assistance while designing and running professional education programmes is based our work in this area, discussion with fellow education providers and literature. To address this, we suggest a situational process management approach for professional education programmes that can extract and store knowledge on processes and best practices and offer them in relevant situations. The approach builds upon our modelling approach for professional education programmes outlined in [16]. The paper provides insights on the development phase, and we plan to evaluate our approach in a user study once development is completed.

The remainder of this paper is structured as follows: Sect. 2 covers related work. Section 3 describes the context of professional education programmes. Section 4 explains our situational process management approach for professional education programmes and its current development status. Section 5 concludes the paper and gives an outlook on future work.

2   Related Work

This paper is concerned with designing and running education programmes, which falls within the instructional design scope. Moreover, we apply techniques from Situational Method Engineering (SME). The following discusses related work from instructional design and existing SME approaches.

ADDIE [5] is probably the most well-known instructional design process. It is an acronym for Analysis, Design, Development, Implementation and Evaluation. The interpretations of ADDIE reach from a waterfall-like process to a description of basic life cycle phases occurring in an instructional design project [3]. The Successive Approximation Model (SAM) is an Agile instructional design process [1]. While ADDIE phases can still be mapped to SAM, it advocates shorter development iterations and early testing by using prototypes and preliminary versions of programmes. Further process models exist like Dick and Carey Model [4] or ASSURE [8]. Our approach does not dictate a specific process but instead suggests processes based on given situations. Hence, these processes can be incorporated as suggestions into our approach.

The IMS Learning Design Specification (IMS-LD) [10] is an XML-based format for describing online learning programmes. In contrast to the modelling language that is the basis for our approach, IMS-LD targets eLearning and the related design/management processes are not covered. STOPS [2] is a curriculum visualisation and development technique. Its focus is on course structures and aspects like educators, time planning or the intended audience are neglected. MISA [14] is an instructional engineering method to build IMS-LD-compliant learning programmes. While we stay agnostic of concrete processes, they define their own design process. In contrast to our approach, the educational design assistant myScripting [13] provides more in-depth assistance in designing learning activities but the process management aspect is not their focus.

SME approaches exist for software engineering projects in general [9] as well as for specific types of projects, e.g. software migration projects [7]. SME approaches also exist in fields outside of software engineering, e.g. Gottschalk et al. [6] apply this technique to business model development and Tsai and Zdravkovic [15] for developing digital business ecosystems. While the terminology, application fields and details of these approaches differ, the core ideas remain the same: Store existing knowledge in a repository, identify situations in which the knowledge is applicable and assist in its application. These core ideas are also the basis for our approach.

3   The 3Ps of Professional Education Programmes

In this section, we provide the context for our work by explaining the 3Ps of professional education programmes: product, people and processes. Most of the presented concepts also apply to other types of education programmes. Nonetheless, there are differences regarding the 3Ps depending on the type of programme, e.g. university study programmes require an accreditation process.

As visualised in the left part of Fig. 1, the **product** is a professional education programme requested by a company and provided by an education provider. Professional education programmes consist of a number of educational activities which address the goals a company is pursuing with such a programme. Usually a programme runs for multiple iterations, each with a new cohort of participants. For instance, new talents are identified and trained regularly in talent development programmes. Programmes are updated based on changing company needs or evaluations, e.g. assessment results or feedback of participants.

We can differentiate between various types of **people** on each side. On the company's side, we can differentiate between clients and participants. Clients are the representatives of a company that request a programme and work together with education providers to create and run it. The participants are the audience for which a programme is intended, e.g. new employees or talents.

On the side of education providers, we can distinguish between designers, educators and managers. Designers are responsible for designing professional education programmes that address the needs of a company. For this, designers closely work together with clients. Once the learning goals of a programme, the intended audience and the client's environment are understood, designers involve educators. Together they develop the educational activities that help reach these learning goals, are suited for the audience and fit the company's environment. Different types of educators exist, e.g. instructors, coaches or subject matter experts, and they are involved in developing activities and their

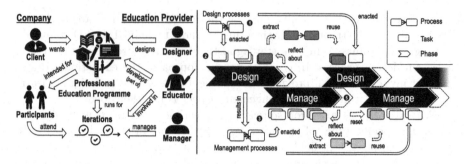

Fig. 1. Visualisation of people and product on the left and processes on the right. Dashed content on the right indicates additions of our approach.

execution. While educators are involved in executing individual activities, programme managers are responsible for the broader management of an iteration. For instance, managers schedule the activities, book rooms, provide participants and educators with information and collect feedback.

Designer, educator and manager are roles and a single person can have multiple roles. Additionally, throughout the lifetime of a programme, the people having these roles change. A designer might manage the first few iterations until a programme is mature enough that someone else can continue managing it.

Regarding the **processes** related to a professional education programme, we distinguish between design and management processes. In the right part of Fig. 1, we visualised their interconnection and already hinted at what is added by our approach. Explanations of our additions (dashed content starting in ❹ and ❺) are given in Sect. 4.

Design processes (see ❶) are typically based on a instructional designer's expertise and/or instructional design processes from literature, such as ADDIE [5], SAM [1], Dick and Carey [4] or ASSURE [8]. Design processes are concerned with analysing what is needed, designing a programme addressing the needs and developing the actual content. Furthermore, design processes also cover the adaption of a programme based on feedback. During the design of a programme, designers and educators perform certain tasks (see ❷). Some of these tasks occur due to the design process, e.g. perform need analysis. In contrast, other tasks are added ad hoc because they were not covered by the initial design process or represent refinements to more actionable tasks. The design phase does not necessarily need to be finished before an iteration of a programme starts. Assume a programme consists of two one-week modules. When the first module runs, the second may still be under development.

A set of management processes may result as part of the design phase (see ❸). Similar to the design phase, various tasks are performed by managers in the manage phase. While some of these tasks result from of the management processes, managers identify and perform additional tasks as they manage a programme. Based on feedback and assessment results, a programme is adapted, which again requires a design phase before the next iteration starts.

4   Situational Process Management for Professional Education Programmes

This section explains how people designing and managing professional education programmes can be supported by suggesting processes, best practices and existing content elements in relevant situations. As mentioned at the end of Sect. 2, our approach follows the core ideas of situational method engineering of externalizing knowledge, giving situation-specific recommendations and assisting in the application. The following gives an overview of how our approach incorporates these ideas and explains the current development status.

4.1   Solution Overview

Figure 2 shows an overview of our situational process management technique for professional education programmes. As a basis for our approach, we propose the Professional Education Programme Modelling Language (PEPML) that allows describing professional education programmes across their entire life cycle.

PEPML focuses on the high-level perspective of professional education programmes and allows the usage of existing tools for detailed planning. For instance, a designer might state that a programme contains an assessment, which is realized as a quiz in a learning management system. In any case, designers create high-level descriptions of programmes, but they are usually spread across multiple informal documents, e.g. slides, spreadsheets or drawings. With PEPML, the high-level description is formalized and the descriptions are reusable. The effort for designers to create such models can be reduced by leveraging information from existing tools. For instance, PEPML allows to specify tasks for any part of an education programme and integrates with existing project management tools to provide more advanced task management capabilities. Additionally, task information can be retrieved from these tools and added to PEPML models. Moreover, PEPML models are persisted in a Neo4j[1] graph database, which makes them queryable. Further details are outlined in [16].

The possibility to query and reuse (parts of) PEPML models is the basis for the knowledge base used for storing and applying gained knowledge from past professional education programmes and iterations. To fill this knowledge base, we suggest a reflection phase after each design/manage phase, as indicated by ❹ and ❺ on the right side of in Fig. 1. In this reflection phase, designers and managers look at the tasks performed in the design/manage phase. Since PEPML allows managing tasks in relation to the programme, it is possible to view tasks based on individual entities of a programme, such as a specific activity like an instructor-led session on a particular topic. During reflection, designers and managers can then state if it was a one-off or recurring task. In the simplest case, recurring tasks can be reset and put into the backlog for the next iteration. Resetting tasks already helps repeating of a programme. Additionally, we allow externalizing the process knowledge represented by these tasks.

---

[1] https://neo4j.com.

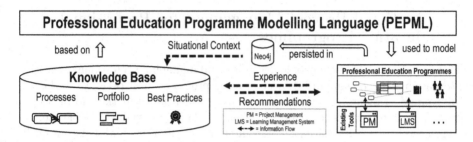

Fig. 2. Overview of our situational process management technique for professional education programmes

A task may be one out of a sequence of tasks always occurring in a specific situation. Such a process can be extracted, the situation in which it applies can be described and both be added to the knowledge base. For instance, a process consisting of tasks like "Ask instructor for availability", "Set Date/Time for Session", "Inform Instructor About Date/Time" and "Send Online Meeting Link" is typical for instructor-led online sessions. We utilize Neo4j's query language Cypher to describe applicable situations since PEPML are persisted in a Neo4j graph database. Parameterized query templates are used to simplify the description of applicable situations. In particular, we have such a query template for describing the type of educational activity. These parameterized query templates reduce the effort of writing a full Cypher query to providing parameter values, e.g. the activity type. PEPML models are queried to check if a particular situation occurs, and the tasks or processes applicable in the respective situation are recommended to the designer or manager. If they follow the recommendation, the respective tasks are added to the task backlog for the next iteration.

In addition to processes, the knowledge base can also contain best practices and a portfolio of existing content elements. A best practice could be a process recommendation, e.g. remind participants about handing in a deliverable. Other types of best practices exist as well, like ensuring in an international programme that online sessions are scheduled during working hours for all participants, using virtual background themes as conversations for online programmes or having a break at least every 90 min. Best practices which are not processes are hard to apply automatically but suggestions can be given. For instance, information on participants could be extracted from a learning management system and reflected in the PEPML model. A suitable timeframe for delivery can be suggested automatically using this information.

With each education programme, education providers also build a portfolio of content elements that designers can reuse in other programmes. Such elements can be catalogued based on topic or type and added to the knowledge base. The portfolio forms the basis for new programmes and can provide alternatives if elements need to be replaced in an existing programme.

4.2 Status of Development

We have developed a metamodel for PEPML and a visual syntax to describe dependencies between elements and the temporal structure of an education programme. To model the dependencies and the temporal structure, we have developed an app for the digital whiteboard Miro[2]. Basing our modelling tool support on Miro makes it also suitable for remote collaboration with clients. We have already successfully used PEPML in the analysis and design of a new professional education programme provided by the Software Innovation Campus Paderborn.

PEPML models are extracted from Miro and persisted in a Neo4j graph database, as indicated in Fig. 2. PEPML has basic support for defining tasks and their relation to entities of an education programme. Additional support for task management is realized by integrating with existing project management tooling. For now, we implemented an example integration with the project management tool OpenProject[3], but it is not a tight coupling to a specific tool.

Similar to the integration with OpenProject, we plan to integrate other existing tools, like learning management systems that manage participants and activities or file storage solutions used for storing and distributing materials. Thereby, designers and managers can rely on existing tooling but simultaneously have the benefits provided by our approach. Tool support for filling the knowledge base and extracting processes by reflecting on done tasks is currently under development.

5 Conclusion and Future Work

Not every professional education programme is developed or run by experienced instructional designers. Hence, it is vital that proven processes, best practices or existing content elements are suggested when relevant. This paper presents our ongoing work towards a situational process management approach for professional education programmes. A modelling language is used to describe professional education programmes on a high abstraction level and manage tasks related to elements of a programme. By reflecting on these tasks, processes that apply in specific situations can be extracted. These processes as well as best practices and existing content elements can be stored in a knowledge base. The models representing professional education programmes are used to suggest applicable elements from the knowledge base. Thereby, this knowledge can be shared and recalled automatically in relevant situations.

In the future, we plan to conduct a user study to evaluate the benefits of our approach. Moreover, by tracking tasks in correspondence to elements of a programme, processes and situational factors could be deduced automatically using process mining techniques.

---

[2] https://miro.com.
[3] https://openproject.org.

References

1. Allen, M.W., Sites, R.: Leaving ADDIE for SAM. American Society for Training and Development, Alexandria (2012)
2. Auvinen, T., Paavola, J., Hartikainen, J.: STOPS: a graph-based study planning and curriculum development tool. In: KOLI CALLING 2014, pp. 25–34. Association for Computing Machinery, New York, NY, USA (2014)
3. Branch, Robert Maribe, Kopcha, Theodore J..: Instructional design models. In: Spector, J. Michael., Merrill, M. David., Elen, Jan, Bishop, M.. J.. (eds.) Handbook of Research on Educational Communications and Technology, pp. 77–87. Springer, New York (2014). https://doi.org/10.1007/978-1-4614-3185-5_7
4. Dick, W., Carey, L., Carey, J.O.: The Systematic Design of Instruction. Pearson Education Ltd., Upper Saddle River (2005)
5. Gagne, R.M., Wager, W.W., Golas, K.C., Keller, J.M., Russell, J.D.: Principles of Instructional Design. Wiley Online Library, New York (2005)
6. Gottschalk, Sebastian, Yigitbas, Enes, Nowosad, Alexander, Engels, Gregor: Situation- and domain-specific composition and enactment of business model development methods. In: Ardito, Luca, Jedlitschka, Andreas, Morisio, Maurizio, Torchiano, Marco (eds.) PROFES 2021. LNCS, vol. 13126, pp. 103–118. Springer, Cham (2021). https://doi.org/10.1007/978-3-030-91452-3_7
7. Grieger, Marvin, Fazal-Baqaie, Masud, Engels, Gregor, Klenke, Markus: Concept-based engineering of situation-specific migration methods. In: Kapitsaki, Georgia M.., Santana de Almeida, Eduardo (eds.) ICSR 2016. LNCS, vol. 9679, pp. 199–214. Springer, Cham (2016). https://doi.org/10.1007/978-3-319-35122-3_14
8. Heinich, R., Molenda, M., Russel, J.D., Smaldino, S.E.: Instructional Media and Technology for Learning. Pearson Education Ltd., Upper Saddle River (2002)
9. Henderson-Sellers, B., Ralyté, J., Ågerfalk, P.J., Rossi, M.: Situational Method Engineering. Springer, Heidelberg (2014). https://doi.org/10.1007/978-3-642-41467-1
10. IMS Global Learning Consortium: Learning Design Specification version 1 (2003). http://www.imsglobal.org/learningdesign/
11. Kuechler, B., Vaishnavi, V.: On theory development in design science research: Anatomy of a research project. Eur. J. Inf. Syst. 17(5), 489–504 (2008)
12. Kyndt, E., Dochy, F., Michielsen, M., Moeyaert, B.: Employee Retention: Organisational and Personal Perspectives. Vocat. Learn. 2(3), 195–215 (2009)
13. Müller, C., Erlemann, J.: Educational design for digital learning with myScripting. In: EDEN Conference 2022 (2022)
14. Paquette, G., de la Teja, I., Léonard, M., Lundgren-Cayrol, K., Marino, O.: An Instructional Engineering Method and Tool for the Design of Units of Learning. In: Learning Design: A Handbook on Modelling and Delivering Networked Education and Training, pp. 161–184. Springer, Heidelberg (2005). https://doi.org/10.1007/b138966
15. Tsai, Chen Hsi, Zdravkovic, Jelena: A Foundation for design, analysis, and management of digital business ecosystem through situational method engineering. In: Serral, Estefanía, Stirna, Janis, Ralyté, Jolita, Grabis, J.ānis (eds.) PoEM 2021. LNBIP, vol. 432, pp. 134–149. Springer, Cham (2021). https://doi.org/10.1007/978-3-030-91279-6_10
16. Wolters, D., Engels, G.: Model-driven Design and Management of Professional Education Programmes. In: ICSOB'22 Companion Proceedings. CEUR Workshop Proceedings, CEUR-WS.org, (in press)

Change Management in Cloud-Based Offshore Software Development: A Researchers Perspective

Muhammad Azeem Akbar[1]([✉]) [ORCID], Kashif Hussain[2], Saima Rafi[3],
Rafiq Ahmad Khan[4], and Muhammad Tanveer Riaz[5] [ORCID]

[1] Software Engineering, LUT University, 53851 Lappeenranta, Finland
`azeem.akbar@lut.fi`
[2] Computer Science, National College of Commerce and Education, Hasilpur 63000, Punjab, Pakistan
[3] Epartment of Informatics and Systems, University of Murcia, Murcia, Spain
[4] Department of Computer Science and IT, University of Malakand, Malakand, Pakistan
[5] Department of Mechanical Mechatronics and Manufacturing Engineering, UET Lahore, Faisalabad Campus, Faisalabad, Pakistan

Abstract. Cloud based Offshore Software Development Outsourcing (COSDO) concept is complex and comes with various challenges, specifically related to the Requirements Change Management (RCM) process. This study aims to investigate the success factors (SF) that could positively influence RCM activities in COSDO firms and to propose a theoretical framework for the investigated aspects. A systematic literature review (SLR) method was adopted to investigate SF. Finally, based on the investigated factors, we developed a theoretical framework that shows the relationship between the identified factors and the implementation of the RCM process in the COSDO domain. The findings of this study could help researchers and practitioners address the key issues of the RCM process in COSDO organizations.

Keywords: Systematic Literature Review (SLR) · Change management · Success factors

1 Introduction

A software development phenomenon, COSDO spanned social, geographic, and temporal borders among its members [1]. More than half the software development industry has adopted COSDO [2–4] because of its financial characteristics. 20% of client software development organizations re-appropriate their improvement activities to vendor associations to benefit from COSDO phenomena, as revealed in a Standish Group study [5]. As a result of the lower development costs, the availability of a skilled labor, and better market access, there has been a noticeable rise in offshore software development outsourcing [5]. Despite this, the COSDO team also deals with questions that aren't

© The Author(s), under exclusive license to Springer Nature Switzerland AG 2022
D. Taibi et al. (Eds.): PROFES 2022, LNCS 13709, pp. 243–251, 2022.
https://doi.org/10.1007/978-3-031-21388-5_17

commonly seen in a collocated setting [6, 7]. Their inability to effectively carry out-growth exercises, is a result of communication and coordination issues [1, 4]. The poor requirement change management could cause system decline [8–10]. Standish Group led a survey of thirteen thousand programming projects and featured that 18% of the tasks were flop because of poor management of requirements change [11].

Models of management that may effectively implement the RCM cycle have been created based on various requirements. Niazi et al. [12], for instance, established a model for RCM utilizing the CMMI level-2 specialized practice known as SP 1.3-1. A request, validation, implementation, verification, and update are all steps in the model's lifecycle. Research undertaken with RCM experts yielded insights into the model's design based on the existing empirical data. RCM problems faced by industry practitioners have been addressed in another study by Keshta and colleagues [14]. Initiate, validate, verify, implement, update, and release are the six primary steps of the Keshta et al. paradigm. However, the model does not allow the execution of RCM operations in large organizations that are internationally scattered [14]. It does, however, provide a detailed guideline on how to make the requested adjustments to the criteria. In overseas software development concept, Akbar et al. [14] develop a change management model in offshore software development domain (Fig. 1). They cover important aspect of change management in overseas software development, but communication aspects does not fit well with this model. Using these models and frameworks, members of the team may more easily adapt to changing requirements, create high-quality products, cut down on development costs, and meet customer expectations [15–17]. The RCM cycle has only been included into the collocated and offshore software development environment by these models and frameworks, but COSD issues have been completely ignored [18].

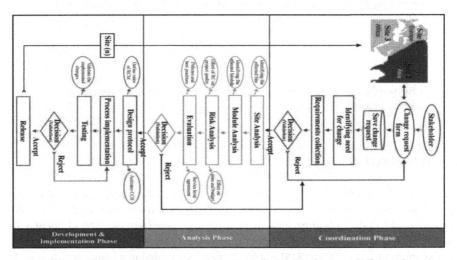

Fig. 1. Change management in outsources software development [reference]

In order to fill this knowledge void, we will design a model for measuring the maturity of software requirements changes and implementations (SRCMIMM). Based on the idea of leaving maturity models in many elements and domains that could affect the RCM program in COSDO environment, the proposed model (SRCMIMM) will be developed. In this article, we have covered the first stage toward the construction of the model, which is the preliminary phase of discussing the success elements of RCM. We followed the step-by-step process of systematic literature review to conduct this study and report on RCM's success factors [26]. Understanding the success aspects of change management can assist the experts in addressing the essential areas of requirement change prior to implementing the RCM method. These research questions were formulated to address the issue under consideration:

[RQ1]: What are the key success factors for RCM in COSDO, reported by researcher?

[RQ2]: What would be an example of a hypothetical RCM success factors framework?

2   Research Methodology

Research Questions
In Sect. 1, we talk about the research questions formulated to perform this study.

Systematic Literature Review (SLR) Process
Considering Chen et al. [27] study, we have selected the most appropriate digital libraries. The selected digital repositories include: "IEEE Xplore", "ACM Digital Library", "Springer Link", "Wiley Inter Science", "Google Scholar" and "Science Direct". There are variety of ways to search in digital libraries. Using RCM and COSDO research publications, phrases from study questions and their alternatives we came-up with a list of synonyms for search terms. The primary keywords and their alternatives were concatenated utilizing the Boolean "OR" and "AND" operators to process the search strings.

In next steps we have performed the quality assessment along with inclusion and exclusion criteria. By conducting the QA check, we examine that according to the AQ checklist, 70% of the selected studies score more than 80%. The detailed results are given at: https://tinyurl.com/m7z4fzwp.

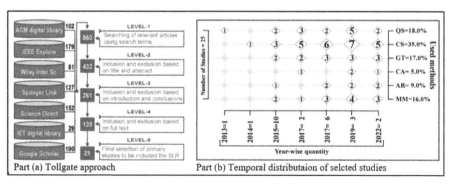

Fig. 2. Literature selection and temporal distribution

Finally, 25 essential studies were shortlisted from total of 860 articles by following the five periods of the tollgate approach (Fig. 2). The Fig. 2 also shows the temporal distribution of selected studies along with research methodology used in those studies. The most common used methods are case studies (CS = 35.0%) and mixed method (MM = 16.0%). List of the selected studies along with quality score is given at: https://tinyurl.com/m7z4fzwp, and each study makes identical with 'SP' to introduce them as SLR primary studies. From 25 primary research, a list of success factors (SF) was compiled. According to the primary studies, the research questions of this study were evaluated. The result is given in Table 1.

3   Results and Discussions

This section presents the findings of the SLR.

3.1   RQ1 (Identified Success Factors)

Using the detailed guidelines provided in Sect. 2 of the SLR technique, our team has conducted an in-depth analysis of the chosen 25 primary studies and identified ten success factors for RCM. Table 1 lists the identified success factors with frequency distribution.

Table 1. Identified success factors

S. No	Success factors	Frequency (N = 25)	Percentage of occurrence
SF1	Management support	12	48
SF2	Strong relationship with practistioners	13	52
SF3	Information sharing	15	60
SF4	RCM expertise	10	40
SF5	Roles and responsibilities	8	32
SF6	Effective RCM leadership	11	44
SF7	RCM process awareness	16	64
SF8	Skilled human resources	14	56
SF9	Standard and procedures	11	44
SF10	3Cs (communication, coordination, control)	18	72

SF1 (Management Support, 48%)

Organizational management must support and commit to requirement change management efforts during the system development process [SP4]. Khan et al. [SP23] emphasized the importance of involving both upper and lower management in the RCM process. For prerequisites and change management, Lavazza [SP10] said that the management's involvement and commitment could be helpful. The following hypothesis has been developed based on the given discussion.

Hypothesis (H1): Management support has a positive association with RCM process in COSDO.

SF2 (Strong Relationship Between Practitioners, 52%)

Effective communication and coordination between team members in a dispersed context are two key indicators of strong working relationships [SP25]. Strong relationship assist towards team, risk and system quality management [SP4]. The following hypothesis has been developed based on the above discussion:

Hypothesis: (H2): Strong relationship between the practitioners could positively impact the RCM activities in COSDO environment.

SF3 (Information Sharing, 60%)

Dispersed team members' ability to exchange program-related information has been identified as a critical component of the RCM's success [SP25]. Data management, coordination and knowledge integration for change management can be simplified with proper information exchange [SP2]. As a result, we believe that information exchange could have a favorable effect on COSDO's RCM efforts.

Hypothesis (H3): The RCM process in a COSDO context benefits from the sharing of information among the team members.

SF4 (RCM Expertise, 40%)

According to Damian et al. [SP3], the level of RCM expertise is defined as the ability of RCM practitioners to successfully and efficiently implement requested requirements modification. According to Khan et al. [SP25], the RCM process's success is dependent on the practitioners' skills level. In order to successfully complete the project activities, the RCM team members must have the necessary skills and knowledge [SP11, SP25]. As a result of this, our working hypothesis is as follows:

Hypothesis (H4): RCM expertise has a positive association with the RCM process in COSDO.

SF5 (Roles and Responsibilities, 32%)

According to Williams et al. [SP2], assigning roles and tasks to the appropriate team members is critical. Furthermore, according to Firesmith et al. [SP5], the roles and duties of the team members must be clearly defined, which is essential for controlling and managing misconceptions during the execution of RCM process activities.

Hypothesis (H5): Roles and responsibilities allocation process positively correlate with RCM activities in COSDO.

SF6 (Effective RCM Leadership, 44%)

Management of change control board (CCB) should have suitable leadership talents and knowledge to assess and deal with change demands, according to Ahmed et al. [SP17]. You'll be able to quickly and effectively respond to the certain modification request [SP10, SP16] because of your leadership qualities. COSDO's RCM process relies heavily on strong leadership to move forward. Therefore, we come up with the following theory.

Hypothesis (H6): Effective RCM leadership has beneficial influence on RCM process in COSDO environment.

SF7 (RCM Process Awareness, 64%)

According to Mavin et al. [SP20], organizational management must promote RCM team members for training and certification. By conducting workshops and seminars, you may successfully convey the RCM practices, and this will help encourage your employees. This is why we came up with the following theory.

Hypothesis (H7): Successful change management in the COSDO context necessitates familiarity with the RCM methodology.

SF8 (Skillful Human Resources, 56%)

The significance of skill human resources has been shed light in different research studies [3, 7, 8]. Minhas et al. [SP21] described that, the practitioners should have expertise and good skills in the computer programming and task the management areas. They further referenced that people with an appropriate skill are the foundations of distributed software development. Therefore, we hypothesize that:

Hypothesis (H8): Key to the success of COSDO's RCM implementation is a well-trained workforce.

SF9 (Standard and procedures, 44%)

According to Khan et al. [SP25], it is critical to use the correct standard and method when implementing RCM process activities. The members of the team should adhere to the established guidelines, frameworks, and standards. Additional research by Khan et al. [25] suggests that the RCM programme may fail because of the lack of established RCM models and standards. Consequently, we hypothesize that:

Hypothesis (H9): Formal RCM standards and procedures have positive association with change management program in COSDO.

SF10 (3Cs "COmmunication, Coordination, Control", 72%)

Knowledge transfer between distributed team members and the method they use to better contact are referred to as 3Cs by Khan et al. [SP23]. Both coordination and control depend on the communication. Strong communication channels could help the distributed teams to properly coordinate and control the RCM activities [3]. Control is "the process of keeping goals, strategies, principles, and quality levels in place" [3]. Coordination and control deals with the key components (i.e., budget, time, and quality), that are essential for the execution of the RCM process [SP25].

Hypothesis (H10):   3Cs "communication, coordination, control" has a positive association with the RCM process in COSDO.

3.2 RQ5 (Proposed Theoretical Framework)

Theoretical framework was proposed for highlighting the association between the independent variables (success factors) and dependent variable (RCM implementation in COSDO) as shown in Fig. 3. The hypothetical relationship between the two types of variables (independent, dependent) is briefly discussed in Sect. 3.1. In addition, we come up with total ten hypotheses (H1–H10) to empirically investigate the association of the reported success factors and RCM implementation process. The empirical study will conduct in the future, where we will comparatively analyze the results of SLR and the hypotheses reported in this study.

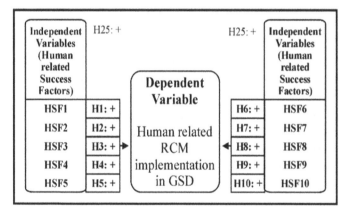

Fig. 3. Proposed theoretical framework

4 Threats to Validity

The first author of this study leads the SLR process and extract data. Thus, there is a possibility of biased data collection as the one member can be prejudiced. But the other authors' participation in the inspection of the SLR results arbitrarily to observe any difficulties that might occur has attempted to reduce the danger in this way.

In most recent studies, the key causes of the observed success variables have not been explored, and this could be a threat to the study's internal validity. There is a good chance that specific types of factors are overrepresented in some research. In addition, because the researchers in the 25 primary papers chosen are primarily from academia, it is possible that they lack familiarity with contemporary RCM process methods in the software development business.

5 Conclusion

Increasing number of global software development (COSDO) projects motivated us to scrutinize the success factors that could positively impact the RCM activities in COSDO environment. Conducting SLR, total of 10 RCM success factors were identified, and five of these factors were deemed the most critical. RCM's important success criteria highlight the areas on which an organization must place a heavy emphasis.

Moreover, the identified factors were also presented in the form of theoretical framework considering ten hypotheses we came up with to show the association of the independent variables (success factors) with the dependent variable (RCM implementation in COSDO). The aim of the theoretical framework is to compare the findings of this study (SLR) and the industrial empirical study that will conduct in the future. The comparative study of both data sets (SLR, empirical) will give insight about the available literature and the views of the RCM practitioners working in COSDO industry. In future, we will design a factors based conceptual model to make RCM process successful in COSDO organizations.

References

1. Niazi, M., El-Attar, M., Usman, M. and Ikram, N. (2012) GlobReq: A Framework for Improving Requirements Engineering in Global Software Development Projects. 4th IEEE International Conference on Global Software Engineering, Ciudad Real, 14–15 May 2012, 166–170
2. Minhas, N.M., Zulfiqar, A.: An improved framework for requirement change management in global software development. J. Softw. Eng. Appl. 7(9), 779 (2014)
3. Shameem, M., Kumar, C., Chandra, B., Khan, A.A.: Systematic review of success factors for scaling agile methods in global software development environment: a client-vendor perspective. In: 2017 24th Asia-Pacific Conference Software Engineering Conference Workshops (APSECW), pp. 17–24. IEEE, December 2014
4. Lai, R., Ali, N.: A requirements management method for global software development." AIS: Adv. Inf. Sci. 1(1), 38–58 (2013)
5. Khatoon, A., et al.: Requirement change management for global software development using ontology. Emerg. Technol. (ICET), In: 2013 IEEE 9th International Conference on. IEEE (2013)
6. Khan, A.A., Basri, S., Dominic, P.D.D.: A propose framework for requirement change management in global software development. In: International Conference on Computer & Information Science (ICCIS), 2012, vol. 2. IEEE (2012)
7. Ramzan, S., Ikram, N.: Requirement change management process models: activities, artifacts and roles. In: IEEE Multi topic Conference, INMIC 2006, Islamabad, 23–24 December 2006, 219–223 (2006). https://doi.org/10.1109/INMIC.2006.358167
8. Lai, R., Ali, N.: A requirements management method for global software development. Adv. Inf. Sci. 1(1) 38–58 (2013)
9. Khan, J.K: Systematic review of success factors and barriers for software process improvement in global software development, IET Softw. (2016) ISSN 1751-8814
10. J. Zhu, et al., "The Requirements Change Analysis for Different Level Users," in Intelligent Information Technology Application Workshops, 2008. IITAW 2008. International Symposium on, 2008, pp. 987–989

11. Khan, A.A., Keung, J., Niazi, M., Hussain, S., Ahmad, A.: Systematic literature review and empirical investigation of barriers for software process improvement in global software development: client-vendor perspective. Inf. Softw. Technol. **87**, 180–205 (2017). .https://doi.org/10.1016/j.infsof.2017.03.006

12. Riaz, M.T., et al.: A wireless controlled intelligent healthcare system for diplegia patients [J]. Math. Biosci. Eng. **19**(1), 456–472 (2022). https://doi.org/10.3934/mbe.2022022

13. Niazi, M., et al.: A model for requirements change management: implementation of CMMI level 2 specific practice. In: International Conference on Product Focused Software Process Improvement. Springer, Berlin, Heidelberg (2008)

14. Khan, A.A., Shuib, B., Dominic, P.D.D.: A process model for Requirements Change Management in collocated software development. In: 2012 IEEE Symposium on E-Learning, E-Management and E-Services (IS3e), IEEE (2012)

15. Akbar, M.A., Shafiq, M., Ahmad, J., Mateen, M., Riaz, M.T.: AZ-Model of software requirements change management in global software development. In: 2018 International Conference on Computing, Electronic and Electrical Engineering (ICE Cube), pp. 1–6. IEEE November 2018

16. Akbar, M.A., et al.: Multicriteria decision making taxonomy of cloud-based global software development motivators. IEEE Access **8**, 185290–185310 (2020). https://doi.org/10.1109/ACCESS.2020.3030124

17. Akbar, M.A., Mahmood, S., Alsalman, H., Razzaq, A., Gumaei, A., Riaz, M.T.: Identification and prioritization of cloud based global software development best practices. IEEE Access **8**, 191242–191262 (2020). https://doi.org/10.1109/ACCESS.2020.3031365

18. Akbar, M.A., et al.: Requirements change management challenges of global software development: an empirical investigation. IEEE Access **8**, 203070–203085 (2020). https://doi.org/10.1109/ACCESS.2020.3035829

19. Riaz, M.T., Ahmed, E.M., Durrani, F., Mond, M.A.: Wireless android based home automation system. Adv. Sci. Technol. Eng. Syst. J. **2**(1), 234–239 (2017)

Half-Empty Offices in Flexible Work Arrangements: Why Are Employees Not Returning?

Darja Smite[1,2(✉)] ⓘ, Nils Brede Moe[1,2] ⓘ, Anastasiia Tkalich[1] ⓘ,
Geir Kjetil Hanssen[1] ⓘ, Kristina Nydal[1], Jenny Nøkleberg Sandbæk[1],
Hedda Wasskog Aamo[1], Ada Olsdatter Hagaseth[1], Scott Aleksander Bekke[1],
and Malin Holte[1]

[1] SINTEF Digital, Trondheim, Norway
{nils.b.moe,anastasiia.tkalich,geir.k.hanssen}@sintef.no,
hedda.aamo@live.no, malin@byremoholte.no
[2] Blekinge Institute of Technology, Karlskrona, Sweden
darja.smite@bth.se

Abstract. Although the forced working from home during the pandemic crisis seem to have ended, many knowledge workers choose to continue working predominantly from home as a partial or permanent practice. Related studies show that employees of companies from various industries, diverse in size and location, prefer to alter working in the office with working at home, coined as hybrid or flexible working arrangements. As a result, offices remain empty, managers are confused, and organizational leaders do not know what to do with the often-expensive rental contracts. In this short paper, we investigate the employee presence in the offices in two software companies and dive deeper into the reasons behind the preferences to work remotely, and practices that help to attract employees back into the offices. The latter are based on the qualitative analysis of interviews and survey responses. Our findings suggest that between the fall of 2021 and the summer of 2022, the offices were half-empty and that, on average, the daily office presence varies between 13–30%. The peaks of office presence in both companies are on Wednesdays, reaching up to 50% during weeks with low virus spread in one company, and in the spring months in 2022 in the other company. The reasons for remote work include behavioral and practical motivations, factors related to office equipment and facilities, and the nature of the work tasks.

Keywords: Remote work · Work from home · WFH · Hybrid workplace

1 Introduction

The forced work from home (WFH) during the pandemic in many software companies demonstrated that perceived productivity not only remains stable, but in some cases improves [1]. As a result of the better-than-expected experiences with remote working, many employees choose to continue WFH if not full time, then at least part-time, altering

© The Author(s), under exclusive license to Springer Nature Switzerland AG 2022
D. Taibi et al. (Eds.): PROFES 2022, LNCS 13709, pp. 252–261, 2022.
https://doi.org/10.1007/978-3-031-21388-5_18

the days in the office with days at home [2], which is referred to as a *hybrid model* or *flexible work arrangement* [3]. As offices remain half-empty, there is a growing realization that flexible work arrangements are here to stay [3, 4].

While there are many benefits of WFH [2, 5, 6], remote communication weakens the connection between colleagues [7, 8] and makes non-verbal signals harder to notice, even in video meetings [9]. Communication challenges significantly complicate the team managers' job, which often depends on the ability to observe, communicate in-the-moment feedback with team members, engage in conversations, and debate [3]. This is not only about Tayloristic managers who rely on command and control, but equally about participative and supportive leadership styles prevalent in agile environments. Besides, face-to-face interactions are important for commitment, assistance, collaboration, and knowledge sharing [9]. Similarly, innovation depends on face-to-face contact with customers and colleagues, who generate ideas in planned and spontaneous brainstorming sessions and conversations [3]. Such cooperation finds place in the hallways, by the coffee machines, water coolers, copiers or between meetings [3, 9]. Evidently, attracting the employees back into the offices is of crucial importance, but how to achieve this when even onboarding is performed remotely and the degree of flexibility the company offers becomes the make-or-break point for many job seekers? Motivated by the hybrid future challenges, in this short paper, we seek to answer the following RQs:

RQ1: *How often are employees present in the office?*

RQ2: *What hinders and motivates employees to visit the office?*

The rest of the short paper is organized as follows. In Sect. 2 we outline the background and motivation for our study. Section 3 details the methodology and describes the empirical cases. In Sect. 4 we share our findings, discussed in Sect. 5.

2 Background

A growing number of organizations implement flexible work arrangements for their employees, including Google, Telenor, Microsoft, and Spotify. Further, a large amount of research studying WFH have concluded that remote work per se does not hinder software engineers [10] and is here to stay [1, 4, 6, 11]. Yet, However, little literature has attempted to predict how flexible arrangements should be performed in practice.

Researchers report more effective individual task solving and work coordination when WFH due to better focus time, fewer interruptions, more time to complete work, more efficient meetings, and more comfortable work environments [5, 12]. In our earlier study of pandemic WFH, we found fewer distractions and interruptions, increased scheduling flexibility, and easier access to developers [1]. Ford et al. report that a more flexible schedule and lack of commute improved work-life balance [5]. On the other hand, working in isolation is not challenge free. Tasks that require coordination or brainstorming are not easy to perform virtually [1]. A study of remote coordination when co-located teams work exclusively from home [6] found that coordination needs increase when working remotely since group cohesion and communication are impaired, and these challenges will likely persist in hybrid work. Similar concerns arise from our work [1] that found remote work to weaken socialization and informal communication, team cohesion, problem-solving, and knowledge sharing. Alienation of colleagues and weakening of the knowledge networks has been found over time as employees continue working remotely [7]. Some companies introduce work policies that constrain the number of WFH days or introduce mandatory office days [13]. However, forced office presence can backfire with increased attrition as a study suggests that 40% of employees who currently WFH, even if only one day a week, would seek another job if employers require a full return to the office [2]. Thus, there is a growing interest in research that would shed light on why employees prefer to work remotely.

3   Methodology

This short paper presents a multiple-case holistic study [14], in which we study one phenomenon, the role of office-based work, in two companies. We collected data from two companies, Knowit and Sparebank 1 Dev, developing software-intensive products, that implemented WFH during the pandemic, and reopened the offices in fall 2021 with an episodic WFH advice during winter 2022. We ended data collection in the summer of 2022. The choice of the companies was driven by convenience sampling, i.e., both companies are a part of an ongoing research project and had readily available data that helps to answer our research questions.

Knowit is a large IT consultancy company with a large presence in Nordic countries and other parts of Europe. The focus of this study was Knowit Objectnet, a subsidiary with approximately 175 consultants, located in Oslo. Consultants mostly work for clients, often at the client site, but they may also WFH, or from the main Oslo office. In April 2022 they moved to a brand new office downtown, which no longer offers free parking, deliberately has fewer work places than employees and is designed and equipped for physical meetings and socializing. But this does not mean that the management prefers remote working.

Sparebank 1 Dev is a Fintech company developing software for Norwegian Banks. The organization offers a wide area of services and caters to both the consumer and professionals. Counting both their in-house employees and consultants, Sparebank 1 had 650 employees at the moment of our study. The teams had considerable freedom in their work, and the company regularly performed surveys to understand the work-from-home situation. The bank offices were renovated during the pandemic.

Data Collection and Analysis. Data collection in Knowit was done by a team of summer internship students (authors five-ten) under supervision (authors one-four), while the second author collected data in Sparebank 1 Dev. We collected office presence data from desk booking records at Knowit and access card entries at Sparebank 1 Dev, extracted and analyzed in Excel quantitatively (Figs. 1 and 2). Qualitative data containing personal preferences for working in the office or WFH was obtained from interviews in Knowit and employee surveys in Sparebank 1 Dev. In Knowit, we performed 12 semi-structured interviews, which were transcribed and analyzed using thematic analysis (See a summary of data sources in Table 1). Thematic analysis was done through open and axial coding with a constant comparison [15] resulting in a set of hypotheses and 32 themes. In Sparebank 1 Dev, we surveyed personal experiences receiving 244 responses from 650 employees (36%). Reasons for working remotely were extracted and comparatively analyzed together with responses from the qualitative interviews conducted in Knowit.

Table 1. Overview of the data sources.

Company	Data collection	
	Office presence	Reasons for remote working
Knowit	Archival data from a desk booking system Seatit during 2021–10–13–06–04–2022	12 semi-structured interviews about remote work preferences and office presence in June 2022
Sparebank 1 Dev	Access card data during 2021–10–01–30–04–2022	244 survey responses on remote work preferences and office presence October and December 2021

4 Results

4.1 Office Presence

Our analysis of the office presence in both companies shows that the offices during the studied time period varied but has been relatively low (see Fig. 1 and Fig. 2). In the fall 2021 the office presence in Knowit was below 25% and below 50% in Sparebank 1 Dev. One exception in Sparebank 1 Dev was the third week of October when the company organized an after-work social event with food, drinks and activities.

In winter, the new pandemic wave started and employees were advised to WFH, which is evident in the low office presence during January 2022. In spring 2022, the office presence in Knowit returned to the level of the fall 2021 and started to spike to around 60–70% on certain days in the end of March motivated by the office-based social events. In Sparebank 1 Dev, January and February showed low office presence, which returned in the beginning of March to the level evidenced in the fall 2021 (around 50%).

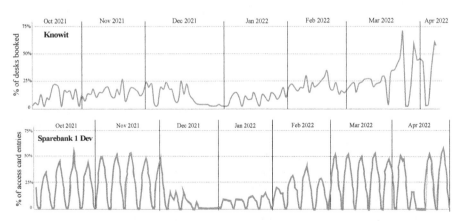

Fig. 1. Overview of office presence in Knowit (desks booked per day, excluding days with no presence) and Sparebank 1 Dev (access entries per day, including weekends and holidays).

When plotting the average number of office visitors from October 2021 to April 2022 during the different workdays, patterns across the companies varied. In Knowit, the week started with the lowest office presence on Monday (13%), and the highest on Wednesday (19%), followed by Friday (18%, the afterwork day). In contrast, the office presence in Sparebank 1 Dev was evenly distributed with the highest presence on Wednesdays and the lowest on Fridays. In general, it is worth noting that the weekly patterns in the two companies are quite different. We believe this is because in Knowit we collected data about the desks booked, while in Sparebank 1 Dev we solicited data from the access card entries, which represents the office presence more accurately.

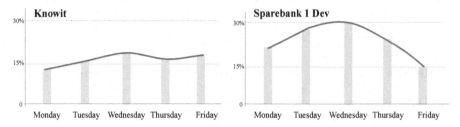

Fig. 2. Average office presence during the week.

4.2 Factors that Motivate Remote Working

In the following, we summarize the key factors that we found to be linked with the motivation of software developers to work remotely.

Long or inconvenient commute to the office was the main reason for WFH in Sparebank1 Dev (over 1/2 of respondents). 1/3 commuted to work by train, 1/3 by tram or bus and 2/3 required more than 1,5h to get to work one way. In Knowit, commute was also an important factor that motivated WFH. After moving into a new building without a parking lot, employees had to walk, bike, or use public commute, which was more difficult than driving for some. Commute time also made a difference. Two interviewees admitted that living closer would make them visit the office more, as one said: "*I use an express bus about 45–50 min to work and over 1h back. It affects my preferences for WFH.*"

Superior Ability to Focus At Home: Home office environment was reported to be superior in providing the ability to concentrate as reported by the survey respondents from Sparebank1 Dev. One respondent commented: "*For me, the noise [in the office] is a real problem. I use a lot of energy just to keep my concentration*".

Better-Equipped Home-Office: In Knowit and Sparebank 1 Dev, company management provided financial support for purchasing office equipment for WFH (desks, chairs, and monitors) that remained at homes after the reopening of the offices. Thus, many informants mentioned better conditions for working at home.

Convenience for Running Personal Routines at Home: Some interviewees mentioned various ways their needs are difficult to meet in the office. For example, for one interviewee, it was about the gym and exercising. Convenience for completing personal issues when working from home was also mentioned in Sparebank 1 Dev's survey.

Habit of Working From Home: Besides, the very habit of WFH motivated during the pandemic times resulted in many continuing to work remotely, as reported by a large number of respondents in the Sparebank1 Dev's survey. As a respondent commented: *"I believe that people have become comfortable with home offices and the extra time it brings to the family etc.".*

Schedule Full of Online Meetings: We learned that some in Sparebank1 Dev found it impractical to commute to the office when their workdays are packed with online meetings. As a respondent commented, *"[We have] challenges with equipment in meeting rooms, not adapted for having [hybrid] meetings. When you are a presenter, you need two screens. So, when there are many meetings it is more practical to sit at home."*

Other Reasons. A few participants also mentioned better coffee machines, food, lighting and air ventilation at home, and the good weather conditions. As one of the interviewees described: *"When the weather is nice, I rather stay at home".*

4.3 Factors that Motivate Office Presence

In the following, we summarize the key factors that we found to be linked with the motivation to work in the office.

Social Interaction with Colleagues: Many informants in both companies revealed that the prime purpose for coming into the office is to meet colleagues and get to know new people. To make offices more attractive, both companies invested into more social zones. A few interviewees said that being in the office provided the unique feeling of inspiration from interactions with colleagues that is absent when WFH. A recently hired developer from Knowit explained, *"I love being in the office. I enjoy working with people. I like meeting other people. I absolutely depend on that to do a good job, I depend on being happy, so I want to be in the office as much as possible."*

Presence and Availability of Colleagues in the Office: Many commented about the desk booking system that allowed checking who else is planning to be in the office on a particular day. Colleagues' presence had a profound influence on the personal choices: people were more likely to come in when others reported to be onsite and when their calendars did not show that they were fully booked, and vice versa. As an interviewee from Knowit explained: *"It's not only about knowing that Erik will be at work, but also that Erik actually has time for visitors".* A product manager further explains *"If I see that my colleague booked a desk, I book one next to him".*

Tasks that Require Interaction: Several interviewees mentioned that the nature of work and the nature of daily tasks might have a large influence on their decision to come to the office. For example, some meetings were easier to conduct and more productive when held in person, while individual tasks felt more appropriate for focused work in isolation at home. As one interviewee explained: *"So I'm trying to set up this work-from-home day for focused work, I need concentration then. The meetings are also best held in the office".* These onsite meetings included planning meetings, brainstorming meetings, first customer meetings, workshops, and task assignment meetings.

Enhanced Work/Life Balance: A few mentioned the need to come to the office to differentiate between work and home and improve the work/life balance. An interviewee who preferred the office explained: *"It's a lot easier for me to separate work from not working when I'm in the office [...]. When I'm at home, [...] it blurs a little"*.

Other Reasons: Finally, some of the interviewees mentioned reasons that would occasionally influence their choice for commuting to the office, such as the need to leave the house and additional errands planned that require commuting anyway, which all increased the likelihood of working in the office but were not permanent motivators. Besides, a few research participants speculated that better food in the canteens, coffee machines and availability of a gym in the office would make them change their mind and come more often to the office.

5   Concluding Discussion

In this short paper, we explored the state of office presence in two Norwegian companies, the reasons for continuing working remotely and factors that motivate office presence, after the reopening of the society (see a summary of our findings in Table 2). The current work policies in both companies allowed employees to spend two days at home and three days at the office, which were subject to negotiation in the team, and with the customers and the manager. At Knowit, employees also need to have a suitable home-office to be allowed to work from home.

Employee Presence in the Office (RQ1): Our findings provide field evidence that supports the results of surveying employee preferences for continuing to work remotely [2, 13]. We found that the offices in both companies were half-empty with the lowest attendance in the winter months, Jan-Feb 2022. The office presence increased only in Knowit due to the long-term negative impacts of remote working and the importance of social interaction. However, it is also fair to state that we are still witnessing the transition from the forced WFH during the pandemic to what we believe will be the hybrid work arrangements. As a respondent from Sparebank 1 Dev explains: *"It's difficult to go from 100% home office to 100% office in such a short time, now Norway just opened too, and before that there was a lot of infection, so a longer transition phase is needed"*.

Factors that Influence Where People Work From (RQ2): We identified factors that motivate remote work and factors that motivate office presence. The reasons can be behavioral, practical or task-related. The main driver of WFH is the commute. One implication is that if a company wants a high office presence, they need to be located in a place that is easy and fast to reach. However, it might be also fair to expect that companies situated in large cities, in general, might resort to low office presence, as found in a study comparing employee preferences for WFH in large cities vs smaller towns [13]. The main driver for being at the office is socialization. If one's colleagues are not there, it is more likely that one will stay at home. We also found that, besides being able to see who else is planning to be at the office, it is also important to see colleagues' availability and thus the ability to socialize. Seat booking systems and solutions inside the joint digital calendars can thus be used to increase the awareness of who is available in the office.

Further, as we found that social activities right after work motivate people to come to the office, social arrangements can be used as a tool to increase office presence. While

Table 2. Factors motivating remote work and office presence.

Factors motivating remote work			Factors motivating office presence		
	Knowit	Sparebank 1 Dev		Knowit	Sparebank 1 Dev
Long or inconvenient commute to the office	X	X	Social interaction with colleagues	X	X
Superior ability to focus at home (noise and interruptions in the office)	X	X	Presence of colleagues in the office and their availability	X	X
Better-equipped home office	X	X	Tasks that require interaction	X	
Convenience for running personal routines while at home	X	X	Enhanced work/life balance	X	
Habit of working from home		X	Need to leave the house	X	
Schedule full of online meetings		X	Additional errands planned that require commuting anyway	X	
Better conditions at home: coffee, food, lighting or ventilation		X			
Good weather conditions	X				

all developers and team members appreciate focused time alone, they also appreciate being with their colleagues. Our findings indicate that employees might be more likely to work onsite in the offices that satisfy the majority of their needs, including zones for collaboration and social interaction and silent zones for focused, undisturbed work, good quality office equipment, and good quality food in the canteen.

Yet, our findings are likely to indicate that hybrid work arrangements, in which the office days are mixed with the WFH days, are likely to remain the trend for the future, since this is an easy way to satisfy the diverse needs of the employees. This is also consonant with prior studies that demonstrated that WFH has both its advantages and disadvantages [1, 3, 5, 7, 10, 12]. A fair implication is that companies might consider repurposing their office space on the days the offices are mostly empty, since the office presence never reaches 100%. The solutions to this problem include hot desking, having onsite work divided into shifts, moving to smaller offices or maybe renting out company offices to startups or partners on the days with the lowest attendance. However, we also warn that employee preferences might change, as we transition away from the pandemic and as the habit of working in the office resurface.

5.1 Future Work

Our exploratory findings show a need for a deeper understanding of what are good teams and company strategies when introducing flexible work arrangements. It is evident that when software developers, product owners, or managers know that their colleagues will be working onsite, it is more likely that they will show up themselves. Therefore, more research is needed to study desk booking systems and other systems providing visibility into the office presence. Further, the current task a team member is working on affects the preferences for where to work from. Our related study [16] confirms that developers chose to perform tasks with vague requirements in co-location while individual tasks that require focus are best performed at home. Future research shall explore how to plan and organize a hybrid work week optimized for individuals, the team, and the company. As long commute time is the main driver for working from home, more research is needed to understand how team members' geographical distance to the office affects hiring and team composition strategies. Should companies that expect a high office presence employ people only living near the office? Should companies compose teams based on the member location and with similar office presence preferences in mind? Finally, future research shall also explore how to onboard new team members, given that traditionally new hires are onboarded through close onsite mentoring requiring high office presence both from the new people and their senior team members.

Acknowledgements. We thank Knowit AS and Sparebank 1 Dev for their engagement in our research, and the Norwegian Research Council for funding the research through the projects Transformit (grant number 321477) and 10xTeams (grant number 309344).

References

1. Smite, D., Tkalich, A., Moe, N.B., Papatheocharous, E., Klotins, E., Buvik, M.P.: Changes in perceived productivity of software engineers during COVID-19 pandemic: the voice of evidence. J. Syst. Softw. **186**, 111197 (2022)
2. Barrero, J.M., Bloom, N., Davis, S.J.: Let Me Work From Home, or I Will Find Another Job. University of Chicago, Becker Friedman Institute for Economics Working Paper, 2021–87, (2021)
3. Gratton, L.: How to do hybrid right. Harv. Bus. Rev. **99**(3), 66–74 (2021)
4. Šmite, D., Moe, N.B., Klotins, E., Gonzalez-Huerta, J.: From forced working-from-home to voluntary working-from-anywhere: two revolutions in telework. J. Syst. Softw. **195**, 111509, (2022)
5. Ford, D., et al.: A tale of two cities: software developers working from home during the covid-19 pandemic. ACM Trans. Softw. Eng. Methodol. **31**(2), 1–37 (2022)

6. Santos, R.E., Ralph, P.: Practices to improve teamwork in software development during the COVID-19 pandemic: an ethnographic study. CHASE arXiv preprint arXiv:2203.09626 (2022)
7. Yang, L., et al.: The effects of remote work on collaboration among information workers. Nat. Hum. Behav. **6**, 43–54 (2021)
8. Blanchard, A.L.: The effects of COVID-19 on virtual working within online groups. Group Process. Intergroup Relat. **24**(2), 290–296 (2021)
9. Fayard, A.L., Weeks, J., Mahwesh, K.: Designing the hybrid office. from workplace to "culture space." Harv. Bus. Rev. (2021)
10. Russo, D., Hanel, P.H., Altnickel, S., Van Berkel, N.: The daily life of software engineers during the covid-19 pandemic. In: 2021 IEEE/ACM 43rd International Conference on Software Engineering: Software Engineering in Practice (ICSE-SEIP), pp. 364–373 (2021)
11. Ozkaya, I.: The future of software engineering work. IEEE Softw. **38**(5), 3–6 (2021). https://doi.org/10.1109/MS.2021.3089729
12. Oliveira, Jr. E., et al.: Surveying the impacts of COVID-19 on the perceived productivity of Brazilian software developers. In: Proceedings of the 34th Brazilian Symposium on Software Engineering, pp. 586–595 (2020)
13. Smite, D., Moe, N.B., Hildrum, J., Huerta, J.G., Mendez, D.: Work-from-home is here to stay: call for flexibility in post-pandemic work policies. *arXiv preprint* arXiv:2203.11136 (2022)
14. Yin, R.K.: Case Study Research: Design and Methods. Sage, Thousand Oaks (2009)
15. Seaman, C.B.: Qualitative methods in empirical studies of software engineering. IEEE Trans. Softw. Eng. **25**(4), 557–572 (1999)
16. Sporsem, T., Moe, N.B.: Coordination strategies when working from anywhere: a case study of two agile teams. In: Stray, V., Stol, K.J., Paasivaara, M., Kruchten, P. (eds.) Agile Processes in Software Engineering and Extreme Programming. XP 2022, LNBIP, vol. 445. Springer, Cham. (2022). https://doi.org/10.1007/978-3-031-08169-9_4

Refactoring and Technical Department

Technical Debt in Service-Oriented Software Systems

Nikolaos Nikolaidis[1]([✉]) [iD], Apostolos Ampatzoglou[1] [iD],
Alexander Chatzigeorgiou[1] [iD], Sofia Tsekeridou[2] [iD], and Avraam Piperidis[2]

[1] University of Macedonia, Thessaloniki, Greece
nnikolaidis@uom.edu.gr
[2] NetCompany-Intrasoft, Athens, Greece

Abstract. Service-Oriented Architectures (SOA) have become a standard for developing software applications, including but not limited to cloud-based ones and enterprise systems. When using SOA, the software engineers organize the desired functionality into self-contained and independent services, that are invoked through end-points (API calls). At the maintenance phase, the tickets (bugs, functional updates, new features, etc.) usually correspond to specific services. Therefore, for maintenance-related estimates it makes sense to use as unit of analysis the service-per se, rather than the complete project (too coarse-grained analysis) or a specific class (too fine-grained analysis). Currently, some of the most emergent maintenance estimates are related to Technical Debt (TD), i.e., the additional maintenance cost incurred due to code or design inefficiencies. In the literature, there is no established way on how to quantify TD at the service level. To this end, in this paper, we present a novel methodology to measure the TD of each service considering the underlying code that sup-ports the corresponding end-point. The proposed methodology relies on the method call graph, initiated by the service end-point, and traverses all methods that provide the service functionality. To evaluate the usefulness of this approach, we have conducted an industrial study, validating the methodology (and the accompanying tool) with respect to usefulness, obtained benefits, and usability.

Keywords: Technical debt · Service analysis · Endpoint analysis · Quality

1 Introduction

The notion of Technical Debt (TD) was introduced by Ward Cunningham [1] to describe the shipment of first-time code with inefficiencies, due to early deployment. To quantify the amount of technical debt, various types of TD and ways of identification / quantification have been proposed in the literature. Since one of the most recognized types of TD, both in industry [2] and academia [3] is the code TD, a significant number tools [4] have been developed to quantify code TD: i.e., identify code inefficiencies and estimate the required effort for fixing them. The main *mechanism beneath code TD identification / quantification is source code static analysis*, pointing to classes that violate certain

© The Author(s), under exclusive license to Springer Nature Switzerland AG 2022
D. Taibi et al. (Eds.): PROFES 2022, LNCS 13709, pp. 265–281, 2022.
https://doi.org/10.1007/978-3-031-21388-5_19

pre-defined quality rules. For example, calculate specific metric scores (e.g., cognitive complexity or lines of code) that when surpass a certain threshold an inefficiency is recorded.

One of the most known tools for TD identification / quantification is SonarQube, which is able to quantify the technical debt of projects written in almost any programming language. SonarQube counts the number of inefficiencies and calculates the remediation time that is needed to bring the code to an optimum (or near-optimum) state. According to Tamburri et al. [5] this process is, and should be, a continuous practice, since the concept of an optimum state is constantly changing. However, despite the support for various languages and programming paradigms, the ***approach for the quantification of technical debt remains unchanged, regardless of the system architecture*** (e.g., whether the software is service-based or monolithic).

Lately, the Service-Oriented Architecture (SOA) has become quite popular due to its ability to create quick and easy applications by using existing micro-services [6]. In the SOA model, services form self-contained units of software that communicate across different platforms and languages to form applications. Communication takes place through their end points, while a loose coupling is promoted to either pass data or coordinate activities. Several studies have assessed different kinds of technical debt quantification in SOA, introducing several approaches [7, 8, 9]. Most of these ***research approaches treat each service as a black-box*** and quantify TD, based on the effort to compose these services. For instance, by focusing on their interface: e.g., the amount of exchanged data, the different types of data, the number of different services, etc. On the other hand, on the limited cases that TD quantification treats services as a white-box, the amount of TD is calculated again with SonarQube (or similar tools)—***considering as the unit of analysis either the whole project or isolated classes***, without taking into account the fact that the project's architecture differs substantially than a software project that is not based on services.

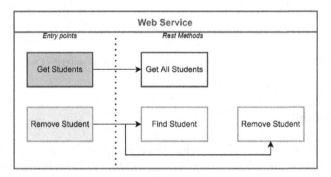

Fig. 1. Generic SOA structure example.

To address the specificities of developing service-based systems, when it comes to maintainability assessment, our paper introduces the SmartCLIDE approach that is tailored for such systems. One of the most prominent characteristics of service-based systems is that they encapsulate, to some extent, traceability in their design: i.e., they *offer end-points that deliver a very specific functionality, and this stands for an entry point to the method call sequence in the code that offers this functionality*–see Fig. 1. By considering that maintenance tickets, coming either from the customer or the preventive maintenance team, are usually describing the problem in a natural language [10], it becomes evident that a specific requirement can be easily spotted. Next, given the identification of the corresponding end-point, the effort estimation for serving the ticket can be more accurately performed, by focusing only on the parts of the system that are successively invoked through the end-point. In other words, *using end-points as the units of analysis for technical debt quantification, in service-based software system, seems as a promising and more accurate alternative compared to working at the class- or at the system-level*. As a first step towards this approach, we have developed a methodology and a supporting tool (in the form of Eclipse Theia extension) that quantifies the amount of TD that a developer will face when performing maintenance to all parts of the system that are invoked through a specific end-point of a given web service. To assess the TD at the method level, we relied on SonarQube so as to identify code inefficiencies, reuse the estimated remediation time, enabling the TD quantification of each endpoint. To validate both the methodology and the accompanying tool, we conducted an empirical study, involving 15 developers, working in 5 companies, spread across Europe. The evaluation targeted the exploration of current approaches for TD quantification in SOA systems, the validation of the approach, and the usability assessment of the tool.

2 Related Work

Technical Debt Quantification: One of the most known studies in the field of TD management has been performed by Alves et al. [11], who performed a systematic mapping study on over 100 primary studies. Alves et al. described the different types of TD and the strategies for identifying TD items. Based on their results, it becomes evident that the majority of the top indicators of TD presence is the existence of "code smells". The same conclusion has also been validated by the first secondary study on TD management, by Li et al. [12]. The identification of code smells is the basis of TD quantification, by the majority of TD tools. Due to existence of various such tools, a recent direction has pursued the identification of the best and more accurate one [4, 12, 13]. Even though there have been a lot of studies and even methodologies that combine different tools [14], there isn't still a consensus on the quantification of TD. Nevertheless, according to a recent analysis of TD quantification tools [4], it seems that the most popular TD quantification tool is SonarQube [15], which is widely known to track the quality and maintainability of source code. The tool quantifies TD by multiplying the number of issues from each category, with the time that is needed to resolve these issues. To provide TD in monetary terms, effort in time can be multiplied with an average man-hour cost. The origins of SonarQube lie on the SQALE method, to provide a pyramid of issues that aids in TD prioritization.

Technical Debt in SOA and Services: Bogner et al. [16] conducted a large-scale survey in order to find the TD management techniques used in service- and microservice-based systems. The results suggested that SonarQube is the most used tool, followed by

FindBugs. Moreover, 67% of the participants have responded that they do not treat maintainability differently, compared to non-service-based software development. However, an important fraction of the participants, mentioned that they should. Finally, 26% of the participants apply somewhat different controls, and approximately 7% mentioned significantly different treatments. Therefore, the authors concluded that it is very important to distinguish between the service-based and the non-service systems. Additionally, based on other studies, it becomes evident that the only analyzed code part of the web services is the interface of the different web services [17, 18]. For instance, Ouni et al. [17] created a machine learning approach to detect defects in the interfaces of web services. The results suggested that this methodology is promising for specific types of services; however, for others (e.g., REST) the methodology is not applicable. Regarding the TD management of microservice-based application, we can find a variety of studies that are focused on defining what can be considered as technical debt in SOA and how it can be quantified. For the quantification of TD in service-based systems all related studies focus outside the code of each service and explore the composition of the services [19]. For instance, de Toledo et al. [8] organized an industrial case study to identify (among others) what is TD in SOA. The results of the study suggested that, as TD we can characterize: (a) the existence of too many point-to-point connections among services; (b) the insertion of business logic inside the communication layer; (c) the lack of a standard communication model; (d) the weak source code and knowledge management for different services; and (e) the existence of different middleware technologies. Even though these issues are related more to the composition of services, it is clear that there is a need for TD evaluation, within the source code of each service. Similarly, the study by Pigazzini et al. [7] suggests that the existence of: (a) cyclic dependency; (b) hard-coded end-points; and (c) shared persistence can be characterized as indicators of poor quality in SOA. Nevertheless, we need to again make clear that for this study each end-point is treated as a black box, even though it's internals are critical in case of future changes. Furthermore, Taibi et al. [9] conducted a similar study and reported additional quality indicators. Among them, as the most important ones, the authors characterize: (a) hardcoded endpoints; (b) no API-gateway; (c) inappropriate service intimacy; and (d) cyclic dependency. Finally, some studies report as the main TD indicator the easiness of changing a microservice for another [9, 19].

3   SmartCLIDE Approach for Calculating TD of Services

In this section, we present the proposed approach for quantifying TD in service-based applications, bringing two important advancements, compared to the state-of-the-art: (a) in our approach services are not treated as black-boxes; and (b) we refine the unit of analysis from the project or class level, to the service level.

The *SmartCLIDE methodology* for quantifying the amount of TD that is accumulated within software services is straightforward. Since a service has a number of different entry points (e.g., end-points), we propose that each one of these end-points deserves its own evaluation of TD. In a way, each entry point could be treated as a different application, since it provides a distinct functionality. The benefit lies in the fact that TD analysis can highlight individual end-points which are in need of improvement, rather than blaming the entire project. The methodology is based on the generation of the call graph of the services end-points. With the term call graph, we refer to the user-defined methods that are being called successively from a given point in the code. This information is critical in order to report only the TD issues appearing in the methods invoked by the given end-point. By knowing the total TD issues reported for all the invoked methods, we are able to quantify the amount of TD that a developer will face, when maintaining the specific end-point from end-to-end, as effort (time) and in monetary terms. To be able to quantify the TD of each endpoint, we had to overcome two major challenges. First, the call graph construction should be initiated from a given starting point (e.g., method). To resolve this issue, the code of the target project should be parsed. To this end, we used the `JavaParser` library [20] which is a very well-known parsing library for Java projects (the downside is that currently only projects written in the Java programming language are supported). Given a source file, or in our case a project, the different syntactic elements are recognized and an `Abstract Syntax Tree` (AST) is generated. This AST is then analyzed by the `JavaSymbolSolver` and locates the declarations associated with each element. We should also note that `JavaParser` makes use of the Visitor design pattern to traverse the created AST and execute the desired operation on the visited nodes. In particular, we developed a new Visitor that finds the annotations of each user-declared method, to identify the methods that all end-points start from. We have been able to find the end-points of projects that use the `JAX-RS` specification, or the `Spring Boot framework`. Once the end-points of the project are known, we then created a Visitor that finds all the methods that are being called successively. For each method, we retain the file path as well as the methods' starting and ending lines.

Illustrative Example: In this subsection, we present an illustrative example through an open-source Java e-commerce software. The `Shopizer`[1] project contains a large number of endpoints as it exposes its functionalities through a RESTful API. As a first step, we analyzed the entire project with SonarQube. The project-level analysis yields all code inefficiencies and the time that is needed to resolve them, as follows:

```
TD: 478.8h / 14362.5€
Number of Issues: 3426
```

By applying the proposed methodology, we were able to map the total TD to the project end-point, and identified cases for which the total number is not representative. Below, we report our calculations for two endpoints: namely, `Shipping Modules` and `List Permissions`. The call graphs for the two end-points are presented in Fig. 2 and Fig. 3, respectively. By applying the proposed methodology for the two cases, we have calculated TD, as follows:

It goes without saying that by focusing TD quantification at the end-point level, a more accurate information is provided, allowing stakeholders to take more informed decisions: while the entire project appears to suffer from a large number of issues, the

---

[1] https://github.com/shopizer-ecommerce/shopizer.

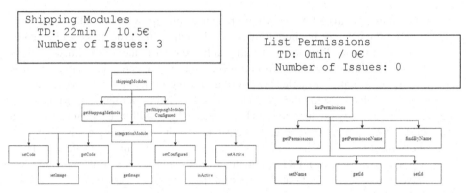

Fig. 2. Shipping modules example call graph   **Fig. 3.** List permissions call graph.

List Permissions end-point is code technical debt free (no TD-related issues); whereas the Shipping Modules end-point is responsible only for the very limited amount of three technical debt-related issues, not raising any alarm for the maintenance team. Therefore, we argue that differentiating between the healthy and problematic parts of a service-based project can help developers prioritize their refactorings, improve their effort estimation, and improve their decision-making processes.

SmartCLIDE Eclipse Theia Extension: The proposed approach for quantifying the TD of ser-vice-based systems is part of the SmartCLIDE project, and has been integrated into the SmartCLIDE IDE, as an Eclipse Theia Extension. Eclipse Theia is a web-based IDE that acts as a code editor, in which a developer is able to create and add extra functionalities as extensions or plugins. We chose to create an extension, due to the extra available functionalities that it offers, and the customizable User Interface (UI). With the only drawback being that the extensions in Theia cannot be dynamically added, as Theia needs to be built from the beginning with the selected extensions. But since the proposed approach is part of the SmartCLIDE IDE, this is not an important drawback, in the sense that the Theia image needs only to be built once, and then installed with the desired functionality. Moreover, with respect to the backend part of the system that undertakes the actual analysis, we have developed a web service that exposes all the necessary functionalities via a RESTful API.

The SmartCLIDE Eclipse Theia extension is an official Eclipse Research Lab project, and is freely available through the Eclipse Research Labs Git repository[2]. For research purposes, we provide online an already deployed instance of the Eclipse Theia, containing the proposed extension[3]. Once the Eclipse Theia is opened, the extension can be reached under the menu "View" through the "SmartCLIDE TD and Reusability" option. After that, the user is able to provide the URL of the git repository that he / she wants to analyse (GitHub, GitLab, etc.). Also, the project key of the SonarQube installation is required so that a new analysis is generated according to the git owner and git name (e.g., owner:name). By providing these values the user is able to start a new

---

[2] https://github.com/eclipse-researchlabs/smartclide-td-reusability-theia.
[3] http://195.251.210.147:3131.

analysis for a new project or load an existing analysis, through the "New Analysis" and "Project Analysis" buttons.

In Fig. 4, we present the analysis, i.e., the amount of TD for the entire project along with all the reported issues (SonarQube). By starting an "Endpoint Analysis" the user can take advantage of the proposed approach. The GUI action, enables the backend service, which locates all the end-points of the provided project and presents the results for them (Fig. 5). The extension is populated with all the end-points, along with the quantified TD amount for each service, as well as the number of issues that have been identified in the method call chain for each end-point. Finally, if the user expands a specific end-point, he / she will get access to the list of issues related to the specific endpoint, along with their criticality and remediation time.

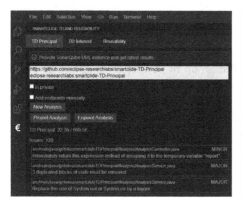   

Fig. 4. Tool instance of project analysis   **Fig. 5.** Tool instance of endpoint analysis.

Finally, through the Eclipse Theia Extension, the user can specify one or more end-points, getting results only on the selected endpoints—see "Add endpoints manually" in Fig. 6 providing the method and filename. We should note that since a method name is not sufficient (there can be many methods with the same name), we require the full method signature. The method signature has the following format:

```
[accessSpecifier] [static] [abstract] [final] [native] [synchronized]
returnType methodName ([paramType [paramName]]) [throws exceptionsList]

private void getGivenEndpointsFromAllFiles
(List<RequestBodyEachEndpoint> requestBodyEachEndpointList) throws File-
NotFoundException, IOException
```

4 Validation Study Design

In this section we report the protocol that we have followed for validating the proposed approach and the accompanying tool, in an industrial setting. To evaluate the current status of TD quantification in software-based systems, as well as the proposed approach and tool we have performed an empirical study, designed and reported, based on the guidelines of Runeson et al. [21].

Research Objectives: The goal of the validation is three-fold: (a) explore and assess the current state-of-practice for approaches and tools that can be used to quantify the TD of service-based systems; (b) validate the proposed approach; and (c) evaluate the developed Eclipse Theia Extension; leading to three research questions:

[RQ1] What are the adopted approaches and tools for TD quantification in service-based software development, in the context of the studied organizations?
[RQ1] How is the proposed approach evaluated by practitioners in terms of usefulness and ease-of-usage?
[RQ3] Does the developed endpoint-level analysis tool meet the expectations of the practitioners?

Study Design: The validation study was conducted with the participation of 15 developers in the field of software services. The group of developers is spread to 5 software industries across Europe (2 Large and 3 Small-Medium Enterprises). In terms of demographics: 4 participants have a low experience as backend developers (with about 1–3 years of experience), 4 of them are medium experienced (with about 4–8 years of experience) and 7 are highly experienced (with over 8 years of experience). The validation study was conducted in the form of a half-day workshop—see Table 1. The same workshop structure was replicated 5 times, one for every involved industry.

Table 1. Workshop Activities.

Activity	Duration
Introduction /Goals of the workshop	20 min
Interviews for RQ_1	20 min (for each participant)
Demonstration of end-point level analysis	20 min
Break	20 min
Interviews for RQ_2	30 min (for each participant)
Task RQ_3	20 min (for each participant)
Interviews for RQ_3	30 min (for each participant)

First, the researchers' team has first given a short introduction of TD in case some of the participants were not familiar with the terminology. Subsequently, the first part of the workshop that was aiming to understand the current practices, along with their benefits and limitations, was carried out so as to get acquainted with the TD practices that our study participants are aware of and use. The data collection was made in the form of interviews. At this point we need to note that a major parameter for opening up the workshop to 5 industries was the nature of RQ1, which required a broad recording of practices in SOA-based projects, obtained by various companies. For better organization and time monitoring, we have split each interview into three blocks. The questions asked during the interviews can be found as supplementary material[4].

Being aware of the current technical debt quantification status, we continued by presenting the proposed approach and the developed Eclipse Theia Extension. We demonstrated the approach and tool on how to quantify the technical debt amount for each end-point of the service, along with the examples presented in Sect. 3. Assuring that all participants have understood in sufficient detail the SmartCLIDE approach for TD quantification, and after a short break, we proceeded to the second round of interviews, aiming to shed light on RQ2. Finally, in order to assess the usability of the Eclipse Theia Extension, we needed to involve the participants in a simple task, so that they get a hands-on experience with the tool. In particular, each participant was asked to do the following actions through the Eclipse Theia Extension, for a private service of their own: (a) get and check the project analysis report; (b) get and check the end-point analysis report for all the endpoints; and (c) provide one or more end-points and get and check the analysis report. After completing the given task, the subjects participated in a final interview round, aiming to the evaluation of the functionality and usability of the tool (answer RQ3). The first block of this interview guide was related to functionality, whereas the second to usability. Usability evaluation was performed, based on the System Usability Scale (SUS) instrument [22].

Data Collection: To validate the proposed TD quantification approach and the corresponding tool implementation, we have relied on both quantitative and qualitative analysis. To synthesize qualitative and quantitative findings, we have relied on the guidelines provided by Seaman [23]. On the one hand, to obtain ***quantitative results***, we employed descriptive statistics. For usability, we assessed the total SUS score, along with the most common scales for interpretation, in terms of acceptance, adjective, and grade. On the other hand, to obtain the ***qualitative assessments***, we use the interviews data, which we have analyzed based on the Qualitative Content Analysis (QCA) technique [24], which is a research method for the subjective interpretation of the content of text data through the systematic classification process of coding and identifying themes or patterns. In particular, we used open coding to create categories, and abstraction. To identify the codes to report, we used the Open-Card Sorting [25] approach. Initially we transcribed the audio file from the interviews and analyzed it along with the notes we kept during its execution. Then a lexical analysis took place: in particular, we have counted word frequency, and then searched for synonyms and removed irrelevant words. Then, we coded the dataset, i.e., categorized all pieces of text that were relevant to a particular theme of interest, and we grouped together similar codes, creating higher-level categories. The categories were created during the analysis process by both the 3rd and the 4th author, and were

---

[4] https://www.dropbox.com/s/vagrr2wdc9p6nu9/SupplementaryMaterial.pdf?dl=0.

discussed and grouped together through an iterative process in several meetings of all authors. The reporting is performed by using codes (frequency table) and participants' quotes. Based on Seaman [23] qualitative studies can support quantitative findings by counting the number of units of analysis that certain keywords and compare the counts, or comparing the set of cases containing the keyword to those that do not.

5   Results and Discussion

In this section, we present the findings of our validation study, organized by research question. Along the discussion, codes are denoted with capital letters, where-as quotes in italics. In Table 2, we present the codes that have been identified along the interviews, accompanied by quotes and the number of participants that used them.

Table 2. Codes of the Qualitative Analysis.

Code	Quote	#
Accuracy	"I think it will be really accurate on the end-point understudy" "The challenge would be how it measures these endpoints with accuracy" "Having an approach like this, a developer can estimate the TD for the code path that is going to be executed for an end-point, or for any new feature" "it makes sense, I would try it" "…but is not reliable with the actual transform action that needs to be done: If I have 5 end-points with almost the same issues, I will see the same issues almost 5 times, and 1 fix will delete 5 issues"	14
No service specific TD	"No, not really, we are not changing anything in SOA" "We are interested more in scalability and reliability, but no special treatment for TD"	12
Prioritization	"…lets developers focus only to specific end-points (with the higher TD)" "I think it's a very good approach. It offers the keys that any manager needs in which issues to focus first." "Seems more structured and easier to focus on end-points that matter most" "Measuring each endpoint's TD, as a standalone application would be really helpful for the developers to understand the complexity of each service, to keep an eye on the most complicated ones"	10

(continued)

Table 2. (*continued*)

Code	Quote	#
Vosualization		8
Time Savings	"Probably requires less time to find issues" "if you are interested on specific functionalities its great because it saves you time to find the issues for a specific case"	6
Usefulness	"In terms of usability I think it's easy and helpful" "Seems simple and easy to use" "Its helpful to know how many issues you can met on each flow" "Seems easy and it make a lot of sense. It would be very helpful for services" "The other practices just perform a static code analysis and detect the code-level issues, but do not make the link to higher-level artifacts"	6
Need for Tailoring	"We follow the same model, regardless of business needs or the architecture" "No specific metrics and indicators (e.g., specific SOA-related metrics)"	4
Hidden parts of the system	"A limitation could be that complexity of hidden aspects of the end-point are ignored, such as related classes (i.e., entities or other utility classes)" "A limitation is that it will not count the functions and classes that are not called right now from end-points"	3
Monitoring	"The team could potentially watch the TD graph rate, as the project grows to monitor and deal with bad code early enough"	3
Rationalle	"…the TD analysis matches the thought process of developers" "…it is very close to what I do manually to check the quality the code, before maintenance"	2
Quality gates	"…for each new end-point that is added, in terms of not exceeding the average (or any limit) of TD that the project has configured"	1

Current Approach for Service TD Measurement: The vast majority of the participants in the study (~85%) have performed TD quantification at least one time into their projects; more than half of them rely their assessment on SonarQube. Other options for TD assessment in the participants' group of our study are: SIG, CAST; whereas for more generic quality assessment the participants have used: code review without tooling, Jaccoco, and CheckStyle. In terms of unit of measurement, most of the participants' organizations are recording the number of issues, since only 2 (out of 15) are recording the monetary values of TD, as calculated by SonarQube. The TD management practices target both front- and back-end components, but the majority of the participants of the study (since our goal was to propose a SOA-based approach) are focusing on back-end software development technologies. Additionally, 75% of the participants are willing to (and usually do) apply the suggestions that they receive from the technical debt management tool; whereas the frequency of getting such suggestions vary from a daily basis to a one-off evaluation before the first release of the project. In terms of prioritization, several options have been discussed by the participants, such as based on the tool assessment of criticality, priority to custom rules based on organization's standards, SonarQube severity, build blocking issues only, etc. Finally, based on the policy of the involved organizations, technical debt assessment is performed by project managers, software architects, or team leaders. Regarding the assessment of TD in SOA projects, the participants have claimed that they are not following a different strategy (NO SERVICE-SPECIFIC TD), compared to *"traditional"* software development. With respect to more *"generic"* quality assessment one participant mentioned the different quality properties that are of interest, such as scalability, availability, resilience, etc., but such run-time quality properties usually do not fall in the context of TD Management. In general, the participants are satisfied with process, raising two concerns: *"We have to follow the given model regardless the business needs or the architecture, and sometime this produces delays or inaccuracies"* and *"No specific quality metrics and indicators (e.g., specific SOA-related metrics)"* suggesting the need for some tailoring of the process (NEED FOR TAILORING). On the positive side, the well-established generic (i.e., non-SOA related) benefits of technical debt management have been highlighted, such as *"Automated reports, and in some cases good catches"*, *"Easy to explain and fix, with clear feedback"*, *"The code repo is cleaner and more secure"*, etc.

Evaluation of the Proposed Approach: This section reports on the evaluation of the proposed approach by the practitioners. More specifically, with respect to the accuracy of the results obtained by applying the approach, the mode response value was *"Accurate"* (4.0 out of 5.0), followed by *"Very Accurate"* (5.0 out of 5.0) given by 33% of the respondents. In total 86.6% of the practitioners characterized the results as *"Accurate"* or *"Highly Accurate"*. In terms of usefulness 93% of the participants graded the approach as either "Useful" or "Very Useful" (mode value: "Very Useful"). Finally, in terms of industrial-readiness of the approach, and how frequently would the developers use it in their daily routine, the mode value was "Sometimes" and "Often". Notably, there were no responses for "Never" or "Very Often". One of the main points that have been raised by the participants was the ACCURACY of the results that are obtained through the approach. The majority of the participants were positive in their evaluation on the accuracy of the obtained results (mentioning that *"they make sense"* or that *"they seem as very accurate"*), but some were hesitant: For instance, in terms of double-counting the same issue in the same class for the same end-point (e.g., if two end-points invoke the same method), or that accuracy in any kind (and with any tool) of TD quantification is challenging and probably not accurate. Also, the participants highlighted the USEFULNESS of the approach, e.g., in terms of TD items PRIORITIZATION and TD MONITORING. While discussing the main idea of the proposed approach, i.e., promoting the end-point as the main unit of analysis, some interesting findings have been identified. One of the most positive judgements on this part of the discussion was provided by a practitioner, describing the main benefit of the approach rationale, in terms of ACCURACY, as follows: "*The idea of measuring the TD from the entry point of a web service request is very nice, because any developer is aware of that, but Sonar cannot see that difference (compared to other types of projects). So having a tool like this, a developer can estimate the TD for the code path that is going to be executed for a single end-point, and even for any new feature*". In this round of discussion, it is important to note that no practitioner had a negative comment on the methodology, validating that the approach RATIONALE is conceptually very close to what a developer would do mentally. The importance of PRIORITIZATION management benefits, as well as in terms of bringing a highly systematic and structured process for TD items prioritization is service-based software development, was highlighted.

Finally, we discuss the benefits that the approach brings, compared to the state-of-practice approaches, as well as its limitations. In general, the participants were very positive on the proposed approach, and they acknowledge that it advances state-of-the-art, since "*it keeps all the benefits of existing tools and appends them*". A specific advancement compared to the state-of-the-art, as described by one practitioner suggests that this approach is not a simple source code analysis, but a more tailored and informative one: "*The benefit of the approach is that it focuses on the end-points and the source code that is required to execute them. The other practices just perform a static code analysis and detect the code-level issues, but do not make the very useful linking to higher-level artifacts*". Nevertheless, some participants mentioned that the proposed approach might lack in terms of ACCURACY since it does not evaluate some HIDDEN PARTS OF THE SYSTEM, such as "*related classes (i.e., entities or other utility classes)*", or "*functions and classes that are not called right now from end-points*", or "*configuration classes*". In addition, one practitioner brought up an interesting future feature of the approach that increases its potential. The suggestion would be to incorporate QUALITY GATES in the approach: i.e., check the quality of the code of every new end-point (compared to some pre-configured threshold) before the pull request before merging, and accept or reject it. Finally, one participant mentioned that the USEFULNESS of this approach might depend on the goals of the quality assessment: e.g., if the quality assurance team is interested in a panoramic view of the project quality, then the proposed approach is not useful. However, if the team wants to focus on some specific functionalities, the proposed approach "*is great because it saves you time to find the issues for a specific one case*" (TIME SAVINGS).

Evaluation of the Eclipse Theia Extension: In terms of ***Functional Suitability***, a high-level representation of the results is presented in Fig. 6. The stacked bar chart corresponds to the evaluation in a 0 to 10 scale of each main functionalities offered by the tool. As we can see there are no features of the tool that have been evaluated with a grade lower than 5, by any participant. The features that were best received by the practitioners were the two ways of VISUALIZATION of the results (light blue and orange bars). The two ways of visualization (at service and at project level) have received a similar evaluation. The slightly more positive evaluation of the visualization at the system level can probably be attributed to the habitual tendency of developers to check quality assurance evaluations at the project level. Nevertheless, the fact that the novel way of representation was as well adopted, as the one dictated by a habit of 5–10 working years, is a very positive indication for the success of the proposed approach. Regarding the ACCURACY of TD quantification, we can observe that it corresponds to the feature with most participants votes higher or equal to 8 out of 10 (sum of green, orange, and light blue bars)—meaning that only two low evaluations (dark blue, red, or yellow bars) have been assigned to this feature. Regarding the addition of end-points and new projects the results were similar and rather balanced. This is a bit unexpected finding, in the sense that these features were considered as trivial from the researchers' team.

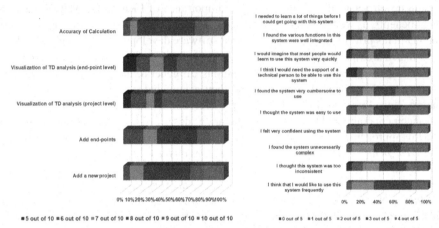

Fig. 6. Functionality analysis.   **Fig. 7.** SUS analysis per question

To further interpret the aforementioned results, next, we present the main outcomes of the qualitative analysis. First, regarding the addition of a new project, the participants believed that: (a) it was not really obvious how to fill in the needed information in the GUI; and (b) how to add a private repository. On the other hand, the addition of a new end-point and the execution of the analysis was characterized as extremely user-friendly. Nevertheless, a suggestion to select the end-points from a drop-down menu seemed to be favorable among the participants. However, as a tentative improvement, the participants mentioned that an Abstract Syntax Tree-like structure for choosing the method instead of copying and pasting text (i.e., the signature of the method) would be preferable. As an overall comment, the participants mentioned that: (a) a better space organization would make the visualization of the results easier to read. For instance, a pagination library could have been used in reporting the results per service or the issues that service suffers from; and (b) the use of different colors in the GUI would lead to more distinguishable items. For example, a different color per issue or service would be very helpful "*to catch the eye*". In terms of missing functionalities, the participants explained that enabling the customization of the rule-set of SonarQube through the Theia Extension would be very helpful, since many times organizations create custom ruleset and replace the default configuration of SonarQube. With respect to desired functionalities, the participants noted that future versions of the extension, could: (a) provide various sorting / filtering options (e.g., by criticality); (b) enable the navigation to the location of the code smell through GUI interaction (e.g., when clicking on the issue or the class, the corresponding part of the code to open in the Theia Editor); (c) provide help on how TD Principal is calculated and configure the constants (e.g., remediation times, default costs); (d) integrate Continuous Integration features to enable the quality gates and the continuous and automated monitoring of TD (e.g., link with Jenkins or build tools); and (e) export reports and import past analysis from previous versions or commits provide more detailed explanations on the issues.

6 Threats to Validity and Conclusions

Construct validity reflects to what extent the phenomenon under study really represents what is investigated according to the research questions [21]. To mitigate construct validity threats, we established a research protocol to guide the case study, which was thoroughly reviewed by two experienced researchers in the domain of empirical studies. Additionally, during the data collection process we aimed at data triangulation to avoid a wrong interpretation of a single data source. Another threat is the fact that the tool and the approach have been evaluated separately, and without a long-term usage of the tool before the study; this has introduced both negative or positive bias. On the one hand (negative bias), the evaluation of the stakeholders was probably stricter, since the users were completely inexperienced with the tool, they have probably faced more usability issues, compared to an evaluation that would have been performed after some training or self-training period. Therefore, we believe that the presented results, correspond to the worst-case scenario of usage and evaluation. On the contrary (positive bias), the evaluation might have been positively biased by using only a demo session, in which unclear parts were explained by the researchers, making them easier to understand by the practitioners. In terms of *external validity* (i.e., the generalizability of the findings derived from the sample [21]), it is difficult to claim that the same results would be derived in other companies. However, emphasizing on analytical generalization we can report on mitigation actions, which allow us to argue that the findings are representative for other cases with common characteristics (especially for RQ_2 and RQ_3). Specifically, the participants of the study were professional software engineers with various years of experience in software development. Regarding RQ_1, however, the results might be difficult to generalize outside the five involved companies. Finally, the *reliability* of an empirical study concerns the trustworthiness of the collected data and the analysis performed, to ensure that same results can be reproduced [21]. We support the reliability of our study by creating a rigor case study protocol and interview guides, which were tested through pilots. To minimize potential reliability threats during the data collection process, we preferred to ask open-ended questions and we requested motivation for the provided answers. To assure the correct and unbiased data analysis, three researchers collaborated during the whole analysis phase. Finally, we have internally archived all collected data (both raw and coded), due to a non-disclosure agreement with our industrial partners. On the other hand, interview guides are presented in Section IV.

Conclusions: Service-based software systems have been widely adopted because of their inherent benefits including, but not limited to, reliability, scalability, platform independence, agility and easy maintenance. As in any other software system, the code behind services needs to be maintained to adapt to new requirements and fix bugs. To assess the maintainability of services the Technical Debt metaphor can be used; however, it should be adapted to the particular features of Service-Oriented Architecture. In this paper, we have introduced an approach and an accompanying tool (in the form of an Eclipse Theia extension) to quantify TD in service-based applications, refining the analysis from the project or class level, to the individual service level. An industrial validation study with 15 engineers from 5 companies revealed the importance of assessing TD for service-based systems at the level of services. In particular, the results suggested that the proposed approach can be considered as more accurate compared to the 'traditional' project-level approaches. The main benefits are related to TD prioritization and monitoring, time savings, and is perceived as useful by the practitioners. The tool has been evaluated as highly usable.

Acknowledgment. Work reported in this paper has received funding from the European Union's Horizon 2020 research and innovation programme under grant agreement No 871177 (project: SmartCLIDE).

References

1. Cunningham, W.: The WyCash portfolio management system. In: Proceedings on Object-Oriented Programming Systems, Languages, and Applications, p. 29 (1992)
2. Zazworka, N., Spínola, R.O., Vetro', A., Shull, F., Seaman, C.: A case study on effectively identifying technical debt. In: Proceedings of the 17th International Conference on Evaluation and Assessment in Software Engineering, New York, USA, Apr 2013
3. Amanatidis, T., Mittas, N., Moschou, A., Chatzigeorgiou, A., Ampatzoglou, A., Angelis, L.: Evaluating the agreement among technical debt measurement tools: building an empirical benchmark of technical debt liabilities. Empir. Softw. Eng. **25**(5), 4161–4204 (2020). https://doi.org/10.1007/s10664-020-09869-w
4. Avgeriou, P.: An overview and comparison of technical debt measurement tools. IEEE Softw. (2021)
5. Tamburri, D.A., Kruchten, P., Lago, P., van Vliet, H.: What is social debt in software engineering? In: 6th International Workshop on Cooperative and Human Aspects of Software Engineering (CHASE), pp. 93–96 (2013)
6. Zimmermann, O.: Microservices tenets. Comput. Sci. Res. Dev. **32**(3–4), 301–310 (2016). https://doi.org/10.1007/s00450-016-0337-0
7. Pigazzini, I., Fontana, F.A., Lenarduzzi, V., Taibi, D.: Towards microservice smells detection. In: Proceedings of the 3rd International Conference on Technical Debt, Jun 2020
8. Soares de Toledo, S., Martini, A., Przybyszewska, A., Sjøberg, D.I.K.: Architectural Technical Debt in Microservices: A Case Study in a Large Company. In: IEEE/ACM International Conference on Technical Debt (TechDebt), vol. 2019, pp. 78–87 (2019)
9. Taibi, D., Lenarduzzi, V., Pahl, C.: Microservices Anti-patterns: A Taxonomy. Springer International Publishing, pp. 111–128 (2020)
10. Hasan, M., Stroulia, E., Barbosa, D., Alalfi, M.: Analyzing natural-language artifacts of the software process. In: International Conference on Software Maintenance, pp. 1–5 E. (2010)
11. Alves, N.S., Mendes, T.S., de Mendonça, M.G., Spínola, R.O., Shull, F., Seaman, C.: Identification and management of technical debt: A systematic mapping study. Inf. Softw. Technol. **70**, 100–121 (2016)

12. Li, Z., Avgeriou, P., Liang, P.: A systematic mapping study on technical debt and its management. J. Syst. Softw. **101**, 193–220 (2015)
13. Lefever, J., Cai, Y., Cervantes, H., Kazman, R., Fang, H.: On the lack of consensus among technical debt detection tools. In: Proceedings of the International Conference on Software Engineering (SEIP), pp. 121–130 (2021)
14. Tsoukalas, D., et al.: Machine Learning for Technical Debt Identification. IEEE Trans. Softw. Eng. (2021)
15. Campbell, G.A., Papapetrou, P.P.: SonarQube in action. Manning Publications (2013)
16. Bogner, J., Fritzsch, J., Wagner, S., Zimmermann, A.: Limiting technical debt with maintainability assurance: an industry survey on used techniques and differences with service- and microservice-based systems. In: International Conference on Technical Debt (2018)
17. Ouni, A., Daagi, M., Kessentini, M., Bouktif, S., Gammoudi, M.M.: A machine learning-based approach to detect web service design defects. In International Conference on Web Services (ICWS), pp. 532–539 (2017)
18. Král, J., Zemlicka, M.: Popular SOA antipatterns. In: 2009 Computation World: Future Computing, Service Computation, Cognitive, Adaptive, Content, Patterns (2009)
19. Alzaghoul, E., Bahsoon, R.: Evaluating technical debt in cloud-based Architectures using real options. In: 2014 23rd Australian Software Engineering Conference (2014)
20. Smith, N., Van Bruggen, D., Tomassetti, F.: Javaparser: visited. Leanpub, Oct 2017
21. Runeson, P., Höst, M., Austen, R., Regnell, B.: Case Study Research in Software Engineering – Guidelines and Examples. John Wiley & Sons Inc. (2012)
22. Brooke, J.: System Usability Scale (SUS): A quick-and-dirty method of system evaluation user information. Taylor & Francis (1996)
23. Seaman, C.B.: Qualitative methods in empirical studies of software engineering. IEEE Trans. Software Eng. **25**(4), 557–572 (1999)
24. Elo, S., Kyngäs, H.: The qualitative content analysis process. J. Adv. Nurs. **62**(1), 107–115 (2008)
25. Spencer, D.: Card Sorting: Designing Usable Categories. Rosenfeld Media, Apr 2009

An Investigation of Entropy and Refactoring in Software Evolution

Daniel Keenan, Des Greer[(✉)] [ID], and David Cutting [ID]

Queen's University Belfast, BT7 1NN Belfast, UK
{dkeenan21,des.greer,david.cutting}@qub.ac.uk

Abstract. As software evolves, the source code tends to become more complex and therefore harder to maintain, something that is exacerbated by poor development practice, where a disorderly development process is more likely to yield a disorderly and more complex result. Disorder in source code evolution may be quantified by using source code change entropy, a measure of the scattering pattern of code changes, i.e., how widely spread throughout the codebase are individual changes. Refactoring is an important activity for improving the structure of existing code and reducing its complexity, but it is unclear if refactoring can effectively counteract software entropy. Understanding how or if refactoring can reduce entropy could provide insights on software evolution and help reduce maintenance cost.

We empirically investigate how entropy at the system and file level evolves in software systems and how it is influenced by refactoring activities as well as non-refactoring changes. We identify refactorings in the version history of open-source projects through the analysis of source code and change metadata. We observe that system-level entropy fluctuates up and down, but remains relatively stable over time on average. We also observe that file-level entropy tends to decrease over time in response to both refactorings and non-refactoring changes, challenging the findings of previous studies. We observe factors which may lessen the utility of existing entropy metrics and suggest future avenues for exploring this intriguing but little-studied concept in software evolution.

Keywords: Software evolution · Software entropy · Refactoring · Mining software repositories

1 Introduction

Software systems evolve continuously over time through different kinds of changes. These may include introducing new features to satisfy users and keep the product competitive, fixing bugs to solve errors or security vulnerabilities, and carrying out maintenance activities, such as adapting the product to work in a new environment. With pressures from end-users, software practitioners often end up taking expedient approaches to deliver new functionality, incurring technical debt, and not prioritising refactoring activities in favour of new

© The Author(s), under exclusive license to Springer Nature Switzerland AG 2022
D. Taibi et al. (Eds.): PROFES 2022, LNCS 13709, pp. 282–297, 2022.
https://doi.org/10.1007/978-3-031-21388-5_20

development. Such poorly managed change processes lead to the degradation of the source code structure, orderliness, and overall quality, therefore increasing complexity and making maintenance an increasingly arduous task.

The second law of thermodynamics states that a closed system naturally tends to degenerate into a more disordered state over time. This is the notion of entropy, which has also been extended to software systems. Jacobson et al. [10] has stated: "As a system is modified, its disorder, or entropy, tends to increase. This is known as software entropy". There are different specific notions of software entropy, but in essence they all measure complexity and disorder, which by their nature undermine a system's maintainability over time. Lehman [13] defined his second law of software evolution as follows: "As an E-type system evolves, its complexity increases unless work is done to maintain or reduce it". This law acknowledges that it is possible to work against the natural growth of software entropy. Refactoring is one way to achieve this.

Hassan and Holt [8] introduced the concept of software entropy that is concerned with the amount of disorder in the development process, rather than the more traditional approach of measuring the complexity of source code. This is source code change entropy (for brevity, referred to in this paper simply as 'entropy'), which adapts Shannon entropy [16] as a way to quantify the scattering pattern of source code changes. The intuition is that the more scattered across the codebase changes are, the harder they are for developers to recall, leading to diminished comprehension of the system. Indeed, code scattering has been recognised as a significant barrier in software evolution [15]. Code scattering together with code tangling causes poor traceability because of the difficulty of reading dispersed code, decreasing code quality, and more difficult software reuse and maintenance [6].

Greater disorder ('chaos') in the development process will lead to greater disorder in the outputs of that process, i.e., the source code itself. File entropy is an individual file's contribution to entropy in a given period of time, and Hassan showed that file entropy is a more accurate metric for predicting faults in files than using the number of prior modifications or prior faults in the file [7].

File entropy has been shown to increase after non-refactoring changes and decrease after refactoring activity [3,4]. These approaches identified refactorings by inspecting commit notes to find keywords such as 'refactoring' and 'cleanup', which indicate refactoring-related changes. Limitations of this approach, as acknowledged by Canfora et al. [3,4], are that it misses refactorings not explicitly mentioned in the commit notes, and that non-refactoring changes may also be present within a refactoring commit. In another study on refactoring practice, [14] it was found that commit messages are unreliable indicators of refactoring activity. A better approach would be to analyse the source code itself, facilitated by automatic detection of refactorings. In this paper, RefactoringMiner [17], a refactoring mining library for Java projects, is used. To the best of our knowledge, it has not yet been applied in a study on entropy.

We build upon the work of previous studies on entropy, especially those by Canfora et al. [3,4], and empirically investigate how entropy varies as software systems evolve, as well as the effect of refactorings on file entropy compared to non-refactoring changes. We compute system- and file-level entropy over successive periods within the Git version histories of 10 open-source Java projects. We identify refactorings by analysing changes in source code, leveraging RefactoringMiner to do this automatically. We then compare the file entropy before and after refactorings, as well as between periods of no refactoring, to better understand how file entropy varies and how it is influenced by refactoring.

The paper is structured as follows. The next section introduces the notion of entropy as applied in this paper. Section 3 details the research questions and methodology used. Section 4 presents and discusses the results of our investigation and discusses threats to validity. Section 5 outlines how the work relates to existing work in this domain. Section 6 summarises the contributions and discusses directions for future work.

2   Background on Entropy

This section explains the concept of entropy as it relates to this investigation. This includes a discussion of Shannon entropy and its derivative, source code change entropy.

2.1   Shannon Entropy

Shannon [16] defined entropy in the context of information theory. Shannon entropy is defined as follows. For a discrete random variable X, with possible outcomes $x_1, x_2, ..., x_n$, the entropy of X is defined as:

$$H(X) = -\sum_{i=1}^{n} P(x_i) \log P(x_i) \tag{1}$$

Here, $P(x_i)$ is the probability of outcome x_i occurring. The logarithmic base used corresponds to the unit used for measuring information. Base 2 is traditionally chosen, relating to the unit of 'bits'. Shannon entropy quantifies the average amount of information required to represent an outcome drawn from the probability distribution. It can also be understood as the average level of 'surprise' inherent in the possible outcomes. As an example, consider a coin with probability p of landing on heads and probability $1-p$ of landing on tails. When $p = 0.5$, there is the greatest average level of surprise, as no outcome is more likely than another. When $p = 0.9$, the average level of surprise is lower, since, while it is possible for the coin to land on tails, it is much more likely to land on heads. When $p = 1$ or $p = 0$, there is no surprise, as the outcome is certain.

For a given number of possible outcomes, entropy is maximum when all outcomes have an equal probability of occurring $P(x_i) = \frac{1}{n}$. Conversely, when a single outcome x_a has a probability of occurring $P(x_a) = 1$, and all others have $P(x_i) = 0$, then entropy is minimum (0 bits). Having more possible outcomes increases the maximum potential entropy. For example, a fair coin toss has entropy of 1 bit, whereas rolling a fair six-faced die has entropy of 2.58 bits.

2.2 Source Code Change Entropy

Hassan et al. [8] brought Shannon entropy into the context of software evolution by deriving from it the metric of source code change entropy, which is defined as follows. For a software system S composed of a set of source files $f_1, f_2, ..., f_n$, the entropy of a period in its evolution is defined as:

$$H(S) = -\sum_{i=1}^{n} \frac{chglines(f_i)}{chglines(S)} \log_2 \left(\frac{chglines(f_i)}{chglines(S)} \right) \quad (2)$$

where $chglines(f_i)$ is the number of line changes made to the file f_i, and $chglines(S)$ is the sum of the line changes made to each file in the system S.

This system-level metric can then be adapted to the level of an individual file, where the file's contribution to the total entropy of a period is quantified. The entropy of a specific file f_i in a given period is defined as:

$$H'(f_i) = H(S) \cdot \frac{chglines(f_i)}{chglines(S)} \quad (3)$$

Entropy measures how 'scattered' changes are in terms of the distribution of line changes across files. Entropy increases with both the number of files changed and how evenly distributed the line changes are across the changed files. When most line changes are concentrated in a small number of the files in a change, entropy is low. Conversely, when line changes are scattered across many files in similar proportions, entropy is high. If no more than one file is changed, entropy is minimised. If multiple files are changed, each by an equal number of lines, entropy is maximised for that number of changed files. The potential maximum entropy increases with the number of files changed. It should be emphasised that entropy does not quantify the magnitude of changes, but the pattern of their occurrence.

Hassan's hypothesis was that the more scattered across the codebase changes are, the more difficult they are for developers to keep up with and recall later, deteriorating the shared understanding of the system and increasing the likelihood that bugs will be introduced. Moreover, intuitively, a well-structured and readily extensible codebase should be conducive to changes which have a low entropy footprint. In other words, when fewer lines of existing code need to be changed to realise new functionality, entropy should be lower.

3 Research Questions and Methodology

The aim of this investigation is to analyse how entropy changes within systems as they evolve and how refactoring affects entropy. The intuition is that developer understanding of a system breaks down more as entropy increases, so it should be controlled. Our research questions and corresponding null hypotheses are defined formally below.

3.1 Research Questions

RQ1: How does system entropy change over time?

Our conjecture is that system entropy increases over time due to the increased scattering of changes occurring as a system evolves, becomes increasingly complex, and falls further into disorder.

Null hypothesis H_{01}: system entropy does not significantly change over time.

RQ2: How do non-refactoring changes affect file entropy?

To meaningfully investigate how refactoring affects file entropy, we need to establish how non-refactoring changes affect file entropy. Our conjecture is that non-refactoring changes increase file entropy due to the increasingly scattered changes that must be made when the file is not being refactored to be more maintainable.

Null hypothesis H_{02}: there is no significant difference in file entropy before and after a non-refactoring change.

RQ3: How do refactorings affect file entropy?

Our conjecture is that refactorings decrease file entropy due to the files being more maintainable after refactoring, reducing the scattering of changes necessary to realise new functionality.

Null hypothesis H_{03}: there is no significant difference in file entropy before and after a refactoring.

RQ1 is an exploratory question, intended to help us understand more about entropy at the system level. RQ2 and RQ3 concern file-level entropy and reiterate questions posed by [3,4].

3.2 Systems Studied

We applied the following criteria to select suitable software systems for analysis: *the system must:*

1. be publicly available;
2. have its source code under Git version control;
3. be composed of at least 90% Java code;
4. have at least 10,000 physical lines of Java code;
5. have a version history of at least 1,000 commits;
6. have at least 10 contributors.

Criterion 1 was applied to support the replication of experiments. Criterion 2 was a necessary constraint of using RefactoringMiner, which only works with projects under Git version control. Criterion 3 was applied to ensure that the systems were mostly Java-based, since RefactoringMiner only supports analysis of Java code. Criteria 4 and 5 were applied to ensure the systems were of reasonably substantial size and evolutionary history, respectively; we assumed that small or little-developed systems would be unlikely to exhibit a level of

Table 1. Software systems analysed in this investigation

System	kLoC (Java)	Size	# Commits	# Contributors
Apache Dubbo	274	Large	4,785	346
Fresco	136	Large	2,963	205
Glide	104	Medium	2,592	131
Hystrix	79	Medium	2,109	109
MPAndroidChart	43	Medium	2,070	69
Nacos	212	Large	3,645	199
Retrofit	37	Medium	1,879	154
SirixDB	180	Large	2,652	38
Termux App	30	Intermediate	1,082	57
Zerocode	25	Intermediate	1,357	43

developmental complexity worth analysing. Criterion 6 was applied to ensure these were 'industrial' projects, worthy of being contributed to by many developers, as opposed to personal projects. 10 systems that met the criteria were arbitrarily chosen and are listed in Table 1. System size was classified using the kLoC-based thresholds proposed by Boehm [2]. Only physical lines of Java code were counted.

3.3 Filtering of Source Files Considered

It is important that only relevant source files are considered when computing entropy. The specific file types that may be appropriate to include vary by project but should exclude configuration files, test files, and documentation, in our view. This is because the development of these files is not guided by the same design principles and patterns as functional code, so it is not appropriate to relate the patterns of changes applied to them to the software's maintainability. As we analysed Java-based systems exclusively, we considered only Java source (.java) files.

Excluding test files from our analysis proved challenging, as each system may store test files in various codebase-specific locations, and it is not always clear whether a file exists for testing purposes. For example, some files contain test utilities and runners but do not contain tests themselves. We used a lightweight, generalised approach of excluding files whose path contains any of the following patterns:

- `Test.java`
- `Tests.java`
- `Tester.java`
- `Testers.java`
- `test/`

- `tests/`
- `tester/`
- `testers/`
- `androidTest/`

These represent common naming conventions for test files and locations. While not an infallible approach, it should be reliable enough to remove almost all test files from consideration.

3.4 Filtering of Refactoring Types Considered

Canfora et al. [3] acknowledged that "ideally, to identify refactorings, it would be appropriate to analyze a source code change, and determine if such a change is related or not to refactoring". With RefactoringMiner, we achieved this programmatically. RefactoringMiner is capable of classifying a wide range of refactoring types, including high-level refactorings, such as class extractions, and low-level refactorings, such as reordering parameters. To designate a period as containing a refactoring for a given file, we had to decide which refactoring types were appropriate to consider. We believe that certain low-level refactoring types (e.g., simple renames) are not substantial enough to meaningfully influence entropy, and, due to their prevalence, including them would result in almost every period being designated as containing a refactoring. Below is the list of refactoring types we chose to consider (grouped by program element):

- superclass: extract
- subclass: extract
- class: extract
- interface: extract
- attribute: extract, merge, split, move, replace, move and rename, pull up, push down
- method: extract, inline, merge, move, extract and move, move and inline, move and rename, pull up, push down
- miscellaneous: introduce polymorphism

3.5 Dividing Version Histories into Periods

The version history of each project had to be divided into periods for which entropy would be computed and the presence of refactorings would be determined. Different approaches exist for defining what constitutes a period in this context. For example, a time interval or a specified number of commits. We discounted a time-based approach on the basis that our analysis of how the software is evolved should be independent of real-world time, so as to not be influenced by the level of development activity at a given time, which would naturally fluctuate (e.g., dropping during holiday periods).

For a consistent and time-independent approach, we defined a period as a sequence of 100 commits, as it is not disproportionate to the length of the version histories in our systems for analysis (mean = 2,513 commits). If the total number of commits is not a factor of 100, then the final (most recent) period in a version history will have fewer than 100 commits. As a technicality, only non-merge commits are considered; merge commits (i.e., those with two parents) are discarded before the division into periods. This is because merge commits yield duplicate changes during the file/line change extraction process. On the same basis, RefactoringMiner also disregards merge commits.

3.6 Performing Analysis and Collecting Data

A Java-based software tool was written to perform analysis. It uses the JGit library to mine the version history of a system, extracting the necessary information about file/line changes occurring in each period to compute system- and file-level entropy. The tool also leverages RefactoringMiner to detect and mark periods containing refactorings. The tool's source code and the data generated using it are available on GitHub.[1] To address RQ1, for each system, we computed the system-level entropy according to (2) for each period in its version history. To address RQ2, for each system, the following approach was applied.

Given a file and the sequence of periods in which it was changed p_1, p_2, ..., p_n:

1. let fe_1, fe_2, ..., fe_n be the file-level entropy of the file, computed according to Eq. (3), for each period in which it was changed
2. calculate the percentage change in file entropy between each pair of adjacent periods p_i and p_j where neither period contains a refactoring of the file

Repeat the above steps for each file in the system, and then calculate the median, across all files, of the percentage change in file entropy between each pair of adjacent periods not containing refactorings of the file. To address RQ3, for each system, we applied a similar approach to [3] to calculate average entropy before and after refactorings, defined as follows.

Given a file and the sequence of periods in which it was changed p_1, p_2, ..., p_n:

1. let fe_1, fe_2, ..., fe_n be the file-level entropy of the file, computed according to Eq. (3), for each period in which it was changed
2. let pr_1, pr_2, ..., pr_m be the periods in which a refactoring was applied to the file
3. for each period in which a refactoring was applied to the file, pr_i:
   (a) calculate the mean file entropy across each previous period not containing a refactoring of the file, up to the previous period in which the file was refactored or the beginning of the project (this is the *mean file entropy before refactoring*)
   (b) calculate the mean file entropy across each subsequent period not containing a refactoring of the file, up to the next period in which the file was refactored or the end of the project (this is the *mean file entropy after refactoring*)

---

[1] https://github.com/Daniel-Keenan-QUB/entropy-project.

4. calculate the percentage change between the mean file entropy before refactoring and the mean file entropy after refactoring

Repeat the above steps for each file in the system, and then calculate the median,
across all files, of the percentage change between the mean file entropy before
refactoring and the mean file entropy after refactoring.

4   Results

4.1   RQ1: How Does System Entropy Change over Time?

In all systems studied, the system entropy exhibited no significant consistent
trend of continuous increase or decrease. Figure 1 shows the entropy variation
for the studied systems. The pattern observed was that entropy tends to fluctuate
up and down within a range of values but remains relatively stable on average
within that range throughout the life of the project. To quantify the variation
in entropy over time for each system, the line of best fit was calculated (using
the 'least squares' method) for the entropy data points. Half of the systems
had a best fit line gradient that was negative, and the other half had a positive
gradient, but in all cases the gradient was very shallow. The lowest gradient was
−0.07 and the highest gradient was 0.19. The mean gradient across all systems
was 0.04. This value is close to zero, reflecting the relative stability of entropy
over time, irrespective of system size. Thus, we cannot refute the null hypothesis
H_{01} that system entropy does not significantly change over time.

Table 2. File entropy for non-refactoring periods and before/after refactoring periods
(significant in bold)

System	Median % change in file entropy between adjacent periods (Wilcoxon 1-Sample)		
	a) Non-refactoring	b) Refactoring	c)= a − b (Wilcoxon 2-Sample)
Apache Dubbo	**−15.21(p≪0.001)**	−28.64(p = 0.815)	**−13.43(p = 0.019)**
Fresco	**−10.83(p≪0.001**	**−48.03(p = 0.021)**	**−37.20(p<0.001)**
Glide	**−19.68(p≪0.001)**	−21.71(p = 0.252)	−2.03(p = 0.453)
Hystrix	**−1.11(p≪0.001**	−45.00(p = 0.677)	−43.89(p = 0.084)
MPAndroidChart	**−12.91(p≪0.001)**	−13.17(p = 0.747)	−0.26(p=0.627)
Nacos	**−21.45(p = 0.012)**	**−67.43(p≪0.001)**	**−45.98(p≪0.001)**
Retrofit	**−5.92(p ≪0.001)**	+ 18.46(p = 0.165)	**+ 24.38(p = 0.156)**
SitrixDB	**+ 0.65(p≪0.001**	−35.24(p = 0.220)	**−35.89(p=0.001)**
Termux App	−28.46(p = 0.777)	**−62.07(p = 0.040)**	−34.24(p = 0.127)
Zerocode	−50.30(p = 0.254)	−38.47(p = 0.507)	+ 11.83(p = 0.509)

Fig. 1. System-wide entropy over time

4.2 RQ2: How Do Non-refactoring Changes Affect File Entropy?

Table 2 shows the median percentage change in file entropy between adjacent non-refactoring periods. Referring to the first column of figures, in 9 out of 10 systems, file entropy follows a decreasing trend between each non-refactoring period. On average, file entropy decreases by approximately 17% between periods in which the file was changed but not refactored. Using a one-sample Wilcoxon test ($\alpha = 0.95$)to determine if the change in file entropy is significantly different from zero in each system, we find that all except Termux App and Zerocode show significance. This provides evidence to reject the null hypothesis H_{02} that there is no significant difference in file entropy before and after a non-refactoring change. We infer that, in our sample, file entropy generally decreases after a non-refactoring change.

4.3   RQ3: How Do Refactorings Affect File Entropy?

Table 2 b) shows the median percentage change in file entropy in after a refactoring period. The median values all show a negative trend except for Retrofit. However, a Wilcoxon signed-rank test shows a p-value <0.05 in only Nacos and Termux. Thus, the data does not confidently support the hypothesis that there is a falling file entropy following refactoring periods. It might also be informative to compare the paired samples of non-refactoring periods and refactoring periods for average file entropy change. Table 2 c) shows the difference between medians for the two samples. In 8 out of 10 systems, file entropy follows a decreasing trend when comparing the mean before and after a refactoring of the file. Retrofit and Zerocode were exceptions. On average, mean file entropy is approximately 34% lower in the periods following a refactoring compared to those before.

Using a Wilcoxon Two Sample test ($\alpha = 0.95$), to test the null hypothesis that there is no difference between average file entropy change between non-refactoring and refactoring periods, as shown in Table 2, we find that 5 systems (Apache Dubbo, Fresco, Nacos, Retrofit SirixDB) suggest that we refute the null hypothesis but the other 5 do not (Glide, Hystrix, MPAndroidChart, Termux App and Zerocode).

4.4   Discussion

Regarding RQ1, we conjectured that system entropy would increase with time, since the disorder of changes should grow as the system becomes more complex, but what we observed instead was levels of entropy fluctuating within a range and not tending to increase or decrease in general. On reflection, dividing a version history into segments based on a fixed length of time or number of commits represents a high degree of arbitrariness. These approaches have been used in previous studies, such as [4] and [8], so we assumed that this approach would be good enough for our measurements, but it may not be the most appropriate way to measure entropy. A period in which development includes more features (by necessity or coincidence), and therefore spans more parts of the codebase than usual, is not necessarily a cause for concern in itself. An entropy increase (and subsequent decrease) would be expected in this case, and not inherently indicative of poor management of code structure or change. If entropy is to be an indicator of either of these, then system-wide entropy measures over arbitrary periods may be of limited practical interest.

Regarding RQ2, we conjectured that changes not related to refactoring would increase file entropy, since the scattering of changes would increase generally while the file is not being refactored to be more maintainable (this is what [4] observed). What we observed instead was file entropy tending to decrease over time. We believe this may be explained by the fact that most files see fewer changes later in their existence. When they are newly created, there is a high initial entropy footprint for the file. As it ultimately takes shape and stabilises in its functionality, it may see few changes, if any, for the rest of the project's life. Assuming most files follow this pattern, their individual contribution to entropy will naturally decrease over time.

Interestingly, Canfora et al. [4] observed the opposite trend, that is non-refactoring changes lead to an increase in file entropy, in their initial study of entropy. This may be explained by their measurement technique. If it is assumed that they measured the difference in file entropy between each non-refactoring period and the period following it, then one may expect moving from a non-refactoring period to a refactoring period to exhibit an increase in entropy, and the converse to exhibit a decrease in entropy, based on the intuition that refactorings themselves tend to have high entropy by nature. They acknowledge the need to exclude refactoring periods themselves in their follow-up paper [3] but do not repeat the investigation of how non-refactoring changes affect file entropy. The two projects analysed in their case study are also older and have longer commit histories than ours, and were not under Git version control at the time.

Regarding RQ3, we conjectured that refactorings would decrease file entropy, since changes would be less scattered as a file becomes easier to maintain due to being refactored. We observed that this was the case, consistent with Canfora's findings in both previous studies [3,4]. However, as discussed previously, we observed that file entropy generally decreases between periods over time even in the absence of refactorings. If our conjecture about the reasons for file-specific entropy diminishing over time holds true, then it challenges previous findings by showing that the relationship between refactorings and reductions in file entropy is non-causative, i.e., file entropy is decreasing no matter what.

5 Threats to Validity

This section discusses the main threats to the validity of our study.

5.1 Internal and Construct Validity

The software for extracting change information from system version histories is fallible, but to maximise confidence, it was carefully scrutinised, verified with unit tests, and manually tested on controlled samples (in a test repository) before being applied to external systems. A crucial factor in the construct validity of our findings for RQ2 and RQ3 is the accuracy of refactoring detection. Tsantalis et al. [17] provide confidence of this by reporting a precision of 98% and recall of 87% for RefactoringMiner, the library on which we rely for refactoring detection. A mitigation to this threat is that we believe our approach is more accurate than previous studies that relied relied on documentation and human judgment to identify refactorings [3,4]. Additionally, we are limited to the, albeit extensive,

22 refactorings detectable by RefactoringMiner that were deemed appropriate for our investigation.

A factor that will pollute results but is not explicitly mentioned in previous studies, is the inclusion of test files in entropy computations. We believe that test files are not relevant to the measurement of entropy, so they should be deliberately excluded from analysis. Our results would be less accurate if any test files were not excluded and/or any non-test files were excluded by accident. We acknowledge that our approach to test file exclusion makes assumptions about naming conventions that will not hold in all cases. A better, albeit manual, way to identify test files may be to inspect each system and determine the conventions for naming and storing test files before exclusion.

Since changes are quantified by analysing each commit and determining the differences in its source code compared to its parent, the pattern in which commits are made influences the emerging pattern of changes. For example, a developer may implement a feature by making small, frequent commits to a feature branch before it is ultimately merged into the master branch. This practice ensures code is regularly backed up and allows for work-in-progress commits; the developer need not worry about each commit being deployable. The issue with this pattern when computing entropy is that 'intermediate' commits containing changes which are subsequently overwritten or discarded represent a contribution to entropy which is actually subsequently invalidated, and their inclusion pollutes the measurement. Variance in commit etiquette, e.g., between developers' styles, policies on projects, and merging strategies, will influence the level of this pollution and may be difficult to control for.

5.2   External and Conclusion Validity

While we analysed more systems than previous studies [3] and [7], it must be acknowledged that our sample is small and of limited diversity. Our sample included intermediate, medium, and large systems, but no very large systems. We analysed systems with between 1,000 and 5,000 commits, but there exist systems with commit counts in the order of 10,000 and 100,000. For example, the IntelliJ IDEA Community Edition project on GitHub has 349,905 commits at the time of writing. These systems could exhibit different trends in entropy, as they have evolved through many more commits. Due to constraints inherent to the tooling used in our study, we analysed only Java-based systems, but systems developed using other languages may exhibit different entropy trends due to differences in language features, coding standards, paradigms, etc. To reinforce the generalisability of our findings, future studies should strive for a sample size in the region of 50-100, with greater variety in system size, version history length, and development languages. Furthermore, we have limited our investigation to open-source software, which means that the findings and conclusions may not apply to other settings.

6   Related Work

Bianchi et al. [1] defined software entropy as a class of metrics aimed at assessing source code quality degradation. These metrics consider the entropy of the source code itself in terms of the links between components, rather than considering the entropy of the code change process. Hassan & Holt [8] introduced software entropy as a measure of the disorder in a code change process by adapting Shannon entropy [16] to quantify the pattern of code changes. They carried out follow-up studies [7,9] which showed that file change entropy is correlated with the presence of bugs, and that file-level entropy is a better predictor of faults in files than historical predictors, such the number of prior modifications and prior bugs.

D'Ambros et al. [5] evaluated a range of defect-prediction approaches, including Hassan's 'entropy of changes', and found that software entropy performed less well than most other metrics and exhibited the highest variability in performance. This observation on variability aligns quite well with our interpretation of the findings of our investigation; excessive 'arbitrariness' of the measurement targets for entropy may play a part in this.

Canfora et al. [4] investigated the relationship of file-level software entropy with refactorings and non-refactoring changes, and found that entropy tends to increase following non-refactoring changes and decrease following refactorings. They also carried out a more in-depth follow-up study [3] investigating the relationship between software entropy and four different factors: refactoring activities, the number of active contributors to a source code file, the participation of classes in design patterns, and the different kinds/topics of changes occurring. They reinforced their finding from the previous paper that entropy tends to decrease following refactoring activity but did not repeat their investigation of variance in entropy following non-refactoring changes. Our findings challenge any interpretation from these studies that refactoring practices are the cause of decreasing entropy.

Kaur et al. [11] applied the software entropy metrics to a subsystem of Android and found that they were unsuitable for bug prediction. This contrasted with a previous study by the same authors which found that the metrics were suitable for predicting bugs in a subsystem of Mozilla. This apparent variation in performance has been seen in other studies, as mentioned earlier. Kaur et al. [12] applied the software entropy metrics with a range of machine learning techniques, and suggest GEP and SVR as stable regression techniques for bug prediction using software entropy.

7   Conclusion and Future Work

As an exploratory research question, we investigated system entropy trends over time in a sample of Java-based systems. Using a commit count-based approach to define periods, we observed that entropy remains surprisingly stable over time and does not tend to grow continuously. There may be an undesirable level of arbitrariness in dividing version histories using this approach, and the system-level metric may primarily reflect the amount of development activity occurring in a given period and not sufficiently reflect a 'disorder' of code changes.

Hassan [7] showed a correlation between file entropy and fault-proneness, highlighting a need to control entropy. Canfora et al. [3] showed a correlation between refactorings of a file and reduction in its entropy, suggesting that refactoring may be an effective countermeasure to the entropy of files. We used modern tooling available to enhance the methodology of Canfora et al. and repeat their investigations into how file entropy varies in response to refactorings and non-refactoring changes. Our results challenged previous findings by showing that, rather than non-refactoring changes increasing file entropy and refactorings reducing it, file entropy follows a decreasing trend over time irrespective of the presence of refactorings. We conjecture that this is due to files naturally seeing fewer modifications later in their existence, meaning their contribution to entropy in given periods will tend to reduce compared to newer files that are being more actively developed.

We propose that there may be value in experimenting with different 'targets' on/over which to measuring entropy. We suspect that system-level entropy is highly sensitive to the natural variation in the source files worked on at different times which may devalue its practicality as an indicator of potential future problems. Instead, we would suggest that entropy may be most appropriately computed over cohesive change sets. That is, for example, a full feature implementation or maintenance activity, isolated from any other changes. Our intuition is that lower entropy exhibited in the implementation of a feature reflects software which is more readily extensible. In this way, the notion of 'the entropy necessary to realise a feature' becomes reflective of the quality of the software itself. It would be valuable to investigate the effectiveness of this approach to measuring entropy. For example, could the entropy of feature implementations be a predictor of faults in those same features?

Software entropy, as a measure of the disorder in code change patterns, is an intriguing and relatively little-studied concept. There remains a strong need to critically evaluate its ability to accurately capture the disorder of a development process, potentially investigate relationships with well-established software quality attributes, such as coupling and cohesion, and ultimately determine whether it truly holds enough utility to be considered and monitored in real-world development settings. To our knowledge, metrics for software entropy of this kind have not been tested in any industrial collaborations. A more comprehensive study, ideally with some industry input, is required. There is also a clear need to perform a sensitivity analysis of the entropy metrics. It may be necessary to adapt existing entropy metrics or propose new ones which are robust to the confounding factors discussed in this paper. Nonetheless, software entropy provides a useful measure for considering the impact of code changes and the type of code change.

References

1. Bianchi, A., Caivano, D., Lanubile, F., Visaggio, G.: Evaluating software degradation through entropy. In: 7th IEEE International Software Metrics Symposium, p. 210. IEEE Computer Society (2001)
2. Boehm, B.W.: Software Engineering Economics. Prentice Hall (1981)
3. Canfora, G., Cerulo, L., Cimitile, M., Penta, M.D.: How changes affect software entropy: An empirical study. Empir. Softw. Eng. **19**(1), 1–38 (2014)
4. Canfora, G., Cerulo, L., Penta, M.D., Pacilio, F.: An exploratory study of factors influencing change entropy. In: The 18th IEEE International Conference on Program Comprehension, pp. 134–143. IEEE Computer Society (2010)
5. D'Ambros, M., Lanza, M., Robbes, R.: Evaluating defect prediction approaches: A benchmark and an extensive comparison. Empir. Softw. Eng. **17**(4-5), 531–577 (2012)
6. França, J.M., Dos Santos, C.A.R., de Oliveira, K.S., Soares, M.S.: An empirical evaluation of refactoring crosscutting concerns into aspects using software metrics. In: 2013 10th International Conference on Information Technology: New Generations, pp. 674–679. IEEE (2013)
7. Hassan, A.E.: Predicting faults using the complexity of code changes. In: 31st International Conference on Software Engineering, pp. 78–88. IEEE (2009)
8. Hassan, A.E., Holt, R.C.: The chaos of software development. In: 6th International Workshop on Principles of Software Evolution, pp. 84–94. IEEE Computer Society (2003)
9. Hassan, A.E., Holt, R.C.: Studying the chaos of code development. In: 10th Working Conference on Reverse Engineering, pp. 123–133. IEEE Computer Society (2003)
10. Jacobson, I., Christerson, M., Jonsson, P., Övergaard, G.: Object-oriented Software Engineering - A Use Case Driven Approach. Addison-Wesley (1992)
11. Kaur, A., Chopra, D.: Reasons for non-applicability of software entropy metrics for bug prediction in android. Int. J. Comput. Syst. Eng. **10**(6), 1170–1175 (2016)
12. Kaur, A., Kaur, K., Chopra, D.: An empirical study of software entropy based bug prediction using machine learning. Int. J. Syst. Assurance Eng. Manage. **8**(2s), 599–616 (2017)
13. Lehman, M.M.: On understanding laws, evolution, and conservation in the large-program life cycle. J. Syst. Softw. **1**, 213–221 (1980)
14. Murphy-Hill, E.R., Parnin, C., Black, A.P.: How we refactor, and how we know it. IEEE Trans. Software Eng. **38**(1), 5–18 (2012)
15. Sehgal, R., Nagpal, R., Mehrotra, D., et al.: Measuring code smells and anti-patterns. In: 2019 4th International Conference on Information Systems and Computer Networks (ISCON), pp. 311–314. IEEE (2019)
16. Shannon, C.E.: A mathematical theory of communication. Bell Syst. Tech. J. **27**(3), 379–423 (1948)
17. Tsantalis, N., Mansouri, M., Eshkevari, L.M., Mazinanian, D., Dig, D.: Accurate and efficient refactoring detection in commit history. In: Proceedings of the 40th International Conference on Software Engineering, pp. 483–494. ACM (2018)

"To Clean Code or Not to Clean Code" A Survey Among Practitioners

Kevin Ljung and Javier Gonzalez-Huerta[✉] [ID]

Blekinge Institute of Technology, 371 79 Karlskrona, Sweden
`javier.gonzalez.huerta@bth.se`

Abstract. Context: Writing code that is understandable by other collaborators has become crucial to enhancing collaboration and productivity. Clean Code has become one of the most relevant software craftsmanship practices and has been widely embraced as a synonym for code quality by software developers and software development organizations all over the world. However, very little is known regarding whether developers agree with Clean Code principles and how they apply them in practice.

Objectives: In this work, we investigated how developers perceive Clean Code principles, whether they believe that helps reading, understanding, reusing, and modifying Clean Code, and how they keep their code clean.

Methods: We conducted a Systematic Literature Review in which we screened 771 research papers to collect Clean Code principles and a survey among 39 practitioners, some of them with more than 20 years of development experience.

Results: So far, the results show a shared agreement with Clean Code principles and their potential benefits. They also show that developers tend to write "messy" code to be refactored later.

Keywords: Clean code · Survey · Code quality

1 Introduction

The development of software systems has turned into a collective endeavor that, in some cases, involves thousands of engineers, distributed globally into hundreds of teams that have to work with code written by others. In this scenario, writing code that is understandable by others becomes crucial. The selection of identifiers, or the length of methods and classes, are, among others, principles that developers should have in mind when writing their code.

However, there are no measures that can assess the quality of code universally, and there is a lack of standards for code quality. Even the understanding of what code quality is somehow diffuse [9].

Clean Code [27] has become one of the most relevant craftsmanship practices for developers worldwide, and several research studies have analyzed its nature and effects. The principles and practices described in the book have been widely embraced as a synonym for code quality by many software developers

© The Author(s), under exclusive license to Springer Nature Switzerland AG 2022
D. Taibi et al. (Eds.): PROFES 2022, LNCS 13709, pp. 298–315, 2022.
https://doi.org/10.1007/978-3-031-21388-5_21

and software development organizations worldwide. However, the evidence of its use in practice, how developers perceive its principles, and how they apply them is scarce in the software engineering literature.

There are several studies reporting the benefits of Clean Code (e.g., [14,20]), how to support it (e.g., [21]), analyzing challenges and hindrances of its adoption in practice (e.g., [30]), or how refactoring might impact the "the cleanliness" and the quality of code (e.g., [2–5,7,12,13,18,29,31,33,36,39]). However, it is still unclear how professional developers perceive Clean Code.

In this paper, we report a Questionnaire Survey study that explores the practitioners' perceptions regarding Clean Code. The goal of the survey is to gain an understanding of: (i) the degree of agreement with its principles and practices amongst practitioners; (ii) whether they believe that Clean Code can help them be more efficient and effective while reading, understanding, reusing and maintaining code; (iii) and how developers keep their code "clean".

To gather a more complete list of Clean Code principles and practices, we conducted a Snowballing [37] Systematic Literature Review using a hybrid method [28], in which we selected 28 papers in addition to the Clean Code seminal book [27].

The remainder of the paper is structured as follows: Sect. 2 discusses related works in the area. Section 3 describes the details of the Systematic Literature Review and the Questionnaire Survey planning and execution. Section 4 reports the results of the study. Section 5 discusses the main findings. In Sect. 6 discusses the limitations and threats to the validity. Finally, Sect. 7 draws the main conclusions and discusses further works.

2   Related Work

The Clean Code seminal book somehow refines one of the aspects of Software Craftsmanship, with a deep emphasis on writing high-quality, understandable code, all surrounded by a shared professional culture.

Since its publication in 2009 there have been several research studies assessing its benefits (e.g., [14,20]), how to support it (e.g., [21]), analyzing challenges and hindrances to its adoption in practice (e.g., [30]), or different aspects of refactoring and how it impacts on Clean Code or code quality (e.g.,[2–5,7,12, 13,18,29,31,33,36,39])

Several studies also assess what affects code readability, understandability, and maintainability (e.g. [5,8,13,17,21–23,32]) and complexity (e.g., [1]). Börstler et al. [9] also carried out an exploratory study focusing on understanding code quality.

Some other studies, like the ones reported by Stevenson et al. [35], or Yamashita and Moonen [38], follow a similar methodology, a questionnaire survey study, but with a different focus: code quality aspects or whether developers care about code smells.

However, we know very little about the practitioners' perceptions of the Clean Code and whether and how they use it in practice [30]. It is still unclear how professional developers perceive Clean Code, whether they agree with its principles and practices, and whether they believe that Clean Code can help them to be more efficient and effective while reading, understanding, reusing and maintaining code. To the best of our knowledge, this is the first attempt that aims at understanding developers' perceptions of clean code and how they keep their code clean.

3   Research Methodology

In this paper, we employ two research methods: (i) a Snowballing Systematic Literature Review (SLR) [37] with a hybrid search method [28] and (ii) a Questionnaire Survey developed following the guidelines by Kitchenham and Pfleeger [19].

We focus on the following research questions:

- **RQ1:** Do developers agree with Clean Code principles?
- **RQ2:** Do developers believe that clean code eases the process of reading, understanding, modifying, or reusing code?
- **RQ3:** How do developers keep their code "Clean"?

3.1   Systematic Literature Review Planning and Execution

To gather a more complete list of clean code principles, going beyond the ones presented by *"Uncle"* Bob Martin in his Clean Code seminal book [27], we conducted the SLR using snowballing [37]. The objective of this SLR is not to analyze or describe the *state-of-the-art* regarding the Clean Code, but rather to identify Clean Code principles in addition to the ones presented in the Clean Code book. We employed a hybrid approach, combining the database search to define the start set with the iterative citations and references analysis (snowballing) [28]. The list of clean-code principles is the one used to survey practitioners, investigating the developers' degree of agreement with Clean Code principles.

Inclusion Criteria - We defined the following inclusion criteria[1]:

- Is the paper published in a peer-reviewed English-language journal, conference or workshop proceedings indexed in Google Scholar?
- Does the paper include the terms "clean code" or "code quality" in the title, abstract, or full text?
- Is the paper published after 2009?
- Does the paper define principles and practices of clean code or report their usage in practice?

---

[1] We applied the abovementioned inclusion and exclusion criteria to define the start set and during the snowballing iterations.

We opted for excluding papers written before and during 2009 since the Clean Code book was originally published in 2009.

Exclusion Criteria - We also defined the following exclusion criterion:

– Is the paper talking only about static analysis techniques without a strong emphasis on their use in practice?

The only exception to the criteria above is the inclusion of the Clean Code book [27], which appears in Table 2 as B.

To define the start set (seed), we carried out a database search in March 2021 using Google Scholar with the search string: "clean code" OR "code quality". The automated search on Google Scholar found 723 papers that were analyzed applying the abovementioned inclusion criteria, which resulted in the inclusion of 9 papers as starting set (designated as S01 to S09 in Table 1).

We then performed four snowballing iterations summarized in Table 1 and stopped when we achieved saturation (i.e., we did not find new papers to include), applying the inclusion and exclusion criteria listed above, resulting in the inclusion of 18 papers. Each snowballing iteration consisted of backward (i.e., references analysis) and forward snowballing (citations analysis), which improve precision and recall, respectively. In the citation analysis, we found that some papers had hundreds of citations, most of them irrelevant, and therefore we narrowed the scope of the citations inspection to the ones that included "clean code" OR "code quality", similar to the one used in the start set definition.

Table 1. SLR snowballing iteration statistics and results

Stage	Citations and references screened	Papers included
Seed		S01 [21], S02 [30], S03 [9], S04 [23], S05 [14], S06 [24], S07 [5], S08 [13], S09 [26]
Iteration 1	23 references and 6 citations	P1 [35], P2 [34], P3 [38], P4 [1], P5 [8], P6 [22], P7 [7], P8 [3], P9 [2], P10 [18], P11 [12]
Iteration 2	10 references and 6 citations	P12 [31], P13 [33], P14 [29], P15 [36]
Iteration 3	0 references and 3 citations	P16 [4], P17 [32], P18 [17]
Iteration 4	0 references and 0 citations	

3.2   Questionnaire Survey Design and Execution

The Questionaire Survey allowed us to gather developers' opinions regarding Clean Code practices, their benefits, and the way they keep their code "clean". The survey was designed following the guidelines by [19]. The questionnaire contained a mixture of closed and open questions to understand the participants' views and opinions better. However, for the sake of brevity and clarity, the results presented in this paper focus only on the closed questions.[2]

The closed questions in the questionnaire mainly were seven items Likert-scale questions, including a neutral response, which avoids forcing a positive or negative choice, which seems adequate for an exploratory survey. The survey questions were grouped into pages to prevent respondents from being overwhelmed with a long list of questions.

Before its distribution, we conducted a pilot to assess the questionnaire, by sending it to one developer with more than 20 years of experience in industry that is also an experienced researcher. The questionnaire was completed, and the main feedback was regarding some questions that focused on assessing the time developers would save in tasks when code is clean vs when code is not so clean, the structure of some multiple choice questions regarding qualities, and small language corrections. We first removed the questions that aimed at quantifying the savings in time when dealing with clean code and then corrected all the other reported issues before sending out the survey.

The questionnaire was developed, spread out, and analyzed using *Questback* survey software[3]. The questionnaire was distributed by email and using social networks, as well as shared with contacts within some companies we collaborated with, who redistributed the survey internally within their respective organizations. Therefore we used non-probabilistic convenience sampling with snowballing [25].

Following the guidelines in [25] the *Target Audience, Unit of Analysis, Unit of Analysis, Unit of Observation,* and *Search Unit* are software developers with industrial experience, whilst the *Source of Sampling* are the authors' contacts in Swedish and Spanish software industry.

The survey began on April 19th, 2021 and had a programmed end on May 18th, 2021. The Total Gross Sample was 645 potential invitees. A total of 110 respondents (i.e., 17.05%) started the questionnaire (Net Participation). However, only 39 completed the questionnaire (35.35% of the Net Participation). The completion rate from the Total Gross Sample was 6.05%.

We examined the partially completed questionnaires and found out that there was a wide range of cases, but mostly few questions were answered. Therefore we decided to exclude the non-completed questionnaires from the analysis.

Finally, aiming to answer our research questions, we applied the Wilcoxon test to check if the responses for a given question were greater or smaller than the neutral value = 4 (i.e., agreement or disagreement) to see if the differences were statistically significant.

---

[2] The questionnaire is available for download in the companion materials in Zenodo DOI: 10.5281/zenodo.6973656.

[3] https://www.questback.com.

4 Results

4.1 SLR Results: Clean Code Principles

In Table 2 we report the Clean Code principles extracted from the papers included in the SLR. We also list the papers in which each principle is mentioned, and whether the papers report evidence of their usage in practice. Most of the principles listed in Table 2 come from the Clean Code book, with one exception: *Minimize Nesting* [32]. The principles listed in Table 2 were the input for the creation of the survey questionnaire questions that aim at answering RQ1. As an additional result, we observed very little evidence of the usage of Clean Code principles in practice.

4.2 Survey Results

Demographics As shown in Fig. 1, from the 39 participants that have completed the survey, the majority are in the age group 31–40 (Fig. 1.(a)), 36 are male 3 are female (Fig. 1.(b)), a big proportion have more than 20 years of experience (Fig. 1.(c)), and most of them, i.e., 22 participants, have a BSc degree (Fig. 1.(d)). Only 4 participants reported not having any higher education degree (i.e., No HE degree in Fig. 1.(e)).

Figure 1.(e), shows the degree of familiarity of the participants with Clean Code. For presenting the results to Likert questions[4], we show on the right and with green colors the number of participants agreeing with a particular statement; on the right and with brown colors, we show the participants that disagree with a particular statement. Finally, in the center and with a grey color, we show the number of participants that neither agree nor disagree with a particular example. As can be seen in Fig. 1.(e), most respondents are familiar with the Clean Code concept.

Based on these demographics, although the number of participants is not very big, we believe the participants constitute a relevant group of respondents for addressing the research questions.

RQ1: Do Developers Agree with Clean Code Principles? Fig. 2 shows the developers' degree of agreement with the *General*, *Naming*, and *Function an Method* Principles. The majority of the participants tend to agree with the principles listed, being OCP - Open Closed Principle [27] and Extract Try-Catch block [27] the most controversial in these groups. The Wilcoxon signed-rank test results ($p - value < 0.05$) show that the answers were significantly greater than the neutral value (i.e., the answers were greater than the neutral value equals 4) for all the principles listed in Fig. 2. These results confirm that the participants agree with these Clean Code principles[5].

---

[4] As the one shown in Fig. 1.(e).

[5] The complete results of the Wilcoxon signed-rank test are available in the companion materials in Zenodo DOI: 10.5281/zenodo.6973656.

Table 2. Clean Code Principles extracted from the SLR, including sources where the principle is mentioned, and wether there is evidence of its usage in practice

Type	Principle	Source
General	The Boy Scout Rule	B, P02, S05
	Minimize nesting	P17
	KISS - Keep It Simple, Stupid!	B, P01, S02
	OCP - Open Closed Principle	B, P01, S06
	Separate constructing a system from Its use	B
Naming	Use meaningful names	B, S01, S02, S04, S06
	Use intention-revealing names	B
	Pronounceable names	B
	Searchable names	B
	Avoid disinformation	B
	Avoid mental mapping	B
Function and Method	Do one thing	B, P02,S06
	Command query separation	B
	Extract Try-catch block	B
	Have no side effects	B, S06
	DRY - don't repeat yourself	B, S02, S07, P09, P11, P14, P17
	Function arguments	B, S06
	Structured programming	B
	Methods/functions should be small	B,S06, P01*
Comments	Amplification	B
	Clarification	B
	Explain yourself in code	B
	Explanation of Intent	B
	TODO comments	B
	Warning of consequences	B
Formatting	Team coding standards	B, S03, S08, S09, P17
	Horizontal formatting - indentation	B
	Dependent functions	B
	Vertical distance and ordering	B
	Organizing for change	B
Object and Data Structures	Data/Object Anti-Symmetry	B
	Law of Demeter	B
Error Handling	Prefer exceptions to returning error codes	B
	Don't pass null	B
	Don't return null	B
	Write your try-catch statement first	B
Unit Tests	Keeping tests clean	B
	One assert per test	B
	Single concept per test	B
Class	Class organization	B
	High cohesion	B, S02, S03, S04, S05, S06, S08, P01*, P8, P9, P11, P12, P14, P16
	Low coupling	B, S02, S03, S04, S05, S06, S08, P1*, P8, P9, P11, P14, P16
	Encapsulation - separation of concerns	B, P11, P14
	Isolating from change	B
	SRP - Single responsibility principle	B, S02, S06, S07, S08, P01*, P3, P16
	Minimal classes and methods	B
	One level of abstraction per function	B, P4*, P14, P16
	Classes should be small	B, S02, S06, P01*

* Reports evidence of the use of the principle in practice.

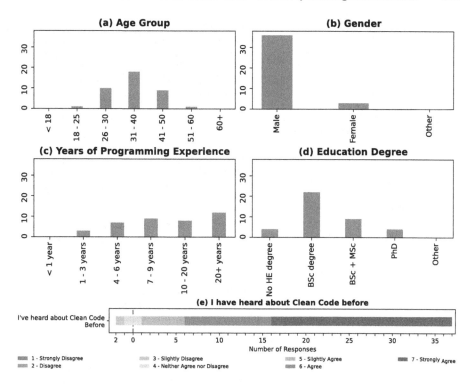

Fig. 1. Participants' demographics including age group, gender, years of programming experience, education, and familiarity with clean code.

Similarly, Fig. 3 shows the degree of agreement with the *Comments*, *Formatting* and *Object and Data Structures* Clean Code principles. Although there are some disagreements with the Comments principles. Again, the Wilcoxon signed-rank test results are statistically significant ($p - value < 0.05$), confirming that the participants tend to agree with these principles.

Finally, Fig. 4 shows the degree of agreement with the Error Handling, Unit Test, and the Class Clean Code principles. In this case, all the principles were statistically significant except two: *Write Your Try-Catch First* ($p - value = 0.47$) and *One Assert Per Test* ($p - value = 0.41$). Therefore we can conclude that developers agree with the majority of the Clean-Code principles except 2 (*Write Your Try-Catch First* and *One Assert Per Test*).

RQ2: Do Developers Believe that Clean Code Eases the Process of Reading, Understanding, Modifying, or Reusing Code? As shown in Fig. 5, participants agree that Clean Code eases the different code-related development activities, i.e., reading, understanding, reusing and maintaining the code. The participants also believe that Clean Code improves the quality attributes of the code, i.e., understandability, reusability, and maintainability (see Fig. 5.(b)). They also agree that reading, reusing, and modifying Clean Code takes a shorter

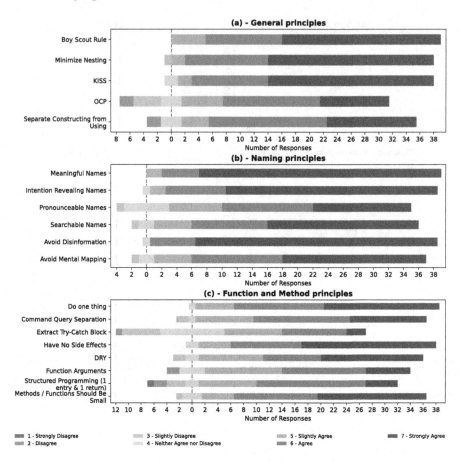

Fig. 2. Developers' degree of agreement with the General, Naming, and Function, and Method Principles.

time than working with "messy" code. The Wilcoxon signed-rank test results $(p - value < 0.05)$ show that the answers were significantly greater than the neutral value for all these questions.

RQ3: How Do Developers Keep Their Code "Clean"? Figure 6 shows the participants' responses to the questions regarding how they deal with Clean Code:

- whether respondents find it more difficult to write clean code initially as compared to writing "messy" code to be later refactored.
- their perceptions about the impact that refactoring has on code quality.
- whether they believe that requirements need to be clear to be able to write Clean Code initially.
- whether they believe that it is easier to write clean code at the beginning (i.e., in early phases) of a project.

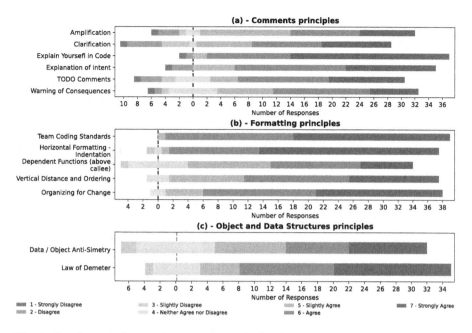

Fig. 3. Developers' degree of agreement with the Comments, Formatting and object and Data Structures Principles.

- whether writing clean code makes it easier to modify the code later.
- whether they perceive they have less time to write clean code towards the end of a project due to deadlines (i.e., time pressure).

Participants generally agree with all the statements. They seem to only disagree with the one about their perception regarding the impact of time pressure at the end of a project and their ability to write clean code. Indeed the Wilcoxon signed-rank test results ($p - value < 0.05$) show that the answers were significantly greater than the neutral value for all these questions but the last one. In this case, we also ran the test with the symmetric hypothesis (to check whether the disagreement was statistically significant) since the visual inspection of Fig. 6 seems to have more disagreeing answers. However, the results were not statistically significant ($p - value > 0.05$).

5 Discussion

RQ1: Do Developers Agree with Clean Code Principles? As reported in Sect. 4.2, the participants agree with most of the Clean Code principles; there are only two in which the statistical test did not find any agreement: *Write Your Try-Catch First* and *One Assert Per Test*. *Write Your Try-Catch First* might be controversial since it probably dictates too much about how to do Test-Driven Development (TDD) (or one can argue that it forces you even to do it). TDD

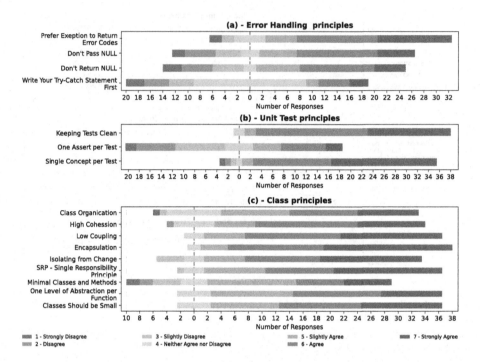

Fig. 4. Developers' degree of agreement with the Error Handling, Unit Test, and the Class Clean Code principles

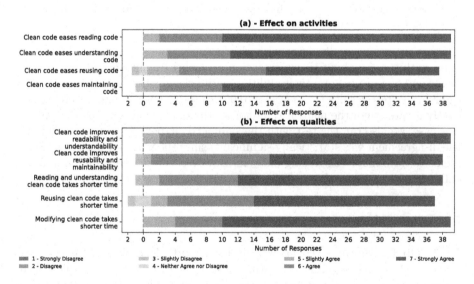

Fig. 5. Developers' perceptions regarding whether Clean Code eases the tasks of reading, understanding, reusing, and maintaining the code, its impact on readability, understandability, and maintainability, and whether it is faster to interact with Clean Code.

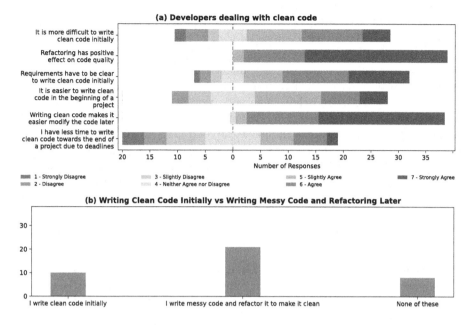

Fig. 6. Participant's perceptions regarding how they deal with Clean Code.

is not just tests-first or test-last but making sure developers take fine-grained develop-test steps and shorten the feedback loops [16]. One might prefer the exception to be thrown until they have finished writing and testing the actual code.

Regarding *One Assert Per Test*, although it has been found that the usage of asserts has a direct impact on the number of defects [10], having more than one does not seem to have an impact on the number of defects [11]. Similarly, using multiple asserts does not seem to have a relationship with code complexity either [6], and might be a source of test clones. The *Comments* principles probably generate reluctance since the principles advocate for not commenting on the code but instead writing "clean" and "clear", self-explanatory code. In the open questions, some of the participants refer to the use of comments to clarify what the code does, which contradicts the Clean Code principles. However, most participants tend to agree with the *Comments* principles.

RQ2: Do Developers Believe that Clean Code Eases the Process of Reading, Understanding, Modifying, or Reusing Code? As shown in Fig. 5, developers believe that Clean Code eases the different code-related developer activities, i.e., reading, understanding, reusing and maintaining the code. The participants also agree with the fact that Clean Code improves the quality attributes in the code (i.e., understandability, reusability, and maintainability). Although there are results that report improvements in maintainability (e.g., [7]), there are also other studies that report that the impact on understandability is not that obvious. For example, Ammerlan et al.,[5] report that understandability can sometimes be hindered when we refactor to clean our code.

We also asked our participants in the questionnaire survey if they believe that it takes a shorter time to read, understand, modify, or reuse clean code compared to unclean code. The respondents strongly agreed with this. Only some developers disagreed that clean code would take a shorter time to read and understand than unclean code. Arif and Rana [7] reported that if developers remove code smells in advance and make the code clean, it will take 7% less effort to add new features to the code than with unclean code. Other research studies (e.g., [20]) suggest that Clean Code has an impact on the time required to change current functionality, although it does not seem to have an impact on the time used to implement new significant functionality or solve bugs, or to solve small coding tasks. Therefore more research seems to be required to analyze these phenomena in industrial settings.

RQ3: How Do Developers Keep Their Code "Clean"? As shown in Fig. 6, participants first acknowledge that they find it more difficult to write Clean Code and that they tend to write "messy" code that they refactor later. All participants agree with the fact that refactoring has a positive effect on code quality and, therefore, helps keep the code clean. Refactoring is probably the most popular technique to keep the code clean and repay Technical Debt [14]. However, it can also negatively affect code quality and introduce Technical Debt Items [39]. In the open questions, in the question *"What are/would be the challenges with refactoring unclean code to become clean code?"*, some participants mentioned *"Breaking the Functionality"*. However, Clean Code has a strong emphasis on testing and having enough test coverage might solve that issue since tests are the "safe net" when refactoring [15].

In addition, we also found that developers agreed that the requirements must be specified clearly to write clean code. Only a few developers disagreed with the previous statement. Therefore, the findings in the literature and our results seem aligned. Lucena and Tizzei [26] also mention that writing more precise requirements helped the team to reduce Technical Debt and to keep their code clean. It also showed that the development had a more sustainable velocity and could deliver a more valuable project to the customer when applying these practices.

There was a mixture of opinions regarding whether participants feel they have less time to write clean code towards the end of the project due to deadlines (or when they approach deadlines). These results somehow contrast previous works (e.g., [30]), in which time pressure was one of the main reasons for developers not writing clean code.

6   Threats to Validity

In this section, we discuss threats to construct, internal, and external validity, as well as reliability.

Construct Validity concerns mapping the constructs (research questions) to the questions in the survey questionnaire. The results and discussion are reported per research question to clarify this mapping. However, it is still possible that some of the questions do not connect to the construct.

Internal Validity is mainly affected by the fact that we derive the findings and conclusions from several questions by "merging" or "abstracting out" the conclusions. This might open the door to researcher bias since we might cherry-pick and give more value to some questions. We have tried to minimize this threat by describing and analyzing the questions separately and using the Wilcoxon signed-rank test to check the significance of each variable individually. Another potential threat to the internal validity is the participants' degree of familiarity with the different clean code principles. We only investigated the fact that the participants were generally familiar with clean code but not whether they knew about each principle. This threat could have been minimized by offering the participants the opportunity of clicking "Unknown" for these principles they were unfamiliar with. However, we tried to partially minimize the threat by including a brief explanation for each principle that the participants could access while answering the survey[6].

The selection of participants in this study is another threat to the internal validity. The survey was shared through social networks (i.e., LinkedIn, Twitter) and using the authors' industrial contacts. This sharing strategy results in a limited selection procedure. In addition, more than half of the participants did not finish the questionnaire (we discarded their responses), which also represents a self-selection protocol and might bias the results. Respondents with more negative views toward Clean Code or less mainstream opinions might have left the questionnaire unfinished. Finally, there might be a tendency to respond with best practices instead of reporting bad behaviors. Once distributed, the researchers had little control over the questionnaire, which had only a closing deadline, which somehow mitigates some validity threats.

External Validity is concerned with the potential generalizability of the results. The number of respondents compared to the potential target population (the software developers working in the industry around the world) is minimal. However, it is in line with similar studies in the area. We could have exposed the survey during a more extended period to have more participants, improving generalizability. However, we designed the survey to close automatically after a

---

[6] The additional explanations for each principle is available in the companion materials in Zenodo DOI: 10.5281/zenodo.6973656.

certain period (i.e., one month). The question is whether the sample is representative of the *Target Audience* [19]. However, the respondents' experience is higher as compared to other studies (e.g., [35,38]).

Reliability to enhance reliability, we have published the multiple choice questions and the results of the statistical test as companion materials in Zenodo. We have not published the answers to the open questions since, in some cases, those can help identify the respondents' affiliation, which would break the anonymity clauses on the pre-questionnaire consent form.

7   Conclusions and Further Work

This paper reports a Questionnaire Survey with 39 participants that explores how professional developers perceive Clean Code. To collect Clean Code principles beyond the seminal book, we conducted a Snowballing Systematic Literature Review using a hybrid search strategy. We screened 771 research papers: 723 papers to define the start set and 48 papers in the four snowballing iterations. The Systematic Literature Review resulted in including in the questionnaire one more Clean Code principle not listed in the seminal book (i.e., *Minimize Nesting*).

The survey results indicate that developers tend to agree with most of the Clean Code principles, except for two, namely *Write Your Try-Catch First* and *One Assert Per Test*. The results also indicate that developers believe that Clean Code eases reading, understanding, reusing and maintaining the code. They also believe clean code improves readability, understandability, reusability and maintainability. Moreover, clean code is perceived to shorten the time required to read, understand, reuse, and modify the code (in this case, empirical evidence exists that confirms and disproves these results). Our results also indicate that developers tend to write "messy" code that they refactor later and perceive refactoring positively affecting code quality. They find it more challenging to write clean code initially than to write messy code to be refactored later. The results also show that developers perceive that at the beginning of a project seems to be easier to write clean code. There is no consensus on whether time pressure impacts the time they can devote to writing Clean Code.

These results are the first step toward understanding what principles developers are more prone to adopt and how they try to clean their code. Our results can also help us to understand the support they need and the potential risks they might incur when refactoring. However, these results are only valid in the context of the study, and it is, at this point, difficult to establish generalizations. Therefore there is still a need to conduct similar studies, or replications of this survey in other contexts, even among contributors to Open-Source systems, to strengthen the evidence.

Acknowledgements. This research was supported by the KKS foundation through the SHADE KKS Hög project (Ref: 20170176) and through the KKS SERT Research Profile project (Ref. 2018010) Blekinge Institute of Technology.

References

1. Ajami, S., Woodbridge, Y., Feitelson, D.G.: Syntax, predicates, idioms - what really affects code complexity? Empir. Softw. Eng. **24**, 287–328 (2019). https://doi.org/10.1007/S10664-018-9628-3
2. Almogahed, A., Omar, M., Zakaria, N.H.: Impact of software refactoring on software quality in the industrial environment: A review of empirical studies. In: Knowledge Management International Conference (KMICe), pp. 25–27, Miri Sarawak, Malaysia (2018)
3. Almogahed, A., Omar, M., Zakaria, N.H.: Categorization refactoring techniques based on their effect on software quality attributes. Int. J. Innov. Technol. Exploring Eng. (IJITEE) **8** (2019)
4. Alomar, E.A., Alrubaye, H., Mkaouer, M.W., Ouni, A., Kessentini, M.: Refactoring practices in the context of modern code review: An industrial case study at xerox. In: 43rd International Conference on Software Engineering (ICSE), pp. 348–357. IEEE, Madrid, Spain (Virtual Event) (2021)
5. Ammerlaan, E., Veninga, W., Zaidman, A.: Old habits die hard: Why refactoring for understandability does not give immediate benefits. In: 22nd International Conference on Software Analysis. Evolution, and Reengineering (SANER), pp. 504–507, Montreal, QC, Canada (2015)
6. Aniche, M.F., Oliva, G.A., Gerosa, M.A.: What do the asserts in a unit test tell us about code quality? a study on open source and industrial projects. In: 17th European Conference on Software Maintenance and Reengineering (CSMR), pp. 111–120. Genova, Italy (2013)
7. Arif, A., Rana, Z.A.: Refactoring of code to remove technical debt and reduce maintenance effort. In: 14th International Conference on Open Source Systems and Technologies (ICOSST), IEEE, Lahore, Pakistan (2020)
8. Avidan, E., Feitelson, D.G.: Effects of variable names on comprehension: An empirical study. In: 25th IEEE/ACM International Conference on Program Comprehension (ICPC), pp. 55–65. Buenos Aires, Argentina (2017)
9. Börstler, J., et al.: "i know it when i see it" - perceptions of code quality. In: 2017 ITiCSE Conference - Working Group Reports, pp. 70–85. ACM, Bologna, Italy (2017)
10. Casalnuovo, C., Devanbu, P., Oliveira, A., Filkov, V., Ray, B.: Assert use in github projects. In: 37th IEEE International Conference on Software Engineering (ICSE), pp. 755–766. IEEE, Florence, Italy (2015)
11. Counsell, S., Hall, T., Shippey, T., Bowes, D., Tahir, A., MacDonell, S.: Assert use and defectiveness in industrial code. In: IEEE 28th International Symposium on Software Reliability Engineering Workshops (ISSREW), pp. 20–23. IEEE, Wuhan, China (2017)
12. Dallal, J.A., Abdin, A.: Empirical evaluation of the impact of object-oriented code refactoring on quality attributes: A systematic literature review. IEEE Trans. Softw. Eng. **44**, 44–69 (2018). https://doi.org/10.1109/TSE.2017.2658573
13. Dibble, C., Gestwicki, P.: Refactoring code to increase readability and maintainability: A case study. J. Comput. Sci. Coll. **30**(1), 41–51 (2014)
14. Digkas, G., Chatzigeorgiou, A.N., Ampatzoglou, A., Avgeriou, P.C.: Can clean new code reduce technical debt density. IEEE Trans. Software Eng. **48**, 1–18 (2020). https://doi.org/10.1109/TSE.2020.3032557
15. Fowler, M., Beck, K.: Refactoring Improving the Design of Existing Code. Addison Wesley, 2nd edn. (2018)

16. Fucci, D., Erdogmus, H., Turhan, B.: A dissection of test-driven development?: Does it really matter to test-first or to test-last? IEEE Trans. Software Eng. **6**, 1–20 (2015). https://doi.org/10.1109/TSE.2016.2616877

17. Johnson, J., Lubo, S., Yedla, N., Aponte, J., Sharif, B.: An empirical study assessing source code readability in comprehension. In: IEEE International Conference on Software Maintenance and Evolution (ICSME), pp. 513–523. IEEE, Dallas, TX, USA, Sep 2019

18. Kim, M., Zimmermann, T., Nagappan, N.: A field study of refactoring challenges and benefits. In: ACM SIGSOFT 20th International Symposium on the Foundations of Software Engineering (FSE), p. 1. ACM Press, Cary, NC, USA (2012)

19. Kitchenham, B.A., Pfleeger, S.L.: Principles of survey research: Part 3 - constructing a survey instrument. In: ACM SIGSOFT Software Engineering Notes, p.20 (2002). https://doi.org/10.1145/511152.511155

20. Koller, H.G.: Effects of Clean Code on Understandability An Experiment and Analysis. Master's thesis, Department of Informatics, University of Oslo (2016)

21. Latte, B., Henning, S., Wojcieszak, M.: Clean code: On the use of practices and tools to produce maintainable code for long-living. In: Collaborative Workshop in Evolution and Maintenance of Long-Living Systems EMLS2019, Stuttgart, Germany, vol. Vol-2308, pp. 96–99 (2019), 'CEUR-WS.org'

22. Lee, T., Lee, J.B., Peter, H.I.: Effect analysis of coding convention violations on readability of post-delivered code. IEICE Trans. Inf. Syst. **98**, 1286–1296 (2015). https://doi.org/10.1587/transinf.2014EDP7327

23. Lerthathairat, P., Prompoon, N.: An approach for source code classification to enhance maintainability. In: 2011 Eighth International Joint Conference on Computer Science and Software Engineering (JCSSE), Nakhon Pathom, Thailand, pp. 319–324 (2011)

24. Lerthathairat, P., Prompoon, N.: An approach for source code classification using software metrics and fuzzy logic to improve code quality with refactoring techniques. In: Zain, J.M., Wan Mohd, W.M., El-Qawasmeh, E. (eds.) ICSECS 2011. CCIS, vol. 181, pp. 478–492. Springer, Heidelberg (2011). https://doi.org/10.1007/978-3-642-22203-0_42

25. Linåker, J., Sulaman, S.M., Höst, M., Mello, R.M.D.: Guidelines for conducting surveys in software engineering v. 1.1. Tech. rep., Department of Computer Science, Lund University, Lund, Sweden (2015)

26. Lucena, P., Tizzei, L.P.: Applying software craftsmanship practices to a scrum project: an experience report. In: 1st Workshop on Social, Human and Economics Aspects of Software (WASHES), Maceió, Brazil, arxiv.org/abs/1611.05789 (2016)

27. Martin, R.C.: Clean Code - A Handbook of Agile Software Craftmanship. Prentice Hall (2009)

28. Mourão, E., Kalinowski, M., Murta, L., Mendes, E., Wohlin, C.: Investigating the use of a hybrid search strategy for systematic reviews. In: Empirical Software Eninneering and Measurements (ESEM), Toronto, ON, Canada (2017)

29. Pantiuchina, J., et al.: Why developers refactor source code. ACM Tran. Softw. Eng. Methodology (TOSEM) **29** (2020). https://doi.org/10.1145/3408302

30. Rachow, P., Schroder, S., Riebisch, M.: Missing clean code acceptance and support in practice - an empirical study. In: Proceedings - 25th Australasian Software Engineering Conference, pp. 131–140. IEEE, Adelaide, Australia (2018)

31. Sae-Lim, N., Hayashi, S., Saeki, M.: Toward proactive refactoring: An exploratory study on decaying modules. In: Proceedings - 2019 IEEE/ACM 3rd International Workshop on Refactoring (IWOR), pp. 39–46. IEEE, Montreal, QC, Canada (2019)

32. Sedano, T.: Code readability testing, an empirical study. In: 29th Conference on Software Engineering Education and Training (CSEE&T), pp. 111–117. IEEE, Austin, TX, USA (2016)

33. Sharma, T., Suryanarayana, G., Samarthyam, G.: Challenges to and solutions for refactoring adoption: An industrial perspective. IEEE Softw. **32**, 44–51 (2015). https://doi.org/10.1109/MS.2015.105

34. Steidl, D., Deissenboeck, F., Poehlmann, M., Heinke, R., Uhink-Mergenthaler, B.: Continuous software quality control in practice. In: IEEE International Conference on Software Maintenance and Evolution (ICSME), Victoria, BC, Canada, pp. 561–564 (2014)

35. Stevenson, J., Wood, M.: Recognising object-oriented software design quality: a practitioner-based questionnaire survey. Softw. Quality J. **26**, 321–365 (2018). https://doi.org/10.1007/s11219-017-9364-8

36. Vakilian, M., Chen, N., Negara, S., Rajkumar, B.A., Bailey, B.P., Johnson, R.E.: Use, disuse, and misuse of automated refactorings. In: International Conference on Software Engineering (ICSE), pp. 233–243. Zurich, Switzerland (2012)

37. Wohlin, C.: Guidelines for snowballing in systematic literature studies and a replication in software engineering. In: 18th International Conference on Evaluation and Assessment in Software Engineering (EASE), London, UK, pp. 1–10 (2014)

38. Yamashita, A., Moonen, L.: Do developers care about code smells? an exploratory survey. In: 20th Working Conference on Reverse Engineering (WCRE), pp. 242–251. IEEE, Koblenz, Germany (2013)

39. Zabardast, E., Gonzalez-Huerta, J., Smite, D.: Refactoring, bug fixing, and new development effect on technical debt : An industrial case study. In: 46th Euromicro Conference on Software Engineering and Advanced Applications (Euromicro-SEAA), pp. 376–384. IEEE, Kranj, Slovenia (Virtual Event) (2020)

Software Business and Digital Innovation

Counter the Uncertainties in a Dynamic World: An Approach to Creating Outcome-Driven Product Roadmaps

Stefan Trieflinger[1]([⊠]), Dominic Lang[2], and Jürgen Münch[1]

[1] Reutlingen University, Alteburgstraße 150, Reutlingen, Germany
{stefan.trieflinger,juergen.muench}@reutlingen-university.de
[2] ETAS GmbH, Borsigstraße 24, 70469 Stuttgart, Germany
Dominic.lang2@bosch.com

Abstract. Context: Nowadays the market environment is characterized by high uncertainties due to high market dynamics, confronting companies with new challenges in creating and updating product roadmaps. Most companies are still using traditional approaches which typically fail in such environments. Therefore, companies are seeking opportunities for new product roadmapping approaches. **Objective:** This paper presents good practices to support companies better understand what factors are required to conduct a successful product roadmapping in a dynamic and uncertain market environment. **Method:** Based on a grey literature review, essential aspects for conducting product roadmapping in a dynamic and uncertain market environment were identified. Expert workshops were then held with two researchers and three practitioners to develop best practices and the proposed approach for an outcome-driven roadmap. These results were then given to another set of practitioners and their perceptions were gathered through interviews. **Results:** The study results in the development of 9 good practices that provide practitioners with insights into what aspects are crucial for product roadmapping in a dynamic and uncertain market environment. Moreover, we propose an approach to product roadmapping that includes providing a flexible structure and focusing on delivering value to the customer and the business. To ensure the latter, this approach consists of the main items outcome hypothesis, validated outcomes, and discovered outputs.

Keywords: Product roadmap · Roadmapping · Product management · Product discovery · Problem discovery · Solution discovery · User research · Ux · Customer value · BANI

1 Introduction

Nowadays, the market environment for the development of digital products or services is characterized by high dynamics, rapidly evolving technologies, and shifting user expectations [1–3] In addition, disruptive approaches threaten established market participants and try to drive them out of the market [4, 5]. Often this situation is referred to with the

© The Author(s), under exclusive license to Springer Nature Switzerland AG 2022
D. Taibi et al. (Eds.): PROFES 2022, LNCS 13709, pp. 319–333, 2022.
https://doi.org/10.1007/978-3-031-21388-5_22

acronym BANI [6, 7, 8, 9]. BANI stands for Brittle, Anxious, Non-Linear, and Incomprehensible, which is intended to describe and emphasize the uncertainty in today's market more clearly. Brittle describes the strong fragility and instability of a system (e.g., a business model) due to the high dynamics and the associated uncertainty in the market. A system that is brittle often seems strong and is often trimmed for maximum efficiency, but it can break down all at once. One example, therefore, is the cultivation of monocultures, which is very efficient and successful but brittle since a simple change in climate or plant disease can destroy it instantly. Anxious means the fear of making decisions in a dynamic market environment. This usually leads to passivity, as managers and leaders feel perplexed and helpless and conclude that if they don´t make decisions, they can´t make wrong decisions. However, such an approach usually leads to stagnation while the world keeps in change and evolving. This behavior will lead to the circumstance that such a company will not acquire new abilities to survive in a dynamic and uncertain market environment. Finally, non-linear means that cause and effect appear to be incoherent or disproportionate. Reasons for this could be, that other factors (e.g., rapidly changing customer behavior or disruptive approaches) distort the cause and effect, or that a delay between the visible cause and the visible effect appears. This can also be found in the last part of BANI, which is incomprehensible. Incomprehensible refers to the difficulty of interpreting phenomena such as the underlying reasons why a feature is not used by the customers or why something worked and something else did not, even if obviously it should be the other way round. Often such situations involve a large amount of data, which makes it almost impossible to analyze and understand such phenomena [6–9].

Against this backdrop, companies are increasingly struggling to create reliable product planning [10]. In order to plan the future product portfolio, product roadmaps are widely used [11–13]. The basic purpose of product roadmaps is to serve as a guide for the product team in order to achieve the corporate vision, allowing them to recognize and act on events that require a change of the strategic direction. Consequently, product roadmaps are strategic communication tools, that map out the vision and direction of a company and the work that is required to get there [2, 3]. Moreover, a product roadmap aims to create alignment and a common understanding of the future direction to gather support and to be able to coordinate the effort among all stakeholders [14]. However, most companies are using a traditional format of product roadmaps that consist of a fixed-time-based chart that provides a forecast of specific products, features, or services, including concrete release dates. Such a format is called feature-driven product roadmaps [2, 3]. However, feature-driven roadmaps lack two main factors that are crucial to surviving in the BANI world. On the one hand, feature-driven product roadmaps consider only outputs such as products or features, not the outcome to be delivered to the customer and the business by providing an output. On the other hand, the structure of feature-driven product roadmaps in the BANI world leads to frequent adjustments to the product roadmap. This results in a high effort, and the roadmap loses trust among its stakeholders. Another problem of feature-driven product roadmaps is that management or experts often decide which features will be included in the product roadmap without considering the problems and needs of the customers. This is because the creation of traditional feature driven product roadmaps does not include a process for identifying customer needs and validating feature ideas to fulfill those needs [2, 3]. A detailed discussion of the problems caused by the use of feature-driven product roadmaps in the BANI world can be found in Münch et al. [3].

For these reasons, feature-driven product roadmaps work well in market environments that are predictable, stable, and reliable, which can not be assumed for the BANI world [3, 5, 15]. Consequently, using feature-driven product roadmaps in the BANI world leads to several problems. First, feature-driven roadmaps are just a scheduled list of products or features that are subject to many changes due to the high uncertainty in the BANI world. These frequent adjustments lead to the fact that stakeholders, employees, and external partners lose trust in the reliability of the product roadmap. Second, feature-driven roadmaps are often understood as a commitment to developing the features they contain. This leads to a shift in focus from the current needs and problems of the customers to the functionality of a product or service with its features. Therefore, the criterion of success is no longer customer satisfaction, but on-time delivery to the customer. This approach leads to the risk that the company moves in the wrong direction and, in the worst case, runs out of business. Third, feature-driven roadmaps often include unrealistic expectations (e.g., delivering many and extensive features in a too short development period). This tends to force the product team to sacrifice product quality in order to meet these expectations. In addition, meeting these expectations puts a lot of stress on the product team which lowers the atmosphere and morale of the product team [16].

By experiencing these problems, many companies have realized that new approaches and procedures regarding the development and handling of product roadmaps are required. However, many companies are struggling to transform their traditional product roadmapping practice to the requirements of the BANI world [10, 14]. Existing literature or practical case studies offers little help on what the BANI world requires for a successful product roadmapping. In order to close this gap, this paper aims to provide good practices that are essential to the success of product roadmapping in the BANI world. The paper is organized as follows: Sect. 2 covers related work. Section 3 discusses our research approach, while Sect. 4 presents our results in form of the good practices as well as a proposed product roadmap format for use in the BANI world. Section 5 addresses the validation of our approach, and Sect. 6 discusses the threats to the validity of our study. Finally, in Sect. 7 a summary is given, and further research is outlined.

2   Related Work

In the scientific literature, few authors considered practical experiences and lessons learned regarding product roadmapping.

Wilby [17] reports on his practical experience regarding the adaption of the roadmap during the agile transformation of Borland Software Corporation. Wilby describes the following requirements of the roadmap: 1) the roadmap should be a living document designed to answer key strategic questions; 2) the roadmap should be reviewed and updated quarterly; 3) the roadmap should include a written distribution plan in order to keep all employees and stakeholders up to date; 4) the roadmap should provide the flexibility to maximize the advantages of agile development. In order to meet these requirements, Borland Software reviewed and changed the roadmap in a two-day workshop with different key members of the department's product management, engineering, marketing, sales, and support. After the introduction of the "agile roadmap", the greatest perceived benefit was that communication barriers between the different teams were overcome. Furthermore, the author firmly believes that the introduction of the "agile roadmaps" has positively affected the development and delivery of a better product-market fit.

De Oliveira et al. [18] analysed three roadmapping project and identified the following learning points: 1) the conduction of individual interviews can be more efficient that workshops with large groups for gathering information regarding the development and updating of a roadmap, 2) Some experts prefer to meet via online conference calls due to agenda issues, lack of initial interest, or unclear facts concerning the project, 3) splitting the roadmapping process into shorter and focused workshops can reduce uncertainties and ensure flexibility to cope with unexpected issues, 4) the project team receives insights while conducting and evaluating expert interviews that prepare them to facilitate workshops and ensure that the most important issues are addressed, 5) the project team should apply an interview protocol and use strategic management tools in order to define the information that should be considered during the interviews, 6) the roadmap architecture is an ideal standard framework for conducting interviews and supports organizing and consolidating data into a preliminary roadmap.

Moreover, many authors describe challenges regarding product roadmapping [3, 4, 19]. One example is the study by Lehtola et al. [20] which describes the challenges of a Finnish software product company that developed and evaluated its own roadmapping process in its organization. In this context, the authors identified the following findings. 1) Roadmapping strengthened the link between business decisions and requirements engineering, 2) product managers consider roadmaps as tools for communicating their ideas to stakeholders, 3) the point of view of engineering was less taken into account compared to that of other stakeholders, 3) Stakeholders of the roadmap complained that roadmaps were immediately outdated, 4) practitioners missed ways to link product development resources to roadmaps and 5) practitioners wrote product roadmaps for a shorter time period than that required. Besides this, the authors mentioned that if just one person or function of the company is responsible for the roadmapping process, the other stakeholders may not see the benefits from their viewpoints and therefore may feel unmotivated.

With regard to the construction and handling of product roadmaps, the scientific literature predominantly covers the reporting of practical experience and the challenges associated with them. However, this is done on a very abstract level. This means that the scientific literature does not provide detailed insights into what aspects need to be considered in order to develop successful product roadmaps in a dynamic and uncertain market environment. This is the focus of the study at hand.

3 Research Approach

The overall goal of our research is to support practitioners that operate in the software-intensive business in developing product roadmaps in a dynamic market environment with high uncertainties. In order to achieve our objective, we formulated the following research questions:

- **RQ1:** What good practices are recommended when developing product roadmaps in a dynamic and uncertain market environment?
- **RQ2**: How does a product roadmap for a dynamic and uncertain market environment look like?

We developed the results of this study within expert workshops attended by one practitioner operating in a large software-intensive company and two researchers. We define an expert as a person that has authorization to a certain field and is involved in decision making processes based on his or her position. We selected the practitioner since he has many years of experience in leading an agile product team and extensive knowledge of the issue of product roadmapping.

The expert workshop was held on 21 July 2022 via the online tool Zoom and lasted 3 h. In order to discuss the development of the good practices systematically, we have taken the following approach: The first task was for the participants to share and discuss their previously experienced challenges related to product roadmapping. Therefore, each participant had 10 min to write down his or her experiences. Afterward, each participant presented their previously experienced challenges and discussed them with the other participants. After each participant had presented their challenges, we presented the challenges that we had identified through the grey literature review mentioned above. Then, the mentioned challenges were summarized in order to build a common context including the motivation for why the good practices, as well as the product roadmap format, should be developed. Subsequently, the development process of these artifacts starts which contains the following tasks: 1) What are the most important aspects of product roadmapping in a dynamic and uncertain market environment from the point of view of the participants? 2) what structure is appropriate for a product roadmap for a dynamic and uncertain market environment and 3) what elements should be included in the roadmap? Each participant was given 10 min to answer this question, which was followed by a 30-min discussion with all participants. To enable participants to collaborate as well as to document their ideas and input of the participants we used the online tool "Mural". In this context, the blind mode provided by Mural was activated to prevent participants from influencing each other while working on the tasks. Activation of this mode has the effect that each participant could see the answers of the other participants only after the time to complete the task had expired. Within the 30-min session between the participants, one researcher acted as moderator, while another researcher documented the key statements. Both researchers were excluded from the discussions.

4 Results

In order to answer RQ1, we developed the good practices presented below within expert workshops. The good practices are intended to help managers and product managers to get a better understanding of what aspects are supportive for a successful product roadmapping in a dynamic market environment. These insights should help companies to transform their often traditionally applied product roadmapping practices to the requirements of a dynamic and uncertain market environment.

4.1 Good Practice for Conducting Product Roadmapping

Good Practice 1: Connect the Corporate Visions to the Product Roadmap via Product Strategy: In order to identify the items that should be put on the roadmap it is highly beneficial to derive the items directly from the company's product strategy, which should be determined by its vision. In developing and revising the product roadmap, the vision and strategy provide guidance and direction to the product teams in making decisions. The product teams can also benefit from making use of a product vision. A product vision describes the ultimate reason for the development of the product as well as the positive changes the product should bring about. When creating the product vision, care should be taken to ensure that the product vision reflects the current problems and needs of the customers. This encourages a shift in discussion from "What should we develop" to "would decision A or decision B support us more in achieving the product vision? To unfold a product vision's full effect, it is crucial that it is communicated and lived throughout the whole company. This motivates and inspires the various teams and external stakeholders to participate in order to make the product vision a reality.

Good Practice 2: Identify Outcomes and Include them in the Product Roadmap: A suitable product roadmap for a dynamic and uncertain market environment should contribute to delivering value to the customer and the business. Therefore, the product roadmap should not only describe what should be developed but also why it should be developed. In order to achieve this, it is necessary that outcomes are included in the product roadmap. Outcomes help clearly communicate the goals and purpose of the next product version to all stakeholders and support including customer-oriented content for the next release. It should be noted that each outcome should contribute to fulfilling the product vision. One suitable method to uncover outcomes is the Jobs-to-be-done framework [21]. The framework says that people buy products and services to get a job done, i.e., to solve a problem. On this base, the framework aims to identify customer needs as well as underserved areas. In this context, it is not enough to scratch the surface, but the underlying needs and desires of the customers must be identified and understood.

Good Practice 3: Fail Cheap by Spending Effort at the Latest Possible Point in Time: IN a dynamic and uncertain market environment, it only seems possible to plan a maximum of three months in advance. This can be observed and gets even enforced by the fact that many companies nowadays work in a quarterly cadence in order to respond to the challenges of the BANI environment. One of these challenges is the high volatility of the market which increases the likelihood of planning and long-term preparation becomes a waste of resources. Therefore, it is considered as good practice to invest as little effort as possible into roadmap items and only focus your work on detailing out them when they are successfully tested and close in time. Therefore, only those items on the product roadmap that are next for implementation should be more detailed and broken down to a feature level. This provides the flexibility to react to changes in the market (e.g. changing customer behaviour) rapidly and efficiently since items can be replaced or removed from the roadmap with low loss of effort. For example, the long-time horizon should include outcomes that are formulated as hypotheses, the mid-term time horizon contains confirmed outcomes with possible solution hypotheses that have to be validated, and the short-term time horizon include only validated outputs such as products or features.

Good Practice 4: Change your Roadmap only Systematically and Transparently: Often, unfounded changes to the roadmaps cause those employees and stakeholders to lose trust in the product roadmap. In order to counter this circumstance, a product roadmap should be stable in a way that changes are only carried out justifiably and systematically. This requires a regular cadence for reviewing and updating the product roadmap involving all people involved in product planning (e.g., product managers, product owners, marketers and distributors, and engineers). This helps to get a better understanding of what contents of the product roadmap should be adjusted and avoid that uncertain features being seen as delivery promises.

Good Practice 5: Consider the Confidence for Each Roadmap Item: Confidence means the probability that a product or feature on the product roadmap will achieve the expected objectives or outcomes to acceptable costs as well as the confidence to deliver the corresponding output. Consequently, the factor of confidence should influence the decision of whether a feature should be developed or not. Hence, the short time horizon should only include those items that are deemed to have high confidence in achieving their respective goals. A possible approach to work with confidence is to rate it by using a Likert-type scale as shown in Table 1.

Table 1. Confidence levels

Confidence level	Description
1	Declining
2	Hesitant
3	Undecided
4	Confident
5	Convinced

Good Practice 6: Integrate Product Discovery Activities into the Product Roadmapping Process: Discovery in this case means the ability of a company to identify needs and validate features on the product roadmap with regards to their ability to respond to those needs before they are developed. This includes the identification and researching of customer problems as well as finding solutions to those problems that are useful, feasible and economically viable. Consequently, a benefit of product discovery activities is to avoid developing features that customers do not want or need. Concrete examples for the conduction of product discovery activities are interviews with customers, rapid prototyping, or customer focus groups. We consider the consequent integration of such discovery activities into the roadmapping process as a success factor since it supports the identification, validation, and detailing of the roadmap items. Additionally, this ensures that only validated solution outcomes that provide a valuable outcome enter the implementation backlog, leading to waste avoidance. A possible approach to how Design Thinking can systematically improve the roadmapping process is presented later in this work with regards to RQ2.

Good Practice 7: Make Sure that Priorities are Set by the Market and not by Management or Experts: IN practice, it often occurs that management or experts (e.g., product managers or product owners) decide what should be delivered first. This brings the risk of not developing those features first that deliver the most value to the customer and jeopardizing the opportunity to develop them later. Therefore, a well-established product roadmap prioritization process is essential for the success of the product roadmap and the development of innovative and customer-oriented products. Overall, there are a variety of prioritization techniques that help to avoid biases with different approaches such as mapping-based techniques (Assumption Mapping or the Systemico Model), scoring-based techniques (e.g., Opportunity Scoring or the RICE scoring model), or game-based techniques (e.g., Buy a feature or Feature Buckets) [22]. In this context, it should be noted that each product manager has his own preferences and can choose his prioritization method accordingly. For example, product manager A prefers a games-based technique, while product manager B favors a scoring-based technique. However, what needs to be ensured when applying the technique selected is that the customer value, as well as the ability to develop the product, must be taken into consideration.

Good Practice 8: Create Alignment Around the Product Roadmap: A product roadmap is almost useless without alignment and buy-in from the key stakeholders. Alignment around the product roadmap is essential to ensure that each employee is aware of the outcomes of the product roadmap that should be achieved so that all product development activities can be orchestrated to achieve those outcomes. Therefore, we recommend sharing the roadmap internally and externally to get employees and customers excited about the features planned to come next. However, in this context, it is crucial to consider the audience for which the product roadmap is shared. The reason for this is that different stakeholders require different information. For example, the management will be interested in objectives and how to achieve them at an abstract level, while engineering or marketing, and sales need detailed information in order to perform their activities. Sharing the product roadmap with customers brings the advantage that feedback can be gathered early so that the customer feels involved and committed to the company. However, it has to be considered that all stakeholders require individual but consistent representations of a common roadmap that reflects their information needs. For this purpose, the creation of a central roadmap that enables to derive different representations for various groups of stakeholders is recommended. Besides this, various methods to achieve alignment exists. Examples, therefore, are the application of OKRs, the conduction of the method Shuttle Diplomacy, or the Behavioural Change Stairway Model [23].

Good Practice 9: Assign Responsibility and Ownership of the Product Roadmap to Product Management: Responsibility answers the question of who is responsible for placing items on the roadmap and conduction of the roadmapping process. The term ownership means who is accountable, i.e., signs off and approves the product roadmap. Especially the ownership has a strong influence on how the roadmapping process is lived and which values are practiced (e.g., management decides about the content of the roadmap vs. product discovery is being conducted). Therefore, the owner of the product roadmap has a high impact on the success of the entire product roadmapping process.

Since product management usually has the task of shaping the future of a product or product portfolio as well as coordinating the various interests of all stakeholders involved, it is advisable to assign responsibility to product management. Also, the ownership should be with product management to fully enable them to take responsibility, increase their independency from stakeholders in a hierarchy and let them act according to market demands. In addition, this approach enables product management to define suitable validation measures and conduct them most quickly (without lengthy discussions with other parties). The management should focus on steering the entire company's direction by providing a vision and strategy while giving autonomy and trust to the product management on the future direction of the product portfolio.

4.2 Proposed Product Roadmap Format for a Dynamic Market Environment

In the following, we provide answers to RQ2 by presenting a product roadmap format that emerged from the expert workshops. This product roadmap format aims to provide a flexible structure as well as on delivering value to the customer and the business. The former is intended to react rapidly to changes and adjust the roadmap accordingly, while the latter strives to steer the focus on developing products that customers really want and need. This roadmap format served as the starting point in the expert workshops for discussions and was adjusted based on the feedback from the participants. This revised version will be presented below.

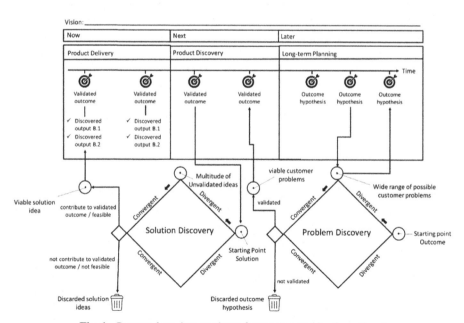

Fig. 1. Proposed product roadmap format (created by the authors)

The roadmap, as shown in Fig. 1, indicates the time horizon by the three columns "Now", "Next", and "Later". The "Now" column indicates what validated outcomes are currently being tackled with which outputs, i.e., which features are currently being implemented by the team. The "Next" column describes which validated outcomes are planned to tackle next, i.e., for which outcomes possible solutions will be researched. The "Later" column contains outcome hypotheses that are not validated and that are therefore prioritized lower for now but that should be considered in more detail at a later point in time. One key aspect of this is, that the team focuses the efforts on outcomes that are closer in time but still has an outlook on things to come without spending much effort.

To identify the corresponding roadmap items (outcome hypothesis, validated outcomes, and discovered outputs), we propose applying the double diamond process from design thinking [24]. Overall, this process consists of the two phases "finding the problem" and "finding the solution". The phase "finding the problem" focuses on identifying and understanding problems from the Customer's perspective, while the phase "finding the solution" addresses the identification of concrete solutions in the form of a product, service, or feature for the previously identified problems. The separation of problem identification and solution finding is intended to counteract the behaviour of focusing too early and exclusively on an identified solution. This means the risk of focusing on the first idea and rushing to implement it. As a result, no other potential solutions are accepted and consequently, solutions that contribute more to solving the customer's problem are not considered. In the worst case, starting with the solution idea without understanding the customer problem first, might lead to implementing outputs with no customer value. Therefore, the separate consideration should ensure that the first step is to systematically capture the problem, and subsequently the creation of possible solutions is considered.

The process of creating and maintaining a product roadmap, as shown before, starts with the identification of possible customer pain points (outcomes) that are formulated as outcome hypotheses (see column "Later"). If necessary, the term outcome can also be defined more broadly in the sense of a customer outcome (pain point, need, desire) or a business outcome (that needs to be converted into customer outcomes). The outcome hypothesis articulates the overreaching problem to be solved and sets the scope for the next steps. The collection of possible customer pain points takes place in the first divergent phase in the diamond "finding the problem". Divergent means that a wide range of possible problems is collected to find the most relevant customer problems. Typical examples of methods in this phase are conducting customer interviews, workshops, or customer focus groups. After finishing the collection, the large number of problems found is reduced by rating and validating them (see convergent section of the diamond "finding the problem"). The validated problems can then be formulated as validated outcomes and added to the "Next" column of the roadmap. The problems (outcome hypothesis) that are not validated are discarded. In this case we recommend documenting the reasons why the hypothesis is discarded so that decisions can be traced at any time.

Regarding the decision on which outcome hypotheses can be selected to be validated from the "Later" column in order to get shifted to the "Next" column, we recommend that each company choose their individual set of prioritization criteria like clarity about the customer need or potential value to be created [25]. This includes also defining a minimum priority in order to invest effort in addressing the customer problem. The outcome hypotheses with a priority higher than this minimum are validated and then assigned to the "Next" column, while the outcome hypotheses with lower prioritization are assigned to the "Later" column. This fact might also lead to realizing the roadmap in a non-sequential order since outcome hypotheses with higher priority might be inserted before outcome hypotheses that are in the roadmap for a long time already. Nevertheless, this only happens in the back part of the roadmap and does not majorly affect the "Now" and "Next" columns. In order to ensure this, the validation and testing of hypotheses should always be considered as an important aspect in prioritization, so that only customer problems that are very well understood and whose effects are proven should have high priority.

The next step focuses on determining solutions for the validated outcomes listed in the "Next" column. This is done in the diamond "finding the solution". Therefore, as in the diamond "finding the problem", the collection of ideas is conducted divergently, i.e., by applying a broad perspective and with the aim of collecting as many ideas as possible (see divergent phase of the diamond "finding the solution"). To collect a large number of ideas, it is advisable to use techniques such as visual brainstorming. The result of this stage is a multitude of unvalidated ideas. Subsequently, these unvalidated ideas must be reduced into a smaller number of conceivable solutions in a converge section. For this purpose, the feasibility and technological implementation are discussed for each idea, as well as the costs in relation to the value generated. This includes conducting experiments (such as the development of minimum viable products (MVPs) or prototypes) to verify that the solution idea contributes to the achievement of the corresponding outcome. In this context, it is recommended to formulate a hypothesis that includes a measure to verify this assertion as well as an indicator when the measure is reached. The feasible ideas that contribute to the achievement of the corresponding outcome is moved to the "Now" column, otherwise, the solution idea is discarded. If a solution is discarded, we recommend to document the hypotheses. This approach ensures that only validated outputs are released for implementation. It should be noted that the product delivery track ("Now" column) and product discovery track ("Next" column) take place in parallel. This means that, for example, in the first quarter the product delivery track implements those features that have already been successfully tested and at the same time the discovery track identifies which outputs should be developed for the second quarter as well as which outcomes should be defined in the long-term. Finally, it should be noted that after the implementation of the validated output, it should be tracked whether it is used by the customers and contributes to solving the identified problem.

5   Validation

The good practices and the proposed product roadmap format were developed with the aim of supporting practitioners to conduct their product roadmapping in a dynamic and uncertain market environment. Hence the practical value of our results should guide the validation process. Therefore, we organize a workshop with four practitioners from Germany that aims to discuss the comprehensibility and usefulness of the results of this study. We have ensured through preliminary discussions that each participant is involved in the roadmapping process in the respective companies. Furthermore, we have included a heterogeneous set of practitioners, i.e. we made sure that the participants work in different companies of various sizes. This was done with the intention of ensuring that the results of this study are developed not only on the basis of the knowledge and experience of participants of large companies but also from the perspective of participants from small and medium-sized companies. The workshop was held online on 02 August 2022 with a duration of 2 h. It should be noted that while these practitioners are from our network, they are not involved in the development of the findings of this study or otherwise in our research. During the workshop, we presented our results in order to collect feedback from the participants. One researcher acted as a facilitator to initiate and lead the group discussions. The discussions revealed that, from the participant's point of view the good practices, as well as the proposed product roadmap format, is comprehensible and useful. Nevertheless, some practices have been reformulated to clarify their utility. The application of design thinking in order to identify the items on the product roadmap was also perceived as useful. The use of the design thinking process to identify the items on the product roadmap was also perceived as useful as well as the presentation using the double diamond diagram was found to be understandable. Practitioners' criticisms focus on the fact that when using this model, every employee involved must have a deep understanding of how to apply design thinking. On the one hand, this means costs for trainings to ensure that any employee who does not already have this ability can acquire it. On the other hand, this limits hiring opportunities because not every potential product management candidate has this skill. In this context, it should be noted that the participants' companies are struggling to find employees for product management at all. Therefore, a further requirement would make it more difficult to find employees. An overview of the participants in the workshop to validate the results is shown in Table 2. The column "experience" refers to the amount of years in which the participants have been involved in product roadmapping activities.

Table 2. Participants in the workshops to validate the results

Participant	Position	Experience
Participant 1	Product owner	5 years
Participant 2	Product manager	3 years
Participant 3	Product manger	2 years
Participant 4	Head of product management	8 years

6   Threats to Validity

In order to discuss the validity and trustworthiness of our study, we applied the framework provided by Yin [26]. This framework consists of four aspects 1) construct validity, 2) internal validity, 3) external validity, and 4) reliability. Each aspect is discussed below.

Construct Validity: The construct validity is threatened by the risk that the experts participating in the workshops misunderstood the goal of developing the good practices and the proposed product format. To counteract this, the purpose and goal of the expert workshops were developed with the participants before embarking on answering the research questions. Technical terms were defined and explained throughout the expert workshop to ensure that all participants use the same terms with the same meanings. In addition, participants had the opportunity to ask questions at any time during the workshop. **Internal validity:** Concerning internal validity, there is the threat that the opinions and views of the experts used to develop the artifacts in this study may be incorrect or only valid only in a particular context. Therefore, we conducted preliminary interviews with each participant prior to the workshop to ensure that they are suitable to participate in our workshop. In addition, we recruited several experts from various companies and industry sectors in the software-intensive business. This was done with the intention to ensure that multiple perspectives were incorporated into the development of the results of this study and that incorrect assumptions or approaches were discussed and corrected. Consequently, the good practices and the content of the proposed product roadmap format were not finally documented until all practitioners agreed. **External validity:** The results of this study were developed with the help of the views and opinions of three practitioners operating in the software-intensive business in Germany. This limits the scope of the study to German companies that operate in such environments. Moreover, all participants originate from German companies. Therefore, the impact of cultural differences cannot be excluded. **Reliability:** In order to support the reliability of our results, two moderators were established in order to reduce research bias. Another threat is that the participants in the expert workshops provide input that does not fully reflect their company´s experience and reality. This is mitigated by the fact that the participants had no incentive or motivation to report false facts.

7 Summary

In this paper, the authors present good practices for product roadmapping as well as a proposed product roadmap format for operating in the BANI world. The BANI world is characterized by high market dynamics, which cause high uncertainties. The development of the good practices as well as the proposed product roadmap format is motivated by the fact that previous studies have shown that companies operating in the BANI world often use so-called feature-driven product roadmaps. Feature-driven roadmaps are not suitable for operation in a dynamic and uncertain market environment. The reason for this is that feature-driven roadmaps are too static to conduct frequent adjustments that are necessary to operate in the BANI world. Moreover, feature-driven roadmaps focus only on outputs such as products and features and do not consider outcomes that should be delivered to the customer and the business. Therefore, the results of this study should support practitioners to escape feature-driven product roadmaps by shifting their mindset to outcome-driven. This includes identifying problems of (potential) customers and deriving hypotheses for possible solutions and validating which solution solves the previously identified customer problem most effectively and efficiently. In order to achieve this, our results provide insights into what aspects are critical for this purpose, which structure and elements a roadmap for the operation in the BANI world should at least contains, and an approach to create these items. Moreover, we conducted an initial validation of the artifacts developed in this study by having them reviewed by five practitioners operating in a dynamic and uncertain market environment. This set of practitioners perceived the good practices as well the roadmap format as comprehensible and useful. Nevertheless, further research is required in order to increase the validity of the results of this study. Therefore, we plan to further validate the results with more participants from various companies.

References

1. Suomalainen, T., Abrahamsson, P., Similä, J.: Software product roadmapping in a volatile business environment. J. Syst. Softw. **84**(6), 958–975 (2011)
2. Lombardo, C.T., McCarthy, B., Ryan, E., Conners, M.: Product roadmaps relaunched - How to set direction while embracing uncertainty. O'Reilly Media Inc, Gravenstein Highway North, Sebastopol (2017)
3. Münch, J., Trieflinger, S., Lang, D.: What's hot in product roadmapping? Key practices and success factors. In: Proceedings of the International Conference on Product-Focused Software Process Improvement (profes), pp. 401–416. Springer, Cham (2019). https://doi.org/10.1007/978-3-030-35333-9_29
4. Kim, E., Yao, S., Agogino, A. M.: Design roadmapping: challenges and opportunities. In: Proceedings of the 20th International Conference on Engineering Design (ICED), pp.85–94. Vol 6: Design Methods and Tools-Part 2, Milan (2015)
5. Münch, J., Trieflinger, S., Lang, D.: Why feature-based roadmaps fail in rapidly changing markets: a qualitative survey. In: Proceedings of the International Workshop on Software-intensive Business: Start-ups, Ecosystems and Platforms (SiBW), pp. 202–218. CEUR workshop proceedings, Aachen (2018)
6. De Godoy, M. F, Fernandes, M., Ribas Filho D.: Facing the BANI World. International Journal of Nutrology 14.02 (2021)
7. Grabmeier, S.: BANI versus VUCA: a new acronym to describe the world. https://stephan-grabmeier.de/bani-versus-vuca/. Accessed 05 Aug 2022
8. Think Insights: BANI: A new framework to make sense of a chaotic world. https://thinkinsights.net/leadership/bani/. Accessed 05 Aug 2022
9. Temmen, M.: BANI vs VUCA— a new acronym for a new world. https://marian-temmen.medium.com/bani-vs-vuca-a-new-acronym-for-a-new-world-59c7be2dddce. Accessed 05 Aug 2022
10. Münch, J., Trieflinger, S., Lang, D.: DEEP: the product roadmap maturity model: a method for assessing the product roadmapping capabilities of organizations. In: Proceedings of the 2nd ACM SIGSOFT International Workshop on Software-Intensive Business: Start-ups, Platforms, and Ecosystems, pp. 19–24. Association for Computing Machinery, New York (2019)
11. Phaal, R., Farrukh, C JP, Propert, D.: Characterisation of technology roadmaps: purpose and format. In: PICMET'01. Portland International Conference on Management of Engineering and Technology. Proceedings, vol. 1: Book of Summaries (IEEE Cat. No. 01CH37199), pp. 367–374. IEEE (2001)
12. Arslan, M., Haug, F., Heitger, N., Kraemer, L.: Don't get stuck in complexity: coping with strategic complexity in the context of Product Generation Engineering. Sci. Soc. Innov. Value Creation **3**, 1–14 (2016)
13. Kostoff, R.N., Schaller, R.R.: Science and technologies roadmaps. IEEE Trans. Eng. Manage. **48**(2), 132–143 (2001)

14. Trieflinger, S.: Münch, J., Lang, D.: The product roadmap maturity model DEEP: validation of a method for assessing the product roadmap capabilities of organizations. In: Proceedings of the International Conference on Software Business (ICSOB), pp. 97–113. Springer, Cham (2019). Doi: https://doi.org/10.1007/978-3-030-33742-1_9

15. Münch, J., Trieflinger, S., Bogazköy, E., Eißler, P., Roling, B., Schneider, J.: Product roadmap formats for an uncertain future: a grey literature review. In: Proceedings of the 46th Euromicro Conference on Software Engineering and Advanced Applications (SEAA), pp. 284–291. IEEE (2020)

16. Cagan. M.: Inspired: How to Create Tech Products Customers Love. Wiley, Hoboken, New Jersey (2018)

17. Wilby, D.: Roadmap transformation: from obstacle to catalyst. In: 2009 Agile Conference, pp. 229–234 (2009)

18. De Oliveira, M.G., Freitas, J.S., Pereira, B.S., Guerra, P.V.: Exploring the involvement of experts in strategic roadmapping with large groups. IEEE Trans. Eng. Manage. **69**(1), 56–66 (2020)

19. Komssi, M., Kauppinen, M., Töhönen, H., Lehtola, L.: Integrating analysis of customer´s process into roadmapping: the value-creation perspective. In: Proceedings of the 19th IEEE International Requirements Engineering Conference (RE), pp. 57–66. IEEE (2011)

20. Lehtola, L., Kauppinen, M., Kujala, S.: Linking the business view to requirements engineering: long-term product planning by roadmapping. In: Proceedings of the 13th IEEE International Conference on Requirements Engineering (RE'05), pp. 439–443. IEEE (2005)

21. Ulwick, A.: Jobs to Be Done - Theory to Practice. IDEA BITE PRESS (2016)

22. How to prioritize your product roadmap when everything feels important: a grey literature review. In: Proceedings of the International Conference on Engineering, Technology and Innovation (ICE), pp. 1–9. IEEE (2021)

23. Trieflinger, S., Münch, J., Bogazköy, E., Eißler P., Schneider, J., Roling, B.: Product roadmap alignment–achieving the vision together: a grey literature review. In: Proceedings of the International Conference on Agile Processes in Software Engineering and Extreme Programming-Workshops (XP), pp. 50–57. Springer, Cham (2020)

24. Design Council: Eleven lessons: managing design in eleven global brands – A study of the design process. https://www.designcouncil.org.uk/fileadmin/uploads/dc/Documents/Ele venLessons_Design_Council%2520%25282%2529.pdf. Accessed 10 Aug 2022

25. Lang, D., Spies, S., Trieflinger, S., Münch, J.: Tailored design thinking approach-a shortcut for agile teams. In: Proceedings of the International Conference on Software Business (ICSOB), pp. 37-49. Springer, Cham (2021)

26. Yin, R.K.: Case Study Research: Design and Methods, 5th edn. SAGE Publications Inc., London (2014)

Designing Platforms for Crowd-Based Software Prototype Validation: A Design Science Study

Sebastian Gottschalk[✉], Sarmad Parvez, Enes Yigitbas, and Gregor Engels

Software Innovation Lab, Paderborn University, Paderborn, Germany
{sebastian.gottschalk,enes.yigitbas,gregor.engels}@uni-paderborn.de,
sparvez@mail.uni-paderborn.de

Abstract. Designing a software product based on early user feedback aligns it faster with the user's needs rather than validating them after the development. This feedback can be provided iteratively on software prototypes before the development to judge the idea behind the product and save development resources. Here, crowdsourcing techniques can be used to collect feedback from many potential users. However, less research focused on software support for this crowd-validation process. Therefore, we conducted a design science research study with three design cycles to develop a platform for software developers to support the prototype validation process using the crowd. We present abstracted design knowledge in the form of design principles and an overall solution concept together with a situated implementation of design features and a software artifact. Our research contributes knowledge to software designers in research and practice designing new and extending existing tools with iterative crowd-validation support.

Keywords: Prototype validation · Software product design · Crowd-based validation

1 Introduction

Nowadays, the constantly chaining VUCA (Volatility, Uncertainty, Complexity, Ambiguity) world has a high impact on developing new software products. Due to the increasing market uncertainties [27] and the wish for users to get integrated solutions for their problems instead of rare software products [40], early feedback from potential users in the market is essential for building successful software products. This feedback can be used to validate the most important assumptions about the software product before the actual development [22]. This validation can be used to decide to go or go not with an overall idea and guide the further

This work was partially supported by the German Research Foundation (DFG) within the CRC "On-The-Fly Computing" (CRC 901, Project Number: 160364472SFB901) and the German Federal Ministry of Education and Research (BMBF) through Software Campus grant (Project Number: 01IS17046).

© The Author(s), under exclusive license to Springer Nature Switzerland AG 2022
D. Taibi et al. (Eds.): PROFES 2022, LNCS 13709, pp. 334–350, 2022.
https://doi.org/10.1007/978-3-031-21388-5_23

development of certain software features. This is especially important in highly competitive markets like mobile ecosystems with millions of already developed software products (i.e., apps) [2].

This validation of the product, in turn, is possible with product discovery that aims to "quickly separate the good ideas from the bad to answer the question of which products, features or services should be developed to fulfill the needs of the customer" [29]. This discovery process, in turn, could be guided by management tools like Product Board[1]. Within the discovery, the current ideas about the product can be visualized using UI prototypes and evaluated by potential users. Those visualizations can be supported by prototyping tools like Figma[2]. However, a key challenge of effective product discovery is the access to the potential users during the discovery [29].

The access to users can be supported by using crowdsourcing. Crowdsourcing proposes the outsourcing of different activities to a large undefined set of users by using an open call [21]. To support such open calls, digital platforms for organizing the crowdsourcing and providing access to the crowd worker like Amazon Mechanical Turk Platform[3] have been established. Here, the crowd could also be used to support the different stages of the product development [41] like the product discovery. However, to the best of our knowledge, there is a gap in how to design platforms that support the prototype development based on the iterative feedback from a crowd of potential users and reduce uncertainties in product discovery. Therefore, we aim to gain knowledge about designing such a platform for crowd-validation by answering the following research question (RQ): *How to design platforms that integrate crowdsourcing techniques in the iterative validation of prototypes?*

To answer the research question, we conducted a design science research (DSR) study [20] with three design cycles to develop abstracted design knowledge and a situated implementation. In this paper, we present the evolvement of our existing study in [15], where we conduct the first design cycle. In contrast to that, this paper shows two additional design cycles that were evaluated using user studies. For the abstracted design knowledge, we have developed nine design principles and an overall solution design. In this design, the software developers iteratively validate their prototypes with the potential users (i.e., the crowd). For that, they receive the individual answers to predefined questionnaires together with support for aggregation and visualization. Moreover, incentive processes for motivating the users and approval processes for supporting secrecy are included. For the situated implementation, we have developed concrete design features and an instantiation of a platform prototype. We evaluated both with an expert workshop and two user studies. With both contributions, we support software designers in research and practice to extend their software with crowd validation.

In the following, we first show the research background of our approach in terms of crowdsourcing and design principles (Sect. 2). Based on that, we intro-

---

[1] Product Board Tool: https://www.productboard.com/.

[2] Figma Tool: https://www.figma.com/.

[3] Amazon Mechanical Turk Platform: https://www.mturk.com/.

duce our research approach with the methodology and the conducted process (Sect. 3). Next, we show our abstracted design knowledge with the design principles and the overall solution design (Sect. 4). Based on that, we derive a situated implementation with the design features and the platform prototype (Sect. 5). Moreover, we show the user evaluation with the setting, the conduction, the interpretation, and current threats to validity (Sect. 6). Finally, we draw a conclusion and provide future work (Sect. 7).

2   Research Background

To build the foundation of our approach, we have provided a research background. For that, we present the usage of crowdsourcing in software development and explain design principles for digital platforms.

2.1   Crowdsourcing of Software Products

The development of software products is a resource-intensive task that can be improved with the iterative feedback of potential customers [37]. To gather that feedback, one concept is crowdsourcing which describes the outsourcing of value-creating activities from a company to a large undefined set of users by using an open call [21]. Crowdsourcing has been established in different research directions like crowd testing, crowd funding, crowd ideation, crowd logistic, crowd production, crowd promotion, and crowd support over the last years [9]. Here, the sub directions of crowd tests and ideation are mostly related to the solution for our approach.

Crowd Testing can be used to evaluate different running software products with the users. Here, CrowdStudy [31] is an approach to allow developers to test the usability of their web interfaces with the crowd workers of Amazon Mechanical Turk. Mechanical Turk is also used by CrowdCrit [24] to support designers to validate created posters in the form of uploaded images.

Crowd Ideation can be used to generate new and improve existing ideas for software products with the users. Here, a recent study by Shixuan et al. [13] analyses the cognitive load during the idea generation and convergence with the crowd under the manipulation of the task complexity, the idea representation, and the procedural guidance. Another study by Zaggl et al. [46] focuses on integrative solutions by reusing the already existing public knowledge of the crowd. ERICA [35] is a tool to use expert knowledge to validate diverse crowd answers. However, none of the approaches directly focused on the application area of prototypes.

2.2   Design Principles for Digital Platforms

In order to develop abstracted design knowledge, design science research (DSR) [34] has been established as one often used method. With DSR, a class of problems is solved by focusing on a specific problem and abstracting the results of the solution. To make those abstracted knowledge transferable to different problems, design principles (DP) can be used. Here, DPs capture and codify that knowledge in an explicit way by focussing on the implementer, the aim, the user, the context, the mechanism, the enactors, and the rationale [17]. DPs can be designed in a supportive way based on identified knowledge sources and the derivation of design requirements at the beginning or in a reflective way by extracting them directly from an instantiated software artifact [28]. Moreover, DPs can be formalized in different abstraction levels, directly impacting the researchers' reusability and practitioners' applicability [43]. Recently, DPs for different software tools and crowd interactions have been proposed.

For **Software Tools**, those DPS describe the design knowledge from which features can be derived. Here, the Crowd-based Business Model Validation System [7] provides DPs to validate uncertainties in the business model development using crowdsourcing. Based on that, the Hybrid Intelligence Decision Support System for Business Model Validation [8] combines crowdsourcing with machine learning aspects to improve the validation. Moreover, a recent study by Schoormann et al. [38] works on DPs for tools to reflect sustainability in design thinking projects, where prototyping plays a major role. Last, a study by Reibenspiess et al. [36] designs DPs for an intrapreneurial platform to generate ideas.

For **Crowd Interactions**, those DPs describe the design knowledge from which interactions can be derived. Here, an approach by Tavanapour et al. [39] provides DPs for crowd collaboration based on different intrinsic and extrinsic incentives. Moreover, a study by Chasin et al. [6] builds DPs for managing digital community currencies on software platforms. However, none of those developed DPs of the approaches directly focused on the application area of prototypes.

3   Research Approach

To answer our research question, we use design science research (DSR). For that, we explain the underlying methodology and show our applied process.

3.1   Design Science Research Methodology

For our research, we use DSR as it aims to solve a class of problems by developing a solution to a specific problem and then generalize that gained knowledge [16] based on the development and evaluation of a corresponding software artifact [34]. Here, we aim to solve the problem of crowd-validation of mobile application prototypes but also ensure that they can be generalized to related application areas. For this, we use design principles (DP) to codify the knowledge in a transferable way [17]. Moreover, we base our DSR on the opportunity creation theory (OCT) [1] as kernel theory to stick in line with similar approaches like business model validation [7] or venture ideation [42] from digital entrepreneurship [30]. Here, OCT originally states that businesses (and their products) are co-created under high uncertainty [42]. Therefore (product) development is an entrepreneurial process where assumptions have to be validated directly with the customer using exploration and exploitation.

According to Gregor and Hevner [16], we position the contribution type of our design principles as operational principles that can be transferred to other domains together with our software prototype as situated implementation of the artifact. Moreover, we use an exaptation according to the knowledge contribution framework by a refinement of the existing concept of crowdsourcing.

3.2   Design Science Research Process

For DSR, we use the cycle of Kuechler and Vaishnavi [20]. The cycle, as shown in Fig. 1, consists of the following five iteratively conducted steps. First, we identify the *(1) Awareness of [the] Problem* based on a real-world problem and provide a *(2) Suggestion* of a possible solution. Next, we work on the *(3) Development* of the software artifact and conduct an *(4) Evaluation* of it. Based on the evaluation results, another iteration is conducted, and/or our research contributions as *(5) Conclusion* are provided.

In the **First Cycle**, which was presented in [15], we got aware of the problem by conducting a literature review and tool analysis in the application areas of lean development, UI prototyping, and crowdsourcing to derive initial design requirements (DR) for our approach. Based on mapping the theoretical and empirical DRs, we suggested our first design principles (DPs) together with a preliminary concept. Out of that DPs we developed the first design features (DFs) and instantiated them in a software prototype. Last, we evaluated them in an online expert workshop (n = 6), where we explained the overall concept, showed the software platform, and asked for feedback. Subsequently, we gave the experts access to the platform. We sent out a questionnaire to rate the importance of the DPs and provide feedback on the overall idea, the proposed solution, the current drawbacks of the platform, and additional feedback.

In the **Second Cycle**, we took the lessons learned from the expert workshop together with additional literature to revisit the underlying DRs. Based on that, we also revisited our DPs and the suggested concept. This lead also to a redevelopment of the DFs and a complete new instantiation of the software prototype. We evaluated the DPs and the prototype in a student seminar on the lean development of mobile applications. Here, the students (n = 14) were divided into different groups (g = 6) to develop an idea for an app within the seminar iteratively. Here, one student per group needed to upload their prototype with questions to the platform. Next, every student gave feedback on two predetermined prototypes by answering the questions that could be used to improve the prototypes. Last, the students evaluated the prototype of the platform on the platform itself by rating the importance of the DPs together with feedback on the overall idea, the proposed solution, current drawbacks of the platform, and additional feedback.

In the **Third Cycle**, which results are also shown within this paper, we took the lessons learned from the user study to revisit our DRs. Out of that, we improved the DPs and the overall solution concept. Moreover, we improved the DFs and the existing software platform based on those changes. We evaluated the DPs and the prototype similar to the second cycle in a student lecture for

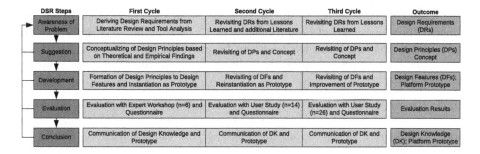

Fig. 1. Research approach (based on Kuechler and Vaishnavi [20])

the systematic development of AR/VR applications. Within the lecture, the students (n = 26) had a mini project where they needed to develop such an AR/VR application in a group (g = 8). Again, one student needed to upload the prototype, each student needed to evaluate two predefined prototypes, and all students needed to evaluate the DPs together with the platform.

4   Abstracted Design Knowledge

To make our study results transferable, we have developed abstracted design knowledge with the design principles and the overall solution design.

4.1   Design Principles (DPs)

We codify our knowledge during the design study within the DPs. Here, each DP shows a certain aspect of the platform and is based on the revisited DRs during the three cycles. Here, those DRs were derived from a literature review and tool analysis on the topics of lean development, UI prototyping, and crowdsourcing [15]. In the following, we show the nine DPs together with references to literature and tools that build the foundation for the mapped DRs.

DP1: User Variety states that *the solution should provide functions for integrating different internal and external users (e.g., platform user, crowd worker) to allow developers to participate with a heterogeneous group of users within the validation process.* In literature, this is reasoned by the fact that developers in the early product development have high uncertainties that can be validated by testing the underlying assumptions [4]. By using the knowledge of a crowd, the assumptions can be proofed [25], and the biases of the developers can be reduced [5]. Here, the users can come from internal sources like employees or external sources like Amazon Mechanical Turk[4].

DP2: Task Iteration states that *the solution should provide functions for conducting tasks iteratively to allow developers an incremental improvement of the*

---

[4] Amazon Mechanical Turk: https://www.mturk.com.

prototypes over time. In literature, this is reasoned by the fact that user feedback support the adjustment of product features [37] and the business model [27] to the market. For that, that feedback can be provided by a crowd of users like with ClickWorker[5] where the rapidness of the given feedback is a critical factor of success [4].

DP3: Prototype Diversity states that *the solution should provide functions for integrating different types of prototyping (e.g., mockups, click dummies) to allow developers a flexible choice for their current validation developments.* In literature, this is reasoned by the fact that because depending on the stage of the product development, also different prototypes like textual descriptions, images, or click dummies can be used [23]. Here, different prototypes can ensure the refinement of the product features or business model over time [32]. For the visualizations, also external tools like Figma[6] can be used.

DP4: Feedback Diversity states that *the solution should provide functions for integrating different types of feedback (e.g., free texts, ratings) to allow developers a flexible choice for their current validation challenges.* In literature, this is reasoned by the fact that depending on the type of the development stage also, different types of feedback are necessary [3]. Depending on the type of test, that feedback can consist of qualitative or quantitative information [32]. Different types of feedback are also integrated within the prototyping tool of UIGiants[7].

DP5: Filter Mechanisms states that *the solution should provide functions for the filtering between users and tasks to allow developers and users to shortlist evaluations based on specific criteria (e.g., skill set, interests).* In literature, this is reasoned by the fact that to ensure the quality of the feedback, the tasks must be just conducted by users of a relevant target group of the developer [26]. Conversely, users should see only tasks in which they are interested [19]. Amazon Mechanical Turk also uses two-sided filtering between the task provider and the crowd worker.

DP6: Aggregation Mechanisms states that *the solution should provide functions for aggregating and visualizing the feedback to allow developers to provide understandable and traceable improvements to the prototypes.* In literature, this is reasoned by the fact that depending on the number of individual user feedback, it can be a time-consuming and challenging activity to process them. Here, the feedback should be provided to the developer in an aggregated form for fast processing [14]. Moreover, appropriate visualizations should support the developers in interpreting the feedback [44]. ClickWorker also aggregates the results of conducted tasks from different crowd workers.

DP7: Incentive Mechanisms states that *the solution should provide functions for supporting extrinsic and intrinsic incentives (e.g., rank lists, money) to allow*

---

[5] ClickWorker: https://clickworker.com.

[6] Figma: https://www.figma.com.

[7] UIGiants: https://www.uigiants.com.

developers to motivate users in the validation process. In literature, this is reasoned by the fact that giving valuable feedback is time-consuming and should ideally be done regularly [37]. Therefore, users should be offered extrinsic incentives like money or intrinsic incentives like fame [18]. While money is used as an extrinsic incentive by Amazon Mechanical Turk, intrinsic incentives like ratings and views are used by social media platforms like YouTube[8].

DP8: Non-disclosure Mechanisms states that *the solution should provide functions for integrating non-disclosure agreements to allow developers to protect their prototypes from user thefts.* In literature, this is reasoned by the fact that developing new ideas is a creative and challenging activity that often needs the collaboration of various stakeholders [10]. Depending on the trust between the developers and the users, non-disclosure agreements can be necessary for a more intensive idea exchange [12]. Those agreements are also often requested by clients on projects with a larger volume on the micro job platform Fiverr[9].

DP9: Governance Mechanisms states that *the solution should provide functions for integrating governance into the process to allow the platform owner to take necessary actions against developers and users that misusage the validation process.* In literature, this is reasoned by the fact that providing valuable interactions between the developers and the users is the key task for the platform to stay successful. Good governance of those interactions will let the users stick much longer on the platform [11]. Here, governance in terms of policies, regulations, and accountability should be provided by the platform [33]. This, in turn, exists in nearly every platform like Innocentive[10], which aims to solve problems by finding innovative solutions.

4.2   Solution Design Concept

Out of the codified DPs, we conceptualize a solution design as shown in Fig. 2. It consists of the three roles of the *Developer*, the *User*, and the *Platform Owner* and the five components of the *Task Creation*, the *Task Conduction*, the *Task Evaluation*, the *Task Incentivisation*, and the *Task Approval*.

In the beginning, different *Developers* and *Users* (i.e., DP1) register to the platform, each with a specific profile. After that, the *Developer* creates a new or iterates an existing task (i.e., DP2) in the *Task Creation* by creating different types of prototypes (i.e., DP3), preparing different types of questions (i.e., DP4), and selecting specific criteria for users (i.e., DP5). Next, the *User* selects different tasks (i.e., DP5) in the *Task Evaluation*, depending on the approval process, executes the prototype (i.e., DP3), and provides feedback (i.e., DP4). This feedback is aggregated and visualized (i.e., DP6) in the *Task Evaluation* and displayed to the *Developer*. Based on that, the *Developer* can provide intrinsic and extrinsic incentives (i.e., DP7) to the *Users* in the *Task Incentivisation*.

---

[8] YouTube: https://www.youtube.com/.
[9] Fiverr: https://www.fiverr.com.
[10] Innocentive: https://www.innocentive.com.

Moreover, the *Developer* can decide on an automatic selection of access to the prototypes with or without the usage of a non-disclosure agreement (i.e., DP8) in the *Task Approval*. Moreover, a manual selection is possible where the users ask for approval and get access to the prototype. Last, the *Platform Owner* governs the whole platform against misuse (i.e., DP9) by moderating users and tasks.

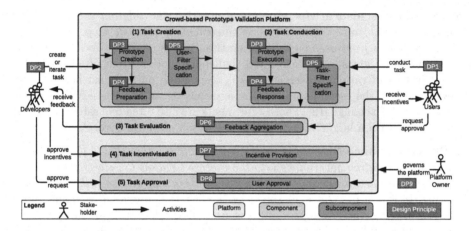

Fig. 2. Solution design for a crowd-based prototype validation platform

5 Situated Implementation

To demonstrate our approach, we have developed a situated implementation. For that, we show our revisited design features and the software platform.

5.1 Design Features (DFs)

We represent the features of our platform using DFs. Here each DP is translated to a set of DFs that can be directly implemented in the platform. In the following, we describe the DFs for each of the nine derived DPs.

For the **DP1: User Variety**, we allow the registration of developers and users both by a registration form (DF1) and a single sign-on service (DF2). Moreover, we provide user profiles with specific information like skills (DF3) and a messaging system between different users (DF4). As **DP2: Task Iteration**, we provide the creation of tasks with essential information (DF5), the provision of feedback with a questionnaire (DF6), and the representation of feedback (DF7). For the **DP3: Prototype Diversity**, we allow the provision of prototypes as textual descriptions (DF8), uploaded images (DF9), and integration of external prototyping tools (DF10). In addition to that, the **DP4: Test Diversity** contains the test of single prototypes (DF11), the comparison of multiple prototypes (DF12), and the usage of split-tests (DF13). Here, also the questionnaire allows multiple types of questions like stars rating, thumbs-rating, radio buttons, and free text fields (DF14).

For the **DP5: Filter Mechanisms**, we support the adding of required user profile criteria to the tasks (DF15) and the shortlisting of tasks by the preferences of the users. As **DP6: Aggregation Mechanism**, we provide visualization charts of aggregatable answers to questions (DF16), investigation of individual feedback of each user (DF17), additional feedback for revealing unconsidered questions (DF18), and the comparison of split-test results (DF19). Based on that, the **DP7: Incentive Mechanism** allows the extrinsic motivation of sending virtual money (DF20) and the intrinsic motivation of publicly displaying the user's trustworthiness (DF21). As **DP8: Non-Disclosure Mechanisms**, we support the direct approval of tasks to all users (DF22), the deposit of a non-disclosure agreement that the users have to accept (DF23), and the manual approval of users (DF24). Finally, for the **DP9: Governance Mechanism**, we provide an admin control panel (DF25) together with the reporting of tasks and users (DF26).

5.2   Implemented Platform Prototype

Out of the developed DFs, we have implemented a software platform to test the features and the underlying principles with real users. While for the first cycle, we developed a rapid prototype to test the overall idea, the second cycle was reimplemented in a scalable and extensible way so that improvements to the third cycle could be easily added.

For the implementation, our Crowd-based Prototype Validation (CBPV) Platform uses Angular[11] in the frontend, NestJS[12] in the backend, and PostgreSQL[13] as a database. Based on those core techniques, we build a microservice architecture so that new DPs and DFs can be easily implemented. Screenshots of our current version applied to the self-evaluation of the platform can be seen in Fig. 3. Here, the **a) Task Creation** shows the creation of tasks (i.e., DF5), the choice of a basic test for a single prototype (i.e., DF11), and the usage of uploaded images (i.e., DF9). The **b) Task Conduction** shows the provision of feedback (i.e., DF6) and the usage of star ratings (i.e., DF14). The **c) Task Evaluation** shows the representation of the feedback (i.e., DF7) and the aggregation of numerical feedback to questions (i.e., DF16).

6   Evaluation Results

As evaluation, we have conducted a user study for the third design cycle. For that, we explain the setting of our study, describe the derived results, analyze and interpret those results, and point out potential threats to validity.

---

[11] Angular: https://www.angular.io.

[12] NestJS: https://www.nestjs.com.

[13] PostgreSQL: https://www.postgresql.org.

6.1   Setting

We conducted our user study in a student lecture for developing AR/VR applications at Paderborn University. Here, the lecture aims to give students an overview of the different topics in the systematic development of AR/VR applications, together with the skill-set to develop such an application from scratch. For that, those students had a mini-project where they grouped themselves into teams of 3–4 students to develop a prototype of their application.

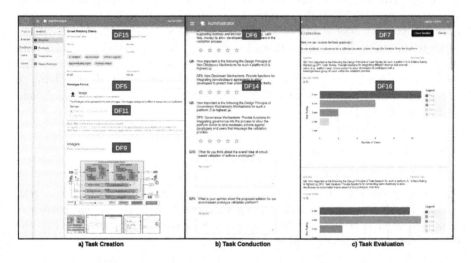

a) Task Creation   b) Task Conduction   c) Task Evaluation

Fig. 3. Platform prototype applied to the self-evaluation of the concept

At the beginning of the mini-project, the teams developed an idea (e.g., a JengaVR game, a smARt note app, an ARmomix cooking app) for the application. For that, they created a description, first screenshots, or a mockup of Figma together with a questionnaire of open questions for which they wanted to receive feedback. After that, one student from each team $(g = 8)$ uploaded their idea in the form of a prototype on the situated implementation of the CBPV Platform. Next, each student $(n = 26)$ provided feedback on the prototypes of two other groups by executing the prototypes and filling out the questionnaires. Here, the matching of the students to prototypes was made by us manually to provide a similar amount of feedback for every team. Last, the platform should be self-evaluated by every student (see Fig. 3 for an excerpt). Here, the prototype consists of images of the platform where the instantiations of the DPs on the platform are labeled. Moreover, the questionnaire provided a 5-stars rating question for each DP and four free text questions on the overall idea, the proposed solution, current drawbacks of the platform, and additional feedback.

6.2   Results

We present the user study results by referring to the created prototypes and filled-out questionnaire by most students (n = 20) during the self-evaluation. For that, we divide between quantitative and qualitative results.

For the **Quantitative Results**, we have answers for the 5-stars rating questions for the nine DPs that mostly relate to the abstracted design knowledge of the prototype validation. An overview of those results as boxplots is shown in Fig. 4. As an overall impression, we see that nearly every DP is rating as crucial for such a platform. The variety of users (i.e., DP1) and iteration of tasks (i.e., DP2) should be provided by every platform. Also, the diversity of prototypes (i.e., DP3) and feedback (i.e., DP4) together with the aggregation of feedback (i.e., DP6) that are specific for prototype crowd-validation are rated as essential. The same holds for providing overall governance (i.e., DP9). The function for filtering (i.e., DP5) and incentives (i.e., DP7) are rated lower by the students as they got predetermined prototypes to validate and no additional incentives for the validations. Last, a higher discrepancy exists for the non-closure agreements (i.e., DP8), which some students could interpret as just additional overhead.

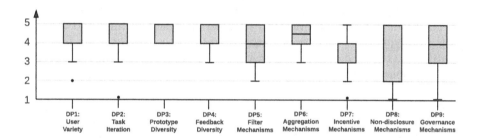

Fig. 4. Evaluated importance of design principles based on boxplots

For the **Qualitative Results**, we have answers for the free text fields of the additional questions for the concept that are mostly related to the situated implementation of the platform prototype but can partially also be abstracted to the design knowledge. An overall impression of that feedback was that most of the students liked the overall idea of the platform. Just one student was curious if the additional effort would be worth the feedback, and one student commented that crowd validation should be just done in addition to regular customer interviews. Most of the feedback was regarding some general issues with the current version of the platform prototype, like better support for mobile web browsers, UI issues, simplified account management, or bug fixes. However, some feedback also suggested improvements to the most important features of the users, the prototypes, and the feedback. For the users, there was feedback to create groups for collaborative working on the prototypes and invite links to share the prototype with colleagues. For the prototypes, there was feedback to add additional types of non-visual prototypes and directly create clickable mockups on the platform. For the feedback, there was feedback for "if not, why" questions and blocks for Likert scale questions. Last, there was the wish to integrate the prototypes and the questions deeper.

6.3   Discussion and Implications

We interpret the user study results by analyzing the created prototypes by the teams and the filled-out questionnaire by the students. Out of that, we provide an analysis of the abstracted design knowledge and the situated implementation.

The **Abstracted Design Knowledge** refers to the developed design principles and the overall solution design. We currently see no major issues with the current set of principles. However, some DPs could be slightly improved in the future. For the variety of the users (i.e., DP1), the external users, and in the iteration of tasks (i.e., DP2), the incremental improvements could be described more precisely. Moreover, the deeper integration of prototypes (i.e., DP3) and feedback (i.e., DP4) could be mentioned. Next, the reasoning for the incentivization (i.e., DP7) and the non-disclosure agreements (i.e., DP8) could be improved. Last, based on the analysis of the created prototypes, a minor design principle that could be investigated in the future would be guidance in creating a task (e.g., choosing the best type of prototype, generating good questions for feedback).

The **Situated Implementation** refers to the design features and the platform prototype. Here, we currently see a need to fix the current issues that were identified by the students. Moreover, we want to work on specific features that were mentioned during the evaluation. For that, in addition to single sign-on services (i.e., DF2) we want to allow the sending of invitation links for concrete task evaluations. Moreover, we want to allow the sharing of prototypes with other developers at the task creation (i.e., DF5). To improve the diversity of the prototypes, we want to add an internal prototyping tool in addition to the external one (i.e., DF10). Furthermore, the diversity of the feedback should be supported by multi-questions based on Lickert scales (i.e., DF14). As a larger project, we want to combine the creation of prototypes and the provision of questions deeper based on the integrated prototyping tool. Last, we want to implement the guidance in task creation as mentioned as a possible DP above.

6.4   Threats to Validity

We discuss our threats to validity according to Yin [45], who divides between Constructs Validity, Internal Validity, External Validity, and Reliability. **Construct Validity** refers to guaranteeing that the most verifiable case study results are based on the research question. To achieve that, we clarify the goal and purpose to the students of the lecture and provide additional explanations of the platform together with an email address for solving occurring problems. Nevertheless, there can be misunderstandings of the purpose, especially on the transferability of the DPs to different application domains. **Internal Validity** refers to establishing trustworthiness due to casual relationships during the case conduction. A threat here is the non-systematic literature review in the first cycle.

While we cover different areas and use a technique like snowballing to reduce that threat, we can not completely ensure missing some literature. However, those issues should be reduced by conducting multiple design cycles. **External Validity** refers to the extent to which the results can be applied to other cases. A threat here is the evaluation in a student lecture and seminar because of the biased view of the students. While we conducted two different user studies to reduce this bias, additionally evaluations with other target groups are necessary in the future. Moreover, we reduced this bias by interviewing experts in the first design cycle. **Reliability** refers to the reproducibility of repeating the case study. For that, we record the whole expert workshop and export the raw data of all data created in the two user studies. While this increases the reliability of the study result, it could also harm the experts and students of providing negative feedback.

7 Conclusion and Future Work

The gathering of early feedback from users is vital to develop successful products. This feedback can be provided iteratively by a large number of crowd workers. However, currently, it is unclear how to design platforms for such a crowd-validation of software products. Therefore, we have conducted a design science study with three design cycles to develop abstracted design knowledge (i.e., design principles, concept) and a situated implementation (i.e., design features, platform prototype) for a platform that solves that challenge. Our research contributes knowledge to software designers in research and practice designing new and extending existing tools with iterative crowd-validation support.

Our future work around the crowd-validation of software products is threefold: First, we want to improve the abstracted design knowledge and situated implementation based on interviews (e.g., interviewing experts from the industry). Second, we want to transfer the design knowledge to other application areas (e.g., validating prototypes in AR/VR). Third, we want to compare our solution against other existing approaches (e.g., combining a prototyping tool and questionnaire to manually collect feedback).

References

1. Alvarez, S.A., Barney, J.B., Anderson, P.: Forming and exploiting opportunities: the implications of discovery and creation processes for entrepreneurial and organizational research. Organ. Sci. **24**(1), 301–317 (2013)
2. App Annie Inc: The State of Mobile 2021 (2021). www.appannie.com/en/go/state-of-mobile-2021/
3. Bland, D.J., Osterwalder, A.: Testing Business Ideas. Wiley, Hoboken (2020)
4. Blank, S.: Why the lean start-up changes everything. Harv. Bus. Rev. **91**, 63–72 (2013)
5. Burmeister, K., Schade, C.: Are entrepreneurs' decisions more biased? An experimental investigation of the susceptibility to status quo bias. J. Bus. Ventur. **22**(3), 340–362 (2007)

6. Chasin, F., Schmolke, F., Becker, J.: Design principles for digital community currencies. In: Proceedings of HICCS, vol. 53. AIS (2020)

7. Dellermann, D., Lipusch, N., Ebel, P.: Developing design principles for a crowd-based business model validation system. In: Maedche, A., vom Brocke, J., Hevner, A. (eds.) DESRIST 2017. LNCS, vol. 10243, pp. 163–178. Springer, Cham (2017). https://doi.org/10.1007/978-3-319-59144-5_10

8. Dellermann, D., Lipusch, N., Ebel, P., Leimeister, J.M.: Design principles for a hybrid intelligence decision support system for business model validation. Electron. Mark. **29**(3), 423–441 (2019)

9. Durward, D., Blohm, I., Leimeister, J.M.: Crowd work. Bus. Inf. Syst. Eng. **58**(4), 281–286 (2016)

10. Ebel, P., Bretschneider, U., Leimeister, J.M.: Leveraging virtual business model innovation: a framework for designing business model development tools. Inf. Syst. J. **26**(5), 519–550 (2016)

11. Evans, D.S., Schmalensee, R.: Matchmakers: The New Economics of Multisided Platforms. Harvard Business Review Press, Boston (2016)

12. Fanimokun, A.O., Castrogiovanni, G., Peterson, M.F.: Developing high-tech ventures: entrepreneurs, advisors, and the use of non-disclosure agreements (NDAs). J. Small Bus. Entrepreneurship **25**(1), 103–119 (2012)

13. Fu, S., et al.: Exploring idea convergence and conceptual combination in open innovative crowdsourcing from a cognitive load perspective. In: Proceedings of HICCS, vol. 52. AIS (2019)

14. Geiger, D., Seedorf, S., Schulze, T., Nickerson, R.C., Schader, M.: Managing the crowd: towards a taxonomy of crowdsourcing processes. In: Proceedings of AMCIS 2011. AIS (2011)

15. Gottschalk, S., Aziz, M.S., Yigitbas, E., Engels, G.: Design principles for a crowd-based prototype validation platform. In: Wang, X., Martini, A., Nguyen-Duc, A., Stray, V. (eds.) ICSOB 2021. LNBIP, vol. 434, pp. 205–220. Springer, Cham (2021). https://doi.org/10.1007/978-3-030-91983-2_16

16. Gregor, S., Hevner, A.R.: Positioning and presenting design science research for maximum impact. MIS Q. **37**(2), 337–355 (2013)

17. Gregor, S., Kruse, L., Seidel, S.: Research perspectives: the anatomy of a design principle. J. Assoc. Inf. Syst. **21**, 1622–1652 (2020)

18. Hammon, L., Hippner, H.: Crowdsourcing. Bus. Inf. Syst. Eng. **4**(3), 163–166 (2012)

19. Kittur, A., Chi, E.H., Suh, B.: Crowdsourcing user studies with Mechanical Turk. In: Proceedings of the SIGCHI Conference on Human Factors in Computing Systems (CHI), p. 453. ACM (2008)

20. Kuechler, B., Vaishnavi, V.: On theory development in design science research: anatomy of a research project. Eur. J. Inf. Syst. **17**(5), 489–504 (2008)

21. Leimeister, J.M.: Crowdsourcing. Controlling Manag. **56**(6), 388–392 (2012)

22. Lindgren, E., Münch, J.: Raising the odds of success: the current state of experimentation in product development. Inf. Softw. Technol. **77**, 80–91 (2016)

23. Linsey, J., Clauss, E., Kurtoglu, T., Murphy, J., Wood, K.L., Markman, A.B.: An experimental study of group idea generation techniques: understanding the roles of idea representation and viewing methods. J. Mech. Des. **133**(3) (2011)

24. Luther, K., et al.: Structuring, aggregating, and evaluating crowdsourced design critique. In: Proceedings of the 18th ACM Conference on Computer Supported Cooperative Work & Social Computing, pp. 473–485. ACM (2015)

25. Maalej, W., Nayebi, M., Johann, T., Ruhe, G.: Toward data-driven requirements engineering. IEEE Softw. **33**(1), 48–54 (2016)

26. Mao, K., Yang, Y., Wang, Q., Jia, Y., Harman, M.: Developer recommendation for crowdsourced software development tasks. In: Proceedings of the IEEE Symposium on Service-Oriented System Engineering, pp. 347–356. IEEE (2015)

27. McGrath, R.G.: Business models: a discovery driven approach. Long Range Plan. **43**, 247–261 (2010)

28. Möller, F., Guggenberger, T.M., Otto, B.: Towards a method for design principle development in information systems. In: Hofmann, S., Müller, O., Rossi, M. (eds.) DESRIST 2020. LNCS, vol. 12388, pp. 208–220. Springer, Cham (2020). https://doi.org/10.1007/978-3-030-64823-7_20

29. Münch, J., Trieflinger, S., Heisler, B.: Product discovery - building the right things: insights from a grey literature review. In: Proceedings of ICE/ITMC, pp. 1–8. IEEE (2020)

30. Nambisan, S.: Digital entrepreneurship: toward a digital technology perspective of entrepreneurship. Entrep. Theory Pract. **41**(6), 1029–1055 (2017)

31. Nebeling, M., Speicher, M., Norrie, M.C.: CrowdStudy. In: Proceedings EICS, p. 255. ACM (2013)

32. Olsson, H.H., Bosch, J.: Towards continuous customer validation: a conceptual model for combining qualitative customer feedback with quantitative customer observation. In: Fernandes, J.M., Machado, R.J., Wnuk, K. (eds.) ICSOB 2015. LNBIP, vol. 210, pp. 154–166. Springer, Cham (2015). https://doi.org/10.1007/978-3-319-19593-3_13

33. Parker, G., van Alstyne, M., Choudary, S.P.: Platform Revolution: Platform Revolution: How Networked Markets Are Transforming the Economy - and How to Make Them Work for You. W.W. Norton & Company, New York (2016)

34. Peffers, K., Tuunanen, T., Rothenberger, M.A., Chatterjee, S.: A design science research methodology for information systems research. J. Manag. Inf. Syst. **24**(3), 45–77 (2007)

35. Quoc Viet Hung, N., Chi Thang, D., Weidlich, M., Aberer, K.: ERICA. In: Proceedings of the 38th International ACM SIGIR Conference on Research and Development in Information Retrieval, pp. 1037–1038. ACM (2015)

36. Reibenspiess, V., Drechsler, K., Eckhardt, A., Wagner, H.T.: Tapping into the wealth of employees' ideas: design principles for a digital intrapreneurship platform. Inf. Manag., 103287 (2020)

37. Ries, E.: The Lean Startup: How Today's Entrepreneurs Use Continuous Innovation to Create Radically Successful Businesses. Crown Business, USA (2014)

38. Schoormann, T., Hofer, J., Knackstedt, R.: Software tools for supporting reflection in design thinking projects. In: Proceedings of the HICSS 2020. AIS (2020)

39. Tavanapour, N., Bittner, E.A.C.: Towards supportive mechanisms for crowd collaboration – design guidelines for platform developers. In: Zaphiris, P., Ioannou, A. (eds.) HCII 2019. LNCS, vol. 11591, pp. 353–372. Springer, Cham (2019). https://doi.org/10.1007/978-3-030-21817-1_27

40. Teece, D.J.: Business models, business strategy and innovation. Long Range Plan. **43**(2–3), 172–194 (2010)

41. Tran, A., Hasan, S.U., Park, J.Y.: Crowd participation pattern in the phases of a product development process that utilizes crowdsourcing. Ind. Eng. Manag. Syst. **11**(3), 266–275 (2012)

42. Vogel, P.: From venture idea to venture opportunity. Entrep. Theory Pract. **41**(6), 943–971 (2017)

43. Wache, H., Möller, F., Schoormann, T., Strobel, G., Petrik, D.: Exploring the abstraction levels of design principles: the case of chatbots. In: Proceedings of WI 2022. AIS (2022)

44. Xu, A., Huang, S.W., Bailey, B.: Voyant: generating structured feedback on visual designs using a crowd of non-experts. In: ACM Conference on Computer Supported Cooperative Work & Social Computing, pp. 1433–1444. ACM (2014)
45. Yin, R.K.: Case Study Research: Design and Methods, Applied Social Research Methods Series, vol. 5. Sage, Los Angeles (2009)
46. Zaggl, M.A., Sun, Y., Majchrzak, A., Malhotra, A.: Integrative solutions in online crowdsourcing innovation challenges. In: Proceedings of HICCS, vol. 54. AIS (2021)

Rapid Delivery of Software: The Effect of Alignment on Time to Market

Kouros Pechlivanidis$^{(\boxtimes)}$ and Gerard Wagenaar

Department of Information and Computing Sciences, Utrecht University,
Princetonplein 5, 3584 CC Utrecht, The Netherlands
{k.pechlivanidis,g.wagenaar}@uu.nl

Abstract. In Scrum, teams working collaboratively on interdependent
pieces of software face alignment issues as they need to coordinate their
work. Organisations aim to minimise time to market of their products,
which makes it relevant to identify how alignment issues affect time to market. Currently, empirical evidence of the effect of implementing alignment
activities on delivering software is scarce. This research aims to identify
those alignment activities that shorten the time to market of backlog items.
First, examination of key concepts led to a grounded choice of alignment
activities taken into account. Use of alignment activities in development of
features was identified by sending feature owners a close-ended questionnaire on the alignment of their collaborating Scrum teams. The cycle times
of backlog items were measured by using the application programmable
interface of the agile tool used for tracking backlog items. Results show that
when user stories were developed using a shared Definition of Ready, process and lead time decreased significantly. Process and lead time also differed between user stories implementing a different number of shared feedback sessions, where using two shared feedback sessions per sprint resulted
in the lowest process and lead time.

Keywords: Agile · Agile tools · Alignment · Scrum · Scrum
collaboration · Time to market

1   Introduction

Before agile software development methods emerged, the dominant approach
used for managing the software engineering process was the Waterfall method
[22]. This model dictates a sequential design process, from requirement analysis to system maintenance. Various comparative studies discuss the differences
between traditional sequential phased approaches and agile methods. McCormick
[13] states that using an agile method in the software engineering process results
in faster delivery of a software solution. Almeida [1] adds that implementing agile
methods allows greater flexibility and responsiveness to changing requirements.
The most widely adopted framework implementing agile principles is Scrum [18].
Scrum implements the advantages of agile methods discussed above by applying
an iterative, incremental process skeleton [16].

© The Author(s), under exclusive license to Springer Nature Switzerland AG 2022
D. Taibi et al. (Eds.): PROFES 2022, LNCS 13709, pp. 351–365, 2022.
https://doi.org/10.1007/978-3-031-21388-5_24

Whereas Scrum in its early years would only be applied in a single team at a single location, its rapid rising crossed both the single team as well as the single location boundary. Hossain et al. [9], already in 2009, made a plea for more empirical study to understand Scrum practices in teams at different locations, more notably globally distributed projects. The introduction of Scrum frameworks like SAFe[1] or LeSS[2] emphasize the need for guidance in scaling Scrum from a team to an organizational level.

Collaboration, co-ordination and communication were already key elements in Scrum teams in their single context [17]. Working with multiple teams working at multiple locations also brings the 3 C's to a new level, where especially co-ordination, the process of managing dependencies among activities, requires attention. Edison et al. [8] identified nine categories of challenges that organisations are confronted with when applying large scale agile development methods with inter-team Collaboration as one of them. Vlietland and Van Vliet [23] identified issues in interdependent Scrum team chains, with alignment being the most prominent one. Vlietland and Van Vliet [24] even suggest that Scrum's focus on independent agile teams causes issues: *"The focus on the single backlog in combination with the 'owned' IT applications likely results in a bounded Scrum team focus rather than a feature delivery focus. Such focus likely results in collaboration (related) issues."* (p.3). Alignment issues between interdependent Scrum teams even may cause features to be delayed [23]. Cohen et al. [5] concludes that in today's intensive competitive environment, each day of delay reduces the delivered business value of a product.

However, empirical evidence of the effect of coordinating alignment activities on improvements in delivering working software are scarce, if not absent. At the same time, this is something software engineering is looking for: *"... the software-intensive systems industry is under severe pressure to improve their capability to deliver on ... software needs"* [3, p. 82]. This study aims to do so by answering the question: *"What effect does alignment between interdependent Scrum teams have on time to market of backlog items?"*. Its answer will scientifically contribute to an empirical foundation for the use of agile methods, Scrum especially. At the same time it guides managers operating in a chain of Scrum teams in selecting effective alignment activities.

The remainder of this paper is structured as follows: Section 2 presents related work, laying the foundation for the research approach discussed in Sect. 3. Section 4 proposes hypotheses used to structure our research. Section 5 presents the study results. The study is concluded in Sect. 6 by summarizing the key takeaways and discussing future research avenues.

2   Background and Related Work

In this section, the context of our work will be introduced by examining related work with regard to alignment activities in Scrum teams (Sect. 2.1) and the time

---

[1] https://www.scaledagileframework.com/.
[2] less.works.

to market of backlog items (Sect. 2.2). At the same time, both sections introduce key concepts in our research, also to support the research approach in Sect. 3.

2.1 Related Work and Key Concepts Alignment Activities

In our introduction we identified alignment of codependent Scrum teams as a main issue of applying Scrum at an organisation level. Yet, alignment is necessary to reduce the amount of unnecessary work done [15]. Several models have been put forward to describe coordination in multiple Scrum teams.

Formal methods and automated tools do not aid in predicting software development performance, where the role of formal coordination and informal coordination and communication do account for variation in the software development performance [14]. Although this statement was not drawn up in the context of agile software development - the Agile Manifesto hadn't been written by then - its validity has not really been contradicted. More recent work, such as that of Strode [19,20] on the effectiveness of coordination, confirms the observation. Her work describes and distinguishes several strategies of coordination, now in an agile context. However, in this work strategies are characterized rather than practices identified.

Edison et al. [8] do include in their systematic literature review a list of practices that could be used for inter-team coordination. Examples are: Common goal for the sprint, synchronised sprint cycle, collaborative platform, PO coordination meetings, and many others. Most practices were based on observation from one or two case study organizations. Results were also based on organizations using one or another framework, which causes this work to be characterized as a kind of top-down approach. In contrast, practices that could be identified as just being used, regardless of (organizational) influences, constitute a more bottom-up approach.

In various (other) studies, Scrum activities and artifacts that influence alignment have been suggested. Table 1 specifies a list of activities we derived from them. We draw here mainly on the work of Vlietland and Van Vliet [24], but added specific alignment activities from other sources.

We assume activities A1-A3 and A7-A8 to be self-explanatory. Applying predefined workflow stages (A4) means that the status of product backlog items are similar for all of the teams involved, for instance defined/build/tested [24]. Aligning the Scrum heartbeat (A5) indicates the length of a sprint being the same for all teams. Feedback moments (A6) are Scrum meetings where communication with external stakeholders takes place, most notably a Sprint Planning Meeting or a Sprint Review Meetings.

2.2 Related Work and Key Concepts Time to Market

Rapid delivery of a software product with a short Time to Market (TtM) requires interdependent Scrum teams to align on activities and deliverables [23]. Studies providing quantitative measures of TtM are scarce. However, TtM was identified to be a key performance indicator for measuring software development processes

Table 1. List of alignment activities

Index	Activity	Source
A1	Using a shared Definition of Ready	[24]
A2	Using a shared Definition of Done	[24]
A3	Using a shared Product Backlog	[6]
A4	Applying predefined workflow stages	[24]
A5	Aligning the Scrum heartbeat	[7,11]
A6	Planning shared feedback moments	[24]
A7	Sharing information on a centralized (digital) work space	[17]
A8	Communicating testing activities through the entire chain of Scrum teams	[23]

at a large organization [21]. This factor, among others, allowed for a coherent analysis across all organizational boundaries to achieve an end-to-end monitoring of the software development processes, thus improving capabilities to identify potentials for improving process and system quality.

To operationalize TtM in our research, two options are available. First, process time of a backlog item could be the time between starting development on the work item and finishing the work item following the Definition of Done (DoD). Alternatively, lead time is defined as the time between creation of the backlog item and completion of the item according to the DoD [10]; this option is more or less equal to the one in Sürücü et al. [21]: Time in days from creating user stories to delivering a system. Usually, lead times are used when trying to shorten the TtM. However, Kim et al. [10] argue that the proportion of process time to lead time is an important metric that can be used when measuring the efficiency of the process. This proportion determines how much time the backlog item is in queue before development starts. A visualisation of process time and lead time is shown in Fig. 1. We will use both in the remainder, also to allow for drawing conclusions about similarities and/or differences between them.

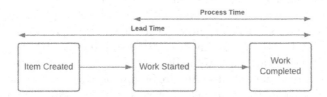

Fig. 1. Process times and lead times (based on Kim et al. [10])

3   Methodology

In this section, we introduce our approach to answer the research question. Section 3.1 discusses how TtM of backlog items was retrieved. Section 3.2 elaborates on the method used for measuring alignment in a chain of interdependent Scrum teams.

3.1   Extracting Empirical Data

With the aim of managing the decision making process in Agile teams, organisations use agile project management tools [2,12]. Common software tools for managing the agile software development process are Rally, Trac, Mingle, Scrum-Works, VersionOne, JIRA, MS Team Foundation Server, XPlanner and Assembla [2]. Organisations expect agile tools to contain a broad set of functionalities, including features for bug tracking, backlog management and burn-down chart visualization [25]. Moreover, most tools provide functionality for time tracking of user stories. By using such functionality, organisations can record the process and lead time of backlog items.

The data set used for analysis was collected data from an international enterprise operating in the logistics sector; for confidentiality reasons we will refer to this company as LogCom. LogCom has a data solutions department consisting of approximately hundred employees. The department is divided into Scrum teams with data engineers, data scientists, machine learning operation engineers and business intelligence specialists. The dedicated Scrum teams work together on user stories to create, deploy and maintain a platform that provides the organisation insights derived from its data. As a result, multiple Scrum teams in a highly interdependent environment collectively build software systems, in a large organisation that deals with complex logistic processes.

LogCom uses the Rally platform developed by Broadcom Inc. to manage agile processes [4]. Rally allows collaboration between multiple agile teams by providing a central hub for tracking work in shared backlogs. Users of Rally can use entities called projects to create a hierarchical structure of teams. LogCom uses projects to represent organisational components, such as departments or development teams. Each user story has a project assigned to specify which Scrum team is responsible for completing the user story. The user stories that are part of the product backlog have one of five workflow stages:

- Undefined: A user story is created, but does not yet implement the criteria from the Definition of Ready (DoR).
- Defined: A user story is created and satisfies the DoR. Development on a user story can be started.
- In Progress: Development on a work item has started, but is not yet finished.
- Completed: Development on a user story has finished, but the product owner (PO) still needs to evaluate whether the produced solution satisfies the DoD.
- Accepted: A delivered work item satisfies the DoD and is accepted by the PO.

In Rally, user stories can be containerized into features, where each feature contains at least one user story. Thus, a feature is a logical collection of user stories that aim towards satisfying the same business need. LogCom facilitates alignment at feature level, meaning all user stories with the same parent feature are developed using the same alignment activities. As our work focuses on aligning interdependent Scrum teams, we only consider features that have user stories assigned to at least two different Scrum teams.

Rally offers a Web Services Application Programmable Interface (WSAPI) to expose information to third party applications. A Python API consumer has been developed to request data from the WSAPI. Process times and lead times will be calculated for all of the collected user stories. Each user story has a creation date, in progress date and accepted date saved as date time attribute. Following the definition of lead times and process times by Kim et al. [10], the lead time of a user story can be calculated with the following formula:

$$LeadTime = UserStory.AcceptedDate - UserStory.CreationDate$$

Similarly, the process time of a user story can be retrieved by subtracting the in progress date from the accepted date:

$$ProcessTime = UserStory.AcceptedDate - UserStory.InProgressDate$$

Table 2 lists all the fields captured in the resulting data set, together with a brief description and example value of the recorded variables.

Table 2. User story set

Variable name	Variable description	Example value
FeatureID	Unique identification code for feature	F8103
UserStoryID	Unique identification code for user story	US90033
CreationDate	Date and time the user story was created	2021–04-08T12:03:40.222Z
InProgressDate	Date and time the user story was moved to the in progress state	2021–04-13T15:42:19.520Z
AcceptedDate	Date and time the user story was moved to the accepted state	2021–04-26T08:11:05.954Z
LeadTime	User story lead time in days	17.84
ProcessTime	User story process time in days	12.69

3.2 Questionnaire

To enrich the data set described in Table 2 with data on alignment, a questionnaire was distributed.

The questions used in the questionnaire are deducted from the list of alignment activities. As LogCom already implements an aligned Scrum heartbeat throughout the organisation, activity A5 (Aligning the Scrum heartbeat) will be excluded in the list of questions. Additionally, Rally uses predefined workflow stages to manage the product backlog. Because of this, a question on A4 (Using predefined workflow stages) will also be excluded from the questionnaire. The questionnaire introduces each activity with a brief definition of the activity, supported by literature. The questions asked in the questionnaire can be found in Table 3.

Table 3. Questionnaire implementation

Activity	Question
A1	When working on the specified feature, did the collaborating Scrum teams implement a shared Definition of Ready?
A2	When working on the specified feature, did the collaborating Scrum teams implement a shared Definition of Done?
A3	When working on the specified feature, did the collaborating Scrum teams use a shared Product Backlog?
~~A4~~	~~When working on the specified feature, did the collaborating Scrum teams use the same predefined workflow stages?~~
~~A5~~	~~When working on the specified feature, did the collaborating Scrum teams use an aligned Scrum heartbeat?~~
A6	When working on the specified feature, how many shared feedback sessions did the collaborating Scrum teams plan per sprint?
A7	When working on the specified feature, did the collaborating Scrum teams actively use a centralized work space to share information on?
A8	When working on the specified feature, was the entire chain of Scrum team involved in setting up testing environments?

Each feature has an owner assigned. Selective sampling is chosen as sampling method for the questionnaire. As feature owners are involved in feature production, it is appropriate to send the questionnaire to them. The survey starts by explaining the study objectives, the time the survey would take and an informed consent form. Participants were then asked to respond to statements about how collaborating Scrum teams aligned during feature development. The questions used in the questionnaire are deducted from the list of alignment activities suggested in Table 1.

4   Hypotheses

To further describe how the the implementation of various alignment activities relates to the time to market of backlog items, hypotheses will be proposed. Vlietland and Van Vliet [24] substantiate that misalignment causes features to be delayed. As a result, the hypotheses have been formulated to test whether the implementation of alignment activities causes features to be delivered faster.

- $H1_A$: User stories that were developed implementing A do not have a shorter lead time compared to those that were not.
- $H2_A$: User stories that were developed implementing A do not have a shorter process time compared to those that were not.

H1 and H2 will be tested for all activities found in Table 1 measuring a dichotomous variable (A1, A2, A3, A7, A8). Hypotheses for the activity measuring a discrete variable (A6) were formulated as follows:

- $H3_{A6}$: There are no differences in lead time between user stories implementing a different amount of shared feedback sessions.
- $H4_{A6}$: There are no differences in process time between user stories implementing a different amount of shared feedback sessions.

5   Results

Before analysing the results, inaccurate measurements of process and lead time were removed. Measurements are considered inaccurate if the recorded metric is smaller than one day, due to the unlikeliness of a user story being started and finished according to the DoD in one day. The inaccuracy of these records can be attributed to multiple factors:

- Developers started working on the user story but forgot to update the user story state in Rally, resulting in process time shorter than a day.
- The Scrum team worked on a task that was not defined as a user story in Rally. To make work visible, the Scrum team created a user story in Rally, putting it on accepted after making it. Hence, the lead time for such a story is shorter than a day.

5.1   Process and Lead Times: Descriptive Statistics

Process times of 219 user stories were recorded after the removal of 55 inaccurate process time measurements. In total, the 219 selected user stories had 8 parent features (M = 27.38, SD = 17.84). Figure 2 visualises the distribution of process times.

After removing 32 inaccurate lead time measurements, the data set containing lead times consisted of 242 user stories with 8 parent features (M = 30.25, SD = 20.15). Figure 3 gives an overview of the distribution of lead times.

5.2   Questionnaire: Descriptive Statistics

The questionnaire was filled in by the appropriate stakeholder for the selected features (N=8). Figure 4 shows a stacked count plot visualising the answers given to the Boolean questions by the respondents. Since A6 (The amount of shared feedback moment) describes a discrete variable, this activity is not shown in the figure. For A6, an average of 2.5 feedback sessions per sprint was recorded (SD = 2.07).

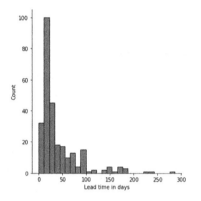

Fig. 2. Distribution of user story lead times

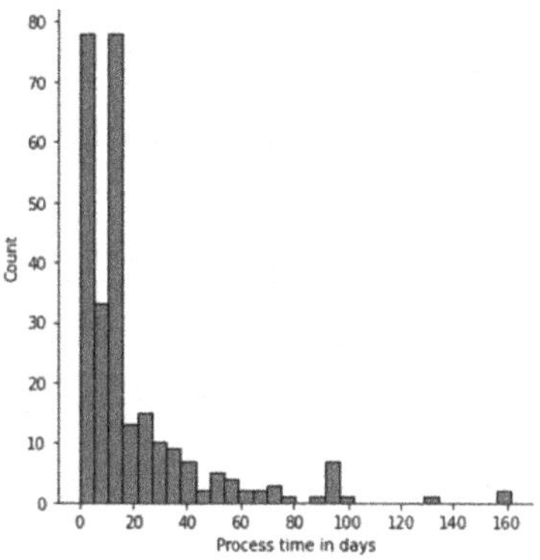

Fig. 3. Distribution of user story process times

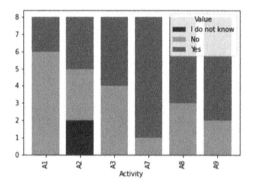

Fig. 4. Count of activity implementations

5.3 Combining Empirical Data and Questionnaire Results: Descriptive Statistics

A more detailed overview of the process times, lead times and group size for each activity is shown in Table 4 and Table 5. For activities A1, A2, A3, A7 and A8, groups with value 1 implement the activity, where as groups with value 0 do not implement the activity. For A6, the group value indicates the number of shared feedback moments.

5.4 Inferential Statistics

Figure 2 and Fig. 3 show that the populations for both process times and lead times are not normally distributed. Hence, the non-parametric Mann-Whitney U Test and Kruskal-Wallis H Test were used. All statistical tests were performed using significance level $\alpha = .01$.

A Mann-Whitney U Test show that user stories that were developed implementing a shared Definition of Ready (Mdn = 15.11) have a shorter lead time

Table 4. Descriptive statistic of lead time

Activity	Group	Mean	Standard deviation	N
A1	1	23.42	16.99	40
	0	45.67	43.38	202
A2	1	44.23	45.11	129
	0	41.58	45.28	54
A3	1	47.33	43.58	144
	0	34.16	35.81	98
A6	5	33.55	23.64	69
	4	28.73	22.60	19
	3	25.05	14.54	44
	2	18.62	7.24	21
	1	112.27	42.15	13
	0	57.23	53.32	76
A7	1	42.54	41.71	232
	0	29.25	16.58	10
A8	1	40.28	39.27	199
	0	49.93	48.19	43

Table 5. Descriptive statistic of process time

Activity	Group	Mean	Standard deviation	N
A1	1	12.42	7.38	34
	0	25.09	26.19	185
A2	1	18.26	14.03	113
	0	29.39	37.13	52
A3	1	22.51	20.64	123
	0	23.92	29.12	96
A6	5	23.99	24.78	63
	4	14.26	11.37	13
	3	17.46	12.64	44
	2	11.29	2.95	21
	1	91.50	29.35	12
	0	19.17	14.66	66
A7	1	23.49	25.14	209
	0	15.50	7.97	10
A8	1	20.33	18.55	178
	0	35.28	40.10	41

compared to those that were not (Mdn = 28.13) (U = 2413). Thus, $H1_{A1}$ will be rejected. Similarly, user stories that were developed implementing a shared Definition of Ready (Mdn = 12.01) have a shorter process time compared to those that were not (Mdn = 13.85) (U = 2214). Thus, $H2_{A1}$ will be rejected.

Furthermore, a Kruskal-Wallis H Test demonstrates that there are differences in lead time between user stories implementing a different number of shared feedback sessions. Thus, we reject $H3_{A6}$. Likewise, there are differences in process time between user stories implementing a different number of shared feedback sessions. The lowest TtM was realised when teams implemented two shared feedback moments per sprint. Thus, we reject $H4_{A6}$.

Table 6 and Table 7 show the more elaborate results of hypotheses testing.

Table 6. Statistical test results for process time hypotheses

Index	Hypothesis	Test Result	p < .01
$H2_{A1}$	User stories that were developed implementing a shared Definition of Ready (Mdn = 12.01) do not have a shorter process time compared to those that were not (Mdn = 13.85)	U = 2214	Yes
$H2_{A2}$	User stories that were developed implementing a shared Definition of Done (Mdn = 12.00) do not have a shorter process time compared to those that were not (Mdn = 12.06)	U = 2792	No
$H2_{A3}$	User stories that were developed using a shared Product Backlog (Mdn = 13.97) do not have a shorter process time compared to those that were not (Mdn = 12.96)	U = 6225	No
$H2_{A7}$	User stories that were developed while actively using a centralized digital work space to share information on (Mdn = 13.03) do not have a shorter process time compared to those that were not (Mdn = 12.98)	U = 1084	No
$H2_{A8}$	User stories that were developed while communicating testing activities to the entire chain of Scrum teams (Mdn = 13.01) do not have a shorter process time compared to those that were not (Mdn = 13.19)	U = 3206	No
$H4_{A6}$	There are no differences in process time between user stories implementing a different amount of shared feedback sessions	HA(5) = 36.57	Yes

Table 7. Statistical test results for lead time hypotheses

Index	Hypothesis	Test Result	p < .01
H1$_{A1}$	User stories that were developed implementing a shared Definition of Ready (Mdn = 15.11) do not have a shorter lead time compared to those that were not (Mdn = 28.13)	U = 2413	Yes
H1$_{A2}$	User stories that were developed implementing a shared Definition of Done (Mdn = 27.88) do not have a shorter lead time compared to those that were not (Mdn = 18.85)	U = 3828	No
H1$_{A3}$	User stories that were developed using a shared Product Backlog (Mdn = 31.48) do not have a shorter lead time compared to those that were not (Mdn = 18.85)	U = 8729	No
H1$_{A7}$	User stories that were developed while actively using a centralized digital work space to share information on (Mdn = 27.14) do not have a shorter lead time compared to those that were not (Mdn = 22.30)	U = 1261	No
H1$_{A8}$	User stories that were developed while communicating testing activities to the entire chain of Scrum teams (Mdn = 27.16) do not have a shorter lead time compared to those that were not (Mdn = 24.86)	U = 3870	No
H3$_{A6}$	There are no differences in lead time between user stories implementing a different amount of shared feedback sessions	H(5) = 53.49	Yes

6   Conclusions, Discussion and Future Work

In this paper, we empirically measured the effect of alignment in a chain of Scrum teams on the TtM of backlog items. First, a list of activities relating to the latent variable alignment were identified from examining related work. Subsequently, their application was tested in a chain of Scrum teams. While at the same time, process and lead times were retrieved by consuming the REST API of an agile platform. Significant lower process and lead times were found for the user stories that were developed using a shared DoR. Differences in process and lead time were found between user stories implementing a different number of shared feedback sessions.

Our findings are in line with the suggestions made by Vlietland and Van Vliet [24], who suggest that alignment issues in interdependent Scrum teams result in delivery delays. Our results provide a crumb of empirical quantitative evidence with regard to the effect of alignment activities, an area in which this kind of proof is not too abundant. Practitioners, for instance Scrum masters or agile coaches, may find our results supportive for the use of a DoR or the implementation of a certain number of Scrum events, for instance Sprint Reviews. On the contrary, we would not like our results to lead to abolition of alignment activities for which we currently did not find support in our research.

6.1 Limitations

Our findings are subject to limitations which are in turn threats to the validity of our research.

We are aware of the limited scope of our research: One organization, LogCom, with several Scrum teams, yet one software product. This necessitates us to be hesitant with regard to the generalizability of our results.

We removed outliers in the Rally data as some values were simply impossible. We came up with explanations, such as the proposition that developers might forget to update the status of a user story in the agile tool. In the end we did not use around 20% of the process times and slightly over 10% of the lead times data. Hence, the recorded TtM may show inaccuracies due to our interventions.

Furthermore, the results of the questionnaire are subject to the respondents understanding of the question. We tried mitigating this limitation by providing a definition of the activities before asking questions on activity implementation. Moreover, there might be more alignment activities not uncovered in existing work. This may have resulted in an incomplete list of observable activities used to measure the latent variable alignment.

6.2 Future Work

When addressing the discussed limitations, the methods used in our work can still serve as an inspiration for future studies. One future research avenue is to empirically test the construct validity of the found alignment activities and to use qualitative research to enrich the current activity list. A next step in our research will be to use the findings from Vlietland and Van Vliet [24] to empirically test the total set of collaboration issues in chains of Scrum teams (coordination, prioritization, alignment, predictability, visibility). For this research avenue, the alignment activities described in this research paper can be used as a framework for assessing alignment.

References

1. Almeida, F.: Challenges in migration from waterfall to agile environments. World J. Comput. Appl. Technol. 5(3), 39–49 (2017)
2. Azizyan, G., Magarian, M.K., Kajko-Matsson, M.: Survey of agile tool usage and needs. In: 2011 Agile Conference, pp. 29–38 (2011)

3. Bosch, J.: Speed, data, and ecosystems: the future of software engineering. IEEE Software **33**(1), 82–88 (2015)
4. Broadcom: Rally Software. www.broadcom.com/products/software/value-stream-management/rally Accessed 19 Nov 2021
5. Cohen, M.A., Eliasberg, J., Ho, T.-H.: New product development: the performance and time-to-market tradeoff. Manage. Sci. **42**(2), 173–186 (1996)
6. Cristal, M., Wildt, D., Prikladnicki, R.: Usage of scrum practices within a global-company. In: 2008 IEEE International Conference on Global Software Engineering, pp. 222–226 (2008)
7. Deemer, P., Benefield, G., Larman, C., Vodde, B.: The scrum primer (2010). www.brianidavidson.com/agile/docs/scrumprimer121.pdf
8. Edison, H., Wang, X., Conboy, K.: Comparing methods for large-scale agile software development: a systematic literature review. IEEE Trans. Softw. Eng. **99**, 1–1 (2021)
9. Hossain, E., Ali, M., Paik, H.: Using Scrum in Global Software Development: a systematic literature review. In: 2009 Fourth IEEE International Conference on Global Software Engineering, pp. 175–184 (2009)
10. Kim, G., Humble, J., Debois, P., Willis, J.: The DevOps handbook: How to Create World-Class Agility, Reliability, and Security in Technology Organizations. IT Revolution, p. 486 (2016)
11. Leffingwell, D.: Mastering the iteration: an agile white paper [white paper] (2007). www.hosteddocs.ittoolbox.com/mastering-the-iteration-an-agile-white-paper.pdf
12. Lin, J., Yu, H., Shen, Z., Miao, C.: Studying task allocation decisions of novice agile teams with data from agile project management tools. In: Proceedings of the 29th ACM/IEEE International Conference on Automated Software Engineering, pp. 689–694 (2014)
13. McCormick, M: Waterfall vs. agile methodology (2012). www.mccormickpcs.com/images/WaterfallvsAgileMethodology.pdf
14. Sawyer, S., Guinan, P.: Software development: processes and performance. In: IBM Syst. J. **37**(4), 552–569 (1998)
15. Scheerer, A., Hildenbrand, T., Kude, T.: Coordination in large-scale agile software-development: a multiteam systems perspective. In: 2014 47th Hawaii International Conference on System Sciences, pp. 4780–4788 (2014)
16. Schwaber, K.: Agile project management with Scrum. Microsoft press (2004)
17. Sharp, H., Robinson, H.: Three 'C' of agile practice: collaboration, coordination and communication. In: Agile software development, pp. 61-85. Springer, Berlin (2010). https://doi.org/10.1007/978-3-642-12575-1_4
18. Stavru, S.: A critical examination of recent industrial surveys on agile method usage. J. Syst. Softw. **94**, 87–97 (2014)
19. Kuhrmann, M., et al. (eds.): PROFES 2018. LNCS, vol. 11271. Springer, Cham (2018). https://doi.org/10.1007/978-3-030-03673-7
20. Strode, D., Huff, S.: A Coordination perspective on agile software development, pp. 64–96 (2015)
21. Sürücü, C., Song, B., Krüger, J., Saake, G., Leich, T.: Establishing key performance indicators for measuring software-development processes at a large organization, pp. 1331–1341 (2020)
22. Szalvay, V.: An introduction to agile software development. Danube technologies, vol. 3 (2004)
23. Vlietland, J., van Vliet, H.: Improving it incident handling performance with information visibility. J. Softw. Evol. Process **26**(12), 1106–1127 (2014)

24. Vlietland, J., van Vliet, H.: Towards a governance framework for chains of scrum teams. Inf. Softw. Technol. **57**, 52–65 (2015)
25. Abraham, A., Gandhi, N., Hanne, T., Hong, T.-P., Nogueira Rios, T., Ding, W. (eds.): ISDA 2021. LNNS, vol. 418. Springer, Cham (2022). https://doi.org/10. 1007/978-3-030-96308-8

Exploring the "Why", "How", and "What" of Continuous Digital Service Innovation

Jenny Elo[(✉)] [ID], Kaisa Pekkala[ID], Tuure Tuunanen[ID], Juuli Lumivalo[ID], and Markus Salo[ID]

University of Jyväskylä, Jyväskylä, Finland
`jenny.m.elo@jyu.fi`

Abstract. Today's rapidly advancing technologies and highly competitive and dynamic markets make continuity essential in organizations' service development and innovation activities. However, little is known about why and how organizations organize for continuous digital service innovation (DSI) and what follows. To address this gap, this paper explores the "why," "how," and "what" of continuous DSI. We present findings from a thematic analysis of 23 semi-structured interviews with six case organizations to shed light on the external and internal drivers (why), principles, practices, methods (how), and outcomes (what) of continuous DSI for organizations. We observe that, externally, continuous DSI is driven by the rapid and dynamic changes in the business environment, rapid technological advancements, and customers' expectations of continuity. Multiple customer, profitability, performance, and technology-related objectives exist internally. The organization for continuous DSI emphasizes customer- and other stakeholder-related principles and practices, as well as continuity-related principles and practices for the development and innovation activities. In addition, we find that service organizations implement various methods for continuous DSI. The effects of continuous DSI on organizations include diverse customer, development and innovation, communication, and collaboration-related outcomes. We contribute by offering a novel, practice-based understanding of continuous DSI in organizations, which may inform future research on this emerging phenomenon.

Keywords: Continuous digital service innovation · Service-dominant logic · Innovation process · Qualitative research

1 Introduction

In today's digitalized world, services are increasingly characterized by digital technologies that present organizations with novel opportunities for value creation and innovation [1, 2]. Over the past two decades, driven by such technological advancements and the ever-growing demands of competitive and dynamic market environments, service organizations have become increasingly interested in utilizing lightweight and iterative development methods (e.g., Agile, Lean) for systems and software [3–5], with recent developments in the field focusing on continuity in organizations' service development

© The Author(s), under exclusive license to Springer Nature Switzerland AG 2022
D. Taibi et al. (Eds.): PROFES 2022, LNCS 13709, pp. 366–381, 2022.
https://doi.org/10.1007/978-3-031-21388-5_25

and innovation activities. As the latest phenomenon, the DevOps (development and operations) approach [6] has attracted increasing interest from practitioners and researchers, especially within the software engineering (SE) community [7, 8]. With DevOps, organizations aim to eliminate silos, align actors' incentives, and achieve a continuous flow in their service development and innovation processes to propose customers with value rapidly while maintaining high service quality [5, 9, 10]. The resulting process, which we refer to as "continuous digital service innovation" (DSI), has become essential for service organizations to remain competitive and ultimately survive in today's markets.

To date, the research on continuous methods (e.g., DevOps) has primarily focused on software-intensive organizations or focused on service organizations' IT functions with little attention to continuity from the entire organization's perspective [8, 11, 12]. Although some valuable openings have been made [e.g., 10, 12], we argue that there is a scant understanding of why and how different digital service organizations organize for continuous DSI and what follows. Moreover, there is currently no established definition of continuous DSI to guide research on the phenomenon.

To address this gap, this paper explores continuous DSI in six Finnish service organizations. Based on the service-dominant (S-D) logic-founded understanding of service innovation [see 13, p. 161], we propose a working definition of continuous DSI as *the continuous rebundling of diverse resources to create novel resources that are beneficial to actors in a digital service context*. We employ a qualitative research approach [14] with the primary goal of exploring and explaining the drivers (why), principles, practices, methods (how), and outcomes (what) of continuous DSI for organizations. More specifically, we present the findings from a thematic analysis of 23 semi-structured interviews with industry informants addressing the following research questions:

RQ1. Why do digital service organizations organize for continuous DSI?

RQ2. How do digital service organizations organize for continuous DSI?

RQ3. What are the outcomes of continuous DSI for organizations?

As our main finding, we present a preliminary framework that identifies six dimensions of continuous DSI in organizations. Thus, we contribute to research and practice by increasing our understanding of continuous DSI and how organizations' organize for this in practice. As digital service organizations increasingly need to ensure continuity both in terms of day-to-day operations and long-term growth and survival, such insights should be of great interest to SE and information systems (IS) researchers and practitioners alike. We hope to generate interest in and discussion of continuous DSI among SE and IS scholars, as we believe these domains hold valuable knowledge and theories to advance the understanding of this multifaceted, socio-technical phenomenon.

The remainder of our paper proceeds as follows. First, we present the theoretical background upon which the working definition of continuous DSI is based, including the concepts of DSI, continuity in DSI, and methods/approaches to continuous DSI. Second, we present the methodology with descriptions of the data collection and analysis. Then, we present our findings, followed by a discussion and conclusion.

2 Theoretical Background

2.1 Digital Service Innovation (DSI)

The theoretical understanding of DSI in our study is founded on S-D logic [15–17], which has been found to be a particularly suitable lens for studying and understanding service innovation [e.g., 13, 18, 19]. S-D logic views service as a co-created process in which actors apply their resources (e.g., competencies such as knowledge and skills) for the benefit of others (or themselves) [15]. The traditional view of services (plural) as intangible outputs (similar to products) is replaced with the concept of service (singular), that is, the process of reciprocal value creation between actors [20], allowing for a broader and more systemic view of service innovation in organizations [19].

Although service innovation can also be used to describe the outcome of innovation, S-D logic emphasizes innovation as a dynamic and interactive process driven by actors' collaborative efforts to find or develop novel ways for value creation [13, 20–22]. By enabling new and better ways for actors to co-create value [13, 21], service innovation supports the creation of novel and/or improved service offerings, processes, and business models for organizations [22, 23]. Building on these notions, we signify DSI as a process rather than an outcome in our research. More specifically, we build on the definition provided by Lusch and Nambisan [13, p. 161] and understand DSI as "the rebundling of diverse resources that create novel resources that are beneficial (i.e., value experiencing) to some actors" in a digital service context. "Digital" denotes the core or enabling role of digital technologies (artifacts) as part of the service. The following subsections expand on the concept of DSI by examining continuity in this context from a theoretical and practical perspective.

2.2 Continuity in DSI

The notion of continuity is built into the S-D logic view of service innovation. That is, innovation in S-D logic is not seen as an exceptional event but as a continuous and systemic process based on the complex interactions between actors, activities, and resources [24]. Similarly, Nambisan et al. [1, p. 226] underlined that DSI "involves the continuous matching of the potential (or capabilities) of new and/or newly recombined digital technologies with original market offerings." Furthermore, reconciling notions of continuous innovation in the innovation management literature, Lianto et al. [25, p. 773] defined continuous innovation as a "continuous process in building and shaping innovation capabilities to increase a company's potential to produce innovation performance (combination of incremental or radical innovation) continuously." Continuous DSI can therefore be understood as a continuous process and activity in organizations in which diverse resources are rebundled to generate short- and long-term benefits (for individuals and organizations), as well as the continuous building of capabilities to enable this.

Furthermore, the expression 'continuous' is often connected to the extent to which innovation occurs, that is, incremental (small and gradual change) versus radical innovation (significant change) [26]. The general perception seems to be that the two go hand in hand. For example, Lianto et al. [25, p. 772] described continuous innovation as a "continuous process in generating incremental or radical innovation combinations."

Also, Steiber and Alänge [27] found it irrelevant to distinguish between radical innovation and incremental improvement, as continuous innovation activities are typically a combination of both. Similarly, we find that the concept of continuous DSI is ideal for characterizing all the continuous development and innovation activities that occur in the described continuous manner in organizations enabling the emergence of novel resources that are beneficial to actors, be they new capabilities for the organization or novel value proposed to customers through an offering not previously available to them (i.e., improvement in the existing service or a completely new service).

2.3   Methods/approaches to Continuous DSI

Looking into the practical side of continuous DSI, over the past two decades, traditional service development methods (e.g., Waterfall) based on rigid step-by-step development projects, usually ending with the first major release of a system, have increasingly been replaced in organizations with lightweight and iterative development methods for systems and software [3, 5, 9]. The first wave in the industry gave rise to a broad spectrum of agile methods (e.g., eXtreme Programming, Scrum) aimed at facilitating organizations and individuals' flexibility in coping with recurrent changes in the business environment [12]. Whereas research and practice around agile methods initially focused on the software development context, in recent years, there has been a recognized need for a more holistic approach, that is, scaling the agile concept to span the whole organization. This has led, for example, to the introduction of the Scaled Agile Framework (SAFe) and the concept of 'Enterprise Agile' [11, 12]. Further, the Lean approach [28] has attracted interest from organizations as a means of optimizing resources, eliminating "waste," and achieving a continuous flow of development and innovation through all functions of an organization [11, 12].

As the most recent phenomenon, the DevOps approach [6], built on the abovementioned agile and lean principles, has gained popularity as a means of increasing the flexibility and efficiency of service development and innovation processes in organizations through the continuous delivery of relevant features demanded by customers [7]. DevOps signifies an organizational shift aimed at aligning actors' incentives (especially those of development and operations), fostering continuous collaboration, and relying on various continuous practices (e.g., continuous integration, deployment, and delivery) that shorten the time between committing a change and deploying it to production while ensuring high service quality [9]. DevOps enables the management of service throughout its lifecycle, offering automating solutions for the build, test, and deployment processes [5]. Consequently, DevOps allows organizations to propose value quickly and continuously to customers and increases the awareness of customer needs through frequent releases and rapid and continuous feedback [8].

To optimize the whole, DevOps should be applied to the entire organization, not just development and operations [6, 10]. To this end, Fitzgerald and Stol [11, 12] propose the term 'BizDev' to emphasize the need for continuity and alignment between business and development functions within organizations. Adopting a holistic approach and drawing on the lean concept of 'flow,' they identify a set of continuous practices (activities) towards continuous development and innovation, assigning them under the umbrella term 'Continuous*.' The authors emphasize that tight integration between different continuous functions is required to create an end-to-end flow between customer demand and the rapid delivery of service [11, 12].

3 Methodology

We follow a qualitative interpretive research approach [14, 29] with the primary goal of exploring and explaining the drivers (how), principles, practices, methods (how), and outcomes (what) of continuous DSI for organizations. Our research objective benefits from a qualitative and exploratory approach, as little extant research and understanding exists on the topic. In addition, the qualitative approach was deemed effective in addressing the "why," "how," and "what" questions guiding our research.

3.1 Data Collection

The data were collected by employing semi-structured interviews with six medium-sized and large service organizations in Finland (Table 1). As a common criterion, organizations were expected to strive towards continuity in their service development and innovation activities and operate in the context of digital or digitally enabled services.

Table 1. Organizations and informants.

Industry	Size	*	Informant roles
IT services and consulting	23,000 + employees (global; 20 countries)	4	Lead Business Developer, Head of Advisory (Design and Innovation), Head of Innovation, Head of R&D
Telecommunications, ICT, and online services	5,000 + employees	2	5G Development Director, Startup Analyst
Industrial and fiber laser equipment	70 + employees (Finland); global parent company 4,800 + employees	4	CEO, Senior Global Service Account & Market Manager, Director (Infrastructure and Service), Product Line Manager
HR service solutions	300 + employees	6	Development Director, Business Development Manager, Development Manager (2), HR Manager, Director (Industry)
Textile rental service	4000 + employees (global; 24 countries)	3	Development Manager, Service Owner, Director (Service Concepts)
Language services and language management solutions for digital environments	150 + employees plus 2 000 + freelance experts	4	Service Manager, Account Manager, Solution Architect, Chief Solutions Business Officer

* Number of informants

Still, the cases ought to differ from each other to enable an understanding of how different types of organizations organize for continuous DSI (i.e., to avoid industry bias).

Informants from each case organization represented various roles and were selected with the company representatives based on their knowledge and suitability. A common expectation was an understanding of both the strategic-level objectives and the operational-level activities related to the service development and innovation areas. Two to six people from each company were interviewed between August and October 2021, resulting in a data set of 23 interviews (13 males, 10 females; ages 25 to 57 years; average working experience in the company/the current role 9 + years).

All interviews followed the same interview guide [30], which included four main themes (1. Current state and perspectives on service development and innovation within the organization 2. Perceptions of continuity and how it is reflected in practice in the development and innovation activities, 3. Focal (internal/external) stakeholders, and 4. Digital technologies and continuous service innovation) with complementary open-ended questions. Semi-structured interviews were considered particularly suitable for the data collection, as they allowed the informants to speak freely and share their knowledge and experiences and welcomed the emergence of new perspectives. However, the themes and questions guided the discussion appropriately to gain a sufficient understanding of the topics of interest. The interviews lasted from 45 to 80 min and were conducted via an online video conferencing tool due to the COVID-19 pandemic. The interviews were recorded and transcribed.

3.2 Data Analysis

The analysis was carried out as a thematic analysis [31], which allows the identification and interpretation of thematic structures by searching for common features, relationships, and comprehensive models from the data. To support the reliability of the study [32], the analysis was performed by two authors. The first author was primarily responsible for coding and analysis; however, weekly discussions (four 1.5-h meetings) were held about the progress of the analysis by the two authors. The coding and interpretations were reviewed and assessed at each phase by the second author. The progress of the analysis was also discussed with the other authors, especially at later stages of the analysis and in formulating the framework.

Following the guidelines of Braun and Clarke [31], the analysis began by carefully reading each transcript to understand its context and content. After familiarizing themselves with the data, the authors discussed based on their notes and impressions and agreed on rules for the analysis. Preliminary themes were also discussed. The second phase of the analysis was initiated by open coding of one of the transcripts by the first author. The test coding was reviewed with the second author, and the necessary modifications to the coding as well as questions were addressed. The qualitative data analysis tool Atlas.ti was utilized to perform the open coding. The inductive coding process resulted in 1,066 quotations and 766 determined codes. The codes were at first descriptive of the informants' descriptions, but very similar codes were combined in the later phases resulting in a final number of 405 codes. In the third phase, we combined the codes to form first-order categories that were further assigned under second-order themes and then third-order dimensions to construct the preliminary framework describing the "why," "how," and "what" of continuous DSI.

4 Findings

The findings of our analysis have been compiled into a preliminary framework depicting the "why," "how," and "what" of continuous DSI (Fig. 1). Six representative dimensions emerged from the analysis: (1) *external drivers (why)*, (2) *organizational drivers (why)*, (3) *strategic principles (how)*, (4) *operational practices (how)*, (5) *methods/approaches/techniques (how)*, and (6) *outcomes (what)*. Each dimension includes a list of identified themes (bolded titles) and categories, followed by numbers that describe the number of codes they comprise. Next, we present the meaning and interesting first findings for each dimension.

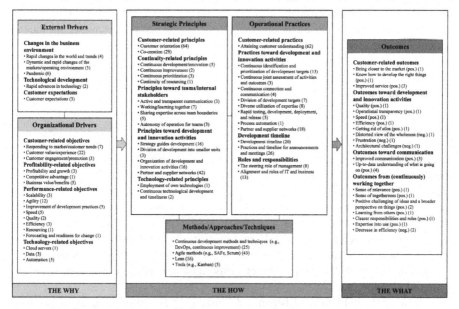

Fig. 1. The "why," "how," and "what" of continuous DSI.

4.1 The Why of Continuous DSI

External drivers represent the factors from outside organizations that guide operations towards continuous DSI. In this regard, the industry informants shared their experiences, for example, of the demands of the ever-changing business environment and its impact on the continuous need to assess and stay up to date with operations. Many of the informants described today's operating environments as dynamic and complex. Furthermore, the market and customer needs are constantly evolving, necessitating continuity.

Also, rapidly emerging and changing trends and circumstantial factors (e.g., COVID-19 pandemic) emerged as matters that demand continuity and timeliness in operations.

> The truth is that the operating environment changes so enormously all the time and all the trends and others that affect it. (Informant 3)

The informants also reported the continuous advancements in technology to increase the opportunities and expectations for continuous DSI without overlooking the influence of external expectations toward continuity (e.g., from customers).

> Technology is advancing so strongly now that what was brand new two years ago is now ancient and no one wants to invest in it anymore, and then these changes make everything change all the time. (Informant 19)

Organizational drivers explain the internal objectives that drive continuous DSI in organizations. Our preliminary findings highlight four themes for organizational drivers: customer-related, profitability-related, performance-related, and technology-related objectives. Regarding the first, our findings underline, for example, the objective of proactive, fast, and flexible responding to market/customer needs and the importance of promoting customer value and experience through continuous DSI.

> As a service provider, you should always be able to be up-to-date and respond to those very rapidly changing [customer] needs. (Informant 7)

The profitability objectives comprise organizations' targets for profitability and growth, competitive advantage, and business value, which are sought through implementing continuous DSI. Within performance objectives, the pursuit of agility appears to be linked to the pursuit of continuous DSI in organizations. The industry informants emphasized the importance of flexibility and agility at the team and the entire organization level. This effort connects to, among other things, the objective of circulating ideas more widely and continuously with customers and of engaging customers in development at the early stages. Furthermore, one reported aim was to establish clear decision-making points, through which ideas are promoted and tested as soon as possible to determine whether the ideas are worth more investment.

> We've tried to make the development more agile and such that ideas would be circulated a little more with the customers as well so that the customer would be involved as early as possible...And then achieve such decision-making points, where we can either decide not to continue developing the idea, or decide that yes, this looks good, and let's continue. (Informant 11)

Further, the objectives of speed, efficiency, and quality of development, and forecasting and readiness for change emerged as internal drivers for continuous DSI. The technology-related objectives were related to transferring the technical architecture to the cloud, continuous and fast utilization of data, and automation of development/processes (e.g., data processing).

Collecting data and then getting a continuous flow of data from those products...we should be able to quickly collect data from all the necessary sources, process it and give as simple an answer as possible to the customer. (Informant 3)

4.2 The How of Continuous DSI

Answers to the "how" question were sought through exploring the strategic principles, operational practices and methods, approaches, and techniques of continuous DSI in organizations. The strategic principles represent common understandings and fundamental guidelines that communicate an organization's strategy for organizing operations. Our analysis identified five themes: customer-related, continuity-related, teams/internal stakeholders-related, development and innovation activities-related, and technology-related principles.

First, our findings emphasize the organizations' fundamental orientation towards customers. The principle of co-creation also emerged from the discussions.

I think there are quite a few different principles that we do that we work by...but I would say the good place to start is always with the customer and everything that we are doing we are doing because we are trying to find value for a customer. (Informant 17)

We now want to do more with customers close to the market with this co-creation model as well. (Informant 5)

Whereas some organizations are well advanced in this process, others are only beginning to think about/looking for systematic and continuous ways to benefit from this.

It's always a certain challenge, that customer orientation; maybe we quite easily start from our own needs. In that we have a challenge, that how to actually listen to the customer and get ahead of the customer more. This is the learning place for us. (Informant 12)

The principles linked to continuity concerned, among others, continuous development and innovation, and continuous improvement, prioritization, and resourcing.

We try to review and prioritize continuously. So even if some X project was taken as a priority last month, if we look at it today and see that hey, this is no longer on the priority list, we have also learned that hey, we can put it aside and take on the more important priority at the top of the list. (Informant 3)

The found principles toward teams/internal stakeholders included active and transparent communication, the culture of working/learning together, sharing expertise across team boundaries, and autonomy of operation for teams.

The development is going is more towards cross functional cooperation, agile development, trying something on a small scale before launching on a global level. So, the basics of agile development work. (Informant 16)

Principles toward development and innovation activities, in turn, included informants' common descriptions of the strategy's important role in guiding DSI by providing a common direction that is then broken down into smaller objectives and activities.

Of course, everything is connected to our strategy. That strategy is then divided into smaller strategies or goals. (Informant 18)

Another interesting finding is the organization of development and innovation activities within the organizations. Some case organizations seem to operate with service development and innovation linked closely together, while others have separate innovation units where continuous innovation and proof-of-concept/value are conducted (via Lean Startup). The latter seems to be more common, especially in larger organizations. From the perspective of organizing for continuous DSI, this preliminary finding reveals exciting opportunities for further examination. Further, as technology-related principles, continuous technological development and timeliness were mentioned as important.

Operational practices are understood as concrete activities that companies implement in continuous DSI. Our findings highlight four themes connected to this. First, customer-related practices include various forms of attaining customer understanding in organizations (e.g., continuous market feedback and continuous testing). However, a shared experience seems to be that more systematic ways of gaining such understanding are being sought, and continuity is not yet where it could be in practice.

So now we're learning this model, how do we sort of see how this big vision, how to break it down into small, reasonably sized pieces. And then that we can also reflect often enough on what needs to be done and changed. And on the other hand, get the constant feedback from the market. (Informant 5)

Regarding development and innovation practices, we found that characteristics of continuous DSI include continuous identification and prioritization of development targets, continuous joint review of activities and outcomes, continuous connection and communication, division of development targets (into smaller units), diverse utilization of expertise, rapid testing, development, deployment, and release, and process automation. Our analysis also shows interesting findings related to the development timeline. Although there are differences in practices within the organizations, what was common was the annual refinement of development and strategy, the semi-annual or quarterly reviews of the portfolio and targets, the general cyclical development toward the strategic objectives, eight-week sprints, and weekly joint meetings bringing together different stakeholders.

Furthermore, roles and responsibilities were seen as part of practices, as they were often related to organizing in practice in the informants' descriptions. In connection with this, the steering role of the management, the visioning of long-term goals at the management level and the active support of the management to the teams emerged as important practices.

The senior management routinely does two things. One, they're very engaged themselves on emerging trends, development efforts and supportive of the team and the business looking at new ways, new areas, new things, new skills. They're constantly looking at that and supportive of it...The support is a huge thing. (Informant 9)

The connections and roles of IT and business included different experiences in organizing activities within organizations. We find that the different operating cycles and methods followed by IT and business functions, as well as the alignment of IT and business in continuous DSI, are especially interesting areas for future exploration.

Lastly, several different methods, approaches, and techniques connected to the enactment of continuous DSI emerged in the analysis. Our first observation is that approaches, especially on the business side, are often ambiguous, and followed practices are often a combination of different methods (e.g., Agile and Lean). Agility and agile methods generally seem to guide the operations on the business side, whereas continuous approaches such as DevOps are familiar on the IT/software development side. On the other hand, the type of service also affects the methods that can be used and how they can be used.

4.3   The What of Continuous DSI

The "what" of continuous DSI explores the outcomes (i.e., consequences) of continuous DSI for organizations. Further analysis is needed to determine potential cause-and-effect relationships. However, thus far, four themes emerged from the analysis: customer-related outcomes, outcomes toward development and innovation activities, outcomes for communication, and various experienced outcomes related to working together, which is one of the characteristics of continuous DSI described by informants. The customer-related outcomes included mentions of continuous DSI directed at operating close to the market and contributing to improved know-how to develop "right things" and propose relevant value and better service to customers.

It has probably helped in knowing how to develop the right things. And maybe then the solutions that have been brought to the market, they have probably taken off better then. (Informant 11)

Continuous DSI was also reported to positively affect development and innovation itself, for example, through improved quality, operational transparency, speed, efficiency, and elimination of silos.

[It makes] our service more efficient, easier and of higher quality (Informant 6)

In my opinion, we have gotten rid of silos very well. (Informant 3)

However, adverse outcomes were also found, such as a distorted picture of the wholeness, frustration, and architectural challenges.

It may cause slight frustration, because you yourself have worked in environment A, and the other has worked in environment B, so it is very likely that these have not met at any point, and recognizing and understanding each other's operating environment, its logic, then it brings, can bring challenges. (Informant 3)

There are quite big problems there, which in my opinion are primarily related to company and business architecture. And how to solve architectural problems across different units...the typical enterprise architecture function is now in a bit of a bad situation because of that, because all the agile, DevOps and others are so popular that such a cementing function, no one likes. That is found so legacy and terribly old fashioned and all that. But on the other hand, you can't build a house if you don't have an architecture... (Informant 13)

Continuous DSI was also reported to facilitate communication and contribute toward an up-to-date understanding of what is going on.

In a certain way, this has dismantled such, or lowered the threshold to be in contact with different parties within the organization, even in everyday matters. (Informant 3)

Finally, several positive consequences were found from working closely together, such as a sense of relevance and togetherness, positive challenging and a broader perspective on things, learning from others, more explicit responsibilities and roles, and better use of expertise.

So yes, the fact that we are in constant contact...yes, of course it brings that sense of relevance. (Informant 4)

You get a bit of a broader perspective on things, maybe sometimes being challenged and things like that, that's good... It's also good, of course, that you get to learn from others. (Informant 8)

However, a potential decrease in efficiency from increasingly working together was also reported.

In a certain way it also slows things down, "the more cooks there are in the kitchen", then it might not always be the most efficient so to speak, so it's maybe something that could still be improved. (Informant 3)

5   Discussion

This paper explores and explains continuous DSI in organizations. The presented framework describes six dimensions—external drivers (why), organizational drivers (why), strategic principles (how), operational practices (how), methods, approaches, and techniques (how), and outcomes (what) of continuous DSI in organizations. As an answer to our first research question, we identify a variety of external and internal drivers for continuous DSI within organizations. Whereas external drivers such as the rapid and dynamic changes in the business environment and rapid technological advancements are frequently presented in the existing literature as motivations for continuous development and innovation, our study is one of the first to reveal the internal drivers for continuous DSI. Multiple customer, profitability, performance, and technology-related objectives exist within organizations. For example, the objective of meeting market/customer needs and ensuring customer experience/value through continuous DSI emerged as highly relevant for organizations, as did performance-related objectives such as speed and agility in operation.

In response to the "how" question, the examined principles, practices, and methods provide insight into how various digital organizations organize around continuous DSI. As previous research has primarily focused on software-intensive organizations operating web or SaaS applications [8], our research provides interesting insights into how continuous DSI is approached and managed in different digital service contexts (such as services combining digital and physical elements) and supports an understanding of continuity as a matter for the entire service organization [e.g., 10, 11]. We find, for example, that the organization for continuous DSI emphasizes customer- and other stakeholder-related principles and practices, as well as continuity-related principles and practices for the development and innovation activities, all of which present intriguing future research opportunities. In addition, we find that service organizations employ a variety of methods for continuous DSI. On the business side of operations, agility and agile methods appear to guide operations, whereas on the IT/software development side "continuous" approaches such as DevOps are prevalent. Still, these methods are all associated with the pursuit of continuity and continuous DSI in the informants' descriptions. This also creates intriguing opportunities and a need for additional research, such as regarding the definition of continuity and the methods utilized by various digital service organizations. What constitutes continuous? What is the relationship between agility and continuity, which appear so intertwined in our informants' descriptions but are frequently discussed as distinct phenomena in the literature? In addition, how do differences in applied methods and approaches manifest themselves in various organizational functions, and what are the implications? Our findings provide initial thoughts on the subject, but additional research is called for.

Thirdly, the outcomes of continuous DSI demonstrate some of its potential effects within organizations. We find that continuous DSI produces diverse customer, development and innovation, communication, and collaboration-related outcomes in organizations. However, it should be noted that the presented findings and framework are also considered preliminary in this regard. The examples from the interviews are not exhaustive, and additional research is required to provide a more comprehensive view of the positive and negative effects of continuous DSI to enforce / mitigate in organizations.

While preliminary, our findings contribute to research and practice in multiple ways. First, we offer a valuable, practice-based understanding of the continuous DSI phenomenon in organizations. For practice, our research provides organizations with a foundation on which to reflect on their personal objectives and drivers, as well as approaches toward continuous DSI. For research, we introduce continuous DSI as a fruitful ground for novel research contributions, particularly for SE and IS researchers. The working definition and conceptualization of continuous DSI presented in this paper can guide such future research on this interdisciplinary phenomenon. However, it is important to view this definition as preliminary and our work surrounding it continues. To this end, we contend that future development on the phenomenon should be based around the S-D logic's [15–17] process-based understanding of service innovation combined with the tangible continuous development methods and practices [e.g., 11, 12] and the context of digital services having digital technologies at their core. In addition, the existing literature on continuous innovation (innovation management) and digital innovation (IS) should be considered.

Lastly, our paper reveals additional avenues for future research on the phenomenon. For example, while our analysis and presentation of the external and internal drivers remains descriptive at this stage, future research could investigate how the external and internal drivers are connected (e.g., whether external drivers influence the emergence of internal drivers), which types of drivers best explain the pursuit of continuity in DSI and why, and how the drivers are realized as outcomes through the continuous DSI process. Future research could also seek to explain how and why the outcomes identified in our analysis occur in order to provide insights for promoting the positive and mitigating the negative outcomes. In relation to this, as part of our ongoing research effort, we have recently completed a second set of interviews with the case organizations (51 interviews) to further focus on the continuous DSI activities in practice and to identify factors enabling and hindering the continuous DSI activities within the organizations, as well as with customers and partners, as part of the continuous DSI process. With this, we aim to provide organizations with additional insights for managing continuous DSI.

6 Conclusion

This study represents the first step in theory building to increase the understanding of how digital service organizations organize for continuous DSI. The proposed working definition and preliminary framework for continuous DSI provide a foundation for further theoretical development on the topic that should aim to establish stronger links between theory and practice. As limitations, we acknowledge that while the presented drivers, organization, and outcomes provide an intriguing first understanding of continuous DSI in organizations, the findings should be considered preliminary. Second, we recognize that our study examined a limited number of organizations. While we included service organizations from a variety of industries to avoid industry bias and obtain a diverse perspective on continuous DSI, we acknowledge that additional research is required to generalize and theorize the findings. Considering this, we intend to establish continuous DSI as an engaging, interdisciplinary topic to which the SE, IS, and service research disciplines, among others, can contribute.

Acknowledgement. This research is partly funded by the Foundation for Economic Education, Finland [grant number 34014860].

References

1. Nambisan, S., Lyytinen, K., Majchrzak, A., Song, M.: Digital innovation management: reinventing innovation management research in a digital world. MIS Q. **41**, 223–238 (2017). https://doi.org/10.25300/MISQ/2017/41:1.03
2. Yoo, Y., Henfridsson, O., Lyytinen, K.: The new organizing logic of digital innovation: An agenda for information systems research. Inf. Syst. Res. **21**, 724–735 (2010). https://doi.org/10.1287/isre.1100.0322

3. Conboy, K.: Agility from first principles: Reconstructing the concept of agility in information systems development. Inf. Syst. Res. **20**, 329–354 (2009). https://doi.org/10.1287/isre.1090.0236
4. Agerfalk, P.J., Fitzgerald, B., Slaughter, S.A.: Introduction to the special issue--flexible and distributed information systems development: state of the art and research challenges. Inf. Syst. Res. **20**, 317–328 (2009). https://doi.org/10.1287/isre.1090.0244
5. Humble, J., Molesky, J.: Why enterprises must adopt devops to enable continuous delivery. Cutter IT J. **24**, 6–12 (2011)
6. Debois, P.: Devops: a software revolution in the making? Cutter IT J. **24**, 3–5 (2011)
7. Stahl, D., Martensson, T., Bosch, J.: Continuous practices and devops: beyond the buzz, what does it all mean? In: 2017 43rd Euromicro Conference on Software Engineering and Advanced Applications (SEAA), pp. 440–448 (2017). https://doi.org/10.1109/SEAA.2017.8114695
8. Lwakatare, L.E., Kuvaja, P., Oivo, M.: An exploratory study of DevOps: extending the dimensions of DevOps with practices. In: The 11th International Conference on Software Engineering Advances. IARIA, pp. 91–99 (2016)
9. Mäkinen, S., et al.: Improving the delivery cycle: A multiple-case study of the toolchains in Finnish software intensive enterprises. Inf Softw Technol. **80**, 175–194 (2016). https://doi.org/10.1016/j.infsof.2016.09.001
10. Osmundsen, K., Bygstad, B.: Making sense of continuous development of digital infrastructures. J. Inf. Technol. **37**, 144–164 (2022). https://doi.org/10.1177/02683962211046621
11. Fitzgerald, B., Stol, K.J.: Continuous software engineering: a roadmap and agenda. J. Syst. Softw. **123**, 176–189 (2017). https://doi.org/10.1016/j.jss.2015.06.063
12. Fitzgerald, B., Stol, K.J.: Continuous software engineering and beyond: Trends and challenges. In: 1st International Workshop on Rapid Continuous Software Engineering, RCoSE 2014 - Proceedings. Association for Computing Machinery, pp. 1–9 (2014). https://doi.org/10.1145/2593812.2593813
13. Lusch, R.F., Nambisan, S.: Service innovation: a service-dominant logic perspective. MIS Q. **39**, 155–175 (2015)
14. Myers, M.D.: Qualitative Research in Business & Management. Sage Publications, London (2020)
15. Vargo, S.L., Lusch, R.F.: Evolving to a new dominant logic for marketing. J. Mark. **68**, 1–17 (2004)
16. Vargo, S.L., Lusch, R.F.: Institutions and axioms: an extension and update of service-dominant logic. J. Acad. Mark. Sci. **44**(1), 5–23 (2015). https://doi.org/10.1007/s11747-015-0456-3
17. Vargo, S., Lusch, R.: Service-dominant logic: continuing the evolution. J. Acad. Mark. Sci. **36**, 1 (2008). https://doi.org/10.1007/s11747-007-0069-6
18. Ordanini, A., Parasuraman, A.: Service innovation viewed through a service-dominant logic lens: a conceptual framework and empirical analysis. J. Serv. Res. **14**, 3–23 (2011). https://doi.org/10.1177/1094670510385332
19. Akaka, M.A., Vargo, S.L.: Technology as an operant resource in service (eco)systems. IseB **12**(3), 367–384 (2013). https://doi.org/10.1007/s10257-013-0220-5
20. Barrett, M., Davidson, E., Prabhu, J., Vargo, S.L.: Service innovation in the digital age: key contributions and future directions. MIS Q. **39**, 135–154 (2015)
21. Vargo, S.L., Wieland, H., Akaka, M.A.: Innovation through institutionalization: a service ecosystems perspective. Ind. Mark. Manage. **44**, 63–72 (2015)
22. Edvardsson, bo., Tronvoll, B.: A new conceptualization of service innovation grounded in S-D logic and service systems. Int. J. Qual. Serv. Sci. **5**, 19–31 (2013). https://doi.org/10.1108/17566691311316220
23. Ostrom, A.L., et al.: Moving forward and making a difference: Research priorities for the science of service. J. Serv. Res. **13**, 4–36 (2010). https://doi.org/10.1177/1094670509357611

24. Mele, C., Colurcio, M., Spena, T.R.: Alternative Logics for Innovation: a call for service innovation research. In: Proceedings of the Naples Forum on Service Conference (2009)
25. Lianto, B., Dachyar, M., Soemardi, T.P.: Continuous innovation: a literature review and future perspective. Int. J. Adv. Sci. Eng. Inf. Technol. **8**, 771–779 (2018). https://doi.org/10.18517/ijaseit.8.3.4359
26. Hyland, P., Boer, H.: A Continuous Innovation Framework: Some Thoughts for Consideration. In: Prepared by Causal Productions [for] Continuous Innovation Network. CINet, pp. 389–400 (2006)
27. Steiber, A., Alänge, S.: A corporate system for continuous innovation: the case of Google Inc. Eur. J. Innov. Manage. **16**, 243–264 (2013). https://doi.org/10.1108/14601061311324566
28. Poppendieck, M., Poppendieck, T.: Lean software development: an agile toolkit. Addison-Wesley (2003)
29. Creswell, J.W.: Research Design: Qualitative, Quantitative, and Mixed Methods Approaches. Sage Publications Ltd., Thousand Oaks, CA (2014)
30. Patton, M.Q.: Qualitative Research & Evaluation Methods. Sage Publications, Inc (2002)
31. Braun, V., Clarke, V.: Using thematic analysis in psychology. Qual. Res. Psychol. **3**, 77–101 (2006)
32. Nowell, L.S., Norris, J.M., White, D.E., Moules, N.J.: Thematic analysis: striving to meet the trustworthiness criteria. Int. J. Qual. Methods. **16**, 1–13 (2017). https://doi.org/10.1177/1609406917733847

Why Traditional Product Roadmaps Fail in Dynamic Markets: Global Insights

Stefan Trieflinger[1]([⊠]), Jürgen Münch[1], Dimitri Petrik[2], and Dominic Lang[3]

[1] Reutlingen University, Alteburgstraße 150, 72768 Reutlingen, Germany
{stefan.trieflinger,juergen.muench}@reutlingen-university.de
[2] University of Stuttgart, Keplerstr. 17, 70174 Stuttgart, Germany
dimitri.petrik@bwi.uni-stuttgart.de
[3] ETAS, GmbH, Borsigstraße 24, 70469 Stuttgart, Germany
dominic.lang2@bosch.com

Abstract. Context: Companies that operate in the software-intensive business are confronted with high market dynamics, rapidly evolving technologies as well as fast-changing customer behavior. Traditional product roadmapping practices, such as fixed-time-based charts including detailed planned features, products, or services typically fail in such environments. Until now, the underlying reasons for the failure of product roadmaps in a dynamic and uncertain market environment are not widely analyzed and understood. **Objective:** This paper aims to identify current challenges and pitfalls practitioners face when developing and handling product roadmaps in a dynamic and uncertain market environment. **Method:** To reach our objective we conducted a grey literature review (GLR). **Results:** Overall, we identified 40 relevant papers, from which we could extract 11 challenges of the application of product roadmapping in a dynamic and uncertain market environment. The analysis of the articles showed that the major challenges for practitioners originate from overcoming a feature-driven mindset, not including a lot of details in the product roadmap, and ensuring that the content of the roadmap is not driven by management or expert opinion.

Keywords: Product roadmap · Product management · Agile methods · UX

1 Introduction

For each company, it is essential to provide a strategic direction in which the product offering will be developed over time. For the development and visualizing of the future product strategy usually, product roadmaps are used in practice. A product roadmap describes how an organization intends to achieve a product vision and the way that is required to get there [1, 2]. However, especially the software-intensive business is characterized by high market dynamics, rapidly evolving technologies as well as fast-changing customer behavior. These factors impact the level of certainty, forcing companies to change the mindset of their approaches to developing and maintaining product roadmaps [3]. A recent study reveals that firms use fixed-time-based charts including

© The Author(s), under exclusive license to Springer Nature Switzerland AG 2022
D. Taibi et al. (Eds.): PROFES 2022, LNCS 13709, pp. 382–389, 2022.
https://doi.org/10.1007/978-3-031-21388-5_26

specific planned products including concrete release dates over a long-time horizon. Such roadmaps are called feature-driven product roadmaps. Feature-driven roadmaps can be considered traditional since it is driven by features to inform stakeholders about the market launch of certain features, products, or services to a certain time point [4]. However, in a dynamic and uncertain market environment with associated uncertainties, it is almost impossible to predict which products, features, or services will satisfy the needs of the customers, especially in the mid and long term. Therefore feature-driven product roadmaps work well in market environments that are stable, predictable, and reliable but are not suitable for a dynamic and uncertain market environment [5]. In the scientific literature, several authors deal with the issue of product roadmapping but do not provide detailed insights into the challenges of product roadmapping and the underlying reasons why practitioners face these challenges [6]. This indicates an existing research gap and justifies further empirical research on the challenges of using product roadmapping. To close this gap, the paper at hand aims to identify and understand current challenges and pitfalls with product roadmaps in practice.

2   Research Approach

We conducted our grey literature review according to the guidelines of Garousi et al. [7]. These guidelines helped us to conduct the study in a systematic and reproducible manner. Overall, the guidelines consist of three main phases 1) planning the review, 2) conducting the review, and 3) reporting the review. Our activities in each of these phases.

2.1   Planning the Review

Need and Aim of the Grey Literature Review: First of all, we assess whether a grey literature review is the appropriate research method for our study. Therefore, we used the checklist according to Garousi et al. [7]. The justification for conducting a GLR is as follows: First, we conduct a Systematic literature review, [6] which showed that most papers discuss the issue of product roadmapping at an abstract level and therefore provide little insights. Furthermore, we conduct an expert interview study that revealed a high level of practitioners' interest in the issue of product roadmapping in a dynamic and uncertain market environment. Therefore, insights regarding product roadmapping would be particularly useful for product managers, product owners, or similar roles. From the scientific point of view, the findings of the grey literature review represent a transfer of novel knowledge to the scientific community. These insights can be used to apply abductive reasoning and extend the existing scientific literature. Based on our study goals we have defined the following research questions:

- **RQ:** What challenges in product roadmapping are reported in the grey literature

Identification of the Search String: The identification of our search string was conducted in a brainstorming session in which three researchers participated. As the first step, we create a list of search terms that seemed to be relevant to our search. Subsequently, we validated these search terms within an initial search and adjusted them iteratively. This validation leads to the following final search terms.

A1: Innovation, A2: Product*, A3: Agile, A4: Outcome*Driven, A5: Outcome*Oriented, A6: Goal*oriented, A7: Theme*, A8: Roadmap*

The complete string used in our study was: (A1 OR A2 OR A3 OR A4 OR A5 OR A6 OR A7) AND A8.

Definition of Inclusion and Exclusion Criteria: To filter irrelevant from relevant articles, we defined the inclusion and exclusion criteria as shown in Table 1.

Table 1. Inclusion and exclusion criteria

Inclusion	• The topic of the article discusses challenges of product roadmapping in a dynamic and uncertain market environment
	• The article was published in English
	• The URL is working and freely available
Exclusion	• The source is non-text-based
	• The article contains duplicated content of a previously examined article
	• The article is not related to software development

2.2 Conducting the Review

Study Selection Process: Data was collected using the above search string in the Google search engine (www.google.com). The search was conducted on January 17, 2020, and yielded 426 results. Since new articles may be published after this search, we performed an update on July 20, 2022, using the same search string. This leads to the additional inclusion of 196 articles published between 17 January 2020 and 20 July 2022. In addition, we performed a snowballing process i.e., we considered articles that were recommended in our identified articles. This resulted in the inclusion of 66 additional articles. Thus, we subjected a total of 622 articles to our aforementioned selection process, which resulted in the identification of 193 relevant articles. In the next step, we categorized these 193 articles according to their subject areas. This leads to the identification of the following subject areas 1) product roadmap processes 2) product roadmapping formats, 3) challenges and pitfalls regarding product roadmapping, 4) product roadmap prioritization techniques and 5) alignment of various stakeholders around the product roadmap. Consequently, each category was analysed individually. It should be noted that this paper focuses on the results of the subcategory challenges and pitfalls regarding product roadmapping, which includes 40 relevant articles. Moreover, we conducted a quality assessment according to Garousi et al. [7]. The reason,therefore, is that grey literature is not peer-reviewed like scientific literature. The procedure and results of the quality assessment can be found on Figshare [8].

3 Results

First, we determined the origin of the authors of the relevant articles. For this purpose, we extract the author's respective place of work by researching social media networks such as LinkedIn or Twitter. This was done with the intention to identify to what extent the results obtained can be generalized. As a stopper, we defined that the author has been employed in the specified country for at least one year. This was done to ensure that the author reported his or her perception based on the impressions gained from the country concerned. The set of authors are heterogeneous and includes North America, Europe, South Africa, and Australia. The most frequently common countries are the United State of America, 2) the United Kingdom, and 3) Canada. In the following, our challenges are identified and the underlying reasons and consequences for each challenge are described.

Feature-Driven Mindset: First of all, several authors reported that product roadmaps often consist of features, including exact delivery dates, on a timeline over a long-time horizon (usually one year) [9, 10]. Such a roadmap format is called feature-driven product roadmaps. The first problem with feature-driven roadmaps is that all the details in a feature-driven roadmap are planned upfront. However, such detailed feature planning upfront does not work in a dynamic and uncertain market environment [11]. The reason for this is that features estimate beyond the next release tend to change as new risks or dependencies are uncovered [12]. Therefore, feature-driven product roadmaps are usually often subjected to frequent adjustments [13]. These adjustments are associated with a high effort since all the features that have been worked out in detail including their associated responsibilities have to be rescheduled [2]. Another problem with feature-driven product roadmaps is that, when customers or stakeholders see a feature to be delivered on a specific date in the product roadmap, they will interpret this as commitment, and expectations are raised [14]. However, the uncertainty that comes with developing products in a dynamic market environment makes it very likely that features will not be delivered as planned and communicated. This applies in particular to features planned in the mid and long term in the product roadmap [15]. This leads to the circumstance that customers or stakeholders perceive the non-delivery as a broken promise and are disappointed and dissatisfied [2]. Third, feature-driven roadmaps consider features, but they do not include the value to be delivered by the feature to the customer and the business [9]. This can lead to the problem that the features planned on the product roadmap do not contribute to the solution of customer problems and are therefore not bought or used by customers [2].

Too Many Details in the Product Roadmap: Another problem is the inclusion of too many details in the product roadmap This means for example very detailed descriptions of user stories, requirements, or resources. [16]. The main reason for including too many details in the product roadmap is that product managers feel obliged to include the wishes of every stakeholder in the product roadmap [11]. However, including too many details blurs recognizing the strategy to achieve the product vision of a company. This causes the product roadmap to be difficult to understand by all stakeholders, leading to misunderstanding and a decrease in the execution of the product strategy [17] In addition, if the underlying reason for conducting the planned product development in the roadmap is buried under details, it will be difficult to generate enthusiasm and excitement across the employees [15].

Individual Opinions Decide Which Items will be Included in the Product Roadmap: IN many companies' management or experts (e.g. product managers, product owners, etc.) decide which items to place on the product roadmap [18]. The problem with this approach is that only individual opinions determine the content of the product roadmap, but the perspective of the perspectives of the customers are not included [19]. This approach can lead to the development of products based on false assumptions and use cases [20]. In the worst case, this can lead that the team members feeling unappreciated and, losing their commitment to the company [21].

Not Reviewing and Updating the Roadmap: Furthermore, several authors point out that the creation of the product roadmap is seen as a one-time activity rather than a continuous process [22]. This means that often companies create and work on their product roadmap at the beginning of the year and use them subsequently as a fixed document with no further changes [23]. However, the problem is that priorities, resources, budget, and external factors such as competitors or major customers can change at any time, affecting the content of the product roadmap [24]. Therefore, it is crucial to continuously review and update the product roadmap at a short time interval (e.g., every week or as a cadence of stakeholder meetings takes place [23]. Otherwise, the company forgoes the opportunity to incorporate findings into the product development process after the time the product roadmap is created [22].

Lack of an Enterprise-Wide Known Product Vision: Wick [25] points out that many companies do not have a product vision or companies have a product vision but never use it [25]. The danger of not having or communicating a product vision is that the teams involved in product development are unclear about the overall goal of developing the planned products in the product roadmap. First, this situation makes it difficult for the teams to identify and prioritize measures that contribute to product success [26]. Consequently, the teams will not be able to identify which measures contribute most to achieving the product vision and will struggle to prioritize various measures [11].

Identification and Implementation of Customer Feedback Channels: Another problem is that companies often struggle to identify and implement data collection channels for customer feedback [17]. Umbach [27] reports that one reason for this is that often product managers stay in their office and do not leave the building to talk to (potential) customers. Datta [12] added that another reason is that in the race to meet deadlines, product teams do not have enough time and resources to devote to identifying customer feedback channels. The risk of not involving customer feedback in the product roadmapping process is that the development of the product roadmap will be based on assumptions without validation [28]. This affects that may products are included in the product roadmap and developed that do not create the intended change in customer behaviour (e.g., the start of using a certain product instead of another product from a competitor). Consequently, these products will not succeed on the market [12].

The Use of the Wrong Product Roadmapping Tool: Kabisch [22] points out that many product roadmap tools include the mapping of features on a timeline. As described above such a product roadmap format is called feature-driven. If a company uses such a tool, it will adapt its product roadmapping to the proposed format of the tool. As a result, the company will be operating in a dynamic and uncertain market environment with an inappropriate product roadmap format with all its disadvantages [22] In addition, Dhiman [23] points out that many companies are using Excel or PowerPoint which are not suitable for creating and handling a product roadmap. The main reason for this is that these tools are too static, making it difficult and exhausting to create or update the product roadmap.

Unrealistic Expectations: Another pitfall is to make unrealistic and arbitrary expectations on the roadmap [17, 23, 29] Setting unrealistic expectations can originate from various sources, for example from management to the operational level but also from product management to software development. In general, such behaviour will result in damaging the relationship between the expectation setter and recipient [24]. A typical example of the setting of unrealistic expectations is the specification of non-realistic release dates[29].

Lack of Criteria for the Conduction of the Product Roadmap Prioritization Process: Another problem is that often product managers prioritize their roadmap items based on individual opinions. This includes views of the management or various members of the product team as well as customer requests [27]. However, this includes the pitfall that often subjective opinions are influenced by personal bias and often present only a single point of view. Therefore, there is a low probability that these opinions reflect the most important current customer problems and are therefore inappropriate for application in the prioritization process of the product roadmap. According to Semick [17], this circumstance is because product managers often have no idea which prioritization technique to use.

Creation of a Single Product Roadmap for all Stakeholders: Dhiman [23] points out that a common mistake in the creation of the product roadmap is to create a single product roadmap. The problem with this approach is that a product roadmap is an artefact that needs to be refereed by many stakeholders such as the CEO, CPO, marketing, sales engineering as well as customers. This means that the information that is focused on and emphasized should be tailored to the stakeholder to whom the product roadmap is presented [30]. Therefore, creating a single roadmap will not be sufficient for informing and collecting feedback from these stakeholders [23].

Considering the validity of the results it should be mentioned that Google does not allow the user access to all articles that match our search string. Therefore, it is not known whether the articles returned by the Google search engine are representative of the overall population of the articles. Moreover, the results of this study refer to the challenges and pitfalls of product roadmapping by practitioners operating in a dynamic and uncertain market environment. Therefore, the results are not transferable to companies participating in a stable market environment.

4 Summary

In this study, we conducted a grey literature review to identify challenges that companies face in developing and maintaining product roadmaps in a dynamic and uncertain market environment. The study revealed that the main challenge of product roadmapping is a feature-driven mindset. A feature-driven mindset means that discussions about detailed outputs guide the roadmapping process, but the outcomes that should be delivered to the customers and the business are not considered. This leads to the creation of so-called feature-driven product roadmaps that contain detailed planned features over a long-time horizon. However, through the high market dynamics, such feature-driven product roadmaps are subjected to frequent ad-hoc adjustment that leads to a decrease in reliability. The findings of our study confirm the results from the expert interviews conducted by Münch et al. [5]. Therefore, it can be concluded that the problems identified by Münch et al. in 2019 are currently valid. Moreover, it can be said that these problems apply not only to the German-speaking regions but also in an international context.

References

1. Lombardo, C.T., McCarthy, B., Ryan, E., Conners, M.: Product roadmaps relaunched - How to set direction while embracing uncertainty. O'Reilly Media Inc, Gravenstein Highway North, Sebastopol, CA, USA (2017)
2. Cagan. M.: Inspired: How to create tech products customers love. Wiley & Sons, Inc Hoboken, New Jersey (2018)
3. Suomalainen, T., Abrahamsson, P., Similä, J.: Software product roadmapping in a volatile business environment. J. Syst. Softw. **84**(6), 958–975 (2011)
4. Münch, J., Trieflinger, S., Lang, D.: What's hot in product roadmapping? Key practices and success factors. In: Franch, X., Männistö, T., Martínez-Fernández, S. (eds.) PROFES 2019. LNCS, vol. 11915, pp. 401–416. Springer, Cham (2019). https://doi.org/10.1007/978-3-030-35333-9_29
5. Münch, J., Trieflinger, S., Bogazköy, E., Eißler, P., Roling, B., Schneider, J.: Product roadmap formats for an uncertain future: a grey literature review. In: Proceedings of the 46th Euromicro Conference on Software Engineering and Advanced Applications (SEAA), pp. 284–291. IEEE (2020)
6. Münch J., Trieflinger S., Lang, D.: Product Roadmap – From vision to reality: A systematic literature review. In: ICE/IEEE ITMC: International Conference on Engineering, Technology and Innovation, IEEE (2019)
7. Garousi, V., Felderer, M., Mäntylä, M.V.: Guidelines for including grey literature and conducting multivocal literature reviews in software engineering. Inf. Softw. Technol. **106**, 101–121 (2019)
8. Figshare: Quality   Assessment   conducted   by   the   authors: https://figshare.com/s/9471896af513b54b38ee Accessed 1 Aug (2022)
9. Kazmi, R.: https://www.koombea.com/blog/common-product-roadmap-mistakes/. Accessed 20 Aug (2022)
10. Sahu,   S.:   https://www.linkedin.com/pulse/product-roadmap-dilemma-suchismita-sahu/. Accessed 20 Aug (2022)
11. Pereira, D.: https://medium.com/serious-scrum/why-most-roadmaps-make-poor-results-inevitable-dd3372b183c8. Accessed 20 Aug (2022)
12. Datta, A.: https://rangle.io/blog/building-product-roadmaps/. Accessed 20 Aug (2022)

13. Marshall, J.: https://www.productplan.com/blog/5-things-that-can-ruin-your-product-roadmap/. Accessed 20 Aug (2022)
14. Gilley, C.: https://uservoice.com/blog/organizational-alignment-roadmap. Accessed 20 Aug (2022)
15. Gottesdiener, E.: https://medium.com/@ellengott/7-ways-of-creating-and-sustaining-an-agile-product-roadmap-9e4410a25a60. Accessed 20 Aug (2022)
16. Mc Closkey, H.: https://www.usertesting.com/blog/agile-product-roadmap . Accessed 20 Aug (2022)
17. Semick, J.: https://productschool.com/blog/product-management-2/nine-roadmap-mistakes/. Accessed 20 Aug (2022)
18. Rex, A.: https://www.mindtheproduct.com/escape-from-the-feature-roadmap-to-outcome-driven-development/. Accessed 20 Aug (2022)
19. Pragmatic: https://www.pragmaticinstitute.com/resources/articles/product/pitfalls-in-product-decision-making/ Accessed 20 Aug (2022)
20. The Product´s Manager Toolbox:. https://theproductmanagerstoolbox.com/product-roadmap-challenges/. Accessed 20 Aug (2022)
21. ProductPlan:. https://www.productplan.com/webinars/feature-less-roadmap/. Accessed 20 Aug (2022)
22. Kabisch, E.: https://productcrunch.substack.com/p/escaping-the-roadmap-trap. Accessed 20 Aug (2022)
23. Dhiman, M.: https://www.mindtheproduct.com/mistakes-to-avoid-while-creating-a-product-roadmap/. Accessed 20 Aug (2022)
24. ProductPlan:. https://www.productplan.com/learn/reasons-product-roadmaps-fail/. Accessed 20 Aug (2022)
25. Wick, A.: https://www.ba-squared.com/blog/happens-dont-product-vision/. Accessed 20 Aug (2022)
26. Wong, A.: https://productmasterynow.com/blog/tei-154-pitfalls-that-can-trap-new-product-managers-with-aero-wong/. Accessed 20 Aug (2022)
27. Umbach, H.: https://medium.com/fresh-tilled-soil/dear-product-roadmap-im-breaking-up-with-you-a47cfa6ca4f7. Accessed 20 Aug (2022)
28. Bowler, M.:. https://www.productledalliance.com/the-common-pitfalls-preventing-product-managers-reaching-their-highest-potential/. Accessed 20 Aug (2022)
29. Naji, C.: https://www.modernanalyst.com/Resources/Articles/tabid/115/ID/3831/7-Tactics-to-Solve-Common-Product-Roadmap-Problems.aspx. Accessed 20 Aug (2022)
30. ProductPlan: https://www.productplan.com/learn/product-roadmap-sharing-mistakes/. Accessed 20 Aug (2022)

Understanding Low-Code or No-Code Adoption in Software Startups: Preliminary Results from a Comparative Case Study

Usman Rafiq$^{(\boxtimes)}$ ⓘ, Cenacchi Filippo ⓘ, and Xiaofeng Wang ⓘ

Faculty of Computer Science, Free University of Bozen-Bolzano, Bolzano, Italy
{urafiq,filippo.cenacchi,xiaofeng.wang}@unibz.it

Abstract. Low-code or no-code application development is a new jargon in the software development community. In response, large and medium-sized companies, are seen triggered to join the bandwagon. Existing research on why small and innovative companies, like software startups, apply this paradigm is limited. The current literature shows that software startups are different from established software companies in terms of their focus on innovation, market-driven context, limited resources, and uncertainty. Therefore, in this paper, we study and report our initial understanding of why software startups apply low-code or no-code. We studied two cases, in the first phase, to address the research question. Our preliminary results show that software startups apply this paradigm in an ad-hoc manner and use it for experimentation, prototyping, and idea validation. On the flip side, large companies enjoy a stable workflow of low-code or no-code development. The motivations include achieving rapid product development, fast feedback, and empowering business users. These results provide a good starting point for discussion and demand for further research. Including additional data, particularly, more cases, therefore, is our essential next step to get a deeper understanding and report final results.

Keywords: Low code · No code · LCNC · LCAP · Startup · Digital transformation

1 Introduction

Recent years have seen a continuing surge in demand for digitalization and automation. As a result, software companies are striving to find possible ways to deliver requirements rapidly and economically [1]. In addition, such companies are hit hard by the challenge of recruiting software developers, showing a gap in the demand and supply of tech talent acquisition [2]. This challenge is considered the biggest challenge to economic growth, which can affect the delivery timeline of the software applications as well [3].

© The Author(s), under exclusive license to Springer Nature Switzerland AG 2022
D. Taibi et al. (Eds.): PROFES 2022, LNCS 13709, pp. 390–398, 2022.
https://doi.org/10.1007/978-3-031-21388-5_27

To mitigate such barriers, companies have started embracing a relatively new way of software development, known as *Low-Code Application Development (LCAD)* or sometimes referred to as *No-Code Application Development (NCAD)*. This paradigm is introduced with an intent to promote digitalization and hyper-automation by enabling quick development and delivery of software applications [3]. It claims to facilitate developers as well as end-users, to contribute to the software development process with minimal effort. End users participating in the development process are assumed to have no prior knowledge of development and are known as *citizen developers* [3,4].

LCAD/NCAD is gaining unprecedented traction since its inception [8]. Several research surveys, conducted by known technological and market research firms, such as Gartner and Forrester, forecast this paradigm to continue to boost in the upcoming years [5,7,9]. In the same vein, Gartner predicts that by 2023, over 50% medium to large enterprises will adopt LCAD/NCAD and by 2024, the adoption rate will surpass 65% [9].

While the research highlights the adoption of such technologies by established companies, it lacks in reporting the adoption for small and innovative companies like for example, software startups. Recently, considerable scientific literature has started emerging (e.g. [4,11–14]), intending to understand LCAD/NCAD, their challenges, characteristics, taxonomy and relevancy with model-driven engineering. However, as we could tell, no empirical studies have been reported on a comparative understanding of adoption for startup and established companies. On the contrary, even though the research on software startups is emerging [10], it does not take account of LCAD/NCAD so far. Therefore, there might be varying determinants and contexts for both types of companies to adopt and practice LCAD/NCAD. This is the gap that the current research intends to address. Therefore, the guiding research question for our study is:

RQ: Why do software startups apply low-code or no-code application development?

To answer the research question, we performed a comparative case study and studied two companies, initially, as part of our ongoing research project. In our sample, the first company is a software startup with a functional product. The second case is a large and well-established company, which is studied to make a comparative assessment. We conducted semi-structured interviews to collect the data. Later, we analyzed the data using thematic analysis and reported our comparative understanding of low-code adoption.

The remainder of the paper is structured as follows. Section 2 reports the background and related work. Section 3 describes the research methodology that we used to answer the research question and related validity threats. Likewise, Sect. 4 reports our preliminary findings while Sect. 5 summarizes further steps required to conclude the research.

2   Background and Related Work

Low-Code or No-Code Application Development (LCAD/NCAD).
Originally inspired by model-driven engineering principles, LCAD facilitates
developers, of varying expertise, in developing applications rapidly [4]. The term,
low-code, was first coined by Forrester in 2014 [15] and a more detailed definition
was provided in 2017. Oftentimes, low-code and no-code, both are considered as
related terms [12]. Practitioners also indicate other synonyms like zero-code,
what you see is what you get, drag and drop, and visual programming, to refer
to low-code [13]. However, low-code and no-code are two common terminologies.
It is claimed that no-code requires no prior knowledge of programming. While
on the other hand, in low-code, a developer might need to write code or scripts.
For some authors, like [9] and [14], no-code is a subset of low-code and it is not
thought of as a separate market segment.

Much of the research on LCAD/NCAD has been carried out in recent years
and yet it is emerging. Sahay et al. [4] reported a comparison of available
LCAD platforms. Luo et al. [13] studied the characteristics and challenges of
LCAD/NCAD. A similar study is carried out by Alamin et al. [8] where authors
studied the perspective of developers in the adoption of this paradigm. In the
same vein, Ruscio et al. [12] made a comparison of it with model-driven engineering. However, the literature lacks in making a comparison of its adoption by
startups and established companies.

Software Startups. Software startups are often characterized as companies with limited resources [10], trying to develop market-driven requirements
under uncertain environments [18]. These young companies yield innovation and
empower the economy by developing software-intensive applications [10]. However, products are generally developed by applying tailored software engineering practices. Startups constantly face multiple challenges during this development. Time pressure, technology uncertainty, team formation, and fast-growing
markets are some major challenges in the startup context [16]. However, in
recent years, practitioners promoted the use of lean startup methodology to
find a product-market fit [17]. In this methodology, a startup hypothesizes an
idea, builds a minimum viable product, and based on the feedback, adjusts its
directions.

3   Research Method

Our study aims to understand the LCAD/NCAD adoption in context-specific
settings. We base our assumption on the fact that software startups are significantly different entities when compared with established software companies
[10,18,21]. These realities make our study exploratory and therefore, the case
study approach seems to be a good fit for this research. The existing body of
research on startups suggests them as good candidates for low-code or no-code
adoption. However, the existing literature lacks reporting on such practices for

startups. Going in the same vein, we further need a multiple-case study app-roach [19] to guide our research. It is planned because a comparative assessment of startup and established companies is aimed to answer the research question.

In the first phase of this research, therefore, we analyze and report two cases, aliased as C1 and C2 to protect anonymity. Our unit of analysis is the company itself. We approached the cases through personal email and LinkedIn invitations. While we found the established company (C2) easily, we had great difficulty in identifying the startup (C1) with experience in LCAD/NCAD. Moreover, we also looked for a startup with a functional product, software as the main business, and paying customers. Once found, we verified through available online information that the startup company (C1) is venture-backed, growing fast, and fulfills our criteria of case selection. We conducted semi-structured interviews to collect the data. The participants were asked about the company or team background, experiences, common practices, benefits, barriers, and lessons learned regarding LCAD/NCAD. Both interviews were conducted in English through Microsoft TEAMS. Each interview lasted 60 min approximately and it was recorded after the consent of the interviewees.

After data collection, we systematically analyzed the transcribed interviews using thematic analysis [20]. We started by reading the interviews, extracting related data, coding the chunks found useful according to the research question, and classifying codes into themes. During this process, we followed the open coding technique. The process had several iterations and it was performed by the first author, however, outcomes were discussed in joint meetings as the analysis process evolved. We used Nvivo to manage the analysis procedure. Lastly, we narrated the results for each case and made a cross-case comparison according to the guidelines provided by Yin [19].

3.1 Threats to Validity

Regarding validity threats to our study, one of the threats is the generalizability of the findings. In our comparative study, we tried to understand the adoption of LCAD/NCAD in startup companies and compare it with established ones. We feel that more cases, particularly from varying business domains, should be included in the sample to produce more concrete results. Though, as a first step, we included one case from each group to get clues on the differences in practices. Another threat to the validity of our findings is construct validity. We mitigated this threat by applying triangulation during the data collection and analysis phase. In this regard, we also developed the interview guide and provided questions to interviewees beforehand. Likewise, the analysis results were discussed among all authors. Lastly, one threat is related to the selection of a real startup. We reduced this threat by establishing criteria for a startup selection.

4 Preliminary Results

Case (C1) is a venture-backed software startup that works in a digital health care setup and offers services for practitioners and patients. The startup was launched six years ago and it pivoted multiple times before achieving the problem-solution fit. Currently, the startup is striving to acquire the market. It has two co-founders, working as Chief Executive Officer (CEO) and Chief Technology Officer(CTO) respectively. The CEO (interviewee) is a tech enthusiast with a background in the medical field but holds extensive experience in software product management and launching. The CEO also possesses hands-on experience in LCAD/NCAD. Similarly, the CTO is an experienced software developer.

Our data analysis revealed a few remarkable findings about startup company *C1*. Findings suggest that the startup is using both LCAD and NCAD in developing several applications. It is somewhat different from *C2* where only LCAD is in practice. Interestingly, we also observe that LCAD/NCAD paradigm in *C1* is mainly adopted for prototyping, experimenting with new features, and building internal products and a by-product. The following excerpt explains different usages of LCAD/NCAD: "*It is used for various purposes. First of all, on prototyping, second of all on designing, and third of all on conducting the service*". The use of LCAD/NCAD for these purposes was indicated at three separate instances in the data. However, surprisingly, we also noticed that it is not used for the main product itself. When asked about it, the CEO highlighted the domain limitation of LCAD/NCAD platforms: "*basically, you can't find the platforms or ready solutions, at least for our product, because our product has no similar products in the world*".

While discussing the scarcity of resources in a startup environment, the CEO alluded to the lack of technical resources as a primary reason for this adoption. For example, in one instance, the CEO explained the scenario for early-stage startups in the following words: "*because they plan to struggle with their own, let's say assumptions. To create a prototype, I need to hire developers and create it so in this sense*". The CEO further compared this with the traditional software development approach and highlighted the need for deep development knowledge for the later case: "*you have to discover, you have to learn and you have to try and then see how to do it traditionally because the traditional way you cannot do this like without deep knowledge*".

We did not notice any particular workflow to develop applications in the startup company. Therefore, in contrast to the company *C2*, the practice of LCAD/NCAD in startup *C1* is pretty ad-hoc, non-consistent, and significantly different. However, on the question of the overall process they follow to develop, the CEO mentioned the use of design thinking: "*It's always the design thinking, you brainstorm You make a prototype. You validate, you deliver*". Alongside this, the difference applies to the platforms used by the company as well. We found in the data that the startup is using multiple LCAD/NCAD tools. When we asked the reasons, the CEO explained it in detail: "*I used to read articles and make researches on which platforms can be easier to penetrate for myself. This is because I don't want to spend time and money on creating prototypes. So I made the research, and these platforms showed the best match for myself because still I need to iterate(product ideas) fast and I need to make things today and test them tomorrow, so I don't want to go deep (on a technology)*". This excerpt shows that according to the need and within scarce resources, the startup searched the internet for the appropriate LCAD/NCAD tools for a better fit.

Overall, we found that the key motivations behind this adoption include reduced time to market, rapid problem/idea validation, and lastly mitigating the absence of developers during the early times of the startup. In the same vein, the CEO mentioned one of the significant challenges in the adoption of LCAD/NCAD i.e. needs to educate investors as well as other team members to adopt these technologies. The CEO revealed that if, as a startup founder, you intend to use LCAD/NCAD as the paradigm to develop the idea then investors won't fund the startup. It is illustrated in the following words: "*how are you going to spend, for development, for coding and blah...if you say that you are using no and low code technologies to create your business idea, then investors just won't give you money for that*". One possible reason is that investors are not aware of this paradigm and there is a need to educate them on its benefits, as explained by the CEO. The CEO commented: "*This makes it much more complicated to raise money in this market because investors have no clue regarding what this means to develop a product using low and no code*". Ultimately, this challenge restricts startup founders from fully utilizing the power of LCAD/NCAD. According to the CEO, this particularly applies to early-stage startups.

Figure 1 illustrates the overview of preliminary findings explaining why software startups apply LCAD/NCAD and why established companies do. In the figure, C1 and C2 denote startup and established companies, respectively. Similarly, the rectangles indicating C1 or C2 represent primary types of LCAD/NCAD workflows, determinants of its usage, and lastly, types of products benefiting from it. In addition, the bordered lines as well as rectangles show expected or realized benefits and domain areas where LCAD/NCAD is in practice.

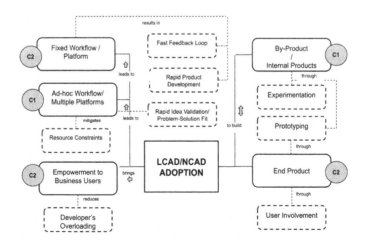

Fig. 1. Overview of preliminary findings

Case (C2) is an established firm with international clients and multiple-site offices. It offers software services, such as ERP, CRM, business intelligence, and service management. The company works as an official partner of Microsoft. The interviewee belongs to a five-member Business Intelligence (BI) team, headed by a team leader, with the responsibility to develop and manage solutions for customers within and outside the work group. The team consists of people with software development and business background. The business resources are responsible to educate customers on the developed solutions. The interviewee has an informatics background with a professional degree and holds several years of experience in development.

Our analysis suggests that rapid application development, faster feedback loops, a reduced workload of developers, and empowerment of business users are among the significant reasons for LCAD adoption in this company. The company applies LCAD using Microsoft Power BI tool and facilitates customers in getting self-service analytics at an enterprise scale. The use of this tool is not an option for the company as they are obliged to use it. This is evident from the following excerpt of the team lead: "*We are a partner of Microsoft and Microsoft is pushing in this direction*".

On the other hand, the practice of LCAD in *C2* follows a structural workflow. It starts with aggregating multiple data sources and building a data model. Thereafter, an interface is provided to customers. It is interesting to report that customers, primarily business users from teams like sales, purchase, finance, and management, can generate data visualizations according to their needs. They are educated through training as well as their participation in the system development phase. Therefore, business users don't need to contact the developers again for the new requirements. This ultimately reduces the developer's workload and therefore allows them to focus on the essential part of the system development. Talking about the motivation for using LCAD, the team lead said: "*visualization of the data is not anymore just the task of the IT/ of the developer*". He continued explaining the developer's relief from such requirements change requests: "*each user in his department, I don't know, finance sales purchase, they can create their reports and have not any more to explain all the processes to the IT*". It is further highlighted that empowerment of business users eventually privileges companies with a low number of developers to do large and multiple projects as the technical tasks are now limited because of the LCAD. He put it in this excerpt: "*if you have a low number of technical people with this approach, you can do bigger projects because you have a smaller amount of tasks to handle with the technical people*".

While explaining the outcomes of LCAD adoption, the team lead also expressed that LCAD made the development process faster and less hectic. He expressed his opinion in the following excerpt: "*process is much faster and a lot of effort is not anymore locked*". Perhaps the involvement of business users during the system development as well as empowering them to fulfill their technical requirements are the possible reasons for this rapid application development and fast feedback loops. The data analysis also suggests that users are involved in the process during the prototype building and they start using the system even before the deployment. The following comment illustrates this notion: *"we get really quick feedback because they are doing it on their own so the loop is in-house"*. The team lead added further: *"(for) the technical parts, we are getting really quick answers because they (users) are using it already during and before it goes live"*. Likewise, while comparing the LCAD paradigm with traditional software development, the interviewee further added: *"with this approach (LCAD), they are made part of the project and the feedback is much quicker"*.

Our data analysis further reveals that the company *C2* achieves faster feedback loops by involving business users after developing a solution prototype. The prototype is evolutionary and technical steps, for instance, the essential data model is already built by the development team. Afterward, the users are shown the prototype and they provide feedback. Commenting on this, the team lead said: *"we are preparing prototypes so that the customer can see what are the possibilities"*. According to the team lead, most of the visualization work is developed after involving users. It is expressed in the following statement:*"as just a prototype and I would say 90% of the final solution is then done during the project, especially if we talk about the visualization"*. We also found that the company educates users through training and empowers them by expressing usage scenarios so that users can think out of the box. The interviewee expressed their practice in educating users in the following words: *"for the training and so on, we use this solution and yeah, of course, we have to show examples of what are the possibilities and how it can look like"*.

5 Next Steps

Our preliminary results provide a good starting point for discussion and further research. Therefore, an immediate next step is to refine our understanding of LCAD/NCAD adoption by interviewing more people from selected cases. In this iterative step, we intend to interview CTO from company *C1* and the developer role from company *C2*. Adding other interviewees might provide additional insights on the topic. In the next phase, we plan to include two more cases, one from each category, to produce comprehensive results. Including additional cases to our data, therefore, is our essential next step to get a deeper understanding and report final results.

References

1. Sanchis, R., García-Perales, Ó., Fraile, F., Poler, R.: Low-code as enabler of digital transformation in manufacturing industry. Appl. Sci. **10**, 12 (2019)
2. Torres, C.: Demand for Programmers Hits Full Boil as US Job Market Simmers. Bloomberg, Com (2018)
3. Waszkowski, R.: Low-code platform for automating business processes in manufacturing. IFAC-PapersOnLine. **52**, 376–381 (2019)

4. Sahay, A., Indamutsa, A., Di Ruscio, D., Pierantonio, A.: Supporting the understanding and comparison of low-code development platforms. In: 2020 46th Euromicro Conference on Software Engineering and Advanced Applications (SEAA), pp. 171–178 (2020)
5. Richardson, C., Rymer, J.: The Forrester Wave^{tm}: Low-Code Development Platforms. Forrester, Cambridge, MA, USA (2016)
6. Gartner Gartner forecasts worldwide low-code development technologies market to grow 23% in 2021. https://www.gartner.com/en/newsroom/press-releases/2021-02-15-gartner-forecasts-worldwide-low-code-development-technologies-market-to-grow-23-percent-in-2021
7. Rymer, J., et al.: The forrester wave^{TM}: Low-code development platforms for ad&d professionals, q1 2019. Forrester Report, Forrester (2019)
8. Al Alamin, M., Malakar, S., Uddin, G., Afroz, S., Haider, T., Iqbal, A.: An empirical study of developer discussions on low-code software development challenges. In: 2021 IEEE/ACM 18th International Conference on Mining Software Repositories (MSR), pp. 46–57 (2021)
9. Vincent, P., Iijima, K., Driver, M., Wong, J., Natis, Y.: Magic quadrant for enterprise low-code application platforms. Gartner Report (2019)
10. Unterkalmsteiner, M., et al.: Software startups-a research agenda. E-Inf. Softw. Eng. J. **10**, 89–123 (2016)
11. Bock, A., Frank, U.: Low-code platform. Bus. Inf. Syst. Eng. **63**, 733–740 (2021)
12. Di Ruscio, D., Kolovos, D., de Lara, J., Pierantonio, A., Tisi, M., Wimmer, M.: Low-code development and model-driven engineering: two sides of the same coin? Softw. Syst. Model. **21**(2), 437–446 (2022). https://doi.org/10.1007/s10270-021-00970-2
13. Luo, Y., Liang, P., Wang, C., Shahin, M., Zhan, J.: Characteristics and challenges of low-code development: the practitioners' perspective. In: Proceedings of the 15th ACM/IEEE International Symposium on Empirical Software Engineering and Measurement (ESEM), pp. 1–11 (2021)
14. Prinz, N., Huber, M., Riedinger, C., Rentrop, C.: Two perspectives of low-code development platform challenges-an exploratory study (2022)
15. Richardson, C., Rymer, J., Mines, C., Cullen, A., Whittaker, D.: New development platforms emerge for customer-facing applications. Forrester, Cambridge, MA, USA. vol. 15 (2014)
16. Giardino, C., Bajwa, S., Wang, X., Abrahamsson, P.: Key challenges in early-stage software startups. In: International Conference on Agile Software Development, pp. 52–63 (2015)
17. Ries, E.: The lean startup: how today's entrepreneurs use continuous innovation to create radically successful businesses. Currency (2011)
18. Rafiq, U.: Towards understanding analytics in software startups. In: 2022 IEEE/ACM International Workshop on Software-Intensive Business (IWSiB), pp. 31–38 (2022)
19. Yin, R.: Case study research: design and methods. In: SAGE (2009)
20. Cruzes, D., Dybå, T., Runeson, P., Höst, M.: Case studies synthesis: a thematic, cross-case, and narrative synthesis worked example. Empir. Softw. Eng. **20**, 1634–1665 (2015)
21. Melegati, J., Chanin, R., Sales, A., Prikladnicki, R.: Towards specific software engineering practices for early-stage startups. In: International Conference on Agile Software Development, pp. 18–22 (2020)

Testing and Bug Prediction

Test Case Selection with Incremental ML

Markus Mulkahainen, Kari Systä$^{(\boxtimes)}$, and Hannu-Matti Järvinen

Tampere University Unit of Computing Sciences, Tampere, Finland
{kari.syst,hannu-matti.jarvinen}@tuni.fi

Abstract. *Context:* Software projects applying continuous integration should run the tests very frequently, but often the number of test is huge and their execution takes a long time. This delays the feedback to the developer. *Objective:* Study if heuristic and especially incremental machine learning can help in finding an optimal test set that still finds the errors. *Method:* Several methods for reducing the tests were tested. Each method was applied to the example software its commit history, and the performance of the methods were compared. *Results:* The test set size can be radically reduced with automatic approaches. Furthermore, it was found that the incremental machine learning based test selection techniques eventually perform equally well or better than the best heuristic.

Keywords: Test case selection · Continuous integration

1 Introduction

This paper documents research that has been inspired by a practical need in a company. The research was originally conducted for a master thesis [13], and this paper summarizes the research for an international audience.

Continuous Integration (CI) is a software engineering practice that automates software integration and encourages developers to commit more often. Testing in CI should be automatic [18] and extensive. Every change in the software should be validated in the context of the whole software to maintain quality.

Test suites tend to grow large during the development and lead to long-lasting test suites. In the context of the case company, Space Systems Finland[1], the problem culminates in validation tests, which exercise multiple end-to-end tests, and even the execution of a single test can take a long time. Test case selection and prioritization can be used in such situations to reduce the time for developer feedback.

The case context was satellite instrument control software for the Meteosat Third Generation Sounder (MTG-S) satellites. The instrument, namely Sentinel-4/UVN, is a high-resolution spectrometer and will be used to monitor air quality parameters over Europe, and the case of this paper was a command and control

---

[1] http://www.ssf.fi/.

© The Author(s), under exclusive license to Springer Nature Switzerland AG 2022
D. Taibi et al. (Eds.): PROFES 2022, LNCS 13709, pp. 401–417, 2022.
https://doi.org/10.1007/978-3-031-21388-5_28

software for the Sentinel-4/UVN instrument. The software and its validation tests are programmed in Ada.

Test case selection (TCS) selects a subset of the test suite for repeated testing. Ideally, the selected subset of the tests finds the same number of faults with lesser effort compared with the original test suite. However, the reduced test set may not include all fault-revealing test cases, but TCS discards some of them. Finding the optimal subset in TCS is a non-obvious task, especially in large systems with a large number of test cases. Machine learning (ML) is an interesting approach for this. Because each project is new and different from the others, incremental ML may be more suitable than approaches with a separate learning phase.

The goal of this research was to evaluate different TCS techniques in order to speed up the testing and facilitate continuous integration. Specifically, the research question was *How effective is incremental machine learning for test case selection and how does it compare to heuristics-based methods?*

Machine learning has become more popular in the domains of TCS [2,8,9,17]. These studies have shown promising results in using ML for TCS.

The paper is organized as follows. Section 2 introduces the background and Sect. 3 summarizes the related research. The experiment is described in Sect. 4 and the results are presented in Sect. 5. The results are discussed in Sect. 6. Finally, Sect. 7 gives the conclusions.

2   Background

2.1   Dependency Coverage

All heuristic methods used in this study rely on dependency coverage. A modification can break functionality in the modified module, but also in the modules that depend on the modified module. This can be troublesome as faults can show up in surprising components or sub-systems [19].

A rather safe way to reduce the number of tests, but to still reveal faults in the dependent modules, is to recognize tests that target the modified modules and their dependents and execute them. The aim is to recognize every test case that could be transitively affected by a change. A test case is affected if the test or any of its dependencies is modified [19].

2.2   Machine Learning

The gist of ML is a piece of software, that is capable of improving its performance in a set of tasks, based on experience [12]. In this paper, incremental machine learning means the application of machine learning algorithms so that the model continuously learns from the new input while being used.

Before machine learning techniques can be applied to test cases, the problems need to be coded to the ML algorithm, i.e., they have to be represented as *feature vectors*. The values used in feature vectors are described below.

Seven features are used to represent test cases as feature vectors, namely *statement coverage, modification coverage, similarity score, duration, failure rate, latest pass* and *history length*. The features are somewhat similar to features used in a related study [2]. The following describes how these features are attained.

Statement Coverage is a floating-point number with a closed interval between 0 and 1. It is the total percentage of statements (or lines) covered by a test case. The statement coverage is updated every time the test case is executed and remains unchanged until the test case is re-executed. Line coverage is used instead of statement coverage, because that information was available.

Modification Coverage is similar to statement coverage, but the coverage is calculated over the modified lines of a commit instead of all software code lines. More closely, the modification coverage is calculated as $\frac{|C_t \cap M|}{|M|}$ where C_t is the coverage of the test case and M is the set of modified lines. The test coverage, C_t, is produced by *gcov*-tool. *Git diff* command was used to find M. The full coverage of previous test executions is needed to deduce coverage over the modified lines, e.g. $|C_t \cap M|$. Therefore, the full coverage produced by *gcov*-tool needs to be persisted and transferred between any two commits.

Similarity Score is a similarity measure between a code change (git commit) and a test case, where a higher value means that certain keywords occur more often in both texts suggesting a higher similarity. The similarity score is calculated with TF-IDF transformation and cosine similarity [10]. A similarity score is a floating-point number with a closed interval between -1 and 1.

Duration is the test execution time of the test case in seconds. Duration is updated every time the test case is executed.

Failure Rate is a floating-point number in a closed range between 0 and 1, and it is calculated by $\frac{T_f}{T_p + T_f}$ where T_f is the total number of failures and T_p is the total number of passes of a single test case. Every test execution updates this value because either T_f or T_p is incremented.

Latest Pass is a left-closed and right-unbounded discrete value from 1 to infinity. It is the number of failing test executions that precedes a passing test execution. Every failing test execution increments this value by one and passing execution resets the value back to 1. The initial value 1 is set because of the assumption that initially, every test case is passing.

History Length is a left-closed and right-unbounded discrete value from 1 to infinity which denotes the number of executions for the test case. The initial value is 1 and each test execution increments the value by one.

2.3   Test Case Selection

Test case selection techniques are a group of regression testing techniques where a subset of the test suite is selected for execution. It reduces the execution time, but at the same time risks neglecting *fault-revealing* test cases.

Test case selection techniques have been evaluated in the literature using metrics such as test suite reduction (TSR) and reduction in fault detection effectiveness [3,4,16]. Test suite reduction is expressed as [16]

$$\text{TSR} = 1 - \frac{|T'|}{|T|} \tag{1}$$

where T is the original test suite and T' is the reduced test suite. Reduction in fault detection effectiveness (RFDE) is given as [16]

$$\text{RFDE} = 1 - \frac{|F_{T'}|}{|F_T|} \tag{2}$$

where F_T is the set of faults found by the original test suite T and $F_{T'}$ is the set of faults found by the reduced test suite T'. The test case selection techniques should maximize the test suite reduction and minimize RFDE.

In this study, F_T is unknown, e.g. the number of actual faults in the system is not known. The failing test cases are known, but a failing test does not always reveal one unique fault. One failing test can reveal any number of actual faults. Because F_T is not known, RFDE cannot be used to measure the performance of TCS techniques. Instead, it is assumed that finding the failing test cases helps to find the actual faults in the system. Therefore, TCS techniques are used to find the failing test cases, f_T, from T. The reduced test suite is not wanted to contain anything else but the failing test cases. In addition to TSR, the objective becomes to maximise the proportion of test failures in the reduced test suite T':

$$\frac{|f_{T'}|}{|f_T|} \tag{3}$$

where $f_{T'}$ is the set of failing tests in T', and f_T is the set of failing tests in the original test suite T. The expression 3 can be rewritten with *true positives* (T_p), *false positives* (F_p), *true negatives* (T_n) and *false negatives* (F_n) by using Knauss et al. [7] descriptions:

- T_p: Test cases that were correctly selected to the reduced test suite (predicted to fail and failed).
- F_p: Test cases that were incorrectly selected to the reduced test suite (predicted to fail but passed).
- T_n: Test cases that were correctly omitted from the reduced test suite (predicted to pass and passed).
- F_n: Test cases that were incorrectly omitted from the reduced test suite (predicted to pass but failed).

The expression 3 can be rewritten with T_p, F_p, T_n and F_n:

$$\frac{|f_{T'}|}{|f_T|} = \frac{|T_p|}{|T_p| + |F_n|} \tag{4}$$

which is the same as *recall* in information retrieval theory [5,15]. The same can be done for test suite reduction, and rewrite it with T_p, T_n, F_n and F_p:

$$
\begin{aligned}
\text{TSR} &= 1 - \frac{|T'|}{|T|} = \frac{|T| - |T'|}{|T|} \\
&= \frac{(|T_n| + |F_n| + |F_p| + |T_p|) - (|T_p| + |F_p|)}{|T_n| + F_n + |F_p| + |T_p|} \\
&= \frac{|T_n| + |F_n|}{|T_n| + |F_n| + |F_p| + |T_p|}
\end{aligned}
\tag{5}
$$

There are now two conflicting performance scores for TCS techniques: test suite reduction and recall. The goal is to find a TCS technique that maximises both of these scores. It is not trivial, because increasing one potentially decreases the other and vice versa.

Thus, the Matthews correlation coefficient (MCC) is introduced. MCC was found to be a good surrogate for a combination of test suite reduction and recall. The MCC score is a single value and gives us a more robust way to compare the performances of TCS techniques. B.W. Matthews introduced the MCC-score in 1975 [11] and defined it as:

$$MCC = \frac{|T_p| \times |T_n| - |F_p| \times |F_n|}{\sqrt{(|T_p| + |F_p|)(|T_p| + |F_n|)(|T_n| + |F_p|)(|T_n| + |F_n|)}} \qquad (6)$$

The highest possible MCC score is 1. It is achieved when $F_p = 0$, $F_n = 0$, $T_p \neq 0$ and $T_n \neq 0$. In such a case, there are no incorrect predictions. Selecting only the failing predictions, the "perfect selection" is got. The perfect selection never fully satisfies test suite reduction, e.g. TSR $\neq 1$, but always results in the maximum recall value of 1. In other words, MCC $= 1$ evaluates to the highest possible test suite reduction for a recall of 1.

2.4   Evaluated Algorithms for TCS

In the case study, there were three heuristic methods based on data coverage; the fourth one is a random method.

Random. In the random technique, both the number of tests and the tests themselves are selected randomly. This means that from $|T|$ test cases n random tests are selected. Hence, n (the size of the selected test suite) can have any value between 0 and $|T|$.

Coverage. The coverage technique selects every test case that covers a modified statement as described in Sect. 2.1. The size of the selected test suite varies between 0 to $|T|$ as in the case of the Random technique.

Coverage (H). This technique includes all the cases of the Coverage technique and tests that have failed in the previous iteration. Naturally, the size of the test suite is between 0 to $|T|$.

Coverage (PH). In this technique, the first step is to select the tests in similarly to Coverage(H). Furthermore, if the selection size is greater than 2% of $|T|$, the selected tests are prioritized and n top test cases are selected until the 2% limit is reached. The prioritization step calculates the average of test history and coverage, sorts the test cases descending and selects n top test cases from the sorted list. In this technique, the test suite size falls between 0 and $0.02 \times |T|$.

The machine learning techniques apply binary classification over the test case samples and categorize the samples into bins of passing and failing. The selected techniques, except the unlimited version of *RandomForest(U)*, guarantee 98% test suite reduction.

RandomForest. Select every test case that is predicted failing using random forest classifier from *scikit-learn* toolkit [14]. The random forest implementation follows Breiman's implementation [1]. Furthermore, if selection size is greater than 2% or less than 2, prioritize the test suite T using class probabilities and select 2% of the most promising tests. This means that the size of the test suite is between 2 and $0.02 \times |T|$.

RandomForest(U). As above, but the test suite size is not limited. Hence, prioritisation is not needed and the size of the test suite is between 2 and $|T|$.

LogReg. Select every test case that is predicted failing using logistic regression classifier from *scikit-learn*. If the selection size is greater than 2% or less than 2, use the same prioritisation method as in *RandomForest*. This leads to the test suite size of 2 to $0.02 \times |T|$.

XGBoost. Select every test case that is predicted failing using gradient boosting technique (XGBClassifier) from *xgboost*-library. Also in this case, if the selection size is greater than 2% or less than 2, prioritisation is done as in the case of *RandomForest* resulting in the test suite size between 2 and $0.02 \times |T|$.

3   Related Work

Spieker et al. [17] used reinforced learning and multi-layer perceptron to predict failing test cases based on test history. They actualized both test case selection and prioritization in test suites. The idea was to 1) prioritize the test suite T, and 2) repeat selecting the topmost test from T as long as the summed duration of the selected tests goes under a time threshold M. They used the normalized average percentage of faults detected (NAPFD) to measure the performance of their technique and concluded that approximately 60 CI cycles are needed to perform equally or better than the reference techniques. The reference techniques were a random technique, which ordered test cases randomly, a sorting technique, which ordered recently failed test cases with higher priority, and a weighing technique, which ordered test cases by a weighted sum of the test features. Spieker et al. were the first to apply reinforcement learning in TCS.

Di Nardo et al. [11] applied TCS in an industrial system with real regression faults. They measured reductions in test suite sizes and fault detection effectiveness with their coverage-based TCS techniques. They were barely able to reduce test suite sizes at all. The maximum reduction was 2%. Because of the small reductions, fault detection was not compromised. Di Nardo et al. discussed, that the small reductions in test suite sizes were likely due to modifications to the core components of the software. Such parts are covered by a multitude of test cases. Additionally, Di Nardo et al. examined only four different software versions, and the modifications between versions were arguably large.

Beszédes et al. [6] used priority-based TCS to reduce test suite size in the WebKit web browser engine. In their initial experiments, they selected every test case that covered the modified procedures in the software, or that had failed previously. Using this initial selection, they witnessed a test suite reduction of 79.43% with 95.08% recall on average. In their study, Beszédes et al. used the term "inclusiveness" instead of a recall, but both measures are the same.

When Beszédes et al. applied their selection technique in an actual live system they witnessed a test suite reduction of 51% with 75.38% recall on average. Beszédes et al. extended their selection technique with an extra prioritization step. The prioritization was based on coverage information. With this extra step, Beszédes et al. were able to further reduce the selection size. With this technique, they showed a test suite reduction of over 90% with half the recall compared with the non-prioritized test suite. Thus, the recall was interpreted to be approximately 38%. Comparing this result with the result by Busjaeger and Xie [10], the ML-based TCS technique seems to have superior performance.

Harrold et al. [19] experienced fluctuating test suite reductions with their code-based regression-test-selection technique. Their TCS technique relied on code coverage information. Harrold et al. recorded test suite reductions from 0% to almost 100%. They discussed, that the large reductions were due to small modifications in the software, where only a few methods covered by a few tests were changed. Harrold et al. did not analyze thoroughly the reasons behind the small reductions but mentioned that the location of a change can affect test suite reduction. As Harrold et al. applied their technique over four different software with less than eleven software versions, it is possible that the modifications between two consecutive versions were still quite large. Applying TCS in such versions can bring no reduction in test suite size.

Gligoric et al. [17] used dynamic dependency tracking from tests to files to reduce the number of tests. Their tool, "Ekstazi", can track any changes in files that are dependent on the tests, and execute only part of the test suite that is relevant for a set of file changes. The tool is capable of tracking source code files, but also configuration files. The tool monitors the execution of tests running on JVM and collects the accessed files using bytecode instrumentation and listening to all standard Java library methods that might open a file. After the collection of the dependent files is done, the tool can select a subset of tests to be executed for any change made in the dependent files. Gligoric et al. report, that their tool is capable to reduce end-to-end testing time by 32%.

Yoo et al. [45] used dependency coverage among other features to select and prioritize tests. The optimization technique by Yoo et al. balanced three competing objectives: dependency coverage maximization, historical fault detection maximization and execution time minimization. Yoo et al. reported an average test suite reduction of 68% with their technique.

4 The Experiment

4.1 Data Collection

The research is based on the version control history of an existing project (528 tests and 87 commits – for further details see [13]). The first phase collected data about tests in each commit in the version control history. An essential part of this data collection was re-executing tests for each version of the software. Then, different test case selection algorithms were applied.

Because data was collected by executing the tests, it took a long time. To reduce the time, handling of source modifying commits and test modifying commits were separated. When a commit modifies only test/ directory and not src/ directory at all, a transitive dependency selection includes only test cases that are transitively affected by the modification. This reduced the number of tests to execute. To further optimize the data collection, consecutive instances of test/* modifying commits were merged. This was done as a preprocessing step before running the data collection algorithm. Every commit that had no source or test modifications was also removed since they had no effect on the functionality of the software. The data collection algorithm used is the following:

1. Checkout newest commit
2. Repeat:
    (a) If the current commit has src/* modifications:
        i. Execute test suite
    (b) Else if the current commit has test/* modifications:
        i. Find modified tests through transitive dependency selection (see 2.1)
        ii. Execute modified tests
    (c) Save executed test verdicts, coverage and durations
    (d) Checkout previous commit

The output of this algorithm is an ordered set of tuples $D = \{commit, tests\}$, where *commit* is a commit's checksum (identification in Git) and *tests* is a set of tuples $\{verdict, coverage, duration\}$. *Verdict* is the output: pass or fail, *coverage* is the full gcov-coverage for the test, and *duration* is the length in seconds.

Step 2ai, test suite execution, lasted about 17 h. The algorithm was continuously being executed for approximately two months for the preprocessed version control history. 87 commits ended up in the dataset, where 45 commits had only source code modifications, 17 commits had both test and source code modifications and 25 commits had only test modifications. Unfortunately, the test suite contained many non-deterministic test cases due to differences in the test environments. Those tests were removed from the dataset As a result, a portion of the commits ended up having no faults. These commits were not removed from the dataset.

The characteristics of the collected dataset are shown in Table 1. Note, that the build or execution failures are test cases that had passed at least once before. Every test case that was recently added and had build or execution failures were removed because it was impossible to gather coverage information for them. As soon as the removed tests passed again in the following commits, they were added back to the test suite. The oldest commit in the dataset did not luckily contain any failing tests after the non-deterministic tests were removed.

Surprisingly, many of the test cases failed because of build or execution errors. The reason behind this was not thoroughly studied, but it could possibly relate to differences between the test environments used in this research and the real one. It is also possible that the developers were aware of these build failures all along, and they had no intention to fix them.

Table 1. Charasteristics of the data used in this research.

Modifications	Source code	Source and test code	Test code
Commits	45	17	25
Commits with at			
Least one failing test case	36	14	11
Failing tests	142	124	119
Normal failures	32	66	39
Build or execution failures	110	58	80
Passing tests	22590	8513	7109

More details about the data and its collection can be found in the original thesis [13].

4.2   Test Case Selection

All test case selection algorithms were applied by iterating through the collected data. The algorithm below presents the procedure. The algorithm was run for every test case selection technique t and for every tuple $d \in D$:

1. If $d.commit$ has test/* modifications:
   (a) Let T_{tmod} be the tests selected with transitive dependency selection
2. If $d.commit$ has src/* modifications:
   (a) Let T_{smod} be the tests selected with t according to current knowledge C
3. Let $T' = T_{tmod} \cup T_{smod}$
4. Simulate the execution of T'
5. Update current knowledge C

C represents the current knowledge about the test cases. This includes the coverage, duration, and test verdict histories (history of passes and fails) for every test case. In the first commit, this information is not available, and therefore one commit is needed to initialize the test case selection techniques. During the first commit, the initial coverage, duration, and test verdicts were collected.

In the first step, a transitive dependency selection to the $d.tests$ is applied, if $d.commit$ type is "test" or "source&test". In the second step, the TCS technique

t to *d.tests* using the current knowledge C is applied. The selected tests were saved in T_{smod}. In the third step, the transitively affected tests T_{tmod} and the selected tests T_{smod} are combined. T_{tmod} is empty, if *d.commit* type is "source". T_{smod} is empty, if *d.commit* type is "test", respectively. If *d.commit* type is "source&test", both T_{tmod} and T_{smod} can contain test cases, but not the same test cases. In the fourth step, it is not necessary to execute the reduced test suite T', because it was already done during the data collection phase. Instead, the existing information of T' was used, and current knowledge was updated about test histories.

The last step 5 is rather complex. The selection T_{smod} is turned into feature vectors, but only if *d.commit* type is "source". Using the coverage, duration and verdict the feature vector {*statement coverage, modification coverage, similarity score, duration, failure rate, latest pass*} is created for every test case. This is done for all tests in T_{smod}, and they are saved for the next iteration d_{i+1}. This idea is applied for every source commit, and eventually, the training data accumulates and grows larger. The training dataset is a set of $\{T_{smod_1}, ..., T_{smod_{n-1}}, T_{smod_n}\}$, where n is an index of a source commit. During every iteration, the machine learning model is re-trained with this training dataset.

It is also necessary to calculate the MCC metric, recall and test suite reduction between the steps 4 and 5 if the *d.commit* is a source commit and the commit has at least one failing test case. If there are no failing tests, the output of MCC is undefined, recall is zero, and test suite reduction would be the only indicator worth measuring. Therefore, measuring performances is skipped when the commit has no failing tests. In addition to non-faulty commits, performances in "test&source" commits or "test" commits were not measured either.

5   Results

Test case selection techniques were compared using Matthews correlation coefficient (MCC) values. The boxplot in Fig. 1 shows MCC-scores for each technique over 35 commits. The green triangle is the mean and the orange line is the median. The box presents values from lower to upper quartile. The whiskers display the range of the data, and the dots are outliers. *Coverage(PH)* technique has the highest median and mean MCC-score, and *Random* technique the lowest.

To examine the significance of the techniques, a Kruskal-Wallis test was done for the MCC scores across 35 source-modifying commits with a failing test. The result showed an H-statistic of 117.9 and the p-value of $2.07 \cdot 10^{-22}$ allowing the rejection of the null hypothesis (medians of the groups are equal). To find which of the groups were different, a pairwise posthoc test was done using Dunn's test with Bonferroni adjustment. The pairwise comparison is shown in Fig. 2.

Figure 3 shows MCC-trend for each heuristic (top) and each machine learning technique (bottom) across 35 source modifying commits. All machine learning techniques have fairly low MCC values during the first 19 commits. Towards the end, the machine learning techniques improve.

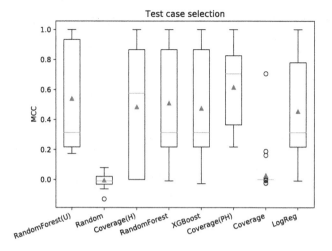

Fig. 1. MCC of each test case selection method over 35 commits.

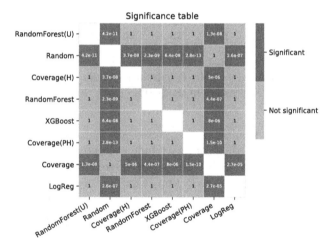

Fig. 2. Pairwise significance analysis using Dunn's test with Bonferroni adjustment. Any value below 0.05 indicates a significant difference in MCC.

6   Discussion

6.1   Test Case Selection

This test case selection case study, compared the performance of eight test case selection techniques. Four of the techniques were based on heuristics, and the rest four were based on machine learning. For each technique three different performance indicators were measured, namely test suite reduction, recall, and Matthews correlation coefficient. The MCC-score was used to differentiate the well and poorly performing techniques in a form of significance analysis using Dunn's test with Bonferroni adjustment (Fig. 2).

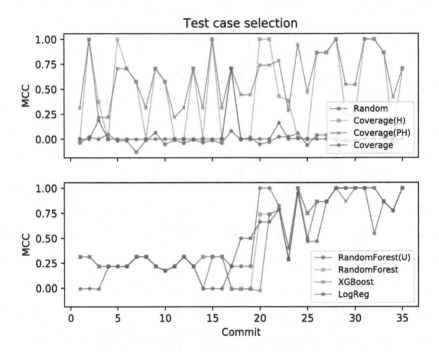

Fig. 3. MCC per method and commit. Trends for heuristics are shown in the top plot, and for machine learning techniques in the bottom plot.

Heuristics. The significance analysis revealed, that *Coverage* and *Random* techniques were outweighed by other techniques. Interestingly, *Coverage* and *Random* techniques did not have a statistical difference in their performances.

The coverage based test case selection (*Coverage*) achieved test suite reduction of 64.7% while having a recall of 39.5% on average. The MCC scores had no significant differences from *Random* technique.

The *Coverage(H)* technique was able to resolve part of the issues of *Coverage*, providing significantly better results. It had an additional way to predict a test failure, namely the *latest pass*. It selected every test case that either covered a modification or failed in the previous commit.

The *Coverage(PH)* technique was the most promising technique among the heuristics of this paper. It used priority-based test case selection over modification coverage and test history. It selected every test case that covered a change or failed in the previous commit. If the selection size was still too large, it reduced the selection by prioritizing the selected tests using failure rate, latest pass, and modification coverage.

Machine Learning. The assumption was that the performance of the machine learning models gradually increases as tests are being executed and new labeled data samples are accumulated in the training dataset. It was interesting to know, whether the machine learning techniques eventually reach the same performance as the heuristics, and if so, then how long time does it take to reach a similar performance? To investigate this, Fig. 3 shows the performance of each technique over time. Indeed, every machine learning technique shows a positive trend for the MCC scores, where the techniques performed better in the end than in the beginning and towards the end they performed equally or better than the heuristics. It looks like that at commit number 20 all techniques gained a positive boost, and they perform better than in commit 19.

During the first 19 commits, the machine learning techniques had fairly low MCC scores possibly due to the low amount of negative samples in the training data. Between commits 20 and 35 however, the machine learning techniques seem to perform better. The Table 2 collects the recall and test suite reduction values of each technique between the commits 20 and 35.

Table 2. Average recall, test suite reduction and Matthews correlation coefficient for each test case selection technique.

Technique	Commits 1-19			Commits 20–35		
	Recall	TSR	MCC	Recall	TSR	MCC
Random	0.316	0.588	−0.010	0.489	0.528	0.003
Coverage	0.553	0.524	0.047	0.215	0.793	0.007
Coverage(H)	0.886	0.523	0.387	0.947	0.778	0.600
Coverage(PH)	0.781	0.988	0.515	0.790	0.986	0.736
LogReg	0.412	0.982	0.189	0.783	0.987	0.771
RandomForest	0.623	0.980	0.220	0.790	0.990	0.854
RandomForest(U)	0.702	0.980	0.255	0.871	0.983	0.881
XGBoost	0.570	0.980	0.203	0.755	0.990	0.798

Comparing the columns of commits 1–19 with columns of commits 20–35, the machine learning techniques had increased their recall but also improved test suite reduction a bit. *RandomForest(U)* technique outperformed *Coverage(PH)* in recall with a slightly lesser test suite reduction. The rest of the techniques also provided competitive results to *Coverage(PH)*. *Coverage(H)* still remained the technique with the highest recall.

The best performing machine learning model was an unlimited random forest (*RandomForest(U)*), which achieved a test suite reduction of 98.2% and recall of 73.1% on average. Towards the end the recall was notably higher, rendering MCC score also higher. This is a promising result for incremental learning-based test case selection and shows that machine learning techniques have the capability to outperform heuristics in a relatively small number of commits.

Spieker et al. [17] used reinforcement learning to select and prioritize test cases, and their technique required 60 consecutive commits to perform equally or better than comparison techniques. The test case selection results in this study suggest, that approximately 20 source code modifying commits to provide similar results with the comparison techniques. The machine learning techniques provided similar or better MCC scores compared to the *Coverage(PH)* technique after 20 commits. This could indicate, that using a different model (e.g. random forest classifier instead of multilayer perception), accumulating training data and re-training the machine learning model in every iteration, and using more features in addition to test histories, such as coverage information and text similarity scores, can help to reach the saturation point faster. The results achieved in this study, are not outright comparable to the results of Spieker et al., because experimentation setups were different, the comparison methods were different and the used measures were different, namely NAPFD and MCC. Also, the results were not validated with other projects but the techniques were applied to a single software project only. Therefore, more investigation is required to compare results more reliably with Spieker et al. and this research.

Busjaeger and Xie [2] used supervised learning and pointwise ranking to prioritize test cases. They were able to select 3% of the topmost test cases and provide 75% recall. Such selection equals to 97% test suite reduction. The results of this study are approximately similar, but the results were achieved with less training data. The results in this study suggest, that even if initial training data does not exist, incremental learning can eventually achieve similar performance to supervised batch learning. The saturation point was at about 20th commit, and then the performance was similar to [2].

In many cases, false positives and false negatives have different impacts. One disadvantage of the MCC score is that it values false positives and false negatives similarly, i.e. it is invariant to the changes in false positives and false negatives when their sum is constant. Small amount of false negatives and a greater amount of false positives is more beneficial than the contrary in test case selection. The MCC score could be biased to penalize false negatives more than false positives, but this is left to future research.

6.2   Threats to Validity

There are many threats to validity. Firstly, all non-deterministic tests were deleted from the test suite before the experiments. This arguably distorts the results. However, the test history features, such as the latest pass and failure rate described in Sect. 2.2 are the key features to explain even the non-deterministic test case failures.

A different test environment was used in the data collection (Sect. 4.1) than in the actual project. These two test environments are similar, but they use a different amount of hardware simulation. This could have brought excessive discrepancies in test verdicts between the test environments.

Because of separating how code (src/*) and test (test/*) commits are handled, the experiment setup became complex. MCC, recall and test suite reduction were calculated for source modifying commits only and ignored the values for the test commit types. Using dependency coverage as a new machine learning feature could have fixed this issue.

Code-coverage-based test case selection is not able to trace every kind of change in the codebase. These are generally the non-instrumental parts of the code repository, such as meta- or configuration files, but also source code. For example, a global variable value change cannot be traced.

The coverage information produced by *gcov*-tool was not accurate when a statement contains line breaks. In such situations, the first line is only detected by gcov, and the rest of the lines are ignored. The software code contained statements that split into multiple lines. Therefore, the coverage-based selection techniques could have been affected.

Finally, the test case selection was applied to one software project only. This suggests that external validity can be affected. The plan included another project but there was not enough time.

7   Conclusions

Because CI aims to provide rapid feedback for the developers, slow testing can be harmful [6]. As software evolves, the test suites become large and at some point, they can no longer be executed in a short time. The aim of this research was to find ways to enhance or speed up testing in order to facilitate CI, and that test case selection techniques can be used to reduce the time required for testing. The incremental machine learning was found especially interesting for its capability to eventually outperform comparison heuristics.

Incremental machine learning was used to predict failing tests out of the test suite using information such as test history, code coverage, and modifications introduced in a commit. With these predictions, the system effectively selected a small number of test cases for execution when a new commit was made to the software repository. The incremental machine learning-based test case selection techniques eventually performed equally well or better than the best heuristic. Similar results have already been suggested by Spieker et al. [17], who used reinforcement learning and neural networks to select a subset of tests based on test history. Their technique required 60 consecutive CI cycles to perform equally well or better than the comparison techniques in NAPFD values. The research reported in this pare was based on the MCC score, and the ML techniques produced equal or better MCC scores than the best heuristic after 20 source code modifying commits. The research supports the results of Spieker et al. and brings in more evidence that when initial training data does not exist, machine learning can be applied incrementally to eventually produce as good or better results as comparison techniques. In addition to that, the results give a cautious hint that accumulating training data and re-training the models in every iteration, using more features such as code coverage and similarity score and using a different classifier, e.g. random forest, can make the models learn faster and predict failing tests correctly earlier.

Despite the positive results in favour of using machine learning in test case selection, the results need further verification. There was a single software project in the case study, and therefore external validity is risked. Secondly, the machine learning models were fully trained in every commit, which can become infeasible when the training data increases.

References

1. Breiman, L.: Random forests. Mach. Learn. **45**(1), 5–32 (2001)
2. Busjaeger, B., Xie. T.: Learning for test prioritization: an industrial case study. In: Proceedings of the 2016 24th ACM SIGSOFT International Symposium on Foundations of Software Engineering, FSE 2016, , New York, NY, USA. ACM, pp. 975–980 (2016)
3. Di Nardo, D., Alshahwan, N., Briand, L., Labiche, Y.: Coverage-based regression test case selection, minimization and prioritization: a case study on an industrial system. Softw. Test. Verification Reliab. **25**(4), 371–396 (2015)
4. Engström, E., Runeson, P., Skoglund, M.: A systematic review on regression test selection techniques. Inf. Softw. Technol. **52**(1), 14–30 (2010)
5. Fawcett, T.: An introduction to roc analysis. ROC analysis in pattern recognition. Pattern Recognit. Lett. **27**(8), 861–874 (2006)
6. Fowler, M., Foemmel, M.: Continuous integration. Thought-Works), 122:14 (2006). http://www.thoughtworks.com/ContinuousIntegration.pdf
7. Knauss, E., Staron, M., Meding, W., Söder, O., Nilsson, A., Castell, M.: Supporting continuous integration by code-churn based test selection. In: 2015 IEEE/ACM 2nd International Workshop on Rapid Continuous Software Engineering, pp. 19–25 (2015)
8. Lachmann. R.: Machine learning-driven test case prioritization approaches for black-box software testing. In: European Test and Telemetry Conference ettc2018, pp. 300–309 (2018)
9. Lachmann, R., Schulze, S., Nieke, M., Seidl, C., Schaefer, I.: System-level test case prioritization using machine learning. In: 2016 15th IEEE International Conference on Machine Learning and Applications (ICMLA), pp. 361–368 (2016)
10. Christopher, D., Raghavan, P., Schütze, H.: Manning. In: Introduction to Information Retrieval, Cambridge University Press, New York, NY, USA (2008)
11. Matthews. B.W.: Comparison of the predicted and observed secondary structure of t4 phage lysozyme. Biochim. Biophys. Acta Protein Struct. **405**(2), 442–451 (1975)
12. Thomas, M.: Mitchell, 1st edn. Machine Learning. McGraw-Hill Inc, New York, NY, USA (1997)
13. Mulkahainen. M.: Test case selection and prioritization in continuous integration environment. Master Thesis, Tampere University, Faculty of Information Technology and Communication, Tampere (2019)
14. Pedregosa, F., et al.: Scikit-learn: machine learning in Python. J. Mach. Learn. Res. **12**, 2825–2830 (2011)
15. Powers, D.: Evaluation: from precision, recall and f-factor to roc, informedness, markedness & correlation. Mach. Learn. Technol. **2**, 01 (2008)
16. Rothermel, G., Harrold, M. J., Ostrin, J., Hong, C.: An empirical study of the effects of minimization on the fault detection capabilities of test suites. In: Proceedings. International Conference on Software Maintenance (Cat. No. 98CB36272), pp. 34–43 (1998)

17. Spieker, H., Gotlieb, A., Marijan, D., Mossige, M.: Reinforcement learning for automatic test case prioritization and selection in continuous integration. In: Proceedings of the 26th ACM SIGSOFT International Symposium on Software Testing and Analysis, ISSTA 2017, New York, NY, USA. ACM, pp. 12–22 (2017)
18. Virmani. M.: Understanding devops & bridging the gap from continuous integration to continuous delivery. In: Fifth International Conference on the Innovative Computing Technology (INTECH 2015), pp. 78–82 (2015)
19. Yoo, S., Nilsson, R., Harman, M.: Faster fault finding at google using multi objective regression test optimisation. In: European Software Engineering Conference and the ACM SIGSOFT Symposium on the Foundations of Software Engineering (ESEC/FSE'11) (2011)

Inferring Metamorphic Relations from JavaDocs: A Deep Dive into the MeMo Approach

Alejandra Duque-Torres$^{(\boxtimes)}$ and Dietmar Pfahl

Institute of Computer Science, University of Tartu, Tartu, Estonia
{duquet,dietmar.pfahl}@ut.ee

Abstract. Identifying and selecting suitable Metamorphic Relations is a complex process since it necessitates a thorough grasp of the system under test and its problem domain. Recently, an approach supporting unit testing at the method level called MeMo was proposed. Through a module called MR-Finder, MeMo infers Equivalent Metamorphic Relations (EMRs) by identifying sentences in Javadoc's comments that describe equivalent behaviours between different methods of the same class. MR-Finder has three main components: *(i)* a predefined set of 10 words that express an equivalence (S10W). *(ii)* A mechanism that measures the semantic similarity between two sentences by using Word Move Distance (WDM). *(iii)* A binary classifier that decides whether a given sentence points to an EMR. The goal of our research is to determine if MeMo's MR-Finder module can be improved. For that purpose, we first re-build the MR-Finder module and use the same dataset provided by MeMo's authors to verify the reported results in the original study and establish the basis for further experiments. Second, we explore two strategies, STRTG No.1 and STRTG No.2, to improve the MR-Finder. In STRTG No.1, we increase the set S10W. In STRTG No.2, we keep S10W unchanged but add a second template sentence to the MR-Finder module. We successfully re-implemented the MR-Finder module and achieved comparable results using the same S10W. Our results indicate that the overall performance of MR-Finder is very likely to improve when the initial set of equivalent words increases, *i.e.*, with STRTG No.1.

Keywords: Software testing · Metamorphic testing · Metamorphic relations

1 Introduction

Software testing is an essential quality assurance activity as it helps to ensure the correct operation and quality of software. One of the major challenges in software testing is known as the test oracle problem. A test oracle determines the correct output of the System Under Test (SUT) for a given input. The test oracle problem arises when the SUT lacks an oracle or when developing

© The Author(s), under exclusive license to Springer Nature Switzerland AG 2022
D. Taibi et al. (Eds.): PROFES 2022, LNCS 13709, pp. 418–432, 2022.
https://doi.org/10.1007/978-3-031-21388-5_29

one to verify the computed outputs is practically impossible [5]. *Metamorphic Testing* (MT) is a software testing technique that attempts to alleviate the test oracle problem [2]. MT differs from traditional test techniques in that, instead of checking the individual outputs of the SUT, it examines the relations between the inputs and outputs of the test runs. These relations are known as Metamorphic Relations (MRs). An MR defines how the outputs should vary in response to a defined change of inputs when executing the SUT [10,15]. If a particular MR is violated for at least one test input (and its change), there is a high probability that the SUT has a fault. On the other hand, if a particular MR is not violated, it does not guarantee that the SUT is fault-free. Therefore, the effectiveness of MT depends largely on the suitability of the MRs used [10].

Identifying and selecting adequate MRs is a complex process since it necessitates a thorough grasp of the SUT and its problem domain. As a result, the automatic identification of MRs is recognised as a big challenge. Some techniques for automatically identifying MRs have been proposed, however, they either focus on specific domains or work under strict assumptions. One of the biggest problems for automatically identifying MRs is knowing what kind of information is needed to infer an MR, as well as where to extract information about SUT to infer a suitable MR. Kanewala et al. [7,9] propose to use code structure information to train Machine Learning (ML) model that predicts whether a method in a newly developed SUT can be tested using a specific MR. In particular, this approach is based on a pre-defined set of six MRs and a classifier trained on the control-flow graph (CFG) extracted from a pool of sample methods. Duque-Torres et al. [4] and Rahman et al. [12] follow the Kanewala et al. approach, but instead of using CFB-based features, Duque-Torres et al. [4] used software metrics extracted from the method's source code, and Rahman et al. [12] use Bag of Words (BoW) model over Javadoc as the feature representation.

Recently, an approach supporting unit testing at the method level called MeMo was proposed by Blasi et al. [1], published in the Journal of Systems and Software, to *"automatically derive metamorphic equivalence relations from natural language documentation, and use such metamorphic relations as oracles in automatically generated test cases"*. MeMo infers MRs by identifying sentences in the comments that describe equivalent behaviours between different methods of the same class. Then, the inferred MRs get automatically translated into executable assertions. In order to see whether and how MeMo's mechanism for inferring MRs can be improved. We decided to perform further research on this.

The rest of the paper is structure as follows: In Sect. 2, we introduce MeMo's approach by Blasi et al. [1]. In Sect. 3, we describe the methodology. In Sect. 4 we present the answers to our research questions, and discuss our results. Section 5 presents the related work. Finally, we conclude the paper in Sect. 6.

2   The MeMo Approach

One approach that has been suggested to automatically identify MRs is MeMo. We focus on automated MR inference from natural language documentation by following the MeMo approach. In this section, we first present MeMo's procedure proposed by Blasi et al. [1] (Sect. 2.1) as well as the dataset used in their study (Sect. 2.2). Then, we summarise the evaluation result reported in the original study (Sect. 2.3).

2.1   MeMo's Procedure

Overall, MeMo's architecture comprises four modules: Comment Processor Module (CPM), Metamorphic Relations Finder Module (MR-Finder), Translator Module (TM), and Executor Module (EM). The CPM parses the input source code and generates a clean version of the Javadoc comments for each method. The MR-Finder analyzes the sentences in the comment and recognizes those that point to an MR. If a sentence points to an MR, the TM interprets and parses the whole comment together with the sentence that points to the MR to generate a Java assertion. The EM embeds the generated assertions into existing code to determine if the MR is maintained at run time. We are only interested in CPM and MR-Finder. We describe them in detail below.

2.1.1   Comment Processor Module (CPM)

Figure 1 shows an example of how looks like Javadoc comments. As shown Fig. 1, the comment begins with a free-text summary description and is followed by tag blocks (@param, @return, @throws, @since, @version, and so on). The official Oracle documentation[1] states that in the method's summary should offer a general description of the method, including any interesting semantic attribute, whereas the tag blocks should express more detailed, narrower information. Based on that, MRs are very likely to occur or be described in method summaries. Therefore, MeMo analyses and infers MRs from the method's summary. The main purpose of the CMP is to generate a clear representation of the Javadoc comments for each method in a given class. It gets rid of formatting information like HTML markup. It saves content using @code and @link inline tags for later use. In addition, the CMP divides each method's cleaned summary text into sentences.

2.1.2   Metamorphic Relations Finder Module (MR-Finder)

As we mention above MRs define how outputs should vary in response to a defined change of inputs when executing the SUT. The MRs explored in MeMo MRs are defined in a different way. The MR definition in MeMo is related to the equivalence of two different functions or methods. For instance, let's consider the function $f(x) = sin(x)$, we know that the $sin(x)$ function is equivalent to the function $cos(\frac{\pi}{2} - x)$. MeMo consider the equivalence between $sin(x)$ and $cos(\frac{\pi}{2} - x)$ as a potential MR. Therefore, one can express a equivalent MR as $sin(x) ==$ $cos(\frac{\pi}{2} - x)$. It is important to highlight that this definition of MR proposed by MeMo, differs from the its traditional definition. In MeMo the MRs needs another function instead of (directly) exploiting knowledge about the original function.

---

[1] https://www.oracle.com/technical-resources/articles/java/javadoc-tool.html#tag.

```
193  /**
194   * Compute a weighted loess fit on the data at the original abscissae.
195   *
196   * @param xval Arguments for the interpolation points.
197   * @param yval Values for the interpolation points.
198   * @param weights point weights: coefficients by which the robustness weight
199   * of a point is multiplied.
200   * @return the values of the loess fit at corresponding original abscissae.
201   * @throws NonMonotonicSequenceException if {@code xval} not sorted in
202   * strictly increasing order.
203   * @throws DimensionMismatchException if {@code xval} and {@code yval} have
204   * different sizes.
205   * @throws NoDataException if {@code xval} or {@code yval} has zero size.
206   * @throws NotFiniteNumberException if any of the arguments and values are
207   * not finite real numbers.
208   * @throws NumberIsTooSmallException if the bandwidth is too small to
209   * accomodate the size of the input data (i.e. the bandwidth must be
210   * larger than 2/n).
211   * @since 2.1
212   */
213  public final double[] smooth(final double[] xval, final double[] yval,
214                   final double[] weights)
```

Fig. 1. Javadoc's comment from Common Math library, class "Interpolation", method "smooth"

Thus, hereinafter we use the expression Equivalent Metamorphic Relation (EMR) instead of MR to refer to the MR definition used in the MeMo approach.

The MR-Finder module determines if a sentence given by the CMP points to an EMR. This module has three main components: (i) a predefined set of 10 words that express an equivalence or equality, e.g., equivalent, equal, similar, etc. (ii) A mechanism that measures the semantic similarity between two sentences. (iii) A binary classifier that decides whether a given sentence points to an EMR or not. The predefined set of 10 words, hereinafter S10W, are: "equivalent", "similar", "analog", "like", "identical", "behaves as", "equal to", "same as", "alternative", "replacement for". Blasi et al. [1] manually identified the S10W by inspecting around 4,741 Javadoc comment sentences selected randomly from the documentation of seven Java projects: Apache Commons Collections, Apache Commons Math, Apache Hadoop, Apache Lucene, Eclipse Vert.x, Google Guava and GWT.

Because the word or term used to describe an equivalence can vary between different comments, using only a set of predefined words to recognise sentences pointing out EMR would restrict MeMo's capabilities. Therefore, identifying EMRs is based on semantic analysis of sentences rather than searching and matching individual words in the comment sentences. The semantic analysis is based on the semantic similarity between two sentences. The most straightforward way to decide whether two sentences are similar is to assume that sentences are similar if they have words in common. However, the most significant limitation of methods that uses that assumption, like Euclidean Distance, Cosine Distance or Jaccard Similarity, is that they do not handle synonym scenario. The Word Move Distance (WMD) is designed to overcome that limitation. WMD uses word embeddings to determine the distance even without a common word. It is assumed that words with similar meanings should have similar vectors.

The mechanism in charge of measuring semantic similarity uses the words in S10W to generate ten template sentences, from now on TS_S10W, with the structure *"This method <S10W> to that method."*. Then, WMD is calculated between each TS_S10W and each sentence in the comment. The similarity score provided by WMD is between 0 and 1. A score of 0 indicates that the sentences are semantically the same, while one means that the sentences do not have any semantic similarity. The binary classifier receives the obtained WDM score and decides whether the given sentence points to an EMR or not. This classifier determines by checking if the WDM score is less than 0.2, which means similarity of at least 80%.

Table 1. Dataset description used by Blasi et al. [1] as well as their result

Library	Dataset info			Results achieved in [1]					
	Classes	Sent$^\perp$	EMR	TP	FN	FP	SP‡	Pre$^\pm$	Rec*
Colb	9	477	19	11	8	0	0	1	0.58
ElasticS	10	228	14	8	6	0	0	1	0.57
GWT	17	448	44	12	31	1	1	0.86	0.27
GraphStr	3	126	11	9	2	0	0	1	0.82
Guava	33	1558	80	9	2	0	0	1	0.82
Hibernate	5	126	5	62	16	2	2	0.94	0.78
JDK	23	3381	72	59	11	2	6	0.88	0.82
Math	9	653	30	26	4	0	2	0.93	0.87
Weka	4	192	6	3	1	2	0	0.6	0.5
Total	113	7189	281	193	81	7	11	0.91	0.69

$^\perp$Sentences, ‡Spurious, $^\pm$Precision,*Recall.

2.2 MeMo's Dataset

To create the ground truth, Blasi et al. manually identify EMRs by inspecting the Javadocs comments of 194 classes from 9 open-source Java libraries and translating them into a code assertion. They provide the constructed ground truth in their GitHub repository[2].

---

[2] https://github.com/ariannab/MeMo/tree/master/expected-equivalences.

The MeMo's approach was evaluated by randomly selecting a reduced set of classes from the ground truth. Table 1 summarises the total number of classes that they select, the total number of sentences among all the comments of the classes selected and the total number the EMRs. Although the authors provided a replication package[3], it is not clear which classes they selected, making exact replication difficult.

2.3   MeMo's Results - Original Study

Table 1 summarises the results achieved by Blasi et al. MeMo was evaluated in terms of effectiveness, and usefulness. Concerning effectiveness, it was computed Precision and Recall. Regarding usefulness, Blasi et al. evaluated whether MeMo assertions improve testing when used as oracles.

It is important to highlight that the evaluation reported by Blasi et al. [1] is not about MR-Finder output but MeMo's final output, *i.e.,* the generation of the assertion. Therefore, when comparing with the ground truth, two type of false negative may occur, non-empty false positive and empty false positive. In the former, MeMo's output is non-empty and does not match the ground truth. In empty false positive or Spurious, MeMo's output is non-empty and the ground truth is empty. Precision and Recall were computed using Eq. (1).

- *True Positive (TP):* MeMo's output is non-empty and matches the ground truth.
- *True Negative (TN):* MeMo's output is empty and matches the ground truth, *i.e.,* the ground true is also empty.
- *False Negative (FN):* MeMo's output is empty but the ground truth is not.
- *False Positive (FP):* MeMo's output is non-empty and does not match the ground truth.
- *Spurious (Sp):* MeMo's output is non-empty and the ground truth is empty.

$$Precision = \frac{TP}{TP + FP + Sp}, Recall = \frac{TP}{TP + FN + Sp} \qquad (1)$$

3   Methodology

Our goal is to investigate whether the MeMo approach of Blasi et al. (i) can be replicated when using our implementation of the pipeline for inferring EMRs, and (ii) can be improved. We aim to answer the following research questions:

RQ$_1$: [Replicability]   *How well does the MeMo approach identify natural language sentences expressing EMR when our processing and training pipeline is used on the full dataset?*

RQ$_2$: [Improvement]   *How to improve the capabilities of the MeMo approach to infer EMR from natural language sentences?*

---

[3] https://github.com/ariannab/MeMo.

3.1 Replicability

In RQ_1, we are interested in checking if the artefacts developed by us achieve better or the same performance as those of Blasi et al. We follow exactly the same steps as Blasi et al. (see Sect. 2.1.2). In the original work, MeMo is implemented in Java and uses open source libraries. In particular, the libraries Standford CoreNLP API and the wmd4j. The CoreNLP API allows to derive linguistic annotations for text, including token and sentence boundaries, parts of speech, named entities, numeric and time values, dependency analysis, etc. wmd4j is a Java library for calculating WMD. Unlike the original MeMo implementation, we use Python. In particular, the open source libraries NLTK (Natural Language Toolkit), Gensim[4], FastText[5], and Word2Vec.wm.distance in Gensim to calculate the WMD score.

NLTK is a collection of libraries and tools for symbolic and statistical natural language processing. Gensim is an open-source framework that uses contemporary statistical machine learning to do unsupervised topic modeling, document indexing, retrieval by similarity, and other natural language processing functions. FastText is an open-source, and lightweight software that enables users to learn text representations and text classifiers.

As we mentioned in Sect. 2.3, the evaluation reported by Blasi et al. [1] is not the output of MR-Finder but the final output of MeMo. Therefore, our evaluation is slightly different. To evaluate our implementation, we use the ground truth provided by Blasi et al., the basic truth is a set of JSON files. Each file contains 7 main fields: *signature, name, wrapper class, target class, isVarArgs, parameter, equivalence*. The *equivalence* field contains the sub-fields: *member, comment, type* and *condition*. We are interested in the sub-fields of the *equivalence* field, *i.e.*, *comment* and *condition*. If the *condition* sub-field is not empty, it means that the comment has a sentence that expresses an EMR. Based on that, we compute Precision and Recall. Below is our definition of TP, TN, FN, and FP.

- *True Positive (TP):* The EMR has been identified and matches the ground truth, *i.e.*, the ground truth has something written in the sub-field condition.
- *True Negative (TN):* The EMR has not been identified and matches the ground truth, *i.e.*, the ground true is empty in the sub-field condition.
- *False Negative (FN):* The EMR has not been identified but the ground truth has something written in the sub-field condition.
- *False Positive (FP):* The EMR has been identified and the ground true is empty in the sub-field condition.

3.2 Improvement

In RQ2, we check if the MeMo approach can be improved in terms of *precision* and *recall*. To do this, we use two different strategies. The first strategy (STRTG No.1) is to increase the number of words in S10W. We first explore how many

---

[4] https://pypi.org/project/gensim.
[5] https://fasttext.cc.

words that express an equivalence can be found in the full dataset. Also, we investigate whether the S10W words are among the top equivalent words in the dataset described in Table 2 in the columns ours. It is important to note that the S10W were obtained from different libraries than those used in the MeMo evaluation.

In STRTG No.1, we follow four steps: *(i)* convert text (comments) into tokens, *(ii)* remove all stop words, *(iii)* lemmatization, and *(iv)* calculate the word frequency. The step *(iii)*, lemmatization, is used to ensure that words that share the same base word are recorded in the frequency as the same word. After this process, we manually filter out the words that express an equivalence. We do this process with the full dataset. We use the open source Regex and NLTK libraries. Regex is for processing regular expressions. Helps convert noise data containing special characters and performs uppercase to lowercase conversion. We use the NLTK library to tokenize the comment into sentences and then into a list of words. With the new S10W, we repeat the process for inferring EMRs with our own artefacts.

The second strategy (STRTG No.2) is to add a second "template sentence" to the mechanism in charge of measuring semantic similarity. This second template sentence, TS_S10W$_2$, has the structure *"Method_A and method_B are <S10W>"*. With both templates, TS_S10W and TS_S10W$_2$, we repeat the process for inferring EMTs by using our own artefacts. In both strategies, STRTG No.1 and STRTG No.2, we report TP, FN, FP, Precision, and Recall.

4   Results and Discussion

4.1   Replicability

RQ$_1$: How well does the MeMo approach identify natural language sentences expressing EMR when our processing and training pipeline is used on the full dataset?

Table 2 reports the number of libraries, number of classes, number of parsed methods, number of methods with comments, number of methods without comments, number of sentences, and number of EMRs, used by Blasi et al. [1] and in this paper. Some information is not provided by the authors, for instance, the number of parsed methods, number of methods with comments, and number of methods without comments. It is notable that in our evaluation, we analyse more classes than the Blasi et al., however, we discard the methods that do not have comments. We believe that the author did the same.

From the Table 2 in the EMRs column, one can see that the number of MRs in our dataset and the original study' dataset do not differ drastically. In fact, 5 of 9 libraries, have the same amount of EMR, and the extra EMRs in our dataset do not exceed more than 5. As for the number of sentences, we expected to have more sentences per library in our dataset as we analysed more classes. This was true for 8 of 9 libraries, where indeed the number of sentences was greater than that used in the [1]. However, the GWT library got 15 fewer sentences than the GWT library used by Blasi et al.. We checked the repository and discovered that

Table 2. Comparison of dataset used in Blasi et al. [1] and the dataset created based on the JSON files

Library	Classes		No. Meth.		Meth. WC$^\perp$		Meth. W/o$^\pm$		Sent*		EMRs	
	Ours	[1]	Ours	[1]	Ours	[1]	Ours	[1]	Ours	[1]	Ours	[1]
Colt	13	9	348	NR!	268	NR!	80	NR!	577	477	21	19
ElasticS	19	10	299	NR!	184	NR!	115	NR!	260	228	14	14
GWT	18	17	273	NR!	253	NR!	20	NR!	433	448	44	44
GraphStr	9	3	187	NR!	154	NR!	33	NR!	381	126	11	11
Guava	78	33	1347	NR!	1118	NR!	229	NR!	2813	1558	81	80
Hibernate	13	5	151	NR!	113	NR!	38	NR!	188	126	5	5
JDK	36	23	1175	NR!	1106	NR!	69	NR!	4393	3381	77	72
Math	29	9	727	NR!	372	NR!	355	NR!	766	653	34	30
Weka	19	4	530	NR!	514	NR!	16	NR!	858	192	6	6
TOTAL	234	113	5037	NR!	4082	NR!	955	NR!	10669	7189	293	281

$^\perp$Total number of methods with comments, $^\pm$Total number of methods without comments *Sentences, **NR!**: Not Reported.

the GWT library was modified after MeMo's paper was submitted. Also, there were some commits pointing to the deletion of some comments. Another possible explanation has to do with the method used during the sentence tokenization process. The authors do not provide information on this. From our side, we use the "sent_tokenize" method of the nltk.tokenize library.

Table 3. Results achieved by Blasi et al. [1] VS our results

Library	Results achieved by Blasi et al. [1]						Our results				
	TP	FN	FP	‡Sp	Pre$^\pm$	Rec*	TP	FN	FP	Pre$^\pm$	Rec*
Colt	11	8	0	0	1	0.58	14	3	3	0.82	0.82
ElasticS	8	6	0	0	1	0.57	10	4	0	1	0.71
GWT	12	31	1	1	0.86	0.27	29	10	5	0.85	0.74
GraphStr	9	2	0	0	1	0.82	8	3	0	1	0.72
Guava	62	16	2	2	0.94	0.78	53	21	7	0.88	0.71
Hibernate	3	2	0	0	1	0.6	3	2	0	1	0.6
JDK	59	11	2	6	0.88	0.82	56	13	8	0.87	0.81
Math	26	4	0	2	0.93	0.87	18	10	6	0.75	0.64
Weka	3	1	2	0	0.6	0.5	5	1	0	1	0.64
Average	21.4	9.0	0.8	1.2	0.9	0.6	21.8	7.4	3.2	0.9	0.7

‡Spurious, $^\pm$Precision, *Recall.

Table 3 reports TP, FN, FP, Precision and Recall of our MR-Finder implementation. Overall, the Precision has satisfactory results, achieving the maximum value, *i.e.*, 1, in 4 of 9 classes, and a minimum of 0.75 over all classes. Our Recall is quite high, too, with a minimum of 0.6. In our context, we want to keep the Recall metric to a minimum value. A high Recall indicates there are several EMRs that could not be identified. When analysing the EMRs that were not identified, we saw the following patterns:

- The sentences that had more than one equivalent word were more likely not to be identified; for instance, the sentence in the Weka library's BinarySparseInstance class: *does **exactly** the **same as** value() if applied to an instance.*
- Sentences with equivalent term *"as"*, for example, in the sentence from Colb library's matrix.linalg.Algebra class: *also known **as** dot product.*
- When the equivalent term is at the very end of the sentence, it is likely that it will not be identified, for instance, in the class matrix.DoubleMatrix2D from the Colb library: *Linear algebraic matrix-matrix multiplication $C = A$ x B **Equivalent to** A.zMult(B,C,1,0,false,false).*
- Sentence with the equivalent term 'synonym', for example, in the graph.Path class of the GraphStream library: *A **synonym** for #add(Edge).*

With regards to *replicability* (RQ_1), our results indicate that we can achieve similar results as Blasi et al. when re-implementing the MR-Finder using different libraries and programming language. In terms of Precision, we achieved the same results for three of nine libraries, better for one of nine, and slightly worse for five of nine libraries. However, when our results get worse, the maximum difference between the Blasi et al. results and ours does not exceed 0.12. In terms of Recall, our results are clearly better for four of nine libraries, equal for one of nine, and slightly worse for four of nine libraries. When our results get worse, the maximum difference between the Blasi et al. results and ours does not exceed 0.23.

4.2   Improvement

RQ_2: How to improve the capabilities of the MeMo approach to infer EMR from natural language sentences?

Table 4 reports the results obtained in RQ_1, and the results obtained in RQ_2. Regarding the analysis for STRTG No.1, we identified eighteen words or terms that express an equivalence in the full dataset. Our results also indicate that the initial ten words, S10W, are among the words found. The eighteen words listed in order from most to least frequent are: *"equivalent"(180)*, *"same" (54)*, *"like" (28)*, *"equal" (27)*, *"identical" (15)*, *"instead" (13)*, *"similar" (9)*, *"equivalently" (9)*, *"exactly as" (3)*, *"synonym" (2)*, *"behaves as (2)"*, *"comparable" (2)*, *"acts as" (2)*, *"replacement for" (1)*, *"preferred" (1)*, *"substitute" (1)*, *"analog" (1)*, *"alternative" (1)*. We call this set of new equivalent words, S18W.

The STRTG No.1 column in Table 4, reports TP, FN, FP, Precision and Recall when repeating the process for inferring EMR by using S18W and our MR-Finder module artefacts. As Table 4 shows, by increasing the initial set of equivalent words, the results improved considerably in terms of FN, Precision

Table 4. Replication results from RQ_1 VS STRTG No.1 and STRTG No.2 from RQ_2

Library	RQ$_1$ results [replicability]					RQ$_2$ results [improvement]									
						STRTG No.1					STRTG No.2				
	TP	FN	FP	Pre$^\pm$	Rec*	TP	FN	FP	Pre$^\pm$	Rec*	TP	FN	FP	Pre$^\pm$	Rec*
Colt	14	3	3	0.82	0.82	16	1	3	0.84	0.94	14	3	3	0.82	0.82
ElasticS	10	4	0	1	0.71	14	0	0	1	1	10	4	0	1	0.71
GWT	29	10	5	0.85	0.74	35	4	5	0.88	0.90	29	10	5	0.85	0.74
GraphStr	8	3	0	1	0.72	10	1	0	1	0.91	8	3	0	1	0.73
Guava	53	21	7	0.88	0.71	65	9	7	0.90	0.88	62	12	7	0.90	0.84
Hibernate	3	2	0	1	0.6	5	0	0	1	1	3	2	0	1	0.60
JDK	56	13	8	0.87	0.81	66	3	8	0.89	0.96	60	9	8	0.88	0.87
Math	18	10	6	0.75	0.64	26	2	6	0.81	0.93	21	7	6	0.78	0.75
Weka	5	1	0	1	0.64	6	0	0	1	1	5	1	0	1	0.83
Average	21.8	7.4	3.2	0.9	0.7	27.0	2.2	3.3	0.9	0.9	23.6	5.7	3.2	0.9	0.8

‡Spurious, $^\pm$Precision, *Recall.

and Recall. As for FN, it is expected that by increasing from S10W to S18W, the module will be able to identify some sentences it could not identify before. For example, when using S10W, the lowest WMD score for sentences with the word "synonym" was 0.38, meaning it did not meet the threshold to be considered an EMR. When using S18W, the lowest score was 0.164, meaning it met the point to be considered a WMD. By lowering the number of FNs and increasing the number of FPs, it is clear that Recall will be positively affected. As Table 4 shown, three out of nine libraries achieved the maximum Recall, *i.e.*, 1. The minimum Recall was 0.88 for the Guva library, and the rest of the libraries achieved a Recall ranging between 0.90 and 0.96.

From the Table 4, one can also see that the Precision increased. This is because the number of TP increased, and the number of FP remained the same. The minimum value of Precision achieved is 0.81 for the Colb library. For the rest of the libraries, the Precision ranges between 0.84 and 1. The same libraries with maximum Precision in RQ1 remained in RQ2 -STRTG No.1. When we inspect the sentences that were marked as FP, we find that they mostly have phrases like: exactly the same and the same. For example, the comment sentence in the Colb library's DoubleMatrix2D method: "Both matrices must have the *same* number of rows and columns". Furthermore, the WDM scores of those sentences are quite close to the decision limit, that is, between approximately 0.193 and 0.198.

The STRTG No.2 column in Table 4, reports TP, FN, FP, Precision and Recall when repeating the process for inferring EMR by using TS_S10W$_2$ and our MR-Finder module artefacts. The table shows that most of the results remained the same, like with TS_S10W in RQ1. Only three libraries benefited from TS_S10W$_2$: Guava, JDK, and Math. Inspecting those libraries, we notice that the sentences that were successfully identified using TS_S10W$_2$, and were not identified in RQ1, are those where the equivalent term is at the end of the sentence, for example, in the class matrix.DoubleMatrix2D from the Colb library: *Linear algebraic matrixmatrix multiplication $C = A$ x B* **Equivalent to** *A.zMult(B,C,1,0,false,false)*.

Regarding to *improvement* (RQ_2), our results indicate that we can achieve better results than in RQ_1. Also, we can achieve more similar results as Blasi et al. when using STRTG No.1, *i.e.,* by using our artefacts and increasing the number of words in S10W. Regarding STRTG No.2, we only improved on three out of nine libraries. However, the improvement is around 0.03 for Precision and 0.06 for Recall. We can conclude that the best way to improve the MR-Finder module is by increasing the initial set of equivalent words. However, it is necessary to consider that increasing S10W could increase the processing time. In our case, the processing time increased by 2490 ms.

4.3   Threats to Validity

In the context of our study, two types of threats to validity are most relevant: threats to internal and external validity. To achieve internal validity, we used the same set of Javadocs provided by Blasi et al. [1]. However, due to the authors randomly taking subsets of the Javadocs provided, it was not possible to do a direct comparison with their results. Another potential validity threat in our study is that we recreated all steps of the MR-Finder approach using different NLP libraries with potentially different parameter settings. Regarding external validity, our study uses the same data provided by the original study. For the sake of generalisability, it would have been preferable to include additional Javadocs or documentation from other programming languages to overcome any potential bias introduced by the selection of Javadocs in the original study. As a consequence, our replication cannot determine the actual scope of the effectiveness of the MR-Finder from MeMo approach.

5   Related Work

Kanewala and Bieman [8], were the first to show that, for previously unseen methods, applicable MRs can be predicted using supervised ML techniques. Their work showed that classification models created using a set of features extracted from CFGs, in particular, features related to CFG' nodes and paths, and a set of predefined MRs are effective in predicting whether a method in a newly developed SUT can be tested using a specific MR taken from the predefined set. Kanewala [7] extend the Kanewala and Bieman [8] approach, by conducting a feature analysis to identify the most effective CFG's related features for predicting MRs. Their results showed that Support Vector Machine (SVM) models built with features based on CFG similarity measurements, in particular using Random Walk Kernel, perform better than SVM models using nodes- and paths-based features with linear kernel. This approach is known as *Predicting Metamorphic Relations*, PMR.

Hardin and Kanewala [6] extended the initial PMR study [8], but instead of using supervising learning techniques, they used semi-supervised learning techniques. Rahman and Kanewala [13] applied PMR approach for predicting three MRs (Permutative, Additive, and Multiplicative) for matrix-based programs. Duque-Torres et al. [3] extended the initial PMR approach to another programming language, Python and C++. Nair et al. [11] explored and compared equivalent and non-equivalent mutants as data augmentation technique to broaden the training set using PMR. Their augmentation approach was tested on the PMR original study dataset [8]. The study demonstrated that equivalent mutants are a valid data augmentation technique to improve the PMR detection rate.

Zhang et al. [14] presented RBF-MLMR, a multi-label technique that predicts MRs using radial basis function neural networks. Instead of using several binary classifiers like in PMR, RBF-MLMR use a neural network to predict all potential MRs for a given method. The major difference between this technique and PMR is the usage of multi-label and neural networks, but it follows the same pipeline as PMR original study. Also, the RBF-MLMR's feature design is CFG's node- and path-based. Duque-Torres et al. [4] follows the PMR idea, but instead of using CFG-based features, they used different software metrics that are extracted from the method's source-code.

Rahman et al. [12] introduce *MRpredT* which is a text classification-based ML approach to predict MRs using software documentation. The idea behind their MRpredT approach is to build a model that predicts whether a method in a newly developed SUT can be tested using a specific MR. A total of 93 program's Javadocs, which handle matrix operations, were used for their study. Overall, the approach follows the same pipeline of PMR approach proposed by Kanewala and Bieman [8], but instead of using features extracted from the programme CFG-based, Rahman et al. use Bag of words (BoW) model as the feature representation. The first step of their method is to extract the Javadoc documentation from the source code using Java Parser and pre-processes them using the lemmatization technique. Then, text feature extraction methods are applied to those pre-processed Javadocs to obtain the feature vectors. These feature vectors of the programs are then supplied into the SVM and Naive Bayes classification algorithms with their associated MR labels. The MR labels are identified manually for all the programs. A disadvantage of MRpredT approach is the need of having a pre-defined set of MRs.

6   Conclusion

MeMo approach is the first approach that attempts to infer EMRs from formal software documentation. We studied its procedure to see whether and how MeMo's approach could be improved. In particular, its module MR-Finder. This module is in charge of determining if a sentence given in a comment points to an EMR. The MR-Finder is based on three main components: *(i)* a predefined set of 10 words that express an equivalence (S10W). *(ii)* A mechanism that measures the semantic similarity between two sentences using WMD. *(iii)* A binary classifier that decides whether a given sentence points to an EMR by checking if the WDM score is less than 0.2

We start by exploring the Javadocs provided by Blasi et al. [1] in their replication package. Next, we implement the components of the MR-Finder module using the Python programming language; our evaluation indicates satisfactory results in precision but not in Recall. We also explore two strategies, STRTG No.1 and STRTG No.2, to improve the MR-Finder. In STRTG No.1, we analyze the words that express an equivalence in the data set to increase S10W. We found 18 words in total; we call them S18W. We repeat the process to infer EMR using S18W. In STRTG No.2, we kept the same S10W but added a second template sentence to the MR-Finder module. We get the best results with STRTG No.1. Our results indicate that the overall performance of MR-Finder is very likely to improve as the initial set of equivalent words increases. However, it is necessary to consider that increasing S10W could increase the processing time. In our case, the processing time increased by 2490 ms.

Acknowledgements. This research was partly funded by the Estonian Center of Excellence in ICT research (EXCITE), the IT Academy Programme for ICT Research Development, the Austrian ministries BMVIT and BMDW, the Province of Upper Austria under the COMET (Competence Centers for Excellent Technologies) program managed by FFG, and grant PRG1226 of the Estonian Research Council.

References

1. Blasi, A., Gorla, A., Ernst, M.D., Pezzè, M., Carzaniga, A.: Memo: automatically identifying metamorphic relations in Javadoc comments for test automation. J. Syst. Softw. **181**, 111041 (2021). ISSN 0164-1212. https://doi.org/10.1016/j.jss.2021.111041
2. Chen, T.Y., Cheung, S.C., Yiu, S.M.: Metamorphic testing: a new approach for generating next test cases. Technical report HKUST-CS98-01, Department of Computer Science, Hong Kong University of Science and Technology, Hong Kong (1998)
3. Duque-Torres, A., Pfahl, D., Claus, K., Ramler, R.: A replication study on predicting metamorphic relations at unit testing level. In: 2022 IEEE International Conference on Software Analysis, Evolution and Reengineering (SANER), pp. 1–11 (2022)
4. Duque-Torres, A., Pfahl, D., Klammer, C., Fisher, S.: Using source code metrics for predicting metamorphic relations at method level. In: 5th Workshop on Validation, Analysis and Evolution of Software Tests, VST'22 (2022)
5. Duque-Torres, A., Shalygina, A., Pfahl, D., Ramler, R.: Using rule mining for automatic test oracle generation. In: 8th International Workshop on Quantitative Approaches to Software Quality, QuASoQ'20 (2020)
6. Hardin, B., Kanewala, U.: Using semi-supervised learning for predicting metamorphic relations. In: 3rd IEEE/ACM International Workshop on Metamorphic Testing (MET), pp. 14–17, MET'18 (2018). ISBN 9781450357296
7. Kanewala, U.: Techniques for automatic detection of metamorphic relations. In: IEEE 7th International Conference on Software Testing, Verification and Validation Workshops (ICSTW), pp. 237–238 (2014). https://doi.org/10.1109/ICSTW.2014.62

8. Kanewala, U., Bieman, J.M.: Using machine learning techniques to detect metamorphic relations for programs without test oracles. In: IEEE 24th International Symposium on Software Reliability Engineering (ISSRE), pp. 1–10 (2013). https://doi.org/10.1109/ISSRE.2013.6698899

9. Kanewala, U., Bieman, J.M., Ben-Hur, A.: Predicting metamorphic relations for testing scientific software: a machine learning approach using graph kernels. Softw. Test. Verif. Reliab. **26**(3), 245–269 (2016)

10. Liu, H., Kuo, F.C., Towey, D., Chen, T.Y.: How effectively does metamorphic testing alleviate the oracle problem? IEEE Trans. Softw. Eng. **40**(1), 4–22 (2014). https://doi.org/10.1109/TSE.2013.46

11. Nair, A., Meinke, K., Eldh, S.: Leveraging mutants for automatic prediction of metamorphic relations using machine learning. In: Proceedings of the 3rd ACM SIGSOFT International Workshop on Machine Learning Techniques for Software Quality Evaluation. MaLTeSQuE 2019, pp. 1–6. Association for Computing Machinery, New York (2019). ISBN 9781450368551. https://doi.org/10.1145/3340482.3342741

12. Rahman, K., Kahanda, I., Kanewala, U.: MRpredT: Using Text Mining for Metamorphic Relation Prediction, pp. 420–424. Association for Computing Machinery, New York (2020). ISBN 9781450379632, https://doi.org/10.1145/3387940.3392250

13. Rahman, K., Kanewala, U.: Predicting metamorphic relations for matrix calculation programs. In: 3rd IEEE/ACM International Workshop on Metamorphic Testing (MET), MET'18, pp. 10–13 (2018)

14. Zhang, P., Zhou, X., Pelliccione, P., Leung, H.: RBF-MLMR: a multi-label metamorphic relation prediction approach using RBF neural network. IEEE Access **5**, 21791–21805 (2017). https://doi.org/10.1109/ACCESS.2017.2758790

15. Zhou, Z.Q., Sun, L., Chen, T.Y., Towey, D.: Metamorphic relations for enhancing system understanding and use. IEEE Trans. Softw. Eng. **46**(10), 1120–1154 (2020). https://doi.org/10.1109/TSE.2018.2876433

An Evaluation of Cross-Project Defect Prediction Approaches on Cross-Personalized Defect Prediction

Sousuke Amasaki[1]($\boxtimes$) iD, Hirohisa Aman[2] iD, and Tomoyuki Yokogawa[1] iD

[1] Okayama Prefectural University, 111 Kuboki, Soja 719-1197, Japan
{amasaki,t-yokoga}@cse.oka-pu.ac.jp
[2] Center for Information Technology, Ehime University, Matsuyama 790-8577, Japan
aman@ehime-u.ac.jp

Abstract. Context: Just-in-time software defect prediction (JIT SDP) helps to prioritize fault-prone commits for efficient software quality assurance. As each commit can be attributed to each developer, JIT SDP can also be personalized to each developer as a personalized defect prediction. A question is whether the commit data of other developers, namely, cross-personalized data, are still valuable for prediction. Cross-project defect prediction (CPDP) approaches are a promising answer. Objective: To clarify the effectiveness of cross-personalized defect prediction with CPDP approaches. Method: An experiment with 23 CPDP approaches was conducted on 9 project datasets. Results: Some CPDP approaches using cross-personalized data were often better than the personalized defect prediction using one's data. Conclusion: It is recommended to use the CPDP approach to achieve better predictions. Turhan09 is our recommendation.

Keywords: Personalized defect prediction · Transfer learning · Comparative study

1 Introduction

Software is prevalent around the world. Safety social systems now depend on the quality of software. Software developers care about their product's quality and try not to induce and leave bugs. Despite their devotion, buggy software is still prevalent around the world.

Resource limitation is one of the reasons for remaining bugs after release. Developers have little time to investigate all software elements and need a measure to find more suspicious elements than the others. *Software defect prediction* (SDP) aims to help prioritize software elements according to their fault-proneness.

Many studies on SDP have been published so far [18,39]. SDP studies target different granularities: source files, classes, functions, methods, and lines. These software elements were measured with static code metrics for building SDPs [24].

© The Author(s), under exclusive license to Springer Nature Switzerland AG 2022
D. Taibi et al. (Eds.): PROFES 2022, LNCS 13709, pp. 433–448, 2022.
https://doi.org/10.1007/978-3-031-21388-5_30

Recent studies also target code changes by developers. Code changes are recorded in a version control system and can be attributed to each developer. Instead of static code metrics, change metrics such as change size and developer experience can be used for prediction.

Just-in-time SDP (JIT SDP) [17] uses code changes by developers for building prediction models at project-level. As each commit is attributed to each developer, JIT SDP models can be built at developer-level. *Personalized defect prediction* [15] aims to improve prediction accuracy by using personalized code change data. On the one hand, the stratification by developers brings homogeneous data by excluding developers' diversity. On the other hand, the stratification decreases the data size supplied for training a prediction model.

Cross-project defect prediction (CPDP) is a research topic that tackles the small amount of training data available using data from other teams/organizations. Although such cross-project data had been used barely (e.g., [4]), cross-project data and target project data usually have different characteristics. Most CPDP approaches thus adapt the cross-project data to a target project data. Recent studies have investigated CPDP approaches on JIT SDP [6,16,36,47].

Cross personalized defect prediction [2] applies the idea of CPDP to personalized defect prediction. The commit data of other developers were considered as cross-personalized data of a target developer. A bare (i.e., straightforward) cross-personalized defect prediction is to use cross-personalized data for training. It is like a JIT SDP, but target developer's data are not used for training. Cross personalized defect prediction is to find a transformation of such data based on the characteristics of the target developer's data. Many CPDP approaches have been proposed for years, and the value of other cross-project defect prediction approaches on cross-personalized defect prediction was still a question.

This paper explored the effectiveness of CPDP approaches where they were applied to cross-personalized defect prediction. The rest of this paper was organized as follows: Sect. 2 describes past studies related to personalized software defect prediction and CPDP. Section 3 gives the motivation of this research and the research questions we addressed. Section 4 explains the methodology we adopted. Sections 5 shows the experiment results with figures and tables, and Sect. 6 answers the research questions. Section 7 discusses the threats to the validity of our experiments. Section 8 provides a summary of this paper.

2   Related Work

Software quality assurance activities suffer from resource shortages and need a measure to prioritize software elements to be examined. Software defect prediction (SDP) aims for quality and efficient prioritization using machine-learning algorithms. In past studies, SDP is thus targeting at different granularity levels such as function and file for the recursive nature of software. As software version control systems had been popular for code management, SDP at the change-level (often called just-in-time (JIT) SDP [17]) got popular in software engineering research. JIT SDP approaches have been widely investigated so far [6,14,21,42,43,47].

JIT SDP can specify who makes faulty changes because code changes are recorded with the authors' information. The relationships between developer characteristics and faults are widely investigated. For instance, Schröter et al. [35] reported that developers' defect densities differed. Rahman et al. [32] also showed that an author's specialized experience in the target file is more important than general experience.

Personalized defect prediction focuses on the diversity of developers. Jiang et al. [15] constructed a personalized defect prediction approach based on characteristic vectors of code changes. They also created another model that combines personal data and the other developers' change data with different weights. Furthermore, they created a meta classifier that uses a general prediction model and the above models. Empirical experiments with OSS projects showed the proposed models were better than the general prediction model. Xia et al. [41] proposed a personalized defect prediction approach that combines a personalized prediction model and other developers' models with a multi-objective genetic algorithm. Empirical experiments with the same data as [15] showed better prediction performance. These personalized defect prediction approaches utilized other developers' data to improve the prediction performance. Ekan and Tosun [7] investigated the performance and the developer characteristics in detail. They identified some characteristics such as experiences that affect the preference of personalized models.

The homogeneity of training data is expected to increase the quality of prediction models. For instance, it was recommended that JIT defect prediction models should regularly be refreshed with recent commits [23]. Personalized defect prediction also follows this idea. However, it reduces the amount of training data and affects the accuracy of prediction models. Cross-project SDP is a research topic that aims to balance that trade-off using data from outside of a target to overcome the small amount of dataset obtained. Many CPDP approaches have also been proposed so far [11,13,46]. Cross-project SDP at the change level has also been investigated and called JIT CPDP [1,6,16,36].

Cross personalized defect prediction follows the idea of JIT CPDP for personalized defect prediction. Instead of using cross-project, developers in the same project are utilized for better prediction. Researchers investigated the effectiveness of cross-personalized defect prediction partially. The personalized defect prediction approaches in the above [15,41] can be considered cross-personalized defect prediction approaches. Because combining defect prediction models based on other projects was studied as a CPDP approach [28].

3   Motivation

In a previous study, the bellwether effect [20], a CPDP approach, was also examined for cross-personalized defect prediction [2]. Some studies [15,41] can be considered cross-personalized defect prediction approaches. These studies were limited to one specific CPDP approach, and no comprehensive and comparative investigation based on not a few approaches has not been conducted so far. Through empirical experiments with 9 project data, we addressed the following research questions:

RQ$_1$. Do CPDP approaches affect the bare cross-personalized defect prediction performance?

RQ$_2$. Which CPDP approaches improve the bare cross-personalized defect prediction performance?

RQ$_3$. Do CPDP approaches contribute to improving personalized defect prediction?

To answer these research questions, cross-personalized defect predictions with 23 CPDP approaches were carried out and compared with each other.

4   Methodology

4.1   Datasets

This study used the same datasets as [2]. The datasets were originally collected by Cabral et al. [5] and provided through a replication package[1]. Table 1 describes the definitions of change metrics in the datasets. The change metrics consist of 14 metrics of 5 dimensions defined in [17].

The datasets were preprocessed before dividing the whole commits into developers' commits. The first step was to recover links between commits and authors, as commits in the datasets had no author information. UNIX timestamps of the commits and their corresponding git repositories were used to identify their authors. Commits with the same timestamp (duplicates) were all removed as it was impossible to connect those commits and their authors. The second step was to cleanse the linked data to filter out suspicious cases. Commits were removed if it has a negative value in a counting metric such as LA in Table 1. We also removed suspicious cases that had zero values only, meaning nothing committed.

Our study focused on personalized defect prediction and used *active developers* data having enough commits for evaluating the performance of CPDP approaches. The other commits were discarded in this study. In [2], the number of commits was used to determine whether a developer was active or not. Active developers must also make enough faulty and no-faulty commits to train a defect prediction model. We adopted a criterion of [2] that active developers must have at least 30 faulty commits and 30 non-faulty commits. Table 2 shows the number of active developers identified and the average commits per developer of the datasets. These numbers varied among the datasets, and it was suitable for evaluation.

---

[1] http://doi.org/10.5281/zenodo.2594681.

Table 1. Changes measures

Dimension	Name	Definition
Diffusion	NS	Number of modified subsystems
	ND	Number of modified directories
	NF	Number of modified files
	Entropy	Distribution of modified code across each file
Size	LA	Lines of code added
	LD	Lines of code deleted
	LT	Lines of code in a file before the change
Purpose	FIX	Whether or not the change is defect fix
History	NDEV	The number of developers that changed the modified files
	AGE	The mean time interval between the last and the current change
	NUC	The number of unique changes to the modified files
Experience	EXP	Developer experience
	REXP	Recent developer experience
	SEXP	Developer experience on a subsystem

Table 2. Statistics of Selected Datasets

Project name	Period	Active developers	Average commits
Brackets	12/2011-12/2017	24	335
Broadleaf	11/2008-12/2017	14	674
Camel	03/2007-12/2017	17	1,509
Fabric8	12/2011-12/2017	10	914
Neutron	12/2010-12/2017	21	196
Nova	08/2010-01/2018	67	230
NPM	09/2009-11/2017	4	1,645
Spring-Integration	11/2007-01/2018	8	878
Tomcat	03/2006-12/2017	9	1,990

4.2 Experiment Design

Cross-personalized defect prediction assumes that an (active) developer needs training data enough from other (active) developers to build prediction models. Although developers' commits in a project can be sorted and used following a timeline, we made experiments straightforward so that cross-personalized defect prediction models were made of all the other developers' commits in the same project. Detailed realistic emulation is our future work. This decision enabled us to use a benchmark framework called CrossPare [12].

Crosspare is a benchmark framework for cross-project defect prediction. This study used 23 out of 24 CPDP approaches implemented. The rest, Nam13 [27], was omitted for the out-of-memory error on a computer. As we focused on cross-personalized defect prediction, the benchmark framework was applied to each project instead of a set of projects. Nine projects were supplied to this experiment and enabled us to observe the stability of performance of CPDP approaches.

Some approaches only transform cross-personalized data and can be combined with arbitrary machine learning algorithms. Therefore, all combinations of the approaches and learning algorithms implemented in CrossPare were evaluated except for SVM for a long-time computation. The adopted approaches were compared with two baselines. The first one is a bare cross-project defect prediction that combines all cross-personalized data and uses a classification algorithm for prediction. This configuration corresponded to a project-level defect prediction and was called a general model in [7]. Another is cross-validation of target data, often called WPDP (within-project defect prediction) in CPDP studies, meaning a normal personalized defect prediction.

4.3   Performance Evaluation

This study adopted AUC (Area Under the Receiver Operating Characteristic Curve) as the performance measure. AUC measure is not sensitive to thresholds that determine faultiness or not. It is also robust to class imbalance, which happened in defect prediction. A classifier is perfect if an AUC value is 1.0. A meaningful classifier results in an AUC value of more than 0.5. If equal or less, the classifier is random guessing at best.

The Scott-Knott Effect Size Difference (ESD) test [37] was used to compare the performance of methods on each dataset statistically. The Scott-Knott ESD test makes some clusters, each consisting of homogeneous configurations (i.e., combinations of a CPDP approach and a machine learning technique) regarding their prediction performance. It corrects the non-normal distribution of an input dataset and merges any two statistically distinct clusters with a negligible effect size into one group. That is, the effect size between two distinct clusters made by the Scott-Knott ESD test is more than negligible. A cluster with the highest performance holds treatments that are clearly better than the others while the performance of those treatments is equivalent.

5   Results

Figures 1, 2, 3, 4, 5, 6, 7, 8 and 9 show the ranking of CPDP approaches on the datasets introduced in Sect. 4.1. The figure shows only the best combination for the approaches accepting arbitrary learning algorithms. The bare (i.e., project-level) cross-personalized defect prediction and the normal personalized defect prediction are named "ALL" and "CV," respectively. That is, if CV were better than ALL, it would imply that personalized defect prediction was more effective than the bare cross-project defect prediction. The differences in colors among the

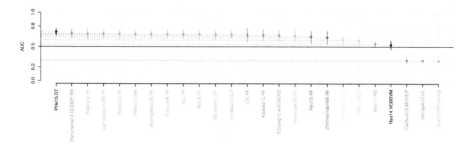

Fig. 1. Ranking of CPDP approaches in AUC (brackets) (Color figure online)

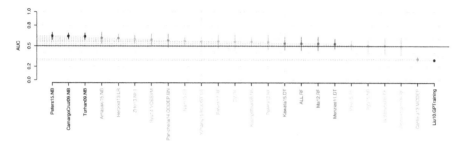

Fig. 2. Ranking of CPDP approaches in AUC (Broadleaf) (Color figure online)

approach names indicate the statistically significant differences in AUCs based on Scott-Knott ESD. The left side is better. The results of these datasets are analyzed below.

Brackets: Figure 1 shows that one baseline named "ALL" (with Random Forests (RF)) was found in the third group. The other named "CV" with RF was in the fourth group. This order implied that the bare cross-personalized defect prediction was better than personalized defect prediction. The group of the bare cross-personalized defect prediction also has 9 CPDP approaches. These CPDP approaches brought no improvement and were ineffective. Two CPDP approaches, PHe15 [9] and Panichella14 [28] were significantly better than the bare cross-personalized defect prediction. The top approach was PHe15 with Decision Tree (DT). Contrastingly, not a few CPDP approaches were still significantly worse than the two baselines. Some approaches performed less than 0.5 of AUC, meaning a random guess.

Broadleaf: Figure 2 shows the ranking on Broadleaf dataset. In contrast to Fig. 1, CV placed in the fifth group while ALL placed in the sixth group. This order implied that the bare cross personalized defect prediction was worse than personalized defect prediction. The group of the bare cross-personalized defect prediction also has 3 CPDP approaches. These CPDP approaches brought no improvement and were ineffective. Fourteen CPDP approaches, namely, Peters15 [31],

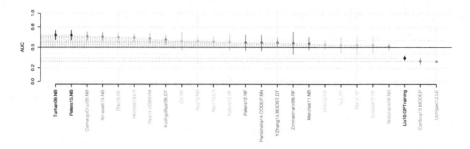

Fig. 3. Ranking of CPDP approaches in AUC (Camel) (Color figure online)

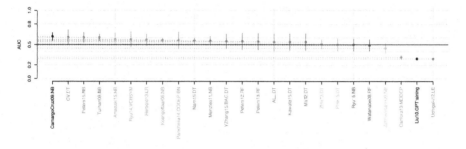

Fig. 4. Ranking of CPDP approaches in AUC (Fabric8) (Color figure online)

CamargoCruz09 [8], Turhan09 [38], Amasaki15 [3], Herbold13 [11], ZHe13 [10], Ryu14 [33], Panichella14, Nam15 [26], YZhang15 [44,45], Peters12 [29], Koshgoftaar08 [19], and Peters13 [30], were significantly better than the bare cross-personalized defect prediction. Furthermore, 8 out of the 14 CPDP approaches were also significantly better than the normal personalized defect prediction. The top group has three approaches, namely, Peters15, CamargoCruz09, and Turhan09. As well as Fig. 1, not a few approaches were worse than the two baselines.

Camel: Figure 3 shows the ranking on Camel dataset. This figure also supported CV in the fifth group against ALL in the seventh group. The group of the bare cross-personalized defect prediction also has 3 CPDP approaches. These CPDP approaches brought no improvement and were ineffective. Sixteen CPDP approaches, namely, Turhan09, Peters15, CamargoCruz09, Amasaki15, ZHe13, Herbold13, Ryu14, Koshgoftaar08, Ryu15 [34], Nam15, Peters13, Peters12, Panichella14, YZhang15, Zimmermann09 [48], and Menzies11 [25], were significantly better than the bare cross-personalized defect prediction. Furthermore, 8 out of the 14 CPDP approaches were also significantly better than the normal personalized defect prediction. The top group has two approaches, namely, Peters15 and Turhan09. Not a few approaches were worse than the two baselines.

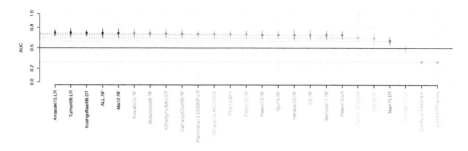

Fig. 5. Ranking of CPDP approaches in AUC (Neutron) (Color figure online)

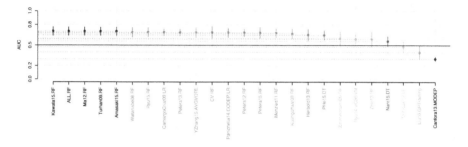

Fig. 6. Ranking of CPDP approaches in AUC (Nova) (Color figure online)

Fabric8: Figure 4 shows the ranking on Fabric8 dataset. This figure also supported CV in the second group against ALL in the fourth group. The group of the bare cross-personalized defect prediction also has 7 CPDP approaches. These CPDP approaches brought no improvement and were ineffective. Eight CPDP approaches, namely, CamargoCruz09, Peters15, Turhan09, Amasaki15, Ryu14, Herbold13, Koshgoftaar08, and Panichella14, were significantly better than the bare cross-personalized defect prediction. Furthermore, CamargoCruz09 was also significantly better than the normal personalized defect prediction. Not a few approaches were worse than the two baselines.

Neutron: Figure 5 shows the ranking on Neutron dataset. In contrast to Fig. 4, ALL in the first group was supported against CV in the fourth group. The group of the bare cross-personalized defect prediction also has 4 CPDP approaches. These CPDP approaches brought no improvement, that is, ineffective. There was no approach above the two baselines. Not a few approaches were worse than the two baselines.

Nova: Figure 6 shows the ranking on Nova dataset. ALL in the first group was also supported against CV in the second group. There was no approach above the two baselines. Not a few approaches were worse than the two baselines.

NPM: Figure 7 shows the ranking on NPM dataset. In contrast to Fig. 6, CV in the fourth group was supported against ALL in the sixth group. The group of

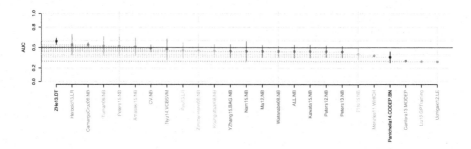

Fig. 7. Ranking of CPDP approaches in AUC (NPM) (Color figure online)

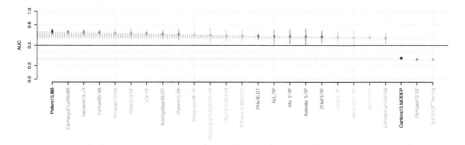

Fig. 8. Ranking of CPDP approaches in AUC (Spring-Integration) (Color figure online)

the bare cross-personalized defect prediction also has 7 CPDP approaches. These CPDP approaches brought no improvement and were ineffective. Ten CPDP approaches, namely, ZHe13, Herbold13, CamargoCruz09, Turhan09, Peters15, Amasaki15, Ryu14, Ryu15, Zimmermann09, and Koshgoftaar08, were significantly better than the bare cross-personalized defect prediction. Furthermore, 6 out of the 10 CPDP approaches were also significantly better than the normal personalized defect prediction. The top group has one approach, namely, ZHe13. Not a few approaches were worse than the two baselines.

Spring-Integration: Figure 8 shows the ranking on Spring-Integration dataset. CV in the third group was supported against ALL in the sixth group. The group of the bare cross-personalized defect prediction also has 4 CPDP approaches. These CPDP approaches brought no improvement and were ineffective. Twelve CPDP approaches, namely, Peters15, CamargoCruz09, Herbold13, Turhan09, Amasaki15, Peters13, Koshgoftaar08, Peters12, Watanabe08 [40], Panichella14, Ryu14, and YZhang15, were significantly better than the bare cross-personalized defect prediction. Furthermore, 4 of the 12 CPDP approaches were significantly better than the normal personalized defect prediction. The top group has one approach, namely, Peters15. Not a few approaches were worse than the two baselines.

Tomcat: Figure 9 shows the ranking on Tomcat dataset. CV in the second group was supported against ALL in the fifth group. The group of the

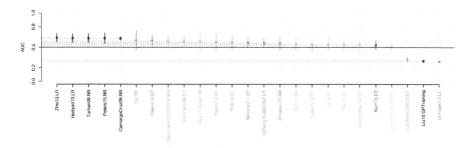

Fig. 9. Ranking of CPDP approaches in AUC (Tomcat) (Color figure online)

bare cross-personalized defect prediction also has 4 CPDP approaches. These CPDP approaches brought no improvement and were ineffective. Fourteen CPDP approaches, namely, ZHe13, Herbold13, Turhan09, Peters15, CamargoCruz09, Peters12, Panichella14, Watanabe08, Ryu14, Peters13, PHe15, Menzies11, YZhang15, and Amasaki15, were significantly better than the bare cross-personalized defect prediction. Furthermore, 5 of the 14 CPDP approaches were significantly better than the normal personalized defect prediction. They were ZHe13, Herbold13, Turhan09, Peters15, and CamargoCruz09. Not a few approaches were worse than the two baselines.

6   Discussion

6.1   RQ$_1$ Do CPDP Approaches Affect Cross-Personalized Defect Prediction Performance?

Some CPDP approaches were grouped with the bare cross-personalized defect prediction noted as "ALL" as shown in Figs. 1, 2, 3, 4, 5, 6, 7, 8 and 9. The other CPDP approaches performed significantly better or worse than the bare cross-personalized defect prediction and formed different groups. Therefore, CPDP approaches could change the bare cross-personalized defect prediction performance.

> **Answer to RQ1:** Yes, not all, but some CPDP approaches significantly changed the bare cross-personalized defect prediction performance positively or negatively.

6.2   RQ$_2$ Which CPDP Approaches Improve the Bare Cross-Personalized Defect Prediction Performance?

Figures 1, 2, 3, 4, 5, 6, 7, 8 and 9 show some groups having CPDP approaches significantly better than the bare cross-personalized defect prediction. However, there was no CPDP approach that was effective on all projects. The bare cross-personalized defect prediction was placed in the first group on Neutron and Nova. Amasaki15, Ma12 [22], and Turhan09 were common between Neutron and Nova and equivalent to the bare cross-personalized defect prediction at most. For the other projects, the most frequently appearing CPDP approaches were Amasaki15, CamargoCruz09, Herbold13, Panichella14, Peters15, Ryu14, and Turhan09. These approaches were better than the bare cross-personalized defect prediction on six projects. Among those CPDP approaches, only Panichella14 appeared as a better one on Brackets dataset, while it was significantly worse on Neutron and Nova. Contrastingly, on Brackets dataset, Amasaki15 and Turhan09 were equivalent to the bare cross-personalized defect prediction. Therefore, they were not the best but the practical choices.

Answer to RQ2: Some CPDP approaches improved the bare cross-personalized defect prediction on some projects but not on all projects. To avoid performance degradation due to the CPDP approach, Amasaki15 and Turhan09 were not the best but the practical choices. These approaches were significantly better on 6 projects and equivalent on 3 projects compared to the bare cross-personalized defect prediction.

6.3 RQ₃ Do CPDP Approaches Contribute to Improving Personalized Defect Prediction?

We found that on 6 out of 9 projects, namely, Broadleaf, Camel, Fabric8, NPM, Spring-Integration, and Tomcat, the normal personalized defect prediction was better than the bare cross-personalized defect prediction, namely, project-level defect prediction. This result revealed the advantage of personalized defect prediction against project-level defect prediction. CPDP approaches improved cross-personalized defect prediction, so their performance was significantly better than the normal personalized defect prediction. The top group on these projects had CPDP approaches only. Especially, Turhan09 was always better than or equivalent to the normal personalized defect prediction. On the rest, namely, Brackets, Neutron, and Nova, the bare cross-personalized defect prediction was better than the normal personalized defect prediction. That is, on all projects, cross-personalized defect prediction was effective.

Answer to RQ3: Yes. There was no project that the normal personalized defect prediction was the best one. Among the CPDP approaches we examined, Turhan09 was the best one.

---

7   Threats to Validity

Internal Validity: One threat is the selection bias of projects. The project data were collected by other researchers for a different purpose. These projects also look diverse regarding size, active developers, and so on. These measures helped to mitigate this threat.

External Validity: The number of software projects was limited and might not represent a typical project distribution enough. Although the diversity of projects helped to mitigate this threat, a different set of projects might lead to a different conclusion.

Construct Validity: The links between developers and commits were based on timestamps, and not a few commit data were dropped off, as shown in Table 2. Although it seems difficult to obtain perfect linking, exploring better linking methods is future work. JIT metrics in Table 1 are common in this research area but not comprehensive. Improving predictive performance with such metrics might change our results.

8   Conclusion

This study evaluated the effectiveness of *cross-project* defect prediction approaches on *cross-personalized* defect prediction. The empirical experiment revealed that some CPDP approaches could achieve better prediction performance than the bare cross-personalized defect prediction, namely, project-level defect prediction. Furthermore, the performance of the normal personalized defect prediction was also surpassed by using CPDP approaches.

An implication for practitioners is to use CPDP rather than the normal personalized defect prediction. Utilizing cross-personalized data based on the characteristics of the developer's data will be beneficial. Especially, Turhan09 was our recommendation among 23 CPDP approaches. It worked at least equivalent to the normal personalized defect prediction and the bare cross-personalized defect prediction.

In future work, experiments with more realistic situations are required. This study used all commits of developers to train personalized defect prediction. One of the purposes of cross-personalized defect prediction is to support developers with a small number of commits. Whether even a small number of commits helps to select cross-personalized data is still a question. Furthermore, a chronological situation along with the timeline is preferable for evaluation. Using developer data of other projects might be an interesting question to be explored.

Acknowledgment. This work was partially supported by JSPS KAKENHI Grant #21K11831, #21K11833, and Wesco Scientific Promotion Foundation.

References

1. Amasaki, S., Aman, H., Yokogawa, T.: A preliminary evaluation of CPDP approaches on just-in-time software defect prediction. In: Proceedings of Euromicro Conference on Software Engineering and Advanced Applications (SEAA), pp. 279–286 (2021)
2. Amasaki, S., Aman, H., Yokogawa, T.: Searching for bellwether developers for cross-personalized defect prediction. In: Proceedings of Product-Focused Software Process Improvement, pp. 183–198 (2021)
3. Amasaki, S., Kawata, K., Yokogawa, T.: Improving cross-project defect prediction methods with data simplification. In: Proceedings of SEAA 2015, pp. 96–103. IEEE (2015)
4. Briand, L.C., Melo, W.L., Wust, J.: Assessing the applicability of fault-proneness models across object-oriented software projects. IEEE Trans. Softw. Eng. **28**(7), 706–720 (2002)
5. Cabral, G.G., Minku, L.L., Shihab, E., Mujahid, S.: Class imbalance evolution and verification latency in just-in-time software defect prediction. In: 2019 IEEE/ACM 41st International Conference on Software Engineering (ICSE), pp. 666–676 (2019). https://doi.org/10.1109/ICSE.2019.00076
6. Catolino, G., Di Nucci, D., Ferrucci, F.: Cross-project just-in-time bug prediction for mobile apps: an empirical assessment. In: 2019 IEEE/ACM 6th International Conference on Mobile Software Engineering and Systems (MOBILESoft), pp. 99–110 (2019). https://doi.org/10.1109/MOBILESoft.2019.00023
7. Eken, B., Tosun, A.: Investigating the performance of personalized models for software defect prediction. J. Syst. Softw. **181**, 111038 (2021)
8. Erika, C.C.A., Ochimizu, K.: Towards logistic regression models for predicting fault-prone code across software projects. In: Proceedings of ESEM 2009, pp. 460–463. IEEE (2009)
9. He, P., Li, B., Liu, X., Chen, J., Ma, Y.: An empirical study on software defect prediction with a simplified metric set. Inf. Softw. Technol. **59**, 170–190 (2015)
10. He, Z., Peters, F., Menzies, T., Yang, Y.: Learning from open-source projects: an empirical study on defect prediction. In: Proceedings of ESEM 2013, pp. 45–54. IEEE (2013)
11. Herbold, S.: Training data selection for cross-project defect prediction. In: Proceedings of PROMISE 2013, pp. 6:1–6:10. ACM (2013)
12. Herbold, S.: CrossPare: a tool for benchmarking cross-project defect predictions. In: Proceedings of ASEW 2015, pp. 90–96. IEEE (2015)
13. Hosseini, S., Turhan, B., Gunarathna, D.: A systematic literature review and meta-analysis on cross project defect prediction. IEEE Trans. Softw. Eng. **45**(2), 111–147 (2019)
14. Huang, Q., Xia, X., Lo, D.: Revisiting supervised and unsupervised models for effort-aware just-in-time defect prediction. Empir. Softw. Eng. **24**(5), 2823–2862 (2018). https://doi.org/10.1007/s10664-018-9661-2
15. Jiang, T., Tan, L., Kim, S.: Personalized defect prediction. In: Proceedings of International Conference on Automated Software Engineering, pp. 279–289 (2013)
16. Kamei, Y., Fukushima, T., McIntosh, S., Yamashita, K., Ubayashi, N., Hassan, A.E.: Studying just-in-time defect prediction using cross-project models. Empir. Softw. Eng. **21**(5), 2072–2106 (2015). https://doi.org/10.1007/s10664-015-9400-x
17. Kamei, Y., et al.: A large-scale empirical study of just-in-time quality assurance. IEEE Trans. Softw. Eng. **39**(6), 757–773 (2013). https://doi.org/10.1109/TSE.2012.70

18. Kamei, Y., Shihab, E.: Defect prediction: accomplishments and future challenges. In: Proceedings of International Conference on Software Analysis, Evolution and Reengineering, pp. 33–45 (2016). https://doi.org/10.1109/SANER.2016.56
19. Khoshgoftaar, T.M., Rebours, P., Seliya, N.: Software quality analysis by combining multiple projects and learners. Softw. Qual. J. **17**(1), 25–49 (2009)
20. Krishna, R., Menzies, T., Fu, W.: Too much automation? The bellwether effect and its implications for transfer learning. In: Proceedings of International Conference on Automated Software Engineering, pp. 122–131 (2016)
21. Li, W., Zhang, W., Jia, X., Huang, Z.: Effort-aware semi-supervised just-in-time defect prediction. Inf. Softw. Technol. **126**, 106364 (2020). https://doi.org/10.1016/j.infsof.2020.106364
22. Ma, Y., Luo, G., Zeng, X., Chen, A.: Transfer learning for cross-company software defect prediction. Inf. Softw. Technol. **54**(3), 248–256 (2012)
23. McIntosh, S., Kamei, Y.: Are fix-inducing changes a moving target? A longitudinal case study of just-in-time defect prediction. IEEE Trans. Softw. Eng. **44**(5), 412–428 (2018). https://doi.org/10.1109/TSE.2017.2693980
24. Menzies, T., Greenwald, J., Frank, A.: Data mining static code attributes to learn defect predictors. IEEE Trans. Softw. Eng. **33**(1), 2–13 (2007)
25. Menzies, T., Butcher, A., Marcus, A., Zimmermann, T., Cok, D.: Local versus global models for effort estimation and defect prediction. In: Proceedings of ASE 2011, pp. 343–351. IEEE (2011)
26. Nam, J., Kim, S.: CLAMI: defect prediction on unlabeled datasets. In: Proceedings of ASE 2015, pp. 452–463. IEEE (2015)
27. Nam, J., Pan, S.J., Kim, S.: Transfer defect learning. In: Proceedings of ICSE 2013, pp. 382–391. IEEE (2013)
28. Panichella, A., Oliveto, R., De Lucia, A.: Cross-project defect prediction models: L'Union fait la force. In: Proceedings of CSMR-WCRE 2014, pp. 164–173. IEEE (2014)
29. Peters, F., Menzies, T.: Privacy and utility for defect prediction: experiments with MORPH. In: Proceedings of ICSE 2012, pp. 189–199. IEEE (2012)
30. Peters, F., Menzies, T., Gong, L., Zhang, H.: Balancing privacy and utility in cross-company defect prediction. IEEE Trans. Softw. Eng. **39**(8), 1054–1068 (2013)
31. Peters, F., Menzies, T., Layman, L.: LACE2: better privacy-preserving data sharing for cross project defect prediction. In: Proceedings of ICSE 2015, pp. 801–811. IEEE (2015)
32. Rahman, F., Devanbu, P.: Ownership, experience and defects: a fine-grained study of authorship. In: Proceedings of International Conference on Software Engineering, pp. 491–500 (2011)
33. Ryu, D., Choi, O., Baik, J.: Value-cognitive boosting with a support vector machine for cross-project defect prediction. Empir. Softw. Eng. **21**(1), 43–71 (2014). https://doi.org/10.1007/s10664-014-9346-4
34. Ryu, D., Jang, J.I., Baik, J.: A hybrid instance selection using nearest-neighbor for cross-project defect prediction. J. Comput. Sci. Technol. **30**(5), 969–980 (2015)
35. Schröter, A., Zimmermann, T., Premraj, R., Zeller, A.: Where do bugs come from? SIGSOFT Softw. Eng. Notes **31**(6) (2006)
36. Tabassum, S., Minku, L.L., Feng, D., Cabral, G.G., Song, L.: An investigation of cross-project learning in online just-in-time software defect prediction. In: Proceedings of International Conference on Software Engineering, New York, NY, USA, pp. 554–565 (2020). https://doi.org/10.1145/3377811.3380403

37. Tantithamthavorn, C., McIntosh, S., Hassan, A.E., Matsumoto, K.: An empirical comparison of model validation techniques for defect prediction models. IEEE Trans. Softw. Eng. **43**(1), 1–18 (2017)
38. Turhan, B., Menzies, T., Bener, A.B., Di Stefano, J.: On the relative value of cross-company and within-company data for defect prediction. Empir. Softw. Eng. **14**(5), 540–578 (2009)
39. Wan, Z., Xia, X., Hassan, A.E., Lo, D., Yin, J., Yang, X.: Perceptions, expectations, and challenges in defect prediction. IEEE Trans. Softw. Eng. **46**(11), 1241–1266 (2020). https://doi.org/10.1109/TSE.2018.2877678
40. Watanabe, S., Kaiya, H., Kaijiri, K.: Adapting a fault prediction model to allow inter language reuse. In: Proceedings of PROMISE 2008, pp. 19–24. ACM (2008)
41. Xia, X., Lo, D., Wang, X., Yang, X.: Collective personalized change classification with multiobjective search. IEEE Trans. Reliab. **65**(4), 1810–1829 (2016)
42. Yang, X., Lo, D., Xia, X., Zhang, Y., Sun, J.: Deep learning for just-in-time defect prediction. In: 2015 IEEE International Conference on Software Quality, Reliability and Security, pp. 17–26 (2015). https://doi.org/10.1109/QRS.2015.14
43. Yang, X., Lo, D., Xia, X., Sun, J.: TLEL: a two-layer ensemble learning approach for just-in-time defect prediction. Inf. Softw. Technol. **87**, 206–220 (2017)
44. Zhang, Y., Lo, D., Xia, X., Sun, J.: An empirical study of classifier combination for cross-project defect prediction. In: Proceedings of COMPSAC 2015, pp. 264–269. IEEE (2015)
45. Zhang, Y., Lo, D., Xia, X., Sun, J.: Combined classifier for cross-project defect prediction: an extended empirical study. Front. Comp. Sci. **12**(2), 280–296 (2018). https://doi.org/10.1007/s11704-017-6015-y
46. Zhou, Y., et al.: How far we have progressed in the journey? An examination of cross-project defect prediction. ACM Trans. Softw. Eng. Methodol. **27**(1), 1–51 (2018)
47. Zhu, K., Zhang, N., Ying, S., Zhu, D.: Within-project and cross-project just-in-time defect prediction based on denoising autoencoder and convolutional neural network. IET Softw. **14**(3), 185–195 (2020). https://doi.org/10.1049/iet-sen.2019.0278
48. Zimmermann, T., Nagappan, N., Gall, H., Giger, E., Murphy, B.: Cross-project defect prediction: a large scale experiment on data vs. domain vs. process. In: Proceedings of ESEC/FSE 2009, pp. 91–100. ACM (2009)

A/B Testing in the Small: An Empirical Exploration of Controlled Experimentation on Internal Tools

Amalia Paulsson[1,2], Per Runeson[1(✉)] ⓘ, and Rasmus Ros[1] ⓘ

[1] Lund University, Lund, Sweden
paulssonamalia@gmail.com, {per.runeson,rasmus.ros}@cs.lth.se
[2] Netlight, Stockholm, Sweden

Abstract. Previous research on A/B testing and continuous experimentation has mostly focused on large-scale settings with company-external customers. However, work efficiency and satisfaction for company co-workers may be highly related to internal tools and their fit-for-use. In this study, we therefore explore A/B testing for online services exclusively used by company co-workers. We A/B tested two versions of Customer Admin, a tool that helps 34 500 IKEA co-workers to interact with customer data. The study comprised i) stakeholder interviews to understand objectives and phrase the experimentation goals, and ii) A/B test execution where data was collected and processed from approximately 350 users for 33 days. While the user base is relatively large for this internal system, the primary metric data collected was too scarce to allow distinction between the two versions. However, secondary metrics and a user questionnaire suggest that the users are more efficient in the new menu design and that the users prefer it to the old. We conclude that A/B testing requires lots of data, making it less feasible for internal users, also for large, global organizations. Thus, we propose combining quantitative and qualitative evaluation of internal tools and propose further research on how to adapt A/B testing for smaller-scale settings.

1 Introduction

The interest for data-driven development is growing globally and A/B testing is a commonly used methodology for large-scale experimentation in the Internet industry [1]. An A/B test is a setup of a controlled experiment—an experiment used to find probable causal relationships, by randomly splitting subjects between versions and instrumenting behavior to determine some evaluation metrics [2]. The value of A/B tests lays in insights into the actual user behaviour, which helps software developers to quickly evaluate design ideas and expand their knowledge about their users.

Even though large actors in the internet industry such as Microsoft, Facebook and Google started applying A/B testing a decade ago, it is still considered to be

© The Author(s), under exclusive license to Springer Nature Switzerland AG 2022
D. Taibi et al. (Eds.): PROFES 2022, LNCS 13709, pp. 449–463, 2022.
https://doi.org/10.1007/978-3-031-21388-5_31

in an early stage of development [3]. Research and practice in online controlled experimentation focuses on external websites and tools, i.e., commercial services where the users are customers to the company, counted in millions, enabling experimentation with statistically significant outcomes. Meanwhile there are multiple types of services that are exclusively used internally, aiming to assist co-workers in managing their tasks. These internal tools evolve continuously and can be critical to the company's operational success, particularly as they contribute to the co-workers (lack of) work efficiency and satisfaction. However, the number of users is much smaller, even for large companies, being questioned for such usage, although there is limited empirical evidence for such claims.

Therefore we explore the feasibility of using A/B testing in the development of internal tools. The overall research question was: *How can A/B testing be effectively applied to the development of internal tools?* We aimed to provide "field-tested and grounded" exemplars of how the problem can be solved [4].

We launched a case study with the multinational retail company IKEA on their internal customer administration tool, called Customer Admin (CA) [5]. We focused on the start menu of the tool, evaluating whether a new implementation would be better for the co-workers, providing more efficient customer service.

Data were collected through interviews with stakeholders to understand the operational conditions and guide the set-up of a feasible set of metrics for experimentation. Next, operational data were collected during 33 days from approximately 350 out of the global 34 500 users in an A/B test, where the original start menu of the CA tool was compared to a redesigned version. The overall evaluation metric was time spent per customer errand.

The contribution of this paper is a thorough exploration of A/B testing for a typical internal user admin tool, with a reasonably large user base. We conclude from the study that the collected data set was not sufficient to statistically reject the hypotheses and thus we propose certain changes to the approach for further application of A/B testing in the small.

2 Background

2.1 A/B Testing and Continuous Experimentation

In essence, an A/B test is an experimentally controlled comparison between two versions of a software, the control (A) version, which usually is the default version, and the treatment (B), which contains a change [6]. This method is often applied to evaluate software updates that are believed to have a positive impact on user behavior, exposing one randomly assigned user group to the existing version and another group to the new version—i.e. the control and the treatment respectively. The primary aim of A/B testing in decision making is to bring insights into the real-world user experience through a direct feedback loop with the users [1]. Giving developers access to continuous flows of data from this feedback loop increases their ability to detect and fix problems, as well as simplifying code and removing unnecessary features [7].

Fabijan et al. [8] defined an A/B testing process, divided into three phases:

- *Ideation*—creating a hypothesis related to some metrics that efficiently encapsulate a relevant problem.
- *Design & Execution*—setting up the experiment and collect data.
- *Analysis & Learning*—interpreting the results and drawing conclusions on how the different versions perform.

Continuous experimentation (CE) is an approach to software development, in which A/B tests are integrated. Fagerholm et al. [9] defined a comprehensive CE framework model, named the RIGHT model. It displays the roles, tasks, technical infrastructure, and information needed to run CE at large scale and integrate it with the development cycle. Fitzgerald and Stol [10] describe many more continuous practices that encompass not only development and operations (DevOps), but also business strategy (BizDev). Ros [11] recently presented an empirically based theory on factors that affect continuous experimentation (FACE), linking DevOps and BizDev aspects together.

In software engineering, a controlled experiment is usually used to tweak the user-facing parts of the software or to validate a new product feature with user data [3]. The metric in the experiment can be anything from the user experience (e.g. clicks), software stack (e.g. duration of a request), or sales process (e.g. conversion rate of potential customers).

2.2   Related Work on Smaller Scale A/B Testing

In their systematic literature review of controlled experimentation [3], Auer, Ros et al. conclude that the research on infrastructure for experimentation primarily focuses on large-scale applications within large organizations, e.g. Microsoft [12]. They further advice that "it should not restrict the community's focus on large scale applications only. The application of continuous experimentation within smaller organizations has many open research questions."

In a business-to-business (B2B) setting, Rissanen and Münch [13] analyzed the development process of two different software products in a medium-sized software company to examine whether CE can be applied in B2B cases. They anticipate three aspects of challenges: technical, customer, and organizational challenges. They advice that major software changes should be avoided to not jeopardize the user experience. Additionally, they stress the organizational challenge to adapt to the experimental mindset and rely on quantitative data rather than opinions when making design decisions.

In another case study Kevic et al. [14] characterize the experimentation process through observation of 21 220 online experiments with Bing—Microsoft's search engine. They discover that experiments can slow down the deployment cycle and argue that practice should focus on identifying experiments worth running and making sure they run smoothly. The efficiency can be increased by tailoring experiments to the characteristics of the code changes, i.e. not phrasing a hypothesis for every little change. Even though their study issues the controlled experimentation method in a large-scale and mature product, these findings would reasonably be further applicable in the context of internal tools.

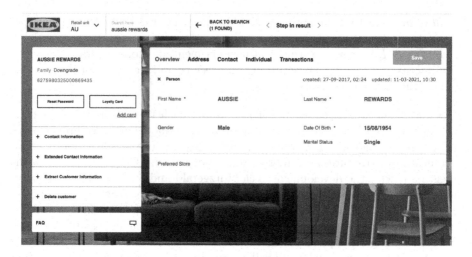

Fig. 1. The original menu design assigned to the control group (A)

2.3   The Case

Customer Admin (CA) is a tool with a user base of 34 500 IKEA co-workers, in the Customer Support Center (CSC) and on the store floor, through which they can interact with customer data. CA consists of an API and a UI and has been created by IKEA Digital's Customer Engagement Team, organized within the INGKA Holding B.V, which is operating close to 400 IKEA stores in more than 30 markets. This project targets the part of CA managing private customers.

CA allows the co-worker to search for a customer, get access to customer information, contact details, transactions with the customer etc. Depending on their role of reader, editor or admin, the user may or may not change and delete information. Figure 1 shows the original version (A) of the start menu and Fig. 2 shows the new version (B), which are compared in our A/B testing.

The A version has five navigation buttons in a top menu and Overview as the default tab. The B version menu displays six navigation buttons in the center section, including a link to the FAQ page. The first four tabs of the A version lead to the same view as the Purchase, Rewards details, Order history and Interactions details, respectively, of the B version.

3   Research Approach

To answer the research question on effectively applying A/B testing to internal tools, we conducted a case study of a proof of concept A/B test implementation in CA, providing a practical example and a base for discussion. The A/B testing process follows the three steps defined by Fabijan et al. [8]: *ideation, design & execution* and *analysis & learning*.

We frame the research in the design science paradigm [4], with its main constituents of *problem conceptualization, solution design*, and *empirical validation*,

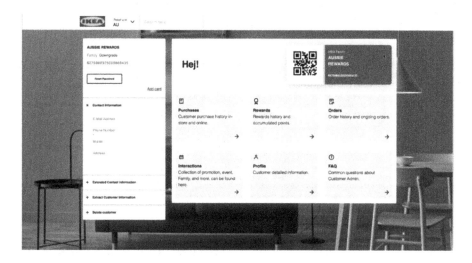

Fig. 2. The test menu design assigned to the treatment group (B)

largely mapping to the three A/B testing steps. Figure 3 depicts an overview of the research, in a visual abstract format, adapted from Storey et al. [15]

The technological rule under study is "to learn about the users of internal tools, apply A/B testing". The problem conceptualization is based on interviews with users of the CA tool, understanding user behaviour and defining evaluation metrics. The proposed solution was to implement established A/B testing practices in the small-scale internal tool case context. The solution was evaluated by execution the A/B tests and analyzing the outcomes.

The study was initiated from the office of INGKA Holding B.V. in Malmö, Sweden. Their staff implemented the versions of the tools. The first author conducted the interviews, implemented the monitoring tools, and performed the analysis. The second and third authors guided the work.

3.1 Ideation: Interviews to Define Goals and Metrics

Firstly interviews were held with six stakeholders in the Swedish office, 1–2) Data Management Leader, 3) a Process Specialist & Sales Coordinator, 4) a Database Specialist, 5) an Engineering Manager, and 6) a Loyalty Leader, all with a connection to CA, either as a user or developer. The interviews laid the groundwork for forming a hypothesis that addressed the actual goal of a new design element. Interview guides are available in a technical report [5].

The interviews were analyzed using Gioia et al.'s three-step model [16] of qualitative analysis, defining 1st order concepts of answers and statements, 2nd order themes with a phrasal description, condensed from 1st order concepts, and finally aggregate dimension from 2nd order themes into overarching statements. The final analysis results are aggregate dimension to be turned into metrics for the A/B testing.

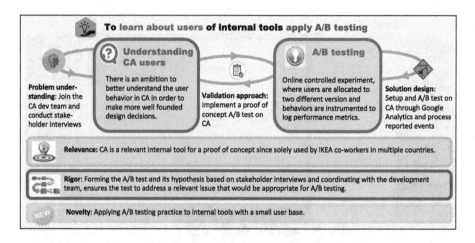

Fig. 3. Visual abstract for the A/B testing for internal tools from a design science perspective.

3.2 Design and Execution

Thereafter the experiment was designed, comparing the two versions in Figs. 1 and 2. For practical reasons, the experimentation was limited to users of the CA client for the Australian market, comprising approximately 350 users. The selection of market was made in agreement with product management and development team members. Even through a larger user group would create more generous amounts of data, it was considered more cautious to conduct the proof of concept test on a small scale. In line with organizational procedures, the Data Management Leader in Australia was informed about the test and the new menu design and communicated the launch to all Australian co-workers.

For each visit, users of the CA Client were randomly exposed to each of the versions of the start menu, 50% on the control and the treatment group, respectively. First, an A/A test was executed during five days to validate the A/B testing platform. Then the A/B experiment was executed during 33 days, given by the time constraints for this study.

The test was monitored using Google Analytics, a web analytics service that denotes tracking website traffic in realtime. The aggregated data was analyzed through post-collection processing script, written in Python, that calculated the evaluation metrics and associated statistics.

3.3 Analysis and Learning

Errands were extracted, containing all events triggered between entering and leaving a customer profile. If no clicks were made between entering and leaving a customer profile, that errand was discarded, assuming that the user had entered wrong customer profile. Each evaluation metric was calculated per errand and 90% confidence intervals were calculated for respective metric. In this project the number of samples and consequently also the variance was different in the control and the treatment. Thus Welch's t-test was applied [17] with a significance level of 10%. This relatively low level was selected due to low traffic, which gave reasons to presume small data volumes.

The data processing script was written and used in an A/A test when all users were still using the original menu. This dry run facilitated testing the script, detecting bugs and other systematic failures. Moreover the standard deviation of respective metric was derived, from which the minimum sample size was calculated as advised by Kohavi et al. [6]: $n = 16\sigma^2/\Delta^2$; where n is the number of observations in each variant, σ is the standard deviation of the of the metric, and Δ is the absolute change to be detected.

4   Results

In this Section, data gathered from the interviews to define goals and metrics for the A/B testing are presented in Sect. 4.1. The data from the A/B test are presented for respective metric in Sect. 4.2. Finally, the hypothesis evaluation is reported in Sect. 4.3.

4.1   Goals and Metrics

The interviews were analyzed as described in Sect. 3.1 , resulting in overall goals for the use of CA. The analysis towards the overall goal is showed in full detail in Fig. 4, while all the four resulting dimensions are summarized in Table 1.

Informant statements addressing the overall objective and purpose of CA are compiled into *1st order concepts*, as shown in Fig. 4. In the *2nd order themes*, three main components were derived from these informant statements: i) making customer data visible and manageable for the co-worker, ii) providing the co-worker with an instrument to manage customer requests, and iii) that it should

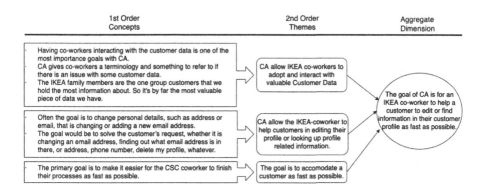

Fig. 4. First order concepts, second order themes and aggregate dimension of the overall goal of CA [16]

Table 1. Dimensions of CA, emerging from the interview analysis

Dimension	Description
Overall goal	The goal of CA is for an IKEA co-worker to help a customer to edit or find information in their customer profile as fast as possible
Use of CA	The most common use case is for a co-worker in the CSC to first locate the right customer, then to look up or update some profile data, that can either be customer information or login credentials
User friendliness	Prioritize and display the most important information will shorten the time spent on an errand, which will improve the usability of CA The "save changes" pop up is a good indication of a completed information update. However, it is not an indication of that the information was correctly updated
Time allocation	An errand usually takes 6 min. Nevertheless there are factors that impact on the time, such as chatty customers or customer search complications

support the co-workers' time efficiency. Lastly, these components are summed in one *aggregate dimension*. All four dimensions emerging from the analysis are shown in Table 1, namely *overall goal, use of CA, user friendliness*, and *time allocation*. The analysis is reported in full detail in the technical report [5].

The interviews revealed *user efficiency* as the main objective of the tool, i.e. its ability to assist the co-workers in finishing their respective tasks as fast as possible. Moreover, clarity and simplicity was stressed, making it intuitive for the co-workers to find what they are looking for. From the insights created during the interviews, a hypothesis was phrased for the proof of concept implementation:

"We predict that a new start menu for co-workers in the Australian market will shorten the average time spent per customer errand because it makes the orientation in Customer Admin easier to comprehend. We will know this is true when we see a decreasing time difference from entering a customer profile and saving a change".

Based on the interviews, a set of metrics were defined to be collected during experimentation, in collaboration with the development team:

- Metric of interest: *Time to save* (sec)
- Key Metrics: *Saved Changes, Time per Errand* (sec), and *Clicks per Errand*

In addition, 25 additional Secondary Metrics were collected on specific types of clicks, which are available in the technical report [5].

Although the time of finding information is quantifiable, it is not necessarily easy to automatically identify at a user click level what overall activities the users perform. For example, as observed from the interviews about the user friendliness dimension in Table 1 the "save changes" pop up is a good indication of a completed update sequence, but it does not indicate a *correct* update.

Secondary metrics, such as page views, average time spent on page and bounce rate, were all automatically tracked and displayed in Google Analytics (GA). Clicks on specific buttons and timestamps of those clicks, however, was not available and had to be customized through different tags in Google Tag Manager (GTM). Similar to the tracking configuration in GA, a tracking code was added into the source code using react-gtm. In GTM, each tag was associated with a trigger that was activated on a specific button. Once a tag was triggered, an event was created in GA.

4.2 A/B Test Data and Statistics

During the 33 days of A/B testing, 14 421 customer errands were identified. Out of those, 396 involved a change to a customer profile, i.e. 12 changes per day.

The null hypotheses that there are no difference between treatment and control were tested, using Welch's t-test [17]. Descriptive statistics and p-values for respective metric are presented in Table 2. The metrics that are significantly differing at a 90% confidence level are marked in bold.

Table 2. Mean values and 90% confidence intervals on the A/B test metrics

Metric name	Mean control (A)	Mean treatment (B)	p-value
Time to save change (sec)	89.8 ± 14.0	90.4 ± 31.4	0.488
Saved Changes	0.0289 ± 0.0032	0.0339 ± 0.0080	0.167
Time per Errand (sec)	232 ± 8	186 ± 15	**0.099**
Clicks per Errand	8.33 ± 0.19	9.03 ± 0.39	**0.00418**

4.3 Hypothesis Evaluation

In the control version (A), it took on average 89.8 s for a user to save a change in a newly entered customer profile, compared to 90.4 s in the treatment version (B). Since the p-value of 0.488 suggest low probability of them differing we can not reject the null hypothesis. Moreover, the average time spent per errand was 232 s in the control (A) and 186 s in the treatment (B), and the average number of clicks per errand was 8.33 in the control and 9.03 in the treatment. Thus, the total time per errand was reduced, but the time to save was slightly increased.

The share of saved changes was higher for the new version. The control (A) had on average a change saved during 2.89% of the visits. In the treatment (B) a change was saved during 3.39% of the visits. Whether this is induced by the changed design cannot be assessed from the collected data.

The main reason for the lack of significance is the limited size of the experiment. Using Kohavi et al.'s minimum sample calculation for experiments [6], the experiment should have to run for 130 days, under the observed frequency of customer errands (12 per day):

$$n = \frac{16\sigma^2}{\Delta^2} = \frac{16 * 99^2}{10^2} = 1568$$

where n is the number of observations in each variant, σ is the standard deviation of the of the metric (here $\sigma = 99$), and Δ is the absolute change to be detected (here we set $\Delta = 10$ s).

To analyze the influence of potential learning effect of the new version, we deployed an Augmented Dickey Fuller (ADF) test. ADF is a unit root test used for determining stationarity in time series data [18]. The ADF tests gave 0 in p-value for both the control and the treatment and hence there is no sign of non-stationarity that would indicate a user learning effect being present.

5   Discussion

In this section we discuss insights from the study, comparing small-scale and large-scale experimentation, related to the CA tool (Sect. 5.1) and to A/B testing on internal tools in general (Sect. 5.2). Recommendations for further implementation and research are discussed in Sect. 5.3 and threats to the validity of our findings in Sect. 5.4.

5.1   Customer Admin User Behavior Insights

As seen in the results, increased time to update a customer profile in the new menu was not statistically significant. On the contrary, the time difference per errand where the time stops whenever the user has left the customer profile (also without saving), indicates that the *new* menu design (B) has shortened the time spent per errand on average 46 s. Here, the standard deviations are significantly smaller due to more use cases, resulting in a bigger sample size.

The observation in the *Use of CA* dimension in Table 1, also indicates that looking up profile data is a more common use case than updating profile data. Thus, the *User friendliness* dimension of Table 1 of prioritizing and displaying the most important information first, argues for the new menu design were those tabs are displayed on the landing page.

Like in large-scale experimentation, capturing the phenomena in quantitative metrics is not easy. The combination of qualitative data from the interviews is needed to get insights, which cannot be gained from the experiment only, particularly if it does not provide significant results.

5.2   A/B Testing Challenges

Challenges encountered during the experiment obviously relate to the traffic flow and data volume. Further, we discuss potential sources of error in the data collection. Thirdly, the network effect across participants, observed in A/B tests in general, is even further emphasized for internal experiments.

Traffic Flow and Data Volume. The low flow of traffic – approximately 12 collected errands per day where the 350 observed users have saved a change – leads to insignificant hypothesis evaluation. In comparison, according to Statista[1] Facebook had on average 1.85 billion daily active users in 2020, Amazon had over 2.44 billion visitors in 2020, and Netflix over 207 million subscribers in the first quarter of 2021. These numbers are hugely exceeding the amount of co-workers at IKEA and potential users of CA. Therefore A/B tests of internal tools will not reach the same level of significance as for external websites. Still the need for understanding the impact of a proposed change remains.

The abundant traffic in external tools allows for collecting enough data in only a few days, unlike for internal tools where it can take months to get a sufficient result. This duration places the users' experiences into jeopardy during the execution phase. It comprises both having the users in a potentially poorer UI and giving the user an ambiguous experience, alternating between two versions.

An option, more viable for internal tools, is to assign co-workers randomly to A and B versions for the full experimental period, rather than for each use of the tool. That would reduce the ambiguity and enable further statistical analysis on learning effects.

Sources of Error in Data Collection. Apart from the insufficient amount of collected data, the quality of the data varied. As observed in the *time allocation* dimension in Table 1, there are multiple factors affecting the time it takes to manage an incoming customer request. These factors are external and cannot be mitigated by the design of the UI. Even though they do not distort the average values, they increase the variance of the test result.

Secondly, as concluded in the *User friendliness* dimension in Table 1, the "save changes" are not necessarily an indication of that the user successfully finished the task of updating a customer detail. This should not affect the A and B versions differently, yet there are reasons to believe that the calculated average time to save a change may be an underestimation for both versions.

Finally there is the uncertainty about whether the user has even located the right customer. As seen in the *Use of CA* dimension in Table 1 occasionally the user does not find the right customer at once. The consequence of this is that those errands presumably take shorter time than an errand were the user lookup or update information, and thereby shorten the average errand time.

These potential data collection errors further stress the need for triangulating the analysis with qualitative understanding of the experimental context.

Internal Tools and the Network Effect. Another challenge that generates a source of error is the users' awareness of being tested. In accordance with IKEA's working process, concerned co-workers have to be briefed about the new version before launch. Even though they were not informed of the test's purpose and how performance was measured, the users' awareness might affect the result.

---

[1] https://www.statista.com.

Since the users are very familiar with the CA tool, they will notice any changes and might inadvertently modify their behavior.

Since co-workers in the same Customer Support Center work in the same office building and inevitably collaborate, the test users influence each other, which violates the stable unit treatment value assumption (SUTVA) [19]. Saveski et al. [19] claim that in an A/B test the treatment should only have an impact on the users being treated, not other users that are in connection with them. In alignment with Backstrom et al. [20] the co-workers' influence on each other would be described through the term "Network Effect" which creates an inter-dependence in the random sample, violating the assumption of independence.

This effect is present also in large-scale A/B testing, but the proportional impact of a connection between two users is much smaller, and fewer users have joint networking opportunities, compared to co-workers within a company.

Tools for Internal Vs. External A/B Testing. When introducing A/B testing on CA as an internal tool, the ideation phase outlined the fundamentals and objectives of CA. To serve the goal in Fig. 4—to shorten the time spent per customer interaction—most metrics of interest were about *minimizing* time or the number of clicks between two specific events. Plausibly, this principle applies for internal tools in general as the users' i.e. co-workers' time efficiency is a matter of interest from a profit perspective.

In contrast, available web analytic services and test tools, e.g. Google Optimize, are designed for the objectives of external websites and their inverted optimization problems, such as *maximizing* pageviews, subscriptions, and conversions, which are common metrics for publishing and e-commerce websites. The process of setting up an A/B test for internal tools is therefore not as straight forward as in the external domain.

5.3   Recommendations

Based on the observations from the case study, we discuss recommended actions to mitigate the identified problems for A/B testing of internal tools.

Expand Data Source. In order to get better significance, the user group could be expanded to include more markets. The enhanced data flow would both increase the significance levels and shorten the execution time needed.

However, there are risks in exposing a larger group of users to the test. If A/B testing behavior becomes more common, the ambiguity of alternating between two UI versions will disturb the user experience. For that reason, it would be sensible to select a more local scope for the market wide tests. On the other hand, a local scope would likely generate a smaller impact on the users' behavior and thereby make it even harder to detect significant differences. To mitigate the alternation problem, we recommend assigning co-workers to A and B groups for the duration of the experiment, but still larger user groups are needed.

Specify Insensitive Metrics. Another way to respond to the scarce data is to include more frequent use cases, for example, the use case where the coworker looks up some customer information. As shown in Table 2, the key metric time per errand provided a comparable measurement with high statistical significance.

As described in Sect. 5.2, time is a unit that is sensitive to disturbance of other factors that are not a part of the UI. Hence, the number of clicks to finish an errand would be a more suitable unit to quantify the co-workers' efficiency. Yet, attention should be payed to that the number of clicks does not take into account the effort the user puts into finding the data field or button, which certainly is a factor in the coworkers' efficiency. A similar problem can be found in external A/B tests of e-commerce websites, where clicks are used as proxies for complete purchases, which is the ultimate goal for the A/B test.

Streamline Setup. In order to minimize the effort and hence the cost of executing the test, the setup should be built so that redundancy is avoided. Foremost it is about choosing web analytic services that efficiently track the data of interest and forward it to platforms and tools that are already deployed and used.

Besides, the analysis scripts should extract as generic metrics as possible that quantify the goal of most UX redesigns. In this case the time spent per errand and the number of clicks could be considered usable metrics in succeeding A/B tests, and hence it is in ambition to reuse the script in the future.

5.4 Threats to Validity

This work contains recommendations on applying A/B tests to the domain of internal tools. The validity of the recommendations is contingent on that the experimentation process is implemented correctly. This internal threat to validity is mitigated by following established procedures for experimentation [6,8]. It is possible that further refinement of the applied statistical methods (such as segmenting the user base or using different metrics) would generate different results in the experiment. Though such refinements requires an ongoing process improvement through conducting plenty of experiments. As such, the question of applicability remains open.

The external validity of our findings is related to the size of the organization. IKEA is a huge corporation, while our study scope is set to 350 co-workers in one unit in one country. Our quantitative findings are relevant for organizations or branches of similar size, while we for the specific case company could have extended the population to more countries or departments.

6   Conclusion and Further Work

We explored *how A/B testing can be effectively applied to the development of internal tools.* We launched an A/B test of two versions of an internal Customer Admin tool. We could not statistically assess the difference with respect to the chosen metric, although the qualitative data helped understand more about the user needs and preferences. Our main finding is problems with scarce data, due to relatively low traffic as a challenge when A/B testing internal tools. Still, the A/B test *helps learn about users of internal tools*, and thus *A/B test can be a recommended practice*.

In order to mitigate the consequences of low traffic, we propose larger test groups and more frequently triggered metrics for evaluation. Moreover sources of error in the used metrics were discussed and the conflict between having independent test users for the sake of statistics and maintaining a coherent working culture where co-workers communicate and collaborate. We also identify that the combination with qualitative data is even more important for A/B testing in the small.

More research is needed before sufficiently validating the technological rule on A/B testing's applicability in the internal domain. Focus should be kept on enhancing rigour by gathering more practical case studies on other types of internal tools. Further, the combination of quantitative and qualitative user studies should be further explored.

Acknowledgment. Thanks to INGKA Holding B.V. (IKEA) employees, Joakim Månsson, Magnus Pettersson and Customer Admin team. The 2nd and 3rd authors were funded by the Wallenberg AI, Autonomous Systems and Software Program (WASP).

References

1. King, R., Churchill, E., Tan, C.: Designing with Data. O'Reilly Media Inc, USA (2017)
2. Kohavi, R., Longbotham, R.: Online controlled experiments and A/B testing. In: Sammut, C., Webb, G.I. (eds.) Encyclopedia of Machine Learning and Data Mining. Springer, Boston, MA. https://doi.org/10.1007/978-1-4899-7687-1_891
3. Auer, F., Ros, R., Kaltenbrunner, L., Runeson, P., Felderer, M.: Controlled experimentation in continuous experimentation: knowledge and challenges. Inf. Softw. Technol. **134**, 106551 (2021)
4. Runeson, P., Engström, E., Storey, M.-A.: The design science paradigm as a frame for empirical software engineering. In: Contemporary Empirical Methods in Software Engineering, pp. 127–147. Springer, Cham (2020). https://doi.org/10.1007/978-3-030-32489-6_5
5. Paulsson, A.: A/B testing customer admin - an empirical validation of controlled experimentation of internal tools, Lund University, Master Thesis LU-CS-EX: 2021–18 (2021)
6. Kohavi, R., Longbotham, R., Sommerfield, D., Henne, R.M.: Controlled experiments on the web: survey and practical guide. Data Min. Knowl. Disc. **18**(1), 140–181 (2008)
7. Fabijan, A., Olsson, H.H., Bosch, J.: Time to say 'good bye': feature lifecycle. In: 42th Euromicro Conference on Software Engineering and Advanced Applications (SEAA), pp. 9–16 (2016)
8. Fabijan, A., Dmitriev, P., Olsson, H.H., Bosch, J.: The online controlled experiment lifecycle. IEEE Softw. **37**(2), 60–67 (2020)

9. Fagerholm, F., Guinea, A.S., Mäenpää, H., Münch, J.: The right model for continuous experimentation. J. Syst. Softw. **123**, 292–305 (2017)
10. Fitzgerald, B., Stol, K.-J.: Continuous software engineering: a roadmap and agenda. J. Syst. Softw. **123**, 176–189 (2017)
11. Ros, R.: Understanding and improving continuous experimentation: from A/B testing to continuous software optimization, Ph. D thesis, Lund University, 2022. https://portal.research.lu.se/sv/publications/understanding-and-improving-continuous-experimentation-from-ab-te
12. Gupta, S., Ulanova, L., Bhardwaj, S., Dmitriev, P., Raff, P., Fabijan, A.: The anatomy of a large-scale experimentation platform. In: IEEE International Conference on Software Architecture (ICSA), pp. 1–109 (2018)
13. Rissanen, O., Münch, J.: Continuous experimentation in the B2B domain: a case study. In: IEEE/ACM 2nd International Workshop on Rapid Continuous Software Engineering. IEEE May 2015
14. Kevic, K., Murphy, B., Williams, L., Beckmann, J.: Characterizing experimentation in continuous deployment: A case study on Bing. In: 39th International Conference on Software Engineering: SE in Practice Track (ICSE-SEIP), pp. 123–132. IEEE/ACM (2017)
15. Storey, M.-A., Engström, E., Höst, M., Runeson, P., Bjarnason, E.: Using a visual abstract as a lens for communicating and promoting design science research in software engineering. In: International Symposium on Empirical Software Engineering and Measurement (ESEM), pp. 181–186. IEEE/ACM (2017)
16. Gioia, D.A., Corley, K.G., Hamilton, A.L.: Seeking qualitative rigor in inductive research: Notes on the Gioia methodology. Organ. Res. Methods **16**(1), 15–31 (2013)
17. Ruxton, G.: The unequal variance t-test is an underused alternative to student's t-test and the Mann-Whitney U test. Behav. Ecol. **17**, 04 (2006)
18. Dickey, D.A., Fuller, W.A.: Likelihood ratio statistics for autoregressive time series with a unit root. Econometrica **49**(4), 1057–1072 (1981)
19. Saveski, M., et al.: Detecting network effects: randomizing over randomized experiments. Series KDD 2017, pp. 1027–1035. New York, NY, USA: ACM (2017)
20. Backstrom, L., Kleinberg, J.: Network bucket testing. In: Proceedings of the 20th International Conference on World Wide Web. Series www 2011, pp. 615–624. New York, NY, USA: ACM (2011)

TEP-GNN: Accurate Execution Time Prediction of Functional Tests Using Graph Neural Networks

Hazem Peter Samoaa[1] , Antonio Longa[2(✉)], Mazen Mohamad[1(✉)],
Morteza Haghir Chehreghani[1(✉)], and Philipp Leitner[1(✉)]

[1] Chalmers—University of Gothenburg, Gothenburg, Sweden
{samoaa,mazenm,morteza.chehreghani,philipp.leitner}@chalmers.se
[2] Fondazione Bruno Kessler and University of Trento, Trento, Italy
alonga@fbk.eu

Abstract. Predicting the performance of production code prior to actual execution is known to be highly challenging. In this paper, we propose a predictive model, dubbed TEP-GNN, which demonstrates that high-accuracy performance prediction is possible for the special case of predicting unit test execution times. TEP-GNN uses FA-ASTs, or flow-augmented ASTs, as a graph-based code representation approach, and predicts test execution times using a powerful graph neural network (GNN) deep learning model. We evaluate TEP-GNN using four real-life Java open source programs, based on 922 test files mined from the projects' public repositories. We find that our approach achieves a high Pearson correlation of 0.789, considerable outperforming a baseline deep learning model. Our work demonstrates that FA-ASTs and GNNs are a feasible approach for predicting absolute performance values, and serves as an important intermediary step towards being able to predict the performance of arbitrary code prior to execution.

Keywords: Performance · Software testing · Machine learning

1 Introduction

Performance is a critical quality property of many real-live software systems. Hence, performance modeling and analysis have gradually become an increasingly important part of the software development life-cycle. Unfortunately, predicting the performance of real-life production code is well-known to be a difficult problem – predicting the absolute execution time of applications based on code structure is challenging as it is a function of many factors, including the underlying architecture, the input parameters, and the application's interactions with the operating system [22]. Consequently, works that attempted to predict absolute performance counters (e.g., execution time) for arbitrary applications from source code generally report poor accuracy [19,21].

© The Author(s), under exclusive license to Springer Nature Switzerland AG 2022
D. Taibi et al. (Eds.): PROFES 2022, LNCS 13709, pp. 464–479, 2022.
https://doi.org/10.1007/978-3-031-21388-5_32

However, recent research has shown that predicting performance characteristics is indeed possible in more specialized contexts, via the application of modern machine learning architectures. For example, Guo et al. successfully predict the execution time of a specific untested configuration of a configurable system [6,7], Samoaa and Leitner have shown that the execution time of a benchmark with specific workload configuration can be predicted [24], and Laaber et al. have shown that a categorical classification of benchmarks into high- or low-variability is feasible [12].

In this work, we demonstrate that another context where performance prediction is possible is the prediction of execution times of functional tests. Test execution times are crucial in agile software development and continuous integration. While individual test cases might have short execution times, software products often have thousands of test cases, which makes the total execution time in the build process high. Researchers have been working on solutions to speed up the testing process by optimizing the code or prioritizing test cases [4,11,18,28]. The goal of this study is to provide the developers with predictions of the execution times of their test cases, and consequently giving them an early indication of the time required to run the cases in the build process. We believe that this would support decisions regarding code optimization and test case selection in early stages of the software life-cycle.

Graphs are mathematical structures used to model pairwise relations between objects. A graph can be used to model a wide number of different domains, ranging from biology [9], face-to-face human interactions [17] and software. Indeed, we propose an approach dubbed TEP-GNN (Test Execution Time Prediction using Graph Neural Networks) that makes use of structural features of test cases (the abstract syntax tree, AST). We enrich the AST with various types of edges representing data and control flow. Following Wang and Jin, we refer to this resulting graph as flow-augmented abstract syntax trees (FA-AST) [30]. We use a graph neural network (GNN) model, GraphConv [20], on the resulting FA-ASTs. We train and test our model on a dataset collected from four well-known open source projects hosted on GitHub: *H2 database*[1], a relational database, *RDF4J*[2], a project for handling RDF data, *systemDS*[3], an Apache project to manage the data science life cycle, and finally the Apache remote procedure call library *Dubbo*[4]. As labelled ground truth data, we collect 922 real test execution traces from these projects' publicly available build systems.

We conduct experiments with our TEP-GNN model to answer the following research questions:

- **RQ1:** How accurately can the absolute execution time of a test file consisting of one or multiple test cases be predicted using FA-ASTs and GNNs?

---

[1] https://github.com/h2database/h2database.
[2] https://github.com/eclipse/rdf4j.
[3] https://github.com/apache/systemds.
[4] https://github.com/apache/dubbo.

- **RQ2:** Does our usage of GraphConv improve execution time prediction compared to a baseline using Gated Graph Neural Networks (GGNN), as frequently used in previous software engineering research [1,5]?

Our results show that using TEP-GNN, test execution time can be predicted with a very high prediction accuracy (Pearson correlation of 0.789). Further, we show that our usage of GraphConv indeed improves the model significantly over GGNN. We conclude that test execution times can indeed be predicted using GNN models with high accuracy, even based on performance counters that have been collected "in the wild" by real projects (as opposed to performance measurements collected on a dedicated performance testing machine). The main novelty of our work lies in the application of a rarely used way of graph-encoding source code (FA-AST), combined with a powerful GNN model (GraphConv), to the problem of performance prediction. Even though test cases are shorter and structurally simpler than arbitrary programs, we see our results as an important stepping stone towards the prediction of the performance of arbitrary software systems prior to execution.

2   The TEP-GNN Approach

In this section, we introduce TEP-GNN. We first provide a general overview of the model and discuss the problem addressed in this paper, followed by a detailed discussion of the main components of TEP-GNN (FA-ASTs and the machine learning pipeline based on the GraphConv [20] higher order GNN).

Fig. 1. Schematic overview of the main phases of TEP-GNN.

2.1   Approach Overview

Our goal in this paper is to predict the execution time of test cases based on static code information alone, i.e., without access to prior benchmarking of the test case or dynamic analysis data. The general procedure of our TEP-GNN approach is sketched in Fig. 1. To process a test file, we first parse it into its AST. Next, we build a graph representation (FA-AST) by adding edges representing control and data flow to the AST. We then initialize the embeddings of FA-AST nodes and edges before jointly feeding a vectorized FA-AST into a GNN.

2.2   Problem Definition

Given a test file (source code containing test cases) C_i and the corresponding run-time value X_i (execution time of all test cases in the file), for a set of test files with known execution times we can build a training set $D = (Ci, Xi)$. We aim to train a deep learning model for learning a function ϕ that maps a test file C_i to a feature vector v mapped to the corresponding value X_i.

2.3   Building Flow-Augmented Abstract Syntax Trees

Recent studies [25] emphasize the importance of the code representation when using deep learning in software engineering. Hence, and given the complexity of predicting performance, prediction based on the syntactical information extracted from ASTs alone is not sufficient to achieve high-quality predictions. In TEP-GNN, the basic structural information provided by the AST is enriched with semantic information representing data and control flow. Consequently, the tree structure of the AST is generalized to a (substantially richer) graph, encoding more information than code structure alone. This idea is based on the earlier work by Wang and Jin [30], who have also introduced the term FA-AST for this kind of source code representation.

```
1  package org.myorg.weather.tests;
2
3  import static
4      org.junit.jupiter.api.Assertions.assertEquals;
5  import org.myorg.weather.WeatherAPI;
6  import org.myorg.weather.Flags;
7
8  public class WeatherAPITest {
9
10     WeatherAPI api = new WeatherAPI();
11
12     @Test
13     public void testTemperatureOutput() {
14         double currentTemp = api.currentTemp();
15         Flags f = api.getFreezeFlag();
16         if(currentTemp <= 3.0d)
17             assertEquals(Flags.FREEZE, f);
18         else
19             assertEquals(Flags.THAW, f);
20     }
21 }
```

Listing 1.1. A Simple JUnit 5 Test Case

AST Parsing. We demonstrate our approach for constructing FA-ASTs for test files using the example of a Java JUnit 5 test case (see Listing 1.1). In this example, a single test case `testTemperatureOutput()` is presented that tests a feature of an (imaginary) API. As common for test cases, the example is short and structurally relatively simple. Much of the body of the test case consists of invocations to the system-under-test and calls of JUnit standard methods, such as `assertEquals`. We speculate that these properties make predicting test execution time a more tractable problem than predicting performance of general-purpose programs, which previous authors have argued to be extremely challenging [19, 21].

A (slightly simplified) AST for this illustrative example is depicted in Fig. 2. The produced AST does not contain purely syntactical elements, such as comments, brackets, or code location information. We make use of the pure Python Java parser javalang[5] to parse each test file, and use the node types, values, and production rules in javalang to describe our ASTs.

---
[5] https://pypi.org/project/javalang/.

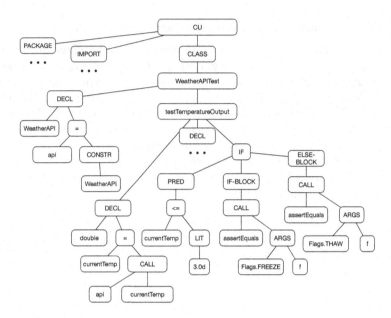

Fig. 2. Simplified abstract syntax tree (AST) representing the illustrative example presented in Listing 1.1. Package declarations, import statements, as well as the declaration in Line 15 are skipped for brevity.

Capturing Ordering and Data Flow. In the next step, we augment this AST with different types of additional edges representing data flow and node order in the AST. Specifically, we use the following additional flow augmentation edges, in addition to the **AST child** and **AST parent** edges that are produced readily by AST parsing:

FA Next Token (b):

This type of edge connects a terminal node (leaf) in the AST to the next terminal node. Terminal nodes are nodes without children. In Fig. 2, an FA Next Token edge would be added, for example, between WeatherAPI and api.

FA Next Sibling (c):

This connects each node (both terminal and non-terminal) to its next sibling, and allows us to model the order of instructions in an otherwise unordered graph. In Fig. 2, such an edge would be added, for example, connecting the first usage of api and with the CONSTR node (representing a Java constructor call).

FA Next Use (d):

This type of edge connects a node representing a variable to the place where this variable is next used. For example, the variable api is declared in Line 10 in Listing 1.1, and then used next in Line 14.

Figure 3 shows an example augmenting the AST in Fig. 2 (and, consequently, the example test case in Listing 1.1). Solid black lines indicate the AST parent and child relationships (for simplicity indicated through a single arrow, read from top to bottom). Red dashed arrows refer to the new edges added to represent the

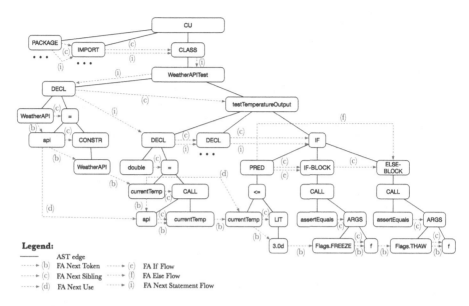

Legend:

——— AST edge

-----► (b) FA Next Token   -----► (c) FA If Flow

-----► (c) FA Next Sibling   -----► (f) FA Else Flow

-----► (d) FA Next Use   -----► (i) FA Next Statement Flow

Fig. 3. Flow-Augmented AST (FA-AST) for the example presented in Listing 1.1. Solid lines represent AST parent and child edges, and dashed lines different types of flow augmentations. (Color figure online)

data and control flow in the FA-AST, with letter codes indicating the edge type. Terminal nodes are connected with FA Next Token edges (b), modelling the order of terminals in the test case. Similarly, the ordering of siblings is modelled using FA Next Sibling edges (c). Finally, data flow is modelled by connecting each variable to their next usage via FA Next Use edges (d). Edge types (e), (f), and (i) represent a control flow statement, which will be discussed in the following. Multiple edges of different types are possible between the same nodes. For example, the terminal nodes `Flags.FREEZE` and `f` are connected via both, an FA Next Token (b) and an FA Next Sibling (c) edge.

Capturing Control Flow. In a second augmentation step, we now add further edges representing the control flow in the test cases. We currently support *if* statements, *while* and *for* loops, as well as *sequential execution*. We currently do not support *switch* statements or *do-while* loops, as these are less common in test cases. Test files containing these elements will still be parsed successfully, but these control flow constructs will not be captured by the FA-AST. Specifically, the following further edges are added: An overview over the additional edges introduced by these control flow statements is given in Fig. 4.

FA If Flow (e):

This type of edge connects the predicate (condition) of the if-statement with the code block that is executed if the condition evaluates to `true`. Every if statement contains exactly one such edge by construction.

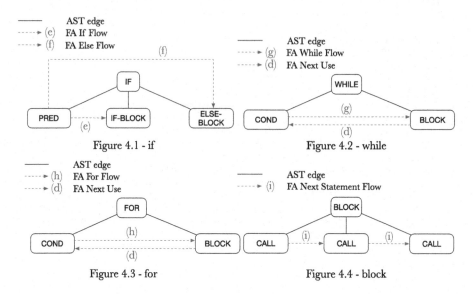

Fig. 4. Additional flow augmentations for different control flow constructs (Color figure online)

FA Else Flow (f):
Conversely, this edge type connects the predicate to the (optional) else code block.

FA While Flow (g):
A while loop essentially entails two elements - a condition and a code block that is executed as long as the condition remains true. We capture this through a FA While Flow (g) edge connecting the condition to the code block, and an FA Next Use (d) edge in the reverse direction. The latter is used to model the next usage of a loop counter.

FA For Flow (h):
For loops are conceptually similar to while loops. We use FA For Flow (h) edges to connect the condition to the code block, and an FA Next Use (d) edge in the reverse direction. Similar to the modelling of while-loops, FA Next Use (d) relates to the usage (typically incrementing) of a loop counter.

FA Next Statement Flow (i):
In addition to the control flow constructs discussed so far, Java of course also supports the simple sequential execution of multiple statements in a sequence within a code block. FA Next Statement Flow edges (i) are used to represent this case. Different from the constructs discussed so far, a code block can contain an arbitrary number of children, and the FA Next Statement Flow edge is always used to connect each statement to the one directly following it.

Referring back to Fig. 3, two types of control flow annotations are visible - the modelling of the if-statement in lines 16 to 19 of the test case on the right-hand side, and various sequential executions (FA Next Statement flow (i)) edges.

Further note how flow annotation adds a large number of edges to even a very small AST, transforming the syntax tree into a densely connected graph. This rich additional information can be used in the next step by our GNN model to predict highly accurate test execution times.

2.4   GNN Model for Test Execution Time Prediction

Once the FA-AST graph has been built for a test file using the three steps discussed above, we use a higher order GNN model to predict the execution time of the Java code. As Fig. 5 shows, we use a 3-layer higher order graph convolution neural network to predict the execution time. Each layer is followed by a ReLU activation function. Since GNN learns node embedding, we use global max pooling to compute a graph embedding. Finally, the graph embedding goes into two Linear layers with a ReLU and a sigmoid activation function to perform the prediction of the test execution time. To train our model we use the mean square error loss.

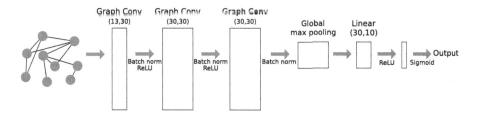

Fig. 5. Architecture of the GNN Model used in TEP-GNN.

3   Evaluation

We now present the results of an experimental evaluation of TEP-GNN based on open source Java projects. As training and test data we make use of existing test suite execution traces from the study subjects' build systems. A replication package containing the scripts used to implement the TEP-GNN approach, all data used in the evaluation, as well as all analysis scripts, are available [8].

3.1   Dataset

Related studies in performance engineering frequently collect their own performance data, for example by repeated execution of the projects on a researcher's laptop [26], in cloud virtual machines [13], or on controlled hardware [27]. To increase the realism of the study we have chosen a different approach – we harvest existing execution traces from an open source build system (GitHub), and extract test execution times from this public data. This data represents actual, real-life test execution times. However, we do not have the option to collect more data on-demand, and we do not know what precise hardware has been used to collect the data.

To collect the data, we searched for projects to serve as study subjects. We applied the following selection criteria: *(i)* projects written in Java; *(ii)* available on GitHub; *(iii)* include test results published on GitHub; and *(iv)* use GitHub shared runners as build system.

Table 1. Overview of study subjects.

Project	Description	Files	Runs	Nodes	Vocabulary size
systemDS	Apache Machine Learning system for data science lifecycle	127	1321	110651	3161
H2	Java SQL database	194	1391	405706	17972
Dubbo	Apache Remote Procedure Call framework	123	524	75787	4499
RDF4J	Scalable RDF processing for Java	478	1055	214436	10755
Total		**922**	**4291**	**806580**	**36387**

Based on these criteria, we selected four projects of diverse application domains, i.e., databases, web servers, and data science life-cycle (systemDS, H2, Dubbo, and RDF4J). These are depicted in Table 1. The first column shows the project's name, the second provides a brief description of the project. The third column shows the number of distinct test files extracted from the project. As for the fourth column, it shows the total number of runs performed in the testing job. The last two columns show the total number of tokens in the entire project test files and the vocabulary size (the number of distinct nodes in the graphs). We observe that RDF4J, a triplestore database used in semantic web contexts [23], contains more test files than the other projects. For the H2 relational database and systemDS we were able to collect the most test runs. Finally, it should be noted that H2 has the highest code density as measured by the number of nodes and the resulting vocabulary size by a wide margin. This indicates that H2 tests are generally larger and more complex than the test cases in the other study subjects.

All data was extracted from GitHub-hosted runners, which are virtual machines hosted by GitHub with the GitHub Actions runner application installed. All shared runners can be assumed to use the same hardware resources, which is available at GitHub's website[6] and each job runs in a fresh instance of the virtual machine. Additionally, all jobs from which the data is extracted uses the same operating system, specifically Ubuntu 18.04. This allows us to minimize bias introduced by variations in execution environment or hardware.

For collecting test execution traces we looked at the latest successful action workflow run for each project. We then extracted the run times from the test report in the workflow, and mined the corresponding source code files from the respective project repositories in order to feed them to the parser. For H2,

---

[6] https://docs.github.com/en/actions/using-github-hosted-runners/about-github-hosted-runners#supported-runners-and-hardware-resources.

some test cases are run several times during the same build job. In these cases, we recorded the average of the run times. As the execution times of tests can vary dramatically between and within projects, to increase the efficiency of the model training, we normalize each execution time to interval $[0; 1]$. Hence, our final dataset includes distinct test files, each associated with one runtime value between 0 and 1. Then after model training, we denormalize the runtime value and present the results based on the original values.

Table 2. Occurrences of control flow nodes in each project

Control flow statement	systemDS	H2	Dubbo	RDF4J
If Statement	166	1322	53	161
While Loop	2	222	3	22
ForStatement	196	1114	42	158
Block Statement	293	2900	116	395
Total	**707**	**5612**	**214**	**736**

Table 2 indicates how prevalent different control flow nodes were in the test cases of our study subjects. For all projects, block statements are the most frequent control flow construct, since sequential executions widely exist in nearly all programs. For loops are substantially more common than while loops, and if statements are also frequent. Do-while loops and switch statements, which are currently unsupported by TEP-GNN, are both quite rare in the tests of our subjects (not shown in the table).

3.2   Results

In this section, we investigate the results of applying TEP-GNN to our dataset, answering RQ1 and RQ2 introduced in Sect. 1.

RQ1: Quality of Predictions. In order to answer the first research question, we combine the collected data for all projects into one dataset entailing 922 code fragments and associated normalized execution times. After that, we apply TEP-GNN as discussed in Sect. 2. For model training, we split the dataset into train and test sets using 80% and 20%, respectively. Each network is trained for 100 epochs. As optimizer we use Adam [10] with a learning rate = 0.001. To evaluate the results of our model, we use a Pearson correlation metric, a measure of linear correlation between two sets of data. In addition, as a loss function, we use mean squared error, which is the average squared difference between the estimated and actual values. All experiments have been executed in a machine equipped with a GeForce 940MX graphics card and 16 GB of RAM.

Results illustrate that our model trained on FA-AST is able to predict test execution times with a very high accuracy, as can be seen in the Pearson correlation (between predicted and actual execution times in the test data set) of

0.789, and a mean squared error of 0.02. These results substantially outperform the accuracy values reported in previous studies that attempted to predict absolute software performance counters [19,21]. We argue that the key innovation that enables this high accuracy is the combination of FA-AST as a powerful code representation model and GraphConv as a modern GNN.

RQ2: Comparison of TEP-GNN Against a Baseline GNN. To validate the suitability of our approach and the selected GNN model, we compare it to a commonly used GNN baseline, called Gated Graph Neural Networks (GGNN) [16]. GGNNs are widely used in studies that attempt to learn code semantics [1, 5]. We compare the methods at two levels – for the entire dataset (similar to the analysis presented for RQ1) and at the level of individual projects.

Comparison for the Entire Dataset. We first apply both TEP-GNN and the baseline method to the dataset consisting of all projects. Figure 6 depicts the respective results. Our model outperforms the baseline, with a Pearson correlation that is higher almost up to 0.1 (i.e., 0.789 versus 0.697). Hence, we conclude that our model and GNN architecture is indeed more appropriate to predict the execution time of test cases than a more standard GGNN approach.

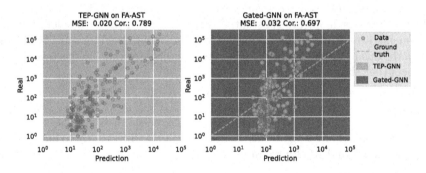

Fig. 6. Comparison of TEP-GNN and a baseline (applying GGNN to the same FA-AST graphs). Dot points show real (y axes) and predicted (x axes) denormalized (original) execution times produced by our model. The dash line refers to the perfect prediction.

Analyzing the results, we observe that TEP-GNN is able to achieve highly accurate predictions in most cases. However, there are rare outliers where our prediction model misses by approximately 20%. The baseline GGNN method, on the other hand, has a tendency to predict fairly uniform execution times between 10^2 and 10^3, almost independent of what the actually observed test execution time is. Hence, it suffers from lower accuracy scores.

Comparison for Individual Projects. In the next step, we conduct a similar analysis, but focused on individual projects. This study answers the question of how well TEP-GNN works if trained on and used by a single project. Thus, we train and test TEP-GNN and the baseline on each of the four projects individually. The results for each project are depicted in Fig. 7.

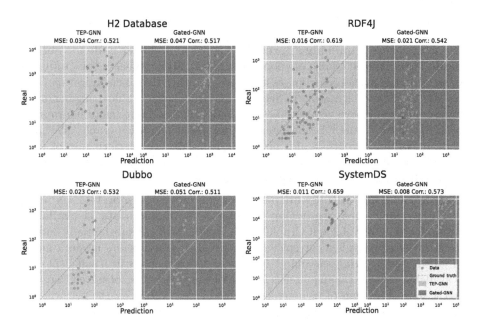

Fig. 7. Overview of TEP-GNN and the GGNN baseline trained for each individual project.

We observe that in general the prediction quality is substantially lower if the model is trained on individual projects, both for TEP-GNN and the baseline. TEP-GNN still outperforms the baseline for each project, but only with negligible prediction performance differences in the case of H2 and Dubbo. For RDF4J, which contains the largest number of test cases (and, consequently, the largest number of graphs to learn from), the difference between our approach and the baseline remains larger.

From these results we conclude that (a) TEP-GNN indeed outperforms the baseline in all the settings we tested, but (b) our approach works best if sufficient training graphs are available in comparison to the size of the graphs and vocabulary (if graphs are complex and/or training data is sparse the difference between our approach and the baseline is insignificant); (c) finally, we conclude that both approaches appear to learn some transferable knowledge even when training on graphs that originate from a different project.

4   Discussion

Our study results show that the accurate prediction of execution times of test suites is possible. This gives developers an early indication of the time required to run the cases in the build process, deciding in the process if techniques such as test case selection are required.

4.1 Lessons Learned

FA-ASTs are a promising approach to represent source code for performance prediction. Unlike previous work [19, 21, 31], our goal in this study was to treat performance prediction as a regression rather than a classification (slow or fast) problem. Our results in Sect. 3.2 indicate that using flow augmentation we are able to achieve good prediction quality. Furthermore, more information could be added to the FA-AST, such as program dependency graphs. We speculate that this approach is also promising to predict the performance of more complex, arbitrary code; however, more specific experiments in this direction need to be carried out as future research.

GraphConv substantially outperforms the more common GGNN models in performance prediction as long as sufficient data is available. As discussed in Sect. 3.2, our GraphConv based GNN model substantially outperforms GGNN, which is a currently commonly used graph neural network model in software engineering research [1, 5]. However, this is only true if sufficient data is available – when training models for individual projects, we observed that, due to the limited amount of training data available in these cases, the performance difference between our GraphConv based model and the GGNN baseline was minimal. We conclude that, as long as sufficient data is available, GraphConv should also be investigated in other software engineering contexts that make use of GNNs.

4.2 Threats to Validity

Internal Validity Threats. A key design choice in our study was the usage of existing, real-world data from GitHub's build system, rather than collecting performance data ourselves (e.g., on a dedicated experiment machine). This has obvious advantages with regards to the realism of our approach, but raises the threat that our training and test data may be subject to confounding factors outside of our knowledge. In particular, prior research has shown that even identically configured cloud virtual machines can vary significantly in performance [14]. However, the high accuracy achieved by our prediction models indicates that this is not a major concern with the data we used.

Another design choice was that we predict execution times for entire test classes (files). More fine-grained predictions (e.g., for individual test cases) would of course be doable. However, individual test cases often have very short execution times in relation to the precision with which build systems typically measure execution times, and the resulting graphs would be very small. We argue that our choice of test class granularity constitutes a good trade-off that is still useful for developers.

External Validity Threats. An obvious question raised by our work is how well the results reported in Sect. 3.2 would generalize to other projects. To mitigate this threat, we have chosen four relatively different Java projects as study subjects following a diversity sampling strategy [2]. However, our study does not allow us to conclude whether the TEP-GNN approach would generalize to other programming languages or closed-source software.

5   Related Work

Predicting Software Performance. Predicting the absolute value of performance, such as execution time, based on the source code alone is challenging. Hence, existing studies often struggle with poor prediction accuracy [19,21]. One way to simplify the problem (and hence make it more tractable) is to convert it into a classification problem. Examples of this approach include Zhou et al. [31], who predict if a program from a programming competition website exceeds the time limit, Ramadan et al. [22], who predict whether a performance change is introduced by a code structure change, or Laaber et al. [12], who have shown that a categorical classification of benchmarks into high- or low-variability is feasible.

However, recent research has shown that predicting absolute performance values can be feasible in more specialized contexts like Guo et al. in the context of configurable system [6,7], and Samoaa and Leitner in the context of benchmark with a specific workload configuration [24].

Graph Neural Networks for Software Engineering. Graph Neural Networks (GNNs) constitute an up-and-coming machine learning model in the context of software engineering research [25]. Li et al. [16] use a GRU cell in gated graph neural networks (GGNNs) for updating the nodes' states. To evaluate their model they run the model on a basic program and try to detect null pointers.

Phan et al. [29] use graph convolutional networks (GCNs) based on compiled assembly code to detect defects on control flow graphs in C. Another application of control flow graphs is using graph matching networks (GMN) between two graphs of binary functions proposed by Li et al. [15]. Other researchers propose the creation of program graphs based on the AST. Allamanis et al. [1] and Brockschmidt et al. [3] use GGNN in C# for naming variables and generating program expressions for code completion respectively.

6   Conclusion and Future Work

In this work, we provide the developers with predictions of the execution times of their test cases, and consequently give them an early indication of the time required to run the cases in the build process. We presented TEP-GNN, an effective method for predicting the execution time of Java test files. Our approach leverages explicitly capturing control and data flow information as augmentations to the program AST. Further, our approach applies high order convolution graph neural networks over this flow-augmented AST (FA-AST). By building FA-AST using original ASTs and flow edges, our approach can directly capture the syntax and semantic structure of test classes. Experimental results on four diverse test subjects demonstrate that by combining graph neural networks and control/data flow information, we can predict absolute test execution times with high accuracy.

As the future work, we plan to further extent the FA-AST model currently used by TEP-GNN, as well as explore other ways of program representation to capture more syntactic and semantic code features. Additionally, we plan to apply our approach to the execution time of general-purpose programs rather than test cases. Finally, we would like to extend our current labeled data set by applying active learning to systematically increase the amount of training data.

Acknowledgements. This work received financial support from the Swedish Research Council VR under grant number 2018-04127 (Developer-Targeted Performance Engineering for Immersed Release and Software Engineering).

References

1. Allamanis, M., Brockschmidt, M., Khademi, M.: Learning to represent programs with graphs (2017). https://arxiv.org/abs/1711.00740
2. Baltes, S., Ralph, P.: Sampling in software engineering research: a critical review and guidelines. EMSE **94**(27) (2022)
3. Brockschmidt, M., Allamanis, M., Gaunt, A.L., Polozov, O.: Generative code modeling with graphs (2018). https://arxiv.org/abs/1805.08490
4. de Oliveira Neto, F.G., Ahmad, A., Leifler, O., Sandahl, K., Enoiu, E.: Improving continuous integration with similarity-based test case selection. In: Proceedings of the 13th International Workshop on Automation of Software Test, pp. 39–45 (2018)
5. Fernandes, P., Allamanis, M., Brockschmidt, M.: Structured neural summarization (2018). https://arxiv.org/abs/1811.01824
6. Guo, J., Czarnecki, K., Apel, S., Siegmund, N., Wąsowski, A.: Variability-aware performance prediction: a statistical learning approach. In: ASE, pp. 301–311 (2013)
7. Guo, J., et al.: Data-efficient performance learning for configurable systems. EMSE **23**(3), 1826–1867 (2018)
8. Samoaa, H.P., Longa, A., Mohamed, M., Chehreghani, M.H., Leitner, P.: TEP-GNN: accurate execution time prediction of functional tests using graph neural networks. Zenodo, August 2022. https://doi.org/10.5281/zenodo.7003881
9. Huber, W., Carey, V.J., Long, L., Falcon, S., Gentleman, R.: Graphs in molecular biology. BMC Bioinform. **8**(6), 1–14 (2007)
10. Kingma, D.P., Ba, J.: Adam: a method for stochastic optimization (2014). https://arxiv.org/abs/1412.6980
11. Knauss, E., Staron, M., Meding, W., Söder, O., Nilsson, A., Castell, M.: Supporting continuous integration by code-churn based test selection. In: 2015 IEEE/ACM 2nd International Workshop on Rapid Continuous Software Engineering, pp. 19–25. IEEE (2015)
12. Laaber, C., Basmaci, M., Salza, P.: Predicting unstable software benchmarks using static source code features. EMSE **26**(6) (2021)
13. Laaber, C., Scheuner, J., Leitner, P.: Software microbenchmarking in the cloud. How bad is it really? EMSE **24**(4), 2469–2508 (2019)
14. Leitner, P., Cito, J.: Patterns in the Chaos - a study of performance variation and predictability in public IaaS clouds. ACM TOIT **16**(3), 15:1–15:23 (2016)
15. Li, Y., Gu, C., Dullien, T., Vinyals, O., Kohli, P.: Graph matching networks for learning the similarity of graph structured objects. In: Proceedings of the 36th International Conference on Machine Learning, vol. 97. PMLR (2019)

16. Li, Y., Tarlow, D., Brockschmidt, M., Zemel, R.: Gated graph sequence neural networks (2015). https://arxiv.org/abs/1511.05493

17. Longa, A., Cencetti, G., Lepri, B., Passerini, A.: An efficient procedure for mining egocentric temporal motifs. Data Min. Knowl. Disc. **36**(1), 355–378 (2022)

18. Marijan, D., Gotlieb, A., Liaaen, M.: A learning algorithm for optimizing continuous integration development and testing practice. Softw. Pract. Exp. **49**(2), 192–213 (2019)

19. Meng, K., Norris, B.: Mira: a framework for static performance analysis. In: CLUSTER (2017)

20. Morris, C., et al.: Weisfeiler and leman go neural: higher-order graph neural networks. In: AAAI, vol. 33 (2019)

21. Narayanan, S.H.K., Norris, B., Hovland, P.D.: Generating performance bounds from source code. In: International Conference on Parallel Processing Workshops, pp. 197–206 (2010)

22. Ramadan, T., Islam, T.Z., Phelps, C., Pinnow, N., Thiagarajan, J.J.: Comparative code structure analysis using deep learning for performance prediction. In: ISPASS, Los Alamitos, CA, USA. IEEE Computer Society, March 2021

23. Samoaa, H., Catania, B.: A pipeline for measuring brand loyalty through social media mining. In: Bureš, T., et al. (eds.) SOFSEM 2021. LNCS, vol. 12607, pp. 489–504. Springer, Cham (2021). https://doi.org/10.1007/978-3-030-67731-2_36

24. Samoaa, H., Leitner, P.: An exploratory study of the impact of parameterization on JMH measurement results in open-source projects. In: ICPE. Association for Computing Machinery (2021)

25. Samoaa, H.P., Bayram, F., Salza, P., Leitner, P.: A systematic mapping study of source code representation for deep learning in software engineering. IET Softw. (2022)

26. Sandoval Alcocer, J.P., Bergel, A., Valente, M.T.: Learning from source code history to identify performance failures. In: ICPE. Association for Computing Machinery (2016)

27. Schulz, H., Okanović, D., van Hoorn, A., Tůma, P.: Context-tailored workload model generation for continuous representative load testing. In: ICPE. Association for Computing Machinery (2021)

28. Spieker, H., Gotlieb, A., Marijan, D., Mossige, M.: Reinforcement learning for automatic test case prioritization and selection in continuous integration. In: ISSTA, pp. 12–22 (2017)

29. Viet Phan, A., Le Nguyen, M., Thu Bui, L.: Convolutional neural networks over control flow graphs for software defect prediction. In: ICTAI (2017)

30. Wang, W., Li, G., Ma, B., Xia, X., Jin, Z.: Detecting code clones with graph neural network and flow-augmented abstract syntax tree. In: SANER (2020)

31. Zhou, M., Chen, J., Hu, H., Yu, J., Li, Z., Hu, H.: DeepTLE: learning code-level features to predict code performance before it runs. In: APSEC (2019)

Improving Software Regression Testing Using a Machine Learning-Based Method for Test Type Selection

Khaled Walid Al-Sabbagh(✉)(ID), Miroslaw Staron(ID), and Regina Hebig(ID)

Computer Science and Engineering Department, Chalmers — University of Gothenburg, Gothenburg, Sweden
{khaled.al-sabbagh,miroslaw.staron,regina.hebig}@gu.se

Abstract. Since only a limited time is available for performing software regression testing, a subset of crucial test cases from the test suites has to be selected for execution. In this paper, we introduce a method that uses the relation between types of code changes and regression tests to select test types that require execution. We work closely with a large power supply company to develop and evaluate the method and measure the total regression testing time taken by our method and its effectiveness in selecting the most relevant test types. The results show that the method reduces the total regression time by an average of 18,33% when compared with the approach used by our industrial partner. The results also show that using a medium window size in the method configuration results in an improved recall rate from 61,11% to 83,33%, but not in considerable time reduction of testing. We conclude that our method can potentially be used to steer the testing effort at software development companies by guiding testers into which regression test types are essential for execution.

Keywords: Software regression testing · Machine learning · Code types · Regression test types

1 Introduction

Modern software development projects evolve rapidly as software engineers add new features, fix faults, or refactor code smells. To prevent faults from breaking existing functionality in the evolving system, software engineers frequently perform software regression testing. A safe and straightforward approach to perform regression testing is to execute a pre-defined set of test cases, usually a selection of unit, system and function tests. Such an approach is often referred to as a *retest-all strategy*. Despite benefits in set-up time, this strategy does not take into consideration changes done to the system – these are often tested during system or function test phases. The frequent execution of these retest-all test suites can also be extremely time and resource consuming. As a remedy to this, a number of Test Case Selection (TCS) methods have been developed, e.g., selecting tests based on their relevance to the modifications made in the SUT (System Under Test), in this way reducing the time and cost of testing.

© The Author(s), under exclusive license to Springer Nature Switzerland AG 2022
D. Taibi et al. (Eds.): PROFES 2022, LNCS 13709, pp. 480–496, 2022.
https://doi.org/10.1007/978-3-031-21388-5_33

A recent family of approaches for TCS employs statistical models to predict test cases based on their historical verdicts [11], [3], and [16]. These approaches are based on the assumption that a dependency between code changes and test case execution results (pass/fail) exists. For example, Knauss et al. [11] proposed an automatic recommender that analyzes the frequency in which test cases fail on a particular day given code changes made to software modules, achieving 78% reduction in the studied test suite. Similarly, one of the first implementations of ML for test case selection was presented in our previous work [3], where we introduced a TCS method that utilizes textual analysis and a conventional tree-based model to predict test case execution results.

All of these approaches create a prediction model using historical test execution results and the code changes against which these tests were exercised. However, there are several inherent challenges to the application of these approaches. One of the major challenges is the need to develop a database of source code changes over time and a database of the related test case verdicts.

In response to this challenge, we have been investigating strategies for applying test selection without the need to use historical information about test execution results. Instead of the historical verdicts, we focus on the relation between types of code changes (e.g., including new conditional statements) and type of regression tests (e.g., statement test, [1]). We have constructed a facet-based taxonomy of dependencies between code changes and test cases of specific types [2]. The knowledge presented in the dependency taxonomy is used to instrument tools for TCS by only analyzing the content of code changes, and thus determine which set of test types will be affected by the change. We address the following research question:

How to reduce the time of regression testing by selecting only the most relevant test types?

We address this question by developing a machine learning-based method (and a tool) – HiTTs (*Human-in-the-loop Approach for Test Type Selection*)– that automatically identifies types of code changes and then selects the relevant types of tests. By using test types and source code changes types, we do not require historical data about the test case verdicts and therefore, HiTTs can be used already from the start of software development.

We work closely with a large power supply provider that develops software solutions to revise the taxonomy and validate the results. To evaluate our method, we used an embedded system that is owned and developed by our industrial partner. The results of this study show that our method has promising potentials in reducing the regression testing time at a high fault detection rate.

2   Related Work

Previous studies have been conducted to examine SW regression testing approaches, as surveyed in [8] and [9]. The majority of these approaches differ from our approach in their used artifacts (i.e., they require information about test cases) and the underlying concepts (i.e., they operate on a test level granularity). Unlike our approach, existing approaches require updating dependency graphs or coverage information to select or prioritize tests. In this section, we discuss some of these approaches and report their time usage of testing.

Greedy-Based: Chi et al. [7] proposed an algorithm that traces method call sequences under each test case to construct a call graph. The call graph is then used to sample the testing order based on method call sequence coverage criterion. The method was valuated and compared for effectiveness in terms of fault detection and time usage against 22 state-of-the-art techniques. The results showed that the algorithm outperformed the other 22 techniques in terms of fault detection, but not in time usage. Specifically, the proposed technique was found to take 20,5% more than the next best technique compared for effectiveness.

Similarity-Based: De Oliveira Neto et al. [13] conducted a case study to investigate the efficiency of 3 similarity-based approaches for test selection, namely, the Normalised Levenshtein, Jaccard Index, and Normalised Compression Distance. The results showed that using the Normalized Levenshtein and Jaccard Index outperformed the Normalised Compression Distance in terms of their coverage rate of test requirements, dependencies, and steps. Specifically, the Normalized Levenshtein reduced the amount of executed tests by 65% and could still cover distinct combinations of test dependencies required to execute test cases. In terms of the saved time, the results showed that the Normalized Levenshtein reduced the testing time by 15,1% compared to random selection.

ML-Based: Bertolino et al. [6] proposed an approach that seeks to find transitively dependent classes on changed ones in new versions of the SUT along with their associated test classes. The approach prioritizes the selected tests based on several code and test metrics which then get fed into an ML model for training. The evaluation of the approach was done by comparing 10 ML algorithms using 6 Java projects in terms of the Rank Percentile Average metric and the sum of time required for ranking the selected tests. The results showed that using the MART algorithm outperforms the others in terms of Rank Percentile Average, whereas the Coordinate ASCENT performed best in terms of ranking time.

Graph-Based: Orso et al. [14] proposed a two-phase algorithm that builds a graph representation of the SUT and then identifies, based on information on changed classes, the parts of the SUT that need to be tested. As a result, tests that traverse the changed parts of the SUT are selected for execution. The authors compared the regression testing time of their approach against a retest-all baseline on 3 programs. The results showed that using their approach reduced the regression testing time between 5.9% to 89.7%, with an average of 42.8%.

3   Core Concepts and Background

This section presents core concepts and defines several types of code changes and tests presented in [2].

3.1   Core Concepts

We use the definition of a software program P to be a collection of lines of code $L < L_1, \ldots, L_n >$. P' denotes a modified revision of P, and includes one or more combinations of added/removed/modified L, distant from P. We use the term 'revision' to refer to a modified version of P. A test case, denoted by tc, is a specification of the inputs and expected results to verify that P' complies without issues. The result of executing a tc is referred to as 'test case verdict' (passed or failed) and is denoted with te. A set of test cases $T = < tc_1, tc_2, \ldots >$ is the test suite for testing P'. Regression test selection refers to the strategy of testing that given a P' selects a subset of tc that is crucial for execution.

3.2   The Dependency Taxonomy

The method presented in this study is based on the knowledge depicted in the dependency taxonomy that we created in collaboration with SW testers from the industry [2]. Each branch in the taxonomy refers to a single dependency between a test and a code change type, where a dependency means that a change in a code type results in a failure of tests of a specific type. In this study, we utilize and validate 8 dependency links from the original taxonomy since our industrial partner could only provide us with information about 4 test types.

Figure 1 illustrate the 8 dependency links between the test and code types. All dependencies in the original taxonomy were identified from two sources of information - SW testers and literature studies. The solid connectors in Fig. 1 correspond to dependencies that were identified by testers, whereas dotted lines correspond to dependencies that were identified from the literature. Table 1 summarizes the definitions of the 4 test types depicted. We refer the reader to [2] for more details about each type of code and test.

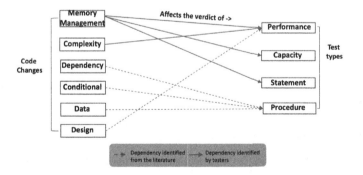

Fig. 1. The taxonomy of dependency between code and test types.

Memory management: This category concerns the management of system memory during run-time. Changes in this category include introducing/fixing memory leaks, buffer overflow, dangling pointers, and resource interference with multi-threading.

Design: This category involves changes that include code refactoring, adding or removing methods, classes, interfaces, enumerators, or code smells.

Complexity: This category represents changes that add to or reduce the time complexity of the SUT. It includes changes such as adding or removing loops, conditional statements, nesting blocks or recursive functions.

Dependency: This category describes a change where a dependency between a module/fragment/library is added/modified. It can be importing a new library, a namespace, or a class.

Conditional: This category occurs when a logical operator or in a conditional statement is added/modified.

Data: This category involves changing 1) function parameters, 2) value assignment to variables, 3) casting, 4) array allocations, or 5) declaring variables.

Table 1. Definitions of test case types in the taxonomy of dependency.

Test case type	Definition
Statement	Constructed to force execution of individual statements.
Performance	Evaluate the degree to which a test item accomplishes its designated functions within a given time.
Capacity	Evaluate the level at which increasing load affects a test item's ability to sustain required performance.
Procedure	Evaluate whether procedural instructions for interacting with a test item to meet user requirements

4   Research Design

In this section, we describe how our method was designed and implemented.

4.1   HiTTs Implementation

The basic idea behind HiTTs is to utilize the relations presented in the dependency taxonomy for automating the classification of L in P' into several code types, and as a result select regression test types that are sensitive to the changes introduced in the code. To achieve this, we use a three-phase process, which we call 1) Annotation and Training, 2) Calibration, and 3) Selection (Fig. 2).

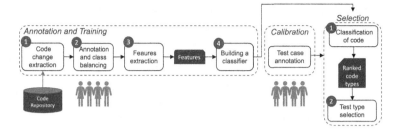

Fig. 2. Human in the loop for test type selection.

Annotation and Training (Phase 1): The first phase in HiTTs consists of 4 steps that concern the extraction of code changes, annotation and class balancing, features extraction, and building a classifier. A step-by-step description of each step in this phase is as follows:

1. **Code change extraction:** the method starts by extracting historical code changes between pairs of consecutive versions of P, P' from the version control system (e.g., git). Only modified and added L at different P' are retained, whereas all deleted L are discarded since the scope of this study is to identify regression tests that will react to new/modified code changes. The tool then parses the content of extracted L and filters out all L that belong to configuration files (e.g., .xml and .json), comments, empty and unit test L. Once the filtering step is complete, we save the extracted set of L for each P' in a 'csv' file.
2. **Annotation and class balancing:** each L in the 'csv' file is then annotated by two or more SW architects into one of the 6 categories of code change. L that are annotated with the same code types are retained, and the remaining ones get discarded. Once the annotation is complete, we inspect the distribution of instances under the 6 code types. If the number of instances in one code type heavily outnumbers those in the other types, we oversample instances in the minority class to balance out the data. This activity is necessary to mitigate the effect of introducing a classification bias toward one of the classes [4].
3. **Features extraction:** In this step, we transform the collected revision files into feature vectors using the bag of words (BoW) approach. We use a tool that, for each L in the collected revision files:
   - creates a vocabulary for all L (using the BoW technique, with a cut-off parameter of how many words should be included[1])
   - creates a token for words that fall outside of the frequency defined by the cut-off parameter of the bag of words

---

[1] BoW is essentially a sequence of words/tokens, which are descendingly ordered according to frequency. This cut-off parameters controls how many of the most frequently used words are included as features – e.g. 10 means that the 10 most frequently used words become features and the rest are ignored.

- finds a set of predefined keywords in each line,
- checks each word in the line to decide if it should be tokenized or if it is a predefined feature.

The output of this step is a large array of numbers, each representing the token frequency of a specific feature in the bag of words space of vectors.

4. **Building a multi-class model:** the final step in this phase concerns feeding the set of extracted feature vectors into a multi-class ML model for training.

Calibration (Phase 2): In order for HiTTs to select crucial regression test types for execution, it requires knowledge about the types of tc that are available in the suites. Thus, the pool of tc from which HiTTs can operate must include information about the type of the tc. This requires SW architects to calibrate the type of test in every new/existing tc. This can be done, for example, by creating a variable in each test class and use it to tag/calibrate the test type of the tc. Note that this step can be performed independently from phase 1.

Selection (Phase 3): The final phase of HiTTs concerns the analysis of code types that are found in new code revisions and selecting regression test types that are sensitive to the changes. The phase can be described in two steps:

1. **Classification of lines of code:** The first step in this phase utilizes the trained model in phase 1 for classifying L that appear in P' into one of the 6 code types. As soon as the classification is complete, the method measures the count of L under each code type and generates a list of *ranked code types* from highest to lowest in terms of L count.

2. **Test type selection:** The next step in this phase is to select regression test types that are important for execution. For this, HiTTs uses a set of predefined rules that specify which test types are sensitive to what code types. These rules are derived from the taxonomy of dependency (see Sect. 3.2) and their usage is determined by a window size. The larger the window size, the more code types that HiTTs will use for selecting test types. Specifically, HiTTs will select all test types that are in dependency with the code types that fall within the window boundary. For example, a window size of 1 would trigger HiTTs to select test types that are in dependency with the first top ranked code type only. Since the taxonomy of dependency consists of 6 code types, HiTTs can currently utilize a window size between 1 and 6.

Note that the first phase of HiTTs needs to be performed only once for training the classifier. Similarly, the second phase is performed only when a new tc is created or existing tc requires calibration.

4.2   Usage Scenario

In this section, we describe a usage scenario to show how test orchestrators can use HiTTs. The scenario assumes that the first and second phases of HiTTs were performed and a classifier was already built.

Suppose that Bob is a SW architect who is modifying a feature in the SUT. After Bob concludes his implementation, he commits his code changes to the development repository (step 1 in Fig. 3). Lines 3, 4, and 5 in Fig. 3 corresponds to the modified L that Bob submitted in his commit. At this point, HiTTs will analyze Bob's commit by classifying each L into one of the 6 categories of code changes (step 2 in Fig. 3). After classifying the modified/added L, HiTTs will measure the count of classifications made with respect to each code type and accordingly generates a ranked list of code types based on their lines' count. In this example, HiTTs classified two-third of the L in Bob's commit as memory management related and one-third as design. Assuming that the test orchestrators at Bob's company set the window size of HiTTs to 1, then HiTTs will decide to select regression test types that are in dependency with the memory management code only (step 3 in Fig. 3). As a result, performance, load, soak, stress, volume, and capacity tests will be executed to test Bob's commit. Now suppose that the test orchestrators at Bob's company decide to change the window size of HiTTs to 2. In this case, HiTTs will decide to select test types that are dependent on both memory management and design code types. Consequently, performance, load, soak, stress, volume, capacity, back-to-back, portability, and backup and recovery tests will be executed.

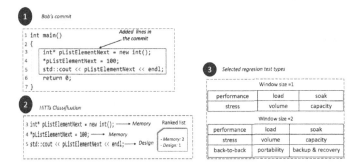

Fig. 3. An illustrative example of a usage scenario for HiTTs.

5   Evaluation of HiTTs

In this section, we present the evaluation results of our method.

5.1   Annotation and Training (Phase 1)

This study was performed over a period of two weeks at a large power supply provider organization that develops software solutions for managing energy consumption in different products. The organization provided us with access to a data-set that belonged to an embedded system written in the C++ language.

Code Change Extraction (Step 1). In this study, a total of 9 code revisions were extracted from the SUT repository. We restricted the extraction of revisions to 9, since we were mainly interested in understanding the effectiveness of our method in reducing the regression testing time. The extracted revisions comprised a total of 2,103 modified and added L from which 1,321 L belonged to source code files ('.cpp' and '.h')[2].

Annotation and Class Balancing (Step 2). Five SW architects that work at the collaborating company were employed to perform the annotations. First, we organized a workshop with the SW architects, where we began by presenting definitions and code examples for each code type in the dependency taxonomy. This was necessary to ensure that all architects posses a good understanding of each type of code change in the dependency taxonomy before starting the annotation. At the end of the workshop, architects were asked to individually annotate each L in the 9 revision files and to send us the annotated L. After receiving the annotated L, we filtered out L that were not mutually annotated by the 5 architects and retained L that were annotated with the same code types. In total, we found 523 L in the annotated files to be similar in their annotation values (level of agreement = 40%). While a common rule of thumb in the literature demands a higher level of agreement between annotators, several studies have shown that comparing annotations by independent and multiple annotators can yield agreement rates as low as 22% [5] and [10].

Figure 4 shows the distribution of code types in the set of annotated L. The Figure shows that the majority of L belonged to the 'Design' code type (25%), whereas the minimal count of L belonged to the 'Conditional' type (4%). The 'Other' category is used by the annotators when encountering L that does not belong to the 6 code categories. Since the distribution of code types is imbalanced, we decided to use the SMOTE module available in the Scikit-learn library [15] to balance the distribution of L in the code types. Applying SMOTE to the data-set resulted in oversampling instances in the minority code types to the same number of instances in the 'Design' code type (the majority class). As a result, we retrieved a total of 903 annotated L.

Features Extraction and Building the Classifier (Step 3). HiTTs employs a textual analysis technique that extracts features from the set of annotated code, where each feature corresponds to a code token that appears in the input file. In this study, we employ the tool proposed by Ochodek et al. [12] to perform the features extraction using the BoW model. Applying BoW on the annotated set of L resulted in a multi-dimensional array that consisted of 895 feature tokens.

HiTTs employs a multi-class classifier that classifies L into one of 6 code change types. This study employed a random forest (RF) model as the multi-classifier in HiTTs. Our choice of using RF was mainly due to the promising

---

[2] Due to non-disclosure agreements with our industrial partner, our data-set can not be made public for replication.

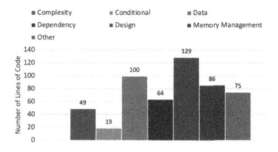

Fig. 4. The distribution of code types in the annotated lines.

potentials that it showed in our recent series of publications (e.g., in [3]). In this study, the hyper-parameters of the RF model were kept in their default state as found in the scikit-learn library (version 0.20.4). The only alteration that we made was in the n_estimator (the number of trees) parameter, where we changed its value from 10 to 100. This was a design choice that we adopted based on our findings in [3], where we experimented the use of an RF model for TCS without tuning the model's parameters. Our findings showed that using an untuned parameters in RF would yield better predictive performance for TCS than other four deep learning and tree-based models.

5.2 Calibration (Phase 2)

In this study, we decided to calibrate tests whose execution verdicts changed from one state to another (e.g., from 'passed' to 'failed'), at least once, during the last six months from the time of conducting this study. This was done to maximize the probability of working with tests that are sensitive to changes in the code-base. As a result, information about 868 tests were extracted from the test logs of the SUT. Architects were required to jointly agree on an ISO test type [1] that best describes each extracted test, and then use that test type for annotation. The keyword 'Other' was used by the architects to annotate tests whose specifications do not match the description of any ISO test types. Four distinct test types were used for annotating the 868 tests. The distribution of the annotated tests was as follows: procedure tests had the highest proportion with a total of 546 tests (62.9%); statement tests had the second highest proportion with 302 tests (34.7%); performance and capacity tests had the lowest proportion with one test respectively; 18 tests (2%) were annotated with the 'Other' keyword. We discarded all tests that were annotated with 'Other', as we do not know which types of code changes would trigger these tests to react.

5.3 Selection (Phase 3)

To evaluate the effectiveness of HiTTs, we extracted code changes committed to the SUT repository and their associated test information after the time of performing the annotation and training phase. A total of 9 code revisions and 26,576 executions of the 868 calibrated tests were extracted. Each code revision was fed into the trained RF model for classifying L into their relevant code types. Figure 5 shows, for each code revision, the number of classified L under each category of code type. All L that were classified as 'Other' by the model were removed from the next step of the selection phase. For the remainder of this paper, we refer to these revisions as 'evaluation revisions'.

5.4 Baseline Construction

To understand whether our method is effective in reducing the regression testing time, we needed to measure and compare its performance against one or more baseline measures. For this purpose, two baselines were used in this study - the actual and retest-all. The actual baseline is a measure of the total time taken to execute all tc that we calculated from the test logs of the build server of the SUT. The retest-all baseline is a measure of the total time taken to execute all available tc under the four test types in similar ratios.

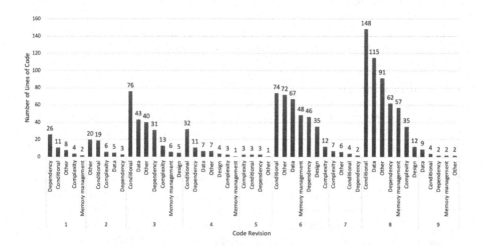

Fig. 5. The distribution of code types in the evaluation revision.

Actual. Table 2 summarizes the information of the execution times of the four test types. The Table shows, for each revision, the number of non-commented lines of code (column 2). The 'actual baseline' column corresponds to the total te time taken to execute all tc of the four test types, as found in the test log files of the SUT. Total execution times spans from 0,91 h to several days. Columns 4 to 7 summarize the actual te for capacity, procedure, statement, and performance tests respectively, whereas columns 8 to 12 show the number of te performed for each test type. By observing the number of te under each test type, we notice that not all test types are executed against the majority of the evaluation revisions. For example, capacity *tc* were only exercised against revisions 1, 2, 3, 5, 8 and 9 (as denoted with '–' in the 'nu. Capacity' column).

Table 2. Information about the actual test execution (in hour) for every revision.

Revision	Lines of code	Actual baseline	Capacity	Procedure	Statement	Performance	nu. Capacity	nu. Procedure	nu. Statement	nu. Performance	nu. Others
1	51	5,73	0,02	3,25	1,77	0,00	5	510	260	–	45
2	53	20,66	0,02	11,02	8,50	0,03	5	1990	1320	5	80
3	201	87,57	0,06	58,23	25,23	0,09	14	9366	1320	14	266
4	65	20,46	0,00	11,68	8,09	0,00	–	2030	2281	–	42
5	10	7,67	0,02	4,08	3,03	0,00	4	816	468	–	44
6	354	22,10	0,00	15,52	5,93	0,00	–	2303	882	–	42
7	19	0,91	0,00	0,91	0,00	0,00	–	192	–	–	–
8	520	12,08	0,03	5,36	6,00	0,00	8	1040	936	–	56
9	19	1,14	0,00	1,14	0,00	0,00	–	240	–	–	–

Retest-All. Since we do not have information about the actual *te* times of every test type across all revisions, we needed to normalize the *te* times of capacity, performance, procedure, statement in order to simulate a retest-all scenario on the 9 evaluation revisions. The normalized *te* times for capacity, performance, procedure, statement tests are presented in Table 2 using the following procedure. First, we calculate the average time required to execute a *tc* under each type in every evaluation revision. Second, for each evaluation revision, we subtract the number of executed tests from those executed against the revision with the highest number of *te*. Third, we multiply the number of missing *te* under each test type with the average *te* time for the same test type. Finally, we add the *te* time of the estimated *tc* to the actual *te* time that we found in the test log data. The advantage of retaining the actual *te* time of existing tests lies in minimizing the probability of using over/under-estimated *te* time. Table 3

Table 3. Normalized execution times (in hour) for each test types in all revisions.

Revision	Retest-all baseline	Capacity	Procedure	Statement	Performance
1	70,63	0,06	56,51	10,09	0,09
2	67,81	0,06	55,38	8,50	0,08
3	87,57	0,06	58,23	25,23	0,09
4	67,97	0,06	55,80	8,09	0,09
5	69,12	0,06	55,51	9,72	0,09
6	71,40	0,06	58,00	9,37	0,09
7	70,44	0,06	56,09	10,35	0,09
8	68,32	0,06	55,44	9,01	0,09
9	70,38	0,06	56,03	10,35	0,09

summarizes the normalized *te* times for all test types across the 9 evaluation revisions. The 'Retest-all baseline' column in Table 3 corresponds to the total *te* time calculated by summing up the normalized values under each test type.

5.5 Results and Analysis

The goal of the evaluation is to identify the total amount of reduced time in performing regression testing. To that end, we compare the testing time required by HiTTs with the two baseline measures. We use a window size of 1, 2, and 3 {*w1, w2, w3*} respectively for the comparison. Results of applying HiTTs with each window size are depicted in Table 4. The Table shows, for each revision and window size, the types of selected *tc* (column 3), the actual failing test types (column 4), the actual *te* time for all *tc* (column 5), the *te* time of a retest-all approach (column 6), the amount of reduced time relative to the retest-all (column 8) and the actual baseline (column 10) time.

The results reported in Table 4 suggest that using any window size in HiTTs reduces the total testing time by more than eight hours across the majority of evaluation revisions. The total reduced time, as measured by correct deselection of passing test types, reached 52,94% when compared with the actual baseline. Similarly, the percentages of improvement in time reduction relative to the retest-all baseline reached between 0,18% and 15,78%. This reduced time can potentially save architects the hurdle of doing large code rework after testing, since bugs found earlier in the development cycle are often easier to fix than bugs found after the time of adding new code. For instance, applying HiTTs with a window size of 1 on revision 8 was found to reduce the testing time by 6,03 h compared with the actual baseline. Hence, instead of waiting for 11,4 h to execute integration and system level tests, architects will wait for 5,37 h to receive feedback about their code. This allows architects to spare 6,03 h for bug fixing, feature development, or executing other types of test suites. Further, by comparing the values in the 'selected test types' and the 'failing test types' columns, we notice that the selection rate of fault-revealing tests was best when using *w2* in HiTTs. However, what stands out in the results is that statement and capacity test types were only selected once for revision 6 when using *w3*. This can be due to missing dependency links in the taxonomy or code types. Hence, future work need to investigate additional dependencies between the capacity and statement tests, and existing code types.

To gain a better understanding of the method's effectiveness, we measured its fault detection capability in terms of recall and precision when using the three window sizes. While precision is the proportion of correctly identified test types, recall is the proportion of relevant test types that were identified as such. Having both precision and recall high ensures the detection of larger amount of test types that will reveal faults in the SUT. Further, we calculated the mean reduced time by HiTTs using the three window sizes and compared the results with the two baselines. Figure 6 shows a bar chart that depicts the results of the comparison. The results indicate that using *w2* or *w3* improves the rate of faults detection by 22,2% compared to when using *w1* (recall improvement from 61%

to 83,33%). Conversely, the precision rate remained unchanged for *w2* (77,78%) and dropped to 69,44% for *w3*. Taken together, these results suggest that using *w3* leads to the least effective performance of HiTTs, whereas *w2* yields the highest performance. On the other hand, the mean reduced times attained when using *w1* or *w2* was found to be similar, which implies that using either of the two window sizes leads to a similar reduction rate of the testing time.

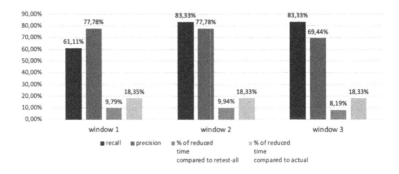

Fig. 6. Mean performance and reduced testing time using three windows.

RQ. How to reduce the time of regression testing by selecting only the most relevant test types?
The results confirm that using our method with a window size of 2 reduces the time of regression testing by 9,94% on average compared to a retest-all approach and by 18,33% compared to the testing approach adopted by our industrial partner.

---

6   Threats to Validity

We use the framework in [17] to discuss the limitations of our paper.

External Validity. We evaluated the effectiveness of HiTTs on 9 revisions that belong to a single industrial system. Thus, we cannot claim that our findings generalize well to other types of systems. However, we increase the likelihood of drawing a representative sample by using all revisions that were committed to the development repository after the time of building HiTTs. Further, we trained the classifier in HiTTs on a small sample of data, which could have resulted in a lower classification performance than what we could achieve with a larger sample. However, our evaluation shows that the performance of HiTTs is high.

Construct Validity. The dependency links used for defining the static rules of procedure tests were drawn from the literature, and thus not validated. However, our evaluation results showed that HiTTs was effective in selecting this type of tests across the 9 evaluation revisions.

Table 4. The evaluation results of HiTTs compared to two baselines.

Window size of 1, 2, and 3

Revision	Window	Selected test types	Failing test types	Actual baseline	Retest-all baseline	Reduced time (retest-all)	% of reduced time (retest-all)	Reduced time (actual)	% of reduced time (actual)
1	w1	Procedure	Procedure, Statement	5,04	66,74	0,14	0,22	0,02	0,40
	w2	Procedure	Procedure, Statement	5,04	66,74	0,14	0,22	0,02	0,40
	w3	Procedure, Performance	Procedure, Statement	5,04	66,74	0,06	0,08	0,02	0,40
2	w1	Procedure	Procedure, Statement	19,56	64,02	0,14	0,22	0,05	0,24
	w2	Procedure, Performance	Procedure, Statement	19,56	64,02	0,06	0,09	0,02	0,10
	w3	Procedure, Performance	Procedure, Statement	19,56	64,02	0,06	0,09	0,02	0,10
3	w1	Procedure	Procedure, Statement	83,61	83,61	0,15	0,18	0,15	0,18
	w2	Procedure	Procedure, Statement	83,61	83,61	0,15	0,18	0,15	0,18
	w3	Procedure	Procedure, Statement	83,61	83,61	0,15	0,18	0,15	0,18
4	w1	Procedure	Procedure	19,77	64,04	8,24	12,86	8,09	40,93
	w2	Procedure	Procedure	19,77	64,04	8,24	12,86	8,09	40,93
	w3	Procedure	Procedure	19,77	64,04	8,24	12,86	8,09	40,93
5	w1	Performance	Procedure	7,13	65,37	9,77	14,95	3,05	42,76
	w2	Performance, Procedure	Procedure	7,13	65,37	9,77	14,95	3,05	42,76
	w3	Performance, Procedure	Procedure	7,13	65,37	9,77	14,95	3,05	42,76
6	w1	Procedure	Procedure	21,45	67,51	9,51	14,09	5,93	27,65
	w2	Procedure	Procedure	21,45	67,51	10,50	15,55	5,93	27,65
	w3	Procedure, Performance, Capacity, Statement	Procedure	21,45	67,51	0,00	0,00	0,00	0,00
7	w1	Performance	Procedure	0,91	66,59	10,41	15,63	0,00	0,00
	w2	Performance. Procedure	Procedure	0,91	66,59	10,41	15,63	0,00	0,00
	w3	Performance. Procedure	Procedure	0,91	66,59	10,41	15,63	0,00	0,00
8	w1	Procedure	Procedure	11,40	64,60	9,16	14,17	6,03	52,94
	w2	Procedure	Procedure	11,40	64,60	9,16	14,17	6,03	52,94
	w3	Procedure	Procedure	11,40	64,60	9,16	14,17	6,03	52,94
9	w1	Procedure	Procedure	1,14	66,53	10,50	15,78	0,00	0,00
	w2	Procedure	Procedure	1,14	66,53	10,50	15,78	0,00	0,00
	w3	Procedure	Procedure	1,14	66,53	10,50	15,78	0,00	0,00

Internal Validity. An internal threat is the presence of undetected defects in the tools that we used for features extraction, code change extraction, and baseline measurements. To increase our confidence in the tools' implementation, we tested our code on smaller examples. The results might differ if we employ other types of models. However, in this study we were only interested in understanding the effectiveness of HiTTs in reducing the regression testing time.

Conclusion Validity. There is a probability that some tests failed due to non-deterministic executions (i.e., flaky tests) or environmental factors (e.g., a hardware element goes offline). As a result, the test execution times that we used for calculating the baselines may belong to tests that failed due to factors unrelated to code changes, and thus lead us to wrong conclusions. To minimize this threat, we collected data of several thousand test executions and minimized the probability of selecting tests that have non-deterministic behaviors.

7   Conclusion and Future Work

In this paper, we introduced HiTTs - a machine learning based method that selects regression test types based on their relation with code types that appear in new revisions without the need of history test information. The presented method was evaluated on an industrial data-set for effectiveness in reducing the regression testing time and faults detection. The results of the study are encouraging: 1) for the subject considered, our method showed considerable time reduction in regression testing - up to 52,94%, 2) increasing the window size of HiTTs to a medium level improves the effectiveness rate of faults detection and still reduces the total time of regression testing.

The results of our study suggest several avenues for future work. First, working on refining and extending the taxonomy to capture more dependencies between the statement and capacity test types and existing code types is needed to improve the effectiveness of the method in TCS. Second, we plan to extend HiTTs by adding an ensemble of classifiers to predict the verdict of tests that belong to each selected test type. This allows HiTTs to operate on a finer-level of granularity (i.e., test case level). Finally, future work needs to compare the effectiveness of HiTTs with state-of-the-art approaches for TCS.

References

1. Iso/iec/ieee int. standard - software and systems engineering - software testing-part 1: Concepts and definitions. Technical report (2020)
2. Al-Sabbagh, K., Staron, M., Hebig, R., Gomes, F.: A classification of code changes and test types dependencies for improving machine learning based test selection. In: Proceedings of the 17th International Conference on Predictive Models and Data Analytics in Software Engineering, pp. 10–19 (2021)
3. Al-Sabbagh, K.W., Staron, M., Hebig, R., Meding, W.: Predicting test case verdicts using textual analysis of committed code churns. In: (IWSM Mensura 2019), vol. 2476, pp. 138–153 (2019)
4. Batista, G.E., Prati, R.C., Monard, M.C.: A study of the behavior of several methods for balancing machine learning training data. ACM SIGKDD Explorations Newsl **6**(1), 20–29 (2004)
5. Bayerl, P.S., Paul, K.I.: What determines inter-coder agreement in manual annotations? a meta-analytic investigation. Comput. Linguist. **37**(4), 699–725 (2011)
6. Bertolino, A., Guerriero, A., Miranda, B., Pietrantuono, R., Russo, S.: Learning-to-rank vs ranking-to-learn: strategies for regression testing in continuous integration. In: Proceedings of the ACM/IEEE 42nd International Conference on Software Engineering, pp. 1–12 (2020)
7. Chi, J., Qu, Y., Zheng, Q., Yang, Z., Jin, W., Cui, D., Liu, T.: Relation-based test case prioritization for regression testing. J. Syst. Softw. **163**, 110539 (2020)
8. Dahiya, O., Solanki, K.: A systematic literature study of regression test case prioritization approaches. Int. J. Eng. Technol. **7**(4), 2184–2191 (2018)
9. Durelli, V.H., et al.: Machine learning applied to software testing: a systematic mapping study. IEEE Trans. Reliab. **68**(3), 1189–1212 (2019)
10. Esuli, A., Sebastiani, F.: Proceedings of the 5th conference on language resources and evaluation (2006)
11. Knauss, E., Staron, M., Meding, W., Söder, O., Nilsson, A., Castell, M.: Supporting continuous integration by code-churn based test selection. In: 2015 IEEE/ACM 2nd International Workshop on Rapid Continuous Software Engineering, pp. 19–25. IEEE (2015)
12. Ochodek, M., Staron, M., Bargowski, D., Meding, W., Hebig, R.: Using machine learning to design a flexible loc counter. In: 2017 IEEE Workshop on Machine Learning Techniques for Software Quality Evaluation, pp. 14–20. IEEE (2017)
13. de Oliveira Neto, F.G., Ahmad, A., Leifler, O., Sandahl, K., Enoiu, E.: Improving continuous integration with similarity-based test case selection. In: Proceedings of the 13th International Workshop on Automation of Software Test, pp. 39–45 (2018)
14. Orso, A., Shi, N., Harrold, M.J.: Scaling regression testing to large software systems. ACM SIGSOFT Soft. Eng. Notes **29**(6), 241–251 (2004)

15. Pedregosa, F., et al.: Scikit-learn: machine learning in Python. J. Mach. Learn. Res. **12**, 2825–2830 (2011)

16. Wang, K., Zhu, C., Celik, A., Kim, J., Batory, D., Gligoric, M.: Towards refactoring-aware regression test selection. In: 2018 IEEE/ACM 40th International Conference on Software Engineering (ICSE), pp. 233–244. IEEE (2018)

17. Wohlin, C., Runeson, P., Höst, M., Ohlsson, M.C., Regnell, B., Wesslén, A.: Experimentation in software engineering. Springer Science & Business Media (2012)

Early Identification of Invalid Bug Reports in Industrial Settings – A Case Study

Muhammad Laiq[1]([✉]), Nauman bin Ali[1], Jürgen Böstler[1],
and Emelie Engström[2]

[1] Blekinge Institute of Technology, Karlskrona, Sweden
{muhammad.laiq,nauman.ali,jurgen.bostler}@bth.se
[2] Lund University, Lund, Sweden
emelie.engstrom@cs.lth.se

Abstract. Software development companies spend considerable time resolving bug reports. However, bug reports might be invalid, i.e., not point to a valid flaw. Expensive resources and time might be expended on invalid bug reports before discovering that they are invalid. In this case study, we explore the impact of invalid bug reports and develop and assess the use of machine learning (ML) to indicate whether a bug report is likely invalid. We found that about 15% of bug reports at the case company are invalid, and that their resolution time is similar to valid bug reports. Among the ML-based techniques we used, logistic regression and SVM show promising results. In the feedback, practitioners indicated an interest in using the tool to identify invalid bug reports at early stages. However, they emphasized the need to improve the explainability of ML-based recommendations and to reduce the maintenance cost of the tool.

Keywords: Bug reports · Invalid bugs · Machine learning · Valid bugs · Bug classification · Software analytics

1 Introduction

Bug reports are submitted to describe undesired behavior of software products. For large projects, the number of such reports may be high [6]. However, not all of the submitted bug reports may be valid, i.e., indicate an actual deviation from acceptable system behavior. For example, for Mozilla and Firefox 31% and 77% of the submitted bug reports were resolved as invalid, respectively [6].

Invalid bug reports may cause a lot of unnecessary effort. In addition to the direct cost of managing them, they make the process of identifying and prioritizing valid bug reports challenging. In large companies, manually checking the validity of each bug report is laborious and error-prone. A tool that determines the likelihood of a bug report's validity may significantly reduce the maintenance cost by assisting practitioners in prioritizing the resolution of bug reports.

Previous research on handling invalid bug reports has primarily focused on the open-source software (OSS) context. Fan et al. [6], He et al. [9] and Zanetti

© The Author(s), under exclusive license to Springer Nature Switzerland AG 2022
D. Taibi et al. (Eds.): PROFES 2022, LNCS 13709, pp. 497–507, 2022.
https://doi.org/10.1007/978-3-031-21388-5_34

et al. [19], for example, proposed automated approaches to predict the validity of newly submitted bug reports in OSS. However, OSS differs from closed-source contexts in facets such as bug handling processes, development processes, level of detail in bug reports and skills and motivation of submitters and testers. In addition, the proportion of invalid bug reports in closed-source contexts is smaller [2]. Thus, it is unclear how well the prediction algorithms and approaches developed for OSS contexts will work on closed-source data.

Furthermore, research on determining bug reports' validity is limited to evaluating ML techniques on prediction accuracy. However, companies consider a number of other factors in their adoption decisions [1]. Thus, this study adapts the technology adoption framework proposed by Rana et al. [14] to investigate important factors practitioners are concerned about when deciding to adopt an ML-based solution for determining the validity of bug reports.

In this paper, we report an industrial case study characterizing the challenge of invalid bug reports and evaluating a state-of-the-art ML-based approach to address some of the challenges in a closed-source context.

RQ1: What are the characteristics of invalid bug reports in a closed-source context? We explore the prevalence and the characteristics of valid and invalid bug reports, such as the amount and lead time.

RQ2: How effective are existing approaches at predicting bug reports' validity when applied in a large-scale closed-source context? We are interested in utilizing existing approaches to determine the validity of bug reports in a large-scale closed-source context.

RQ3: What are the important factors for practitioners when deciding to adopt an ML-based tool for the validity prediction of bug reports? We aim to evaluate the proposed approach and identify practitioners' adoption concerns for an ML-based approach to predict invalid bug reports.

2   Research Method

To answer the research questions (stated in Sect. 1), we conducted an industrial case study [15]. We broadly followed a two step approach. First, we manually analyzed bug reports to investigate the prevalence and characteristics of invalid bug reports using descriptive statistics and graphs. Then, we applied existing ML-based approaches to determine the validity of incoming bug reports in a large-scale closed-source context. We assessed ML models' accuracy on a telecommunication company's two products (see Sect. 2.3).

2.1   Case Description

The case company is a large telecommunication vendor in Sweden, developing and maintaining large critical software products. We collect and analyze data of two large products at the company (see Sect. 2.3 for the products' details).

The company has several hundreds of employees distributed over several countries. The development context of the company is embedded systems. Teams use agile practices and principles in development. Most of the code at the company is written in C++, JavaScript (JS) and Java.

Bug reports about a perceived issue in a product are filed from different sources, e.g., testers, customers, or the developers themselves. As shown in Fig. 1, bug reports are first manually screened by the Change Control Board (CCB) to ensure that only bug reports that describe faults in the code are assigned to a team. Despite this approach, several bug reports related to configuration, insufficient data, or future improvements are still assigned to teams as bug reports (which later turn out to be invalid bug reports). Thus, consuming resources and affecting bug management scheduling and prioritization adversely.

2.2 Invalid Bug Reports

In prior studies [6,9,19], a definition of valid and invalid bug reports was used. It is based on the resolution of bug reports in Bugzilla.

At the case company, valid bug reports describe a fault in the code with one of the following resolutions: already fixed, will be fixed in a future update, the document will be corrected, and will be corrected in a future update. Likewise, invalid bug reports (i.e., not a fault in the code) are those with one of the following resolutions: insufficient information, future requirement, misunderstanding of functionality, no such requirements exist, and configuration issue.

In the present case study, we relied on the case company's definition of a valid bug report.

2.3 Data Collection

We collected bug reports data from BTS for over five years of two products (both products, P1 and P2, had approx. 3500 bug reports, and the percentage of invalid bug reports was 14 and 17, respectively). For the context of this study, we are only using bug reports having a final verdict of being valid or invalid. We also removed duplicate bug reports to avoid potential bias and overfitting.

Furthermore, to collect practitioners' feedback we used both focus groups and a questionnaire. The following six practitioners participated in the focus groups: Two managers with approx. 20 years of experience, a domain expert, and a software engineer with approx. 8 years of experience, a data scientist with 10 years of experience, and a data scientist with 2.5 years of professional experience.

2.4 Development of the Diagnostic and Predictive Tool

We performed three iterations to develop the support tools. In each iteration, we conducted a focus group with practitioners to collect their feedback.

Diagnostic Tool. The tool supports analysis of various characteristics of bug reports: (a) a visualization of data to identify and compare trends in the prevalence of bug reports, e.g., to understand if the number of invalid bug reports is increasing or decreasing, and (b) a grouping of bug reports by origins, priority, lead time, and their mapping to software/system quality characteristics.

Predictive Tool. To answer RQ3, we built a predictive tool that uses a supervised ML-based model to determine the likelihood of the validity of a newly submitted bug report. We collect past bug reports from the Bug Tracking System (BTS) to train an ML-based model using labeled data. Once a new bug report is submitted, we convert information present in the new report into features as input to the predictive tool. The predictive tool then predicts the class of a newly submitted bug report, i.e., valid or invalid. As shown in Fig. 1, the dotted line is used for the predictive tool suggestion to the CCB, development teams, or developers in the decision-making process.

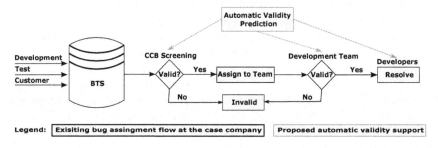

Fig. 1. Existing bug assignment flow at the case company and proposed support

2.5   Feature Selection

We used textual (*Heading*, and *Observation*), categorical (*Priority*), and numerical features (*Submitter Experience*). These features have been commonly used in previous work in the context of bug reports classification [6,9]. Fan et al. [6] used summary, description, and submitter experience with other features in the OSS context to determine the validity of bug reports. Likewise, He et al. [9] applied a deep learning-based approach using summary and description.

The heading is a short description of a bug report, and observation is a detailed explanation of the issue that occurred on the user side. Unlike heading, observation includes steps to reproduce the issue.

The submitter experience can affect the bug reporting quality/validity, i.e., people with less experience are more likely to submit invalid bug reports, such as duplicate ones [4]. In contrast, people with more experience usually provide complete information [11]. Submitter experience is based on historical data and comprises the validity rate and total number of bug reports submitted by an individual. The validity rate is a ratio of valid to total bug reports submitted by a person. Unlike OSS, in a closed-source context, the submitters keep themselves familiar with systems and processes at the company. Thus, we do not use the recent behavior of submitters for the submitter experience feature (i.e., we only used validity rate and total bug reports) as used by Fan et al. [6].

Furthermore, we do not use readability, completeness, and collaboration network dimensions because readability and completeness have negligible significance [6] in distinguishing valid and invalid bug reports, and the collaboration network is not available in the case company. Furthermore, the quality of bug reports in a closed-source context is usually higher than in OSS [2]. Thus, readability and completeness will likely be less important in a closed-source context.

2.6   Experimental Setup

Similar to previous studies [5,6,17], we conducted our experiments using an incremental setup, see Fig. 2. We first sort bug reports chronologically based on their initial submission time. Then we divide them into 11 equal folds. We perform our experiments using ten runs as follows: In the first run, fold-1 is used for training and fold-2 for testing. In the second run, fold-1 and fold-2 are used for training and fold-3 for testing. In the final run, fold-1 to fold-10 are used for training and fold-11 for testing. We then measure the average prediction results over each fold.

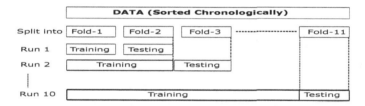

Fig. 2. Experimental setup

2.7   Evaluation Metrics

To evaluate the performance of the models, we choose Area Under the Curve (AUC) of receiver operator characteristic (ROC) [10]. AUC is robust towards imbalanced datasets and unbiased towards classifiers [12,16].

We also measure Matthew's Correlation Coefficient (MCC) [13], F1-score, recall, and precision. These metrics are calculated to compare the reliability of their results with AUC (i.e., underlying evaluation metric) on imbalanced datasets. MCC is a widely used performance evaluation metric in the biomedical field [13]. The metric is suitable for an imbalanced data set [7].

2.8   Technology Adoption Evaluation Framework

The ML-based technique to determine the likelihood of bug reports' validity can be helpful in the practitioners' decision-making process. However, when companies consider adopting such approaches, they also look at further factors. This

Table 1. Factors that effects the adoption of ML-based solution [14]

Factors	Attributes
Need and importance	Need and importance for early detection of invalid bug reports
Potential use-cases of tool	Additional review, deprioritization, and flagging
Familiarity and experience with ML	Understanding of ML-based technology
	Collaborated with academics in ML-based projects
	Tried ML previously and ability to implement in-house
	Ability to interpret and assess results of ML-based tool
Other important aspects, i.e., perceived benefits and barriers and tool availability	Accuracy and explainability of the predictions by tool
	Adoption/operationalization cost of tool
	Buy-in from the concerned stakeholders
	Integration in the current workflow and long term maintenance
	Adaptability to different product units such as P1 and P2
	Ability to handle a large amount of bug reports data
	Integration with existing systems and obtaining results at a low cost
	Availability as an open-source tool

study adapts the technology adoption framework proposed by Rana et al. [14] to investigate such factors (see Table 1) for the ML-based solution to determine the validity of bug reports.

3   Results and Analysis

RQ1: What are the characteristics of invalid bug reports in a closed-source context? We developed a diagnostic tool (see Sect. 2.4) to answer this question. The average lead time for valid and invalid bug reports is similar. For P1, we get around 18, and for P2 around 16 mean calendar days. The average priority for invalid bug reports is medium for both products. This signifies the seriousness of the invalid bug reports problem at the company.

Furthermore, we analyzed the origin of invalid bug reports for P1 and P2 by segmenting the sorted data into yearly chunks and mapping each bug report to the various testing levels used at the company. However, we observed that most faults slip through to later stages for both products, i.e., verification or verification on the target environment. The mapping of software/system quality characteristics yields similar results for P1 and P2, i.e., most of the bug reports are mapped on identical quality characteristics.

RQ2: How effective are existing approaches at predicting bug reports validity when applied in a large-scale proprietary context? To answer this research question, we developed classification models using features described in Sect. 2.5. Table 2 presents the results of Logistic Regression and SVM for both products. At best, we achieve 0.84 AUC using Logistic Regression on P1. Our approach is rather simple, but the results are comparable to previous work in the OSS context, i.e., Fan et al. [6] used 33 features and achieved the 0.73 (lowest) AUC for Netbeans and 0.87 (best) on Firefox dataset. We also trained Decision Tree and KNN; best, we got 0.63 AUC and 0.62 AUC, respectively.

As shown in Table 2, the F1-score, precision, accuracy, and recall results are misleading and biased towards valid class. The possible explanation for these biased results is an imbalanced dataset, i.e., only about 14–17% of the bug reports are invalid in our dataset. In this context, the choice of AUC metric and nMCC is more suitable.

In comparison to the work on invalid bug reports in the OSS context by Zanetti et al. [19], He et al. [9], and Fan et al. [6], our approach is relatively simple. However, it still achieves comparable results in a closed-source context.

Table 2. Model performance: AUC, nMCC, F1-score (F1), Precision (P) and Recall (R) for Valid (V) and Invalid (I) bug reports

Model	Product	Algorithm	AUC	nMCC	F1(I)	P(I)	R(I)	F1(V)	P(V)	R(V)
M1	P1	Logistic regression	**0.84**	0.71	0.42	0.71	0.31	0.94	0.91	0.98
M2	P1	SVM	**0.77**	0.69	0.40	0.60	0.31	0.94	0.91	0.97
M3	P2	Logistic regression	**0.76**	0.62	0.25	0.54	0.17	0.91	0.86	0.97
M4	P2	SVM	**0.71**	0.63	0.30	0.51	0.22	0.91	0.86	0.96

RQ3: What are the important factors for practitioners when deciding to adopt an ML-based tool for the validity prediction of bug reports? We evaluated the proposed ML-based technique with practitioners using an adaption of Rana et al.'s [14] framework (see Sect. 2.8). We collected practitioners' (see practitioner's profile in Sect. 2.3) feedback using a questionnaire and open discussion. A total of six participants were involved in each focus group and a questionnaire was answered by three. Since the number of participants and respondents to the questionnaire were small, we do not claim statistical generalizability. Still, we got useful input for further investigations. The respondents represent different roles and have extensive experience.

Practitioners indicated an interest in having a tool to determine invalid bug reports at early stages. However, they would like to have an explainability aspect in the tool. Further, practitioners indicated that integration with existing systems is possible. However, they highlighted that the tool should be adaptable to other products and handle a large amount of data with low maintenance costs.

4 Discussion

This section discusses our findings and the related work on invalid bug reports.

Identification of Bug Report Validity. There are few studies on determining the validity of bug reports automatically. The most relevant studies to our work are Zanetti at al. [19], Fan et al. [6], and He et al. [9]. However, all three are conducted in the OSS context. Zanetti et al. [19] built collaborative networks on OSS bug reports datasets. The collaborative network was formed based on the bug reports relations., i.e., assigned fixer and its cc email address. Then nine features were obtained from the network as input for an SVM classifier to predict the validity of bug reports. Fan et al.'s [6] approach uses 33 features to determine the validity of the bug reports. These features were extracted in five dimensions: submitter experience, collaboration network, and a bug report's text, completeness, and readability. The approach was applied to an OSS dataset using Random forest and SVM classifier. The model's performance indicates considerable improvement over Zanetti et al.'s [19] approach. However, it is worth noting that the strategy utilizes 33 features that might cause the curse-of-dimensionality [8]. He et al. [9] applied deep learning using convolutional neural networks using only summaries and descriptions of bug reports to identify the validity of bug reports automatically. The approach was evaluated on five OSS projects and results indicate improvements over Fan et al.'s [6] approach.

Our approach is relatively simple and applied in a large-scale closed-source context. The performance of our models is comparable to the work discussed above (see Table 2). Furthermore, we evaluated our approach using Rana et al.'s [14] technology adoption framework for ML-based solutions (see Sect. 2.8).

Prevalence of Bug-Reports. We found that around 14% and 17% of all submitted bug reports are invalid for P1 and P2, respectively. In OSS, Fan et al. [6] reported 31% and 77% of invalid bug reports for Mozilla and Firefox, respectively. In contrast to OSS, the percentage is smaller. A possible explanation for this are the rigorous processes followed in a proprietary context for writing and reviewing bug reports, and the disparity in skills and motivation of submitters [2].

Evaluation Setup. Similar to previous studies [5,6,17], we use an incremental approach. It is suitable in our context since we aim to predict the validity of future bug reports. It also reduces experimental bias [18]. Other approaches might produce better results, however, the selected approach is a realistic simulation of the BTS environment and provides a pragmatic assessment of our experiments.

Benefits of Validity Assessment. Early identification of invalid bug reports has implications for practitioners. For instance, bug reports that are likely to be invalid: (a) could undergo an additional review before assignment, (b) could be deferred, i.e., prioritize valid ones, and (c) could be flagged for downstream developers, indicating that a bug report is likely to be invalid. Practitioners also acknowledged these as relevant use-cases in their feedback.

5   Threats to Validity

In this case study, we evaluate ML-based approaches to validity prediction in large-scale closed source contexts. Both human and technical aspects are considered. The main threats to validity regard the representatives of our case and the validity of the empirical evaluations.

Generalization of Results: We consider that the case company and their two large products are an example of a large-scale closed-source software development context. As the approach delivers similar accuracy as in the OSS context, we are confident that ML-based approaches for validity prediction will likely generalize to other cases similar to the case and context described in this study.

Evaluation of Human Aspects: The main conclusions about the identified use cases for the validity predictions at the case company and the need to improve the prediction model's explainability are based on feedback from a small group of practitioners. The small sample is a threat to generalizability both within the company and externally. We used focus groups to collect data. Two researchers participated in all focus groups to improve the reliability of the collected feedback. One researcher took notes in each focus group, and the other led the discussion. Afterward, the researchers discussed the feedback and documented their interpretation. We also performed member checking by presenting our interpretation and analysis results back to the practitioners. We used an existing adoption framework [14] to guide our feedback collection from the case company. Furthermore, we internally reviewed and revised the questionnaire before sending it to the respondents.

Evaluation of ML Performance: We used AUC and MCC to evaluate the performance of the models, as they produce more reliable results when the data is imbalanced (please see Sects. 3 and 2.7 for a detailed discussion). To have training data with high reliability, we used only bug reports with final validity labels since they often represent the judgment of more than one domain expert. In this study, we did not investigate the impact of "concept drift" [3], i.e., how often the model needs to be retrained to capture major changes in the ways of working, technology, or personnel involved in the bug management process.

6   Conclusion and Contributions

The number of invalid bug reports, estimated severity, and their resolution time indicate a significant source of waste in large-scale closed-source systems. They cost substantial resources and adversely affect the scheduling and resolution of valid bug reports. The main contributions of this work are as follows:

Practical Contributions: We developed a tool that supports exploratory analysis of bug reports by giving practitioners visibility in their current practice and facilitate trend analysis. The tool also has a predictive component that provides practitioners a determination whether a defect report is likely to be valid.

Scientific Contributions: 1) We evaluated the ML-based approaches to validity prediction in a new context, i.e., in a large-scale closed-source context, 2) In previous work, the human aspects/concerns of practitioners are entirely missing. However, we used focus groups and a technology adoption framework to collect practitioners' feedback. We identified that practitioners consider the need to explain the justification for each recommendation by the predictive tool as essential for its widespread adoption.

Acknowledgment. This work has been supported by ELLIIT; the Swedish Strategic Research Area in IT and Mobile Communications.

References

1. Ali, N.B.: Is effectiveness sufficient to choose an intervention? considering resource use in empirical software engineering. In: 10th International Symposium on Empirical Software Engineering and Measurement, pp. 54:1–54:6 (2016)
2. Bachmann, A., Bernstein, A.: Software process data quality and characteristics: a historical view on open and closed source projects. In: Joint ERCIM Workshops on Principles of Software Evolution and Software Evolution, pp. 119–128 (2009)
3. Bennin, K.E., Ali, N.B., Börstler, J., Yu, X.: Revisiting the impact of concept drift on just-in-time quality assurance. In: 20th International Conference on Software Quality, Reliability and Security, pp. 53–59 (2020)
4. Bettenburg, N., Just, S., Schröter, A., Weiss, C., Premraj, R., Zimmermann, T.: What makes a good bug report? In: 16th International Symposium on Foundations of Software Engineering, pp. 308–318 (2008)
5. Bettenburg, N., Premraj, R., Zimmermann, T., Kim, S.: Duplicate bug reports considered harmful...really? In: International Conference on Software Maintenance, pp. 337–345 (2008)
6. Fan, Y., Xia, X., Lo, D., Hassan, A.E.: Chaff from the wheat: characterizing and determining valid bug reports. Trans. Softw. Eng. **46**(5), 495–525 (2018)
7. Halimu, C., Kasem, A., Newaz, S.S.: Empirical comparison of area under roc curve (auc) and mathew correlation coefficient (mcc) for evaluating machine learning algorithms on imbalanced datasets for binary classification. In: 3rd International Conference on Machine Learning and Soft Computing, pp. 1–6 (2019)
8. Han, J., Pei, J., Kamber, M.: Data mining: concepts and techniques. Elsevier (2011)
9. He, J., Xu, L., Fan, Y., Xu, Z., Yan, M., Lei, Y.: Deep learning based valid bug reports determination and explanation. In: 31st International Symposium on Software Reliability Engineering, pp. 184–194 (2020)
10. Huang, J., Ling, C.X.: Using auc and accuracy in evaluating learning algorithms. Trans. Knowl. Data Eng. **17**(3), 299–310 (2005)
11. Just, S., Premraj, R., Zimmermann, T.: Towards the next generation of bug tracking systems. In: Symposium on Visual Languages and Human-centric Computing, pp. 82–85 (2008)
12. Lessmann, S., Baesens, B., Mues, C., Pietsch, S.: Benchmarking classification models for software defect prediction: a proposed framework and novel findings. Trans. Softw. Eng. **34**(4), 485–496 (2008)
13. Matthews, B.W.: Comparison of the predicted and observed secondary structure of t4 phage lysozyme. Biochimica et Biophysica Acta (BBA)-Protein Struct. **405**(2), 442–451 (1975)
14. Rana, R., Staron, M., Hansson, J., Nilsson, M., Meding, W.: A framework for adoption of machine learning in industry for software defect prediction. In: 9th Intern. Conference on Software Engineering and Applications, pp. 383–392 (2014)
15. Runeson, P., Höst, M.: Guidelines for conducting and reporting case study research in software engineering. Empir. Softw. Eng. **14**(2), 131–164 (2009)
16. Tantithamthavorn, C., Hassan, A.E.: An experience report on defect modelling in practice: pitfalls and challenges. In: 40th International Conference on Software Engineering: Software Engineering in Practice, pp. 286–295 (2018)
17. Wang, S., Zhang, W., Wang, Q.: Fixercache: unsupervised caching active developers for diverse bug triage. In: 8th International Symposium on Empirical Software Engineering and Measurement, pp. 1–10 (2014)

18. Witten, I.H., Frank, E.: Data mining: practical machine learning tools and techniques with java implementations. ACM SIGMOD Rec. **31**(1), 76–77 (2002)

19. Zanetti, M.S., Scholtes, I., Tessone, C.J., Schweitzer, F.: Categorizing bugs with social networks: a case study on four open source software communities. In: 35th International Conference on Software Engineering, pp. 1032–1041 (2013)

Posters

RESEM: Searching Regular Expression Patterns with Semantics and Input/Output Examples

Hiroki Takeshige[✉], Shinsuke Matsumoto, and Shinji Kusumoto

Graduate School of Information Science and Technology,
Osaka University, Osaka, Japan
{h-takesg,shinsuke,kusumoto}@ist.osaka-u.ac.jp

Abstract. Regular expression is widely known as a powerful and general-purpose text processing tool for programming. Though the regular expression is highly versatile, there are various difficulties in using them. One promising approach to reduce the burden of the pattern composition is reuse by referring to past usages. Still, several source code-specialized search engines have been proposed, they are not suitable for the scenario of reusing regular expression patterns. The purpose of this study is the efficient reuse of regular expression patterns. To achieve the purpose, we propose a usage retrieval system RESEM specialized in regular expression patterns. RESEM adopts two key features: search by semantics and collecting input/output examples. RESEM will smoothly connect *what to do* to *how to do* in the implementation process of string manipulation.

Keywords: Regular expression · Pattern · Usage search · Input/output example · Dynamic analysis · Semantics

1 Introduction

Regular expression is widely known as a powerful and general-purpose text processing tool for programming. In regular expression, any strings can be expressed in a special character sequence. This paper calls such a character sequence pattern. An example of a pattern is \d+\.\d+[1] which accepts any version number consisting of a major and a minor number.

Though the regular expression is highly versatile, there are various difficulties in using them. One of the reasons is on non-intuitive metacharacters in a pattern [4]. While metacharacters enable flexible text manipulation with only a few characters, they do not intuitively represent what they mean. In addition, it is difficult to analyze and generalize the string to be processed and manipulated [4]. Wang et al. reported that 46% of regular expression-related bugs were caused by incorrect behaviors of patterns [5].

---

[1] \d, +, and \. respectively means a single digit, one or more repetitions of the preceding character, and a single dot.

© The Author(s), under exclusive license to Springer Nature Switzerland AG 2022
D. Taibi et al. (Eds.): PROFES 2022, LNCS 13709, pp. 511–517, 2022.
https://doi.org/10.1007/978-3-031-21388-5_35

One promising approach to reducing the burden of the pattern composition is reusing past pattern usages. Several source code-specialized search engines have been proposed to support the reuse of program APIs [1,6] and code snippets [2,3]. Although these engines can be used to retrieve usages of regular expression, they are not suitable for the scenario of reusing regular expression patterns. The reason is that the existing approach provides *"how to use an API"*, not *"how to compose a pattern using regular expression literals"*. Furthermore, although the existing approach queries code snippets themselves (e.g., API names), we need to query the meaning of the pattern.

The purpose of this study is the efficient reuse of regular expression patterns. To achieve the purpose, we propose a usage retrieval system, RESEM, specialized in regular expression patterns. RESEM adopts two key features: search by semantics and collecting input/output examples. RESEM accepts patterns' meaning or purpose as a search query. This idea enables to query by the semantics of patterns rather than their contents. In addition, multiple sets of input/output examples corresponding to the usages are presented in the search result. The concrete I/O examples are powerful information that helps to understand the pattern. These features reduce the user's burden of analyzing the manipulation and reading special characters. To evaluate the effectiveness of RESEM, we conducted an experiment with 12 subjects. As a result, we confirm that RESEM decreased the time required for describing patterns by 16%. Currently, prototype of RESEM is available on https://tyr.ics.es.osaka-u.ac.jp/resem/.

2   RESEM

2.1   Overview

In order to alleviate the burden of composing regular expressions, this paper proposes a usage retrieval system RESEM specialized in regular expression. RESEM has the following two features. One is that it enables search by the meaning of the pattern (F1). The other is to present an example of inputs and outputs of a pattern (F2). These features make it possible for users who have little experience in using regular expression to search for usages efficiently.

The appearance of RESEM is shown in Fig. 1. Users enter search queries in the upper input area. The search queries are the meaning of the pattern they want. In Fig. 1, "version" is entered to search for a pattern that accepts strings representing a version number. As the first search result, a usage using with the pattern \d+(\.\d+(\.d+)?)? is shown. One usage consists of a pattern, semantics, I/O examples, and code snippet around an API call. The users select the pattern that fits their purpose from the results and use it in their programs.

2.2   F1: Search by Semantics

RESEM accepts the meanings of a pattern as a search query. This feature allows users to search by what they want to achieve rather than how to compose a pattern. For example, considering searching for a pattern that matches the version

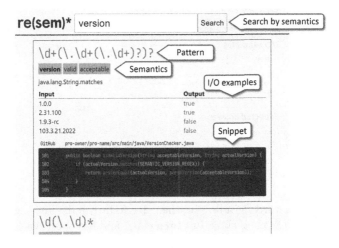

Fig. 1. A screenshot of RESEM

number of software that uses semantic versioning. The users can enter words such as "version" or "semantic" without having to think about how to express numbers or repetitions in regular expression.

In order to realize this feature, RESEM collects meanings of patterns by static analysis. The meanings are collected from identifiers around use of a regular expression API. We assumed that variables storing patterns and input strings, and names of the methods that make API calls are set concerning the meaning of the patterns.

2.3   F2: Presentation of I/O Examples

RESEM outputs usages of regular expression with I/O examples. The examples enable users to imagine easily what the set of strings the pattern accepts without interpreting the special characters it contains. This feature improves the efficiency when the user selects a reference pattern from the search result.

The I/O examples are gathered by dynamically analyzing patterns given to the regular expression API, input strings, and their outputs when the program is tested. The flow of I/O analysis is as follows. First, an instrumentation code is embedded in the regular expression APIs call detected by Sect. 2.2. When the instrumentation code is executed, it writes out the patterns given to the API, input strings, and outputs of the API to a file. Next, the embedded code is executed by software test. Finally, the inputs and the outputs for the patterns are collected by analyzing the output file of the embedded code.

2.4   Collecting from Open Source Projects

We collected usages from public Java projects on GitHub. Because RESEM uses Gradle, a build automation tool, to run test suite, we selected target projects

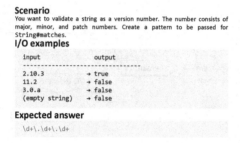

Fig. 2. An example of tasks

which contain the word "gradle" in their README.md. The target regular expression APIs are `String` class, `Pattern` class, and `Matcher` class. As a result, 3,120 usages were collected from 68 projects. The other projects did not output any examples, or failed in running their tests.

3   Experiment

We carried out experiment with subjects to evaluate the effect of presenting usages by our system on pattern description, and to investigate the impression of subjects using the system.

We design the experiment to answer the following questions:

Qa Can RESEM reduce the time to describe patterns?
Qb Can search by semantics (F1) make creating patterns easy?
Qc Can presenting I/O examples (F2) help to select a usage?

To answer Qa, we ask the subjects to perform a string processing task and compare the time required depending on whether RESEM is used. In addition, to answer Qb and Qc, subjects' impressions about RESEM are collected.

3.1   Experiment Design

In this experiment, subjects are asked to perform a task of string processing. The task consists of a scenario for the process and I/O examples.

One of the tasks is shown in Fig. 2. The scenario asks to verify that the input string follows the format of the version number, and provides input examples and expected output to assist in understanding the scenario. The subject creates a pattern according to this scenario. The expected answer for this task is \d+\.\d+\.\d+.

We prepare the scenarios under the following conditions. First, be generic and independent of specific applications. Second, some usages in the RESEM database can be used for reference.

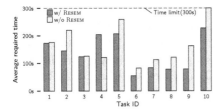
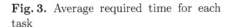

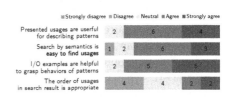

Fig. 3. Average required time for each task

Fig. 4. Result of questionnaire

The first condition is set because a scenario that depends on a specific application is inappropriate for evaluation. Such scenarios can confirm the usefulness only when RESEM is used with the application. To conduct the experiment assuming general situations, we do not make a scenario which depends on specific applications. The second condition is set to focus on the effectiveness of the usage presentation. The aim of RESEM is reuse patterns in past usages. When no usage is useful for a scenario, we cannot evaluate the utility of proposing usages. Therefore, the scenarios are created based on the collected usages.

After completing all tasks, we ask the subjects to answer a questionnaire.

The subjects were 12 people, one graduate school teacher and 11 students. In this experiment, we pay attention to the difference in required time between RESEM users and non-users. The subjects are divided into two groups. One group uses RESEM and the other does not for each task. Both groups can use Web search throughout the experiment. In the grouping, we avoid bias in programming and regular expression skills. In addition, whether a group can use RESEM is switched in half of the tasks so that the experiment results are not affected by the skill difference between the two groups.

3.2   Results and Discussion

The average time required for each task by each group is shown in Fig. 3. The horizontal axis is the number of tasks, and the vertical axis is the average time required for each task. Blue is the group in which the RESEM was available, and gray is the group in which the use was prohibited. The required time for subjects who made an incorrect answer or reached the time limit is treated as 300 s, which is the same as the time limit.

The average required time of the group using RESEM was short for all tasks except for Task 4. The average reduction rate of all tasks was about 16%. Though no person gave the correct answer on task 10 in the group which did not use RESEM, two of six people answered correctly in the group which used it. The task cannot be solved without using lookahead and lookback. Therefore, we expected that some knowledge of these functions was necessary to answer this task by Web search. On the other hand, subjects who used RESEM and correctly answered this task found the effective usage using "alphabet num" as a search query. From this, it can be said that RESEM allows users with little knowledge of regular expression to search for usages that use advanced features.

The questionnaire result is shown in Fig. 4. More than half of the respondents answered that the presented usages were useful, therefore it was revealed that the description support by the usage retrieval was effective. In addition, RESEM's characteristics (F1, F2) were useful because there were many favorable answers to the retrieval by the meaning and the presentation of I/O examples.

On the other hand, more than half of the subjects answered that the order in which search results were displayed was undecided or inappropriate. Therefore, it can be said that the order needs to be improved.

From the results of the subject experiment, we answer Qa, RESEM can shorten the time required for the description of the pattern. The large difference in the difficult tasks suggests that this method can contribute to creating complex patterns that take a long time to be composed in actual development.

As for Qb and Qc, we judged RESEM's features facilitate searching for and selecting usages because of two reasons. First, there were many favorable answers on the retrieval by the meanings and presenting I/O examples. Second, it was effective for the creation of patterns which is difficult to search from the Web.

4   Conclusion

In this paper, we propose a search system RESEM, which realizes semantic search, to support regular expression pattern description. The evaluation experiment was carried out. As a result, RESEM can collect regular expression usages from public projects. We confirmed that the time required for the description of the patterns was reduced by our method.

Acknowledgments. This research was partially supported by JSPS KAKENHI Japan (Grant Number: JP21H04877, JP20H04166, JP21K18302, JP21K11829, JP21K11820, JP22H03567, and JP22K11985).

References

1. Asyrofi, M.H., Thung, F., Lo, D., Jiang, L.: AUSearch: accurate API usage search in GitHub repositories with type resolution. In: Proceedings of International Conference on Software Analysis, Evolution and Reengineering, pp. 637–641 (2020)
2. Chatterjee, S., Juvekar, S., Sen, K.: Sniff: A search engine for java using free-form queries. In: Proceedings of International Conference on Fundmental Approaches to Software Engineerng, pp. 385–400 (2009)
3. Linstead, E., Bajracharya, S., Ngo, T., Rigor, P., Lopes, C., Baldi, P.: Sourcerer: mining and searching internet-scale software repositories. IEEE Trans. Data Mining Knowl. Discov. **18**(2), 300–336 (2009)
4. Michael, L.G., Donohue, J., Davis, J.C., Lee, D., Servant, F.: Regexes are hard: Decision-making, difficulties, and risks in programming regular expressions. In: Proceedings of International Conference on Automated Software Engineering, pp. 415–426 (2019)

5. Wang, P., Brown, C., Jennings, J.A., Stolee, K.T.: An empirical study on regular expression bugs. In: Proceedings of International Conference on Mining Software Repositories, pp. 103–113 (2020)
6. Zhong, H., Xie, T., Zhang, L., Pei, J., Mei, H.: MAPO: Mining and recommending api usage patterns. In: Proceedings of European Conference on Object-Oriented Programming, pp. 318–343 (2009)

Building a Unified Ontology for Behavior Driven Development Scenarios

Konstantinos Tsilionis , Yves Wautelet(✉) , and Samedi Heng

KU Leuven, Leuven, Belgium
{konstantinos.tsilionis,yves.wautelet,samedi.heng}@kuleuven.be

Abstract. Behavior Driven Development (BDD) offers a way to write scenarios in structured natural language on how to successfully fulfill a requirement. We fail to find documentation on how to use existing BDD templates. A set of templates with a clear definition of the keywords to use would provide guidance. This paper empirically explores the keywords found in the different dimensions of BDD scenarios to build a reference set of non-redundant concepts.

1 Introduction and Research Approach

A Behavior Driven Development (BDD) scenario describes a way to *execute the requirement* depicted in a user story. Tsilionis et al. [7] presents the first version of an ontology depicting the keywords most usually found in BDD templates without details on how it was built. This paper describes these; to this end, we applied a method similar as in Wautelet et al. [8] consisting of collecting and associating semantics to the most frequently found keywords in the *GIVEN*, *WHEN* and *THEN* dimensions.

1.1 *Descriptive_Concepts* in BDD Test Scenarios

To build the ontology, the goal is to collect the keywords and thus the concepts that are effectively used in practice when building BDD scenarios and to bring more formality and consistency in their use. The research process first required to collect data; the latter was gathered online in order to list and evaluate the most commonly used BDD test scenario templates. Scenarios are typically structured around the *GIVEN*, *WHEN*, and *THEN* dimensions (these will be referred to as the BDD scenarios' *dimensions* in this study). We consider each keyword found in such BDD templates as a *Descriptive_Concept* (*D_C*) which is a class of concepts containing (as attributes) a dimension (GIVEN, WHEN or THEN), a syntax (i.e. the keyword itself) and a semantic (a definition). The *D_C*-based approach was defined and applied in Wautelet et al. [8]. *D_C* as well as their dimension and syntax attributes can immediately be instantiated when a template is found in a formal or informal source (so typically we have one instance per dimension). Further investigation is generally needed to fill out the *semantic* attribute. We seldom find a definition associated to a keyword so it needs to be associated with it in another way (this is documented in Sect. 2).

© The Author(s), under exclusive license to Springer Nature Switzerland AG 2022
D. Taibi et al. (Eds.): PROFES 2022, LNCS 13709, pp. 518–524, 2022.
https://doi.org/10.1007/978-3-031-21388-5_36

1.2   Building the Dataset

This section depicts the process of collecting data to gather the most commonly used **test scenario templates** used by BDD practitioners. We distinguish between *formal sources* (i.e., published scientific articles and books on BDD, see Appendix A[1]) and *informal sources* (i.e., blogs and forums addressing BDD, see Appendix B). Overall, these primary data sources yielded 120 formal and informal BDD test scenario templates widely used (see Appendix E). The formal sources came from searches on Google Scholar, Limo libis, IEEE Xplore and Springer Link using the keywords "scenario acceptance test", "bdd", "gherkin", "given when then", "behavior driven development", "bdd scenario". The first 10 pages of the returned results, per source, were consulted. The templates extracted from these sources can be found in Appendix A. Informal sources were found them using the same keywords as for formal sources but also including the following ones: "feature file", "bdd feature file", "feature file template", "bdd template", and "scenario template"; we used the Google search engine. As for the formal sources, the first 10 pages of the returned results were consulted. The templates extracted from these sources can be found in Appendix B.

During the elaboration of the dataset, each element that we find in a BDD scenario template that relates to one of the three dimensions becomes an instance of the D_C class. As an example, for the template 'GIVEN $<a\ context>$, WHEN $<an\ event>$, THEN $<an\ outcome>$', we will have three instances: one for *context*, one for *event*, and one for *outcome*. Each of these instances is related to the corresponding dimension of the template; the attribute *dimension* of the D_C class must therefore take one of the values *GIVEN*, *WHEN* or *THEN*. The attribute *syntax* will take the term found within the dimensions themselves (i.e., **context** for GIVEN, **event** for WHEN and **outcome** for THEN). Finally, the attribute *semantic* will be instantiated later through the use of publications addressing agile processes, Goal-Oriented Requirements Engineering (GORE) frameworks and other references in requirements/software engineering.

1.3   Building the Ontology

The elaboration of our data sources (formal and informal) yielded 120 test scenario templates containing multiple keywords. Each keyword has been considered separately and included in a list related to the dimension it supports. From that point, a series of refinements were made to keep the most relevant keywords. Relevant means here precise, specific and complementary to the other keywords ensuring the coherence of all the scenarios' dimensions. More specifically, these refinements were necessary to i) filter-out non-significant/vague/overlapping keywords allowing the remaining ones to serve as the candidate D_C for inclusion in an ontology, and ii) associating a semantic to each of the candidate D_C. The refinement process is described below.

First, on the basis of the dataset, we listed all of the keywords in a table where each dimension is considered separately. The number of occurrences of the keyword in formal and informal sources was noted; In total, 21 different instances were

---

[1] Appendices are consolidated in Appendix_Consolidated_BBD_templates.docx. at: https://data.mendeley.com/datasets/svmcxt5z5f/1.

recorded for the *GIVEN* dimension, 22 for the *WHEN* and 19 for the *THEN* dimension (see Appendix F). Next, informal non-significant and vague terms were removed (e.g. 'Something', 'Scenario', 'It', 'Future', 'Past', 'Present', etc.). We then associated semantics to all of the potential D_C instances. Since no semantics were ever found with the collected templates, we had to find semantics in another way. A first overview has been done in BDD related books to evaluate if more information on templates was available. We looked for definitions of the keywords, found in the previous stage, in a list of sources in the domain of agile processes, GORE frameworks, and software engineering to find a matching semantic. When a match was found between the syntax appearing in a test scenario template dimension and a semantic given in the former sources, we proceeded to a preliminary adoption and did not go through the rest of the sources in the list. The keywords for which we could associate a semantic were allowed to proceed to the next stage as D_C candidates. Otherwise, the keyword was being abandoned and considered irrelevant. The list of sources from the most to the least preferred one were: (i) User Stories Applied: a publication elucidating the ways for improvements in agile processes in requirements engineering [1]; (ii) KAOS: a framework for requirements engineering based on goal modeling [2, 4]; (iii) Requirements Engineering Fundamentals: a study guide for the Certified Professional for Requirements Engineering Foundation Level exam as defined by the International Requirements Engineering Board (IREB) [5]; (iv) BABOK: a professional guide describing the terms and concepts related to the role of a business analyst [3]; and (v) SEVOCAB: a glossary of concepts and their definition in the field of Software and Systems Engineering [6]. Next, we compared the semantics associated to the keywords that were retained in the previous stage. This was done to highlight any similarities/overlapping/mismatches between semantics into a same dimension. Explicitly, every initial semantic overlap between two (or more) keywords was further analyzed. In several occasions, a presumed semantic overlap was eventually being dismissed as one upon further investigation. Each D_C instance candidate was then allowed to pass to the next stage of evaluation. If the semantic overlap was persisting, we were checking whether the use of another source from the aforementioned list could attribute a different semantic definition to either of the two (or more) keywords. The D_C instance of which the semantic was the most alienated to the purpose of the scenario's dimension was taking a new semantic from another source. If no new semantic could be allocated to the keyword through another source, the most generic one was retained. The kept D_C were included to form our base ontology and their semantics were then evaluated one last time on the basis of the secondary data, i.e. the set of test scenario examples. Few D_C remained at the end of this process; they were consolidated as an ontology.

2   Building the Ontology for BDD Scenarios

A Table summarizing the relevant keywords from each BDD scenario template found in the primary data set can be found in Tsilionis et al. [7]. We discuss in this section the choices that have been made to select D_C instances for the 3 dimensions.

2.1 The *GIVEN* Dimension

Syntax Included and Semantic Association: Using the method and the list of sources depicted in Sect. 1.3, the semantics associated to the kept syntaxes were: (i) Context: *The system context is the part of the system environment that is relevant for the definition as well as the understanding of the requirement of a system to be developed* [5]; (ii) Precondition: *A required precondition captures a permission to perform the operation when the condition is true* [4]; (iii) State: *A state defines a period of time in which a system shows a particular behavior and waits for a particular event to occur* [5]; and (iv) Input: *An input represents the information and precondition necessary for a task to begin; it may be: explicitly generated outside the scope of business analysis (e.g. construction of a software application) or generated by a business analyst task* [3].

Comparison of Associated Semantic: A complementarity was noted between the semantics associated to the keywords *Precondition* and *Input*. More detailed, the International Institute of Business Analysis (IIBA) [3] states that an input can be regarded as a precondition to start a task; all in all the *Precondition* encompasses the *Input* but is more general than it so we decided to keep the former as one of the *D_C* candidates to be integrated in the ontology. Additionally, *State* and *Context* are both described in [5] as (system) behavior-communicating elements. However, the former seems to focus on the time-dimension of the system's expressed behavior in-between transitions while the latter focuses on the system's surrounding circumstances to better understand the behavior itself. Therefore, despite their slight initial convergence in their meaning, these two elements seem not to be overlapping each other. To be sure, we allowed the *D_C* class instantiated with both of these keywords to proceed to the next stage so they can be further evaluated semantically based on our assembled BDD scenario examples.

Semantic Evaluation on Examples: The semantics for *Context*, *Precondition*, and *State* were further evaluated on the basis of BDD scenario examples gathered from our secondary dataset. This revealed that the word *Precondition* was used in 59% of the scenarios' instances, compared to a corresponding 25% use of the word *Context* and 16% use of the word *State*. Despite the predominance of the word *Precondition* compared to the other two terms, their semantic interpretation could not be easily differentiated within the examples where it was suggested that *Context* was incorporating a set of necessary *Preconditions* required for the BDD testing phase landing the system in a specific *State*. The *State* is the examples related to a set of *Preconditions* rather than behavior as suggested in its definition. We decided thus to keep the *State* element but to change its semantics to "a set of preconditions" rather than the original semantics that were associated to it in order to match the empirical use of the term. Hence, all three concepts were kept as candidates for the ontology.

2.2 The *WHEN* Dimension

Syntax Included and Semantic Association: Using the method and the list of sources depicted in Sect. 1.3, the semantics associated to the kept keywords were: (i) Event: *Actions and events are the plot of a scenario. They are the steps an actor can take to achieve his goal or a system's response* [1]; (ii) Action: *Actions and events are the plot* *of a scenario. They are the steps an actor can take to achieve his goal or a system's response* [1]; (iii) Interaction: *An interaction is an action that takes place with the participation of the environment of the object* [6]; (iv) Behavior: *Observable activity of a system, measurable in terms of quantifiable effects on the environment whether arising from internal or external stimulus* [6].

Comparison of Associated Semantic: Sevocab [6] details that an *Interaction* can be uni-directionally regarded as an *Action* while the opposite does not seem to hold. Hence, out of the two, the latter being more generic, it seems like the better candidate for a possible integration in the ontology. Moving on, Cohn [1] yields an exact overlap between the semantic definition of *Event* and *Action* so we had to proceed to the next source to see whether the meaning of the two could be extended further. The IIBA [3] describes an *Event* as a *system trigger initiated by humans* whereas Darimont et al. [2] describe an *Action* as *an input-output relation over objects; action applications define state transitions; actions may be caused, stopped by events and they are characterized by pre-, post- and trigger-conditions*. So Darimont et al. [2] present actions to be initiated by events rendering the latter as a trigger of the former; with their semantic being aligned it is equal to take one or the other but one must be selected. So the *Event* was allowed to move on to the next phase of evaluation as a candidate D_C.

Semantic Evaluation on Examples: The words *Event* and *Behavior* were prevalent in the test scenario examples (76% and 22%). Also, 2% of the examples contained the word *Precondition*, but the last one was not part of our primary syntax selection for this dimension so it was not further considered. Given the clear predominance in the use of the word *Event* within the examples, corresponding also to the semantic definition as prescribed in the previous phase, we decided to keep this syntax as candidate for the D_C instance for this dimension. The term *Behavior* was also kept because of the clear difference in its definition with respect to the other concepts.

2.3   The *THEN* Dimension

Syntax Included and Semantic Association: Using the method and the list of sources depicted in Sect. 1.3, the semantics associated to the kept syntaxes were: (i) Outcome: *The business benefits that will result from meeting the business needs and the end state desired by stakeholders* [3]; (ii) Postcondition: *A required postcondition captures an additional condition that must hold after any application of the operation* [4]; (iii) Output: *An output is a necessary result of the work described in the task. Outputs are created, transformed or change state as a result of the successful completion of a task* [3]; (iv) Change: No semantic was found so it was considered non-relevant.

Comparison of Associated Semantic: A semantic complementarity was noted between *Outcome* and *Output* as the IIBA [3] portrays both as the *culminating effect* of a task/operation. This similarity can be problematic as no clear differentiating factor can be found between these D_C instances so we proceeded to the next source seeking whether the meaning of the two can be extended. Sevocab [6] defines *Outcome* as *an artefact, a significant change of state or the meeting of specified constraints* and *Output* as a *a product, result or service generated by a process* or as an *input to a successor* *process*. The latter definition outlines the process-driven nature of an *Output* signaling a temporary result being in a transient state while waiting to contribute as input to the start of the next activity; on the other hand, an *Outcome* is deemed as an enduring effect signifying the achievement of a specific purpose. Considering the culminating disposition of the *THEN* dimension in a BDD scenario, we considered the instance of the *D_C* class associated to the syntax *Outcome* as more relevant for constructing the ontology.

Semantic Evaluation on Examples: Our consulting examples depicted a 57% use of the term *Postcondition* compared to a 29% use of the word *Outcome*. They also showed a 14% use of the word *Event* but as the last one was not part of the selection process for the *THEN* dimension, it was not considered further. Despite the predominance of the term *Postcondition*, we encountered difficulties dissociating it from a *State* in the sense that one or multiple postconditions were required to be satisfied for the achievement of an outcome within the examples. Hence, both *D_C* instances through their associated semantics were considered relevant for the construction of the ontology.

3   Ontology for BDD Test Scenarios

The remaining concepts have been placed in an ontology. From the selection process, two kind of concepts can be distinguished: *user-driven* and *system-driven* scenarios. The former refer to human-related concepts, i.e., the *Context*, the *Event* and the *Outcome*. These are typically instantiated by depicting the behavior taken by the user to achieve the outcome; these are expressed using a pronoun. Conversely, the system-driven concepts refer to software related concepts, i.e. the *Precondition*, the *Behavior* and the *Postcondition*; these are typically instantiated by describing successively the state of the system before, and after the occurrence of a specific event. In the ontology, the keywords *Behavior* and *Event* are difficult to evaluate (and differentiate) in nature without their associated semantics. Moreover, the keyword *Behavior* is misleading since it refers to system behavior in the semantics but, by nature, it is matching to the topic of behavior driven development which is theoretically centered on the user. The true element that assists in the discrimination of instances is the *WHEN* dimension so that particular attention needs to be dedicated to it. We thus change the keyword *Event* to *User_Behavior* and the keyword *Behavior* to *System_Behavior* while keeping their associated semantics. Finally, a *State* is seen as a set of preconditions; this is here also extended to the postconditions. The *State* thus only concern the system-driven context.

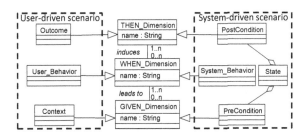

Fig. 1. Ontology for BDD test scenarios.

References

1. Cohn, M.: User Stories Applied: For Agile Software Development. Addison-Wesley (2004)
2. Darimont, R., Van Lamsweerde, A.: Formal refinement patterns for goal-driven requirements elaboration. ACM SIGSOFT Softw. Eng. Notes **21**(6), 179–190 (1996)
3. IIBA, K.B.: A Guide to the Bus. Anal Body of Knowledge. International Institute of Bus (2009)
4. Letier, E., Van Lamsweerde, A.: Deriving operational software specifications from system goals. ACM SIGSOFT Softw. Eng. Notes **27**(6), 119–128 (2002)
5. Pohl, K.: Requirements Engineering Fundamentals: A Study Guide for the Certified Professional for Requirements Engineering Exam-foundation Level-IREB Compliant. Rocky Nook, Inc. (2016)
6. SEVOCAB: Software and Systems Engineering Vocabulary. IEEE Computer Society (2015)
7. Tsilionis, K., Wautelet, Y., Faut, C., Heng, S.: Unifying behavior driven development templates. In: 29th IEEE International Requirements Engineering Conference, RE 2021, pp. 454–455. IEEE (2021)
8. Wautelet, Y., Heng, S., Kolp, M., Mirbel, I.: Unifying and extending user story models. In: Jarke, M., et al. (eds.) CAiSE 2014. LNCS, vol. 8484, pp. 211–225. Springer, Cham (2014). https://doi.org/10.1007/978-3-319-07881-6_15

Quality Metrics for Software Development Management and Decision Making: An Analysis of Attitudes and Decisions

Hannes Salin[1,2]($\boxtimes$), Yves Rybarczyk[1], Mengjie Han[1], and Roger G Nyberg[1]

[1] School of Information and Engineering, Dalarna University, Borlänge, Sweden
`{hasa,yry,mea,rny}@du.se`
[2] Swedish Transport Administration, Borlänge, Sweden
`hannes.salin@trafikverket.se`

Abstract. We combine current literature in software quality metrics with an attitude validation study with industry practitioners, to establish how quality metrics can be used for data-driven approaches. We also propose a simple metric nomenclature and map our findings into a decision making model for easy adoption and utilization of data-driven decision-making methods.

Keywords: Quality metrics · Agile software development · Decision-making · Project management

1 Introduction

Frameworks and established concepts such as Software Development Lifecycles (SDLC) and DevOps, seem to increase in all of IT, where agile methods are natural components of the total software delivery. All of these building blocks of modern software development provide the potential of collecting a broad range of metrics; many of them even by the use of automation. This in turn may enable a strong data-driven approach for software development [11,17]. Data-Driven Decision-Making (DDDM) is the ability to collect, analyse and make decisions based on available data. It seems that there is no clear scientific understanding of the complete utilization of quality metrics in agile software development, and it may even conflict with more traditional methods of quality measurements [10]. Thus, we need a stronger scientific understanding of how to define quality within the context of (hybrid) agile software development. Moreover, for a DDDM process in place, we need adequate and proper data to feed such process for best output. Our contribution consists of an analysis of current definitions of software development quality metrics in the academic literature, combined with an attitude validation study with industry practitioners. We provide a statistical analysis on the results and map metric factors into a decision model. Many different software quality models have been proposed and used in practice, and a comprehensive literature study in the subject is provided by Galli

© The Author(s), under exclusive license to Springer Nature Switzerland AG 2022
D. Taibi et al. (Eds.): PROFES 2022, LNCS 13709, pp. 525–530, 2022.
https://doi.org/10.1007/978-3-031-21388-5_37

et al. [4]. Although the research is extensive regarding the models, these are not frameworks where metrics are mapped into processes or decision-making models, and the metric definitions differs in both nomenclature and structure. Decision-making is often context specific. However, for upper management to better understand goals and expectations in the organization, it would be beneficial to map quality metrics in all decision levels (team, project, management) into a decision model.

2   Method

Our research method consisted of a combination of a literature analysis and a validation survey with industry practitioners. The final stage of the analysis consisted of an article weight computation, in terms of importance, by counting number of citations each study used in their analysis: 1 point for <10 articles cited, and 2 points for >=10 articles cited. Moreover, 1 additional point is given if the study also included any empirical studies for validation. The validation survey consisted of 9 questions based on the findings from the literature analysis. The target group was practitioners from the software development industry: *agile management* (G_1), i.e., product owners and scrum masters, *project management* (G_2), i.e., project leaders, and (G_3), i.e., IT- and engineering managers. There were 6 respondents in each group and all were from two Swedish government agencies and three companies in IT-consultancy and finance sectors respectively. All participants worked in hybrid or agile environments. The questionnaire aimed to measure the level of decision and impact (importance) of the selected metrics from the literature. Before publishing the questionnaire, a pilot with 5 practitioners was conducted to test and adjust the questions and format. The quality notion we use in this work refers to the overall quality a project has. To clarify, we define a metric nomenclature. The fundamental structure is based on the work of Mladenova [13] and López et al. [10]. Three categories are defined: *Project metrics*, e.g. project's risks, plan and budget. *Process metrics*, e.g. team performance, incidents and defects. *Product metrics*, e.g. anything that can be measured of the deployed software, e.g., telemetry. We attribute each metric a *decision factor* and *impact factor*, indicating the perceived level of importance for decision-making, and level of the metric being reliable data for quality indication. We measure these properties in a scale from 1 to 3. We use our quality metric analysis into a managerial decision-making model, and use the same structure as in [1], i.e., a model where three layers of decision-making occur in the organisation: *Operational level*, mapped to G_1, consists of team management decisions and is mostly in an ad-hoc manner with structural decisions on a day-to-day basis. *Tactical level*, mapped to G_2, consists of decisions made with a bearing on the upcoming weeks, months or even up to a year in future and includes understanding of aggregated deliveries in terms of system and software life-cycles, middle-management business decisions, resource management and annual budgets. *Strategic level*, mapped to G_3, consists of highly strategic decisions with a bearing on several years in future, e.g., adoption of new technologies and new business directions.

3 Results

In total we filtered and included 12 primary studies. The main conclusion from the literature analysis was that there are many different software quality factors (often stated within models, e.g. FURPS, SQUALE, IEC/ISO), but very few consider the project-, process-, and product categorization. The resulting analysis is shown in Table 1 where the scores for empirical evaluation (Empirical) is given together with the total score (Total). The chosen metrics for each factor are analyzed further in Table 2. When comparing attitudes of quality versus keeping deadlines (in a scale from 1 to 5), all respondents valued quality over cost (mean 4.22) more than quality over keeping deadlines (mean 3.89). Next, Δ_{G_i} is the difference of group G_i's aggregated decision factor (scale 1 to 3) compared to the aggregated attitude of using the metric in data-driven approaches. Δ is the total difference of all groups aggregated. We investigated possible correlations between project, process, and product metric categories. Since the data points are opinions and not strict interval data, i.e. ordinals, we applied the non-parametric measure of Spearman's rank correlation (ρ) method. All categories correlates as follows: $\rho_{project} = -0.768$, $\rho_{proces} = 0.728$ and $\rho_{product} = 0.882$. We conclude that the weaker correlation on project level may be due to team performance type of metrics only implicitly impact quality decisions and is more difficult to quantify; metric aggregation and long term decision-making would then be more difficult

Table 1. Quality metric factors, mapped into project-, process- and product categories. These factors (and metrics thereof) were indicated as the most important ones from the selected articles in the literature analysis.

Project category	Factor	Research articles	Empirical	Total
	Performance	[3,5,6,9,10,12,15]	3	14
	Reliability	[5,16,18]	3	7
Process category				
	Performance	[3,5,6,8–10,12,15,18]	5	18
	Security	[3,6,10,16]	2	10
	Testability	[3,6,9,12,15,18]	3	12
	Productivity	[3,9]	0	4
Product category				
	Functionality	[5,7–10,18]	3	11
	Performance	[3,5–10,14,15,18]	7	25
	Security	[3,6,10,15,16,18]	4	14
	Reliability	[3,5–10,12,15,18]	6	22
	Maintainability	[3,5,6,8–10,14,15]	5	18
	Testability	[3,6,7,9,10,12,15,18]	4	17
	Satisfaction	[3,6–8,10,18]	3	13
	Business value	[3,6,9,10,18]	2	11

Table 2. Overview of selected quality metrics from the literature study, including factors and surveyed properties from the questionnaire. Δ_{G_i} is the difference in the group's decision factor (Dec.) and the aggregated attitude towards using the metric for data-driven approaches (Data).

Project metric	Factor	Dec.	Imp.	Data.	Δ_{G_1}	Δ_{G_2}	Δ_{G_3}	Δ
Work estimation	Performance	2.17	1.39	1.83	−0.50	−0.33	−0.17	−0.33
Team velocity	Performance	2.22	1.83	2.00	−0.50	−0.33	0.17	−0.22
Risk management	Reliability	2.11	2.33	2.00	0.17	−0.17	−0.33	−0.11
Process metric								
Test automation level	Testability	2.56	2.33	2.56	0.00	0.00	0.00	0.00
Deployment frequency	Productivity	2.33	2.17	2.17	−0.17	−0.33	0.00	−0.17
Lead time for change	Performance	2.28	2.22	2.28	0.33	−0.17	−0.17	0.00
Feature lead time	Productivity	2.06	1.78	2.11	0.17	0.00	0.00	0.06
Product metric								
Bug correction time	Reliability	2.28	2.28	2.17	−0.17	0.00	−0.17	−0.11
Response time	Performance	2.28	2.22	2.33	0.17	−0.33	0.33	0.06
Test coverage	Testability	2.61	2.56	2.72	0.00	0.33	0.00	0.11
Customer satisfaction	Satisfaction	2.72	2.83	2.67	−0.33	0.00	0.17	−0.06
Perceived value	Business value	2.28	2.28	2.22	0.00	0.00	−0.17	−0.06
Number of defects	Reliability	2.67	2.50	2.61	−0.17	0.00	0.00	−0.06
Technical debt[a]	Maintainability	2.56	2.44	2.67	0.17	0.00	0.17	0.11
Mean time to recover	Maintainability	2.06	2.22	2.33	0.33	0.67	−0.17	0.28
Service Level Agreement	Reliability	2.22	2.33	2.39	−0.33	0.33	0.50	0.17
Vulnerability count[a]	Security	2.39	2.50	2.61	0.00	0.33	0.33	0.22
Requirement fulfilment	Functionality	2.11	2.22	2.17	0.00	0.00	0.17	0.06

[a]Refers to classification as both process and product metric.

to perform. Also, as noted in [2] with difficulties in agile quality measurements it may be plausible to conclude that on project level using team performance metrics, the linkage between the final product quality and work estimation is highly unclear. Further research is needed to investigate other type of performance metrics on project level, e.g. motivation and team maturity, although that would require a separate study in itself. In Table 3 all factors are listed with the perceived average decision- and impact factors (denoted *Dec.* and *Imp.*) for each decision-making level (i.e. mapped from G_1, G_2 and G_3), together with the overall importance weight from the literature analysis. We analyzed the correlation between the validation study results and the score of the literature analysis, and preliminary results shows that the strongest correlation (using Spearman's ρ coefficient) is for team level decision-making $\rho_{G_1-dec} = -0.677$, but weak for all other comparisons: $\rho_{G_1-imp} = -0.051$, $\rho_{G_2-dec} = 0.157$, $\rho_{G_2-imp} = 0.327$, $\rho_{G_3-dec} = -0.139$ and $\rho_{G_3-imp} = -0.051$ respectively.

Table 3. Metric factor structure to be used for decision-levels with guiding importance weights from the literature analysis score (Lit.) and validation study averages (Dec. is decision factor and Imp. is impact factor). The highest metrics are highlighted in bold.

Factor	Operational		Tactical		Strategic		Lit
	Dec.	Imp.	Dec.	Imp.	Dec.	Imp.	Score
Performance	2.33	1.96	2.25	2.12	2.13	1.67	19.0
Reliability	2.42	2.42	2.17	2.29	2.38	2.38	14.5
Testability	2.58	2.25	2.50	2.42	**2.67**	**2.67**	14.5
Productivity	2.08	1.92	2.25	2.00	2.25	2.00	4.0
Business value	2.00	2.00	2.33	2.50	2.50	2.33	11.0
Satisfaction	**2.83**	**2.83**	**2.67**	**2.83**	**2.67**	**2.83**	13.0
Maintainability	2.25	2.42	2.17	2.08	2.50	2.50	18.0
Security	2.33	2.50	2.33	2.50	2.50	2.50	12.0
Functionality	2.00	2.00	2.33	2.50	2.00	2.17	11.0

4   Conclusions

Our findings shows that the attitudes towards several metrics found in the literature differs depending on the decision-maker's level (in the model) and that correlations are more diffuse on the strategic decision level. The highest ranked metric factor for all decision levels is *satisfaction*, and for strategic level also *testability*. Our study provides indications of the impact and decision weights of the chosen quality metrics, which can serve as a guideline for industry practitioners in their decision-making processes.

References

1. Aurum, A., Wohlin, C.: Wohlin, c.: The fundamental nature of requirements engineering activities as a decision making process. Inf. Softw. Technol. **45**, 945–954 (2003). https://doi.org/10.1016/S0950-5849(03)00096-X
2. Behutiye, W., et al.: Management of quality requirements in agile and rapid software development: A systematic mapping study. Inf. Softw. Technol. **123**, 106225 (2020). https://doi.org/10.1016/j.infsof.2019.106225. https://www.sciencedirect.com/science/article/pii/S095058491930240X
3. Colakoglu, F.N., Yazici, A., Mishra, A.: Software product quality metrics: a systematic mapping study. IEEE Access **9**, 44647–44670 (2021). https://doi.org/10.1109/ACCESS.2021.3054730
4. Galli, T., Chiclana, F., Siewe, F.: Software product quality models, developments, trends, and evaluation. SN Comput. Sci. **1**(3), 1–24 (2020)
5. Garomssa, S.D., Kannan, R., Chai, I., Riehle, D.: How software quality mediates the impact of intellectual capital on commercial open-source software company success. IEEE Access **10**, 46490–46503 (2022). https://doi.org/10.1109/ACCESS.2022.3170058

6. Haindl, P., Plösch, R.: Value-oriented quality metrics in software development: practical relevance from a software engineering perspective. IET Softw., November 2021. https://doi.org/10.1049/sfw2.12051
7. Kabir, M.A., Rehman, M.U., Majumdar, S.I.: An analytical and comparative study of software usability quality factors. In: 2016 7th IEEE International Conference on Software Engineering and Service Science (ICSESS), pp. 800–803 (2016). https://doi.org/10.1109/ICSESS.2016.7883188
8. Kassie, N.B., Singh, J.: A study on software quality factors and metrics to enhance software quality assurance. Int. J. Productivity Qual. Manage. 29(1), 24–44 (2020). https://doi.org/10.1504/IJPQM.2020.104547. https://www.inderscienceonline.com/doi/abs/10.1504/IJPQM.2020.104547
9. Kupiainen, E., Mäntylä, M.V., Itkonen, J.: Using metrics in agile and lean software development - a systematic literature review of industrial studies. Inf. Softw. Technol. 62, 143–163 (2015). https://doi.org/10.1016/j.infsof.2015.02.005. https://www.sciencedirect.com/science/article/pii/S095058491500035X
10. López, L., et al.: Quality measurement in agile and rapid software development: a systematic mapping. J. Syst. Softw. 186, 111187 (2022). https://doi.org/10.1016/j.jss.2021.111187. https://www.sciencedirect.com/science/article/pii/S0164121221002661
11. Maalej, W., Nayebi, M., Johann, T., Ruhe, G.: Toward data-driven requirements engineering. IEEE Softw. 33(1), 48–54 (2016). https://doi.org/10.1109/MS.2015.153
12. Maddox, M., Walker, S.: Agile software quality metrics. In: 2021 IEEE MetroCon, pp. 1–3 (2021). https://doi.org/10.1109/MetroCon54219.2021.9666049
13. Mladenova, T.: Software quality metrics - research, analysis and recommendation. In: 2020 International Conference Automatics and Informatics (ICAI), pp. 1–5 (2020). https://doi.org/10.1109/ICAI50593.2020.9311361
14. Molnar, A.-J., Neamţu, A., Motogna, S.: Evaluation of software product quality metrics. In: Damiani, E., Spanoudakis, G., Maciaszek, L.A. (eds.) ENASE 2019. CCIS, vol. 1172, pp. 163–187. Springer, Cham (2020). https://doi.org/10.1007/978-3-030-40223-5_8
15. Padmini, K.V.J., Dilum Bandara, H.M.N., Perera, I.: Use of software metrics in agile software development process. In: 2015 Moratuwa Engineering Research Conference (MERCon), pp. 312–317 (2015). https://doi.org/10.1109/MERCon.2015.7112365
16. Siavvas, M., Kehagias, D., Tzovaras, D., Gelenbe, E.: A hierarchical model for quantifying software security based on static analysis alerts and software metrics. Softw. Qual. J. 29(2), 431–507 (2021). https://doi.org/10.1007/s11219-021-09555-0
17. Svensson, R.B., Feldt, R., Torkar, R.: The unfulfilled potential of data-driven decision making in agile software development. In: Kruchten, P., Fraser, S., Coallier, F. (eds.) XP 2019. LNBIP, vol. 355, pp. 69–85. Springer, Cham (2019). https://doi.org/10.1007/978-3-030-19034-7_5
18. Tsuda, N., et al.: Wsqf: comprehensive software quality evaluation framework and benchmark based on square. In: 2019 IEEE/ACM 41st International Conference on Software Engineering: Software Engineering in Practice (ICSE-SEIP), pp. 312–321 (2019). https://doi.org/10.1109/ICSE-SEIP.2019.00045

Are NLP Metrics Suitable for Evaluating Generated Code?

Riku Takaichi[1(✉)], Yoshiki Higo[1], Shinsuke Matsumoto[1], Shinji Kusumoto[1], Toshiyuki Kurabayashi[2], Hiroyuki Kirinuki[2], and Haruto Tanno[2]

[1] Graduate School of Information Science and Technology,
Osaka University, Suita, Osaka, Japan
`r-takaic@ist.osaka-u.ac.jp`
[2] Nippon Telegraph and Telephone Corporation, Minato, Tokyo, Japan

Abstract. Code generation is a technique that generates program source code without human intervention. There has been much research on automated methods for writing code, such as code generation. However, many techniques are still in their infancy and often generate syntactically incorrect code. Therefore, automated metrics used in natural language processing (NLP) are occasionally used to evaluate existing techniques in code generation. At present, it is unclear which metrics in NLP are more suitable than others for evaluating generated codes. In this study, we clarify which NLP metrics are applicable to syntactically incorrect code and suitable for the evaluation of techniques that automatically generate codes. Our results show that METEOR is the best of the automated metrics compared in this study.

Keywords: Automated metric · Code generation · Deep learning

1 Introduction

Code generation is a technique that generates program source code without human intervention. It significantly changes the software process and is known as a promising way to reduce the burden of programming on developers [14]. In recent years, there has been much research on automated methods for writing code, such as code generation [1,4,14]. In these studies, automated metrics (hereinafter, referred to it simply as "metrics") are used to evaluate generated code, and several metrics for code evaluation have already been proposed [13,15]. These metrics use abstract syntax trees or program dependency graphs, assuming that code is syntactically correct. However, research on code generation is still in its infancy, and it is not uncommon for syntactically incorrect code to be generated. For example, 7.0 % of code generated by SNM [14] and 90 % of code by Coarse-to-Fine [4], which are recently proposed code generation models, are syntactically incorrect. Therefore, metrics for code that assume that generated code is syntactically correct may not be usable.

In some cases, metrics used in natural language processing (NLP) are used to evaluate the code generation techniques in place of metrics for code [12]. For

© The Author(s), under exclusive license to Springer Nature Switzerland AG 2022
D. Taibi et al. (Eds.): PROFES 2022, LNCS 13709, pp. 531–537, 2022.
https://doi.org/10.1007/978-3-031-21388-5_38

example, BLEU is frequently used to evaluate the quality of generated code. However, this metric has limitations when used in code evaluation [5,13]. It is thus still unclear which metrics are suitable for evaluating code without assuming the syntactic correctness of the code.

In this study, we clarify which metrics are suitable for evaluating code, and in particular, can be applied to syntactically incorrect code. More specifically, we focus on the code generation task by deep learning, and clarify which metrics are suitable for evaluating code that are automatically generated from requirements written in natural language.

Currently, it is difficult to generate complete code from requirements described using natural language [7]. When using code generation, human modification of the generated code is required to make the code meet the requirements. Therefore, it is desirable that the generated code be easy to modify into code that satisfies the requirements. The suitability of metrics for generated code can be evaluated by the ease with which the generated code can be modified into code that satisfies the requirements.

In this study, we measure the ease of modifying various examples of generated code into code that satisfies given requirements. The results suggest that METEOR is the best metric that correlates with the ease of modifying generated code and is thus the most suitable for evaluating code created via code generation [3].

2   Research Questions

RQ1: Which metrics can be used to evaluate the ease of modifying generated code in terms of modification time?

The ease of modifying generated code can be evaluated in terms of the time a developer take to modify it. To evaluate the ease of modification of generated code in terms of modification time, we investigate which metrics can evaluate the ease of modification. More specifically, we examine the correlation between the time it takes a developer to modify generated code into code that satisfies their requirements and the evaluation values of metrics.

RQ2: Which metrics can be used to evaluate the ease of modifying generated code in terms of the size of changes to the code needed to modify it?

The ease of modification of generated code can also be evaluated by the amount of modification of the code by a developer. When evaluating the ease of modification of generated code by the amount of modification, we investigate which metrics can evaluate the ease of modification. As in RQ1, we examine the correlation between the amount of modification and the evaluation values of metrics, where the strongest correlation between these is considered indicative of ease of modification. In this study, the amount of modification is defined as the number of tokens to modify the generated code.

3 Background

3.1 Code Generation

Code generation is a method by which source code is written automatically. It can be classified in terms of the following elements:

- Input, for example, requirements written in natural language [7], DSL [10], or input/output examples [9].
- Approach, for example, translation-based [7] or search-based [11].

This study focuses on translation-based code generation using deep learning, which takes requirements written in natural language as input.

3.2 Edit Distance

The edit distance is the minimum number of edits (insertions, deletions, or substitutions) required to make one sequence X equivalent to another sequence Y.
The normalized edit distance (NED) between X and Y is computed as

$$\mathrm{NED}(X,Y) = \frac{\mathrm{EditDistance}(X,Y)}{\max\left(\mathrm{length}(X), \mathrm{length}(Y)\right)}$$

where $\mathrm{EditDistance}(X,Y)$ is the edit distance between the sequence X and Y. Here, $\mathrm{length}(S)$ refers to the length of the sequence S. The value of normalized edit distance is between 0 and 1. In this study, the edit distance is calculated by considering the code as a sequence of tokens.

3.3 Metrics

Metrics are used for the automated evaluation of the quality of translation results. Ideally, automated evaluations should correlate highly with human evaluation because metrics are meant to be a feasible alternative to human evaluation. The metrics used in this study are as follows:

BLEU [8] is an metric for evaluating the quality of natural language machine translation results. It is calculated using the n-gram of two sequences.
STS [13] is calculated using the edit distance.
ROUGE-L [6] is calculated using the length of the longest common subsequence.
METEOR [3] is an metric for evaluating the quality of automated translation results in the field of NLP [2]. In this study, a code was regarded as English text because a code is usually written using English words.

These metrics are between 0 and 1. A higher value means a higher evaluation. BLEU, STS, and ROUGE-L were selected because there are studies that used them to evaluate code [12,13]. METEOR was selected because it is designed to address BLEU's weaknesses [2].

4   Experiment

We conducted an experiment to measure the ease of modifying code created with a code generation model to code satisfying given requirements. The ease of modification we measured involves either the modification time or the modification amount. The higher these, the lower the ease of modification. The amount of modification is measured by the normalized edit distance between generated code and modified code. We also examine the correlation between the ease of modification and evaluations of the generated code using metrics. The stronger the negative correlation, the more suitable the automated evaluation value is for evaluating code generated from requirements described in natural language.

4.1   Code Generation Model

We created a code generation model using a deep neural network for NLP available on GitHub[1]. The code generation model was trained on the dataset ReCa [7] comprising requirement text, correct code, and test cases used in programming contests. The dataset includes 5,149 requirements and 16,673 Python code. The code generation model was trained using 300 data entries for testing, 200 for validation, and the remainder for training.

The input of the model is text that has been preprocessed with lowercasing, lemmatization, and removing stopwords. The original text before preprocessing is requirement text written in English. The output of the model is tokens of Python code. It can be automatically transformed into actual Python code. The generated code may not satisfy the requirement described in the input text. The correct code satisfies the requirement and passes the test cases.

4.2   Measuring Ease of Modification

We conducted an experiment with human subjects to measure the ease of modification of generated code. In this experiment, 10 data entries were randomly sampled from the 300 test data. The sampled data have an average of 53.4 test cases per requirement. The subjects were 11 people, one associate professor and ten students. Each subject had a different skill level in Python. A cheat sheet with the code that might be needed when modifying the generated code was supplied for the subjects who were less skilled. Each subject experiments with the 10 sampled data. The experimental steps are as follows:

STEP-1 [Understanding Requirements]. Subjects receive the requirements text and test cases. They understand the requirements by reading the text.

STEP-2 [Modifying Generated Code]. Subjects receive the generated code. They modify the generated code to satisfy the requirements given in STEP-1.

STEP-3 [Testing]. Subjects check whether the code modified in STEP-2 passes all the test cases given in STEP-1. If it passes, STEP-3 is completed. Otherwise, they return to STEP-2 to modify the generated code once more.

---

[1] https://github.com/nazim1021/neural-machine-translation-using-gan.

We count the seconds from STEP-2 to the end of STEP-3 and took this value to be the time developers took to modify the generated code. In the above steps, the modified generated code is called "modified code". We cannot obtain both the modification time and the modified code if the subject cannot successfully modify the generated code so that the requirements are met.

4.3 Results

Table 1 lists the Pearson's correlation coefficients between the evaluation value of each metric and the ease of modification (such as the modification time and the modification amount), with p-values. According to the results in Table 1, the correlation between the evaluation and the modification time and modification amount is strongest for METEOR. However, it is only weakly correlated with modification time.

Table 1. Correlation between metrics and the ease of modification

Metric	RQ1: the modification time		RQ2: the amount of modification	
	COR	p-value	COR	p-value
BLEU	−0.181	0.117	−0.392	4.64×10^{-4}
STS	−0.100	0.389	−0.555	1.99×10^{-7}
ROUGE-L	0.011,5	0.921	−0.481	1.08×10^{-5}
METEOR	−0.251	0.028,6	−0.696	3.03×10^{-12}

Answer to RQ1 and RQ2: Among the examined metrics, METEOR is the best metric to evaluate the ease of modifying generated code in terms of the modification time and the modification amount. In addition, BLEU, which is widely used to evaluate generated code, is not a good metric in these context.

5 Conclusion

The purpose of this study was to clarify which NLP metrics can be applied to syntactically incorrect code. We investigated which metrics strongly correlate with the evaluation values obtained in the experiment with subjects. The results of the study showed that METEOR has a relatively strong correlation with both amount of modification and the time required to modify code created by code generation to meet the given requirements. We conclude that METEOR is a better metric for generated code than the frequently used BLEU. However, metrics may not be suitable for evaluating generated code because of its weak correlation with the modification time. In addition, note that there are limitations in applying these results to real projects because the subject experiment in this study was conducted using programming contest data.

For future research, we are going to examine the evaluation values that correlate stronger with the coding time reduced by using the generated code. This is why we plan to compare the time required for subjects to read the requirements and write a program with the time required for them to modify generated code to satisfy the requirements.

Acknowledgements. This research was supported by JSPS KAKENHI, Japan (grant numbers JP20H04166, JP21K18302, JP21K11820, JP21H04877, JP22H03567, and JP22K11985).

References

1. Ahmad, W., Chakraborty, S., Ray, B., Chang, K.W.: Unified pre-training for program understanding and generation. In: Proceedings of Conference of the North American Chapter of the Association for Computational Linguistics: Human Language Technologies (2021)
2. Banerjee, S., Lavie, A.: METEOR: An automatic metric for MT evaluation with improved correlation with human judgments. In: Proceedings of ACL Intrinsic and Extrinsic Evaluation Measures for Machine Translation and/or Summarization (2005)
3. Denkowski, M., Lavie, A.: Meteor universal: language specific translation evaluation for any target language. In: Proceedings of Workshop on Statistical Machine Translation (2014)
4. Dong, L., Lapata, M.: Coarse-to-Fine decoding for neural semantic parsing. In: Proceedings of Annual Meeting of the Association for Computational Linguistics (2018)
5. Karaivanov, S., Raychev, V., Vechev, M.: Phrase-based statistical translation of programming languages. In: Proceedings of ACM International Symposium on New Ideas, New Paradigms, and Reflections on Programming and Software (2014)
6. Lin, C.Y.: ROUGE: a package for automatic evaluation of summaries. In: Proceedings of ACL Text Summarization Branches Out (2004)
7. Liu, H., Shen, M., Zhu, J., Niu, N., Li, G., Zhang, L.: Deep learning based program generation from requirements text: are we there yet? IEEE Trans. Softw. Eng. **48**(4), 1268–1289 (2022)
8. Papineni, K., Roukos, S., Ward, T., Zhu, W.J.: Bleu: a method for automatic evaluation of machine translation. In: Proceedings of Annual Meeting of the Association for Computational Linguistics (2002)
9. Parisotto, E., Mohamed, A., Singh, R., Li, L., Zhou, D., Kohli, P.: Neuro-symbolic program synthesis. In: Proceedings of International Conference on Learning Representations (2017)
10. Rabinovich, M., Stern, M., Klein, D.: Abstract syntax networks for code generation and semantic parsing (2017). https://arxiv.org/abs/1704.07535
11. Spector, L.: Autoconstructive evolution: Push, PushGP, and Pushpop. In: Proceedings of Genetic and Evolutionary Computation Conference (2001)
12. Svyatkovskiy, A., Deng, S.K., Fu, S., Sundaresan, N.: Intellicode compose: code generation using transformer. In: Proceedings of ACM Joint Meeting on European Software Engineering Conference and Symposium on the Foundations of Software Engineering (2020)

13. Tran, N., Tran, H., Nguyen, S., Nguyen, H., Nguyen, T.: Does BLEU score work for code migration? In: Proceedings of IEEE/ACM International Conference on Program Comprehension (2019)
14. Yin, P., Neubig, G.: A syntactic neural model for general-purpose code generation. In: Proceedings of Annual Meeting of the Association for Computational Linguistics (2017)
15. Zhao, G., Huang, J.: Deepsim: deep learning code functional similarity. In: Proceedings of ACM Joint Meeting on European Software Engineering Conference and Symposium on the Foundations of Software Engineering (2018)

Automated and Robust User Story Coverage

Mickael Gudin and Nicolas Herbaut[✉][iD]

Centre de Recherche en Informatique Université Paris 1 Panthéon-Sorbonne, Paris,
France
nicolas.herbaut@univ-paris1.fr

Abstract. Current practices in software testing such as Test Driven
Development or Behavior Driven Development aim at linking code to
expected behavior. In this context, code coverage is widely used to
improve code quality, reduce bugs and ssure requirements satisfaction.
Even if change tracking software allows finely analyzing code evolution,
associating a particular code chunk to the requirements at the origin of
the code modification is difficult for a large code base. In this preliminary
work, we propose a new "user story coverage" metric that reports lacking requirement coverage quality, to help developers focus their efforts
on enhancing unit and integration tests. We propose a methodology to
compute this metric in a robust and automated fashion and evaluate its
feasibility on open-source projects.

Keywords: Requirements · Code coverage · Abstract-syntax-tree ·
Software quality

1 Introduction

In the software industry, testing best practices such as Test-Driven Development
(TDD) or Behavior-Driven Development (BDD) are now mainstream. TDD's
goal is to have consistent test cases with the produced code whereas BDD's goal
is to have consistent test cases with the expected behavior, which is the actual
business needs [1]. In the unit testing phase, developers use the code coverage
metric to assess how well the code base is tested, as a high coverage rate is
deemed to make a software program less error-prone [2].

Another common practice is the use of software configuration management
(SCM), to track code changes and facilitate collaboration. A good practice in
SCMs is to have traceability between requirements and implementation [3],
through commit messages. Commits often mentions the *issue ID*, which in turns
contains a reference to the business needs behind the code modification, commonly formalized as User Stories (US) in agile teams. This precious traceability
information, however, tends to degrade over time. The reason is that SCM-
provided tools, such as blame, are line-centric: newer commits mask the previous
ones, effectively breaking the traceability chain. As a consequence, there is no

© The Author(s), under exclusive license to Springer Nature Switzerland AG 2022
D. Taibi et al. (Eds.): PROFES 2022, LNCS 13709, pp. 538–543, 2022.
https://doi.org/10.1007/978-3-031-21388-5_39

easy way, given a chuck of code, to backtrack to the requirement which led to its inclusion into the codebase.

This paper fills the gap in requirements to code traceability code by combining unit test coverage, SCM history and issue tracker data to compute a new metric, *User Story coverage*, which can be considered as a proxy to assess *Requirement coverage*. In the rest of the paper, we present some background, methods, evaluation and discussion before concluding.

2   Background and Related Work

Requirements and User Story Coverage. In this paper, we make the assumption that issues contains User Stories, which is a form of requirement expressed from the perspective of an end-user goal. Agile teams often use USs as a proxy for proper requirements to facilitate developers' understanding of the desired features [4].

A semi-automated requirement coverage tool was proposed in [5], where authors demonstrated the feasibility of the concept. The main difference with our approach is that we rely on robust code differencing to prevent recent commits masking previous ones, and we also make the hypothesis that the process linking requirements and code are fully automated, through commit messages containing *issue IDs* pointing to USs.

In [6], authors present a new metric based on the Requirements Traceability Matrix (RTM) to better allocate testing efforts based on requirements coverage. We have a related goal, but we do not assume the existence of an RTM and use the existing unit tests to cover testing intents.

Robust Code Differencing. Code differencing is commonly performed through a text-based approach with `git diff` and `git blame` commands relying by default on the Myers algorithm [7]. Abstract syntax tree (AST)-based tools are the current state-of-the-art and bring more accurate differences, which are especially efficient at detecting refactoring and minor code modification [8].

In this paper, we decided to use vanilla GumTree for the AST-based approach and compare it with a text-based approach, leaving out considering recent enhancements in this field for future work.

3   Methods and Evaluation

In this section, we detail how we built the proof of concept[1] to compute the requirement coverage metric. To aggregate the code chunks to a given requirement, we aggregate the code of all commits that references the corresponding issues. We implemented two coverage approaches as two code chunks aggregation techniques: line-based and method-based which are in turn based on unit test coverage metrics: line coverage and method coverage.

---

[1] https://github.com/nh-group/dextorm.

3.1   US Coverage Metric Computation

Data Collection. Data collection uses 3 different data sources: The Issue Manager (IM), Repository and Code Coverage (CC) from unit tests. In this section, we present the data sources and the different steps that lead to the generation of US Coverage data (Fig. 1).

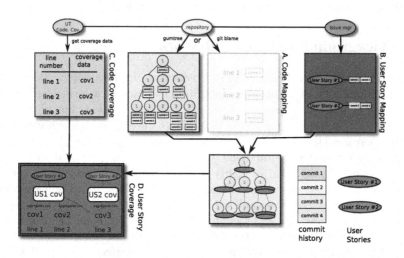

Fig. 1. High-level architecture

Code Mapping. Code mapping aims at correlating each code chunk with a commit from the repository. This operation is trivial when using the `blame` command, but offers poor precision: since (1) each line of code is associated with exactly one commit and (2) whenever any token from the line is modified by a commit, the line becomes associated with the said commit. This means that refactoring, reformatting and commenting on a line will destroy the connection between the statements and the associated commit, hence the user story.

For this paper, we developed a more robust method to compute Code Mapping, relying on GumTree. This method reads the git history for each file, and analyze each modification done on the file, producing ASTs labeled with the commit and line. More precisely, for each file F, for each commit t, we compare the two versions of the file F_{t-1} and F_t, before and after commit t. We subsequently parse the files as AST T_{t-1} and T_t, and compute the mapping M_t between T_{t-1} and T_t. If there is a mapping between nodes $N \in T_{t-1}$ and $M \in T_t$, we add all the labels of N to M. If no mapping exists, then M is labeled with commit t.

US Mapping. First, we connect to the issue manager and assemble every issue corresponding to the project. The user can apply specific filters (e.g., date, label, issue status) to restrict which issues are included in the analysis. Then, we scan the whole history of the project, and gather commit messages containing references to IM issues. We finally associate each commit with the corresponding US.

Code and User Story Coverage. Due to lack of space, we do not present the full description of the US coverage metric, but instead intuitions and usage examples. The *line-based User story coverage metric* is the ratio of the number of lines associated with a US, which are marked as covered by unit tests, over the total number of lines associated to the US. Likewise, *method-based User story coverage metric* follows the same principle based on method coverage.

3.2   Illustrative Example

To illustrate our approach, we take the example of a US where some contact information is retrieved from a phone number, implemented in *commit1*.

```
1  public class ContactService {
2      RepositoryContact repo = new RepositoryContact();
3
4      public Contact findContactWithPhoneNumber(String
5      number) {
6          return repo.getContactWithPhoneNumber(number);
7      }
8  }
```

Listing 1.1. commit 1

```
1  +++ a/ContactService.java
2  --- b/ContactService.java
3  @@ -2,9 +2,6 @@ public class ContactService {
4      RepositoryContact repo = new RepositoryContact
       ();
5
6      public Contact findContactWithPhoneNumber(
        String number) {
7  +        if(number != null && number.length() == 10)
         {
8  +            return repo.getContactWithPhoneNumber(
          number);
9  +        }
10 +        return null;
11 -        return repo.getContactWithPhoneNumber(
          number);
12     }
13 }
```

Listing 1.2. commit2 (patch format)

Assuming that the US coverage is 100% in commit1, it would stay at 100% in commit2 when computed with GumTree, since line 6 of Listing 1.1 would still be associated with commit1, thanks to Gumtree being resistant to code moves.

If we were to use `git blame` however, the result would change drastically: none the news lines in Listing 1.2 would be associated with commit 1 and with the US anymore: since `git blame` is line-based, the US would not be covered at all, since no line linked with commit1 would be executed in the unit tests.

3.3   Performance Evaluation

We evaluated the presented US coverage computation techniques on several real-world open source projects RxJava, Shenyu and dnsjava, which use GitHub SCM to support both issues and version tracking:

We carried out computations on an Intel Xeon W-10855M CPU @ 2.80 GHz with SSD and 32 GB of RAM. We used the Java Microbenchmark Harness and

Table 1. Performance and runtime comparison

Project	DA	Scope	Execution time (s)	# Classes	# Versions	# NCLOC	# Issues	GitBlame Loss ratio	GitBlame method loss ratio
RxJava	GitBlame	Instructions	337.54	2941	6001	368,268	3096	7.84%	23.89%
		Methods	52.59						
	GumTree	Instructions	5384.89						
		Methods	5360.19						
Apache/shenyu	GitBlame	Instructions	32.28	1807	2488	100,399	1559	4.48%	20.96%
		Methods	15.42						
	GumTree	Instructions	846.75						
		Methods	841.76						
dnsjava	GitBlame	Instructions	15.91	277	2066	22,308	147	6.25%	25.62%
		Methods	8.63						
	GumTree	Instructions	101.17						
		Methods	105.25						

we report the execution time with the AverageTime method over 10 executions
for each combination.

We show static metrics for each project (number of classes, number of versions, number of significant line of codes and number of collected issues) and
the computation runtime for each combination of diff algorithms (GitBlame
and GumTree) and scope (instruction-based or method-based). We also report
two performance metrics: the gap between the most accurate coverage computation method (GumTree algorithm computed on instructions) and another
reference method: G_i (GitBlame Loss ratio, which represents the normalized
average difference between GumTree and GitBlame coverage with instruction
scope) and I_i (GitBlame Method Loss Ratio, that represent the normalized
average difference between instruction-based coverage for the GumTree algorithm and method-based coverage for GitBlame). We define these metrics as:

$$G_i = \sqrt{\sum_{i \in I} (c_i^{g,\text{inst}} - c_i^{b,\text{inst}})^2 / \#I}, \text{ and } I_i = \sqrt{\sum_{i \in I} (c_i^{g,\text{inst}} - c_i^{b,\text{meth}})^2 / \#I}$$

where I is the set of the issues for the project, $c_i^{g,\text{inst}}$ (resp., $c_i^{b,\text{inst}}$) is the coverage ratio reported by GumTree (resp., GitBlame) for issue i with the instruction
scope and $c_i^{b,\text{meth}}$ is the coverage ratio for the method scope for the GitBlame
algorithm.

4   Discussion

As we can see from Table 1, computations using the GitBlame algorithm outperform GumTree by one order of magnitude and shows a coverage precision loss
of 4.48% to 7.84%. The main factor explaining this is the necessity for GumTree
to compute as many diff trees as there are revisions for each file with an $\mathcal{O}(N^2)$
worst-case complexity (with N equals the number of nodes in the AST), while
git blame relies on a diff algorithm [9] requiring only O(M) space (where M is the
number of tokens of the file). Interestingly, using the method scope (based on
comparing method signatures), does not provide a large benefit in runtime for
the GumTree algorithm, since the main bottleneck is the computation of AST
mappings that need to be computed anyway. For GitBlame, however, the time
reduction seems significant (from 50% to 84% improvement) while increasing the
loss ration from 20.96% to 25.62%. While the precision erosion is substantial, it

stays limited. This suggests that we could use both approaches conjointly: using GumTree with instructions (the slowest but most precise) in an off-line setting (e.g., on a software factory while computing the other continuous integration tasks), along with GitBlame with methods (the fastest, bit least precise) on the developer's workstation for a fast feedback loop.

5   Conclusion

In this article, we proposed a methodology to compute a proxy for requirement coverage that we called *User Story coverage*. Thanks to AST-based code differencing and data aggregation from issue manager, SCM and unit tests coverage, the metric can be automatically obtained robustly. As future work, we plan to integrate this metric in an IDE and follow a design science approach to evaluate how it can improve code quality throughout the development lifecycle. We also expect performance improvement through more advanced AST-based code differencing techniques.

References

1. Zampetti, F., Di Sorbo, A., Visaggio, C.A., Canfora, G., Di Penta, M.: Demystifying the adoption of behavior-driven development in open source projects. Inf. Softw. Technol. **123**, 106311 (2020). https://doi.org/10.1016/j.infsof.2020.106311
2. Bach, T., Andrzejak, A., Pannemans, R., Lo, D.: The impact of coverage on bug density in a large industrial software project. In: 2017 ACM/IEEE International Symposium on Empirical Software Engineering and Measurement (ESEM), pp. 307–313 (2017)
3. Standard for configuration management in systems and software engineering. IEEE Standard 828–2012 (2012)
4. Cohn, M.: User stories applied: For agile software development. Addison-Wesley Professional (2004)
5. Mordinyi, R., Biffl, S.: Exploring traceability links via issues for detailed requirements coverage reports. In: 2017 IEEE 25th International Requirements Engineering Conference Workshops (REW)
6. Ziftci, C., Kruger, I.: Getting more from requirements traceability: requirements testing progress. In: 2013 7th International Workshop on Traceability in Emerging forms of Software Engineering (TEFSE) (2013). https://doi.org/10.1109/tefse.2013.6620148
7. Nugroho, Y.S., Hata, H., Matsumoto, K.: How different are different diff algorithms in git? Empirical Softw. Eng. **25**(1), 790–823 (2020)
8. Falleri, J.-R., Morandat, F., Blanc, X., Martinez, M., Monperrus, M.: Fine-grained and accurate source code differencing. In: Proceedings of the 29th ACM/IEEE International Conference on Automated Software Engineering, pp. 313–324 (2014)
9. Myers, E.W.: An o(ND) difference algorithm and its variations. Algorithmica **1**(1), 251–266 (1986)

Tidy Up Your Source Code! Eliminating Wasteful Statements in Automatically Repaired Source Code

Takumi Iwase[✉], Shinsuke Matsumoto, and Shinji Kusumoto

Graduate School of Information Science and Technology,
Osaka University, Osaka, Japan
{tk-iwase,shinsuke,kusumoto}@ist.osaka-u.ac.jp

Abstract. Automated program repair (APR) is a concept of automatically fixing bugs in source code to free developers from the burden of debugging. One of the issues facing search-based APR is that repaired code contains wasteful or meaningless statements that do not affect external behavior. This paper proposes a concept named *source code tidying* that eliminates wasteful statements in source code repaired by search-based APR. Our proposed method applies pre-defined tidying rules to repaired code and evaluates the effect of tidying using source code metrics such as lines of code. By repeating this process based on a genetic algorithm, unnatural and full of wasteful source code is gradually brought close to natural with preserving its behavior. Our method will be involved in a process of APR by improving the readability of repaired code.

Keywords: Automated program repair · Source code tidying · Wasteful statements · Dead code · Refactoring

1 Introduction

Automated program repair (APR) is a concept of automatically fixing bugs in source code to free developers from the burden of debugging [5]. APR can be broadly classified into search-based [6] and semantics-based [9] approaches. This paper focuses on genetic algorithm-based APR (GA-APR), one search-based APR that introduces bio-inspired evolution into program repair. GA-APR takes as input source code containing one or more bugs and test cases. GA-APR repeatedly applies tiny modifications to the buggy code until all test cases pass. While the semantics-based approach is limited to a specific type of bug, such as conditional bug [12], the search-based approach has the significant advantage of generality in that it can theoretically fix any kind of bug.

One of the issues facing GA-APR is that repaired code contains wasteful or meaningless statements that do not affect external behavior. Usually, GA-APR repeatedly applies predefined modifications without considering semantic information. Typical modifications include insertion/deletion/reuse of AST nodes

© The Author(s), under exclusive license to Springer Nature Switzerland AG 2022
D. Taibi et al. (Eds.): PROFES 2022, LNCS 13709, pp. 544–550, 2022.
https://doi.org/10.1007/978-3-031-21388-5_40

[6], insertion/deletion of method calls [2], and modification of variable names or operators [1]. These blind and random modifications lead to a problem that repaired source code tends to be far from the source code written by developers. For example, repetitive insertion of AST nodes will generate wasteful statements such as "n++; n--;", which negate each other, or "n++; n=10;", in which the former statement is overwritten. There is also a case where only an empty block "{}" is left due to repetitive deletion. The number of applied modifications will increase if a bug is difficult to repair. Many modifications make repaired code full of wasteful statements. As a result, overall repair performance (i.e., search performance) will gradually decrease with increasing the generations because wasteful statements affect the performance of compilation and test execution.

This paper proposes a concept named *source code tidying* that eliminates wasteful statements in source code repaired by GA-APR. We define wasteful statements as executable statements that do not affect external behavior. This definition includes not only dead code [4,10], which is a well-known concept of unused and unreachable code, but also used and reachable but unnecessary. Our proposed method applies predefined tidying rules to repaired code and evaluates the effect of tidying using source code metrics such as lines of code. By repeating this process based on a genetic algorithm, unnatural and full of wasteful source code is gradually brought close to natural with preserving its behavior. Our method will be involved in a process of GA-APR by improving the readability of repaired code.

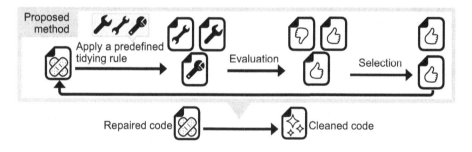

Fig. 1. Overview of proposed method

2   Proposed Method

2.1   Overview

The purpose of the proposed method is to *tidy* source code that contains wasteful statements. We define wasteful statements as executable statements that do not affect external behavior and *tidy* as eliminating these wasteful statements. Figure 1 shows an overview of the proposed method. The input is repaired source code by GA-APR, and the output is tidied source code which is same behavior as the input. The proposed method consists of three iterative processes using genetic algorithm: tidying, evaluation, and selection. First, the source code is partially tidied by a randomly selected rule from predefined tidying rules. At this time, the decision on which rule to use is made several times. This results in multiple tidied source codes from a single source code. Next, evaluate each partially tidied source code. As fitness, we use metrics such as lines of code and cyclomatic complexity. Then, *good* source codes are selected to the next tidying based on fitness. If the fitness does not improve after repeating these processes, the iteration finishes and the proposed method outputs source code with the best fitness.

The proposed method has two features: tidying rules can be added, and the source code is tidied based on GA. Even if the proposed method fails to tidy some source codes, the proposed method will be able to tidy them by adding rules. GA-based tidying enables natural tidying as humans do.

2.2   Tidying Rules

Table 1 shows the tidying rules adopted in this paper. If rule affects the behavior of source codes when applying, it does not apply. For example, the swap rule for D1 in Table 1 does not apply to "n++; m=n;". Tidying rules are broadly classified into two. One is "direct rules", which directly eliminate wasteful statements. The other is "detour rules", which add or swap statements in the opposite direction to wasteful statements elimination. Wasteful statements in repaired source codes may not be adjacent. Direct rules eliminate adjacent wasteful statements and cannot eliminate nonadjacent wasteful statements. Therefore, we adopted detour rules in the role of gathering scattered wasteful statements. Detour rules are a major difference from related works, and we believe it works effectively for tidying of repaired source codes.

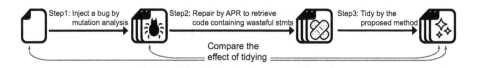

Fig. 2. Overview of experiment

3   Preliminary Experiment

3.1   Overview

We conduct a preliminary experiment using a programming contest as the subject. Figure 2 shows an overview of the experiment. This experiment consists of three steps. First, we inject bug into bug-free source codes (S_{origin}) and obtain bug-injected source codes ($S_{mutated}$). Next, we repair $S_{mutated}$ by APR and obtain bug-repaired source codes ($S_{repaired}$). Finally, we tidy $S_{repaired}$ by the proposed method and obtain tidied source codes (S_{tidied}). We compare S_{tidied} with S_{origin} and $S_{repaired}$ to confirm effectiveness of tidying.

3.2   Experimental Procedure

Table 2 shows a list of the experimental settings and each step is described below.

Step1: Bug injection. S_{origin} are correct answers for twenty 100-point tasks of the past AtCoder Beginner Contest (ABC), held at AtCoder[1]. We inject bug into these correct answers. Mutation analysis [8] is used for the bug injection. In

Table 1. Tidying rules (Rn: direct rule, Dn: detour rule)

ID	Rule	Before	After	ID	Rule	Before	After
R1	Eliminate unary operator stmts that negate each other	`n++;` `n--;`		D1	Swap two stmts that have no order dependence	`n++;` `m--;`	`m--;` `n++;`
R2	Eliminate overwritten stmts	`n++;` `n=1;`	`n=1;`	D2	Inline a stmt located below control stmt	`if(m>0){` `  n--;` `}else{` `}` `n++;`	`if(m>0){` `  n--;` `  n++;` `}else{` `  n++;` `}`
R3	Eliminate a block without having control stmt	`{ n++; }`	`n++;`	D3	Inline a stmt located above control stmt that has no dependence on condition	`n++;` `if(m>0){` `  n--;` `}else{` `}`	`if(m>0){` `  n++;` `  n--;` `}else{` `  n++;` `}`
R4	Eliminate an empty block stmt	`n++;` `{ }` `n--;`	`n++;` `n--;`				
R5	Omit a control stmt whose condition is always true or false	`if(true){` `  n++;` `}`	`n++;`	D4	Copy return stmt located below control stmt	`if(m>0){` `  n++;` `}` `return n;`	`if(m>0){` `  n++;` `  return n;` `}` `return n;`
R6	Merge a duplicate return stmt	`if(m>0){` `  n++;` `  return n;` `}` `return n;`	`if(m>0){` `  n++;` `}` `return n;`				

---

[1] https://atcoder.jp/.

Table 2. Experimental settings

Parameter	Setting
S_{origin}	ABC[a] 100-point tasks
Number of tasks	20
Applied mutations	5 operations (see Table 3)
Used APR tool	kGenProg [7]
Number of $S_{repaired}$	76
Fitness in prop. method	Lines of code

[a] https://atcoder.jp/

Table 3. Mutation operations

Operation	Before	After
Replace + and -	n = a + b	n = a - b
Replace * and /	n = a * b	n = a/b
Replace % to *	n = a % b	n = a * b
Negate condition	if (n > 0)	if (n <= 0)
Change boundary	if (n > 0)	if (n >= 0)

mutation analysis, a single line in source code is modified by mutation. Table 3 shows the mutations adopted in this experiment. There are multiple operators and conditions that can be modified in a source code. We use all candidates and one candidate is used to generate one $S_{mutated}$. Therefore, multiple $S_{mutated}$ are generated from one S_{origin}. A total of 76 $S_{mutated}$ are generated from 20 S_{origin}.

Step2: Apply APR. The APR tool to repair $S_{mutated}$ is kGenProg [7]. Source codes of programming contest are simple and unlikely to contain wasteful statements when repaired. This makes it difficult to confirm effectiveness of the proposed method. Therefore, we generated multiple bug-repaired source codes from a single $S_{mutated}$. This increases the probability of generating source code with a lot of wasteful statements. The most wasteful source code is selected as $S_{repaired}$ among these multiple bug-repaired source codes.

Step3: Apply proposed method. The proposed method is applied to 76 $S_{repaired}$. As mentioned earlier, source codes for programming contest are simple. With metrics other than the lines of code (LOC), it is difficult to make a difference before and after tidying. Therefore, we use LOC as fitness in the proposed method.

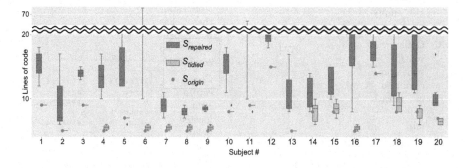

Fig. 3. Number of lines before and after tidying per subject

3.3 Results and Discussion

The Effect of Tidying: We confirm how many wasteful statements have been eliminated by the proposed method. Figure 3 shows LOC before and after tidying for each subject. The horizontal axis represents each subject, and the vertical axis represents LOC. The red dots represent LOC of S_{origin}. LOC decreased in all subjects, and we confirmed some source code tidied to LOC of S_{origin}. Next, manual check was carried out for each S_{tidied}. In 66 of the 76 source codes, wasteful statements were completely eliminated. Some source code had a different number of lines from S_{origin}, but no wasteful statements. This is because structure of conditional branches changed due to repair by APR. In the remaining 10 source codes, wasteful statements were not eliminated completely. The reason is the lack of tidying rules. By adding rules, we can eliminate wasteful statements in these source codes. From the above results, we consider that the proposed method can eliminate wasteful statements of source code.

4 Conclusions and Future Work

In this paper, we proposed the method to tidy APR-generated unnatural source code into natural source code. The proposed method tidies source code based on GA. We devised detour rules that do not directly eliminate wasteful statements. We conducted experiment using programming contest as subject. The obtained results showed that the proposed method could eliminate wasteful statements.

In future work, we expand tidying rules to improve the generality of the proposed method. This paper only focuses on fundamental arithmetic operators and basic control statements. Tidying rules for method invocation are necessary to apply our method to more practical source code. We consider that the key is checking the program dependences [3] and side-effect [11] of each statement.

Acknowledgments. This research was partially supported by JSPS KAKENHI Japan (Grant Number: JP21H04877, JP20H04166, JP21K18302, JP21K11829, JP21K11820, JP22H03567, and JP22K11985).

References

1. Assiri, F.Y., Bieman, J.M.: An assessment of the quality of automated program operator repair. In: Proceedings of International Conference on Software Testing, Verification and Validation, pp. 273–282 (2014)
2. Dallmeier, V., Zeller, A., Meyer, B.: Generating fixes from object behavior anomalies. In: Proceedings of International Conference on Automated Software Engineering, pp. 550–554 (2009)
3. Ferrante, J., Ottenstein, K.J., Warren, J.D.: The program dependence graph and its use in optimization. ACM Trans. on Program. Lang. Syst. **9**(3), 319–349 (1987)
4. Fowler, M.: Refactoring: Improving the Design of Existing Code. Addison-Wesley Professional, Boston (1999)

5. Gazzola, L., Micucci, D., Mariani, L.: Automatic software repair: a survey. IEEE Trans. on Softw. Eng. **45**(1), 34–67 (2019)
6. Goues, C.L., Nguyen, T., Forrest, S., Weimer, W.: GenProg: a generic method for automatic software repair. IEEE Trans. on Softw. Eng. **38**(1), 54–72 (2012)
7. Higo, Y., et al.: kGenProg: a high-performance, high-extensibility and high-portability APR system. In: Proceedings of Asia-Pacific Software Engineering Conference, pp. 697–698 (2018)
8. Jia, Y., Harman, M.: An analysis and survey of the development of mutation testing. IEEE Trans. on Softw. Eng. **37**(5), 649–678 (2010)
9. Nguyen, H.D.T., Qi, D., Roychoudhury, A., Chandra, S.: Semfix: program repair via semantic analysis. In: Proceedings of International Conference on Software Engineering, pp. 772–781 (2013)
10. Romano, S., Vendome, C., Scanniello, G., Poshyvanyk, D.: A multi-study investigation into dead code. IEEE Trans. on Softw. Eng. **46**(1), 71–99 (2020)
11. Rountev, A.: Precise identification of side-effect-free methods in java. In: Proceedings of International Conference on Software Maintenance, pp. 82–91 (2004)
12. Xuan, J., Martinez, M., et al.: Nopol: automatic repair of conditional statement bugs in java programs. IEEE Trans. Softw. Eng. **43**(1), 34–55 (2017)

Tutorials

Utilizing User Stories to Bring AI Ethics into Practice in Software Engineering

Kai-Kristian Kemell[1]([✉])(iD), Ville Vakkuri[2](iD), and Erika Halme[3](iD)

[1] University of Helsinki, Helsinki, Finland
`kai-kristian.kemell@helsinki.fi`
[2] University of Vaasa, Vaasa, Finland
[3] University of Jyväskylä, Jyväskylä, Finland

Abstract. AI ethics is a research area characterized by a prominent gap between research and practice. With most studies in the area being conceptual in nature or focused on technical ML (Machine Learning) solutions, the link between AI (Artificial Intelligence) ethics and SE (Software Engineering) practice remains thin. Establishing this link, we argue, is vital going forward. While conceptual discussion is required to define AI ethics, much progress has already been made in this regard. Similarly, though technical ML solutions are also required for practical implementation, ML systems are ultimately still software, and thus SE cannot be forgotten. In this paper, we propose one way of bringing AI ethics closer to conventional SE practice: utilizing user stories to implement AI ethics by means of Ethical User Stories (EUS). EUS can be used to formulate both functional and non-functional requirements, although an ethical framework is required produce them. By treating AI ethics as a part of the development process in this fashion, as opposed to a separate task, it can ideally become a part of SE for ML systems.

Keywords: Artificial Intelligence · AI ethics · User story · Ethical user story · Ethical tool

1 Introduction

Implementing ethics in practice is challenging in SE. In practice, doing so often means converting abstract ethical principles into tangible requirements. This requires extensive ethical consideration and discussion, which developers can seldom devote time to among their other work. Ethical guidelines are a typical way of approaching ethics in SE, though such documents seem to see little use. For example, it has been argued that one of the more prominent such documents, the ACM Code of Ethics, has had very little impact on practice in SE [9].

Arguably the most topical research area related to ethics in SE has recently been AI ethics, following rapid advances in AI technology in the past two decades. For example, issues such as bias and data privacy, even though not exclusive to AI systems, have received notable media attention following ethical shortcomings in

© The Author(s), under exclusive license to Springer Nature Switzerland AG 2022
D. Taibi et al. (Eds.): PROFES 2022, LNCS 13709, pp. 553–558, 2022.
https://doi.org/10.1007/978-3-031-21388-5_41

such systems out on the field. Thus far, discussion in the area has been predominantly conceptual, focusing on defining what is AI ethics and what issues should be addressed. On the other hand, empirical studies have been rare [7,11,13]. Studies discussing the current state of pracitce in the area point towards guidelines having had limited impact on practice in the context of AI ethics as well (e.g., [14–16,18]).

Indeed, despite various ethical issues being acknowledged, tackling these issues in practice remains one of the key challenges in the area [14]. For example, guidelines, which have been the most common tools for implementing AI ethics, are abstract and difficult to utilize in practice. Guidelines merely present sets of ethical principles to tackle but often fall short when it comes to providing instructions for doing so. Translating abstract ethical principles into tangible requirements is a difficult task. [10,14] Aside from guidelines, various specific ML techniques for implementing AI ethics exist [11,13], such as techniques related to bias detection, which are arguably useful for their intended purposes, but require their users to already know what ethical issues they are tackling and how. However, SE process related tools, such as practices or methods, are lacking.

To help tackle this issue by better linking AI ethics with conventional SE, we discuss the idea of utilizing of user stories for implementing AI ethics. We argue that user stories can function as a way of converting AI ethics principles into tangible requirements. However, rather than doing so directly through AI ethics guidelines, we utilize a recent method for implementing AI ethics, ECCOLA [17], to support the creation of such user stories. Such Ethical User Stories (EUS) are one way of linking ethics more closely to conventional SE practice. EUS is a concept we have begun to explore in an existing paper through empirical evidence [5]. Though this approach is not exclusive to AI ethics and can be of interest when it comes to ethics in SE in general, AI ethics is arguably one of the areas where such approaches are most needed currently.

2   Background and Related Work

2.1   AI Ethics

Though discussion on ethical issues related to AI systems is highly active, bringing this discussion into practice is a prevalent issue [14]. This discussion on AI ethics has recently converged around a set of recurring *principles*, which in practice are umbrella concepts comprising various more specific issues [4,6,11]. Some issues are more tangible and consequently have more tangible solutions, while others are more abstract or general and require far more effort to implement in practice.

To provide a practical example of these principles, let us briefly discuss *fairness* as a principle. Fairness deals with diversity, inclusiveness and, equality. In practice this manifests as the prevention, monitoring or mitigation of unwanted bias and discrimination in AI/ML systems. [6] Fairness could be argued to be one of the more practical principles in terms of its technical implementation.

This is highlighted by various existing papers proposing technical ML solutions dedicated to tackling bias in ML [11,13].

Yet, in part, it is exactly this focus on technical tools and conceptual discussion that is currently a large problem in AI ethics, we argue. Whereas numerous technical ML tools for implementing AI ethics exist, and while the conceptual discussion on the topic is highly active, few empirical studies exist [7,11,13]. To this end, the point of view of SE is also largely still missing [14,17]. Technical ML solutions are ultimately specific solutions for specific problems, and only as far as ML is considered. Yet ML is but a part of any AI system, and engineering AI systems is still SE at the end of the day.

2.2   User Stories

User stories are a commonly utilized tool for formulating requirements in SE [3], and particularly in Agile development [2]. Having originated from eXtreme Programming XP, user stories are now utilized in most Agile approaches [12]. Though the purpose of user stories is to help formulate and communicate requirements, their implementation in practice varies in form. I.e., there are various templates and approaches used to formulate user stories.

User stories commonly take on the form of a card or a sheet of paper, such as a post-it note, or more formally a user story template. Of course, this may also be done using digital tools. They are written using natural language and their purpose is to communicate the goals of the system that is being developed [19]. One of the more popular approaches to user stories formulates them as follows: "As a [user], I want to [capability], so that [receive benefit]" [2]. Many variants of this three-part-template exist. On the other hand, for example, Lucassen [8] proposes a four-part one that consists of format, role, means, and end.

2.3   Related Work: Implementing AI Ethics

This topic is at the intersection of user stories in the context of ICT-related ethics and implementing ethics in practice, with AI ethics being the specific context here. Though this idea of using user stories to implement ethics is not exclusive to AI ethics, it is currently an area for tools to implement ethics are sorely needed. Overall, the idea of utilizing user stories to for the purpose of implementing ethics seems to be quite novel.

In terms of implementing AI ethics in practice, empirical studies are scarce. Guidelines have been the most common approach to doing so [6], but are argued to not work [10], given the limited impact they have had on practice [14]. Technical tools for ML, on the other hand, are highly specific [11]. Focus on SE in implementing AI ethics has been lacking [14], which we argue is currently a key gap in the area. As far as SE methods are concerned, we are only aware of a method for implementing ethics we ourselves have proposed, ECCOLA [17], as well as one other method, RE4AI [1]. On the other hand, general-purpose tools and methods related to ethics are numerous in fields such as design.

3   Devising Ethical User Stories Using the Ethical Framework Method

Ethical User Stories (EUS), in brief, are user stories devised to help tackle and formalize ethical issues in SE, from the point of view of a particular ethical framework. EUS are a novel concept we have begun to explore in an existing paper [5], which provides empirical evidence of EUS in practice.

Figure 1 describes the process of devising EUS. EUS are formulated based on the case at hand, like user stories in general. However, when devising EUS, an ethical framework must be present to motivate and direct ethical consideration. The ethical framework provides the lens through which ethics is approached in the particular project context. EUS are then written like a conventional user story, aside from them also including ethical consideration or being motivated by ethical consideration. EUS can be used to formulate both functional and non-functional requirements.

The ethical framework used to create EUS can be any ethical tool: a method, a set of guidelines, or even an ethical theory. The purpose of the ethical framework is to define what is 'ethical' in the given context, as well as to provide guidance for, e.g., which ethical issues should be tackled. To this end, the framework of choice would ideally be as closely related to the context at hand as possible (e.g., AI ethics framework for AI ethics, as opposed to a generic one).

Below, we provide a tangible example of an EUS. In this case, a large number of EUS were devised for a real use case of Smart terminal[1] using an AI ethics method, ECCOLA [17], as the ethical framework. This is a part of a larger research endeavor on the topic (see footnote) that we are currently working on, which this paper provides an initial look at.

ECCOLA is an empirically tested developer-focused AI ethics method that is presented in card-format. Each ECCOLA card discusses an AI ethics principle or issues related to a principle. Thus, EUS devised using ECCOLA can typically be linked to a specific card, as seen in Fig. 2. Figure 2 showcases the relevant ECCOLA card and an EUS discussing features related to the card.

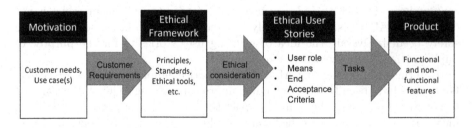

Fig. 1. Process of devising ethical user stories

---

[1] Ethical User Stories in SMART Terminal Digitalization Project: Use Case Passenger Flow: https://doi.org/10.48550/arXiv.2111.06116.

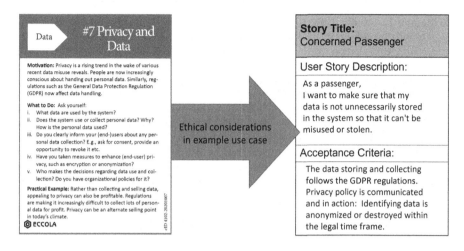

Fig. 2. Example of an ethical framework and the resulting EUS (from real case)

4 Summary

AI ethics is an area of research where the gap between research and practice remains prominent. In particular, the link between AI ethics and SE practice is thin [14]. Studies in the area are generally either conceptual in nature or most focused on technical tools for ML. Engineering ML systems is still SE, and focusing purely on the ML components results in a narrow focus.

We propose Ethical User Stories (EUS) as one tool for bringing AI ethics closer to conventional SE practice. User stories are commonly used SE tools in Requirements Engineering. By incorporating ethical issues into this process through an ethical framework, we argue that user stories could help implement ethics in practice. We provide some initial empirical evidence of their use in an existing paper [5].

In this light, we strongly urge future research to conduct further empirical studies in AI ethics, particularly with a focus on solutions for tackling AI ethics in practice in SE. Such studies should focus on incorporating AI ethics as a part of SE practice. EUS provide one example of how this could perhaps be done.

References

1. Siqueira de Cerqueira, J., Azevedo, A., Tives, H., Canedo, E.: Guide for artificial intelligence ethical requirements elicitation - re4ai ethical guide. In: Proceedings of the 55th Hawaii International Conference on System Sciences, January 2022
2. Cohn, M.: User Stories Applied: for Agile Software Development. Addison-Wesley, Boston (2004)
3. Dimitrijević, S., Jovanović, J., Devedžić, V.: A comparative study of software tools for user story management. Inf. Softw. Technol. **57**, 352–368 (2015)
4. Hagendorff, T.: The ethics of AI ethics: an evaluation of guidelines. Mind. Mach. **30**(1), 99–120 (2020)

5. Halme, E., et al.: How to write ethical user stories? impacts of the ECCOLA method. In: Gregory, P., Lassenius, C., Wang, X., Kruchten, P. (eds.) XP 2021. LNBIP, vol. 419, pp. 36–52. Springer, Cham (2021). https://doi.org/10.1007/978-3-030-78098-2_3

6. Jobin, A., Ienca, M., Vayena, E.: The global landscape of AI ethics guidelines. Nat. Mach. Intell. **1**(9), 389–399 (2019)

7. Johnson, B., Smith, J.: Towards ethical data-driven software: Filling the gaps in ethics research & practice. In: 2021 IEEE/ACM 2nd International Workshop on Ethics in Software Engineering Research and Practice (SEthics), pp. 18–25 (2021)

8. Lucassen, G., Dalpiaz, F., Van Der Werf, J.M.E., Brinkkemper, S.: Forging high-quality user stories: towards a discipline for agile requirements. In: 2015 IEEE 23rd International Requirements Engineering Conference (RE), pp. 126–135. IEEE (2015)

9. McNamara, A., Smith, J., Murphy-Hill, E.: Does ACM's code of ethics change ethical decision making in software development? In: Proceedings of the 2018 26th ACM ESEC/FSE, pp. 729–733. ESEC/FSE 2018, ACM, New York, NY, USA (2018)

10. Mittelstadt, B.: Principles alone cannot guarantee ethical AI. Nat. Mach. Intell. **1**, 501–507 (2019)

11. Morley, J., Floridi, L., Kinsey, L., Elhalal, A.: From what to how: an initial review of publicly available AI ethics tools, methods and research to translate principles into practices. Sci. Eng. Ethics **26**(4), 2141–2168 (2020)

12. Schön, E.M., Thomaschewski, J., Escalona, M.J.: Agile requirements engineering: a systematic literature review. Comput. Stand. Interf. **49**, 79–91 (2017)

13. Sloane, M., Zakrzewski, J.: German AI start-ups and "ai ethics": Using a social practice lens for assessing and implementing socio-technical innovation. In: 2022 ACM Conference on Fairness, Accountability, and Transparency, FAccT 2022, pp. 935–947. Association for Computing Machinery, New York, NY, USA (2022)

14. Vakkuri, V., Kemell, K., Kultanen, J., Abrahamsson, P.: The current state of industrial practice in artificial intelligence ethics. IEEE Softw. **37**(4), 50–57 (2020)

15. Vakkuri, V., Kemell, K.-K., Abrahamsson, P.: Implementing ethics in AI: initial Results of an Industrial Multiple Case Study. In: Franch, X., Männistö, T., Martínez-Fernández, S. (eds.) PROFES 2019. LNCS, vol. 11915, pp. 331–338. Springer, Cham (2019). https://doi.org/10.1007/978-3-030-35333-9_24

16. Vakkuri, V., Kemell, K.-K., Jantunen, M., Abrahamsson, P.: This is just a prototype: how ethics are ignored in software startup-like environments. In: Stray, V., Hoda, R., Paasivaara, M., Kruchten, P. (eds.) XP 2020. LNBIP, vol. 383, pp. 195–210. Springer, Cham (2020). https://doi.org/10.1007/978-3-030-49392-9_13

17. Vakkuri, V., Kemell, K.K., Jantunen, M., Halme, E., Abrahamsson, P.: ECCOLA-a method for implementing ethically aligned AI systems. J. Syst. Softw. **182**, 111067 (2021)

18. Vakkuri, V., Kemell, K.K., Tolvanen, J., Jantunen, M., Halme, E., Abrahamsson, P.: How do software companies deal with artificial intelligence ethics? A gap analysis. In: The International Conference on Evaluation and Assessment in Software Engineering 2022, pp. 100–109. EASE 2022, Association for Computing Machinery, New York, NY, USA (2022)

19. Wang, X., Zhao, L., Wang, Y., Sun, J.: The Role of requirements engineering practices in agile development: an empirical study. In: Zowghi, D., Jin, Z. (eds.) Requirements Engineering. CCIS, vol. 432, pp. 195–209. Springer, Heidelberg (2014). https://doi.org/10.1007/978-3-662-43610-3_15

Workshop on Engineering Processes and Practices for Quantum Software (PPQS'22)

Workshop on Engineering Processes and Practices for Quantum Software (PPQS'22)

Co-located with PROFES 2022, Finland

Mahdi Fehmideh[1], Muhamed Waseem[2], Aakash Ahmad[3], and Naveed Ikram[4]

[1] University of Southern Queensland, Australia
Mahdi.Fahmideh@usq.edu.au

[2] Wuhan University, China
m.waseem@whu.edu.cn

[3] Lancaster University Leipzig, Germany
a.ahmad13@lancaster.ac.uk

[4] EYCON PVT Limited, Pakkistan
naveed.ikram@riphah.edu.pk

Abstract. This report provides a synopsis of a planned workshop titled Workshop on Engineering Processes and Practices for Quantum Software (PPQS'22). The PPQS'22 workshop, as a pioneering effort aims to organise a community of researchers and practitioners on process-centered development of quantum software systems and applications. The workshop will have a keynote session from industry expert, presentation of an accepted article, followed by plenary discussion and will be held on November 21, 2022 as a co-located event of the International Conference on Product-Focused Software Process Improvement in Jyväskylä, Finland.

Keywords: Quantum software engineering · Quantum computing · Software process

1 Introduction to the Workshop (PPQS'22)

Quantum Software Engineering (QSE) is a recent genre of Software Engineering (SE) discipline - relying on engineering processes and practices - to design, develop, validate and evolve quantum software (QSW) systems effectively and efficiently [1]. Traditional SE processes and practices can still be useful in QSE context. However, they need to be augmented with the unique characteristics of quantum software [2].

The Workshop on Engineering Processes and Practices for Quantum Software (PPQS'22) is as a pioneering effort that aims to establish a community, fostering academic research and industrial solutions, focused on QSE principles and practices for process-centric design, development, validation, deployment and maintenance of quantum software systems and applications [3]. The workshop intends to attract publishable, applicable research as empirical studies, industrial experience reports, and solution proposals etc. on process-centric QSE.

Keynote Session: The workshop will open with a Keynote presentation by industry representative (Dr. Valtteri Lahtinen the CSO and co-founder of Quanscient [4]). The focus of the keynote will be Process-centered and iterative development of quantum software systems.

Accepted Workshop Paper(s): The workshop received one submission as a full paper. The research area is relatively young and rapidly evolving with much less research on processes and practices of quantum software engineering when compared to classical software engineering processes. The submitted paper was reviewed by at-least two experts and both recommended their acceptance along with comments, inviting the authors to improve their work in the final version.

Paper title: *Classical to Quantum Software Migration Journey Begins: A Conceptual Readiness Model*

Paper focus and contributions: The research presents a readiness model that can help an organization assess its capability of migration from classic software engineering to quantum software engineering. The model is based on the existing multi-vocal literature, industrial empirical study, understanding of the process areas, challenging factors and enablers that could impact the quantum software engineering process.

Plenary Discussion: The discussion among workshop participants also welcomes other participants at PROFES to share their ideas, experiences, and open discussion on the software engineering processes and practices for quantum computing platforms. The workshop can also help to streamline the points and agenda for future research on processes and practices for quantum software systems.

2   Program Committee

Mahdi Fahmideh, University of Southern Queensland, Australia
Muhamemd Waseem, Wuhan University, China
Aakash Ahmad, Lancaster University Leipzig, China
Naveed Ikram, Ripah International University, Pakistan
Liang Peng, Wuhan University, China
Zularnain Hashmi, Terablu, Pakistan
Rabie Ramadan, University of Ha'il, Saudi Arabia
Arif Ali, University of Oulu, Finland
Amna Asif, Lancaster University, Leipzig

References

1. Piattini, M., Serrano, M., Perez-Castillo, R., Petersen, G., Hevia, J.L.: Toward a quantum software engineering, IT Prof. **23**(1), 62–66 (2021)
2. Gemeinhardt, F., Garmendia, A., Wimmer, M.: Towards model-driven quantum software engineering. In: IEEE/ACM 2nd International Workshop on Quantum Software Engineering (Q-SE), pp. 13–15, IEEE (2021)

3. Ali, S., Yue, T.: Modeling quantum programs: Challenges, initial results, and research directions. In: Proceedings of the 1st ACM SIGSOFT International Workshop on Architectures and Paradigms for Engineering Quantum Software, pp. 14–21 (2020)
4. QUANSCIENT. Simulations for the Industry 4.0. https://quanscient.com/

Classical to Quantum Software Migration Journey Begins: A Conceptual Readiness Model

Muhammad Azeem Akbar[1]([✉]), Saima Rafi[2], and Arif Ali Khan[3]

[1] Department of Software Engineering, LUT University, Lappeenranta, Finland
azeem.akbar@lut.fi
[2] Department of Informatics and Systems, University of Murcia, Murcia, Spain
[3] M3S Empirical Software Engineering Research Unit, University of Oulu, 90570 Oulu, Finland
arif.khan@oulu.fi

Abstract. With recent advances in the development of more powerful quantum computers, the research area of quantum software engineering is emerging. Quantum software plays a critical role in exploiting the full potential of quantum computing systems. As a result, it has been drawing increasing attention recently to provide concepts, principles, and guidelines to address the ongoing challenges of quantum software development. The importance of the topic motivated us to voice out a call for action to develop a readiness model that will help an organization assess its capability of migration from classic software engineering to quantum software engineering. The proposed model will be based on the existing multivocal literature, industrial empirical study, understanding of the process areas, challenging factors and enablers that could impact the quantum software engineering process. We believe that the proposed model will provide a roadmap for software development organizations to measure their readiness concerning to transformation from classic to quantum software engineering by suggesting best practices and highlighting important process areas, challenges, and enablers.

Keywords: Quantum software engineering · Readiness model · Process areas · Challenges · Enablers · Best practices

1 Introduction

Quantum computing promises to solve many problems more precisely than possible with classical computers, e.g., simulating complex physical systems or applying machine learning techniques [1, 2]. Presently, that quantum computing has become widespread in developing more powerful quantum computers, and their need in terms of quantum software and applications, development process and frameworks, quantum software architectures and styles are becoming increasingly important [3, 4]. Quantum computing is a technological revolution that demands a new software engineering paradigm to develop and conceive quantum software systems. Quantum software engineering calls for novel techniques, tools, processes, and methods that explicitly focus on developing software systems based on quantum mechanics [5]. Though, the development of such

© The Author(s), under exclusive license to Springer Nature Switzerland AG 2022
D. Taibi et al. (Eds.): PROFES 2022, LNCS 13709, pp. 563–573, 2022.
https://doi.org/10.1007/978-3-031-21388-5_42

quantum applications is complex and requires experts with knowledge from various fields, e.g., physics, mathematics, and computer science [6, 7].

Quantum software engineering is an emerging research area investigating concepts, principles, and guidelines to develop, maintain, and evolve quantum applications [8, 9]. Therefore, it is important to enhance the quality and reusability of the resulting quantum applications by systematically applying software engineering principles during all development phases, from the initial requirement analysis to the software implementation [10]. In classical software engineering, software development processes often document the different development phases a software artefact or application goes through [11, 12]. Furthermore, such software development process also summarizes best practices and methods that can be applied in the various phases and corresponding tools [9, 13]. Hence, they can be used for educating new developers by providing an overview of the development process or serving as a basis for cooperating with experts from different fields [14]. Today's quantum applications are often hybrid, consisting of quantum and classical programs [15]. Thus, the development process for quantum applications involves developing and operating both kinds of programs. However, existing lifecycles from classical software engineering [16] and quantum software development process [13, 17] only target one of these kinds and do not address the resulting integration challenges.

Furthermore, the execution of the quantum and classical programs must be orchestrated, and data has to be passed between them [18]. The workflow process is a means for these orchestrations to provide benefits, such as scalability, reliability, and robustness [19]. Thus, to transform from classic to quantum software development process, we need to analyze the software development community's tools, standards, and guidelines. Stefano et al. [20] highlighted that *"the challenge of quantum software engineering is to rework and extend the whole of classical software engineering into the quantum domain so that programmers can manipulate quantum programs with the same ease and confidence that they manipulate today's classical programs."* Ahmad et al. [21] presented the architectural view of quantum software engineering architecture (Fig. 1). The presented architecture view helps to reflect in designing and envisioning an overall system, to avoid errors and future bugs in quantum system. Hence, the role of architecture is empowered in quantum software applications to abstract complexities of source code modules and their interactions as architectural component and connectors [22].

Motivation Scenario

Despite the significance of quantum software engineering, no standards and models are available to handle quantum software development processes. For example, if an organization want to transform from classic to quantum software development, they need guidelines and strategies to put the process on the right path. Thus, it is required to estimate all aspects of a software development process like time, cost, integration aspect, scope, quality, human resources, risk, communication, stakeholders, and procurements. The transformation from classic to the quantum system is a challenging exercise due to issues such as:

Little research has been conducted on the development of models and strategies. The problems faced by organizations during the implementation of quantum software development activities are quite different from the traditional or classical paradigm.

Therefore, existing literature doesn't examine the transformation from classic to quantum software engineering in sufficient detail as there is little research that highlights the important process areas and challenges to address for the adoption of quantum software development. Therefore, *lack of proper guidelines* that help practitioners to implement quantum technology for software development. Presently, there are no assessment tools and frameworks for determining an organization's readiness concerning transforming from a classic to a quantum software development process. No such practices are available that assist practitioners in improving quantum software engineering in their organization.

Moreover, there is a *lack of a roadmap* to help organizations choose the appropriate patterns, particularly for their problems. No study *addresses the project management changes* caused due to the migration from classic to quantum software engineering. Thus, it is demanded to deeply study the important process areas, challenges, enablers, and guidelines that could influence the adoption of quantum software development. Furthermore, discussing the different software artefacts usually constituting a quantum application and presenting their corresponding process areas is required. It is *critical to identify the plug points* between the classic and quantum software modules to enable their integration into overall application, for execution of hybrid quantum applications. To address all the highlighted concerns, there is need of practically robust roadmap and guidelines to assist the practitioners to make the migration from classic to quantum software development successful. Hence, the readiness model is one of the key instruments

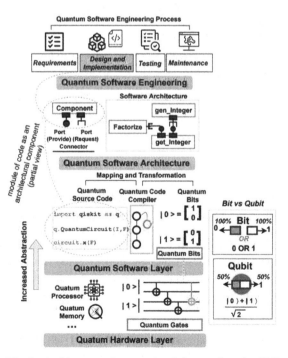

Fig. 1. Architecture of quantum software engineering [21]

to assists software development organizations to assess the capability of an organizations concerning to transform from classic software engineering to quantum software engineering.

Readiness Models and Standards

A readiness model is a technique to assess an organization or team based on the specified criteria to represent their level of readiness. Readiness models are intended to help organizations appraise their process readiness and develop it for improvement. They serve as points of reference for different stages of readiness in an area. Software engineering readiness models intend to help organizations move from ad-hoc processes to mature and disciplined software processes [23].

In software engineering research, a readiness model has been utilized in several studies. It was used by Niazi et al. [24] to assess organizational readiness in terms of software process improvement. Their readiness model has several levels: aware, defined, and optimizing. Critical factors and barriers support each level. The researchers validated their readiness model by performing case studies in three software organizations. Similarly, Ali and Khan [25] presented a model to measure the readiness of a software organization to form outsourcing relationships. They utilized critical partnership factors to develop a readiness model and examined their practical implementation. Their readiness model has several levels: contract, success, readiness, conversion and maturity. Similarly, Khan et al. [26] proposed a software outsourcing vendor readiness model (SOVRM). The readiness levels of the SOVRM consist of critical barriers and critical success factors. Similarly, a recent study conducted by Sufi et al. [27] proposed security requirements engineering readiness (SRERM). The levels of SRERM are based on security requirements categories. All the above-discussed readiness models followed the capability maturity model Integration (CMMI) staged representation structure and considered the critical barriers and success factors as the key process areas (KPA's). The software engineering institute developed CMMI almost twenty years ago [28].

CMMI helps organizations to streamline process improvement. It clearly shows what organizations should do to mature software processes. CMMI model is integrated into five maturity levels, i.e., (initial, managed, defined, quantitatively managed, and optimizing). CMMI had proved itself for decades yet has had no meaningful impact in providing detailed information about broader technology space such as quantum computing in implementing strategies and key practices.

ISO/IEC 15504 Information Technology: SPICE is an international framework for accessing software development [29]. It provides a detailed description of standard documents for the software development process and related management functions within an organization. It includes two dimensions, i.e., capability dimension and process dimension. It also introduces assessment indicators that help an organization with brief guidelines to assess the quality of their management process. To see in terms of improving quantum computing process areas, SPICE does integrate existing process improvement methodologies. Still, it does not provide an explicit process improvement path regarding quantum software.

International Standards Organization (ISO) 9000/9001: ISO 9000 is a series of standards in quality management that helps organizations maintain their customer and other stakeholder needs related to a product or service [30]. It helps organizations to document the elements needed for quality software systems effectively. ISO 9001 consists of generic standards that are not specific to the only software industry and can be applied to different types of organizations. These standard guidelines focus on the industry's manufacturing and services aspects, including quality standards. However, it still lags behind process improvement aspects of software systems while using quantum technology.

Several readiness and maturity models have been proposed by researchers and practitioners in the traditional software development domain, providing a framework to assess an organization's current effectiveness and supporting figuring out what capabilities they need to acquire next to improve their performance. Indeed, this apparent popularity of these models out on the field has partly motivated us to propose a readiness model in the context of transformation from classic to quantum software development. In an area where we struggle with a gap between research and practice, we argue that looking at frameworks, models, and other tools actively used out on the field is a good starting point for further steps. Thus far, guidelines have been used to make quantum software engineering more tangible, but further steps are still needed, and a robust readiness model could be one such step.

2   Call for Action

We propose developing a readiness model to provide a roadmap for migrating from classical to quantum software development. Such a readiness model would help the field move from ad hoc implementation of quantum software development to a more mature process. Furthermore, we argue that this model should not be an effort for a single researcher or research group but a multidisciplinary project that builds on a combination of theoretical models and empirical results. The research work is classified in four steps to developing the proposed readiness model.

Step 1: This step will give a broad overview of the available literature and identify the key process areas and challenging factors that can influence the transformation from classic to quantum software development process. To meet this objective, we plan to conduct a multivocal literature review (MLR) which is a viable approach to extracting data from the grey and white literature. As the topic under investigation is not maturely studied in mainstream research, thus the grey literature could give critical insights about it. The key finding of this step revolves around the following questions.

[What process areas of transformation from classic software development to quantum software development are reported in the existing literature?.

[What are the key challenging factors of transforming the classic software development process to quantum, reported in the literature?.

[What enablers are essential for transforming the existing classic to quantum software development process, reported in the literature?

Step 2: This step leads to empirically Quantum Software Engineeringvalidating the literature findings (Steps 1) with industry practitioners by conducting the questionnaire survey, case study, and interviews. This step aims to confirm significant process areas and challenges identified in step 1 and to enlist additional influencing areas towards transforming the traditional software development process into quantum. In this step, we will find the answers to the following questions:

[What process areas are critical to consider while transforming from classic to quantum software development process?].

[What are the key challenges faced by industrial practitioners while transforming the existing classic software development process to quantum software development?].

[What enablers are essential for transforming the existing classic to quantum software development process? discussed in real-world practice?].

Step 3: This step will investigate best practices against each identified challenging factor and enabler (in Steps 1 and 2). To achieve this step, we will conduct MLR to investigate the state-of-the-art best practices reported in grey and formal literature. Furthermore, we will empirically explore the best practices against each challenging factor and enabler by conducting a questionnaire, case study, and interviews. This step will answer the following questions:

[What best practices address the challenging factors (Step 1), reported in the literature and real-world industry?].

[What are the best practices to achieve the enablers identified in Step 2, reported in the literature and real-world industry?].

Step 4: Finally, a readiness model will be developed to assist the software development organizations in assessing, adapting and improving their process toward the migration from classic to quantum software development paradigm. To develop the readiness model, we will consider the findings of steps 1, step 2, and steps 3.

The readiness model will consist of three components, i.e., the assessment component, factors component (process areas, challenges, enablers), and guidelines component. The identified best practices will be mapped against each enabler and challenging factor to achieve that certain level. If an organization wants to move to the next level, they need to address each enabler and challenging factor by implementing its respective best practices.

The developed readiness model will help the organizations assess their ability with respect to the transformation from classic to quantum software development and provide a roadmap to improve their capability concerning the adoption of quantum software development.

To check the practical robustness of the model, we will conduct case studies in software development organizations and update them according to their suggestions. The final model will be available for software development organizations to adopt and improve their adaptability and executability concerning to quantum software development process.

[How to develop and evaluate the effectiveness of the proposed model?].

[What would be the readiness levels of the proposed model?].

[How to check the robustness of the proposed model in the real-world industry?].

3   Architecture of Proposed Model

The basic architecture of the proposed quantum software engineering readiness model (QSERM) will be designed based on Process areas and their associated challenges and key enablers identified from literature and industry practices. To align identified components in the structured model, we will use the concept of existing software engineering standards such as CMMI, IMM and SPICE. Figure 2 shows the relationship between key components of the proposed model. It depicts the proposed model's complete component, highlighting how the results of existing models, literature and industry findings will be used to design the key components of the proposed QSERM.

The four components of QSERM are:

- Readiness level component
- Process areas
- Challenge
- Key enablers

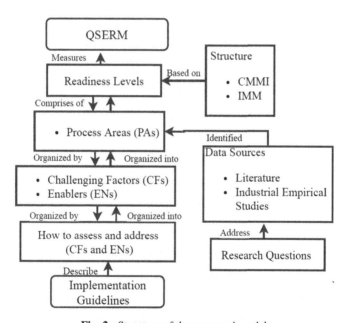

Fig. 2. Structure of the proposed model

3.1   Readiness Level Component

The proposed model consists of readiness levels based on the standard model for software engineering i.e., CMMI. Several adjustments are required in the structure of CMMI to make it applicable for quantum software applications. The structure of each readiness level is given in Fig. 3, and brief explanation is given below:

Process Areas (PAs): Process areas are the building blocks that indicate the areas an organization should focus on to improve software processes. These areas consist of a cluster of related practices that when implemented collectively, satisfy the goals related to that area. Therefore, we will identify the process areas related to quantum software engineering to improve the software development process.

Challenging Factors (CFs): The architecture of the proposed model consists of various process areas. The identified challenging factors will be mapped to all maturity levels and process areas associated with each level. This formulation has been used previously by many researchers. Therefore, we can justify the use of challenging factors in our study.

Enablers (ENs): The Key enablers will be identified to support the proposed model to accomplish the goals associated with all five maturity levels of QSERM. To justify the use of key enablers, it provides the best support to perform essential tasks. We will perform an SLR study to identify the key enablers from software engineering experts working with quantum development.

Fig. 3. Structure of each readiness level

The proposed QSERM will be based on five readiness levels (Fig. 4). Each readiness level encompasses specific process areas. The process areas highlight the important zones that need to be addressed by an organization. Furthermore, important, challenging factors and enablers will be aligned with each process area. To achieve a higher level, an organization must address all the process areas of a readiness level. And to address all the process areas, organizations must address all the challenging factors and enablers.

The best practices will be mapped against each challenge and enabler, which will assist the organizations in addressing them effectively. For example, if organization-A wants to move to level 2, they need to address all the process areas of level 1. To achieve this, they need to address all the challenging factors and enablers of level-1 by implementing their associated best practices.

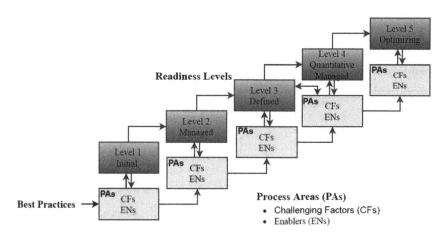

Fig. 4. Example of proposed readiness model

3.2 Assessment Dimension

To evaluate the model, we will use the Motorola assessment tool [31]. Many researchers in software engineering field have used this tool to evaluate their proposed readiness model. Therefore, we have selected the same tool for the evaluation of QSERM. This tool will assist the organization in identifying the areas that need further improvement. The three dimensions of the Motorola assessment tool are:

Approach: Emphasize the top management's commitment to implementing the specific practice.

Deployment: Focus on the consistent and uniform practice implementation across quantum project areas.

Results: Assess the breadth and consistency of the results of deployed practice across different project areas.

4   Expected Outcomes

Since in the early stage, the study will highlight only a few contributions. One of the contributions is identifying process areas, challenges, enablers, and associated practices that will help quantum software development. The process areas consist of a cluster of related practices that, when implemented collectively, satisfy the goals related to that area. The second contribution is to develop a quantum software engineering readiness model. This model will assist organisations in assessing readiness and suggest guidelines for successfully adopting the quantum software engineering paradigm. And the third contribution is to help organizations in "identifying", "analyzing" and "mitigating" the challenges faced during the migration from classic to quantum software engineering. The novelty of this research work is the development of a readiness model that will state activities, guidelines or roadmap that can be assist in migrating from classic to quantum software development.

Acknowledgement. This research is supported by the PHP Foundation with the grant 20220006.

References

1. Outeiral, C., et al.: The prospects of quantum computing in computational molecular biology. Comput. Mol. Sci.. **11**(4), e1481 (2021)
2. De Stefano, M., et al.: Software engineering for quantum programming: How far are we?," J. Syst. Softw. **190**, 111326 (2022)
3. Häner, T., Steiger, D.S., Svore, K., Troyer, M. J. Q. S. and Technology, "A software methodology for compiling quantum programs. Quant. Sci. Technol. **3**(2), 020501 (2018)
4. Ahmad, A., Khan, A.A., Waseem, M., Fahmideh, M., Mikkonen, T.: Towards process centered architecting for quantum software systems. In: IEEE International Conference on Quantum Software (QSW) (2022)
5. Gemeinhardt, F., Garmendia, F., Wimmer, M.: Towards model-driven quantum software engineering. In: Towards Model-Driven Quantum Software Engineering. pp. 13–15 (2021)
6. Nita, L., et al.: Education, "The challenge and opportunities of quantum literacy for future education and transdisciplinary problem-solving, Res. Sci. Technol. Educ. pp. 1–17 (2021)
7. Altman, E., et al.: Quantum simulators: architectures and opportunities. PRX Quant. **2**(1),017003 (2021)
8. Piattini, M., Peterssen, G., Pérez-Castillo, R.: Quantum computing: a new software engineering golden age, ACM SIGSOFT Softw. Eng. Notes **45**(3), 12–14 (2021)
9. Zhao, J.: Quantum software engineering: landscapes and horizons. In: Serrano, M.A., Pérez-Castillo, R., Piattini, M. (eds.) Quantum Software Engineering. Springer, Cham (2020). https://doi.org/10.1007/978-3-031-05324-5_2
10. LaRose, R.J.Q.: Overview and comparison of gate level quantum software platforms. Qunat. Comput. **3**, 130 (2019)
11. Akbar, M.A., et al.: Improving the quality of software development process by introducing a new methodology–AZ-model. IEEE Acces **6,** 4811–4823 (2017)
12. Mohammed, N.M., Munassar, A., Govardhan, A.: A comparison between five models of software engineering. Int. J. Comput. Sci Iss. **7**(5), 94 (2010)
13. Weder, B., Barzen, J., Leymann, F., Salm, M., Vietz, D.: The quantum software lifecycle. In: APEQS 2020: Proceedings of the 1st ACM SIGSOFT International Workshop on Architectures and Paradigms for Engineering Quantum Software, pp. 2–9 (2020)
14. Campbell, E., Heyfron, L..E.: An efficient quantum compiler that reduces T count, Quant. Sci. Technol. **4**(1) (2018)
15. Leymann, F., Barzen, J.: Hybrid quantum applications need two orchestrations in superposition: a software architecture perspective (2021)

16. Akbar, M.A., et al.: Statistical analysis of the effects of heavyweight and lightweight methodologies on the six-pointed star model. IEEE Access **6**, 8066–8079 (2018)
17. N. Dey, M. Ghosh, Kundu, S.S., Chakrabarti, A.: QDLC--the quantum development life cycle (2020)
18. Weder, B., Breitenbücher, B., Leymann, F., Wild, K.: Integrating quantum computing into workflow modeling and execution. In: 2020 IEEE/ACM 13th International Conference on Utility and Cloud Computing (UCC), pp. 279–291 (2020)
19. Weder, B., Barzen, J., Leymann, F., Vietz, D.: Quantum software development lifecycle. In: Serrano, M.A., Pérez-Castillo, R., Piattini, M. (eds) Quantum Software Engineering. Springer, Cham (2022). https://doi.org/10.1007/978-3-031-05324-5_4
20. Bettelli, S., Calarco, T., Serafini, L.: Toward an architecture for quantum programming. Mol. Opt. P. Phys. **25**(2), 181–200 (2003)
21. Ahmad, A., Khan, A.A., Waseem, M., Fahmideh, M., Mikkonen, T.: Towards Process centered architecting for quantum software systems. In: 2022 IEEE International Conference on Quantum Software (QSW), pp. 26–31 (2022)
22. Murali, P., Linke, N.M., Martonosi, M., Abhari, A.J., Nguyen, N.H., Alderete, C.H.: Full-stack, real-system quantum computer studies: Architectural comparisons and design insights. In: ISCA 2019, Proceedings of the 46th International Symposium on Computer Architecturepp, pp. 527–540 (2019)
23. VTetlay, A., John, P.: Determining the lines of system maturity, system readiness and capability readiness in the system development lifecycle. In: 7th Annual Conference on Systems Engineering Research 2009 (CSER 2009) (2009)
24. Niazi, M., Wilson, D., Zowghi, D.: Organisational readiness and software process improvement. In: Münch, J., Abrahamsson, P. (eds.) PROFES 2007. LNCS, vol. 4589, pp. 96–107. Springer, Heidelberg (2007). https://doi.org/10.1007/978-3-540-73460-4_11
25. Ali, S., Khan, S.U.: Software outsourcing partnership model: an evaluation framework for vendor organizations. J. Styst. Softw. **117**, 402–425 (2016)
26. Khan, S.U.: Software outsourcing vendors readiness model (SOVRM). In: Profes Doctoral Symposium, Keele University (2011)
27. Mufti, Y., Niazi, M., Alshayeb, M., Mahmood, S.: A readiness model for security requirements engineering. IEEE Acces. **6**, 28611–28631 (2018)
28. Paulk, M.C., Curtis, B., Chrissis, M.B., Weber, C.: Capability maturity model, version 1.1. IEEE Softw.**10**(4), 18–27 (1993)
29. ISO.ISO/IEC 15504-4: Information Technology—Process Assessment—Part 4: Guidance on Use for Process Improvement and Process Capability Determination. International Organization for Standardization (2004)
30. Committee, I.T.: ISO 9000: 2005 quality management systems–fundamentals and vocabulary. Technical report, International Organization for Standardization **55**, 89 (2005)
31. Daskalantonakis,, M.K.: Achieving higher SEI levels. IEEE Softw. **11**(4), 17–24, (1994)

1st Workshop on Computational Intelligence and Software Engineering (CISE 2022)

1st Workshop on Computational Intelligence and Software Engineering (CISE 2022)

Pasquale Ardimento[1] , Akhtar Jami[2] , and Michele Scalera[1]

[1] Department of Informatics, University of Bari Aldo Moro, Via Orabona 4,
Bari, Italy
{pasquale.ardimento,michele.scalera}@uniba.it
[2] Department of Computer Science, National University of Computer and
Emerging Sciences, Pakistan
akhtar.jamil@nu.edu.pk

Abstract. In the last decades, despite the introduction of innovative approaches and paradigms useful in the SE (Software Engineering) field, their technological transfer on a larger scale has been very gradual and still almost limited. This is due to the critical aspects in SE with respect to other well-founded engineering disciplines since SE is strongly influenced by social aspects (i.e., human knowledge, skills, expertise, and interactions) that are highly context-driven, non-mechanical and strongly based on context and semantic knowledge. The rise of artificial intelligence (AI) has the potential to define effective approaches for improving software quality allowing a growth in the project success rates. AI can provide the capabilities to assist software teams in many aspects, from automating routine tasks to providing project analytics and actionable recommendations, and even making decisions where non-trivial context detection and information processing are needed. Recent works reported that several software engineering problems could effectively tackled using a combination of AI techniques such as NLP, machine learning, fuzzy logic, multi-objective search, metaheuristics, and clustering algorithms.

1 Introduction

The overall goal of this interdisciplinary workshop is to raise the level of engagement and discussion about SE and AI communities to identify opportunities to improve the quality of scientific results and improvements on software product development. A further goal of the workshop is to identify opportunities to improve the quality of scientific discourse and progress on human aspects within software processes, as well as to identify opportunities able to assist researchers about how to make decisions where non-trivial context detection and information processing in the context of software engineering. To achieve these goals, it is important to bring together researchers and practitioners who face the problem of integrating AI methods in software processes and have tried effective methods to resolve it.

1.1 Target Audience

The objective of this workshop is to foster the integration between SE and AI communities to improve research results, teaching and mentoring, and ultimately industrial practice.

2   Workshop Papers

Below is the list of accepted papers.

2.1   Paper 1: Technical Debt Forecasting from Source Code Using Temporal Convolutional Networks

This paper was written by Lerina Aversano (University of Sannio, Department of Engineering), Mario Luca Bernardi (University of Sannio, Department of Engineering), Marta Cimitile (Unitelma Sapienza University Rome) and Martina Iammarino (University of Sannio, Department of Engineering).

ABSTRACT: Technical Debt describes a deficit in terms of functions, architecture, or integration, which must subsequently be filled to allow a homogeneous functioning of the product itself or its dependencies. It is predominantly caused by pursuing rapid development versus a correct development procedure. Technical Debt is therefore the result of a nonoptimal software development process, which if not managed promptly can compromise the quality of the software. This study presents a technical debt trend forecasting approach based on the use of a temporal convolutional network and a broad set of product and process metrics, collected commit by commit. The model was tested on the entire evolutionary history of two open-source Java software systems available on Github: Commons-codec and Commons-net. The results are excellent and demonstrate the effectiveness of the model, which could be a pioneer in developing a TD reimbursement strategy recommendation tool that can predict when a software product might become too difficult to maintain.

2.2   Paper 2: Adagio: a bot for AuDio processing AGainst vIOlence

This paper was written by Vito Nicola Convertini, Giuseppe Pirlo, Ugo Lopez, Antonella Serra, and Rosa Conte (all from University of Bari Aldo Moro).

ABSTRACT: Within social networks, audio is a vehicle for violent, bullying or generally unwanted content. This research intends to propose an automatic tool for extracting text from an audio stream. Microsoft azure cognitive cloud services, and in particular, Speech SDK and bot SDK are used for extraction and recognition tasks. The extracted text can then be analyzed using techniques and algorithm known for analyzing critical situations such as violence or bullying but is applicable in any context.

2.3   Paper 3: End Users' Perspective of Performance Issues in Google Play Store

This paper was written by Anam Noor (Mohammad Ali Jinnah University), Muhammad Daniyal Mehmood (Mohammad Ali Jinnah University), and Teerath Das (University of Jyvňäskylä).

ABSTRACT: The success of mobile applications is closely tied to their performance which shapes the user experience and satisfaction. Most users often delete mobile apps from their devices due to poor performance indicating a mobile app's failure in the competitive market. This paper performs a quantitative and qualitative analysis and investigates performance-related issues in Google Play Store reviews. This study has been conducted on 368,704 reviews emphasizing more 1- and 2-star reviews distributed over 55 Android apps. Our research also reports a taxonomy of 8 distinct performance issues obtained using manual inspection. Our findings show that end-users recurrently raised Updation (69.11%), Responsiveness (25.11%), and Network (3.28%) issues among others. These results can be used as preliminary steps towards understanding the key performance concerns from the perspective of end users. Furthermore, our long-term objective will be to investigate whether developers resolve these performance issues in their apps.

2.4   Paper 4: Predicting Bug-Fixing Time: DistilBERT Versus Google BERT

This paper war written by Pasquale Ardimento (University of Bari Aldo Moro).

ABSTRACT: The problem of bug-fixing time can be treated as a supervised text categorization task in Natural Language Processing. In recent years, following the use of deep learning also in the field of Natural Language Processing, pre-trained contextualized representations of words have become widespread. One of the most used pre-trained language representations models is named Google BERT (hereinafter, for brevity, BERT). BERT uses a self-attention mechanism that allows learning the bidirectional context representation of a word in a sentence, which constitutes one of the main advantages over the previously proposed solutions. However, due to the large size of BERT, it is difficult for it to put it into production. To address this issue, a smaller, faster, cheaper, and lighter version of BERT, named DistilBERT, has been introduced at the end of 2019. This paper compares the efficacy of BERT and DistilBERT, combined with the Logistic Regression, in predicting bug-fixing time from bug reports of a large-scale open-source software project, LiveCode. In the experimentation carried out, DistilBERT retains almost 100% of its language understanding capabilities and, in the best case, it is 63.28% faster than BERT. Moreover, with a not time-consuming tuning of the C parameter in Logistic Regression, the DistilBERT provides an accuracy value even better than BERT.

2.5   Paper 5: Proposing Isomorphic Microservices Based Architecture for Heterogeneous IoT Environments

This paper was written by Pyry Kotilainen, Teemu Autto, Teerath Das, Viljami Järvinen and Juho Tarkkanen (all from University of Jyväskylä).

ABSTRACT: Recent advancements in IoT and web technologies have highlighted the significance of isomorphic software architecture development, which enables easier deployment of microservices in IoT-based systems. The key advantage of such systems is that the runtime or dynamic code migration between the components across the whole system becomes more flexible, increasing compatibility and improving resource allocation in networks. Despite the apparent advantages of such an approach, there are multiple issues and challenges to overcome before a truly valid solution can be built. In this idea paper, we propose an architecture for isomorphic microservice deployment on heterogeneous hardware assets, inspired by previous ideas introduced as liquid software. The architecture consists of an orchestration server and a package manager, and various devices leveraging WebAssembly outside the browser to achieve a uniform computing environment. Our proposed architecture aligns with the long-term vision that, in the future, software deployment on heterogeneous devices can be simplified using WebAssembly.

3   Workshop Organization

- Pasquale Ardimento, organizing chair (University of Bari Aldo Moro, Italy)
- Akhtar Jamil, organizing chair (National University of Computer and Emerging Sciences, Pakistan)
- Michele Scalera, organizing chair (University of Bari Aldo Moro, Italy)

Technical Debt Forecasting from Source Code Using Temporal Convolutional Networks

Aversano Lerina[1] , Mario Luca Bernardi[1] , Marta Cimitile[2] ,
and Martina Iammarino[1](✉)

[1] Engineering Department, University of Sannio, Benevento, Italy
{aversano,bernardi,iammarino}@unisannio.it
[2] Unitelma Sapienza University, Rome, Italy
marta.cimitile@unitelmasapienza.it

Abstract. Technical Debt describes a deficit in terms of functions, architecture, or integration, which must subsequently be filled to allow a homogeneous functioning of the product itself or its dependencies. It is predominantly caused by pursuing rapid development versus a correct development procedure. Technical Debt is therefore the result of a non-optimal software development process, which if not managed promptly can compromise the quality of the software. This study presents a technical debt trend forecasting approach based on the use of a temporal convolutional network and a broad set of product and process metrics, collected commit by commit. The model was tested on the entire evolutionary history of two open-source Java software systems available on Github: Commons-codec and Commons-net. The results are excellent and demonstrate the effectiveness of the model, which could be a pioneer in developing a TD reimbursement strategy recommendation tool that can predict when a software product might become too difficult to maintain.

Keywords: Technical debt · SonarQube · Software quality metrics · Process metrics · Feature selection · Temporal convolutional network

1 Introduction

The term "Technical Debt" (TD) was first coined by programmer Ward Cunningham in a 1992 article stating that while an organization may be able to save money in the short term by writing imperfect code, over time, interest from TD will build up, just like with monetary debt, making the initial problem increasingly expensive to solve [13].

With his metaphor, Ward describes debt as the natural result of writing code on something that you don't have an adequate understanding of. He doesn't talk about poor code which - according to him - represents a very small part of the debt. Instead, it speaks of the disagreement between the needs of the business

© The Author(s), under exclusive license to Springer Nature Switzerland AG 2022
D. Taibi et al. (Eds.): PROFES 2022, LNCS 13709, pp. 581–591, 2022.
https://doi.org/10.1007/978-3-031-21388-5_43

and how the software was written. Consequently, in terms of quality, TD may be viewed as a collection of design decisions that, as they build up over time, make the system challenging to maintain and develop. It stands for something that has a detrimental impact on a system's internal and non-functional properties, particularly its maintainability and evolvability [19].

There are effective tools, such as CAST[1], and SonarQube[2], which are mostly used due to their features and functionality, to measure and track TD in source code [4]. But these tools are no longer sufficient because they only allow you to identify the debt once it has been introduced, and sometimes it may be too late to remedy it.

More research is needed because to date few studies have focused on predicting TD [5,6,21-23]. Therefore, this study aims to test a model based on a temporal convolution neural network on two open-source software systems to forecast the progress of the TD according to the variation of the product and process metrics considered. Given a certain instant t in the history of a software system, the model is capable of verifying whether the TD at instant $t+1$ will remain stable or will undergo an increase or decrease in its value, even before the developer makes the change, and then commit.

This document is structured as follows. Related works are listed in the following section. Section 3 describes the approach in each phase, while the experimental results are in Sect. 4. Finally, Sect. 5 presents the conclusions and future work.

2   Related Work

Numerous research has been undertaken and published in the literature on the methodology that might support developers and project managers in estimating and measuring TD [3,8,9,15,18]. The authors of the study [11] made a comparison based on the functionality and popularity of all existing tools capable of identifying TD. Authors in [19] meticulously mapped out the TD and its management. This study has shown that more empirical research with solid supporting data is needed to fully understand the management process as a whole. Therefore, the opinion has become widespread that in addition to monitoring the TD it has become of fundamental importance to predict its progress to adopt preventive strategies that avoid compromising the quality of a software system.

Numerous research has looked at the relationship between the TD's presence and the quality of the source code, establishing the quality measures of the TD indications. [14,20,25]. In [10] the main goal was to predict changes in qualitative properties, such as CK metrics or other traits closely associated with TD. The results show that when the measure of technical debt worsens, so do the software quality metrics.

Few studies have focused on TD forecasts. Tsoukalas et al. conducted three different studies on the subject, in the first [22] they presented an empirical

---

[1] https://www.castsoftware.com.

[2] https://www.sonarqube.org.

analysis on TD prediction using time series and creating a repository containing 750 commits at weekly intervals, which belong to five software systems. This model was found to be able to predict only 8 weeks into the future. In the second study, [23] they used multivariate methods of Machine Learning, expanding the dataset to 15 systems, but always considering commits at intervals. The results show that linear regularization models perform better over short periods while Random Forest regression as a predictor works better over extended periods. Finally, the most recent study [24] investigated whether clustering may be thought of as a method to increase the accuracy of TD prediction. They gathered information from several software products and organized it into clusters based on similarities. The results are encouraging and allow for the assignment of known clusters to unknown software systems to anticipate TDs.

Therefore, we propose a method for predicting the variation of TD in the code of software systems, using finely collected data relating to a big set of metrics.

3   Approach

The model's function is to forecast the TD's trend in the code. In particular, given a specific Java class to a specific commit, the model can forecast whether the TD would remain stable, rise or decrease in the following commit based on the metrics gathered. This section describes the approach proposed, presenting the data extraction and collection process, the set of features considered, the predictive model with the parameters set, and finally the metrics used to validate the performance of the predictive model.

3.1   Data Collection and Extraction

Figure 1 shows the four main steps used to extract and collect the data used to conduct the study. The first step has been to extract the history of changes to the software system from Github. In particular, the source code, revision data, and logs were extracted. Those information have been used in the second phase of the process, in which the source code for each commit has been analyzed to detect the measures showing the TD's existence and its value; revision data made it possible to collect the metrics of the quality indicators of the source code and the extraction of the logs has been used to collect data necessary for obtaining the process metrics. Respectively, the tools that have been used are Sonarqube, CK tool[3], and some python scripts. The third step consisted of the integration of all the extracted information, to allow the creation of a dataset for each software system, in a single CSV file in which there is the history in terms of changes (commits) made for each java class considered, with the metrics of the attachments considered. The next step involved the creation of a set of ethical traces, in a normalization and data windowing phase, where each line of the trace represents an instance of the system that has been assigned a label

---

[3] https://github.com/mauricioaniche/ck.git.

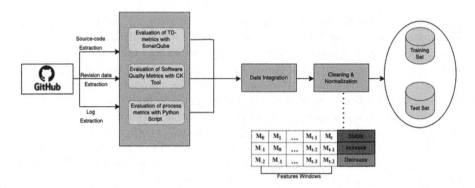

Fig. 1. Process of extraction and collection of data

indicating the value of the TD. In particular, to prepare the data and better represent their temporal evolution, we used the sliding window methodology, setting 5 or 10 as the window size.

Finally, Table 1, shows the characteristics of the software systems considered, Commons-codec[4] and Commons-net[5].

Table 1. Characteristics of the software systems considered

System Name	Numbr of classes	Number of commit	Commit time-interval
Commons-Codec	2266	340	25 April 2003 | 6 September 2022
Commons-Net	2612	819	3 April 2002 | 6 September 2022

3.2 Features Model

A very large set of metrics has been used to train the predictive model, which can be divided into two main groups, product metrics, and process metrics.

In the first group, there are the metrics resulting from the analysis of the source code, which can be considered indicators of the TD, such as bugs and code smells. These identify the presence of the TD because they compromise the understanding and maintainability of the code and indicate the need for refactoring [2,7,16]. In addition to these, indicators closely related to the quality of the code were also considered for the product metrics, such as the metrics defined by Chidamber and Kemerer [12] that evaluate the cohesion, complexity, coupling, and size of the code, and other quantitative metrics related to methods, fields and other constructs present in the source code.

To the second group belong four metrics that refer to the quality with which the developers have worked, such as the cost and effort of the activities, taking into account their experience.

---

[4] https://github.com/apache/commons-codec.
[5] https://github.com/apache/commons-net.

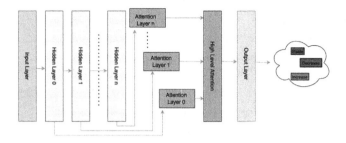

Fig. 2. Predictive model architecture

Table 2 describes in detail the set of features considered. More specifically, the first column indicates whether the metrics refer to product metrics - more specifically related to TD or software quality -, or process metrics. In the second column, there is the name followed by a short description of the metric.

3.3 Predictive Model

For the prediction, we have chosen a Temporal Convolutional Network (TCN), built to have very long historical dimensions [1]. With its broad receptive fields and temporality, it is a version of convolutional neural networks that use convolutions and random dilations to adapt to sequential data.

More specifically, in Fig. 2 we report the proposed architecture, which is composed of an input level, n hidden layers, an attention level, a batch normalization level, and the final output level. Respectively, the first is composed of as many nodes as there are attributes received at the input, while the hidden levels are used to interpret the relationships between the data by returning the weighted sum of the inputs after the calculation of the activation function. With the levels of attention, we introduce in the model the hierarchical mechanism of attention [26] to model relationships, regardless of the distance, while reducing the impact of unstable gradients with the level of normalization, we can achieve more precision during both the testing and validation phases. Finally, the final level is made up of three neurons, like the three classes, which represent the three values that the progress of the TD can assume in the code (stable, increase, decrease).

The model has been created in Python, using the Keras[6] and Tensorflow[7] APIs.

3.4 Experimental Setting

To prevent wasting time and resources and to avoid over-adaptation, we have imposed a limit of 50 epochs for the trials and introduced an early stop for

---

[6] https://keras.io.
[7] https://www.tensorflow.org.

Table 2. Feature set considered

Kind	Name	Description
Product Metrics TD Related	Bugs	Quantity of Bugs
	Code Smell	Quantity of code smells
	Classes	Quantity of classes: nested interfaces, classes, annotations and enumerations.
	Vulnerabilities	Quantity of vulnerabilities.
	Functions	Methods that are actually present in the classes, omitting any that are found in nameless
	Ncloc	Quantity of lines of code.
	Comment lines	Quantity of lines with comments and commented code inside.
	Comment lines density	Comment line density = Comment lines / (Code lines + Comment lines) * 100 With such a formula, values equal to: a) 50% mean that the number of lines of code equals the number of comment lines b) 100% indicates that the file contains only comment lines
	Complexity	The number of linearly distinct paths through the source code serves as a measure of the cyclomatic complexity of a particular portion of code. The complexity will be 1 if the source code lacks any decision points, such as IF or FOR loops. There will be two possible paths if the code contains a single IF with a single condition.
	Cognitive complexity	Evaluation of how difficult it is to comprehend control flow
	Sqale rating	The score assigned to the technical debt ratio. It is divided into several intervals: A = 0–0.05, B = 0.06–0.1, C = 0.11–0.20, D = 0.21–0.5, E = 0.51–1.
	Sqale debt ratio	Remediation cost / Development cost, which can be expressed as: Remediation cost / (Cost for developing 1 line of code * Total of lines of code). Ratio of the cost of developing the software to the cost of repairing it.
Product Metrics Software Quality Related	Weight Method Count per Class	Weighed sum of a class's methods, where each method's weight is determined by a custom complexity factor.
	Lack of Cohesion of Methods	The ability of a method to only access class characteristics is expressed by the cohesiveness of the method. The fact that there are numerous methods to access similar features is what causes the lack of cohesiveness.
	Coupling Between Objects	Number of a class's collaborations, or the number of other classes it is associated with
	Response for a class	A measurement of the "volume" of communication between classes. High values result in an increase in the class's design complexity and testing effort.
	Depth of Inheritance Tree	Maximum separation between a node (a class) and the tree's root, which represents the hereditary structure. The number of methods a class can inherit increases with the depth of the hierarchy.
	Number of static invocation	How often do static methods make invocations
	Number of methods	Quantity of methods
	Number of fields	Quantity of fields
	Number of unique words	Total of words that are unique
	Non-Commented, non-empty Lines of Code	Quantity of code lines, excluding blank lines.
	Parenthesized expressions	Quantity of expressions in parentheses.
	Math Operations	Quantity of mathematical operations
	Anonymous classes, subclasses and lambda expressions	Quantity of anonymous declarations of classes or subclasses
	String literals	Quantity of string literals. Repetition counts the number of times that a string appears.
	Usage of each variable	Determine how much of each variable is used in each method.
	Usage of each field	Determine how much of each field is used in each method
	Comparison	Quantity of comparisons
	Try/catches	Quantity of try and catches
	Variables	Total of variables
	Modifiers	Total of public / private / abstract / protected / native modifiers of classes / methods.
	Returns	Number of returns instructions.
	Numbers	Total of numbers
	Loops	Total of loops (for, while, do while, generalized for)
	Max nested blocks	The highest number of blocks nested together.
Process Metrics	Seniority of Developers	Calculate the difference between the commit date and the dates of the commit that preceded it in the repository to get the developer seniority for a specific commit in terms of days.
	Ownership of the commit	The group of developers who together made at least 50% of the most important single changes to a particular file.
	Number of Files Owners	The collection's cardinality for a certain file and commit.
	Owned File Ratio	calculates the ratio of modifications made by developer d_j on file f_j to all changes ($cdot$) made by other users from the beginning of the observation period on the same file in the commit interval $[c_s, \ldots, c_k]$

the target measure. In this approach, training can be terminated if no improvement occurs, and the model can then be put away for testing. Additionally, the experiments' environment involved optimizing the network architecture's hyperparameters. The parameters shown in Table 3 have all been put together in every possible combination, but only the best combination will be reported in the Results Section.

To validate the performance of the model we used the F1 score, which represents the accuracy and the weighted and harmonic average of the recall.

Finally, in addition to testing the model on the complete set of metrics collected, we also tested the predictive model after making the selection of features, to compare the results. In particular, we applied a hierarchical cluster analysis, based on the Spearman coefficient, to evaluate the redundancy and collinearity measures between the [17] features. Thanks to this method, metrics with high redundancy and collinearity values were grouped into a single cluster and by choosing 0.50 as the pruning threshold we reduced the number of features considered.

In detail, we have eliminated the threshold crossing features common to the two systems: Nloc, Complexity, Functions, Code Smell, RFC, WMC, LOC, ComparisonQty, MaxNestedBlocks, TotalMethods, PublicMethods, StaticFiels, FinalFields, AssignmentsQty, VariablesQty, NumbersQty and Owner of the commit. In this way, the model that follows the selection of characteristics considers 42 characteristics instead of the initial 58.

Table 3. Hyperparameter optimization

Parameter	Description	Range
Network Size	Indicates how many learning parameters the network contains.	Small-Medium
Activaction Function	Describes the transformation of the input to the output using a weighted sum	RELU
Learning Rate	The learning rate is a hyperparameter that determines how much to alter the model each time the model weights are updated in response to the predicted error	$3 \div 6$
Number of layers	Number of levels considered	$6 \div 8$
Batch size	The number of samples that are processed before the model is changed	128–256
Dropout Rate	Indicates the rate of randomly selected neurons that are ignored during training	0.15–0.20
Optimization Algorithms	It is used to reduce losses by altering neural network characteristics like as weight and learning speed	SGD
Timestamp	Window size	5–10

4   Experimental Results

Table 4 reports the results of the best permutations of the proposed predictive approach. The first column contains the name of the analyzed system, the second indicates whether the feature selection has been made or not. The third to eighth columns show the parameters for which the optimization has been done, while the last two columns show the value of the F1-Score metric in percentage, used to validate the model, and the training times in seconds for the epoch.

As can be seen, for both systems the parameters with which the network obtained the best result are the same, both on the original dataset and on the one on which the selection of characteristics was made.

More specifically, for Commons-codec the results are very good, in fact, in both cases, the model has got an F-Score of 99%, 99.47% on the dataset with 58 features, and 99.50% on the reduced one. The result that it is necessary to underline is the training time which in the case of the feature selection is reduced by 60%, going from 253 s to 80 s. This shows the efficiency of the model and the chosen metrics.

In the case of Commons-net, an F1-score of 97% is reached, 97.63% in the case without feature selection, and 96.91% on the reduced dataset. Therefore, with this system, there has not been an improvement in performance in terms of the F1 score, but here too there is a significant reduction in the training time necessary for the model to learn the data. A decrease of 40% is noted, passing from 355 s to 210 s per epoch.

For the Commons-codec system, in Fig. 3 we also report the trend of the accuracy and the loss during the training and validation of the model for the best permutation carried out on the dataset with feature selection. The graphs show the epochs on the abscissa axis and the values on the ordinate axis. In particular, the first graph compares the accuracy during the training in pink, with the accuracy during the validation phase in green. While the second compares the loss during the training in pink, with the loss during the validation vase in green. The graphs show that the accuracy and the loss during training improve considerably between the first and third epochs, and then settle down. Instead, the values during the validation phase are good already from the first epoch and remain stable for the entire duration of the permutation.

Table 4. Best permutation results

Project	Feature Selection	Network Size	Learning Rate	Batch Size	Number of Layers	Dropout Rate	Timestamp	F1-Score	Training Time
Commons-codec	NO	Small	3	128	6	0.15	10	99.47 %	252,80 s
Commons-codec	YES	Small	3	128	6	0.15	10	99.50 %	79.62 s
Commons-net	NO	Small	3	128	6	0.15	10	97.63 %	355.01 s
Commons-net	YES	Small	3	128	6	0.15	10	96.91 %	210.97 s

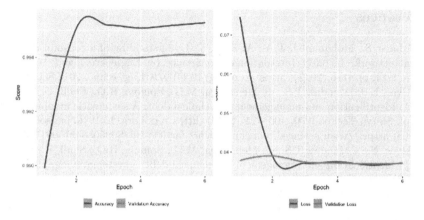

Fig. 3. Precision and loss plots of the best Commons-Codec permutation with feature selection

5   Conlusions and Future Works

Technical Debt refers to the idea that organizations will have to pay later for a fundamentally flawed, little-known, or "quick and sporadic" solution to a software development problem. Technical debt is generated for various reasons related to processing, people, and technical factors, reducing the quality and maintainability of the code. This is why it has aroused great interest, making it a hot topic in the literature. A lot of research has focused on its identification, management, or resolution, but as far as we know, there have been relatively few contributions to its prediction. In this regard, this study aims to investigate the extent to which the use of deep learning models represents an accurate approach for predicting TD in open-source software projects. Specifically, we present a Temporal Convolutional Network-based model that can forecast the progress of the TD in each class of a software system, commit by commit, given the TD information, the software quality, and the process metrics. The model has been tested on two Java software systems, Commons-codec and Commons-net, for each of which a dataset has been created which contains all its evolutionary history in terms of class, commit by commit, with all the metrics collected. To date, no study has focused on the prediction of the TD commit by commit. The experiment has been originally run on a metric model with 58 different features and, after a feature selection process, they were reduced to 42, resulting in exceptional prediction model performance and much shorter lead times. The results are good because both in the first and in the second case, for Commons-codec we have got an F-Score of 99%. For Commons-net the approach has reached 97%. The model has so far proved very effective in anticipating the growth of TD in source code and aims to pave the way for the development of a tool for creating recommendation systems and decision-making mechanisms to improve TD reimbursement strategy and predict when a software product may become too difficult to maintain.

References

1. Albawi, S., Mohammed, T.A., Al-Zawi, S.: Understanding of a convolutional neural network. In: 2017 International Conference on Engineering and Technology (ICET), pp. 1–6 (2017). https://doi.org/10.1109/ICEngTechnol.2017.8308186
2. Alves, N.S., Mendes, T.S., de Mendonça, M.G., Spínola, R.O., Shull, F., Seaman, C.: Identification and management of technical debt: A systematic mapping study. Inf. Softw. Technol. **70**, 100–121 (2016). https://doi.org/10.1016/j.infsof.2015.10.008, https://www.sciencedirect.com/science/article/pii/S0950584915001743
3. Alves, N.S., Mendes, T.S., de Mendonça, M.G., Spínola, R.O., Shull, F., Seaman, C.: Identification and management of technical debt: a systematic mapping study. Inf. Softw. Technol. **70**, 100–121 (2016)
4. Amanatidis, T., Mittas, N., Moschou, A., Chatzigeorgiou, A., Ampatzoglou, A., Angelis, L.: Evaluating the agreement among technical debt measurement tools: building an empirical benchmark of technical debt liabilities. Empir. Softw. Eng. **25**(5), 4161–4204 (2020). https://doi.org/10.1007/s10664-020-09869-w
5. Ardimento, P., Aversano, L., Bernardi, M.L., Cimitile, M., Iammarino, M.: Using deep temporal convolutional networks to just-in-time forecast technical debt principal. J. Syst. Softw. **194**, 111481 (2022). https://doi.org/10.1016/j.jss.2022.111481, https://www.sciencedirect.com/science/article/pii/S0164121222001649
6. Aversano, L., Bernardi, M.L., Cimitile, M., Iammarino, M.: Technical debt predictive model through temporal convolutional network. In: 2021 International Joint Conference on Neural Networks (IJCNN), pp. 1–8 (2021). https://doi.org/10.1109/IJCNN52387.2021.9534423
7. Aversano, L., Bernardi, M.L., Cimitile, M., Iammarino, M., Romanyuk, K.: Investigating on the relationships between design smells removals and refactorings. In: 15th International Conference on Software Technologiesp, pp. 212–219 (2020)
8. Aversano, L., Bruno, M., Di Penta, M., Falanga, A., Scognamiglio, R.: Visualizing the evolution of web services using formal concept analysis. In: Eighth International Workshop on Principles of Software Evolution (IWPSE'05), pp. 57–60 (2005). https://doi.org/10.1109/IWPSE.2005.33
9. Aversano, L., Cerulo, L., Palumbo, C.: Mining candidate web services from legacy code. In:10th International Symposium on Web Site Evolution, 2008. WSE 2008, pp. 37–40 (2008). https://doi.org/10.1109/WSE.2008.4655393
10. Aversano, L., Iammarino, M., Carapella, M., Vecchio, A.D., Nardi, L.: On the relationship between self-admitted technical debt removals and technical debt measures. Algorithms **13**(7) (2020)). https://www.mdpi.com/1999-4893/13/7/168
11. Avgeriou, P.C., et al.: An overview and comparison of technical debt measurement tools. IEEE Softw. **38**(3), 61–71 (2021). https://doi.org/10.1109/MS.2020.3024958
12. Chidamber, S.R., Kemerer, C.F.: A metrics suite for object oriented design. IEEE Trans. Softw. Eng. **20**(6), 476–493 (1994). https://doi.org/10.1109/32.295895
13. Cunningham, W.: The WyCash portfolio management system. In: Addendum to the Proceedings on Object-oriented Programming Systems, Languages, and Applications. ACM (1992)
14. de Freitas Farias, M.A., de Mendonça Neto, M.G., d. Silva, A.B., Spínola, R.O.: A contextualized vocabulary model for identifying technical debt on code comments. In: 2015 IEEE 7th International Workshop on Managing Technical Debt (MTD), pp. 25–32 (2015). https://doi.org/10.1109/MTD.2015.7332621

15. Iammarino, M., Zampetti, F., Aversano, L., Di Penta, M.: An empirical study on the co-occurrence between refactoring actions and self-admitted technical debt removal. J. Syst. Softw. **178**, 110976 (2021). https://doi.org/10.1016/j.jss.2021.110976, https://www.sciencedirect.com/science/article/pii/S016412122100073X

16. Iammarino, M., Zampetti, F., Aversano, L., Di Penta, M.: An empirical study on the co-occurrence between refactoring actions and self-admitted technical debt removal. J. Syst. Softw. **178** (2021). https://doi.org/10.1016/j.jss.2021.110976

17. Köhn, H.F., Hubert, L.J.: Hierarchical Cluster Analysis, pp. 1–13 Wiley StatsRef: Statistics Reference Online (2014)

18. Letouzey, J.: The sqale method for evaluating technical debt. In: 2012 Third International Workshop on Managing Technical Debt (MTD), pp. 31–36 (2012). https://doi.org/10.1109/MTD.2012.6225997

19. Li, Z., Avgeriou, P., Liang, P.: A systematic mapping study on technical debt and its management. J. Syst. Softw. **101**, 193–220 (2015). https://doi.org/10.1016/j.jss.2014.12.027, https://www.sciencedirect.com/science/article/pii/S0164121214002854

20. Li, Z., Liang, P., Avgeriou, P., Guelfi, N., Ampatzoglou, A.: An empirical investigation of modularity metrics for indicating architectural technical debt. In: Proceedings of the 10th International ACM Sigsoft Conference on Quality of Software Architectures, pp. 119–128. Association for Computing Machinery, New York, NY, USA (2014). https://doi.org/10.1145/2602576.2602581, https://doi.org/10.1145/2602576.2602581

21. Skourletopoulos, G., Mavromoustakis, C.X., Bahsoon, R., Mastorakis, G., Pallis, E.: Predicting and quantifying the technical debt in cloud software engineering. In: 2014 IEEE 19th International Workshop on Computer Aided Modeling and Design of Communication Links and Networks (CAMAD), pp. 36–40 (2014). https://doi.org/10.1109/CAMAD.2014.7033201

22. Tsoukalas, D., Jankovic, M., Siavvas, M., Kehagias, D., Chatzigeorgiou, A., Tzovaras, D.: On the applicability of time series models for technical debt forecasting. In: 15th China-Europe International Symposium on Software Engineering Education (2019)

23. Tsoukalas, D., Kehagias, D., Siavvas, M., Chatzigeorgiou, A.: Technical debt forecasting: an empirical study on open-source repositories. J. Syst. Softw. **170**, 110777 (2020). https://doi.org/10.1016/j.jss.2020.110777, https://www.sciencedirect.com/science/article/pii/S0164121220301904

24. Tsoukalas, D., Mathioudaki, M., Siavvas, M., Kehagias, D., Chatzigeorgiou, A.: A clustering approach towards cross-project technical debt forecasting. SN Comput. Sci. **2**(1), 1–30 (2021). https://doi.org/10.1007/s42979-020-00408-4

25. Wehaibi, S., Shihab, E., Guerrouj, L.: Examining the impact of self-admitted technical debt on software quality. In: 2016 IEEE 23rd International Conference on Software Analysis, Evolution, and Reengineering (SANER), vol. 1, pp. 179–188 (2016). https://doi.org/10.1109/SANER.2016.72

26. Yang, Z., Yang, D., Dyer, C., He, X., Smola, A., Hovy, E.: Hierarchical attention networks for document classification. In: Proceedings of the 2016 Conference of the North American Chapter of the Association for Computational Linguistics: Human Language Technologies, pp. 1480–1489. Association for Computational Linguistics, San Diego, California (Jun 2016). https://doi.org/10.18653/v1/N16-1174, https://www.aclweb.org/anthology/N16-1174

Adagio: A Bot for Audio Processing Against Violence

Rosa Conte, Vito Nicola Convertini$^{(\boxtimes)}$ [ID], Ugo Lopez [ID], Antonella Serra [ID], and Giuseppe Pirlo [ID]

Università degli Studi di Bari Aldo Moro, Bari, Italy
{vitonicola.convertini,ugo.lopez,antonella.serra,
giuseppe.pirlo}@uniba.it

Abstract. Within social networks, audio is a vehicle for violent, bullying or generally unwanted content. This research intends to propose an automatic tool for extracting text from an audio stream. Microsoft azure cognitive cloud services, and in particular, Speech SDK and bot SDK are used for extraction and recognition tasks. The extracted text can then be analyzed using techniques and algorithm known for analyzing critical situations such as violence or bullying but is applicable in any context.

Keywords: Adagio · Audio extraction · Speech recognition · Microsoft Azure · Speech SDK · Bot SDK

1 Introduction

The rapid increase in the use of Internet technology by all kinds of social groups has created the need to protect individuals from harmful content. Due to the huge number of audio and video files present, there is a need to introduce automatic tools to detect inappropriate content. Furthermore, many films are not violent in the video part, but are violent in the audio part [1]. This makes it essential to improve efficient violence detectors with automatic violence detectors based on digital content. However, the solutions presented in the related works require sophisticated code-side implementations reducing the ability to use sophisticated audio analysis tools to non-professionals.

In this work we present Adagio, a cloud-based speech recognition and content extraction solution that can be easily implemented and customized for each context of use. In particular, the solution is based on the Microsoft Azure services Speech SDK and Bot SDK. Speech SDK exposes many of the Speech service capabilities, to develop speech-enabled applications. The Speech service provides speech-to-text and text-to-speech capabilities with an Azure Speech resource. Microsoft Bot Framework and Azu-re Bot Service are a collection of libraries, tools, and services to build, test, deploy, and manage intelligent bots. The Bot Framework includes a modular and extensible SDK for building bots and connecting to AI services. With these frameworks, Adagio can extract and recognize text containing inappropriate content such as violence or bullying [1].

© The Author(s), under exclusive license to Springer Nature Switzerland AG 2022
D. Taibi et al. (Eds.): PROFES 2022, LNCS 13709, pp. 592–602, 2022.
https://doi.org/10.1007/978-3-031-21388-5_44

2 Related Works

C. Clavel [2] proposed an audio analysis system based on the Gaussian mixture model (GMM) to detect events of interest in non-silent locations. Events such as shouting, gunshots and explosions were considered for the detection of anomalous situations.

In this approach many experimentations are carried out to reduce false rejection (FR) and False Detection (FD) rate. Giannakopoulos T. [3] introduced the vector-based audio feature (SVM) for the classification of violence content using audio extracted from real films and not audio samples. Giannakopoulos T. [4] extended his work by using a multiclass classification algorithm. Each audio segment was classified into six classes, three for violence and three for non-violence. D.Impedovo et al. [5, 6] used feedback-based multi-classifier systems to reduce the misclassified entities. Esra Acar [7] proposed a violent scene detection (VSD) system using two different methods, namely the vector quantization-based (VQ-based) method and the sparse coding-based (sparse coding-based) method. Zaheer et al. [8] used Deep Boltzmann Machines (DBM) for scream detection in different contexts. By using its self-recorded scream dataset 100% accuracy is achieved by the proposed system.

The work is structured as follows. Section 2 describes the related work on audio recognition and classification. Section 3 describes the speaker recognition functionalities used in Adagio using Microsoft Speech SDK. Section 4 describes the NLU used. Section 5 illustrates the use of the Microsoft Bot Framework SDK for the creation and composition of Adagio with the technologies illustrated above.

3 Speaker Recognition in Adagio

The functionality of speaker recognition, in our proposal, is provided through two APIs [9].

Speech Software Development Kit (SDK) [10] is a tool that exposes various features of the Voice service to enable the development of speech recognition-enabled applications. Speech SDK can be found in several programming languages and on all platforms. To configure and subsequently used Speech SDK with Microsoft Visual C++ for Visual Studio 2019 and Visual Studio 2019. Once the tools are installed, we proceeded to install the NuGet Speech SDK package to use it in our code.

.NET Speech SDK can be installed from the command line interface. For microphone input, the Media Foundation collections that are part of Windows 10 and Windows Server 2016 need to be installed. Speech synthesis or speech recognition transcribes audio streams into text that applications, tools, or devices can use or display. Voice translation can be used to translate speech input into a different language with a single call. Speech recognition can be used on a variety of platforms. Specifically, C++ /Windows & MacOS Linux# (Framework &.NET Core)/Windows & UWP & Unity & Xamarin & Linux & macOS, Java (Jre e Android), JavaScript (Browser e NodeJS), Python, Swift, Objective-C, Go (only SR). The input text is a literal value of type string or an SSML language (Speech Synthesis Markup Language) [11].

Voice assistants using Speech SDK enable the creation of natural, human-like conversational interfaces for collected applications and experiences. Speech SDK provides fast and reliable interaction that includes speech synthesis and conversational data [12] in a single connection. The implementation can use Bot Framework [13] of the Direct Line Speech or custom command service for task completion. In addition, voice assistants can use custom voices created in the dedicated portal to add a unique voice output experience. Voice assistant support can be used on all platforms.

Keyword speech recognition is supported within the Speech SDK algorithm and can identify a keyword while speaking followed by an action such as "Hey Siri" or "Alexa."

In addition, the algorithm is ideal for transcribing meetings from both a single device and multiple devices simultaneously. The Speech Recognition Service offers advanced functionality with predefined templates for speech synthesis. The Recognition Service offers a wide range of code-free customization tools that simplify and enable you to create a competitive advantage with customized templates based on your own data that are available only to you or your organization.

Once the "NuGet Speech SDK" package is installed, we begin by creating our first project to use the Speech SDK algorithm.

If we needed to use a specific input device, we would enter and specify the device id using the code: audioConfig = AudioConfig.FromMicrophoneInput ("<device id>");

The capabilities of the Speech SDK algorithm are many. If we want to perform voice recognition directly from an audio file, we can still configure the "AudioConfig" object, but instead of calling the "FromDefaultMicrophoneInput()" function, we will have the "FromWavFileInput()" function and the file path will be passed.

3.1   Continuous Recognition and Dictation Mode

In the previous examples we saw that it is possible to have vocal recognition only at the beginning when we have a single expression. The end of the expression is determined by staying listening to the silence at the end or until a maximum of 15 s of audio is processed. But if we wanted to have a device that continuously recognizes the sound then have continuous recognition, it is needed to have "Recognizing", "Recognized" and "Canceled" events. To stop recognition "StopContinuosRecognitionAsync" must be called [14, 15]. Next, it is necessary to create a property to manage the state of speech recognition [15]. Finally, it is necessary to create the SpeechRecognizer events. Specifically:

- Recognizing: Signal for events containing intermediate recognition results.
- Recognized: Signal for events that contain the results of the final recognition and signal that the recognition was successful.
- SessionStopped: Signal for events indicating the end of a recognition session (operation).
- Canceled: Signal for events containing recognition results cancelled due to a direct cancellation request or transport or protocol error.

Once the configuration is finished, the "StartContinuousRecognitionAsync" function must be called to start the recognition [16]. With the continuous recognition described in the previous paragraph, it is possible to enable dictation processing using the corresponding function. With this mode the instance of "SpeechConfig" interprets textual descriptions of sentence structures such as punctuation. To enable this method, it is necessary to enable: "speechConfig.EnableDictation()".

3.2   Improve Recognition Accuracy and Customized Voice Recognition

Phrase lists [17] are used to identify known phrases within audios such as a person's name, an unwelcome word, or a specific location. If we provide the algorithm with a list of phrases or words, the accuracy of speech recognition can be improved. Anything from a single word or an entire sentence can be added to the list of phrases. Note: The "Phrase List" feature should be used with no more than a few hundred phrases. If we have a larger list of phrases, it is necessary to use a custom template, which we will see in the following paragraphs.

To use the phrase list, it is necessary to create the object 'PhraseListGrammar' and add phrases with 'Add Phase'. All changes made to 'PhraseList-Grammar' become effective at the next speech recognition [15, 18]. If we want to clear the list of phrases and then configure others, we use the function: phraseList.Clear().

3.3   Customized Voice Recognition

When testing the accuracy of Microsoft speech recognition or testing custom patterns, audio data and text data are needed.

The text and audio used to test and train a personalized model must include examples of the heterogeneous set of speakers and scenarios that you want to recognize from the model. Several factors should be kept in mind when collecting data:

- Text and voice audio data must cover the types of verbal statements that users will generate during interaction with the model. For example, a model that increases and decreases temperature requires training on the instructions that users might make to request such changes.
- The data must include all the vocal variances that the model needs to recognize. Many factors can vary the voice, including accents, dialects, language combination, age, gender, vocal tone, stress level, and time of day.

You must include examples of different environments (indoor, outdoor, street noise) in which the model will be used. It is necessary to collect audio using the hardware devices that will be used by the production system. If the model is to identify the voice recorded in the recording devices of varying quality, the audio data provided to perform model training must also represent these different scenarios.

More data can be added to the model later, but it is necessary to keep the dataset heterogeneous and representative of the project needs.

Inclusion of data not included in the recognition requirements of the custom model may harm the quality of recognition overall. Include only the data that the model needs to transcribe.

Files used for training must be grouped by type into a dataset and uploaded as a.zip file, and each dataset must contain only one type of data.

Training with Audio Data

If a data model does not support training with audio data, the voice service will only use the text of the transcripts and ignore the audio. If you change the base model used for training and have audio in the training dataset, you should always check if the newly selected base model supports training with audio data.

Data Uploading

Speech Studio must be used to upload the data.

1. After creating a project, go to the Item Data Sets tab and select Upload Data to start the wizard and create the first data set.
2. Specify whether the dataset will be used for training or testing. Each caricalted dataset must be properly formatted before loading and must meet the requirements per chosen data type.
3. After loading the data set you can:
4. Switch to the "Train custom models" tab to perform training of a custom model.
5. Switch to the "Test models" tab to visually examine quality with audio-only data or evaluate the accuracy with audio and human-labeled transcription data.

The REST API Voice Recognition v3.0 can automate any-any operations related to custom templates. We have used the REST API to load a dataset. This is especially useful when the dataset file exceeds 128 MB, because you cannot upload large files using the Local File option in Speech Studio. We used Azure's BLOB or shared path option in Speech Studio for the same purpose, as described in the previous section. To create and load a dataset, we used a Create Dataset request.

A dataset created using the REST API Speech Recognition v3.0 will not be connected to any Speech Studio project unless you specify a special parameter in the body of the request (see code block later in this section). Connection to a Speech Studio project is not required for model customization operations if they are performed using the REST API. When Speech Studio is accessed, the user interface will send a notification when an unconnected object is found, such as datasets loaded via the REST API without reference to the project. The interface will also offer a connection of such objects to an existing project. To connect the new dataset to an existing project in Speech Studio during loading, use Create Dataset and fill in the body of the request according to the format [15].

Plain Text Data for Training

To improve the accuracy of recognition of specific names or jargon, it is possible to use domain-related phrases and specify phrases in a single file and use text data that are increasingly close to the expected spoken expressions. To create a custom model, we need to provide a list of example expressions. They need not be complete or grammatically correct, a must-no reflect the expected spoken input in the production environment.

Table 1. Text properties for training.

Property	Value
Text encoding	UTF-8 BOM
Number of utterances per line	1
Maximum file size	200 MB

To see whether the data fil o use the list of sentences, it is necessary to create the object is formatted correctly, we need to observe the properties in Table 1.

It is also necessary to specify restrictions:

Avoid repeating characters, words, or groups of words more than three times, as in "aaaa," "yes yes yes," or "that's all there is to it." The Voice service may delete lines with too much repetition. URIs will be rejected.

Structured Text Data for Training

Expressions follow a certain criterion. A common criterion is that expressions differ only by words or phrases in a list.

To simplify the creation of training data and enable custom modeling, structured text in Markdown format can be used to define lists of items. These lists can then be referenced within training expressions. The Markdown format also supports the specification of phonetic pronunciation of words.

The Markdown file must have an md extension. The syntax of Markdown is the same as that of Language Understanding templates, especially list entities and example expressions; an example of the Markdown format [19].

Just as with regular text, training with structured text typically takes several minutes. In addition, sample sentences and lists should reflect the type of spoken input expected in the production environment. Even for the Markdown file there are limits and properties that one must respect.

Data Audio for Test

Audio data are better for testing the accuracy of Microsoft's basic speech recognition model or custom model. Audio data is used to check the accuracy of speech against the performance of the model.

The default audio streaming format is WAV but through GStreamer other formats such as: MP3, OPUS/OGG, FLAC, ALAW nel contenitore WAV, MULAW in WAV container.

4 Definition of the Purpose of Expression (Natural Language Understanding) in Adagio

Natural language Understanding (NLU) is the focus of a conversational bot. It is a machine learning tool whose main purpose is to convert an input from users who speak natural language, into objects in which the bot can understand and react.

NLU engines are unable to understand what the user says on their own, but developers must provide a set of training examples. After the training, the NLU engine gets the ability to identify the words and phrases that the user may say and perform the mapping to a user's intention in the form of purpose, which represents a task or action that the user wants to perform and entities. The file with the lu extension allows the user to create understanding models that define them for the bot developed using Bot framework SDK and Composer. A .lu file contains simple text-based definitions in a Markdown-like format. Purpose represents an activity or action that the user wants to perform, as seen in a user's expressions. Purposes are added to the bot to enable it to identify groups of questions or commands that represent the same intention as the user.

Some examples of hints, taken from Microsoft Ignite documentation [17] are presented in Table 2:

Table 2. Purpose examples.

Intent	Example utterances
BookFlight	"Book me a flight to Maui next week" "Fly me to Maui in the 17^{Th}" "I need a plane ticket next Friday to Maui"
Greeting	"Hi" "Hello" "Good afternoon"
CheckWeather	"What's the weather link in Maui next week?"
None	"I like cookies" "Bullfrogs have been recorded jumping over 7 feet"

When the None (none) purpose is used, it is a mandatory purpose that must be created with expressions outside the domain. Purposes with example expressions are declared.

In which #<intent-name> describes a new purpose definition section and purpose definition are example expressions describing purposes with <utterance>.

An entity definition defines how to recognize a range in an expression as an entity that you can then use in the bot. There are several types of entities, including: machine-learned, precompiled, lists, regular expressions, and templates. Entity definitions in files with the lu extension start the entry with the at () symbol followed by the entity type @ and the entity name. Each entity can also have roles that identify different uses of the same entity. It is also possible to add features that enable a better entity recognition process. The general syntax is specified in the entity definition file [15].

4.1 Machine Learning-Based Entity

Machine learning entities provide examples in which to label example expressions. This type of entity is ideal when identifying data that is not properly formatted but has the same meaning. When a user says something like "I need a flight booked from London to Madrid," LUIS will detect the purpose "bookFlight" and extract both London and Paris as city entities. Roles are essentially an additional layer of contextual information that can be added to machine-learning entities, which also learn from context. The following example expression shows the start and destination roles associated with the city entity [15]. Machine-learned entities can also be complex in which they have a hierarchy of related entities. For example, you can have an entity-like element with the following pizzaOrder child entities: quantity, size, crust, toppings, and so on.

Machine Learning works by taking features and learning how they are related to purposes and entities. Features are the words that make up expressions. Phrase lists allow multiple words to be grouped into a new feature. In this way, machine learning generalizes better from fewer examples. Phrase lists come are global and apply to all models and can also be associated with specific purposes and entities.

Another feature is the addition of metadata. This will allow the parser to properly handle the content of the Language Understanding, and they are added to the beginning of the lu file property [15]. Specifically, the metadata are presented in Table 3:

Table 3. Purpose examples.

Metadata	Description
Name	Application name
Versionid	Specific version name
Culture	Application language
Version schema	LUIS schema is updated for every additional feature and setting. Use the schema version number set when the LUIS model has been created or updated

5 Bot Framework SDK

The bot, accompanied by the Azure Bot service, provides the tools to compile, test, deploy, and manage intelligent bots. The Bot Framework SDK includes a modular and extensible SDK for creating bots and tools for artificial intelligence (Fig. 1). Bots are like robots but can be used for simple tasks such as making dinner reservations or collecting information. Users can converse with a bot using text and speech, and a sophisticated conversation can be established. The bot can be thought of as an application with a conversational interface such as Facebook, Microsoft teams. The bot underlies the input and performs relevant tasks. This can include accessing services on behalf of the user. The bot performs user input recognition to interpret what the user asks or says. It can

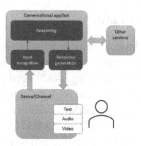

Fig. 1. Bot overview

generate responses by saying what it has done and depending on the configuration users can interact.

Bots are very similar to modern Web applications, which connect to the Internet and use APIs to send and receive messages. The content of a bot varies greatly depending on the type of bot. Modern bot software relies on a range of technologies and tools to provide increasingly complex experiences across a wide range of platforms. However, a simple bot can simply receive a message and send it back to the user with the need for very little code.

Bots can perform the same operations as other types of software: reading and writing files, using databases and APIs, and performing normal computational tasks. The peculiarity of bots lies in their use of mechanisms generally reserved for communication between humans.

Bots can be integrated with other Azure services such as the cognitive services described in the previous paragraphs.

As mentioned earlier, the bot can be linked to all social networks and can be linked to different channels.

To create the bot, you need to assign a virtual machine and use the following software components:

- ASP.NET Core Runtime 3.1
- Bot Framework Emulator
- Knowledge of ASP.NET Core and asynchronous programming in C#
- Visual Studio 2019 or later versions
- Bot Framework models SDK v4 for Visual Studio

In visual studio we have created a new bot project using the Echo Bot template.

Thanks to the template, the newly created project contains within it all the necessary code. To start the bot, it is necessary to open the project without debugging. The application will be compiled and deployed to localhost and the browser will be started to display the "default.htm" page of the application.

6   Conclusions

In this preliminary work, we presented the Adagio. It uses two frameworks hat combined can offer interesting perspective in the extraction and detection of texts from audio.

Through Speech SDK it is possible to start speech recognition and set up a set of phrases and expressions ready to be recognized. If known derogatory words or expressions are set within the training file, it is possible, through the bot synchronized with the social networks of interest, to intercept these expressions. The Bot Framework includes a modular and extensible SDK for building bots and connecting to AI services. The potential of the combination of Speech SDK and Bot SDK finds both law enforcement agencies and forensic experts as natural users. The next step will be to test the performance of the bot on known datasets such as VSD [18], UCF-Crime [19], XD-Violence [20] and then test it in real-life usage contexts connected to social networks of interest.

References

1. Bautista-Durán, M., García-Gómez, J., Gil-Pita, R., Mohíno-Herranz, I., Rosa-Zurera, M.: Energy-efficient acoustic violence detector for smart cities. Int. J. Comput. Intelli. Syst. **10**(1), 1298–1305 (2017). https://doi.org/10.2991/IJCIS.10.1.89
2. Clavel, C., Ehrette, T., Richard, G.: Events detection for an audio-based surveillance system. In: IEEE International Conference on Multimedia and Expo, ICME 2005, vol. 2005, pp. 1306–1309 (2005). https://doi.org/10.1109/ICME.2005.1521669
3. Giannakopoulos, T., Kosmopoulos, D., Aristidou, A., Theodoridis, S.: Violence content classification using audio features. In: Antoniou, G., Potamias, G., Spyropoulos, C., Plexousakis, D. (eds.) SETN 2006. LNCS (LNAI), vol. 3955, pp. 502–507. Springer, Heidelberg (2006). https://doi.org/10.1007/11752912_55
4. Giannakopoulos, T., Pikrakis, A., Theodoridis, S.: A multi-class audio classification method with respect to violent content in movies using Bayesian Networks. In: 2007 IEEE 9Th International Workshop on Multimedia Signal Processing, MMSP 2007 - Proceedings, pp. 90–93 (2007). https://doi.org/10.1109/MMSP.2007.4412825
5. Pirlo, G., Trullo, C.A., Impedovo, D.: A feedback-based multi-classifier system. In: Proceedings of the International Conference on Document Analysis and Recognition, ICDAR, pp. 713–717 (2009). https://doi.org/10.1109/ICDAR.2009.75
6. Impedovo, D., Pirlo, G.: Updating knowledge in feedback-based multi-classifier systems. In: Proceedings of the International Conference on Document Analysis and Recognition, ICDAR, pp. 227–231 (2011). https://doi.org/10.1109/ICDAR.2011.54
7. Acar, E., Hopfgartner, F., Albayrak, S.: Detecting violent content in Hollywood movies by mid-level audio representations. In: Proceedings - International Workshop on Content-Based Multimedia Indexing, pp. 73–78 (2013). https://doi.org/10.1109/CBMI.2013.6576556
8. Zaheer, M.Z., Kim, J.Y., Kim, H.G., Na, S.Y.: A preliminary study on deep-learning based screaming sound detection. In: 2015 5th International Conference on IT Convergence and Security, ICITCS 2015 - Proceedings, October 2015. https://doi.org/10.1109/ICITCS.2015.7292925
9. Microsoft.com: QuickStart: Recognize and verify who is speaking. February 2022 [Online]. https://learn.microsoft.com/en-us/azure/cognitive-services/speech-service/get-started-speaker-recognition?tabs=script&pivots=programming-language-csharp. Accessed 26 Sep 2022.
10. Microsoft.com: What is the Speech SDK? September 24 2022. https://learn.microsoft.com/en-us/azure/cognitive-services/speech-service/speech-sdk?tabs=windows%2Cubuntu%2Cios-xcode%2Cmac-xcode%2Candroid-studio. Accessed 26 Sep 2022
11. Microsoft.com: Improve synthesis with Speech Synthesis Markup Language (SSML). Sep. 20, 2022. https://learn.microsoft.com/en-us/azure/cognitive-services/speech-service/speech-synthesis-markup?tabs=csharp. Accessed 26 Sep 2022)

12. Scalera, M., Serra, A.: Customer centric strategies for value creation: academic experimentation. J. e-Learn. Knowl. Soc. **10**(2), 65–76 (2014). https://doi.org/10.20368/1971-8829/922

13. Microsoft.com.What is the Bot Framework SDK?. Sep. 2022 [Online]. https://docs.microsoft.com/en-us/azure/bot-service/bot-service-overview-introduction?view=azure-bot-service-4.0. Accessed 26 Sep 2022

14. GitHub - vnconvertini/audioprocessingbot. https://github.com/vnconvertini/audioprocessingbot. Accessed 29 Sep 2022

15. Microsoft.com.Improve recognition accuracy with phrase list. Feb. 2022 [Online]. https://learn.microsoft.com/en-us/azure/cognitive-services/speech-service/improve-accuracy-phrase-list?tabs=terminal&pivots=programming-language-csharp. Accessed 26 Sep 2022

16. lu file format - Bot Service | Microsoft Learn. https://learn.microsoft.com/en-us/azure/bot-service/file-format/bot-builder-lu-file-format?view=azure-bot-service-4.0. Accessed 30 Sep 2022

17. Demarty, C.-H., Penet, C., Soleymani, M., Gravier, G.: VSD, a public dataset for the detection of violent scenes in movies: design, annotation, analysis and evaluation. Multim. Tools Appl. **74**(17), 7379–7404 (2014). https://doi.org/10.1007/s11042-014-1984-4

18. Sultani, W., Chen, C., Shah, M.: Real-world Anomaly Detection in Surveillance Videos. January 2018 [Online]. http://arxiv.org/abs/1801.04264

19. Wu, P., et al.: Not only look, but also listen: learning multimodal violence detection under weak supervision. July 2020 [Online]. http://arxiv.org/abs/2007.04687

End Users' Perspective of Performance Issues in Google Play Store Reviews

Anam Noor[1]🆔, Muhammad Daniyal Mehmood[1]🆔, and Teerath Das[2(✉)]🆔

[1] Department of Computer Science, Mohammad Ali Jinnah University,
Karachi, Pakistan
{fa19mscs0018,sp21msse0009}@maju.edu.pk
[2] Faculty of Infromation Technology, University of Jyväskylä, Jyväskylä, Finland
teerath.t.das@jyu.fi

Abstract. The success of mobile applications is closely tied to their performance which shapes the user experience and satisfaction. Most users often delete mobile apps from their devices due to poor performance indicating a mobile app's failure in the competitive market. This paper performs a quantitative and qualitative analysis and investigates performance-related issues in Google Play Store reviews. This study has been conducted on 368,704 reviews emphasizing more 1- and 2-star reviews distributed over 55 Android apps. Our research also reports a taxonomy of 8 distinct performance issues obtained using manual inspection. Our findings show that end-users recurrently raised *Updation* (69.11%), *Responsiveness* (25.11%), and *Network* (3.28%) issues among others. These results can be used as preliminary steps towards understanding the key performance concerns from the perspective of end users. Furthermore, Our long-term objective will be to investigate whether developers resolve these performance issues in their apps.

Keywords: Android mobile apps · Google play reviews · Performance related issues

1 Introduction

Technological breakthroughs have largely influenced modern society, particularly in the field of mobile apps. It is expected that the App Economy will rise to a new peak from \$693 Billion in 2021 to \$935.2 Billion in 2023[1]. The performance aspect of the apps is a significant indicator of their successful growth. Developers implement new resource-intensive features in the apps to meet the end users' requirements showcasing efficient performance. Thus, performance is a crucial parameter for determining the success or failure of any mobile app, as the user experience highly depends on it: the more flawless performance, the better the user-acceptance ratio.

---

[1] https://www.statista.com/statistics/269025/worldwide-mobile-app-revenue-forecast/.

© The Author(s), under exclusive license to Springer Nature Switzerland AG 2022
D. Taibi et al. (Eds.): PROFES 2022, LNCS 13709, pp. 603–609, 2022.
https://doi.org/10.1007/978-3-031-21388-5_45

To date, performance issues have been analyzed in various systems like web applications [1], heterogeneous environments [3], and large scale applications [6]. Further, Liu et al. [4] have explored 70 performance smells in mobile apps and classified them into three broad categories. To the best of our knowledge, one of the studies [2] closely resembles our study. However, the significant difference between the two is that the former [4] analyzed the performance issues in GitHub commits, and the latter explored the reviews of android apps available on the Google Play Store. Our approach is different and novel because we are analyzing performance related issues from end users perspective i.e., exploiting Google reviews of Android apps. Our results shows how the performance reviews vary across different android app categories. Furthermore, we produced a taxonomy of performance issues after manual inspection of 1 and 2-star reviews.

The main **contributions** of this paper are:

- Analysis of performance issues in Google Play Store reviews of 55 Android apps.
- A taxonomy of most common types of performance issue in Android apps.

2   Study Design

The *goal* of this study is to analyze the performance in rich Google reviews, with the *purpose* to comprehend their connectivity with the end-users and attributes of the projects. The *context* of our study is 55 android apps from Google Play Store and examined their 1 and 2- star reviews from the *point of view* of the end users. This research aims to address the following research questions:

RQ1: *To what extent do end users perceive the performance-related issues in Android app reviews?*

RQ2: *What are the performance issues that end users raise in Android apps reviews?*

RQ1 focuses on estimating the prevalence in which the end users consider performance issues in android apps, whereas *RQ2* dedicates to classifying Google reviews with respect to the performance issues as raised by the end users. The design of our study mainly comprises a set of mobile apps distributed across the Google Play Store. The purpose of selecting Google Play Store as our target area of the population lies in its increasingly huge popularity among all the other marketplaces for apps. Figure 1 represents the step-by-step process adopted to get our targeted apps; (i) firstly, we selected the most popular apps from the first quarter of 2021 using different sources[2] (S), which resulted in identifying 55 android apps, (ii) then, we extracted all the reviews of selected apps using a Python script and collected a total of 355,687,535 reviews, (iii) after that, we filtered 368,707 reviews based on their 1 and 2-star reviews. The reason for selecting these reviews is that the end users express their dissatisfaction by giving 1- and 2-star reviews. We inscribed a dedicated script to extract 1- and

---

[2] https://github.com/anam-noor/Replication-package-.

2-star Google reviews from the selected apps. Thus, the final population for this research is 368,707, which is spread over 55 different apps.

The designed variables for addressing RQ1 include (i) *pReviews*: the performance-related reviews out of the total number of reviews (*tReviews*) of android apps, and (ii) android apps categories in the Google play store. For RQ2, the reviews are categorized into different categories addressing performance issues. We identified a review as a performance-related review (*pReviews*) if it contains one of the following keywords: *update, wait, slow, lag, response, time, speed, graphic, perform, hang, memory, leak, connect, image*, not. These keywords were considered by looking, evaluating, and combining mining methodologies from past empirical studies [2,5,7,8] on software performance (both mobile and not mobile-specific). The script ensures all the possible combinations of the upper and lower case keywords.

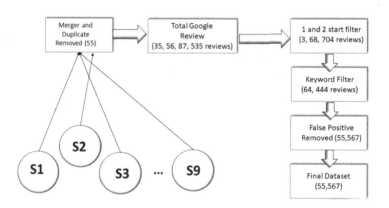

Fig. 1. Google reviews extraction

The matching of the keywords resulted in detecting a set of 64,444 performance-related reviews of 1- and 2-star ratings. After a manual analysis, 8,877 reviews are discarded for being categorized as False Positive. The whole process finally produced a total of 55,567 performance-related reviews.

Furthermore, we investigated the categories of performance concerns by manually labeling the 55,567 reviews. We used manual labeling to categorize performance-related reviews into relevant groups in two phases: the first phase is dedicated to tagging each review with its relevant keywords (e.g., graphics from GUI, slow, and hang). Subsequently, in the second phase, we labeled those tags into more significant groups with an explanatory title (e.g., Memory management issues, Networking issues). The second phase of labeling resulted in 8 different types of categories. The manual inspection of both the phases are conducted by two masters students separately and then supervisor cross check the labels.

3 Results

In this section, we will discuss the results by addressing all research questions of our study, as mentioned in the previous section.

RQ1: *To what extent do end users perceive the performance-related issues in Android app reviews?*

To answer this research question, we primarily compute the ratio of identified number of performance-related reviews (*pReviews*) to the total number of reviews (*tReviews*) present in our dataset. It is interesting to note that all 55 apps in our dataset have at least one performance-related review. A total of 55,567 (15%) performance issues have been identified out of 368,704 reviews.

Table 1 reports the apps categories, the frequency of each app category, total number of reviews (*tReviews*), and performance related reviews (*pReviews*) identified. Performance issues vary across different natures of the applications. For example, the *Entertainment* app category holds the highest percentage of performance-related reviews (22.23%) as shown in Table 1. This is understandable because such apps have a captivating user experience, and users tend to spend more time on these apps due to online sessions. The *Game* app category holds the second highest performance reviews (17.23%) followed by *Shopping* (15.53%) category. The *Game* category mainly relies on the user experience of long sessions, whereas the shopping category is a utility that included in task-based apps with short usage sessions. This shows that performance issues are orthogonal across each category and distributed without the application context.

Table 1. Distribution of performance related issues over various app categories.

App category	App frequency	tReviews	pReviews
Entertainment	4	28,558	6350 (22.23%)
Games	11	116,691	20161 (17.27%)
Shopping	9	80219	12294 (15.3%)
Education	6	31054	4310 (13.87%)
Tools	8	34391	3459 (10.3%)
Lifestyle	6	1918	190 (9.90%)
Books and references	1	684	56 (8.18%)
Food and drink	3	14635	886 (6.05%)
Music and audio	8	60538	2653 (4.35%)

RQ2: *What are the performance issues that end users raise in Android apps reviews?*

To answer this research question, we manually analyzed the 55,567 reviews, which resulted in 8 different performance categories. Table 2 depicts eight categories extracted from the manual inspection along with an example of representative review (the representative review is randomly selected from our observed dataset) and *pReviews* (in terms of frequency percentage) of performance-related reviews for each category. In the following, we will consider each of the listed categories of performance issues obtained from manual analysis.

As mentioned in Table 2, the most frequent concern of end-users while using android apps is the *updation* (69.11%), e.g., "In terms of chat during the games, lags due to update." From the manual inspection of reviews, we derive that the end user's perspective of app performance is of paramount importance for app developers. Some examples of *updation* issues after manual inspection are *"Crashing of apps after update," "App stops working after update"* and *"Features unavailability"*. Therefore, Performance enhancements constitute a significant part of app updates.

The second most common performance-related complaint expressed by end users' is *Responsiveness* (25.6%), which is determined by evaluating Speed, Lag, and Delay keywords. *"Slow apps", "Waiting a long time for an app to load," "App lagging, app stuck," and "App hang"* are all examples of Responsiveness issues. The *Network* (3.28%) related performance issues are also commonly documented by end-users in their reviews, e.g., "The apps seems useless if it does not connect to the server", "Disconnecting from the server" and "Network sharing, and several connection issues". Despite being reported in lesser frequency, *Memory Management* issue ((0.36%)) is still one of the most critical as it can paralyze the app by halting key processes. Examples of such issues are *"Using three times of memory than other apps"* and *"Immediately ate up over 17MB of memory without ever loading"*.

Loading Time of any app plays an important role in the overall app performance for the end user. Loading time makes up for 0.14% of *pReviews*. Some examples are "It takes ages to start the screen" and "Never ending loading time". Moreover, about 0.85% of the *pReviews* are *generic* and do not point to a specific issue category. In these reviews, users do not describe any specific category; instead, they talk in general without explaining the reason. Some examples are *"Improve the app"* and *"Good game but with performance issues"*.

4   Threats to Validity

The use of keyword matching to detect performance-related reviews poses a threat to *construct Validity*. In our study, we assume that a review containing specified keywords should be considered a performance-related review. This approach may omit a few performance-related reviews because we may miss a few keywords. In order to mitigate this threat, we consider all the keywords in the previous studies [2,5,7,8]. False positives have been reduced by manual inspection of extracted reviews.

External Validity threats primarily affect the generalization of our findings, which are related to the representation of different app categories studied in this study. We were able to mitigate this risk by using a relatively large data set (i.e., 368,704 reviews consisting of 55 apps) and picking apps belonging to diverse app categories and built as part of real-world apps (i.e., all apps are released on the Google Play store and are publicly available).

Table 2. Identified categories of performance-related reviews

Performance category	Representative review	pReviews
Updation	*This is horrible, the update ruined everything, when you are done finding what you want to say the meeting is over*	38,404 (69.11%)
Responsiveness	*Hangs at startup logo. Unusable*	14,247 (25.6%)
Network	*Slow server... Always lost connection when almost win*	1,826 (3.28%)
Generic concern	*As game is growing it is becoming very dull performance*	475 (0.85%)
GUI	*Outdated user interface, not quite intuitive and audio*	319 (0.57%)
Memory management	*Don't you guys have any good devs? Your app is full of memory leaks!*	205 (0.36%)
Loading time	*I either receive an error message or it's stuck on a loading screen*	82 (0.14%)
Image	*Image loading is awful on the app. its really frustrating to have to wait over 20 s for images to load*	6 (0.010%)

5   Related Work

Various studies have been done which analyze performance issues in android apps for example Das et al. [2] takes similar approach, but in the context of performance related commits of the android apps having versioning history hosted on GitHub repositories whereas our study focuses on performance issues as per end user reviews. Another study by Liu et.al [4] investigates performance bugs and categorizes them into categories. They identify 70 performance related bugs and characterize these bugs into 3 categories. In our study we not only consider more performance issue categories in our taxonomy but also relate app categories to these issues forming a pattern. Malavolta et al. [5] conducts a similar study but into hybrid mobile apps, by mining free apps and reviews from the Google Play Store.

6   Conclusion and Future Work

This paper reports the results of a study by analyzing performance related reviews in Android apps. We investigated a total of 55,567 Google Play Store reviews which were rated 1 and 2-stars out of 368,704 distributed over 55 apps. We proposed a taxonomy for such reviews using manual inspection and identified a total of 8 performance related issue categories. The main findings of our study show performance issues are mostly found in the app due to *Updation*. In addition to that, we also observed numerous reviews for the *responsiveness* of apps and *Network* related issues. This study will help developers understand different performance bottlenecks in their apps from end users perspective.

Future work aims to exploit these labelled performance issue categories of this study to automatically classify using different machine learning algorithms. It is also interesting to analyze the performance-related reviews using natural language processing techniques. Future work also aims to analyze other aspects of non-functional issues in the google reviews.

References

1. Tarek, M.: Studying the effectiveness of application performance management (APM) tools for detecting performance regressions for web applications: an experience report. In Miryung Kim, Romain Robbes, and Christian Bird, editors. In: Proceedings of the 13th International Conference on Mining Software Repositories, MSR 2016, Austin, TX, USA, May 14–22, 2016, pp. 1–12. ACM (2016)
2. Das, T., Di Penta, M., Malavolta, I.: a quantitative and qualitative investigation of performance-related commits in android apps. In: 2016 IEEE International Conference on Software Maintenance and Evolution, ICSME 2016, Raleigh, NC, USA, October 2–7, 2016, pp. 443–447. IEEE Computer Society (2016)
3. Foo, K.C., Jiang, Z.M., Adams, B., Hassan, A. E., Zou, Y., Flora, P.: An industrial case study on the automated detection of performance regressions in heterogeneous environments. In: Bertolino, A., Canfora, G., Elbaum, S.G., eds. In: 37th IEEE/ACM International Conference on Software Engineering, ICSE 2015, Florence, Italy, May 16–24, 2015, Vol. 2, pp. 159–168. IEEE Computer Society (2015)
4. Liu, Y., Xu, C., Cheung, S.C.: Characterizing and detecting performance bugs for smartphone applications. In Pankaj Jalote, Lionel C. Briand, and André van der Hoek, editors, In: 36th International Conference on Software Engineering, ICSE '14, Hyderabad, India - May 31 - June 07, 2014, pp. 1013–1024. ACM (2014)
5. Malavolta, I., Ruberto, S., Soru, T., Terragni, V.: End users' perception of hybrid mobile apps in the google play store. In Onur Altintas and Jia Zhang, editors, In: 2015 IEEE International Conference on Mobile Services, MS 2015, New York City, NY, USA, June 27 - July 2, 2015, pp. 25–32. IEEE Computer Society (2015)
6. Malik, H., Hemmati, H., Hassan, A. E.: Automatic detection of performance deviations in the load testing of large scale systems. In: Notkin, D., Cheng, B.H.C., Pohl, K., eds. In: 35th International Conference on Software Engineering, ICSE '13, San Francisco, CA, USA, May 18–26, 2013, pp. 1012–1021. IEEE Computer Society (2013)
7. Selakovic, M., Pradel, M.: Performance issues and optimizations in javascript: an empirical study. In: Dillon, L.K., Visser, W., Williams, L.A., eds. In: Proceedings of the 38th International Conference on Software Engineering, ICSE 2016, Austin, TX, USA, May 14–22, 2016, pp. 61–72. ACM (2016)
8. Zaman, S., Adams, B., Hassan, A. E.: A qualitative study on performance bugs. In: Lanza, M., Di Penta, M., Xie, T., eds. In: 9th IEEE Working Conference of Mining Software Repositories, MSR 2012, June 2–3, 2012, Zurich, Switzerland, pp. 199–208. IEEE Computer Society (2012)

Predicting Bug-Fixing Time: DistilBERT Versus Google BERT

Pasquale Ardimento[(✉)] [ID]

University of Bari Aldo Moro, Department of Informatics, Via Orabona 4, Bari, Italy
`pasquale.ardimento@uniba.it`

Abstract. The problem of bug-fixing time can be treated as a supervised text categorization task in Natural Language Processing. In recent years, following the use of deep learning also in the field of Natural Language Processing, pre-trained contextualized representations of words have become widespread. One of the most used pre-trained language representations models is named Google BERT (hereinafter, for brevity, BERT). BERT uses a self-attention mechanism that allows learning the bidirectional context representation of a word in a sentence, which constitutes one of the main advantages over the previously proposed solutions. However, due to the large size of BERT, it is difficult for it to put it into production. To address this issue, a smaller, faster, cheaper and lighter version of BERT, named DistilBERT, has been introduced at the end of 2019. This paper compares the efficacy of BERT and DistilBERT, combined with the Logistic Regression, in predicting bug-fixing time from bug reports of a large-scale open-source software project, LiveCode. In the experimentation carried out, DistilBERT retains almost 100% of its language understanding capabilities and, in the best case, it is 63.28% faster than BERT. Moreover, with a not time-consuming tuning of the C parameter in Logistic Regression, the DistilBERT provides an accuracy value even better than BERT.

Keywords: Google BERT · DistilBERT · Bug-fixing · Deep learning · Software maintenance process · Defect tracking systems

1 Introduction

Software bugs can originate from all stages of the software life cycle. Bug fixing has become an important activity during the software development and maintenance process. A bug report contains a large amount of text information that can help software developers and maintainers understand bugs well and complete bug fixing. Many open-source software projects use bug tracking systems (BTS) to store and manage bug reports, such as Bugzilla. A large number of new bug reports are submitted to BTS every day which contain a wealth of bug knowledge. In recent years, lots of work utilized information retrieval technology to explore these massive bug repositories to help developers understand,

© The Author(s), under exclusive license to Springer Nature Switzerland AG 2022
D. Taibi et al. (Eds.): PROFES 2022, LNCS 13709, pp. 610–620, 2022.
https://doi.org/10.1007/978-3-031-21388-5_46

localize and fix bugs [3,11,13]. However, bug reports are submitted by different users, with free grammar and different structures, including a large number of phrases and short text. The very fast development knowledge in bug repositories shows the characteristics of heterogeneity, diversity and fragmentation. Traditional information retrieval technology is based primarily on statistical methods that treat bug reports as a collection of words, which breaks the context and does not fully explore the semantic knowledge in bug reports. Accurately extracting and expressing rich semantics and knowledge in bug reports is important for various bug analysis activities, such as diagnosis, fixing, testing, and documentation of bugs. For example, when developers encounter software bugs, they usually search various software sources, such as bug libraries, software control versions, etc., to obtain reference solutions. The search results are usually large, and most of them are irrelevant. By understanding the semantic information of the bug report, it will be helpful to recommend a related bug report that is closer and reasonable to the bug content retrieved by the developer, and further study the code repair link of the report to obtain repair suggestions.

Several predictive models have been proposed to automatically predict the time to fix a bug. These approaches share the idea of using all textual information of bug reports and adopt context-free word representations (e.g., the bag-of-words representation model). Recently, two waves arose paving new ways in the field of bug-fixing time. Firstly, the revolution of deep learning used in the field of Natural Language Processing (NLP), thanks to which it is possible having "(1) distributed representations of linguistic entities via embedding, (2) semantic generalization due to the embedding, (3) long-span deep sequence modeling of natural language, (4) hierarchical networks effective for representing linguistic levels from low to high, and (5) end-to-end deep learning methods to jointly solve many NLP tasks" [9]. Secondly, the extraction of semantic features from the textual messages through topic modeling, such as Latent Dirichlet allocation [5], Non-negative matrix factorization [10] and its recent applications [8], and several other techniques initially applied in different domains.

This work focuses on the use of deep learning in the field of NLP. Recently, following the use of deep learning in the field of Natural Language Processing (NLP), pre-trained contextualized representations of words have become widespread. However, current techniques restrict the power of the pre-trained representations, especially for the fine-tuning approaches. The major limitation is that standard language models are unidirectional, but language understanding is bidirectional. The unidirectionality limits the choice of usable architectures during pre-training. Such restrictions are "sub-optimal for sentence-level tasks, and could be very harmful when applying fine-tuning based approaches to token-level tasks such as question answering, where it is crucial to incorporate context from both directions." [14]. BERT, which stands for Bidirectional Encoder Representations from Transformers, is a language representation model whose key novelty consists in applying the bidirectional training of Transformer, an attention-based mechanism that can accurately extract contextual relationships in words to realize unsupervised learning by combining text input and output through the decoder-encoder framework. BERT reads the text from both directions at once (bidirectional) having a deeper sense of language context and flow than single-direction language models. In recent work, the BERT model has been demonstrated to be effective in bug-fixing time prediction problem [4].

However, BERT suffers from fixed input length size limitations, wordpiece embedding problems, and computational complexity [1]. For this reason, in this work it is also used DistillBERT, "a general-purpose pre-trained version of BERT, 40% smaller, 60% faster, that retains 97% of the language under-standing capabilities" [14]. To confirm or reject this statement for the problem of bug-fixing time prediction, performances of the BERT and DistilBERT mod-els on LiveCode, a large-scale open-source project, have been compared. The results obtained show that DistilBERT is better than BERT since it achieves the same accuracy values being greatly faster than BERT. The paper is orga-nized as follows. Section 2 provides the necessary background of BTS, techniques used to analyze the text corpus of a bug report and the approach of the proposed prediction model. In Sect. 3 the results and a discussion of the empirical investi-gation carried out are presented. Section 4, finally, draws some conclusions and future work.

2   Material and Methods

This section provides, in brief, necessary background information about the Bug Tracking Systems and a description of the main components of the proposed classifier model of the bug-fix time prediction process adopted, shown in Fig. 1.

2.1   Bug Tracking Systems

The life cycle of a bug in a BTS can be described as follows. Life cycle starts when the bug is discovered and ends when the bug is closed, after ensuring that it has been fixed. Bug life cycle can be slightly different depending on the BTS used. General BTS as well as Bugzilla BTS, a popular BTS, allow users to report, track, describe, comment on and classify bug reports. A bug report is characterized by several predefined fields, such as the relevant product, version, operating system and self-reported incident severity, as well as free-form impor-tant text fields, such as bug title, called summary in Bugzilla, and description. Moreover, users and developers can add comments and submit attachments to the bug report, which often take the form of patches, screenshots, test cases or anything else binary or too large to fit into a comment.

2.2   Proposed Classifier Model

Figure 1 depicts the main components of the proposed classifier model: dataset extraction (Fig. 1a), dataset generation (Fig. 1b), the classifier architecture (Fig. 1c), and evaluation metrics (Fig. 1d).

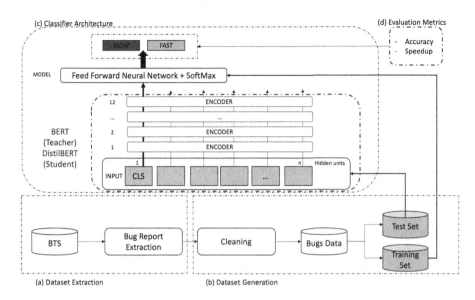

Fig. 1. Overall process and classifier architecture.

2.3   Dataset Extraction

The process deployed for the bug report extraction is shown in Fig. 1a. This preliminary research is focused on bug reports extracted from only one Bugzilla installation. Basically, Bugzilla has been selected because has a wide public installation base and offers a native well documented REST API as a preferred way to interface with Bugzilla from external applications. On Bugzilla's official page there is a list, whose last update is on February 25th, 2021, of 140 companies [7], organizations, and projects that run public Bugzilla installations. The choice of which project to select fell on LiveCode [12], since currently it is a mature and active open-source software project, exposing a public Bugzilla installation. Data were collected by performing a web scraping of bug reports from the Bugzilla platform. This process was made possible by using the APIs made available from Bugzilla, collecting bug reports of the LiveCode project in a JSON file. Only bug reports whose status field has been assigned to VERIFIED and the resolution field has been assigned to FIXED were selected. Since the time spent to fix a bug was not publicly available an additional field, named Days resolution, has been introduced. This field calculates, in calendar days, the time distance between the time where bug field Status was set to RESOLVED and the date where the bug report was assigned for the first time. Calculation in calendar days is due to the absence of information about the actual time spent by developers responsible for fixing bugs. As consequence, the Days resolution field may be not very accurate and potentially affect the results. Fields, such as "Short description", "First comment" and "Comments", containing relevant natural language information to perform fine-tuning on BERT pre-trained model have been selected.

Days resolution field, instead, has been used to discretize resolution time. The remaining fields of the bug report, instead, have been discarded. Finally, all bug reports without both the description and at least one comment were discarded.

2.4 Dataset Generation

The process deployed for the training/test datasets generation is shown in Fig. 1b. Natural language sentences contained in the selected fields have been aggregated into a derived field called Text, since BERT is unable to handle natural language information coming from multiple fields. Bug description and comments usually contain a combination of free unstructured text, code snippets and stack traces, making the data highly noisy; a pre-processing of the input text is required. The following operations were carried out in sequence: URL, symbols and isolated dashes removal; numbers removal; conversion of dashes to underscores. The objectives of the pre-processing task are to reduce the data noise as much as possible but, at the same time, preserve the context of words within sentences. For this reason, common text pre-processing operations that could negatively influence the context of words, such as stop word removal, have been avoided. Text conversion into lowercase letters is an operation not necessary since the uncased version of BERT will be adopted, which performs this operation before the WordPiece tokenization, a technique used by the pre-trained model to segment words into subword-level in Natural Language Processing (NLP) tasks. To address the bug-fixing time prediction issue as the result of a binary text categorization task, it is necessary to discretize the number of days of resolution of each bug into two classes called Fast and Slow. Fast class refers to all bugs that can be fixed in a relatively short time and Slow class to bugs requiring more time and resources. The Days resolution field, representing the time necessary to fix a bug, was discretized in two classes via the median split procedure. In this way, the problem of unbalanced classes was avoided and there was not any need to use balancing techniques.

2.5 BERT

The BERT-based architecture is shown in Fig. 1c. BERT (Bidirectional Encoder Representations from Transformers) is a language representations model that, conceived in late 2018, introduced the key innovation factor to apply the bidirectional training of a Transformer, a popular attention model, to language modeling. Previous approaches, instead, looked at a text sequence either from left to right or combined left-to-right and right-to-left training, as described in [5]. BERT makes use of a Transformer, a model introduced in [6], characterized by a self-attention mechanism that learns contextual relations between words (or subwords) in a text. Generally, a Transformer includes two separate mechanisms: an encoder that reads the text input and a decoder that produces a prediction for the specific task. Since BERT's goal is to generate a language model, only the encoder mechanism is necessary. The input to BERT can be a single sentence or a sentence pair in a sequence of words (e.g., for question answering tasks, the input can be a pair [question, answer]). For a given word, its input representation can be constructed by summing token, segment and position embeddings. The token embedding represents the word vector. The first word is the CLS special token, which can be used for subsequent classification tasks; for the other downstream tasks, the CLS token can be ignored. The segment embedding is used to distinguish between two sentences since pre-training is not only a language modeling but also a classification task with two sentences as input. The positional embedding is used to encode the position of the word to the sentence. The main phases of BERT are pre-training and fine-tuning: during the pre-training, the model is trained using unlabeled data over different pre-training tasks. For fine-tuning, BERT is first initialized with the pre-trained parameters, and all of the parameters are fine-tuned using labeled data from the downstream tasks, term indicating the main supervised tasks of NLP. It is important to note how BERT fine-tuned model performs prediction for a binary text classification task: during the tokenization of the input text, a special token called CLS, which stands for classification, is prepended to the beginning of every sentence. BERT's architecture is composed of a stack of encoders, each encoder generates an embedding that is passed to the next one. The output word embedding of the last encoder, related to the CLS token, can be provided as input to a classifier (a feed-forward neural network with a softmax layer, which normalizes an input vector into a range that leads to a probabilistic interpretation) to perform a classification of the input text. The fine-tuning approach is not the only way to use BERT, since it can also be used as a feature-based approach. It is possible to use the pre-trained version of the model to generate contextualized word embeddings and feed these embeddings to other existing models. The feature-based approach, according to the authors of the model, has certain advantages. First, not all tasks can be easily represented by a Transformer encoder architecture, and therefore require a task-specific model architecture to be added. Second, there are major computational benefits to pre-compute an expensive representation of the training data once and then run many experiments with cheaper models on top of this representation. However, there is the issue of determining which vector, among those provided as output by each encoder, works best as a contextualized embedding.

2.6 DistilBERT

DistilBERT, proposed in [14], is a smaller version of BERT developed based on open-source code and technologies by the team at HuggingFace [2].

DistilBERT uses a technique called knowledge distillation, which approximates BERT, i.e. the large neural network by a smaller one. The idea is that once a large neural network has been trained, its full output distributions can be approximated using a smaller network. Knowledge distillation [6] is a compression technique in which a compact model, the student, is trained to reproduce the behaviour of a larger model - the teacher - or an ensemble of models.

In brief, the student (DistilBERT) has the same general architecture as the teacher (BERT). In the student, the token-type embeddings and the pooler are removed while the number of layers is reduced by a factor of 2. Most of the operations used in the Transformer architecture (linear layer and layer normalisation) are highly optimized in modern linear algebra frameworks and investigations in [14] showed that variations on the last dimension of the tensor (hidden size dimension) have a smaller impact on computation efficiency (for a fixed parameters budget) than variations on other factors like the number of layers. Thus, DistilBERT focuses on reducing the number of layers. In addition to the previously described optimization and architectural choices, an important element in DistilBERT training procedure is to find the right initialization for the subnetwork to converge. Taking advantage of the common dimensionality between teacher and student networks, the student is initialized from the teacher by taking one layer out of two.

3   Empirical Investigation and Results

To conduct the experiment, using the pre-trained model described in Sects. 2.5 and 2.6, additional data operations were required.

3.1   Experimental Settings

The classifier proposed is constructed by using the Python library called Simple Transformers [16], version 0.63.9. This library is based on the Transformers library by HuggingFace. The high-level process of using Simple Transformers models follows the same pattern: (i) initialize a task-specific model; (ii) train the model; (iii) evaluate the model; (iv) make predictions on unlabelled. Google Colaboratory (CoLab) was chosen as execution environment. It is a free Jupyter notebook interactive development environment useful to disseminate machine learning education and research fully configured for deep learning approaches. Colab requires no setup for being used and runs entirely in the cloud. One of the main features of this environment is the possibility to use a cloud GPU to execute notebooks, which speeds up the training process of very complex models like BERT. In the experiment carried out, a free-tier Colab was available. Since it allows access to high-memory Virtual Machines with up to 25 GB RAM, only 300 bug reports were randomly selected out from the entire dataset. This number represents approximately the threshold above which the session ran out of memory in GPU.

To evaluate the model, the accuracy metric is used. It expresses the ratio of the number of correct predictions to the number of instances in the test set, i.e. it denotes the proportion of bugs correctly predicted. As stated above, it was decided to use the Slow labeled class as the positive class, because of its larger impact in terms of cost/effectiveness. In this work, in particular, DistilBERT processes bug report and passes along some information it extracted from it to the next model. The result of DistilBERT's processing is taken as input by a basic Logistic Regression (LR). LR classifies the bug report as either FAST or SLOW (1 or 0, respectively). To improve the performance, a search for the best value of the C parameter, which is the inverse of the regularization strength of a LR, has been made. Any modification of the learning method to improve performance on unseen datasets is called regularization. Regularization is necessary to introduce bias to the model and decrease the variance. Regularization strength applies a penalty to increase the magnitude of parameter values to reduce data overfitting. Smaller values of C specify stronger regularization which will create simple models which underfit the data. For bigger values of C, instead, the power of regularization is lower which implies the model is allowed to increase its complexity, and therefore, overfit the data.

Two different notebooks were created, one for BERT and the other for DistilBERT.

3.2   Results and Discussion

Table 1 shows the result set of the experiment. Both the models, first of all, proved to be very effective in the correct classification of bug reports, accuracy values are 0.91 or 0.92. Thus, performing fine-tuning on a pre-trained deeply bidirectional Transformer is an effective approach to predicting bug-fixing time. Another remark relates to DistilBERT that is faster than BERT [14] and even better performing when combined with both Logistic Regression and the searching for the best value of the C parameter. To evaluate if there is an improvement in the speed of execution of the prediction task, from applying BERT to DistilBERT, Amdahl's law was used. This law is an observation of the improvement in the execution time of a task by speeding up a particular portion of a task. It quantifies performance by comparing two elapsed time values. The equation of speedup is:

$$S = \frac{T_{old}}{T_{new}} = \frac{1}{1 - p + \frac{p}{s}} \tag{1}$$

where

- T_{new} – represents the execution time of the overall task after improvements have been made to some part of the task (in this case the improvement concerns the entire task);
- p – represents the proportion of the task that has been improved, sped up, or parallelized (in this case p is equal to 100%);
- T_{old} – represents the execution time of the overall task prior to any improvements;
- s – represents the factor by which p proportion of the task has been improved or sped up;
- S – represents the theoretical speedup of the overall task (in this case s and S assume the same value).

DistilBert, combined with both Logistic Regression and the tuning of parameter C, takes 199 s instead of 522 in the case of BERT, to execute the prediction task. Applying Amdahl's law the speedup achieved by DistilBert is equal to

2.7236 with a time percentage change of 63.28%. In the case of DistilBert without the tuning of parameter C, the speedup is equal to 2.5566 achieving a time percentage change of 60.89%. DistilBert, thus, in each case is faster than BERT and both the percentage changes represent a significant boost in execution time, are very similar to the result reported in [14] where DistilBERT is faster by 60% than BERT.

However, several limitations to the validity of the results have to be highlighted. First of all, only one project has been used. This project, therefore, is not representative of the population of all open-source software and, thus, the results cannot be generalized to commercial systems that, as known, have different process management of bugs. From a technical perspective, moreover, the hyperparameters tuning has not been carried out for both BERT and DistilBERT. Only the search for the best C parameter value has been carried out. Finally, it is also possible that a bug report, selected as VERIFIED and CLOSED, has been reopened one or more times. When this situation happens, since the bug is treated as a new insertion of a report it introduces a significant noise in the selected dataset.

Table 1. Comparison of accuracy and execution time, expressed in seconds, of BERT, DistilBERT and DistilBERT with the best C on the LiveCode dataset

Models	Accuracy	Execution time
BERT	0.915	542
DistilBERT	0.913	199
DistilBERT with Best C=15.789	0.922	212

4   Conclusions

In this paper, a preliminary assessment of the efficacy of the BERT and DistilBERT pre-trained transformer models in predicting bug-fixing time was performed. These models were applied to the bug reports gathered from a very large open-source software, LiveCode. Both the models proved efficient in predicting bug-fixing time from the reports, with DistilBERT, combined with both a basic Logistic Regression and the best value of the C parameter, attaining the highest accuracy. In the future, an ensemble of the model would be considered to improve predicting performance. Also, strategies to inculcate commonsense knowledge into the model would be considered to improve its generalization ability. A possible avenue of this work is the possibility to perform fine-tuning on BERT pre-trained model; such an approach could provide more accurate estimates of bug resolution time. Additionally, as a more challenging target, it is planned to investigate which sentence embedding (e.g., bug report embedding) works best as a contextualized embedding, among those generated by each encoder layer. To the aim of supporting bug triage a different, but likewise valid, avenue could be the construction of a semi-automatic tool for recognizing neologisms reported in the bug reports. It could support software companies in the creation of neologisms capable of evoking semantic meaningful associations to customers [15], that are the programmers in our case. Furthermore, by using this tool bug reporters and fixers could be inspired and led when they report or comment on a bug report.

References

1. Acheampong, F.A., Wenyu, C., Nunoo-Mensah, H.: Text-based emotion detection: Advances, challenges, and opportunities. Engineering Reports 2 (2020)
2. Aggarwal, A.: Huggingface implmementation of distilbert. https://huggingface.co/docs/transformers/model_doc/distilbert
3. de Almeida, C.D.A., Feijó, D.N., Rocha, L.S.: Studying the impact of continuous delivery adoption on bug-fixing time in apache's open-source projects. In: 2022 IEEE/ACM 19th International Conference on Mining Software Repositories (MSR). pp. 132–136 (2022). https://doi.org/10.1145/3524842.3528049
4. Ardimento, P., Mele, C.: Using BERT to predict bug-fixing time. In: 2020 IEEE Conference on Evolving and Adaptive Intelligent Systems, EAIS 2020, Bari, Italy, May 27–29, 2020. pp. 1–7. IEEE (2020). https://doi.org/10.1109/EAIS48028.2020.9122781
5. Blei, D.M., Ng, A.Y., Jordan, M.I.: Latent dirichlet allocation. In: Dietterich, T.G., Becker, S., Ghahramani, Z. (eds.) Advances in Neural Information Processing Systems 14 [Neural Information Processing Systems: Natural and Synthetic, NIPS 2001(December), pp. 3–8, 2001. Vancouver, British Columbia, Canada]. pp. 601–608. MIT Press (2001). https://proceedings.neurips.cc/paper/2001/hash/296472c9542ad4d4788d543508116cbc-Abstract.html
6. Bucila, C., Caruana, R., Niculescu-Mizil, A.: Model compression. In: Eliassi-Rad, T., Ungar, L.H., Craven, M., Gunopulos, D. (eds.) Proceedings of the Twelfth ACM SIGKDD International Conference on Knowledge Discovery and Data Mining, Philadelphia, PA, USA, August 20–23, 2006. pp. 535–541. ACM (2006). https://doi.org/10.1145/1150402.1150464
7. Bugzilla: Bugzilla installation list. https://www.bugzilla.org/installation-list/ Accessed 09 Sept (2022)
8. Casalino, G., Castiello, C., Buono, N.D., Mencar, C.: A framework for intelligent twitter data analysis with non-negative matrix factorization. Int. J. Web Inf. Syst. 14(3), 334–356 (2018). https://doi.org/10.1108/IJWIS-11-2017-0081
9. Deng, L., Liu, Y. (eds.): Deep Learning in Natural Language Processing. Springer, Singapore (2018). https://doi.org/10.1007/978-981-10-5209-5
10. Lee, D.D., Seung, H.S.: Algorithms for non-negative matrix factorization. In: Leen, T.K., Dietterich, T.G., Tresp, V. (eds.) Advances in Neural Information Processing Systems 13, Papers from Neural Information Processing Systems (NIPS) 2000, Denver, CO, USA. pp. 556–562. MIT Press (2000). https://proceedings.neurips.cc/paper/2000/hash/f9d1152547c0bde01830b7e8bd60024c-Abstract.html
11. Liu, Q., Washizaki, H., Fukazawa, Y.: Adversarial multi-task learning-based bug fixing time and severity prediction. In: 2021 IEEE 10th Global Conference on Consumer Electronics (GCCE). pp. 185–186 (2021). https://doi.org/10.1109/GCCE53005.2021.9621355

12. LiveCode: Livecode bug tracking system - bugzilla installation for livecode project. https://quality.livecode.com/ Accessed 09 Sept 2022

13. Noyori, Y., et al.: Extracting features related to bug fixing time of bug reports by deep learning and gradient-based visualization. In: 2021 IEEE International Conference on Artificial Intelligence and Computer Applications (ICAICA). pp. 402–407 (2021). https://doi.org/10.1109/ICAICA52286.2021.9498236

14. Sanh, V., Debut, L., Chaumond, J., Wolf, T.: Distilbert, a distilled version of BERT: smaller, faster, cheaper and lighter. CoRR abs/1910.01108 (2019). http://arxiv.org/abs/1910.01108

15. Schicchi, D., Pilato, G.: WORDY: A semi-automatic methodology aimed at the creation of neologisms based on a semantic network and blending devices. In: Barolli, L., Terzo, O. (eds.) Complex, Intelligent, and Software Intensive Systems - Proceedings of the 11th International Conference on Complex, Intelligent, and Software Intensive Systems (CISIS-2017), Torino, Italy, July 10–12, 2017. Advances in Intelligent Systems and Computing, vol. 611, pp. 236–248. Springer (2017). https://doi.org/10.1007/978-3-319-61566-0_23

16. simpletransformers: Simple transformers library. https://pypi.org/project/simpletransformers/ (2022). Accessed 09 Sept 2022

Proposing Isomorphic Microservices Based Architecture for Heterogeneous IoT Environments

Pyry Kotilainen[(✉)] [iD], Teemu Autto [iD], Viljami Järvinen [iD], Teerath Das [iD], and Juho Tarkkanen [iD]

University of Jyväskylä, Seminaarinkatu 15, 40014 Jyväskylä, Finland
`pyry.kotilainen@jyu.fi`

Abstract. Recent advancements in IoT and web technologies have highlighted the significance of isomorphic software architecture development, which enables easier deployment of microservices in IoT-based systems. The key advantage of such systems is that the runtime or dynamic code migration between the components across the whole system becomes more flexible, increasing compatibility and improving resource allocation in networks. Despite the apparent advantages of such an approach, there are multiple issues and challenges to overcome before a truly valid solution can be built. In this idea paper, we propose an architecture for isomorphic microservice deployment on heterogeneous hardware assets, inspired by previous ideas introduced as liquid software [12]. The architecture consists of an orchestration server and a package manager, and various devices leveraging WebAssembly outside the browser to achieve a uniform computing environment. Our proposed architecture aligns with the long-term vision that, in the future, software deployment on heterogeneous devices can be simplified using WebAssembly.

Keywords: Isomorphic software architecture · WebAssembly · Internet of Things

1 Introduction

Internet of Things (IoT) and related emerging technologies are already playing a crucial role in almost all domains of daily life, e.g., healthcare, banking, and smart home, among others. In addition, technologies such as cloud computing, virtualisation, and artificial intelligence complement these IoT systems to expand to a wide range of applications. The introduction of edge devices in IoT architecture allows users to acquire desired delay-critical services. This recent transition in IoT development complements the concept of a programmable world, where devices are connected and programmed to fulfil the end user's needs.

The complexity of current IoT systems is increasing at a dynamic pace due to the integration of several software technologies at different levels, complex software architectures, unnecessary use of virtualization, and package handling

© The Author(s), under exclusive license to Springer Nature Switzerland AG 2022
D. Taibi et al. (Eds.): PROFES 2022, LNCS 13709, pp. 621–627, 2022.
https://doi.org/10.1007/978-3-031-21388-5_47

approach [10]. To ease managing complex dependencies and for rapid development of non-trivial applications with a higher level of abstraction language, the
usage of containers has exploded. Even though containers are regarded as a more
lightweight solution than virtual machines, they are generally too resource-heavy
for IoT use-cases and require underlying homogenous architecture. More platform agnostic solutions such as using JavaScript can make the interpreter code
execution slow and resource-heavy due to the dynamically-typed nature [7].

WebAssembly (WASM) is another promising technology used to implement
an isomorphic runtime in web applications. It is a binary instruction format
for a stack-based virtual machine [4], and can be seen as a reliable option to
accomplish dynamic isomorphism, where a standard runtime interpreter is used
to execute the code of the IoT applications. WebAssembly can be used as a common runtime architecture, meaning that the web application can be developed
entirely in various languages and compiled for the WebAssembly interpreter.
Moreover, the use of WebAssembly is not merely limited to web browsers, but
instead the developer community started to realise its significance even beyond
the browser [6,13], i.e., on heterogeneous devices.

In this idea paper, we propose a novel system for isomorphic microservices
deployment on heterogeneous hardware assets leveraging recent developments
in WebAssembly outside the browser. The proposed system consists of a varied
number of heterogeneous devices and a central command and control server, here
referred to as an orchestration server, which also serves software as WebAssembly
modules. The devices leverage a WebAssembly runtime to provide a uniform
and dynamic computing environment for various software modules that can be
deployed on the devices by the server.

The motivation behind our research is the fragmented nature of IoT development. In this paper, we propose a system that allows development in a multitude
of programming languages while deploying on a variety of heterogeneous devices.
The system also aims to solve the problem of configuration and continuous management of a diverse IoT hardware deployment. With the creation of such a
system, we aim to explore the feasibility and limitations of such an approach.

2   Background

In the background section, we will discuss the important concepts used in our
study.

2.1   WebAssembly

Assembly language is a term used for the low-level language that is usually
used as an intermediary between high-level programming languages and machine
code. *WebAssembly* (WASM) is a variation of assembly, targeting a virtual processor, which is used to bring near-native behaviour and compact memory usage
to the browser. WebAssembly Virtual Machines (WASM VM) enable WASM
to operate outside browsers [13], while making reasonable presumptions about

underlying machine capabilities. These VMs can implement a system call interface called WebAssembly System Interface(WASI), which allows WASM VMs to provide capabilities for accessing system resources. WASM's optimised memory usage and near-native performance make it suitable for constrained environments like IoT devices [8].

2.2 Orchestration

Orchestration is a process exploited to automatically configure, manage, and coordinate computer systems, applications, and services. Traditionally, managing these tasks requires a lot of manual effort, and hence can become very cumbersome. Orchestration allows the developers' team to manage these complex tasks and workflows.

An *orchestration server* is responsible for storing, supplying, and executing independent workflows to set up working environments. Orchestration has several use cases, i.e., provisioning, incident response, cloud server management, etc. Key processes can be executed in a streamlined manner to optimise the implementation and reduce DevOps intervention. Orchestration enables the DevOps team to focus on business requirements instead of setting up environments in a repetitive manner. In this paper, we describe an orchestration server to manage all the tasks automatically.

2.3 IoT Device

An IoT device is a networked node, a device capable of having one or more network communication addresses, processing ability and network communication capabilities. In the proposed system, an IoT device can be any hardware/software platform, as long as it can run the host control middleware that will manage the system functions on the device.

3 Architecture

The proposed system shown in Fig. 1 consists of an orchestration server and a variable amount of heterogeneous node devices in the same local area network. An actor (user or another system that interacts with our system) can control the system through the orchestration server.

System functionality can be split into three phases: device discovery, deployment and execution. Upon first discovery, the orchestration server requests configuration information from the device and adds it to the device database the server maintains. Upon a request for deployment, the orchestration server generates a deployment solution, and dishes out the microservices to suitable devices

Aside from communication and application logic, the orchestration server has three components:

- *Device database* contains the hardware configurations of the various devices and is populated by listening to the network and requesting information from devices.
- *Deployment registry* contains all executed deployments by the orchestrator, each deployment listing the devices involved and the services they provide.
- *Package manager* maintains a database of all available WebAssembly software modules which can be sent to the devices. It is also capable of resolving dependencies to provide a complete list of required modules for a given module to run.

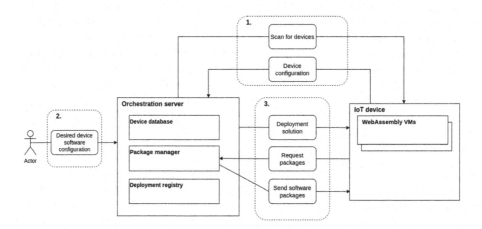

Fig. 1. Proposed architecture

3.1   Device Discovery

The discovery depicted in block 1 of Fig. 1 follows a two-stage process described in the W3C Web of Things specification; Exploration and Introduction [2]. In the Introduction phase devices advertise themselves on the link-local network with mDNS. After the orchestration server receives a new device introduction, the exploration phase begins; The orchestrator queries the capabilities of the device using REST with a well-known URI, and the device replies with an CoRE description [5]. For the applicable parts device description follows WoT-Thing description [3], and additional details of the device, such as which are needed for the deployment solution, follows the OpenAPI specification [1]. Upon receiving the description data, the orchestrator adds the device and its capabilities to the device database.

3.2   Deployment

Deployment is triggered when an actor requests desired functionality, depicted in block 2 of Fig. 1. The Orchestrator looks for suitable deployment solutions for such functionality by comparing available packages, and devices with suitable capabilities on its devices database. Upon finding a solution, a new service namespace is created for a service, which contains a suitable list of devices, their connections and needed packages. For some of the tasks machine- to-machine (M2M) schema can be one-to-many and many-to-many. For the initial MVP only one- to-many requests are supported and within a single namespace, as finding if such rule selection can be generalised and automated needs more research.

After the target devices have been selected, the orchestrator creates a deployment solution manifest based on the capabilities of the devices and metadata of the available software modules. The solution manifest is created on a device basis and contains a list of microservices and their associated modules, configuration for microservices, attribute-based access control rules (ABAC), interconnectivity declarations and security tokens. Deployment manifests are sent to the devices, which then pull the necessary packages from the package repository. This process is depicted in block 3 of Fig. 1.

3.3 Execution

The device host controller, which we are calling hypervisor, configures the downloaded modules and the runtime interface according to the module configuration information and required device-to-device and service-to-service communication. The hypervisor then sets up WASM runtime access controls and runs the software modules in the runtime environment, facilitating communication between devices and services through the runtime.

A new WASM-runtime is created on a service basis, and required modules for running are linked. The deployment configuration can require multiple WASM-runtimes to be run on the device. A simple atomic service, such as "hello world!" would only require one runtime; the hypervisor links the REST API with the declared entry point of the module. Upon receiving a request, the hypervisor runs the entry point function and returns the response as a REST response.

For more complex setups, such as composite services requiring multiple microservices cooperation, the deployment solution contains intra-connectivity declarations. In such cases, the underlying microservice does not need to care about network topology, protocol or node connections, as the complexities are in the hypervisor, which is responsible for setting up services pointing to the correct node. Thanks to the abstractions provided by WASM runtimes, declared entry point functions from other microservices can be called as they would be local; Hypervisor makes a selection based on the deployment solution and its own status checks where to redirect that call, and upon receiving a reply returns the function as it would be local.

3.4 Implementation Considerations

A significant challenge in developing the system is the immaturity of WebAssembly outside the browser. The WebAssembly System Interface (WASI) is under development and the available runtimes have implementations varying in capabilities and provide different ways of granting the WebAssembly modules access outside the runtime.

As a result, most of the work on the devices lies in writing code to augment the interface between the runtime and the platform to allow the WebAssembly modules access to OS/hardware functions. The varying state of available runtimes and their bespoke interfaces also means that the significant amount of boilerplate code required makes changing runtimes challenging. An important consideration is also the platforms which a runtime supports, as there are only a few currently available runtimes capable of running on popular microcontrollers used in many IoT devices.

To minimise potential issues related to network unreliability, the devices use Constrained Application Protocol (CoAP) for M2M communication, which can run over a myriad of protocols and is designed for use with constrained nodes and constrained networks [11]. Also, if the deployment solution declares multiple possible end-points for a service, the hypervisor can select the best-suited device based on multiple rulesets, such as network distance/latency, physical distance, suitability, or best performance/availability. The call can be a one-to-one scenario, or a call to multiple hosts simultaneously in one-to-many scenarios, where the fastest response is used. Furthermore, the hypervisor constantly keeps track of the latency of the external nodes, and if it is over the threshold, it triggers a circuit breaker call, and calls to that end-point are suspended. The best way to handle cases when no endpoint is available is not yet clear.

A suitable method for establishing a secure and trustworthy communication approach must be considered. Common approaches are federated identity in form of security tokens, and client certificates [9].

4   Discussion and Future Work

In this paper, we have introduced a system for isomorphic microservices based architecture for IoT, which aims to offer ease of development. However, Running code as WebAssembly modules in runtime does result in a performance hit compared to native code and requires more both working memory and persistent storage [8]. It also complicates deploying real-time applications. With increasing computational power and memory of IoT devices, the trade-off for ease of development and flexibility of deployment will likely become less and less of a problem.

In future it is also our hope that the functionality of the orchestration server can be expanded. For example, the deployment requests need not be as specific as outlined above. The server could make decisions about device selection and deployment topology based on device availability and their dynamic state according to a deployment task describing desired deployment outcome without necessarily naming specific devices or their arrangement.

Including dynamic state for devices could also enable improved persistence and self-healing properties, as detection of failed devices could trigger a change in deployment topology and either a replacement device could be selected or the responsibilities of the failed device could be moved to a device in the same namespace.

References

1. OpenAPI Specification v3.1.0 — Introduction, Definitions, & More. https://spec. openapis.org/oas/latest.html
2. Web of Things (WoT) Discovery. https://www.w3.org/TR/wot-discovery/
3. Web of Things (WoT) Thing Description 1.1. https://www.w3.org/TR/wot-thing-description11/
4. WebAssembly Core specification. Tech. rep., W3C (2019)
5. Amsüss, C., Shelby, Z., Koster, M., Bormann, C., der Stok, P.V.: CoRE resource directory. In: Internet-Draft draft-ietf-core-resource-directory-26, Internet Engineering Task Force/Internet Engineering Task Force
6. Bryant, D.: Webassembly outside the browser: a new foundation for pervasive computing. Keynote at ICWE **20**, 9–12 (2020)
7. Haas, A., et al.: Bringing the web up to speed with WebAssembly. In: Proceedings of the 38th ACM SIGPLAN Conference on Programming Language Design and Implementation. PLDI 2017, Association for Computing Machinery, New York, NY, USA, pp. 185–200 (2017). https://doi.org/10.1145/3062341.3062363
8. Hall, A., Ramachandran, U.: An execution model for serverless functions at the edge. In: Proceedings of the International Conference on Internet of Things Design and Implementation. IoTDI '19, Association for Computing Machinery, New York, NY, USA, pp. 225–236 (2019). https://doi.org/10.1145/3302505.3310084
9. Li, S., et al.: Understanding and addressing quality attributes of microservices architecture: a Systematic literature review. Inf. Softw. Technol. **131**, 106449 (2021). https://doi.org/10.1016/j.infsof.2020.106449
10. Mikkonen, T., Pautasso, C., Taivalsaari, A.: Isomorphic internet of things architectures with web technologies. Computer **54**(7), 69–78 (2021). https://doi.org/10.1109/MC.2021.3074258
11. Shelby, Z., Hartke, K., Bormann, C.: The constrained application protocol (CoAP). RFC 7252 (2014). https://doi.org/10.17487/RFC7252
12. Taivalsaari, A., Mikkonen, T., Systä, K.: Liquid Software Manifesto: The era of multiple device ownership and its implications for software architecture. In: 2014 IEEE 38th Annual Computer Software and Applications Conference, pp. 338–343 (2014). https://doi.org/10.1109/COMPSAC.2014.56
13. Tomassetti, F.: WASI: How to run WebAssembly code outside of your browser (2021)

Doctoral Symposium

Ethical Tools, Methods and Principles in Software Engineering and Development: Case Ethical User Stories

Erika Halme$^{(\boxtimes)}$

University of Jyväskylä, PO Box 35, 40014 Jyväskylä, Finland
erika.a.halme@jyu.fi
https://www.jyu.fi/en/frontpage

Abstract. The great leap with the development of Artificial Intelligence (AI) and Machine Learning (ML) technology has increased the range of different requirements for software quality, especially in terms of ethics. To implement high-level requirements, like ethical principles, into the workflow of software engineering, new requirements engineer tools are to be developed. Ethical User Stories (EUS) offers a simple way of implementing ethics in software development. This research has investigated the idea of using familiar requirements engineering artifacts, User Stories, to implement ethical principles, into the workflow of software engineering and operationalizing the studied phenomena of EUS. The preliminary results, found through two ongoing empirical studies with a data collection of 600+ EUS, show that EUS is a pressure-free, human-centric and accessible approach to Ethically Aligned Design (EAD) that intertwines with quality characteristics and relieves the developer from the heavy burden of ethical consideration to a smooth workflow of software engineering. An effective EUS is consistent throughout the user story and shares the idea that user-driven ethical motivation generates system functionality or benefits non-functional software design for quality assurance.

Keywords: AI ethics · User stories · Agile software engineering

1 Introduction

AI is a technology that serves a significant role in modern technology and has several benefits. The downside to the technology development is unfortunately witnessed in some real-life cases indicating that AI is failing in many ways. The technology itself may harm people's privacy issues [1] and be even discriminating [2]. These cases and several others has caused different research fields in software engineering to take action to ensure trustworthiness for the technology developed and for ethically aligned software development. As the requirements increase in the high-level of software development, e.g. aligning the ethics to the workflow of software engineers, the engineering methods and tools are modulated within the

© The Author(s), under exclusive license to Springer Nature Switzerland AG 2022
D. Taibi et al. (Eds.): PROFES 2022, LNCS 13709, pp. 631–637, 2022.
https://doi.org/10.1007/978-3-031-21388-5_48

paradigm shift. The research is then motivated by the industry, where EAD [3,4] is challenged. To find out how to implement in practise ethical requirements into the workflow of software engineers, the research in question studies the process of Agile Requirements Engineering (ARE) [5,6], where a basic ARE artifact, User Stories [7], are intensified with AI Ethics principles.

The research so far has studied the phenomena of ethical user stories with the assistance of an EAD method called the ECCOLA method [8]. The ACM code of ethics [9] could have been also chosen for framing the study but due to the different nature of AI technology, AI being probabilistic and not deterministic [10], ECCOLA method, was specifically developed for delivering ethically aligned AI software development and for the reason, chosen for framing the study along with the Agile practises. Agile practises have been considered more people friendly than traditional software development and emphasizing on human values [11] and considered ethical minded approach to software development [12].

This research has been ramified into two empirical studies. The first branch has been studying the functionality and operationalisation of the phenomena of ethical user stories. The second branch took the phenomena into industrial setting to explore the validation of the proof-of-concept artifact, ethical user stories.

2   Related Work

Resent research state that at least 84 public-private AI ethics principles and values initiatives were identified by Mittelstadt [13]. Also, a scoping review by Jobin et al. [14], with an analysis including a search for grey literature containing principles and guidelines for ethical AI, has been made with academic and legal sources excluded [14]. The results present that there was a massive increase (88%) after the year 2016 towards the number of released publications or documents containing ethical principles or guidelines [14]. Indeed, AI Ethics is regarded as necessary today as any information system standard that developers require. What the industry is utilizing or what is the developer's professional knowledge of AI ethics today should be reviewed. The AI ethics research so far has created guidelines, principles, regulations, plans and frameworks for implementing ethical consideration into software development. Even a typology, by Morley et al. have been introduced for developers and practitioners to apply ethics in different phases in machine learning development process [15].

Resent findings in research indicate however that principles and guidelines do not turn easily into practice for developers. [13] There exist a gap between research and practice, where developers consider ethics important in principle, but perceive them to be distant from the issues they face in their work. [10] Still, we cannot say that ethics hasn't been a theme in IT as it has for several decades. [16] Ethics in general has been a study field in IT forming branches like IT ethics, Computer Ethics and lately, AI ethics that can be considered the starting point and path to the EUS research in software engineering. Human values in IT, as already mentioned, has been noticed through the agile manifesto, but recently also in requirements engineering [17,18]. Also, there has been a user story centered research with ethical tuning forming to ethical integration to user stories [19] and ethically-sensitive user story that has been build on a conceptual studies [20]. The field of AI ethics and also requirements engineering is missing empirical studies of ethical user stories that this research has been, in large measures, concentrating on.

3 Methodology

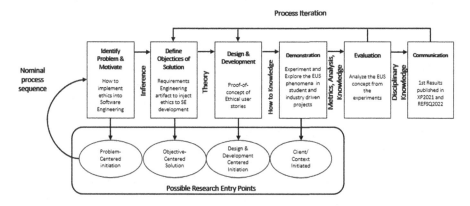

Fig. 1. Overview of the EUS research in compliancy with the Design Science Research Methodology. Adapted from Peffers, Tuunanen, et al. (2007)

In the search for the right research method, we turn to Design Science Research Method (DSRM) as it has origins in Information Systems, Engineering and Requirements Engineering research in general [21]. DSRM was chosen also for the reason that the output of the research was to design an artifact through a process [22]. This research as a whole concentrates on all of these six process steps observed and adapted specifically to this research in Fig. 1 adapted from Peffers et al. [22]. The research takes a problem-centered motivation approach, where the community of software engineering is lacking tools to implement ethics in software engineering development. The output goal is to design and develop an artifact, EUS, concentrating on developing the concept for EUS for practitioners and scholars for communication. Software engineering experimentation by Wohlin [23] is applied to this research as empirical study design guidelines. The following sections review the empirical studies and related research questions following to results and the research outcome and contribution so far.

Empirical Study I. This first experimental study [24], was conducted through a masters level course in the university of Jyväskylä, where students of real-life software development project created 250+ user stories and in the context of this research the user stories were ethically evaluated. The following research question was set for the research as **R1:** How can Non-Functional ethically-oriented User Stories be written with the assistance of the ECCOLA method? [24]

This study was further developed for the EUS operationalisation, where new data collection of 137 user stories were analyzed through an empirical experiment for ethical content. The goal of operationalisation of the phenomena was to find the elements that frame the concept of EUS and also develop the model for writing them. That inspired us to focus the study to find answer to our second research question as **R2:** What is the concept of Ethical User Stories? With supportive questions: "What are the traits/elements/attributes that frames the EUS concept? Results from this are not yet released as the research is still under construction.

Empirical Study II. The context of the second branch empirical study [25] was in a digitalisation project called the Smarter [26]. The goal for the project was to create blueprints for a digitalized and autonomous port terminals with certain requirements, one of them being a trustworthy product outcome and EAD. EUS process and ECCOLA method was then used in the study design for creating project's ethical requirements that proceeded as 273 EUS, jointly developed in several workshops by the project industrial and institutional partners and by the university of Jyväskylä AI ethics laboratory researchers. As this branch of the research is heavily influenced by the industry the research question was partially perceived from the project point-of-view but still keeping along the EUS phenomena with the following research questions **R3:** How to make ethical user stories? [25] **R4:** What are the ethical requirements in the Maritime industry, especially in port terminals when switching over to SMART terminals? [25] Here the research question R3 concentrates on the process of making the ethical user stories rather than finding the functionality like in R1.

The heavy empirical approach points out to the fact that there is a knowledge gap between implementing ethics into the practise of software development as well as in agile requirements engineering research.

4   Preliminary Results

The preliminary results, based on the empirical findings, are listed below. Using the ethical framework in the user story writing process, does not directly affect the ethical outcome but can be seen indirectly when results are analyzed. The compilation of the results is divided between the EUS experimentation and by the operationalisation.

Results From The Experiments: Based on the empirical experiment - using the ethical framework, here the ECCOLA method, in the user story process seems to result in more human-centric user stories [24], which drives the development out of the technology focused consideration and bring human values to the surface to follow EAD in software engineering. The statistical results from the research experimentation is not released yet, but indicate that using the ethical framework in the user story writing process does not produce more ethical user stories but affects positively to the quality of the software development. We could expect that ethics and quality is then intertwined and can be worked in both ways, ethics enhances the quality of software development and quality of work enhances ethics. Still, we considered that in practise, Non-functional user stories can be written with the assistance of the ethical framework [24].

Results From the Operationalisation: The model of writing EUS seems to streamline the ethical consideration to the software development and "liberate the software developers from the ethical theoretizising" [25]. EUS model is an enjoyable learning process for developers, where the Ethical framework is streamlined to developers to progress in the process efficiently [25]. The concept of EUS is still under construction but findings so far indicate that the essence of writing EUS starts from a motivation towards a particular ethical theme and considers the user story outcome on behalf of the user consistently.

5   Expected Contributions

In recent years, AI ethics has been a famous topic globally in different forums. Regardless of the different acts towards trustworthy AI applications and ethically aligned software design, software engineers are lacking tools when ethics are considered. Even the research is lacking with empirical studies for how to implement ethics into the AI software development.

EUS research offers State-of-the-Art tool for software engineers to implement (AI) ethics to software development. The EUS artifact that has been evaluated by practitioners of the field, is now in the progress of operationalizing for further development and use.

Acknowledgements. This research is partially funded by the BusinessFinland program Sea4Value and the Smarter project. The author is grateful for the funder for their support.

References

1. Cambridge Analytica and Facebook: The Scandal and the Fallout So Far. https://www.nytimes.com/2018/04/04/us/politics/cambridge-analytica-scandal-fallout.html. The New York Times (nytimes.com) Accessed 4 Apr 2018

2. Real-life Examples of Discriminating Artificial Intelligence | by Terence Shin | Towards Data Science, https://towardsdatascience.com/real-life-examples-of-discriminating-artificial-intelligence-cae395a90070. The New York Times (nytimes.com) Accessed 4 June 2020

3. AI, H.: High-level Expert Group on Artificial Intelligence (2019)

4. Ethics guidelines for trustworthy ai, https://ec.europa.eu/digital-single-market/en/news/ethics-guidelines-trustworthy-ai. Accessed 26 Apr 2022

5. Schön, E.M., Thomaschewski, J., Escalona, M.J.: Agile requirements engineering: a systematic literature review. Comput. Standards Interfaces. **49**(4), 79–91 (2017)

6. Eberlein, A. and Leite, J.C.S.P.: Agile requirements definition: A view from requirements engineering. In Proceedings of the international workshop on time-constrained requirements engineering (TCRE'02), pp. 4–8 (2002)

7. Cohn, M.: User stories applied: For agile software development. Addison-Wesley Professional (2004)

8. Vakkuri, v., Kemell, K.-K., Jantunen, M., Halme, E., Abrahamsson, P.: Eccola - a method for implementing ethically aligned ai systems. J. Syst. Softw. **182** (2021)

9. Anderson, R.E.: ACM code of ethics and professional conduct. Commun. ACM **35**(5), 94–99 (1992)

10. Vakkuri, V., Kemell, K.K., Kultanen, J., Abrahamsson, P.: The current state of industrial practice in artificial intelligence ethics. IEEE Softw. **37**(4), 50–57 (2020)

11. Miller, K.W., Larson, D.K.: Agile software development: human values and culture. IEEE Technol. Soc. Mag. **24**(4), 36–42 (2005)

12. Judy, K.H.: Agile principles and ethical conduct. In: 2009 42nd Hawaii International Conference on System Sciences, IEEE, pp. 1–8 (2009)

13. Mittelstadt, B.: Principles alone cannot guarantee ethical ai. Nature Mach. Intell. **1**(11), 501–507 (2019)

14. Jobin, A., Ienca, M., Vayena, E.: The global landscape of ai ethics guidelines. Nature Mach. Intell. **1**(9), 389–399 (2019)

15. Morley, J., Floridi, L., Kinsey, L., Elhalal, A.: From what to how: an initial review of publicly available AI ethics tools, methods and research to translate principles into practices. Sci. Eng. Ethics **26**(4), 2141–2168 (2022)

16. Bynum, T.W.: Milestones in the history of information and computer ethics. In: The Handbook of Information and Computer Ethics, vol. 25 (2008)

17. Perera, H., et al.: The impact of considering human values during requirements engineering activities (2021). arXiv preprint arXiv:2111.15293

18. Detweiler, C., Harbers, M.: Value Stories: putting human values into requirements engineering. In REFSQ Workshops **1138**, 2–11 (2014)

19. Kamthan, P., Shahmir, N.: On Integrating Ethicality in User Stories. In: The Thirty Third International Conference on Software Engineering and Knowledge Engineering (SEKE 2021), Pittsburgh, USA (2021)

20. Kamthan, P., Shahmir, N.: On ethically-sensitive user story engineering. In: 2021 4th International Conference on Computer Science and Software Engineering (CSSE 2021) pp. 71–79 (2021)

21. Wieringa, R.J.: Design Science Methodology for Information Systems and Software Engineering. Springer, Heidelberg (2014). https://doi.org/10.1007/978-3-662-43839-8

22. Peffers, K., Tuunanen, T., Rothenberger, M.A., Chatterjee, S.: A design science research methodology for information systems research. J. Manage. Inform. Syst. **24**(3), 45–77 (2007)

23. Wohlin, C., Runeson, P., Höst, M., Ohlsson, M.C., Regnell, B., Wesslén, A.: Experimentation in software engineering. Springer Science & Business Media. (2012). https://doi.org/10.1007/978-3-642-29044-2
24. Halme, E., et al.: How to write ethical user stories? impacts of the ECCOLA method. In: Gregory, P., Lassenius, C., Wang, X., Kruchten, P. (eds.) XP 2021. LNBIP, vol. 419, pp. 36–52. Springer, Cham (2021). https://doi.org/10.1007/978-3-030-78098-2_3
25. Halme, E., et al.: Ethical User Stories: Industrial Study. In: REFSQ Workshops (2022)
26. SMART TERMINALS - SMARTER. https://www.dimecc.com/dimecc-services/smart-terminals-smarter/ Accessed 20 Jun 2021

Architectural Degradation and Technical Debt Dashboards

Dario Amoroso d'Aragona[✉]

Tampere University, Tampere, Finland
dario.amorosodaragona@tuni.fi

Abstract. ***Background.*** Companies frequently try to improve the quality of their software by resolving technical issues that are perceived to have an impact on software quality. Technical information is any information that may be gathered from the source code or the software development process, for instance: code or documentation guidelines, and the use of specific patterns. If these issues are not fixed they may generate technical debt. ***Goal.*** The goal of the Ph.D., which started on January 2022, is to understand which are the causes of Architectural Technical Debt in a real case study and to develop a Dashboard to notify developers as earlier as possible.

Methods and expected contribution. We first plan to investigate the actual production code process and then, and then to work with teams to find the best practices and strategies to easily manage Architectural Technical Debt.

Keywords: Technical debt · Architectural debt · Software quality

1 Introduction

Kruchten et al [4] in their work defined Technical Debt as *"design of implementation constructs that are expedient in short term but that set up a technical context that can make a future change more costly or impossible"*.

The management of Technical Debt is not a trivial task in every context. The field of software quality has reached a good level of maturity and several tools/methods and techniques exist to support developers to manage Technical Debt. However, understanding which are the best practices to adopt in a specific context is challenging. Malakuti et al [8] conduct a study to understand which are the most challenging quest for a company to find the right way to manage Technical Debt. The authors find that the biggest issue is finding the starting point for technical debt management. Other issues that may injure technical debt management are [8]: a) The company's history of quality improvements and its potential (unfavorable) effects on how different people view the efficacy of adopted methods; b) the lack of company-wide understanding of software

This work is funded by the Doctoral School of Industry Innovation (DSII), and ABB.

© The Author(s), under exclusive license to Springer Nature Switzerland AG 2022
D. Taibi et al. (Eds.): PROFES 2022, LNCS 13709, pp. 638–643, 2022.
https://doi.org/10.1007/978-3-031-21388-5_49

architecture and technical debt; c) the adoption of technical debt management techniques that may not always produce the desired results; d) the need for quality improvements outside of software, such as process debt.

Technical debt may exist at the architecture level as well as the coding level. Static code analysis tools are available to detect technical debt at code level. Without running the code, these tools can do static code analysis. These tools' primary function is to identify issues in the source code and show developers various metrics that can be used to fix those issues. One of the most well-known static code analysis tools is SonarQube, for instance. [11] defines Architectural Technical Debt (ATD) in software-intensive systems as a metaphor used to describe the "big" design decisions (e.g., choices regarding structure, frameworks, technologies, languages, etc.) that, while being suitable or even optimal when made, significantly hinder progress in the future. In contrast to other types of technical debt, architectural technical debt has an impact on software architecture rather than the code itself. Architectural Technical debt may be produced as a result of bad decision regarding the design of the software architecture, which has a substantial impact on different system components.

In order to early detect Architectural Technical Debt, and to provide dashboards to make possible stakeholders aware of the amount of accumulated Technical Debt, we are planning to investigate the following Research Questions (RQs):

- **RQ1**: Which are the commons causes of Architectural Technical Debt in a company?
- **RQ2**: Which tools/techniques/best practices the company uses to manage Architectural Technical Debt?
- **RQ3**: Which are the effects of these solutions on the Architectural Technical Debt?
- **RQ4**: How is it possible to improve and reduce the Architectural Technical Debt?
- **RQ5**: What visualization techniques can be adopted to visualize the Architectural Technical Debt?

2 Background and Related Works

Companies typically attempt to enhance the quality of their software by fixing technical problems that are thought to affect software quality. Any information that may be gleaned from the source code or the software development process is referred to as technical information. Examples include the use of particular patterns, adherence to coding or documentation rules, or architectural issues. Such problems cause technical debt if they are not resolved.

Alves et al. [1] proposed a mapping study to identify the various type of Technical Debt and the known solution adopted for each of these. Their results show how Architectural Technical Debt refers specifically to those problems encountered in the architecture of the system (e.g., high coupling, high cohesion, no modularity). These types of issues may affect architectural requirements (performance, robustness, among others).

Brown et al. [3] first and Krutchen et al [5] after in their works have investigated the relationship between the Code Debt [1] and the Architectural Debt. The results show how this type of debt cannot be resolved with simple refactoring in the code but needs more extensive development activities.

Recently, Malakuti et al. [8] have investigated the Technical Debt in their company finding that the cause of Architectural Technical Debt is to be attributed to different factors: *(i)* Changes in Context: changes in the business context, aging technology, ad-hoc approach for supporting multiple hardware/software variants, natural evolution and aging; *(ii)* Business: time and cost pressure, requirements shortfall, misalignment of business goals; *(iii)* Processes and Practices: insufficient processes, insufficient documentation, inadequate software engineering practices, and tools, inadequate planning; *(iv)* People: inexperienced teams, unclear quality-related roles, and responsibilities, insufficient motivation concerning quality improvement, coordination and communication shortfall, and lack of common understanding of technical debt.

Moreover, Malakuti et al.[7] have investigated which are the open challenge in the management of Technical Debt reporting how there is still a lack of a clear taxonomy of debt and their relations, how it is possible to introduce systematic management of each technical debt category, and finally how to manage the relations between the technical debt issues between the technical debt categories. Lenarduzzi et al. [6] proposed a systematic literature review on Technical Debt Prioritization, the findings demonstrate how software companies are under increasing pressure to provide value to customers. Finding a compromise between allocating developer time, effort, and resources to new feature implementation and TD remediation tasks, bug repair, or other system upgrades is crucial. In the work proposed by Besker et al. [2] this concept is summarized as "the pressure of delivering customer value and meeting delivery deadlines forces the software teams to down-prioritize TD refactoring continuously in favor of implementing new features rapidly" Budget, resources, and available time are crucial considerations in a software project, especially at the prioritization stage, as investing time and energy in refactoring tasks typically means that less time can be allocated to other tasks, such adding new features. This is one of the key causes, along with their frequent focus on delivering customer-visible features, explaining why software companies don't always allocate additional funds and resources to fixing Technical Debt in the source code [12].

Additionally, according to Martini, Bosch, and Chaudron [9], TD refactoring activities typically have lower priority than the development of new features, and Technical Debt that is not directly connected to the deployment of new features is frequently put off.

Vathsavayi and Syst [10] echo this notion, stating that "Deciding whether to spend resources for developing new features or fixing the debt is a challenging task." The researchers highlight that software teams need to prioritize new features, bug fixes, and TD refactoring within the same prioritization process.

As the final results of the works proposed by Lenarduzzi et al. [6] the authors demonstrate how studies frequently concentrate their prioritization techniques on prioritization among various TD components, with the aim of determining which item should be refactored first. None of the prioritizing strategies mentioned in the publications analyzed directly discusses how to prioritize between putting time and effort into reforming TD and developing new features.

3   The Proposed Approach

The Ph.D. plan consists of the four following steps:

1. Analysis of Architectural Technical Debt in literature
2. Analysis of the strategies/best tools/practices adopted in the company (ABB) to manage Architectural Technical Debt
   2.1. Analysis of ABB code production process and comparison with the state of the art
   2.2. Analysis of the tools actually used in the CI process.
   2.3. Survey with the developers to investigate why they used that specific tool or why they don't use any tool.
   2.4 . Work with teams to understand how to mitigate the issues that arose.
3. Investigation on the effects of the solutions adopted
4. Implementation of a tool/dashboard that can help the developers to manage technical debt showing the metrics more useful for them according to the previous results.

Step one attempts to answer RQ1. RQ2 is answered in the second step. The third step try to answer RQ3 and RQ4. Finally, the last step answers RQ5.

3.1   Research Methodology

Step 1. The first step is to analyze the Technical Debt in literature, understanding which is the starting point reached now, which are the most common causes of Architectural Technical Debt identified in these last years, which are the best practices identified, and how they are applied in different contexts. The goal is to study in deep all the aspects of Technical Debt, considering all the aspects of the coin. Thus, the issues related to the code, to the architecture, to the lack of knowledge, to the lack of best practices but also the aspect related to the social smells and how this impacts the introduction of Technical Debt in a system.

Step 2. The second step is related to the state of the art of Technical Debt management in the company (ABB). Thus, understand which are the best practices and the tools yet used to take under control the Technical Debt in their code, focusing on which of these tools can be used also to manage Architectural Technical Debt. This step is composed of 4 phases:

- *Phase 1.* In the first phase we will perform a manual analysis of their repositories, of the Continuous Integration tools used, and of the configuration of the pipelines to understand which is their production process;
- *Phase 2.* In the second phase we will perform a manual analysis of the Continuous Integration tools (e.g., Jenkins, Azure pipelines) to understand which tools they have in their production process to manage Technical Debt (e.g., Lattix, SonarQube, Test framework, Lint);
- *Phase 3.* The third phase consists to dispense a survey to the developers to understand why some tools are used at the expense of others, why some teams do not use any tools (if there are), if there is some correlation between the product that the teams are developing and the tools used by them, if there is some adopted tool useful to manage Architectural Technical Debt (eg., to prioritize ATD items; to minimize ATD in source code) and so on;
- *Phase 4.* Finally we want to select a subset of developer teams to work with them improving their Technical Debt management.

Step 3. In the third step, we will evaluate the solutions adopted to understand if they really improve the management of Technical Debt or not. In the latter case, we plan to investigate other solutions, introduce them, and evaluate them. In other words, steps 2 and 3 will be performed in an iterative cycle.

Step 4. Finally, in the last step, we intend to collect all the metrics of the tools introduced in the previous steps that are really useful for developers and show them in a dashboard.

4 Expected Contributions

Our research wants to help developers to manage (eg., prioritize/minimize) Architectural Technical Debt. In the long-term, we expect to find which are the best practices that a company with the same characteristic as the company investigated by us can introduce to take under control the Architectural Technical Debt in their products. Moreover, we guess that the findings of our research will help the community to better understand how Technical Debt grows up in a real case study, which is the impact on a real production process, which solutions can be adopted, which could be the causes of Technical Debt in a company.

References

1. Alves, N.S., Mendes, T.S., de Mendonça, M.G., Spínola, R.O., Shull, F., Seaman, C.: Identification and management of technical debt: a systematic mapping study. Inf. Softw. Technol. **70**, 100–121 (2016). https://www.sciencedirect.com/science/article/pii/S0950584915001743
2. Besker, T., Martini, A., Bosch, J.: Technical debt triage in backlog management. In: 2019 IEEE/ACM International Conference on Technical Debt (TechDebt), pp. 13–22 (2019)

3. Brown, N., et al.: Managing technical debt in software-reliant systems. In: Proceedings of the Workshop on Future of Software Engineering Research, FoSER 2010, at the 18th ACM SIGSOFT International Symposium on Foundations of Software Engineering, Santa Fe, NM, USA, pp. 7-11 (2010)
4. Kruchten, P., Nord, R., Ozkaya, I.: Managing Technical Debt: Reducing Friction in Software Development, Addison-Wesley (2019)
5. Kruchten, P., Nord, R.L., Ozkaya, I.: Technical debt: From metaphor to theory and practice. IEEE Softw. **29**(6), 18–21 (2012)
6. Lenarduzzi, V., Besker, T., Taibi, D., Martini, A., Arcelli Fontana, F.: A systematic literature review on technical debt prioritization: Strategies, processes, factors, and tools. J. Syst. Softw. **171**, 110827 (2021). https://doi.org/10.1016/j.jss.2020.110827, https://www.sciencedirect.com/science/article/pii/S016412122030220X
7. Malakuti, S., Heuschkel, J.: The need for holistic technical debt management across the value stream: Lessons learnt and open challenges (2021)
8. Malakuti, S., Ostroumov, S.: The quest for introducing technical debt management in a large-scale industrial company. In: Jansen, A., Malavolta, I., Muccini, H., Ozkaya, I., Zimmermann, O. (eds.) ECSA 2020. LNCS, vol. 12292, pp. 296–311. Springer, Cham (2020). https://doi.org/10.1007/978-3-030-58923-3_20
9. Martini, A., Bosch, J., Chaudron, M.: Investigating architectural technical debt accumulation and refactoring over time: a multiple-case study. Inf. Softw. Technol. **67**, 237–253 (2015). https://doi.org/10.1016/j.infsof.2015.07.005, https://www.sciencedirect.com/science/article/pii/S0950584915001287
10. Vathsavayi, S., Systä, K.: Technical debt management with genetic algorithms. In: 2016 42th Euromicro Conference on Software Engineering and Advanced Applications (SEAA), pp. 50–53 (2016)
11. Verdecchia, R., Kruchten, P., Lago, P., Malavolta, I.: Building and evaluating a theory of architectural technical debt in software-intensive systems. Journal of Systems and Software 176, 110925 (2021), https://www.sciencedirect.com/science/article/pii/S0164121221000224
12. Vidal, S., Vazquez, H., Diaz-Pace, A., Marcos, C., Garcia, A., Oizumi, W.: JSpIRIT: a flexible tool for the analysis of code smells. In: 2015 34th International Conference of the Chilean Computer Science Society (SCCC), pp. 1–6 (2015). https://doi.org/10.1109/SCCC.2015.7416572

The Impact of Business Design in Improving the Offering of Professional Software Services

Sari Suominen[✉][iD]

Faculty of Information Technology University of Jyväskylä, Seminaarinkatu 15,
40014 Jyväskylä, Finland
sari.s.suominen@jyu.fi

Abstract. Companies offering professional software services face challenges
from many directions. Increased competition put downward price pressure even
as labor shortages drive up costs and the pressure for increasing profits is endless.
Many of the challenges in offering professional software services arise because
of the time and material pricing model. To overcome these problems, this study
brings the business design approach into the context of professional software
services to achieve more scalable and profitable service offering. To develop an
in-depth understanding of business design approach, a multiple case study will be
conducted. The business design framework developed in this study may enable
companies in software industry to develop their professional service offering with
the aim to overcome the problems with labor shortage, profitability, scalability,
efficiency and productivity.

Keywords: Business design · Professional software services · Software
industry · Profitability · Labor shortage · Time and material pricing · Service
productization

1 Introduction

Our economy, markets, and customers' expectations evolve at an exhilarating pace. The
business models and infrastructures that have been the foundation for companies are
not sufficient to meet the demands of today, let alone the demands of tomorrow [5].
One of trends is that the money flows are shifting from agriculture and product-oriented
consumption to consuming services. Services comprise 70 to 80 percent of economics
in mature countries, and many industries have noticed that services are higher-margin
businesses than manufacturing [18].

Digitalization and technology have driven radical transformation and disruption and
in the core of change are the products and services of the software industry [2, 18].
Software industry can be divided into the following segments: professional software
services, software products (including enterprise solutions and packaged software) and
embedded software including services [11]. In this research I will focus on the professional software services, also called human services [17], which form 37 percent of the
revenue in the software industry [10].

© The Author(s), under exclusive license to Springer Nature Switzerland AG 2022
D. Taibi et al. (Eds.): PROFES 2022, LNCS 13709, pp. 644–649, 2022.
https://doi.org/10.1007/978-3-031-21388-5_50

Companies offering professional software services face challenges from many directions. As services are intangible and comparatively little capital is required to produce them, market entry for new competitors is relatively easy [21]. Thus, increased competition creates need to lower prices even as talent shortages drive up costs and the pressure for increasing profits is endless.

The main goal of the research is to provide a cohesive understanding of how the challenges can be overcome utilizing the business design method in respect to the professional software services. Conceptually, I will develop an industry specific business design framework by supplying a solid foundation for practitioners and researchers. The research question is *"How can business design improve the offering of professional software services?"*. I will begin by clarifying what practical challenges I have identified in the professional software service offering. These challenges spring from my own experience from the software industry where I have worked for 20 years in various positions and supported by literature. Furthermore, I propose that by utilizing business design in developing professional software services, a company can be more competitive and profitable.

2 Background

The most common and simplest pricing model for professional software services is the Time and Materials (T&M) pricing, also called the Time and Materials Contracting [4] or Cost-Based pricing [9]. The model involves calculating the cost of the labor (time) and other expenses (materials) and adding a desired margin to cover overhead and profit [9, 14]. When using the T&M pricing, the customer is buying resources to make a system, rather than an outcome or a specific solution as in fixed-price contract [13, 15].

The literature suggests many advantages for using T&M pricing. As the pricing model is simple and it offers a straightforward method to ensure that the costs of producing the service are covered, it is used by many professional software service providers [20]. The pricing offers flexibility, especially when Agile methods are used and when the scope is not predictable [4]. Thus, the customer is allowed to adjust the scope and priorities to their needs during the project [4, 16]. Even though there are obvious benefits for T&M pricing, this research focuses on the challenges and the limitation of the T&M pricing model.

Based on literature, the downsides of using the T&M pricing in offering professional software services are volatile productivity, lack of innovation and efficiency, limited profitability and scalability and labor shortage [4, 15, 16, 20], which are illustrated in Fig. 1. One of the challenges is that the productivity differs greatly depending on who is producing the service, on their know-how, skills, experience and even motivation. The productivity depends on the team build to execute the service and the communication between the customer and the service provider is. Furthermore, as the service provider receives compensation based on hours or man-days, they might not have an incentive to exert effort [16]. This can cause that the service provider is not motivated to improve efficiency or find solutions, that require less work. This eliminates the possibility for innovation and more efficient ways of working. As Lichtenstein [15] states, on the contrast to T&M pricing, fixed-pricing rewards the service supplier as the supplier benefit from cost savings and one the other hand, pays for cost overruns.

Another significant downside of T&M pricing are the limited profits. The intangibility of services and the T&M pricing can be ineffective for service providers that have a profit-maximizing goals [20]. Although, the hourly charge differs by roles and expertise levels, the profits are still limited in relation to billable hours. The scalability can be only done through recruiting more labor and performing more hours. A weakness is also that T&M might overlook the customer's willingness to pay a higher price and the value the service adds to the customers business [20].

Another very critical problem that most of the companies in the software industry are struggling with is the labor shortage. As the talent shortages drive up costs, the software industry is keen to hire more inexperienced talent and to train them. However, the customers often demand experienced teams and individuals as their resource. As the customer is buying resources, they might be very conscious on the resources they are paying for, which means that the T&M pricing can lead to monitoring and controlling the supplier's actions and costs [4, 16] In practice, this complicates integrating new talent to professional software services offerings.

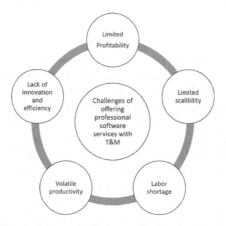

Fig. 1. The challenges of offering professional software services

The challenges are faced everyday by companies offering professional software services. They do not affect only the suppliers, but also their customers, who are relying on getting the right knowhow to boost their business with technology and digitalization. Furthermore, the challenges affect the labor. The shortage of labor is a very major struggle for the whole industry. This leads to overburdening current talent and hampers finding new talent, which is a major obstacle in achieving growth and profitability targets.

3   Business Design

One of the tendencies that shapes the software industry is the coopetition balance between software products and professional software services. This means productization of services and servitization of products [11]. Service productization is determined as "the process for analyzing a need, defining and combining suitable elements into a product-like object, which is repeatable and comprehendible" [8]. The benefits of service productization are more efficient way of working, lower costs, and greater customer satisfaction [14]. Service providers that understand the strategic role of pricing and how the customers value the alternative pricing models, can make better decisions throughout the service development and implementation process [9].

However, service productization has not diminished the challenges for example the labor shortages and the limited profits. My proposition in this study is that the challenges can be overcome by applying the business design approach to the development of professional software service offering.

The practitioners see business design as a customer-centered approach to developing and innovating services. The approach applies design principles and practices to build competitive advantage and profitable and sustainable offerings. Business design is the totality how a company selects its customers, defines and differentiates offerings, builds competitive advantage, creates value for the customer, configures its resources and captures profit [10, 12]. It can be perceived as the gap between business strategy and operational execution. Business design method deepens service productization by adding design practices and principles to the development of services as illustrated in Fig. 2.

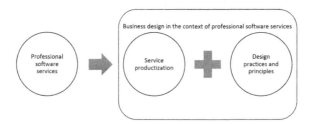

Fig. 2. Business design in the context of professional software services

In literature, business design is often dealt from the designer perspective [1, 6], not from the business perspective. Business design is acknowledged among practitioners in the software industry and discussed commonly in managerial magazines and seminars, but it is not discussed explicitly in the academic literature in the context of software industry.

4   Research Methodology

As I am studying the impacts of using business design in professional software services, which has not been studied nor is the business design term established in the context, the case study method is chosen as the research methodology. Rowley [19] defines case study as "an empirical method aimed at investigating contemporary phenomena in their context". Although case studies as a research method or strategy might been viewed as lacking rigour and objectivity, they do offer insights that might not be achieved with other methods [3, 19].

The case study methodology offers a flexible design strategy, which includes a significant amount of iterations over the steps. The iterations will allow us to evaluate and develop the use of the framework with the business design method. Also, the data collection and analysis can be conducted incrementally [19]. As I am investigating not only use of the business design method but also the impact it has on profitability, I will use mixed methods for data collection, which is typical for the case study method [19, 20].

A multiple case study approach seemed most appropriate because to be able to form a practical and useful framework for companies, I need to discover replicable actions. As Rowley [19] states, the greater the number of case studies that show replication, the more robust are the research outcomes. I will choose from six to ten companies that offer professional software services with time and material pricing. Selecting the most suitable case companies is crucial, and the selection must be determined by the research purpose, questions, propositions and theoretical context [19].

In a case study, the researcher must be familiar with the subject [3], and the researcher has to make a speculation on the basis of the literature and other evidence as to what they expect the finding of the research to be. The data collection and analysis can then be structured to support or refute the research propositions [19].

Software engineering case studies tend to lean towards a positivist perspective, which is suitable for my research as well. A positivist case study searches evidence for formal propositions, measures variables, tests hypotheses and draws inferences from a sample to a stated population [20]. Rowley [19] agrees by adding that the positivist approach provides a firm foundation for understanding and managing issues such as validity and reliability and for structuring data collection and analysis. This makes the positivist approach more straightforward.

However, the literature also stresses that even though the case study method is a flexible and the includes iterations over the steps, there should be a specific objectives set the from the beginning [20]. If the set objectives change, a new case study should be carried out rather than altering changing the existing one.

References

1. De Turi, I., Antonicelli, M.: A nebusiness design tool for digital business model innovation: DEA approach. Can. Cent. of Sci. Edu. (2020). https://doi.org/10.5539/ibr.v13n6p86
2. Engel, C., Ebel, P.: Data-driven service innovation: a systematic literature re-view and development of a research agenda. In: European Conference on Information Systems (ECIS) (2019)
3. Fidel, R.: The case study method: a case study. Libr. Inf. Sci. Res. 6(3), 273–288 (1984)
4. Franklin, T.: Adventures in agile contracting: evolving from time and materials to fixed price, fixed scope contracts. In: Agile 2008 Conference, pp. 269–273, (2008). doi: https://doi.org/10.1109/Agile.2008.88
5. Fraser, H.M.A.: Designing business: new models for success. Des. Manage. Rev. 20(2), 56–65 (2009). https://doi.org/10.1111/j.1948-7169.2009.00008.x
6. Gaglione, S., dil Gaziulusoy, A.: Designers designing business. understanding howdesigners create enterprises. Des. J. 22(sup1), 51–63. (2019)
7. Harkonen, J., Haapasalo, H., Hanninen, K.: Productisation: a review and research agenda. Int. J. Prod. Econ. 164, 65–82 (2015)

8. Harkonen, J., Tolonen, A., Haapasalo, H.: Service productisation: systematising and defining an offering. J. Serv. Manag. **28**(5), 936–971 (2017). https://doi.org/10.1108/JOSM-09-2016-0263

9. Harmon, R., Demirkan, H., Hefley, B., Auseklis, N.: Pricing strategies for information technology services: a value-based approach. In: 2009 42nd Hawaii International Conference on System Sciences, pp. 1–10. IEEE. (2009)

10. Hong C., LiHua T., Ying H.: Business design for an on demand business enterprise. In: IEEE International Conference on E-Commerce Technology for Dynamic E-Business, pp. 349–352. (2004). https://doi.org/10.1109/CEC-EAST.2004.25

11. Hoch, D.J., Roeding, C., Lindner, S.K., Purkert, G.: Secrets of Software Success. Harvard Business School Press, Boston (2000)

12. Hornbach, K.: Competing by business design—the reshaping of the computer industry. Long Range Plan. **29**(5), 616–628 (1996). https://doi.org/10.1016/0024-6301(96)00056-8

13. Lacity, M.C., Willcocks, L.P., Feeny, D.F.: The value of selective IT sourcing. Sloan Manage. Rev. **37**, 13–25 (1996)

14. Levitt, T.: The industrialization of service. Harv. Bus. Rev. **54**(5), 63–74 (1979)

15. Lichtenstein, Y.: Puzzles in software development contracting. Commun. ACM **47**(2), 61–65 (2004). https://doi.org/10.1145/966389.966391

16. Lichtenstein, Y., McDonnell, A.: Pricing Software Development Services. In: Proceedings of the 11th European Conference on Information Systems (ECIS) (2003)

17. Popp, K.: Software industry business models. IEEE Softw. **28**(4) (2011)

18. Reason, B., Lovlie, L., Brand, F.M.: Service Design for Business – A Practical Guide to Optimizing the Customer Experience. John Wiley & Sons, Inc., New Jersey (2016)

19. Rowley, J.: Using case studies in research. Manag. Res. News **25**(1), 16–27 (2002). https://doi.org/10.1108/01409170210782990

20. Runeson, P., Höst, M.: Guidelines for conducting and reporting case study research in software engineering. Empir. Softw. Eng. **14**(2), 131–164 (2009). https://doi.org/10.1007/s10664-008-9102-8

21. Schlissel, M.R., Chasin, J.: Pricing of services: an interdisciplinary review. Serv. Ind. J. **11**(3), 271–286 (1991). https://doi.org/10.1080/02642069100000046

Applications of MLOps in the Cognitive Cloud Continuum

Sergio Moreschini$^{(\boxtimes)}$ (iD)

Tampere University, Tampere, Finland
`sergio.moreschini@tuni.fi`

Abstract. Background. Since the rise of Machine Learning, the automation of software development has been a desired feature. MLOps is targeted to have the same impact on software development as DevOps had in the last decade.
Objectives. The goal of the research is threefold: (RQ1) to analyze which MLOps tools and platforms can be used in the Cognitive Cloud Continuum, (RQ2) to investigate which combination of such tools and platforms is more beneficial, and (RQ3) to define how to distribute MLOps to nodes across the Cognitive Cloud Continuum.
Methods. The work can be divided into three main blocks: analysis, proposal and identification, and application. The first part builds the foundations of the work, the second proposes a vision on the evolution of MLOps then identifies the key concepts while the third validates the previous steps through practical applications.
Contribution. The thesis's contribution is a set of MLOps pipelines that practitioners could adopt in different contexts and a practical implementation of an MLOps system in the Cognitive Cloud Continuum.

Keywords: Software engineering · Machine learning · Mlops

1 Introduction

DevOps [2] is defined as a set of practices to encourage collaboration between application development and IT operations teams. The main purpose of DevOps is to ensure fast release of quality software changes and operating resilient systems. DevOps methodology has become a core concept of the software development lifecycle for practitioners and with the increasing adoption of Machine Learning (ML)-based software the methodology needs to be extended to include the ML development steps that differ from the original software development. The process of including an ML pipeline when developing software needs to be addressed so that the new software system will ensure both long-term maintainability and adaptable nature. These requirements are due to the hybrid nature

Supervisors:
David Hästbacka, Tampere University, david.hastbacka@tuni.fi
Davide Taibi, University of Oulu, davide.taibi@oulu.fi.

© The Author(s), under exclusive license to Springer Nature Switzerland AG 2022
D. Taibi et al. (Eds.): PROFES 2022, LNCS 13709, pp. 650–655, 2022.
https://doi.org/10.1007/978-3-031-21388-5_51

of such ML-based as the long term maintainability is inherited from the DevOps practices, while the adaptable nature is achieved through continuous training of new data continuously provided to the ML algorithm. For this reason, such extension is categorized as an evolution of the classical DevOps and denominated MLOps [7].

With the increasing availability of devices connected to the Internet and the ability to generate data, MLOps has the potential to become the reference model to develop software capable of detecting anomalies, projecting future trends, augmenting intelligence and so much more. However, as most of these devices composing the environment have limited computational power it is important to investigate also how to develop applications along the so-called COgnitive CLoud CONtinuum (COCLCON).

The main goal of this thesis is to study the most common approaches when developing ML-based software in the COCLCON. In this work I will attempt to answer the following research questions:

RQ$_1$. Which MLOps tools and platforms can be used in the COCLCON?
RQ$_2$. What combination of MLOps tools and platforms can be used in the COCLCON optimized pipeline?
RQ$_3$. How to distribute MLOps across the COCLCON?

2   Background

The concept of MLOps is a new hype in academic literature [3]. Even if the problem of automating ML applications was firstly addressed in 2015 [14], the first mentions of the term MLOps itself are from 2018. In the last 4 years, the engagement with the topic grew exponentially, so that at the time of writing there are more than 200 million projects adopting ML on GitHub [15]. Consequently multiple works, both in white and grey literature, tried to define their vision on the concept of MLOps, but many of them differed on multiple aspects mostly related to the pipeline [6,10,15]. One of the main goals of this work is to propose a pipeline which has strong literature foundations, takes into account common practices and the state-of-the-art of MLOps projects and, most important, validates it through practical applications.

2.1   MLOps

Software development has seen its last revolution with the introduction of DevOps. The methodologies proposed by DevOps helped companies to improve results and create a culture based on two fundamental factors: the increased frequency of software releases and the reliability of the produced software. These two factors that once seemed to be opposite of each other started not only to coexist but also to grow together following the dynamic nature of DevOps practices. Such dynamic nature has been represented through the iconic DevOps pipeline which aims to portray the division of application Developers (Dev) and IT Operations (Ops) tasks in teams as an infinite loop.

The increased adoption of ML-based software has created a new figure in the corporate organizational environment: the ML developer. Such a figure actively participates in the development of the software, performing tasks that are parallel to the Dev engineer. The natural evolution of the development cycle for agile software, and therefore of the DevOps pipeline, which includes the development of ML-based software has been defined as MLOps.

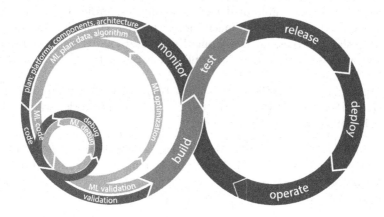

Fig. 1. Proposed MLOps pipeline [10]

The graphical representation for MLOps proposed in [10] is depicted in Fig. 1. Such representation aims at highlight the diversification yet affinity when developing the ML-based software from the software developer and the ML developer perspectives. The main differences between the proposed MLOps pipeline and the original DevOps lie in the Plan and Code phases, moreover, a subsequent phase has been added and defined as Validation.

2.2 Cognitive Cloud Continuum

Another important aspect to take into account is where to deploy the ML-based software. One of the most recent hypes in the cloud computing domain is the concept of Cloud Continuum, which together with the concept of Cognitive Cloud has raised interests of funding agencies [1].

The first definitions of Cloud Continuum were presented in 2016 [4,5]; while the first one presented it as a *"continuum of resources available from the edge to the cloud"* the second focused on computationally related aspects. Since then, more than 30 definitions have been proposed for Cloud Continuum. The definitions have focused on the distribution of resources both from the point of view of the entity responsible for the computation and of the computational power.

The term cognitive was originally used in computer science to refer to the behavior of computers analogous or comparable to the human brain. In the 2010 s, "cognitive computing" became the new research trend aiming to develop novel systems relying on extensive amounts of data from many sources. With the advent of the era of big data, the increasing amount of unstructured data caused problems in information analysis and processing; in this scenario, cognitive computing provided solutions by imitating the human way of thinking.

Analyzing the evolution of both terms, the Cognitive Cloud Continuum is moving towards an extension of the traditional Cloud towards multiple entities. Such entities not only are capable of providing data, store it and processing it, but they are also capable of sensing the environment and, by learning from it, they can adapt the computational load.

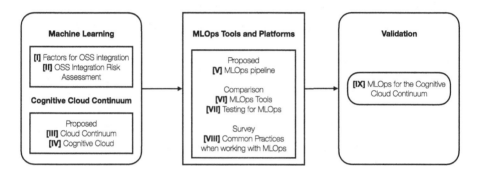

Fig. 2. PhD structure

3   The Proposed Approach

The structure of the PhD is depicted in Fig. 2. It is composed by 3 main steps, divided in 9 sub-steps, that might be submitted as individual publication:

- Step 1: **Analysis of the literature** for ML in the COCLCON
- Step 2: **MLOps: platforms, tools, methods and processes**
  - Proposed MLOps pipeline
  - Comparison of testing and tools
  - Survey on the impact of MLOps in the industry domain
- Step 3: **Applications of MLOps in the COCLCON**
  - Investigation of MLOps tools usage in the COCLCON
  - ML distribution to the different nodes of the COCLCON.

The research method is based on both empirical methodology and practical applications. The empirical methodology includes systematic literature reviews, case studies, surveys, and interviews. Starting from the analysis of the literature I aim at answering RQ1 in the first step. To answer RQ2 I make use of the aforementioned empirical studies; the goal is to provide clear pipeline proposals by finding the optimal combination of tools used at each step of the MLOps pipeline. RQ3 revolves around the concept of Cognitive Cloud Continuum, therefore a fundamental part is the definition of the two concepts composing it. Following this, I aim at investigating MLOps tools and their usage in this particular environment to practically develop an MLOps system in the third step.

Step 1: Analysis of the Literature. The implementation of ML models strongly relies on the capability of importing Open Source Libraries in the same way that Open Source Software (OSS) has been integrated into commercial products. When talking about OSS it is important to estimate factors and metrics to evaluate its reliability of it before embedding it [9]. Some key points desired when integrating OSS are continuous updates and maintainability and based on these it is possible to calculate the risk of abandonment [8]. Once the properly available libraries have been selected the development of the software can begin.

Another important aspect to take into account is the device on which the software needs to be developed, how the calculation needs to be carried out, and in which environment such device is [11,12]. The analysis of the literature focuses on these aspects which are the foundation on which the development of the software lies.

Step 2: Identification of Methods and Tools. Developing software that relies on ML techniques necessitates a different approach when compared to normal DevOps. Among the various reasons, there is one based on the need to include the figure of the ML developer who needs to develop the system in parallel with the software engineer. For this reason, an extension of the DevOps pipeline is required [10].

Once the pipeline is clearly stated, it is important to analyze the state of the art of the current tools for ML-based projects and how they are used [13]. Particular attention needs to be placed on those tools used for testing the overall systems [15]. Furthermore, it is also critical to investigate practitioners' common practices when working with such ML-based systems.

Step 3: MLOps in the COCLCON. In the last step, I aim at using the knowledge acquired in the previous steps to provide an MLOps system capable of delivering applications along the COCLCON.

4   Current Status

The Research work started in January 2021. During this period I investigated Step 1, and Step 2.1. Step 1 consisted of four different works [8,9,11,12] aiming at answer RQ1.

Step 2.1 is the first result towards answering RQ2 and has been achieved through the proposition of an MLOps pipeline published in [10]. The work, not only envisions a pipeline for MLOps but also produces a meaningful comparison to classical DevOps. The publication is the first part of a roadmap for the development of MLOps practices. At the stage of writing, I am currently developing the second part of this step which will result in two publications.

As for the remaining steps I am currently collaborating with different partners to investigate how to properly address problems related to RQ3.

5 Expected Contribution

The main contribution of this thesis is to analyze the evolution of the development process of MLOps, particularly applied in the Cognitive Cloud Continuum. The main contribution of this thesis will be a validated set of MLOps pipelines that companies can adopt in different contexts, together with their pros and cons.

References

1. Cognitive Cloud: Ai-enabled computing continuum from cloud to edge (RIA) (2022). https://ec.europa.eu/info/funding-tenders/opportunities/portal/screen/opportu-nties/topic-details/horizon-cl4-2022-data-01-02, Accessed 07 JULY 2022
2. Bass, L., Weber, I., Zhu, L.: DevOps: a software architect's perspective. Addison-Wesley Professional (2015)
3. Calefato, F., Lanubile, F., Quaranta, L.: A preliminary investigation of MLOps practices in GitHub. In: IEEE ESEM, vol. 22, pp. 283–288 (2022)
4. Chiang, M., Zhang, T.: Fog and IoT: an overview of research opportunities. IEEE Internet Things J. **3**(6), 854–864 (2016)
5. Gupta, H., Nath, S.B., Chakraborty, S., Ghosh, S.K.: SDFog: a software defined computing architecture for QoS aware service orchestration over edge devices. arXiv preprint arXiv:1609.01190 (2016)
6. Gupta, S.C.: MLops: Machine learning lifecycle. https://towardsdatascience.com/machine-learning-lifecycle-in-mlops-era-5b45284c0e34 (2022)
7. John, M.M., Olsson, H.H., Bosch, J.: Towards MLOps: a framework and maturity model. In: Euromicro/SEAA (2021)
8. Li, X., Moreschini, S., Pecorelli, F., Taibi, D.: OSSARA: abandonment risk assessment for embedded open source components. IEEE Softw. **39**(4), 48–53 (2022)
9. Li, X., Moreschini, S., Zhang, Z., Taibi, D.: Exploring factors and metrics to select open source software components for integration: an empirical study. J. Syst. Softw. **188**, 111255 (2022)
10. Moreschini, S., Lomio, F., Hästbacka, D., Taibi, D.: MLOps for evolvable ai intensive software systems. In: SQ4AI@SANER (2022)
11. Moreschini, S., et al.: Cognitive Cloud: the definition. In: DCAI (2022)
12. Moreschini, S., Pecorelli, F., Li, X., Naz, S., Hästbacka, D., Taibi, D.: Cloud Continuum: the definition. In: Under Review (2022)
13. Recupito, et al.: A multivocal literature review of MLOps tools and features. In: SEAA (2022)
14. Sculley, D., et al.: Hidden technical debt in machine learning systems. In: NIPS, vol. 28. Curran Associates, Inc (2015)
15. Symeonidis, G., Nerantzis, E., Kazakis, A., Papakostas, G.A.: MLOps - definitions, tools and challenges. In: 2022 IEEE CCWC, pp. 0453–0460 (2022)

Implementing Artificial Intelligence Ethics in Trustworthy System Development - Making AI Ethics a Business Case

Mamia Agbese[(✉)][iD]

University of Jyväskylä, Seminaarinkatu 15, 40014 Jyväskylä, Finland
mamia.o.agbese@jyu.fi

Abstract. Software businesses struggle to implement AI ethics or ethical requirements in their development and engineering of AI. Current tools mainly focus on the technical level, with scarce resources identified for the different groups across software business organizations. This study focuses on developing a proposed solution, the ethical requirement stack, as a toolkit software businesses can leverage to implement ethical requirements. The tool aims to improve the understanding and visibility of AI ethics by serving as a go-to in interpreting AI ethics guidelines, thereby reducing the gap in transitioning AI ethics from principles to practice.

Keywords: Artificial Intelligence · AI Ethics · Ethical requirements · AI ethics principles · Software businesses · Ethical requirement stack

1 Introduction

As software businesses increase their usage of Artificial Intelligence (AI) in developing software systems, so does the need for them to improve their understanding of applicable ethical requirements [4]. Software systems are still rife with incidents of AI collecting user data from third parties without consent at interaction points, AI proffering sensitive solutions without explanations, AI making decisions on behalf of humans, and autonomous AI accidents [1,5,6]. Suggesting the need for a more hands-on approach to aid the implementation of ethical requirements in their engineering and development. Ethical requirements are requirements for AI systems derived from AI principles or ethical codes (norms) similar to Legal Requirements derived from laws and regulations [7]. Ethical requirements bring the visibility of AI ethics practices to the forefront in software businesses as requirements [7]. AI ethics deals with the moral behavior of humans in the design, usage, and behavior of machines [13]. Jain et al. [8] explain AI ethics as a field of applied moral values that focuses on the various sociotechnical discrepancies or issues generated from the construction and function of AI systems.

© The Author(s), under exclusive license to Springer Nature Switzerland AG 2022
D. Taibi et al. (Eds.): PROFES 2022, LNCS 13709, pp. 656–661, 2022.
https://doi.org/10.1007/978-3-031-21388-5_52

Challenges identified by [4] for the lack of practical approach by most software businesses, and AI practitioners include poor understanding of AI ethics principles and dedicated tools to aid their implementation as ethical requirements [6,7,15]. Baker-Brunnbauer [1] explains that beyond the technical level, middle to higher-level stakeholders' perspectives on ethical requirements are relatively low as they are viewed as unimportant and unprofitable due to inadequate visibility and understanding [1]. In addition, the primary approach to implementing ethics in the form of AI ethics principles serving as guidelines is considered too general, lacking in specificity and tools for these stakeholders [9,10]. Consequently, the implementation of ethical requirements is often relegated to technical teams and dealt with as non-functional requirements with virtually no representation at higher levels [15]. However, the impact of failed AI systems from ethical issues can be catastrophic [6], cutting across the entire organizational structure and not just the technical level. Incidents such as the "Volvo defeat device" scandal [3] have set the precedence for a hands-on approach for implementing ethics practices within organizations. As such, critical stakeholders at levels beyond the technical require tools and practices to inform their understanding and representation of ethical requirements to enable their involvement in implementing AI ethics [1].

To help tackle this challenge, which motivates our research, we focus our study on ethics of practice and our research question (RQ) How to implement ethical requirements or AI ethics principles for trustworthy software systems development Wickramasinghe [16] explains that for AI systems to attain the European Union standard of trustworthy AI, software businesses need to ground their ethics practices or implement them in three components: ethical algorithms, ethical data, and ethical practices. Ethics of data focuses on collecting, analyzing, profiling, advertisements, and usage of data issues. Ethics of algorithms focus on the application, autonomy, and increasing complexity of ML algorithms issues. Ethics of practice focuses on the responsibilities and liabilities of human users (such as developers, adopters, organizations, and system users) involved in the AI life cycle [16].

2   Related Work

Most of the work on implementing ethics towards the development of trustworthy AI focuses mainly on technical frameworks and methods targeted at ethical algorithms and data. This direction may be due to the speed empirical multidisciplinary bottom-up research affords AI implementation as it tends to focus on the technical needs and challenges of AI developers [2]. Morley et al., [12] mapped machine learning initiatives, tools, and methods to implement AI ethics in creating ethical or trustworthy AI. The work by [12] is extensive, with over 100 tools and frameworks identified. However, its translation of AI ethics principles to actionable practices focuses on machine learning development and not on the ethics of practices aspects that involve human users such as developers, adopters, organizations, and system users.

Mökander & Floridi [11] propose ethics-based auditing as a mechanism for implementing AI ethics and helping organizations that design and deploy AI systems to influence ethical requirements challenges. An ethics-based audit involves a structured process where auditors, which could be third-party, assess the safety, security, privacy, and fairness-related claims made in the engineering and development of AI to ascertain its ethical requirements [11]. The process can help assess for consistency with relevant principles or norms. Ethics-based audits can act as a mechanism to help software businesses identify, visualize, and communicate the normative values embedded in their AI system. However, this approach largely targets the technical aspects of ethical requirements. It highlights audit areas such as functionality audits which focus on the rationale behind the decision, code audits which focus on reviewing the source code, and impact audits which focus on the effects of algorithm's outputs [11]. In addition, it also highlights the lack of uniformity around high-level ethics principles as a challenge in determining optimal ethical requirements to be assessed against [11].

On the non-technical side, Baker-Brunnbauer [2] provides the Trustworthy Artificial Intelligence Implementation (TAII) Framework within an organization. The framework aims to decrease entry-level barriers to AI ethics implementation and provides a management perspective on the challenge of implementing AI ethics. It analyses ethical inconsistencies and dependencies along the value chain for AI projects using twelve iterative steps to aid AI ethics implementation. The framework is extensive. However, the TAII is broad in application and skewed towards managerial perspectives. In addition, it requires that ethical requirements are generated in the implementation process, which may cause them to be overlooked if they are not well defined early as integral to the process.

3   Research Gap and Proposed Solution

From the review of literature the following gaps were identified:

- Most tools focus on the technical layer of software businesses, particularly data and algorithm practices.
- A gap exists for tools and practices for levels beyond the technical layer
- Existing tools targeted at these layers are broad and inadequately interpret AI ethics principles as ethical requirements

In closing this gap, the use of literature reviews and empirical practices will be used to develop the conceptual solution, an AI ethical requirement stack. Similar to the concept of a technical stack used as a solution toolkit in projects, the stack aims to represent ethical requirements across the different organizational levels of software businesses. In achieving this stack, ethical requirements will be elicited by associating congruent practices pertinent to AI ethical practices at the targeted layer to help improve understanding and build up a stack of ethical practices. These practices can provide a go-to set of techniques that may simplify implementing ethical requirements at the relevant layer. The approach is not meant to be solely top-down in its approach because, as [2] explains, this approach is more challenging than a bottom-up approach that begins with requirements and settings within specific use cases. Instead, ethical requirements will be identified at the various organizational levels, from the technical to the decision-making level, to help improve the visibility of AI ethics as a culture disseminated across the organization.

The first phase of this research is to systematically analyze the knowledge about ethical requirements studied in its application within software businesses. Consequently, the (RQ) is subdivided into three sub-RQs.

[RQ1] How to identify vulnerabilities or knowledge gaps of AI ethics implementation as ethical requirements within software businesses?

[RQ2] What action can be taken to help mitigate these AI ethics implementation vulnerabilities?

[RQ3] How to measure the effectiveness of the proposed solution to determine the viability?

Depending on the first RQ's results, the dissertation's next part will focus on developing the proposed solution, the ethical requirement stack, and investigating its viability.

4   Methodology

We envisage the development of an artifact as an outcome of the study. Therefore the proposed process will follow a design science research utilizing the Design Science Research Methodology (DSRM) for Information Systems Research proposed by [14]. The DSRM illustrated in (Fig. 1) will be used as a framework for the creation process and proposes an iterative, six-step-process for design science research in IS, consisting of 1) problem identification and motivation, 2) defining objectives of a solution, 3) design and development, 4) demonstration, 5) evaluation, and 6) communication. This process ultimately produces an artifact to solve an identified organizational problem.

Peffers et al. [14] explain that the Design Research process might start with identifying the problem and motivation. They explain that the problem definition can help develop the artifact to provide an effective solution [14]. Problem definition is also helpful in atomizing the problem conceptually to enable a solution that can capture its complexity [14]. This phase reflects the current stage of the research. We are currently in the process of effectively atomizing the problem to enable us to conceptualize a solution that captures its complexity [14]. Conceptualizing the solution allows us to pursue the solution to understand the state of the problem, its importance, and the reasoning associated with our understanding of the problem [14].

Following the completion of this stage, we will proceed to the next stages following the nominal process sequence explained by [14] in (Fig. 1).

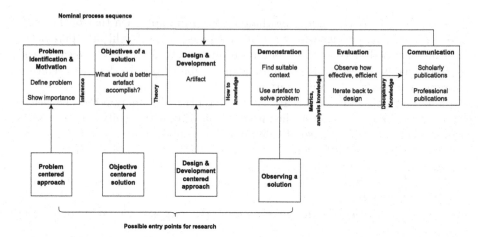

Fig. 1. Illustration of the design science research methodology [14]

5   Preliminary Results

The outcome of the first year, as part of the first phase of the study, is a journal paper evaluating an AI ethical developmental tool, ECCOLA, which we utilized for our study. The evaluation was to determine areas where we could improve the information robustness of method models used by developers at a higher level for implementing ethical requirements. The tool was rigorously evaluated with an Information governance framework, Generally Accepted Recordkeeping Principles (GARP). The findings and recommendations for its improvement to include Information governance practices as a more effective way of implementing ethical requirements are communicated as a research article accepted for publication in the e-informatica software engineering journal.

These findings and new empirical findings will inform the ongoing research.

6   Expected Contributions

This study aims to improve how AI ethics or ethical requirements can be represented and disseminated across software business organizations to help reduce ethical challenges associated with AI using a proposed solution, the ethical requirement stack. The stack can potentially aid stakeholders beyond the technical level of software businesses with a tangible representation of AI ethics, thereby reducing the complexity and ambiguity associated with them. With current tools and methods for implementing AI ethics currently concentrated at the technical stage, a tool presenting AI ethics across the various levels of the organization can help provide a more holistic approach to addressing ethical requirements implementation challenges. The proposed ethical requirement stack can give visibility to ethical requirements that can help bring to the forefront pertinent AI challenges so that the necessary solution needed to address them is implemented. The tool can also enable stakeholders to understand ethical requirements to make more informed decisions. Overall, the study aims to contribute to closing the current gap in transitioning AI ethics principles to practice.

References

1. Baker-Brunnbauer, J.: Management perspective of ethics in artificial intelligence. AI Ethics **1**(2), 173–181 (2021)
2. Baker-Brunnbauer, J.: TAII framework for trustworthy AI systems. ROBO-NOMICS: J. Automat. Econ. **2**, 17 (2021)
3. Barn, B.S.: Do you own a Volkswagen? Values as non-functional requirements. In: Bogdan, C., et al. (eds.) HESSD/HCSE -2016. LNCS, vol. 9856, pp. 151–162. Springer, Cham (2016). https://doi.org/10.1007/978-3-319-44902-9_10
4. Brendel, A.B., Mirbabaie, M., Lembcke, T.B., Hofeditz, L.: Ethical management of artificial intelligence. Sustainability **13**(4), 1974 (2021)
5. Collins, C., Dennehy, D., Conboy, K., Mikalef, P.: Artificial intelligence in information systems research: a systematic literature review and research agenda. Int. J. Inf. Manag. **60**, 102383 (2021)
6. Falco, G., et al.: Governing AI safety through independent audits. Nat. Mach. Intell. **3**(7), 566–571 (2021)
7. Guizzardi, R., Amaral, G., Guizzardi, G., Mylopoulos, J.: Ethical requirements for AI systems. In: Goutte, C., Zhu, X. (eds.) Canadian AI 2020. LNCS (LNAI), vol. 12109, pp. 251–256. Springer, Cham (2020). https://doi.org/10.1007/978-3-030-47358-7_24
8. Jain, S., Luthra, M., Sharma, S., Fatima, M.: Trustworthiness of artificial intelligence. In: 2020 6th International Conference on Advanced Computing and Communication Systems (ICACCS), pp. 907–912. IEEE (2020)
9. Jobin, A., Ienca, M., Vayena, E.: The global landscape of AI ethics guidelines. Nat. Mach. Intell. **1**(9), 389–399 (2019)
10. Mittelstadt, B.: Principles alone cannot guarantee ethical AI. Nat. Mach. Intell. **1**(11), 501–507 (2019)
11. Mökander, J., Floridi, L.: Ethics-based auditing to develop trustworthy AI. Minds Mach. **31**(2), 323–327 (2021)
12. Morley, J., Floridi, L., Kinsey, L., Elhalal, A.: From what to how: an initial review of publicly available AI ethics tools, methods and research to translate principles into practices. Sci. Eng. Ethics **26**(4), 2141–2168 (2020)
13. Müller, V.C.: Ethics of artificial intelligence and robotics (2020)
14. Peffers, K., Tuunanen, T., Rothenberger, M.A., Chatterjee, S.: A design science research methodology for information systems research. J. Manag. Inf. Syst. **24**(3), 45–77 (2007)
15. Vakkuri, V., Kemell, K.K., Kultanen, J., Abrahamsson, P.: The current state of industrial practice in artificial intelligence ethics. IEEE Softw. **37**(4), 50–57 (2020)
16. Wickramasinghe, C.S., Marino, D.L., Grandio, J., Manic, M.: Trustworthy AI development guidelines for human system interaction. In: 2020 13th International Conference on Human System Interaction (HSI), pp. 130–136. IEEE (2020)

Developing a Critical Success Factor Model for DevOps

Nasreen Azad[✉][iD]

Department of Software Engineering, Lappeenranta, Finland
nasren.azad@lut.fi

Abstract. DevOps has presently become a mainstream software development model in the software industry. DevOps is a software engineering paradigm which is adopted and implemented by various software organizations. There is a need for a model which could guide the professionals and practitioners to achieve organizations goals and performance. To address this study objective, we have developed an initial framework for the critical success factors models which will be validated by three research questions.

Keywords: DevOps · Critical success factors · DevOps success factor model

1 Introduction

To compete in a highly volatile market, it is necessary for an organization to release software that is both effective and has the capability to sustain in the competition [5]. For customers, it is important to have new features with efficient software delivery [3]. As the software business has matured over the years, also the requirements for speed and efficiency have changed [8]. As a response to the changing business environment, also the software development life cycles and the development processes have been evolving.

The purpose of the agile practices is to discover user requirements and develop solutions through collaboration with cross-functional teams and end users [9]. Agile practices have some limitations and create complexity while scaling agile development framework [10]. In contrast, DevOps is the combined process of 'development' and 'operations', which is used for the software development to speed up the delivery process with efficiency [13].

DevOps is a widely used development strategy that helps to minimize software development costs through implementation and adoption. The aim of DevOps is to provide continuous development and continuous delivery for the software development process [12]. DevOps allows to make collaboration with development and operations teams within the organization and provide an effective delivery process for software development.

Critical success factors are a management literature concept, which dates back to the beginning of the 1960s [4]. While there is vast literature on the

© The Author(s), under exclusive license to Springer Nature Switzerland AG 2022
D. Taibi et al. (Eds.): PROFES 2022, LNCS 13709, pp. 662–668, 2022.
https://doi.org/10.1007/978-3-031-21388-5_53

critical factors and their role, they can be briefly defined as *"the few key areas of activity in which favorable results are absolutely necessary for a particular manager to reach his goals"* [2, p. 4].

2   Methods and Goals

2.1   Methods

The aim of the research is to provide a deep understanding of DevOps critical success factors in software development practices. To achieve this goal, we will use four research methods in this thesis: Systematic literature review [10], Case study research [11], multivocal literature review [7] and survey methods [6]. We have chosen multiple research methods because the quantitative along with the qualitative analysis will provide an in-depth understanding of the topic at hand by answering the research questions regarding the critical success factors of DevOps project.

For the data collection process, at first we have conducted an SLR by selecting empirical papers on DevOps domain. Second, we have conducted an open ended online questionnaire survey with DevOps professionals. To get more clear idea on the topic we have conducted semi-structured interviews with same DevOPs professionals who participated in survey previously. Our next step would be to design a 7-point Likert scale questionnaire to measure the constructs presented in Fig. 1 and for that we will conduct an online survey to collect approximately 200 responses for our research purpose. We will also conduct a Multivocal literature review to get an overall view of DevOps success factor for organizations.

The research will conduct a thorough study based on Software companies and IT professional's practices on DevOps use. Some of the hypotheses are presented below.

2.2   Hypotheses

H1: Performance engineering factor for DevOps directly impacts DevOps project success.

H2: Integration factor for DevOps process directly impacts DevOps project success.

H3: Build and test automation factor directly impacts DevOps project success.

H4: Infrastructure factor directly impacts DevOps project success.

H5: DevOps as a service factor directly impacts DevOps project success.

H6: Intra organizational collaboration and communication factor directly impacts DevOps project success.

H7: Organizational hierarchy factor directly impacts DevOps project success.

H8: Strategic planning factor directly impacts DevOps project success.

H9: Team dynamics factor directly impacts DevOps project success.

H10: Cultural shift factor directly impacts DevOps project success.

H11: Team Dynamics factor moderately effects the organizational success factors of DevOps project success.

H12: Cultural shift factor moderately effects the organizational success factors of DevOps project success.

In this model, we suggested that technical factors and organizational factors (intra-organizational collaboration, organization hierarchy, and strategic planning) would directly impact DevOps success. The social and cultural factors (team dynamics and cultural shift) would moderate the effects of organizational factors on DevOps success. In addition, social and cultural factors might also impact DevOps success directly.

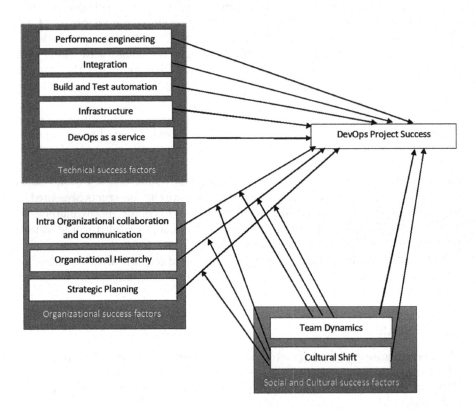

Fig. 1. DevOps critical success factor model (adapted from [1]).

2.3   Research Questions

To address the aim of this research topic we have one key research question (RQ). The key research question is:

RQ What are the critical success factors of DevOps projects?

To understand the key research question, we need to understand three sub-research questions. The sub-research questions are written below.

SRQ1 What are the critical success factors, as reported in the extant research literature, of DevOps projects and how do the findings differ with an MLR literature?

SRQ2 What are the critical success factors of DevOps projects as reported by the professionals?

SRQ3 What are the challenges professionals face in DevOps projects? How do they mitigate the challenges and risks?

3   Results

For the research we have three sub-research questions. The first sub-research questions is about the critical success factors reported on the extant literature and how do the findings differ with MLR literature, the second question describes about the success factors of DevOps reported by the professionals. Third question is about the challenges professionals face during DevOps practices and how they mitigate the risks for the projects.

For the first research question We are still left with the MLR literature review. We believe that after conducting the MLR literature we will get an overall view of Critical success factors of DevOps and that will address the first research question for our study. Then we will design a 7-point Likert scale questionnaire to measure the constructs presented in Fig. 1 and will conduct an online survey to collect data and address our research questions. We will analyse the data with PLS (Partial least square) regression methods to find out what critical factors that impact the success of DevOps projects. Below we discuss our three papers findings.

SRQ1: What are the critical success factors, as reported on the extant research literature, of DevOps projects? Critical success factor for DevOps SLR (ICSOB2021).

> DevOps fills the gap between the development and operations teams and maintains the collaboration among information technology professionals for delivering the software applications. Due to its recent emergence, there are relatively little research done, at least when compared to the other software process models, on DevOps and its successful usage. Previously, some empirical research studies have been conducted on the success factors of DevOps, but a synthesis of these findings is needed. This paper aims to find out various critical success factors of DevOps projects that have been discussed in prior research by following a systematic literature review. Based on our extensive keyword search and after applying inclusion/exclusion criteria, we have included 38 research articles in this paper. The identified critical success factors were categorized into technical, organizational, and social and cultural dimensions. Finally, this study offers a comprehensive framework depicting how the critical success factors impact or drive DevOps success.

SRQ2: What are the critical success factors of DevOps projects as reported by the professionals? Understanding DevOps critical success factors and organizational practices (IWSIB 2022).

> DevOps is a combination of practices and a company culture that aims to minimize the barriers between the operation and development teams in the organization. As its adoption and use in the industry have been growing, different kinds of research are trying to explore DevOps practices, processes and implementations in organizations. Most of the extant research conducted in the past was to investigate how DevOps worked, what impacts it made on the organizations and how the adoption of DevOps played a role in the overall success for companies. This paper presents a qualitative analysis of a dataset collected via an open-ended survey from 15 software professionals who are experienced in DevOps. The focus of the study is on reporting DevOps practices in organizations, and how they impact the success of DevOps. We discuss the DevOps professionals' point-of-view on DevOps practices and align their thoughts through a DevOps model of the critical success factors.

SRQ3: What are the perceived challenges of DevOps projects for professionals? How to mitigate the challenges and risks for DevOps? DevOps challenges in organizations: Through professional lens (ICSOB 2022).

While the success factors of DevOps adoption have been studied in the extant literature, also the perceived challenges that a company faces during the adoption are crucial to discover. This paper explores and highlights these challenges through an open- ended survey (N=15) and in-depth interviews with DevOps professionals (N=16). According to the findings, there are various challenges while implementing DevOps in organizations. The research suggests that (i) lack of team coordination, (ii) risky change and development, (iii) team members expertise level, (iv) lack of focus or differences in development, (v) test and production environment, (vi) poorly defined functional and technical requirements, (vii) poor integration and test process, (viii) pipeline execution problems, (ix) tools integration challenges, (x) people challenges and silo-ed thinking, (xi) debugging challenges due to remote execution, (xii) feature release challenges, (xiii) integrating new standards, (xiv) challenges with clients, (xv) knowledge sharing, (xvi) responsibility distribution issues are the challenges while using DevOps. The found list of perceived challenges will help future research to suggest mitigation and risk management strategies for successful use of DevOps.

4   Conclusion

Our research focus is to understand DevOps critical success factors. To understand DevOps current state, we have conducted a systematic literature review, which has given us an overview of a current research work, findings and gaps that need to be addressed. we have designed a semi- structured questionnaire to conduct interviews with IT professionals from various companies which helped us to validate the success factors we have found in the literature review. We have conducted interviews with DevOps professionals and got insightful information regarding DevOps operations, success factors, DevOps challenges, and risks. Next, we will develop a questionnaire for conducting an online survey with different constructs we have found from our study. Thus, we will test the hypothesis of our proposed model for DevOps success factors for (Fig. 1).

Acknowledgements. The dissertation work is supervised by Sami Hyrynsalmi from LUT University.

References

1. Azad, N., Hyrynsalmi, S.: What are critical success factors of devops projects? a systematic literature review. In: Wang, X., Martini, A., Nguyen-Duc, A., Stray, V. (eds.) ICSOB 2021. LNBIP, vol. 434, pp. 221–237. Springer, Cham (2021). https://doi.org/10.1007/978-3-030-91983-2_17

2. Bullen, C.V., Rockart, J.F.: A primer on critical success factors. Working papers 1220–81. Report (Alfred P. Sloan School of Management. Center for Information Systems Research); no. 69, Massachusetts Institute of Technology (MIT), Sloan School of Management (1981), https://econpapers.repec.org/paper/mitsloanp/1988.htm

3. Colomo-Palacios, R., Fernandes, E., Soto-Acosta, P., Larrucea, X.: A case analysis of enabling continuous software deployment through knowledge management. Int. J. Inf. Manage. **40**, 186–189 (2018)

4. Dickinson, R.A., Ferguson, C.R., Sircar, S.: Critical success factors and small business. Am/ J. Small Bus. **8**(3), 49–57 (1984)

5. Erich, F.M., Amrit, C., Daneva, M.: A qualitative study of devops usage in practice. J. Softw. Evolut. Proc. **29**(6), e1885 (2017)

6. Gable, G.G.: Integrating case study and survey research methods: an example in information systems. Eur. J. Inf. Syst. **3**(2), 112–126 (1994)

7. Garousi, V., Felderer, M., Mäntylä, M.V.: The need for multivocal literature reviews in software engineering: complementing systematic literature reviews with grey literature. In: Proceedings of the 20th International Conference on Evaluation and Assessment in Software Engineering, pp. 1–6 (2016)

8. Järvinen, J., Huomo, T., Mikkonen, T., Tyrväinen, P.: From agile software development to mercury business. In: Lassenius, C., Smolander, K. (eds.) ICSOB 2014. LNBIP, vol. 182, pp. 58–71. Springer, Cham (2014). https://doi.org/10.1007/978-3-319-08738-2_5

9. Krawatzeck, R., Dinter, B.: Agile business intelligence: Collection and classification of agile business intelligence actions by means of a catalog and a selection guide. Inf. Syst. Manag. **32**(3), 177–191 (2015)

10. Petersen, K., Wohlin, C.: A comparison of issues and advantages in agile and incremental development between state of the art and an industrial case. J. Syst. Softw. **82**(9), 1479–1490 (2009)

11. Runeson, P., Höst, M.: Guidelines for conducting and reporting case study research in software engineering. Empir. Softw. Eng. **14**(2), 131–164 (2009)

12. Sacks, M.: Devops principles for successful web sites. In: Pro Website Development and Operations, pp. 1–14. Springer (2012). https://doi.org/10.1007/978-1-4302-3970-3_1
13. Sebastian, I.M., Ross, J.W., Beath, C., Mocker, M., Moloney, K.G., Fonstad, N.O.: How big old companies navigate digital transformation. In: Strategic Information Management, pp. 133–150. Routledge (2020)

Strategic ICT Procurement in Finland: Tensions and Opportunities

Reetta-Kaisa Ghezzi[✉][iD]

University of Jyväskylä, Jyväskylä, Finland
reetta.k.ghezzi@jyu.fi

Abstract. This research proposal targets public sector ICT practices. The goal is to explore in-depth the causes of issues in public ICT. Furthermore, the goal is to fill research gaps in public agency and supplier interrelationships, EA practices, and intended public sector technological solutions. The proposed research binds these areas to establish a coherent framework for how ICT should be built and led in public agencies.

Keywords: Public procurement · Enterprise architecture · Sustainable software · Interoperability

1 Introduction

Half of the ICT projects fail in Finland [5]. Globally the ICT project failure rate varies from 70–90%. Meanwhile, ICT procurement, including services, software, and hardware, is the largest Finnish state procurement category, worth 1,07 billion euros in 2021 [7]. For Finnish municipalities, the same number is 1,14 billion euros [7]. In European Union ICT procurement was worth of 3.8% of total GDP in 2019 [6].

The previous research reveals ICT procurement issues such as ICT projects exceeding original budgets and schedules; systems collapse before launch, project resources being under-evaluated [10], requirements are inadequate and ambiguous [10], and strict parameters set by laws and directives hinder the effectiveness in ICT procurement [14]. However, the causes behind the issues above do not receive attention in previous research. Therefore, one research gap is in the ICT procurement preparation practices and how the inadequate and ambiguous requirements repeatedly pass to the tender phase.

Furthermore, the previous research reveals that in agencies that do not have controlled project management practices, the IT department may find out about ICT procurement after it has been tendered [8]. Naturally, this causes issues in establishing coherent enterprise architecture (EA). In many cases, the technical interoperability with existing EA has not been in ICT procurement criteria in the tender phase, and the problems yield to the post tender phase [8]. The issue of non-existent interoperability is demanding to fix afterward [8]. The research gap in building a coherent EA exists in missing connections between public sector practices to purchase software solutions to the existing EA.

© The Author(s), under exclusive license to Springer Nature Switzerland AG 2022
D. Taibi et al. (Eds.): PROFES 2022, LNCS 13709, pp. 669–674, 2022.
https://doi.org/10.1007/978-3-031-21388-5_54

Furthermore, combining perspective with public agency and supplier relationship is missing from the literature but is altogether vital to understand the ICT procurement landscape. The assumption is that vendors and public agencies may have differing views about the needs.

Therefore, this research agenda paper describes the interconnections of ICT procurement, public EA, and supplier relationships. First, the literature background and motivation for the topic are presented. Second, the research questions and methods are described. Finally, the research agenda is discussed, and final thoughts are presented in conclusions.

2   Background and Motivation

Enterprise Architecture Adoption in Public Sector. For Finland, a certain level of national EA is mandatory, and recommendation JHS179 [13] describes the EA needs in detail. JHS179 has roots in the Open Group Architecture (TOGAF). The problem is that even if TOGAF is well recognized and widely used [4], it has not been adopted thoroughly. Furthermore, TOGAF's practical implications remain unknown because it lacks research, and the situation is similar to JHS179. Bradley et al. [2] prove that EA maturity influences IT resource efficiency when pursuing strategic goals. Finding relies on the considerations where IT planning involves business planning and vice versa, which results in IT decisions becoming more centralized [3,19]. Therefore, EA maturity mapping seems an important topic to cover to understand how EA is established in Finnish public agencies and how a more holistic EA could be formed in the public sector. Furthermore, the acquisition practices miss researched.

Problems in ICT Procurement. Many issues in ICT procurement emerge from under-evaluated project resources, which introduce bottlenecks and prolong the project [10]. Tendering is a critical phase and a vital issue in ICT procurement [12]. Inadequate and ambiguous requirement-set analysis for tender requirements cause exceeding in budget and schedule [10].

Suppliers in ICT Procurement. The cooperation between public agency and vendors aim to build a coherent view of the market, inform the market about the upcoming procurement, and communicate the requirements for participating vendors [12]. Cooperation is vital to plan and execute the procurement in a way that does not violate the nondiscrimination and transparency principles [1]. The previous literature does not offer the perspective that combines and examines the interrelationship between public agencies and vendors. Therefore, the interrelationship must be researched and evaluated thoroughly, as it might reveal the causes behind the recognized issues in ICT procurement.

In addition, public agencies can buy in-house without setting the purchase to tendering, which is a significant but allowed derogation to the Public Procurement Act [18]. In-house procurement divides opinions, and it has its opponents and proponents. Proponent arguments are that in-house procurement aids in controlling and regulating services, it is cheaper to provide services through it, and it is a legislated method to be used in purchases [9]. In opposing arguments, the view is that in-house procurement breaches competition rules by eliminating private undertakings, especially in IT services, it may hinder the adoption of innovative solutions, and the solutions are more expensive than solutions acquired from the market [9].

Technological Point of View. The final piece to cover is the technical point of view. Outside the IT domain, public agency stakeholder groups fail to adopt EA artifacts in practice [17,20]. Public sector software sustainability issues can be overcome with EA, where different services and vendors can quickly deploy and integrate into the ecosystem environment [21]. Nurmi et al. [17] reveal that ecosystem thinking in EA software is missing and needed. An ecosystem, where every piece gives something, may be achieved with services that interact via well-defined APIs but with no direct access to other services [21]. However, the previous literature does not explore how the technological requirements are established holistically, and whether ecosystem-like EA is required in ICT procurement.

To summarize, the holistic approach to composing interoperable technology has been suggested in the literature. However, the practice contribution is missing, revealing a research gap.

3   Research Approach

The research approach is a combination of qualitative and quantitative research methods. The goal is to publish research articles on ICT procurement practices in Finnish public agencies. Semi-structured interviews, case studies, and surveys are the research methods to answer the research questions and create a public ICT management model for the practice.

3.1   Research Questions

The research question (RQ) is *how to build sustainable and efficient public ICT?* The RQ will be examined through three sub-research questions in all of the research articles:

- *RQ1: What are the recognized problems in practice?*
- *RQ2: What are the causes of the problems?*
- *RQ3: What changes are needed to develop the practices?*

3.2   Research Methods

Methods to Examine RQ1. Semi-structured interviews are the best way to address the research gap, why inadequate requirements repeatedly pass to the tender phase and do the existing EA belongs in the selection criteria in new

ICT procurement. Semi-structured interviews, with open-ended questions and rein for free speech, combining structured and non-structured interview methods [15]. Semi-structured interviews offer narrowed focus with pre-formulated questions and the possibility to discuss important topics in detail [15]. The participants receive questions on ICT procurement, the existing EA procedures, and ICT composition in the organization. In the interview situation, the topics are discussed in detail to understand the problems' magnitudes and the causes (RQ2) behind them.

Methods to Examine RQ2. The purpose of case studies is to collect empirical evidence from real people in real organizations to contribute to knowledge generation [15]. The goal is to increase the applicability of the results and to make conclusions about the phenomenon at the general level as well [15]. In detail, the case study type in this research is critical to evaluate the current practices [15].

The goal of the in-house procurement case study is to examine the interrelations between in-house companies and public agencies and whether in-house procurement is problematic or not and to reveal how significantly the public sector relies on in-house procurement. In this research, the focus groups are to largest cities and in-house vendors in Finland, and the data is gathered from the purchase invoice data.

In vendor relationships, the case study is a method to understand the vendor intentions in public procurement and whether they differ from what public agencies wish to receive. Therefore, public agency and vendor interrelationship is examined through semi-structured interviews as a part of the case study and through documents from the public agencies, procurement units, or vendors. In Finland, small, medium, and large-sized ICT vendors participate in ICT procurement, and therefore, the focus group is determined accordingly.

The survey examines public agencies' software requirements to research technological points of view. The survey is an excellent way to reach a large number of participants, has standardized questions, and is ideal for examining ideas and attitudes [16]. In the survey, the wanted technological solutions are explored in the same focus groups as in previous research; Finnish public agencies such as municipalities, cities, welfare organizations, and administrations; most prominent ICT in-house vendors; and ICT vendors who participate in tendering. The intention is to discover the opinions on how public ICT should be composed and with what technologies.

Methods to Examine RQ3. Drawing results from the abovementioned research, design science research (DSR) is drafted to propose a solution to the practice. DSR is a suitable method to create new solutions and knowledge and to establish working solutions to real-world problems [11]. Hopefully, the examinations of ICT procurement practices, EA practices, habits to define needed technologies, and ICT management practices reveal the points for improvement. In DSR, one way to create a working solution is to propose a methodology to achieve the wanted result [11]. The problems seem recognized in Finnish public ICT practices, but a further understanding of how to improve practices is missing, at least in the literature.

4   Discussion

The research question for this research agenda paper is *how to build sustainable and efficient public ICT?*. Problems and causes in ICT procurement and EA practices are evaluated through semi-structured interviews and case studies to examine RQ1 and RQ2. The case studies suit the best to understand the interrelationship between public agencies and suppliers. Furthermore, to examine the different needs and intentions technology-wise, which might cause issues in ICT procurement, the survey is used as a research method to receive comparable and standardized results from all focus groups [16].

Finally, to answer RQ3, the design science research is drafted to create a working solution to real-world problems [11]. The research agenda is planned to build a holistic view of the Finnish public ICT practices, especially acquisition practices. However, the guidelines on what to do and what not to do are missing. Therefore, drafting strategic ICT methods for public agencies seems helpful in practice and theory. The goal is to comprehensively explore ICT practices in the public sector - how knowledge management, project management, public EA with interoperability perspective, ICT supplier management, and ICT procurement practices bind together. These interrelations and missing of them might reveal the fundamental causes why public sector ICT projects often fail. The purpose of the discussed research is to offer to understand methods for the practice and propose how to manage ICT effectively in the public sector. The theoretical implication is to understand the fundamental causes of public ICT issues.

5   Conclusions

This research proposal targets public sector ICT practices. The goal is to explore in-depth, what are the causes of issues in public ICT. Furthermore, the goal is to fill research gaps in public agency and supplier interrelationships, EA practices, and intended public sector technological solutions. Furthermore, the goal is to offer tools to enhance ICT purchasing processes and suggest more effective collaboration practices to enhance the use of resources in society to aid innovation in public sector ICT solutions.

References

1. Directive 2014/24/eu of the European parliament and of the council of 26 february 2014 on public procurement and repealing directive 2004/18/ec (2014)
2. Bradley, R.V., Pratt, R.M.E., Byrd, T.A., Outlay, C.N., Wynn, D.E.: Enterprise architecture, it effectiveness and the mediating role of it alignment in us hospitals. Inf. Syst. J. **22**(2), 97–127 (2012)
3. Bradley, R.V., Pratt, R.M.E., Byrd, T.A., Simmons, L.L.: The role of enterprise architecture in the quest for it value. MIS Q. Executive **10**(2), 73–80 (2011)
4. Cameron, B.H., McMillan, E.: Analyzing the current trends in enterprise architecture frameworks. J. Enterprise Archit., 60–71 (2013)
5. Tietojärjestelmien hankinta suomessa (2013)
6. ICT sector - value added, employment and R&D (2022)
7. Explore public spending (2022)
8. Ghezzi, R.-K.: State of public ICT procurement in Finland (2022)
9. Hartung, W., Kuźma, K.: In-house procurement - how it is implemented and applied in Poland. Euro. Procurement Public Private Partnership Law Rev. **13**(3), 171–183 (2018)
10. Nor Hayati, T., Maharoof, V.M., Burhanuddin, M.A.: Theoretical foundation in analyzing gaps in information communication and technology (ICT) tender process in public sector. J. Eng. Appl. Sci. **13**(6), 407–1413 (2018)
11. Hevner, A.R., March, S.T., Park, J., Ram, S.: Design science in information systems research. MIS, pp. 75–105 (2004)
12. Iloranta, K., Pajunen-Muhonen, H.: Overview of Enterprise Architecture work in 15 countries. Tietosanoma, Helsinki (2012)
13. Jhs 179 kokonaisarkkitehtuurin suunnittelu ja kehittäminen (2017)
14. Keränen, O.: Roles for developing public-private partnerships in centralized public procurement. Industr. Market. Manag. **62**, 199–210 (2017)
15. Myers, M.D.: Qualitative Research in Business and Management. SAGE Publications, London (2020)
16. Nardi, P.M.: Doing Survey Research: a Guide to Quantitative Methods, 4th edn. Routledge, London (2018)
17. Nurmi, J., Penttinen, K., Seppänen, V.: Towards ecosystemic stance in finnish public sector enterprise architecture. In: Pańkowska, M., Sandkuhl, K. (eds.) BIR 2019. LNBIP, vol. 365, pp. 89–103. Springer, Cham (2019). https://doi.org/10.1007/978-3-030-31143-8_7
18. Act on public procurement and concession contracts (2016)
19. Ross, J.W., Weill, P., Robertson, D.C.: Enterprise Architecture As Strategy - Creating a Foundation for Business Execution. Harvard Business School Publishing, Boston (2006)
20. Seppänen, V., Penttinen, K., Pulkkinen, M.: Key issues in enterprise architecture adoption in the public sector. Electron. J. E-gov. **16**(1), 46–58 (2018)
21. Setälä, M., Abrahamsson, P., Mikkonen, T.: Elements of sustainability for public sector software - mosaic enterprise architecture, macroservices, and low-code. Lecture Notes in Business Information Processing, 434 LNBIP, 3–9 (2021)

Leverage Software Containers Adoption by Decreasing Cyber Risks and Systemizing Refactoring of Monolithic Applications

Maha Sroor[✉] [iD]

University of Jyväskylä, Mattilanniemi 2, Jyvaskyla, Finland
maha.m.sroor@jyu.fi

Abstract. Containers are one of the deployment solutions that possess attention. It is always compared to virtual machines (VM). Thus, there is a debate about its capabilities. It supports software agility that helps satisfy users' requirements and shorten deployment time. Many works of literature have discussed the advantages of containers and promoted their role in developing the software industry. However, the actual migration rate in the software market is not as expected compared to the advantages.

This research highlights the barriers to adopting containers. Also, it digs in depth into two main barriers to adoption, namely security risks and refactoring of monolithic applications. It aims to study the impact of cyber risks on the applications' performance. The risks will be studied from a narrow view focusing on sharing resources and a broader view focusing on using malicious container images in project performance. Moreover, it will investigate the requirements and practices of refactoring monolithic applications into a container-based format. This research aims to address the container security risks and provide a systemized refactoring model for monolithic applications. The research is qualitative. The empirical data will be collected from primary studies, surveys, and interviews to explain the container adoption barriers. Providing more understanding of the adoption barriers' causes will help to avoid them, consequently increasing container adoption.

Keywords: Software containers · Security risks · Monolithic applications

1 Related Work

Software applications are an essential element in the software industry. The demand for the applications has increased [1], and requesting advancing features such as usability, integration, simple installation, and robustness also increased [2]. The accelerating demand made applications complex, and the software development process became challenging. As a result, Software companies are trying to adopt agile development methods to ensure accessibility, maintainability, and shorter deployment time [2, 3].

Solutions such as virtual machines (VMs) and containers support software development. VMs are virtual platforms that run individual software applications [4]. VMs can run an entire software environment, including the OS. It extensively utilizes the hardware

© The Author(s), under exclusive license to Springer Nature Switzerland AG 2022
D. Taibi et al. (Eds.): PROFES 2022, LNCS 13709, pp. 675–680, 2022.
https://doi.org/10.1007/978-3-031-21388-5_55

[5]. In comparison, containers are a software development approach that virtualizes an isolated software environment to run applications and their dependencies [6]. Containers are copied into a container image, and users use the container image to update and make changes to applications. Unlike VMs, containers do not run OS but instead, utilize the hosting machine's OS to elasticate resources [7].

Containers and VMs both virtualize an operating software environment but significantly differ in structure. Understanding the differences between both approaches can be noticed in the different behavior with the hosting OS, performance, isolation, and startup time [8]. Table 1 presents a comparison between containers and VMs.

Table 1. Comparison between VMs and containers

	Containers	VMs
Hosting OS	Share OS and kernel, kernel load on physical memory	Has its OS and kernel load on its memory space
Performance	Has the same as the production machine	Has overheads before production
Isolation	Share subdirectories with the host	VM cannot share any files or libraries
Startup time	Few seconds	Few minutes

The advantages of containers are not limited to the advantages mentioned before; they are also flexible, portable, and lightweight [8]. The remarkable advantage of containers is that their structure supports multiple software development approaches, such as modularity [9], component-based software (CBS) [10], and microservices [11]. All these approaches provide autonomous services to satisfy user needs [12] and support agile software development [13].

2   Research Problem

Containers are essential in managing software products and creating new business avenues for vendors. Although they highly support agile software development, many software companies are hesitant to adopt them. The reason is that containers have not reached their maturity compared to VM; for example, containers have challenges with complex networking [14], security issues [15], refactoring monolithic applications [16], and a lack of management tools [17]. This research project will focus on the top significant challenges to increasing container adoption in the software development market: security issues and monolithic applications [6].

Security risks are the primary barrier to container adoption. The containers' threat model has three main players: container, application, and hosting machine [15]. The most critical element in the threat model is the container. Its architectural styles make it the primary security threat because tens of containers can share the operating system and the hosting machine's physical resources. This makes containers more likely to transfer malicious threats to other containers on the same environment, the hosting machine, and applications. Also, if containers are reused, malicious container images would affect multiple projects [18].

There are few papers on the impact of reusing faulty or infected containers on the hosting environment. Also, the impact of faulty and infected containers on the application's operation and performance is not yet explored. The importance of studying the impact will be beneficial when developers start to run the application on production or when injecting a new function into a running system. If the risk likelihood is not calculated accurately and no risk mitigation plan is ready for the high-impact threats, no one will expect the system's performance. The impact might be fatal that the system might hold or even collapse.

Refactoring monolithic applications is another challenge for container adoption. Monolithic applications are complex applications encompassing independent services. They are hard to deploy, upgrade and maintain. Refactoring them into container-based-format does require not only architectural changes but also environmental changes [16].

Most available literature about refactoring monolithic applications discussed the phases before the refactoring process [16] and the deployment process [19]. The literature does not address the requirements, limitations, and best practices for refactoring. The importance of addressing the refactoring requirements, limitations, and practices is to save cost and time. A preliminary analysis before the refactoring process will help determine the refactoring decision's effectiveness.

3   Research Objectives

This research project's holistic goal is to increase container adoption in developing and deploying software applications. The project aims to overcome two main challenges facing container adoption namely cyber risks and refactoring monolithic applications. The project plan is built on two main pillars. The first pillar is reducing cyber risks to a minimum level. It could be achieved by investigating the cyber risks emerging from container architectural style and using container images in multiple projects. After that, connect the security risks to a suitable mitigation plan. The second pillar is to facilitate the refactoring of monolithic applications into containers by systemizing the process. It could be achieved by addressing the basic requirements and limitations of the refactoring process and studying the best practices of the refactoring process. Beating these two challenges will increase container adoption.

4   Research Questions

The research project is conducted in two phases. The theme of phase one is container cyber risks, which will answer RQ1 "How can the architectural style for containers affect software system security?" It will be split into the following three questions.

- RQ1.1: What are the barriers to adopting containers?
- RQ1.2: What role can software containers' architectural styles play in the cyber security of the software application?

- RQ1.3: How can the reuse container affect the software system's security?

The theme of phase two is refactoring the monolithic applications, which answers RQ2 "How to achieve systemization to refactoring monolithic applications into the container-based format?" It will be divided into the following two questions.

- RQ2.1: What are the main requirements to refactor the monolithic applications to container-based applications?
- RQ2.2: what are the best practices to transfer monolithic applications to microservices using containers?

5 Research Approach

This research project is qualitative in nature. As Sect. 4 "research questions" mentions, the project will have two research phases. The first phase aims to answer RQ1. Currently, empirical data is being collected for the first paper. It is a systematic literature review. The paper's primary goal is to overview the advantages of adopting containers and the barriers that obstruct their adoption. It will focus on challenges related to cyber and data security, like compliance with GDPR, EU data, and AI acts.

The second and third papers are complementary to the first paper to answer RQ1. The second paper is qualitative research on the cyber risks emerging from the container architectural style. The paper's primary goal is to highlight the cyber threats resulting from sharing the OS and the host machine's physical resources. The third paper is a survey on the cyber risks that stem from using malicious container images on projects. The paper's primary goal is to identify if malicious images would cause new security threats and how they would impact the performance and operation of the system overall. The empirical data will be collected from companies that adopted containers earlier and have faced cyber risks that emerged from reusing containers.

The second phase aims to answer RQ2. It includes the fourth and fifth papers. The fourth paper is a case study on the requirements and limitations for refactoring monolithic applications. Empirical data will be collected from companies on refactoring requirements in different stages (destructure, reliable base, configuration, logging, and injection). The fifth and last paper is a survey on the best practices for refactoring monolithic applications. It will study the differences and similarities among the refactoring practices. The empirical data will be collected from companies adopting containers in deploying applications.

6 Research Timeline

The research work will be organized into three stages. The first stage is planned from one and a half years to two years. The second stage is planned. It is planned from one year to 15 months. The third stage is dissertation writing. It would last for a year. This research started in August 2022, and the plan and the submission dates might be subject to changes according to the early findings of the research and the availability of the empirical data. Table 2 presents a summary of the research status.

Table 2. Summary of the research status.

	Methodology	Submission date
Paper 1	SLR	June 2023
Paper 2	Qualitative research	March 2024
Paper 3	Survey	September 2024
Paper 4	Case study	March 2025
Paper 5	Survey	September 2025

7 Research Contribution

This research aims to create a new vision for software container utility outside the generic cloud environment. This research will help software engineering researchers to develop their knowledge of the containers' cyber risks that were not explored before in the literature. Also, it will help practitioners to minimize the cyber risk levels and develop more effective risk mitigation plans to protect software applications. Moreover, it will shorten the deployment time for refactoring monolithic applications by following a refactoring model that provides a preliminary analysis of the validity of refactoring.

References

1. Donca, I.-C., Stan, O.P., Misaros, M., Gota, D., Miclea, L.: Method for continuous integration and deployment using a pipeline generator for agile software projects. Sensors **22**, 4637 (2022). https://doi.org/10.3390/s22124637
2. Crnkovic, I.: Component-based software engineering — new challenges in software development. Softw. Focus **2**, 127–133 (2001). https://doi.org/10.1002/swf.45
3. Reifer, D.J.: How good are agile methods? IEEE Softw. **19**, 16–18 (2002). https://doi.org/10.1109/MS.2002.1020280
4. Smith, J.E., Nair, R.: The architecture of virtual machines. Computer **38**, 32–38 (2005). https://doi.org/10.1109/MC.2005.173
5. Zhang, Q., Liu, L., Pu, C., Dou, Q., Wu, L., Zhou, W.: A Comparative Study of Containers and Virtual Machines in Big Data Environment. In: 2018 IEEE 11th International Conference on Cloud Computing (CLOUD). pp. 178–185 (2018). https://doi.org/10.1109/CLOUD.2018.00030
6. Koskinen, M., Mikkonen, T., Abrahamsson, P.: Containers in software development: a systematic mapping study. In: Franch, X., Männistö, T., Martínez-Fernández, S. (eds.) PROFES 2019. LNCS, vol. 11915, pp. 176–191. Springer, Cham (2019). https://doi.org/10.1007/978-3-030-35333-9_13
7. Hoenisch, P., Weber, I., Schulte, S., Zhu, L., Fekete, A.: Four-fold auto-scaling on a contemporary deployment platform using Docker containers. In: Barros, A., Grigori, D., Narendra, N.C., Dam, H.K. (eds.) ICSOC 2015. LNCS, vol. 9435, pp. 316–323. Springer, Heidelberg (2015). https://doi.org/10.1007/978-3-662-48616-0_20
8. Dua, R., Raja, A.R., Kakadia, D.: Virtualization vs containerization to support PaaS. In: 2014 IEEE International Conference on Cloud Engineering. pp. 610–614 (2014). https://doi.org/10.1109/IC2E.2014.41

9. Woodfield, S.N., Dunsmore, H.E., Shen, V.Y.: The effect of modularization and comments on program comprehension. In: Proceedings of the 5th International Conference on Software Engineering, pp. 215–223. IEEE Press, San Diego (1981)

10. Crnković, I.: Component-based software engineering - new challenges in software development. J. Comput. Inf. Technol. **11**, 151–161 (2003). https://doi.org/10.2498/cit.2003.03.02

11. Amaral, M., Polo, J., Carrera, D., Mohomed, I., Unuvar, M., Steinder, M.: Performance evaluation of microservices architectures using containers. In: 2015 IEEE 14th International Symposium on Network Computing and Applications, pp. 27–34 (2015). https://doi.org/10.1109/NCA.2015.49

12. Jaramillo, D., Nguyen, D.V., Smart, R.: Leveraging microservices architecture by using Docker technology. In: SoutheastCon 2016, pp. 1–5 (2016). https://doi.org/10.1109/SECON.2016.7506647

13. Hasselbring, W., Steinacker, G.: Microservice architectures for scalability, agility and reliability in E-Commerce. In: 2017 IEEE International Conference on Software Architecture Workshops (ICSAW), pp. 243–246 (2017). https://doi.org/10.1109/ICSAW.2017.11

14. Watada, J., Roy, A., Kadikar, R., Pham, H., Xu, B.: Emerging trends, techniques and open issues of containerization: a review. IEEE Access. **7**, 152443–152472 (2019). https://doi.org/10.1109/ACCESS.2019.2945930

15. Sultan, S., Ahmad, I., Dimitriou, T.: Container security: issues, challenges, and the road Ahead. IEEE Access. **7**, 52976–52996 (2019). https://doi.org/10.1109/ACCESS.2019.2911732

16. Auer, F., Lenarduzzi, V., Felderer, M., Taibi, D.: From monolithic systems to Microservices: An assessment framework. Inf. Softw. Technol. **137**, 106600 (2021). https://doi.org/10.1016/j.infsof.2021.106600

17. Pahl, C., Brogi, A., Soldani, J., Jamshidi, P.: Cloud container technologies: a state-of-the-art review. IEEE Trans. Cloud Comput. **7**, 677–692 (2019). https://doi.org/10.1109/TCC.2017.2702586

18. Shu, R., Gu, X., Enck, W.: A study of security vulnerabilities on Docker Hub. In: Proceedings of the Seventh ACM on Conference on Data and Application Security and Privacy, pp. 269–280. Association for Computing Machinery, New York (2017). https://doi.org/10.1145/3029806.3029832

19. Kuryazov, D., Jabborov, D., Khujamuratov, B.: Towards decomposing monolithic applications into microservices. In: 2020 IEEE 14th International Conference on Application of Information and Communication Technologies (AICT), pp. 1–4 (2020). https://doi.org/10.1109/AICT50176.2020.9368571

Author Index

Printed in the United States
by Baker & Taylor Publisher Services